AF838615

SHAPING A GENUINE AREA OF FREEDOM, SECURITY AND JUSTICE

This book provides an ambitious assessment of the increasing importance of case law in the field of the Area of Freedom, Security and Justice on the evolution of EU law.

In recent years, the Area of Freedom, Security and Justice (AFSJ) has occupied an increasingly prominent place in the working of the European Union and, by extension, that of the Court of Justice (CJEU). Over three parts, the book looks at the framework of the AFSJ, its workings and, finally, the impact of EU law upon it. The collection provides remarkable insights into the growing importance of the AFSJ and how EU law has evolved in light of this.

Shaping a Genuine Area of Freedom, Security and Justice

Liber Amicorum Vice-President Bay Larsen

Edited by
Koen Lenaerts
Eugene Regan
Ulla Neergaard
and
Karsten Engsig Sørensen

•HART•
OXFORD • LONDON • NEW YORK • NEW DELHI • SYDNEY

HART PUBLISHING

Bloomsbury Publishing Plc

Kemp House, Chawley Park, Cumnor Hill, Oxford, OX2 9PH, UK

1385 Broadway, New York, NY 10018, USA

29 Earlsfort Terrace, Dublin 2, Ireland

HART PUBLISHING, the Hart/Stag logo, BLOOMSBURY and the Diana logo are trademarks of Bloomsbury Publishing Plc

First published in Great Britain 2024

Copyright © Koen Lenaerts, Eugene Regan, Ulla Neergaard, Karsten Engsig Sørensen, and Contributors severally 2024

Koen Lenaerts, Eugene Regan, Ulla Neergaard, Karsten Engsig Sørensen, and Contributors have asserted their right under the Copyright, Designs and Patents Act 1988 to be identified as Authors of this work.

All rights reserved. No part of this publication may be reproduced or transmitted in any form or by any means, electronic or mechanical, including photocopying, recording, or any information storage or retrieval system, without prior permission in writing from the publishers.

While every care has been taken to ensure the accuracy of this work, no responsibility for loss or damage occasioned to any person acting or refraining from action as a result of any statement in it can be accepted by the authors, editors or publishers.

All UK Government legislation and other public sector information used in the work is Crown Copyright ©. All House of Lords and House of Commons information used in the work is Parliamentary Copyright ©. This information is reused under the terms of the Open Government Licence v3.0 (http://www.nationalarchives.gov.uk/doc/open-government-licence/version/3) except where otherwise stated.

All Eur-lex material used in the work is © European Union, http://eur-lex.europa.eu/, 1998–2024.

A catalogue record for this book is available from the British Library.

A catalogue record for this book is available from the Library of Congress.

ISBN: HB: 978-1-50997-511-2
ePDF: 978-1-50997-513-6
ePub: 978-1-50997-512-9

Typeset by Compuscript Ltd, Shannon

To find out more about our authors and books visit www.hartpublishing.co.uk. Here you will find extracts, author information, details of forthcoming events and the option to sign up for our newsletters.

Foreword

In the pages that follow, the reader will find a collection of essays that pay tribute to the stellar legal career of Vice-President Bay Larsen at both national and European level. In his home country, Denmark, Vice-President Bay Larsen chose to dedicate himself to a life of public service, by working for many years in the Danish Ministry of Justice and then, by becoming a judge of the *Højesteret* (the Danish Supreme Court). On 11 January 2006, he became a Judge of the European Court of Justice (the ECJ or the Court), and the fourth Danish national to be appointed to the Court in that capacity following Max Sørensen, Ole Due, and Claus Christian Gulmann.

During his many years of service at the ECJ, Vice-President Bay Larsen contributed tremendously to the development of EU law. His fine analytical skills, strength of legal reasoning and hard work were quickly recognised by his colleagues who twice elected him President of Chamber, and subsequently, Vice-President of the Court.

Quantitatively, the enormous number of cases handled by Vice-President Bay Larsen speaks volumes as to his commitment to his work. He acted as Judge-Rapporteur in more than 500 cases, of which 76 were assigned to the Grand Chamber. Qualitatively, he played a leading role in landmark cases pertaining to almost all areas of EU law. In EU environmental law, for example, suffice it to recall cases such as *Confédération paysanne and Others* and *Blaise*.[1] In the realm of EMU, he was Judge-Rapporteur in the seminal *Gauweiler* and *Weiss* cases, the only references made to date by the *Bundesverfassungsgericht* (the German Constitutional Court).[2] Regarding free movement law, he was Judge-Rapporteur in cases such as *Torresi* and *Cilevičs and Others*.[3]

However, without any doubt, it is in cases relating to the AFSJ that the contribution of Vice-President Bay Larsen has been the most significant and, in particular, in the fields of refugee law and judicial cooperation in criminal matters. Acting as Judge-Rapporteur in more than a hundred such cases, Vice-President Bay Larsen is rightly perceived as one of the leading experts in the field.

His judicial work in this field also mirrors the evolution of the AFSJ. Before the entry into force of the Treaty of Lisbon on 1 December 2009, the AFSJ was only partially 'communitarised', since it combined both the Community method and the method of intergovernmental cooperation. Whilst visas, asylum, immigration and judicial cooperation in civil matters were governed by provisions set out in Title IV of Part Three of the EC Treaty, judicial cooperation in criminal matters remained subject to intergovernmental dynamics under Title VI of the EU Treaty (also known as the 'Third Pillar'). Judicial cooperation in criminal matters was, moreover, subject to the unanimity rule within the Council, making it considerably harder for the EU to pass legislation.

[1] Case C-528/16 *Confédération paysanne and Others*, EU:C:2018:583; Case C-688/21 *Confédération paysanne and Others (In vitro random mutagenesis)*, EU:C:2023:75, and Case C-616/17 *Blaise and Others*, EU:C:2019:800.

[2] Case C-62/14 *Gauweiler and Others*, EU:C:2015:400, and Case C-493/17 *Weiss and Others*, EU:C:2018:1000.

[3] Joined Cases C-58/13 and C-59/13 *Torresi*, EU:C:2014:2088, and Case C-391/20 *Cilevičs and Others*, EU:C:2022:638.

Moreover, in the AFSJ, judicial dialogue was subject to a specific regime.[4] According to ex Article 68 EC, only 'a court or tribunal of a Member State against whose decisions there is no judicial remedy under national law' could engage in a dialogue with the ECJ regarding, for example, the Brussels Regulation and the Directives on Asylum.[5] In the same way, according to ex Article 35 EU, the jurisdiction of the ECJ to issue preliminary rulings regarding questions concerning judicial cooperation in criminal matters was subject to a Member State making a declaration in that regard.[6] Those specificities may explain why in the pre-Lisbon era, the requests for a preliminary ruling relating to the AFSJ were far less numerous than today. Thus, from 1999 to 2009, only 67 orders for reference were made.

That said, because of his expertise and previous experience in dealing with '*home affairs*' issues, Vice-President Bay Larsen was entrusted with cases pertaining to asylum law and judicial cooperation in criminal matters shortly after his arrival in Luxembourg. His work was therefore pioneering in establishing the seminal judgments that would constitute the first generation of cases relating to the AFSJ, such as *Elgafaji*,[7] *Kozlowski*,[8] *Salahadin Abdulla and Others*,[9] *B and D*,[10] and *Kadzoev*,[11] to name just a few.

With the entry into force of the Treaty of Lisbon, the AFSJ was fully 'communitarised' from both a legislative and judicial perspective. The ordinary legislative procedure became the standard decision-making process, meaning that the European Parliament and the Council are now co-legislators and that only a qualified majority vote is required in the Council. Judicially, the preliminary reference mechanism is now open to all courts across the EU. In addition, the Treaty of Lisbon transferred new competences to the EU, allowing it to adopt minimum rules concerning the definition of criminal offences and sanctions in respect of particularly serious crimes with a cross-border dimension. These changes inevitably meant that more AFSJ cases would come before the ECJ. From 2009 to 2019, 648 orders for reference were made, out of which 131 concerned asylum.

Moreover, the refugee crisis of 2015 intensified, albeit temporarily, this trend, as national courts sought guidance from the ECJ in a situation where the asylum systems of some Member States were on the verge of collapsing due to the high volume of cases brought about by that crisis.[12] Vice-President Bay Larsen played a pivotal role during that crisis, being Judge-Rapporteur in important cases such as *AS* and *Jafari*.[13]

This shows that European integration has moved on from the internal market paradigm. It now seeks to establish an area without internal frontiers, where citizens may move freely and securely. Vice-President Bay Larsen has been a key judicial actor in this paradigm shift. The

[4] See, generally, K Lenaerts, 'The Contribution of the European Court of Justice to the Area of Freedom, Security and Justice' (2010) 59 *International and Comparative Law Quarterly* 255.

[5] See, e.g., order in Case C-555/03 *Warbecq*, EU:C:2004:370, para. 15 (holding that 'as the reference to the Court has not been made by a court or tribunal as referred to in Article 68 EC, the Court has no jurisdiction to give a preliminary ruling on the interpretation of [the Brussels I] Regulation').

[6] For example, the ECJ would refer to the declaration made by the Member State concerned in order to hold that it had jurisdiction in the case at hand under ex Article 35 EU. See, for example, Case C-123/08 *Wolzenburg*, EU:C:2009:616, paras 3 and 40.

[7] Case C-465/07 *Elgafaji*, EU:C:2009:94.

[8] Case C-66/08 *Kozlowski*, EU:C:2008:437.

[9] Joined Cases C-175/08, C-176/08, C-178/08 and C-179/08 *Salahadin Abdulla and Others*, EU:C:2010:105.

[10] Joined Cases C-57/09 and C-101/09 *B and D*, EU:C:2010:661.

[11] Case C-357/09 PPU *Kadzoev*, EU:C:2009:741.

[12] See, for example, K Lenaerts, 'The Court of Justice of the European Union and the Refugee Crisis' in K Lenaerts, J-C Bonichot, H Kanninen, C Naômé and P Pohjankoski (eds), *An Ever-Changing Union?: Perspectives on the Future of EU Law in Honour of Allan Rosas* (Oxford: Hart Publishing, 2019) 3.

[13] Case C-490/16 *A.S.*, EU:C:2017:585 and Case C-646/16 *Jafari*, EU:C:2017:586.

case law on the AFSJ is centre stage in the current development of EU law. That is the reason why the editors of this collective volume thought that the best way of honouring the work of Vice-President Bay Larsen was by exploring that area as 'a driving force of EU law'.

This book contains 29 essays that provide the reader with a comprehensive study of the AFSJ. Given that contributors include current and former members of the ECJ and the General Court, legal secretaries and academics, the reader will benefit from a broad array of perspectives and opinions that explore the legal questions and challenges that accompany the establishment and functioning of the AFSJ.

It is divided into four parts. In Part I, the book looks at the key structural features that underpin the AFSJ. For example, it pays special attention to the principle of mutual trust and to the way in which that principle is to interact with fundamental rights. Part II is devoted to exploring the driving principles of the AFSJ, such as the principle of solidarity, the principle of *ne bis in idem* and the principle of non-refoulement. Part III is more specific in that it examines concrete legal problems with which the ECJ has been confronted and looks at the way in which the Court has interpreted relevant instruments of secondary EU legislation. Finally, Part IV looks at the impact of the AFSJ beyond the EU legal order. It examines, for example, how the case law of the ECJ has influenced international refugee law or the case law of the ECtHR.

Written in a clear and entertaining style, this book succeeds in providing a solid analytical basis for future debates about the AFSJ. Above all, it is a token of our collective gratitude to Vice-President Bay Larsen for a professional life devoted to justice, at both national and European level.

Kære Lars, Tak for alt!

Prof. dr. Koen Lenaerts,
President of the Court of Justice of the European Union

Preface

WHILE THE CONSTRUCTION of the internal market has long been the cornerstone of European integration, the Area of Freedom, Security and Justice (AFSJ) has come to occupy an increasingly prominent place in the case law of the European Court of Justice. Indeed, from defining the conditions of mutual trust to upholding the values that are common to Member States, recent developments in the AFSJ have been crucial in shaping EU law. These developments reflect the broadening and deepening relationship between the EU and its Member States, as well as among the latter, arising from the need to define the essential conditions upon which such relationships are founded. Such advances offer an insight into how EU law is currently evolving. The aim of this book is to trace these developments, which illustrate how the AFSJ has become a driving force of EU law.

The beginning of Vice-President Lars Bay Larsen's term as a judge at the Court of Justice of the European Union in 2006 coincided with the entry into force of the Treaty of Lisbon, which integrated what was previously the third pillar of the EU into a single common structure, strengthening the role of the European Union in this area of law. During his almost two decades of serving at the Court of Justice of the European Union, Vice-President Lars Bay Larsen has undoubtedly been influential in this very significant period for EU law, notably in the shaping of the AFSJ. The following contributions from present – and former – colleagues of Vice-President Lars Bay Larsen, as well as representatives from other parts of the European legal community, celebrate his judicial legacy.

The book consists of four parts, with each reflecting on a key aspect of the AFSJ. Part I, entitled 'The AFSJ Framework', explores the specific mechanisms that ensure the application of EU law in this area, and critically examines the distinctive nature of the issues raised therein. Part II, entitled 'The Driving Principles of the AFSJ', presents some of the prominent legal principles at play. Considerations relating to fundamental rights, as well as values common to the Member States, receive particular attention. Part III, entitled 'The Dynamics at Work in the AFSJ', focuses on some of the most significant legislative and jurisprudential developments in the AFSJ. Part IV, entitled 'The Impact of the AFSJ', examines the influence that EU rules and principles constitutive of the AFSJ have on domestic law, the European Convention on Human Rights and international law.

The editors

The editors are grateful for the assistance given by Julien Sterck, Antoine Masson, Michael Ryan and Emma Marie Sejr.

Vice-President Bay Larsen
Biography and Career

BORN IN 1953 in Gladsaxe, Copenhagen (Denmark), Lars Bay Larsen studied at the Københavns Universitet (University of Copenhagen, Denmark). He graduated in political science in 1976. In 1978, he returned to study at the same university, this time enrolling in the Faculty of Law, where he obtained a law degree in 1983.

After leaving the university, he was appointed as an official at the Danish Ministry of Justice where he worked from 1983 to 1985. From 1985 to 1986, he was Head of Section at the Advokatsamfund (Danish Bar Association). After returning to the Danish Ministry of Justice, he served successively as Head of Section from 1986 to 1991, Head of Division from 1991 to 1995, Head of the Police Department from 1995 to 1999, and Head of the Law Department from 2000 to 2003. During that period, he was also Representative of the Kingdom of Denmark on the K4 Committee from 1995 to 2000, the Schengen Central Group from 1996 to 1998, and the Europol Management Board from 1998 to 2000. He was called to the Bar in Denmark in 1991 and, in 2003, his career turned to the judiciary. At that time, he joined the Højesteret (Supreme Court, Denmark) where he served as a judge until 2006.

Mr Bay Larsen's career also illustrates the fruitful complementarity between practice and teaching, since he was a lecturer from 1984 to 1991 and then, from 1991 to 1996, an associate professor in family law at the Københavns Universitet. Since 2008, he has been a lecturer in European criminal law at the université du Luxembourg (University of Luxembourg).

Mr Bay Larsen has been a Judge at the Court of Justice since 11 January 2006. Having been elected by his peers to the position of President of Chamber, he performed that function for two successive terms, from 9 October 2012 to 8 October 2018. Since 8 October 2021, Mr Bay Larsen has been Vice-President of the institution.

© Photo: Jesper Bay

Contents

Personalia

Allegrezza, Silvia is Associate Professor of Criminal Law and Procedure at the University of Luxembourg. Her research focuses on European criminal justice, evidence law, genetics forensics, financial crime, and anti-money laundering integrated strategies. She received a PhD in Criminal Procedure from the University of Bologna, where she lectured until 2014. Since her arrival at the University of Luxembourg, she has led several research projects and written widely on the above. She is a member of the EU Commission experts group on criminal justice and served as Rapporteur for the EU Parliament on anti-money laundering. She has been a Visiting Professor at several institutions around the world, including Paris-Nanterre, Urbino, Rennes, and a Research Fellow at the Max-Plack Institut for the Study of Crime, Security and Law in Freiburg im Breisgau. She is the Director of the Master's Programme in European Economic and Financial Crime as well as the Chair of the Ethics Review Panel of her university.

Bianku, Ledi is an Associate Professor at the University of Strasbourg and an International Judge at the Constitutional Court of Bosnia and Herzegovina. He is also Associate Attorney with Doughty Street Chambers in London and Member of the Ethics Commission of the Prince Albert II Foundation. From 2008 to 2019 he was Judge at the European Court of Human Rights in respect of Albania. He served previously as Member of the Venice Commission for the Democracy through Law (2006–2008) and taught Public International Law, EU Law and Human Rights Law at the Tirana Law Faculty and the Albanian School of Magistrates 1993–2007. He also served as legal adviser for various national and international bodies. Mr Bianku is a graduate from Tirana University and College of Europe in Bruges.

Brière, Chloé is Associate Professor of EU Law and Director of the Institut d'études européennes at the Université libre de Bruxelles. She holds a PhD in Law delivered in 2016 by the Université libre de Bruxelles and the University of Geneva, and she is an alumna of the Erasmus Mundus GEM PhD School 'Globalisation, the EU & Multilateralism'. After defending her PhD, she held positions at the Vrije Universiteit Brussel, Dublin City University and the United Nations Office on Drugs and Crime. Her research notably addresses the EU's external relations in criminal matters, and she has published on the external dimension of the EU's policy against trafficking in human beings (including a monograph with Hart Publishing, 2021) and cooperation in criminal matters between the EU and the UK post-Brexit.

Cassagnabère, Tatiana is Legal Secretary (référendaire) at the European Court of Justice, in the chambers of Mr Bay Larsen. Previously, she was admitted to the Bar in Paris and in Strasbourg, practising law as an attorney in both cities. Mrs Cassagnabère's education includes Professional Lawyer's certification from the École régionale des avocats du Grand Est (ERAGE) in Strasbourg, a Master's Degree in Law from Higher European Studies Institute in Strasbourg, and finally a Bachelor's Degree from the Faculty of Law, Political Sciences and Management, University of Strasbourg.

Christiansen, Per is Cand Jur (1976) and Dr Jur (1988) at the University of Oslo. He has been Secretary to the Board of Governors of the Norwegian Central Bank, Financial Counsellor at

Mission of Norway to the EU, Director General of the Ministry of Finance, Advocate with PricewaterhouseCoopers, and Professor at the University of Tromsø, Faculty of Law. He was a Judge at the EFTA Court from 2011 to 2023.

Grasso, Anna is Legal Secretary (référendaire) at the European Court of Justice, in the chambers of Mr Bay Larsen. Previously, she was admitted to the Paris Bar and studied Law at the University of Florence and at the Sorbonne in Paris. She also graduated from the École nationale d'administration (National School of Administration, France) with an international diploma in public administration.

Gratsias, Dimitrios obtained his Master's Degree in Law from the Ethniko kai Kapodistriako Panepistimio Athinón (National and Kapodistrian University of Athens, Greece) in 1980 and a diplôme d'études approfondies (diploma of advanced studies, DEA) in Public Law from the université de Paris I, Panthéon-Sorbonne (University of Paris I, Panthéon-Sorbonne, France) in 1981. The following year, the Centre universitaire d'études communautaires et européennes (Université Paris I) (University Centre for Community and European Studies, University of Paris I, France) awarded him a diploma in Community Law. In 1985, Mr Gratsias began his professional career at the Symvoulio tis Epikrateias (Council of State, Greece) where he worked as a junior officer until 1992. He was subsequently appointed as a junior member in 1992 and then as a member in 2005. In addition to those functions, he was appointed, in 1998, as a supplementary member of the Anotato Eidiko Dikastirio (Superior Special Court, Greece) for two years (1998–1999) and, in 2006, as a member of the Eidiko Dikastirio Agogon Kakodikias (Special Court for Actions against Judges, Greece) for one year. In 2008, he was a member of the Anotato Dikastiko Symvoulio Dioikitikis Dikaiosinis (Supreme Council for Administrative Justice, Greece). During the 2009–2010 judicial year, he was an inspector of administrative courts. Between 1994 and 1996, Mr Gratsias joined the European Court of Justice as a Legal Secretary (référendaire) in the cabinet of Advocate General Georges Cosmas. Mr Gratsias was a Judge at the General Court between 25 October 2010 and 6 October 2021 where he also took on the functions of President of Chamber for two successive terms, from 18 September 2013 to 30 September 2019. He has been a Judge at the European Court of Justice since 7 October 2021.

Jarukaitis, Irmantas is a Judge of the European Court of Justice (since 2018), Judge (2010–2018) and Vice-President (2012–2017) of the Supreme Administrative Court of Lithuania, Deputy Director General of the European Law Department under the Ministry of Justice (2004–2010), Associate Professor at Vilnius University Faculty of Law.

Jürimäe, Küllike obtained her Law Degree (equivalent to a Master's Degree) at Tartu ülikool (University of Tartu, Estonia) in 1986. She continued her higher education at the Estonian School of Diplomacy, from which she graduated in 1992. In 2003, following a course of study at the Università degli Studi di Padova (University of Padua, Italy) and at the University of Nottingham, United Kingdom, she obtained a European Master's in Human Rights and Democratisation. She was a public prosecutor in Tallinn (Estonia) for five years from 1986. From 1991 to 1993, she was a legal adviser and then, from 1992 to 1993, General Counsel at Eesti Kaubandus-Tööstuskoda (Estonian Chamber of Commerce and Industry). Between 1993 and 2004, she served as a Judge at the Tallinna Ringkonnakohus (Tallinn Court of Appeal, Estonia). Ms Jürimäe was appointed as a Judge at the General Court on 12 May 2004. She has served as a Judge at the European Court of Justice since 23 October 2013 and has been President of Chamber at that court since 8 October 2021. She is also member of the Governing

Board of the Constitutional Law Foundation at the Estonian Academy for Sciences, member of the Governing Council and Director of the Association of European Competition Law Judges, member of Eesti Kohtunike Ühing and member of Eesti Juristide Liit.

Konstadinides, Theodore is Professor of Law at the Essex Law School, University of Essex. His publications cover a broad spectrum of Public Law, encompassing EU Constitutional Law, and Comparative Constitutional Law and Theory. He is notably the author of *Rule of Law in the European Union: The Internal Dimension* (Hart Publishing). He is a member of the executive committee of the UK Association for European Law.

Laurans, Yann graduated in Law from the Université Nancy II (2005) and later became a Doctor of Law of the same university (2009). He qualified as a lawyer in 2012. He has been working as a Legal Secretary (référendaire) in the chambers of Mr Bay Larsen since 2012.

Łazowski, Adam is a Professor of EU Law, Westminster Law School, University of Westminster in London as well as Visiting Professor at the College of Europe (Natolin) and Ivan Franko National University of Lviv (Ukraine).

Lenaerts, Koen obtained a Law Degree in 1977 from Katholieke Universiteit Leuven (Belgium) before continuing his studies at Harvard University, US, where he obtained a Master of Laws in 1978 and a Master in Public Administration in 1979. Returning to Katholieke Universiteit Leuven, he became a Doctor of Laws in 1982. It was at that same university that he started his professional career in 1979 as a lecturer before becoming a Professor of European Law in 1983. During his university career, he also taught at the College of Europe in Bruges (Belgium) from 1984 to 1989 and as a Visiting Professor at Harvard Law School, US, in 1989. Mr Lenaerts began his career at the European Court of Justice as a Legal Secretary (référendaire) to Judge René Joliet, a post which he held from 1984 to 1985 before working as a lawyer at the Brussels Bar from 1986 to 1989. He was appointed as a Judge at the Court of First Instance of the European Communities on 25 September 1989, the date on which that newly created court was established. He served in that capacity for more than 14 years before being appointed as a Judge at the European Court of Justice on 7 October 2003. He was elected by his peers to the office of President of Chamber for two successive terms from 9 October 2006 to 8 October 2012 and subsequently to the office of Vice-President of the European Court of Justice on 9 October 2012. He was elected as President of the European Court of Justice on 8 October 2015 and has held that office since.

Ligeti, Katalin is Professor of European and International Criminal Law and Dean of the Faculty of Law, Economics and Finance at the University of Luxembourg. She has widely published on topics of police and judicial co-operation in criminal matters, EU criminal law, comparative criminal procedure, economic and financial crime as well as information technology and criminal law. She is Vice President in Charge of Scientific Coordination of the International Association of Penal Law (AIDP) and co-coordinator of the European Criminal Law Academic Network. She is also a member of the Board of Directors of the Siracusa International Institute for Criminal Justice and Human Rights, and of the International Penal and Penitentiary Foundation.

Lycourgos, Constantinos obtained a Law Degree in 1985 and, subsequently, a diploma of advanced studies in Community Law in 1987 at université Panthéon-Assas Paris II (University Paris 2 Panthéon-Assas, France), the university at which he presented his doctoral thesis in Law in 1991. Admitted as a lawyer in Cyprus in 1993, he worked as a lawyer at the Nicosia

Bar until 1996, when he was appointed as a special adviser on European affairs to the Cypriot Minister for Foreign Affairs. He held that post until 1999 and, subsequently, the post of adviser on Community Law at the Law Office of the Republic of Cyprus from 1999 to 2002. He was a member of the Cypriot mission responsible for negotiating accession to the European Union between 1998 and 2003 and a member of Greek-Cypriot delegations involved in negotiations for a comprehensive settlement of the Cyprus problem from 2002 to 2014. His expertise led him to serve as a senior lawyer of the Republic of Cyprus from 2002 to 2007 and, subsequently, as a senior counsel of that State from 2007 to 2014. He was head of the European Union Law Section of the Law Office of the Republic of Cyprus from 2003 to 2014, whilst also representing the Cypriot Government before the Courts of the European Union as an agent from 2004 to 2014. Mr Lycourgos was appointed as a Judge at the European Court of Justice on 8 October 2014 and has served as President of Chamber at that court since 8 October 2021.

Masson, Antoine is a Legal Secretary (référendaire) at the European Court of Justice, an associate lecturer at the ESSEC Business School (Paris), the executive director of the Law & Management Research Network and a director of a law book series (Larcier).

Mihăescu-Evans, Bucura C is a Legal Secretary (référendaire) in the cabinet of Judge PG Xuereb at the European Court of Justice. Previously, she worked as a post-doctoral research associate at the University of Luxembourg, where she was in charge with various EU-related teaching, editorial and publishing tasks. In 2014, as a fellow of the Marie Curie INCOOP Program of the European Commission, she defended her PhD on the topic 'The right to good administration at the cross-roads of the various sources of fundamental rights in the EU integrated administrative system' (Nomos, 2015). Prior to joining the University of Luxembourg, she worked in the cabinet of Advocate General Yves Bot at the European Court of Justice. She graduated in EU Law and Political Science from universities in France, England and Luxembourg.

Mitsilegas, Valsamis is Professor of European and Global Law and Dean of the School of Law and Social Justice at the University of Liverpool (UK). He joined the University in September 2022 from Queen Mary University of London, where he was Professor of European Criminal Law and Global Security and held a number of senior leadership positions including Head of the Department of Law (2012–2018). From 2001 to 2005, he served as legal adviser to the House of Lords European Union Committee. He is co-coordinator of the European Criminal Law Academic Network and is currently serving for a fourth term as a member of the European Commission's Expert Group on Criminal Policy. He is the author of nine books and over 150 articles and chapters and the curator of over 20 edited volumes in the fields of European and transnational criminal law, asylum and migration law, and security and human rights. The second edition of his *EU Criminal Law* was published by Hart Publishing in 2022.

Neergaard, Ulla serves as a Professor of EU Law at the University of Copenhagen. Ulla Neergaard's journey began with her appointment as a professor at the University of Copenhagen in 2009. Initially designated as Professor of EU Market Law, she later transitioned to Professor of EU Law. Before this, she was a Professor of Competition Law at the Copenhagen Business School. Also, Ulla Neergaard was a Visiting Professor at the Law Faculty at Oxford University (St John's College) in 2015–2016. Her academic foundation is rooted in the prestigious European University Institute in Florence, where she achieved her PhD. Ulla Neergaard has been an 'expert member' to various boards and committees. These include the Danish Council of Competition, the Danish Energy Regulatory Authority, and the Danish Appeals

Permission Board (Procesbevillingsnævnet). Currently, for example, she serves as an alternate in the board of directors of the Danish Court Administration (Domstolsstyrelsen). Her accolades also include presiding over the International Federation for European Law (FIDE) from 2013 to 2014 and orchestrating the FIDE Congress in 2014. For over a decade, she has helmed the Danish Association for European Law. Ulla Neergaard is involved in different advisory boards of esteemed journals like the *Common Market Law Review*, *Nordic Journal of European Law*, and *Europarättsligt Tidskrift*. She also contributes to the editorial board of *EU-ret & Menneskeret*. Ulla Neergaard's research has carved niches in areas like the interplay between EU Law and Danish law, the foundational pillars of EU Law, and EU legal theory, method and research approaches, as well as the social dimensions of the EU and the many different dimensions of solidarity. She has also delved into contemporary challenges like digitalisation, European sovereignty, colonisation, defence and the implications of COVID-19. Ulla Neergaard has a repertoire of about 170 publications, the majority being international.

Passer, Jan studied at the Universita Karlova (Charles University, Czech Republic) where he obtained his law degree. He also completed a Masters of Laws at the Stockholms universitet (University of Stockholm, Sweden) in 2000. In 2007, he defended his doctoral thesis in law at the Universita Karlova. Since 1997, he has carried out a number of judicial functions in his home country, first as a trainee judge at the Městský soud v Praze (Prague City Court, Czech Republic), a position which he held until 2001, and then as a judge at the Obvodní soud pro Prahu 2 (Prague 2 District Court, Czech Republic), from 2001 to 2005. From 2005 to 2016, he was a judge at the Nejvyšší správní soud (Supreme Administrative Court, Czech Republic). The substantial experience gained during his practice took Mr Passer to teaching. He was a lecturer in, amongst other subjects, EU law at the Universita Karlova from 2001 to 2003, at the Masarykova univerzita (Masaryk University, Czech Republic) from 2006 to 2016, and at the Univerzita Palackého v Olomouci (Palacký University Olomouc, Czech Republic) from 2014 to 2016. That expertise also led him to teach law at the Judicial Academy of the Czech Republic from 2001 to 2016. Mr Passer was appointed as a Judge at the General Court of the European Union on 19 September 2016. He served at the General Court for four years before being appointed, on 6 October 2020, to his current role as a Judge at the Court of Justice.

Peers, Steve is a Professor of Law at Royal Holloway, University of London, United Kingdom. He is the author or co-author of many books and articles on EU Law, including *EU Justice and Home Affairs Law*, 5th edn (Oxford University Press, 2023), and the co-editor of many books on EU Law, including (with T Hervey, J Kenner and A Ward) *Commentary on the EU Charter of Fundamental Rights*, 2nd edn (Hart Publishing, 2021).

Regan, Eugene studied at University College Dublin, where he obtained a Degree in Politics and Economics in 1974 and a Master's Degree in Political Economy in 1975. He completed his university education with a Master's Degree in International and Comparative Law from the Université libre de Bruxelles (Free University of Brussels, Belgium) in 1979. Between 1975 and 1979, Mr Regan worked as an economist with the Irish Farmers' Association (IFA) and as Director of its Brussels Representative Office to the European Economic Community. He was Chief Executive of the Irish Meat Exporters Association from 1980 to 1984. He was a member of the cabinet of Peter Sutherland, then Commissioner for Competition at the European Commission, between 1985 and 1988. He returned to the agricultural sector as Commercial Director of a major Irish export company from 1989 to 1995. Mr Regan qualified as a Barrister at the Honourable Society of King's Inns (Dublin) in 1985. He practised at the Irish Bar in that capacity from 1995 to 2005 and then as Senior Counsel from 2005 to 2015. From 2007 to 2011, he was also a member of Seaned Éireann (the upper house of the Irish Parliament). Mr Regan was appointed a Judge of the European Court of Justice on 7 October 2015 and reappointed for a second term in 2021. He was elected President of the Fifth Chamber by his peers on 9 October 2018. Mr Regan is Vice-President of the Irish Centre for European Law and Bencher of the Honorable Society of King's Inns, Dublin.

Rennemo-Henriksen, Philip is an assistant attorney at the Danish law firm Gorrissen Federspiel. After graduating from the Faculty of Law of the University of Copenhagen in June 2022, Mr Rennemo-Henriksen has since then worked closely with Mr Saugmandsgaard Øe on all kinds of matters related to EU law, providing legal counsel to both Danish and international clients.

Ricci Chiara, Maria graduated in law from the Université catholique de Louvain (Belgium) (2012). She continued her studies at the College of Europe, where she obtained a Master of Arts in European Interdisciplinary Studies (2013). She has been working as a Legal Secretary (référendaire) in the chambers of Mr Bay Larsen for over seven years (2014–2015 and 2017–present).

Rossi, Lucia Serena is a Judge at the European Court of Justice; Professor of EU Law at the University of Bologna. Admitted as a lawyer to the Bologna Bar in 1985, she was Director of the International Research Centre on European Law of the University of Bologna (1998–2018); member of the Joint Managerial Committee of the China-EU School of Law of the China University of Political Science and Law (2011–2013). She has authored 18 books and more than 150 publications.

Safjan, Marek is a former Judge at the European Court of Justice, serving from 2009 to 2024. He is also a Professor Emeritus of the University of Warsaw, where from 1994 to 1997 he was a Vice-Chancellor. In 1997, he was appointed as a Judge of the Polish Constitutional Tribunal and served as its president from 1998 to 2006. He is the author of numerous publications in Civil Law, Medical Law and European Law. Vice-President of the International Academy of Comparative Law from 2010 to 2018.

Saugmandsgaard Øe, Henrik is a partner at the Danish law firm Gorrissen Federspiel. Mr Saugmandsgaard Øe is a former member of the European Court of Justice, where from 2015 to 2021 he fulfilled the role of Advocate General. From 2006 to 2014, he held the position of Danish Consumer Ombudsman.

Schmitt, Pierre is a Legal Secretary (référendaire) at the Court of Justice of the European Union. He graduated in Law at UCLouvain (Belgium) and obtained an LLM in International and Comparative Law at the Vrije Universiteit Brussel (Belgium). From 2005 to 2008, he worked as an attorney, prior to joining the Katholieke Universiteit Leuven (Belgium), where he became a Doctor of Laws in 2015, as a research fellow. Since 2016, he has been working in the chambers of Judge Jan Passer, first at the General Court and, since 2020, at the European Court of Justice.

Sørensen, Karsten Engsig is a Professor at the Department of Law, Aarhus University, Denmark. He holds a Danish Law Degree, an LLM (from Exeter), a PhD (on EU Company Law), and a Danish Dr Jur (on joint ventures). His research is mainly focused on EU Law and Company Law and in particular the regulation of the internal market. He is the coauthor of a comprehensive textbook on EU Law (EU-Retten) which is now in its 8th edition, and he has recently co-edited a book marking the 50 years anniversary of the Danish EU membership.

Sterck, Julien is a Legal Secretary (référendaire) at the European Court of Justice. Previously, he lectured in Ireland and in the United Kingdom. He graduated from the Université Montesquieu – Bordeaux IV and from the University of Kent. He holds a DEA from the Université Paris-X Nanterre and a PhD from University College Dublin and the University of Montesquieu Bordeaux IV.

Storey Hugo is a recently retired Judge of the Upper Tribunal (Immigration and Asylum Chamber) UK, one of the founding members of the International Association of Refugee and Migration Judges (IARMJ) and the honorary and immediate past President of the IARMJ's European Chapter. During his time as a Senior Immigration Judge, he initiated the tribunal country guidance system. From 2015–2022 he headed the judicial work on two projects between IARMJ-Europe and the European Asylum Support Office (EASO) (now European Union Asylum Agency (EUAA)) to review, update and develop core judicial training materials on asylum law in 27 Member States. In an academic capacity, he has published widely on human rights, refugee law, international law and European law issues. A former law lecturer in Leeds, he is a Research Fellow attached to the Refugee Law Initiative (RLI), University of London and, since February 2024, an Adjunct Professor at the Kaldor Centre, University of New South Wales, Sydney, Australia. His book on *The Refugee Definition in International Law* was published by Oxford University Press in October 2023.

Svenningsen, Jesper studied Law at Aarhus Universitet (University of Aarhus, Denmark), at the end of which he obtained the juridisk kandidateksamen in 1989. From 2006 to 2013, he was a Legal Secretary (référendaire) to Judge Lars Bay Larsen at the European Court of Justice. Mr Svenningsen was appointed a Judge of the Civil Service Tribunal on 7 October 2013 and served on that Tribunal until its dissolution on 1 September 2016. He was appointed a Judge at the General Court on 19 September 2016 and was elected President of Chamber by his peers on 30 September 2019.

Thorning, Christian is a senior Danish diplomat and Phd with specialities in EU and International Law. Currently Ambassador of Denmark to Iraq. Formerly, Principal Agent of Denmark before the Court of Justice of the European Union. All opinions expressed herein are personal to the author.

Vajda, Christopher KC was a Judge at the European Court of Justice from 2012 until 2020 (Brexit). He is a member of Monckton Chambers, London, a Visiting Professor at King's College, London, the College of Europe at Bruges and the University of Luxembourg. He is a graduate of the University of Cambridge and obtained a licence spéciale en droit européen at the Institut d'Etudes Européennes in Brussels. He was called to the Bar of England and Wales in 1979 and was appointed a QC in 1997. He is a Bencher of Gray's Inn, London and served as a Recorder of the Crown Court in England (part-time judge) between 2003 and 2012. He is a member of the Luxembourg Bar, of the EU panel of Chairpersons for Arbitrations to which the EU is a party, the Panel of Recognised International Market Experts in Finance (P.R.I.M.E), and the UK Sports Resolutions panel.

Xuereb, Peter George studied at the Università ta' Malta (University of Malta) where he graduated with a Degree in Law in 1977, and studied at the University of London (UK) where he obtained a Master of Laws in 1979. In 1982, he was awarded a doctorate in law by the University of Cambridge (UK). Mr Xuereb started his career as a lecturer at Ealing College of Higher Education (UK) from 1982 to 1984, which he continued at the University of Exeter (UK) from 1984 to 1990, and at Queen Mary and Westfield College, University of London, from 1990 to 1993. Between 1993 and 2016, he taught law as a Professor at the Università ta' Malta, where he was also Head of the Department of European and Comparative Law. At the same time, he was President of the European Documentation and Research Centre at that university. That position provided him with an opportunity to author numerous publications in a variety of fields. He was admitted as an advocate of the superior courts of Malta in 1979. From 1993 to 2016, he combined his academic activities with his work as a legal adviser in the private sector. During the same period, Mr Xuereb also worked as a consultant for the Maltese Parliament. From 1995 to 2016, he contributed to the development of the dissemination of EU Law as President of the Malta European Law Association. On 8 June 2016, Mr Xuereb was appointed as a Judge at the General Court. Since 8 October 2018, he has been carrying out that role at the European Court of Justice.

Ziemele, Ineta PhD (Cantab) is a Professor of International Law and Human Rights at the Riga Graduate School of Law (Latvia) and a Judge at the European Court of Justice former President of the Constitutional Court of Latvia. She is a former Judge at the European Court of Human Rights and President of Section; a corresponding member of the Latvian Academy of Sciences and an editor-in-chief of the *Baltic Yearbook of International Law*.

Part I

The Area of Freedom, Security and Justice Framework

1

The Concept of Public Policy in the Area of Freedom, Security and Justice

KOEN LENAERTS*

I. INTRODUCTION

WHEN DOES A third-country national constitute a 'threat to public policy'? Is it enough for such a third-country national to have been convicted of whatever kind of criminal offence? Is there *a single* concept of 'threat to public policy' that applies across the entire Area of Freedom, Security and Justice (AFSJ) or does the meaning of that concept vary depending on the EU directive or regulation at issue?

The purpose of this contribution is to honour my dear friend and colleague, Vice-President Bay Larsen, by looking at those questions in the light of the relevant case law of the European Court of Justice (ECJ). It is worth noting that Vice-President Bay Larsen acted as reporting judge in some of the cases that will be examined below.[1] This shows that his contribution to the development of EU law in general and to that of the AFSJ in particular has been of tremendous importance throughout his 18-year mandate.

The present contribution is divided into three substantive parts. Part II explores the free-movement origins of the concept of 'threat to public policy', holding that the ECJ has borrowed that concept in order to interpret EU regulations and directives adopted in the AFSJ context. In Part III it is submitted that subsequently, the ECJ has taken some distance from free movement law, by favouring an approach that focuses on the normative environment in which the concept of 'threat to public policy' is applied. That new approach shows that the concept of 'threat to public policy' resulting from free movement law is not the only option available to the EU legislature. On the contrary, the latter may decide to define that concept by referring to standards that are 'markedly less stringent' than those resulting from free movement law,[2] thereby giving more leeway to the Member States when determining the existence of such a threat.[3] Part IV shows, however, that the new approach does not necessarily lead to a different outcome, since

* President of the European Court of Justice and Professor of European Union Law, Leuven University. All opinions expressed herein are personal to the author.

[1] See, in this regard, Case C-380/18 *EP (Threat to public policy)*, ECLI:EU:C:2019:1071; Joined Cases C-381/18 and C-382/18 *GS and VG (Threat to public policy)*, ECLI:EU:C:2019:1072; and Case C-8/22 *Commissaire général aux réfugiés et aux apatrides (Refugee who has committed a serious crime)*, ECLI:EU:C:2023:542.

[2] *GS and VG (Threat to public policy)* (n 1), para 57.

[3] See, in this regard, D Thym, *European Migration Law* (Oxford University Press, 2023) 261 (observing that '[a] common thread of the judgments on migration law is to give states more leeway').

the EU legislature may decide to embrace a definition of 'threat to public policy' that mirrors that applied under free movement law. Finally, a brief conclusion is presented that supports the contention that the concept of 'threat to public policy' in the AFSJ must be defined in a way that ensures both continuity and change. *Continuity* because the way in which the EU legislature defines the concept of 'threat to public policy' must comply with primary EU law and, notably, with the principle of proportionality, understood as a general principle of EU law. *Change* because that concept must be defined in keeping with the degree of discretion that the EU legislature has conferred on national authorities, which may vary across the AFSJ.

II. THE INFLUENCE OF FREE MOVEMENT LAW

In the field of free movement law, the Member States may restrict the freedom of movement and residence of Union citizens on grounds of public policy. In the seminal *Bouchereau* judgment, decided in the 1970s, the ECJ provided two requirements that measures adopted on 'public policy' grounds must fulfil. Those two requirements are still good law today and have been codified by Directive 2004/38.[4]

First, since those measures constitute a derogation from the right to free movement, the concept of public policy is subject to strict interpretation.[5] Not all infringements of the law necessarily entail a threat to public policy, since such a threat must be genuine and sufficiently serious, affecting one of the fundamental interests of society.[6] It is, in essence, this definition of 'threat to public policy' that can be found in Article 27(2) of Directive 2004/38. That said, the ECJ did recognise that 'the particular circumstances justifying recourse to the concept of public policy may vary from one [Member State] to another and from one period to another'. That is why the competent national authorities must enjoy 'an area of discretion' when defining those circumstances, 'within the limits imposed by the [Treaty] and the provisions adopted for its implementation'.[7]

Second, a prior criminal conviction does not suffice as such to justify a public policy restriction on free movement. The past conduct of the person concerned is only relevant if it demonstrates his or her propensity to act in the same way in the future.[8] Subsequently, the ECJ would add that national measures grounded in public policy considerations require a case-by-case assessment, which rules out measures of a general preventive nature.[9] Most importantly, for present purposes, when applying the concept of public policy, the Member State concerned must comply with the principle of proportionality. This means, for example, that it must take into account the social danger brought about by the presence of the person concerned, the nature of the offending activities and the time lapsed between the acts committed and the behaviour of the person concerned.[10]

[4] Directive 2004/38/EC of the European Parliament and of the Council of 29 April 2004 on the right of citizens of the Union and their family members to move and reside freely within the territory of the Member States amending Regulation (EEC) No 1612/68 and repealing Directives 64/221/EEC, 68/360/EEC, 72/194/EEC, 73/148/EEC, 75/34/EEC, 75/35/EEC, 90/364/EEC, 90/365/EEC and 93/96/EEC [2004] OJ L158/77.

[5] Case 30/77 *Bouchereau*, ECLI:EU:C:1977:172, para 33 (referring to Case 41/74 *Van Duyn*, ECLI:EU:C:1974:133).

[6] ibid, para 35.

[7] ibid, para 34.

[8] ibid, para 29.

[9] See eg Cases 67/74 *Bonsignore*, ECLI:EU:C:1975:34; C-482/01 and C-493/01 *Orfanopoulos and Oliveri*, ECLI:EU:C:2004:262, para 68; and C-165/14 *Rendón Marín*, ECLI:EU:C:2016:675, para 61.

[10] See, in this regard, E Guild et al, *The EU Citizenship Directive: A Commentary* (Oxford University Press, 2014) 258–59.

In the AFSJ, the ECJ has drawn on the *Bouchereau* line of case law in order to adopt the same definition of 'threat (or risk) to public policy' as that applied under free movement law. Three examples taken from the case law may illustrate this point.

First, in *Zh and O*,[11] the ECJ was asked to interpret Article 7(4) of the Return Directive,[12] according to which Member States may refrain from granting a period for voluntary departure (or grant a period shorter than seven days), if the person concerned poses a risk to public policy. Given that the Return Directive does not define the concept of 'risk to public policy', that concept had to be examined in the light of the wording of Article 7(4) thereof, its context and the objective it pursues. It followed from that examination that Article 7(4) of the Return Directive constitutes 'a justification for derogating from an obligation designed to ensure that the fundamental rights of third-country nationals are respected when they are removed from the [EU]'.[13] As such, this meant that that provision was to be interpreted strictly. Accordingly, in applying the *Bouchereau* judgment by analogy, the ECJ concluded that the concept of 'risk to public policy', within the meaning of Article 7(4) of the Return Directive, 'presupposes, in any event, the existence [...] of a genuine, present and sufficiently serious threat affecting one of the fundamental interests of society'.[14]

Second, the ECJ reached a similar conclusion in interpreting Article 8(3) of the Reception Directive.[15] In *N*,[16] it held that in order to place or to keep an applicant for international protection in detention 'when protection of national security or public order so requires',[17] such an applicant must constitute 'a genuine, present and sufficiently serious threat affecting one of the fundamental interests of society'.[18] That strict approach was justified because of both the exceptional nature of the detention and the strict limits within which national authorities use detention.

Third and last, in *T*,[19] a case which concerned the interpretation of Article 24(1) of the Qualification Directive,[20] according to which a Member State shall issue to beneficiaries of refugee status a residence permit, 'unless compelling reasons of public order otherwise require'. The ECJ adopted the same definition of 'public order' as that of 'public policy' contained in

[11] Case C-554/13 *Zh and O*, ECLI:EU:C:2015:377.

[12] Directive 2008/115/EC of the European Parliament and of the Council of 16 December 2008 on common standards and procedures in Member States for returning illegally staying third-country nationals [2008] OJ L348/98.

[13] *Zh and O* (n 11), para 48.

[14] ibid, para 60.

[15] Directive 2013/33/EU of the European Parliament and of the Council of 26 June 2013 laying down standards for the reception of applicants for international protection [2013] OJ L180/96.

[16] Case C-601/15 PPU *N*, ECLI:EU:C:2016:84.

[17] It is worth noting that the French concept of '*ordre public*' has not been uniformly translated into the other official languages of the EU. In English, in some cases it is translated using the expression 'public policy' (eg the Return Directive), whilst in others the expression 'public order' is used instead (eg the Qualification Directive and the Reception Directive). In her Opinion in Case C-554/13 *Zh and O*, ECLI:EU:C:2015:94, point 29 ff, AG Sharpston posited that those two expressions 'are not synonyms', since the expression 'public order' has to be interpreted more strictly than that of 'public policy'. However, for present purposes, that semantic debate is, to some extent, rendered moot by the fact that in the cases relating to the concept of 'public order' (which are examined in this contribution), the Court of Justice defined that concept by drawing on the definition of 'public policy' applied under free movement law. See, in this regard, *N* (n 16), para 65, and Case C-373/13 *T*, ECLI:EU:C:2015:413, paras 77–79.

[18] *N* (n 16), para 67.

[19] *T* (n 17).

[20] Council Directive 2004/83/EC of 29 April 2004 on minimum standards for the qualification and status of third-country nationals or stateless persons as refugees or as persons who otherwise need international protection and the content of the protection granted [2004] OJ L304/12, repealed by Directive 2011/95/EU of the European Parliament and of the Council of 13 December 2011 on standards for the qualification of third-country nationals or stateless persons as beneficiaries of international protection, for a uniform status for refugees or for persons eligible for subsidiary protection, and for the content of the protection granted (recast) [2011] OJ L337/9.

Directive 2004/38. It justified its interpretation, holding that 'the extent of the protection a society intends to afford to its fundamental interests cannot vary depending on the legal status of the person that undermines those interests'.[21] Arguably, this would suggest a common definition of 'public policy' (public order) under EU law, despite the fact that, as the ECJ itself acknowledged, those two directives pursue different objectives.

The approach followed by the ECJ in *Zh and O* and *N* may be explained by the fact that the provisions in question constituted either a derogation to the general scheme established by the EU legislature, or imposed a serious limitation on the exercise of the fundamental rights of the applicant for international protection. By contrast, as the cases examined below will show, it seems to me that the ECJ has implicitly abandoned the approach it followed in *T* – according to which there is a unique definition of 'threat to public policy' (public order) for Union citizens and for third-country nationals. This is because, in subsequent case law, the ECJ has consistently emphasised the possibility for the EU legislature to define the concept of 'threat to public policy' differently, allowing room for a larger margin of discretion to the Member States. This does not mean, however, that the *Bouchereau* line of case law is no longer relevant for the purposes of developing and maintaining the AFSJ. However, when compared with the *T* judgment, the approach under which the ECJ draws on free movement law has changed significantly, since the ECJ appears to focus on the specific normative environment in which that concept is to be applied.[22]

III. TAKING SOME DISTANCE FROM FREE MOVEMENT LAW

In *Koushkaki*,[23] the ECJ was asked to interpret the concept of 'threat to public policy', within the meaning of the Visa Code,[24] as a ground of refusal to issue a uniform visa. The ECJ did not apply the *Bouchereau* line of case law, preferring instead to adopt a concept that granted wide discretion to national authorities in assessing the existence of such a threat.[25] The ECJ reached a similar result in *Fahimiam*,[26] which concerned a refusal to issue a student visa as provided for by Directive 2004/114.[27] Referring to Article 6(1)(d) of that Directive, read in the light of Recital 14 thereof, it held that, 'in contrast [...] to Directive 2004/38', the threat does not have to be 'genuine, present and sufficiently serious' but might be only potential. 'That assessment', the ECJ wrote, 'may thus take into account not only the personal conduct of the applicant but also other elements relating, in particular, to his professional career'.[28] In addition, the ECJ observed that, in order to assess whether such a threat exists, national authorities must carry out complex evaluations that seek to predict the foreseeable conduct of the applicant for a visa.[29]

[21] *T* (n 17), para 77.

[22] Opinion of AG Pitruzzella in Case C-380/18 *EP (Threat to public policy)*, ECLI:EU:C:2019:609, para 32.

[23] Case C-84/12 *Koushkaki*, ECLI:EU:C:2013:862.

[24] Regulation (EC) No 810/2009 of the European Parliament and of the Council of 13 July 2009 establishing a Community Code on Visas (Visa Code) [2009] OJ L243/1.

[25] *Koushkaki* (n 23), paras 57–60.

[26] Case C-544/15 *Fahimian*, ECLI:EU:C:2017:255.

[27] Council Directive 2004/114/EC of 13 December 2004 on the conditions of admission of third-country nationals for the purposes of studies, pupil exchange, unremunerated training or voluntary service [2004] OJ L375/12.

[28] *Fahimian* (n 26), para 40. Although that judgment concerned the concept of 'public security' within the meaning of Directive 2004/114, it is worth noting that the concept of 'public policy' is also laid down in both Art 6(1)(d) of that Directive and Recital 14 thereof. In fact, both concepts appear next to each other, meaning that the same findings apply *mutatis mutandis*.

[29] ibid, para 41.

The potential nature of the threat, coupled with the complexity of those evaluations, means that national authorities enjoy a wide margin of discretion in assessing the relevant facts when applying Directive 2004/114.[30] That wide discretion translated into interpreting 'the kindred concept of threat to public [policy] more broadly than it is in the case law relating to persons enjoying the right of free movement'.[31]

Koushkaki and *Fahimian* may be seen as two stepping stones allowing the ECJ to develop a new approach when interpreting the concept of 'threat to public policy' in the AFSJ. That approach is explained by the ECJ in two seminal judgments delivered on the same day. Those two judgments were delivered in the context of three references made by the Dutch Council of State (*Raad van State*), namely *EP (Threat to public policy)* concerning the Schengen Borders Code (SBC),[32] and *GS and VG (Threat to public policy)*, which were joined, both concerning the Family Reunification Directive (FRD).[33]

In *EP (Threat to public policy)*,[34] the ECJ was asked to determine whether a third-country national not subject to a visa requirement constituted a threat to public policy, within the meaning of Article 6(1)(e) of the SBC,[35] because he or she was suspected of having committed a criminal offence. According to that provision of the SBC, a third-country national may only enter into and stay in the territory of the Member States in so far as he or she is not a threat to public policy. If he or she is such a threat, he or she may not enter the EU. If he or she has entered, then his or her stay is illegal and may therefore be subject to a return order. Obviously, if the findings of national authorities are based exclusively on past criminal conduct, the application of the *Bouchereau* line of case law would suggest that such a threat does not exist. However, the ECJ decided to develop a different approach.

At the outset, the ECJ described the evolution of the case law examined above. First, it recalled the concept of 'threat to public policy' within the meaning of the *Bouchereau* line of case law, as codified by Directive 2004/38.[36] Second, referring to *Zh and O*, *N* and *T*, it observed that the concept had been interpreted 'in the same way' in the context of a number of directives adopted in the AFSJ.[37] That was not always the case, however, and the ECJ therefore held, third, that 'any reference by the EU legislature to the concept of "threat to public policy" does not necessarily have to be understood as referring exclusively to individual conduct representing a genuine, present and sufficiently serious threat affecting one of the fundamental interests of the society of the Member State concerned'.[38] To that end, it referred to its previous judgment in *Fahimian*.

Next, that evolution came to demonstrate that it was necessary to develop an approach which focused on the normative environment in which the concept of 'threat to public policy' is applied. This meant that the ECJ had to look at the wording, the context and the objectives pursued by Article 6(1)(e) of the SBC. The wording did not 'expressly' reproduce the

[30] ibid, para 42.

[31] See, in this regard, *EP (Threat to public policy)* (n 1), para 32 (referring to *Fahimian* (n 26), para 40).

[32] Regulation (EU) 2016/399 of the European Parliament and the Council of 9 March 2016 on a Union Code on the rules governing the movement of persons across borders (Schengen Borders Code) [2016] OJ L77/1.

[33] Council Directive 2003/86/EC of 22 September 2003 on the right to family reunification [2003] OJ L251/12.

[34] *EP (Threat to public policy)* (n 1).

[35] That provision reads as follows: 'For intended stays on the territory of the Member States of a duration of no more than 90 days in any 180-day period [ie for short stays] […] the entry conditions for third-country nationals shall be the following: they are not considered to be a threat to public policy […], in particular where no alert has been issued in Member States' national data bases for the purposes of refusing entry on the same grounds'.

[36] *EP (Threat to public policy)* (n 1), para 29.

[37] ibid, para 30.

[38] ibid, para 31.

concept of 'threat to public policy' as set out in Directive 2004/38. Regarding the context, the ECJ observed that, since national authorities enjoy wide discretion in determining whether the conditions to issue a Schengen visa are complied with, they should enjoy the same discretion in determining whether the short stay of a third-country national is illegal. Moreover, Article 6(1)(e) of the SBC was worded differently from Article 8(2) of the SBC, which only applies to 'persons enjoying the right to free movement under [EU] law' and contains the same definition of 'threat to public policy' as that set out in Directive 2004/38. Finally, regarding the objectives pursued by the SBC, the ECJ stressed the fact that border control should help to prevent 'any threat' to public policy. Drawing on the textual, contextual and teleological interpretation of the SBC, the ECJ came to the conclusion that a third-country national who is suspected of having committed a criminal offence may constitute a threat to public policy, *without* national authorities having to establish 'that his or her conduct represents a genuine, present and sufficiently serious threat affecting one of the fundamental interests of the society of the Member State concerned'.[39]

That said, the ECJ added that the concept of 'threat to public policy', within the meaning of Article 6(1)(e) of the SBC, had to be interpreted in keeping with the principle of proportionality, a general principle of EU law. This meant, first, that the criminal offence that the person concerned is suspected of having committed is 'sufficiently serious, in the light of its nature and of the punishment which may be imposed, to justify that national's stay on the territory of the Member States being brought to an immediate end'. Second, any suspicions of national authorities must be based on 'consistent, objective and specific evidence'.[40]

The ECJ followed a similar approach in *GS and VG (Threat to public policy)*. In those cases, it was asked to determine whether a national authority could reject an application for entry and residence, withdraw a residence permit or refuse to renew it on the ground that the person concerned constituted a 'threat to public policy', within the meaning of Article 6(1) and (2) of the FRD. In one case, Dutch authorities decided not to renew – and to withdraw retroactively – the residence permit of the person concerned because a sentence sufficiently severe in comparison with the duration of his stay in the Netherlands had been imposed on him. In the other case, the person concerned applied for a residence permit under the FRD but his application was rejected because he had a criminal conviction imposed during a previous stay in the Netherlands.

Again, the ECJ developed the same approach as that put forward in *EP (Threat to public policy)*, taking some distance from free movement law and focusing instead on the normative environment in which the concept of 'threat to public policy' is applied. First, the ECJ stressed the fact that Article 6(1) and (2) of the FRD do not expressly refer to the definition of 'threat to public policy' as laid down in Directive 2004/38. In particular, Article 6(2) of that Directive states that in withdrawing or refusing to renew a residence permit, national authorities are required to consider 'the severity or type of the offence' at issue and 'the dangers that are emanating' from the person concerned, as well as his or her degree of integration. In that regard, the ECJ held that 'that obligation refers to a standard that is markedly less stringent than the standard resulting from the case law [on free movement]'.[41] Similarly, it noted that the wording of those provisions did not 'establish a link between the concept of "threat to public policy" and the risk of one of the fundamental interests of

[39] ibid, para 46.
[40] ibid, paras 48–49.
[41] *GS and VG (Threat to public policy)* (n 1), para 57.

society being adversely affected'. As to the context, the ECJ pointed out that Recital 14 of the FRD stated that 'the [concept] of public policy may cover a conviction for committing a serious crime'. Most importantly for present purposes, the amended proposal for the FRD had initially based the concept of 'threat to public policy' on the personal conduct of the person concerned. However, that approach was finally rejected by the EU legislature. As to the objectives pursued by the FRD, the ECJ recalled that since authorisation of family reunification is the general rule, Article 6(1) and (2) of the FRD have to be interpreted strictly. That said, and in the light of the foregoing considerations, the ECJ concluded that national authorities are not precluded from applying those provisions 'in reliance solely upon the fact that the person concerned has been convicted of a criminal offence'. This meant that the concept of 'threat to public policy' did not require establishing that 'the individual conduct of that person represents a genuine, present and sufficiently serious threat affecting one of the fundamental interests of the society of the Member State concerned'.

Again, just as it did in *EP (Threat to public policy)*, the ECJ recalled that the FRD had to be interpreted in the light of the principle of proportionality. This meant that a criminal conviction could not, as such, automatically amount to considering the person concerned to be a threat to public policy. In addition, a third-country national is a threat to public policy 'only if [the criminal] offence is so serious, or of such a type, that it is necessary to rule out the residence of that national on the territory of the Member State concerned'. Moreover, in the cases of withdrawal of, or refusal to renew, a residence permit, the EU legislature requires national authorities to carry out an individual assessment of the situation of the person concerned. That assessment should take due account of his or her family relationships, the duration of his or her residence in the Member State and the existence of family, cultural and social ties with his or her country of origin.

IV. UNDERSTANDING THE NEW APPROACH

In *EP (Threat to public policy)* and *GS and VG (Threat to public policy)*, the ECJ focuses on the normative environment in which the concept of 'threat to public policy' is applied. In my view, three implications flow from those two judgments.

First, the ECJ seeks to highlight the distinction between Union citizens and third-country nationals when considering them to be a threat to public policy.[42] To that end, the Treaty provisions on Union citizenship require compliance with the principle of not submitting Union citizens to conditions that are *less favourable* than those applicable to third-country nationals. That principle was explicitly put forward by the ECJ in *Ordre des barreaux francophones et germanophone and Others (Preventive measures for removal)*.[43] There, it held that:

> measures aimed at avoiding the risk of absconding which may be imposed in the context of the expulsion of Union citizens and their family members on grounds of public policy or public security

[42] See, however, E Brouwer, 'Challenges to EU Legality in the Field of Asylum and Migration Law' in C Kilpatrick and J Scott (eds), *Contemporary Challenges to EU Legality* (Oxford University Press, 2021) 59 (who argues that 'when the protection of public order within the EU is at stake, and it is necessary to assess the nature and scope of the threat the presence of an individual on the territory would involve, the nationality or status of this person is irrelevant'). For a summary of the academic debate on this point, see K Eisele, 'Public Security and Admission to the EU of Foreign Students' (2018) *Common Market Law Review* 279, 292–94.

[43] Case C-718/19 *Ordre des barreaux francophones et germanophone and Others (Preventive measures for removal)*, ECLI:EU:C:2021:505.

> *cannot be less favourable* than measures provided for under national law to avoid the risk of third-country nationals absconding, during the period for voluntary departure, where such third-country nationals are subject to a return procedure under Directive 2008/115 on grounds of public policy or public security.[44] (emphasis added)

It follows from this principle that the EU legislature is precluded from adopting a definition of the concept of 'threat to public policy' under which a third-country national is *not* considered to be such a threat, whilst a Union citizen who is in an objectively comparable situation is for the purposes of the relevant provisions of EU law.

However, the same does not hold true the other way around. For example, in relation to family members of Union citizens, the *Bouchereau* line of case law applies, whilst this is not the case in the context of the FRD. Why is that? As explained above, this is due to the choices made by the EU legislature. Also, and perhaps most importantly, the freedom of movement for individuals is one of the foundations of the EU and, as such, 'the provisions laying down [that freedom] must be given a broad interpretation, whereas exceptions to and derogations from that freedom must be interpreted strictly'. In the realm of free movement law, the policy choices of the EU legislature are severely limited by the Treaties. This is, however, not the case in the AFSJ, whose establishment and development cannot be driven at the level of primary EU law, but requires activating the political process.

That said, there are cases where it is impossible to draw a distinction between Union citizens and third-country nationals when considering them to be a threat to public policy. In particular, where the threat to public policy is a health threat caused by the conduct of Union citizens and third-country nationals alike, the case law suggests that the definition of 'threat to public policy' under free movement law applies. This is, for example, the case of a pandemic of a scale such as that of COVID-19 since, as human beings, we all may catch and pass on that virus. In *NORDIC INFO*,[45] the ECJ was asked to determine whether Belgium was permitted to reintroduce internal border controls temporarily – as provided for by Articles 25 to 28 of the SBC – on public health grounds connected with combating the COVID-19 pandemic. Pursuant to Article 25(1) of the SBC, that reintroduction is only allowed, 'where […] there is a serious threat to public policy or internal security'. The ECJ began by noting that, in some circumstances, a health threat may amount to a threat to public policy and/or internal security.[46] It then went on to interpret the concept of 'serious threat to public policy', within the meaning of Article 25(1) of the SBC, as follows. '[It] entails the existence – in addition to the disturbance of the social order which any infringement of the law involves – of a genuine, present and sufficiently serious threat affecting one of the fundamental interests of society'.[47] Thus, the ECJ adopted the same definition of that concept as that applied under free movement law.[48] In the case at hand, the ECJ found that the COVID-19 pandemic constituted a serious threat, since it was:

> liable to affect one of the fundamental interests of society, namely that of ensuring the lives of citizens while preserving the proper functioning of the healthcare system and the provision of care

[44] ibid, para 57.

[45] Case C-128/22 *NORDIC INFO*, ECLI:EU:C:2023:951.

[46] ibid, para 126 (referring to Case C-137/09 *Josemans*, ECLI:EU:C:2010:774, para 65).

[47] ibid (referring to *N* (n 16), paras 65–66).

[48] It is worth noting that, in *NORDIC INFO* (n 45), para 126, the ECJ also referred to Case C-331/16 and C-366/16 *K and HF (Right of residence and alleged war crimes)*, ECLI:EU:C:2018:296, para 42, which is a case concerning the interpretation of Directive 2004/38.

appropriate to the population, and also affects the very survival of a part of the population, in particular the most vulnerable.[49]

As to the second implication, the new approach developed by the ECJ in the two judgments mentioned above does not necessarily rule out the application of the *Bouchereau* line of case law. The textual, contextual and teleological interpretation of the EU provision in question may militate in favour of applying that line of case law. This is precisely what the ECJ did in *Commissaire général aux réfugiés et aux apatrides (Refugee who has committed a serious crime)*.[50] This case concerned Article 14(4)(b) of the Qualification Directive (recast),[51] according to which a Member State may revoke, end or refuse to renew refugee status 'when [the third-country national], having been convicted by a final judgment of a particularly serious crime, constitutes *a danger to the community* of that Member State' (emphasis added). *Again*, in that case, the ECJ recalled the definition of 'threat to public policy' under free movement law. *Again*, the ECJ stressed the fact that this definition is not the only option available to the EU legislature in the AFSJ. *And again*, the ECJ proceeded to examine in detail the normative environment in which the concept of 'danger to the community' is applied. Regarding the wording of that provision, the ECJ inferred from the verb 'constitute' that the 'danger' had to be 'genuine' and 'present'. Next, regarding the normative context, the ECJ observed that the Qualification Directive (recast) lays down measures with varying degrees of intensity that national authorities may adopt against beneficiaries of refugee status. They range from refusing to issue a residence permit (Article 24), revoking refugee status (Article 14(4)), to ordering the refoulement of a refugee where it is not prohibited by the Geneva Convention (Article 21). It is worth noting that both Articles 14(4)(b) and 21(2)(b) are worded in identical terms, which means that those two provisions must be interpreted consistently. Moreover, the ECJ observed that in *T*, it had already interpreted the concept of 'compelling reasons of public order' set out in Article 24(1) of the Qualification Directive. That provision states that national authorities shall issue to beneficiaries of refugee status a residence permit, 'unless compelling reasons of public order otherwise require'. As mentioned above, in *T*, the ECJ interpreted that provision by referring to free movement law. It held that those compelling reasons 'only [exist] where the third-country national concerned constitutes a genuine, present and sufficiently serious threat affecting one of the fundamental interests of society'. Whilst it is true that Articles 14(4)(b) and 21(2)(b) of the Qualification Directive mention 'danger to the community' instead of 'public order', this did not justify applying a different standard between that provision and the other two. This was because revoking, ending or refusing to renew refugee status – and indeed, ordering the refoulement of a refugee – is 'subject to rigorous conditions that are more onerous than those that apply' when refusing to issue a residence permit. Stated differently, the more onerous the measure is, the more rigorous the conditions for its application are. Thus, the conditions for identifying the existence of a threat to public order (in order to refuse to issue a residence permit) cannot be more rigorous than those for identifying a danger to the community (in order to revoke refugee status or to order the refoulement of a refugee). Compliance with the internal coherence of the Qualification Directive thus required the application of the same standard for those three

[49] *NORDIC INFO* (n 45), para 127.
[50] *Commissaire général aux réfugiés et aux apatrides (Refugee who has committed a serious crime)* (n 1).
[51] See n 20.

provisions. This was corroborated by the teleological interpretation of the Qualification Directive (recast), which requires Article 14(4)(b) of that Directive to be interpreted strictly. Accordingly, the ECJ held that:

> a measure referred to in Article 14(4)(b) of Directive 2011/95 may be adopted only where the third-country national concerned constitutes a genuine, present and sufficiently serious threat to one of the fundamental interests of the society of the Member State in which he or she is present.

Third and last, the principle of proportionality operates as a limit to the choices made by the EU legislature. It may decide to depart from the concept of 'threat to public policy' under free movement law. However, in so doing, it may not grant national authorities a margin of discretion that, for example, does not guarantee compliance with fundamental rights. The judgments of the ECJ in *Zh and O* and *N* illustrate this point. Had they been decided following the new approach, I am certain that the ECJ would have reached the same outcome, ie adopting the same definition of 'threat to public policy' (public order) as that applied under free movement law. This is because both the normative environment of the EU provision at issue and the principle of proportionality played a decisive role in the reasoning of the ECJ.[52] In *Zh and O*, the ECJ interpreted Article 7(4) of the Return Directive in the light of its wording, its context and the objectives it pursues. It also held that the application of that provision is conditional on a 'case-by-case assessment' and compliance with the principle of proportionality, which rules out any general practice or any assumption in order to examine the existence of a risk to public policy. The conduct of the third-country national had to pose a 'genuine and present risk to public policy'. Moreover, the ECJ noted, in the light of a contextual interpretation of that provision of the Return Directive, that the 'risk to public policy' had to be understood in the sense of 'threat'. All these elements pointed towards adopting the same definition of 'risk (threat) to public policy' as that applied under free movement law.

Similarly, in *N*, the reasoning of the ECJ is developed in keeping with the principle of proportionality. In that case, the ECJ was asked to examine the validity of point (e) of the first subparagraph of Article 8(3) of the Reception Directive in the light of the fundamental right to liberty enshrined in Article 6 of the Charter. As mentioned above, according to that provision, an applicant for international protection may be detained 'when protection of national security or public order so requires'. Pursuant to Article 52(1) of the Charter, that examination required the ECJ to determine whether point (e) of the first subparagraph of Article 8(3) of the Reception Directive complied with the principle of proportionality. In that context, the ECJ stressed the fact that, because of the importance of the fundamental right to liberty and the gravity of the interference with that right, limitations on its exercise 'must apply only in so far as is strictly necessary'. That was the reason why the Reception Directive lays down a 'strictly circumscribed framework', which subjects detention to a series of conditions that are accompanied by significant legal and procedural safeguards and limits. Moreover, 'detention is to be used only as a last resort'. Logically, since that framework seeks to circumscribe strictly the powers of national authorities to detain an applicant for international protection, the concept of 'public order' had to be interpreted strictly. A strict version of the principle of proportionality thus requires the application of that concept as defined under free movement law.

[52] *N* (n 16).

V. CONCLUSION

The new approach to interpreting the concept of 'threat to public policy' in the AFSJ is, first and foremost, methodological. The ECJ has developed a new framework of analysis which highlights the fact that the AFSJ is different from free movement law. It is important to examine the normative environment in which that concept is applied before drawing on free movement law. This means, in essence, that the ECJ rejects an automatic transplantation of the *Boucherau* line of case law into the AFSJ.

In my view, this is correct because, unlike the Treaty provisions on free movement and Union citizenship which directly confer rights upon individuals, the development and establishment of the AFSJ require the active intervention of the EU legislature. In that area, the concept of 'threat to public policy' is subject to the policy choices of the EU legislature. That is why the ECJ is right in focusing on the normative environment in which that concept is applied. However, when defining the margin of discretion enjoyed by national authorities in assessing the existence of such a threat, those policy choices are circumscribed by primary EU law. As a result, the EU legislature enjoys a 'spectrum of choice' within which it may define that concept.

At one end of that spectrum, where Union citizens and third-country nationals are in an objectively comparable situation, the concept of 'threat to public policy' in the AFSJ may not impose stricter standards than those applicable under free movement law. Union citizenship, which 'is intended to be the fundamental status of nationals of the Member States',[53] would oppose such a difference in treatment. The EU legislature is therefore precluded from adopting a definition of that concept under which a third-country national is not considered to be a threat to public policy, whilst a Union citizen who is in an objectively comparable situation constitutes such a threat, for the purposes of the relevant provisions of EU law.

At the other end of the spectrum, where the EU legislature decides to endorse less stringent standards than those applicable under free movement law, the principle of proportionality is of paramount importance for ensuring that granting a wider margin of discretion to national authorities does not allow room for arbitrary decisions. Moreover, the principle of proportionality also permits 'variable geometry' within the AFSJ, since compliance with that principle may impose different requirements depending on the EU act in question and even depending on the provision in question within the same EU act. For example, when deciding whether a third-country national who is suspected of having committed a crime constitutes a threat to public policy for the purposes of Article 6(1)(e) of the SBC, compliance with the principle of proportionality only requires national authorities to determine whether the crime is so serious that it is necessary to rule out residence of that national on the territory of the Member State, and to rely on consistent, objective and specific evidence that provides grounds for suspecting that he or she has committed such a crime. By contrast, in the context of the FRD, the existence of a threat to public policy requires more than those suspicions. It requires the third-country national concerned to have been actually convicted of a serious crime, and compels national authorities to look at the individual situation of the person concerned. Similarly, the concept of 'threat to public policy' may vary in the application of the SBC, depending on whether the provision at issue refers only to the situation of

[53] See, to that effect, Cases C-34/09 *Ruiz Zambrano*, ECLI:EU:C:2011:124, para 41; and C-673/20 *Préfet du Gers and Institut national de la statistique et des études économiques*, ECLI:EU:C:2022:449, para 49 and the case law cited.

third-country nationals,[54] only to that of persons enjoying the right to free movement,[55] or to that of both categories.[56]

In my view, the judgments of the ECJ in *EP (Threat to public policy)* and *GS and VG (Threat to public policy)* constitute two positive and important developments that highlight the specific features of the AFSJ. Those features require both continuity and change: the EU legislature must continue to develop that area in keeping with primary EU law, and notably with the principle of proportionality, whilst allowing room for change in so far as its policy choices may take some distance from free movement law.

[54] See Art 6(1)(e) of the SBC.
[55] Recital 27 and Art 8(2) of the SBC.
[56] See Art 25 ff of the SBC, in the context of the COVID-19 pandemic.

2

Judicial Cooperation in Criminal Matters: Two Sides of Institutional Evolution

EUGENE REGAN*

I. INTRODUCTION

COUNCIL FRAMEWORK DECISION 2002/584/JHA of 13 June 2002 on the European arrest warrant (EAW) and the surrender procedures between Member States (the EAW Framework Decision)[1] was the first measure implementing the principle of mutual recognition in criminal matters. The attacks of 11 September 2001 significantly accelerated the Commission's publication of its initial proposal on 27 November 2001,[2] as well as the Council's adoption of the instrument less than seven months later.

In criminal matters, mutual recognition obliges Member States to accept judgments handed down in other Member States, and to give them effect on their territory, as if they were national judgments. Simple in its operation, mutual recognition has radical implications in practice, which were nicely summed up by the Court in the case *GK and Others (European Public Prosecutor's Office)*, in which Judge Lars Bay Larsen acted as reporting judge:

> The principle of mutual recognition of judgments and judicial decisions implies that there is mutual trust as to the fact that each Member State accepts the application of the criminal law in force in the other Member States, *even though the implementation of its own national law might produce a different outcome*.[3] (emphasis added)

As long as their national laws are perfectly aligned, mutual recognition poses no particular problem for Member States. It is in the event of divergence between their national laws that Member States will have to *trust each other*. This issue of mutual trust is particularly sensitive in the field of criminal law, which directly affects sovereignty. Understandably, where Member States are required to mutually recognise their judgments in criminal matters, they need to be reassured about the operation of each other's criminal justice systems, particularly with regard to respect for fundamental rights.

* Judge at the European Court of Justice. The views expressed in this chapter are strictly personal.

[1] [2002] OJ L190/1. The deadline for transposing the EAW Framework Decision expired on 31 December 2003 pursuant to Art 34(1) thereof.

[2] Commission, 'Proposal for a Council Framework Decision on the European arrest warrant and the surrender procedures between Member States' COM (2001) 522 final.

[3] C-281/22 *GK and Others (European Public Prosecutor's Office)*, ECLI:EU:C:2023:1018, para 57.

In this context of mutual recognition, mutual trust takes on two different and yet interdependent meanings. According to one approach, mutual trust is the result of the adoption of common standards by the EU legislature, which facilitate the proper functioning of mutual recognition. Indeed, the EU legislature has endeavoured to adopt common minimum rules on the rights of victims and on the rights of suspected or accused persons. Such common standards increase mutual trust of Member States in the operation of their respective criminal justice systems, making it easier for them to recognise, and give effect to, national laws that diverge from their own. Under this approach, mutual trust is a structural *precondition* for mutual recognition to function properly, which is reflected in Recital 10 of the EAW Framework Decision: 'the mechanism of the [EAW] is based on a high level of confidence between Member States'.

According to a second approach, mutual trust is an *obligation* imposed on Member States by EU law. In *Opinion 2/13* on the accession of the EU to the ECHR, the Court famously stated:

> [T]he principle of mutual trust between the Member States is of fundamental importance in EU law, given that it allows an area without internal borders to be created and maintained. That principle requires, particularly with regard to the area of freedom, security and justice, each of those States, save in exceptional circumstances, to consider all the other Member States to be complying with EU law and particularly with the fundamental rights recognised by EU law.[4]

Here, mutual trust means that Member States are under the obligation to presume that other Member States respect fundamental rights. Consequently, they are not entitled, in principle, to invoke a breach of fundamental rights in order to avoid complying with their obligation to recognise the criminal judgments of other Member States. However, this presumption is not irrebuttable: sometimes, Member States do breach fundamental rights. In *Aranyosi and Căldăraru*, the Court clarified the conditions under which a breach of fundamental rights can frustrate an obligation of mutual recognition in criminal matters. Indeed, if certain conditions are met, Member States are released from their obligation of mutual trust and, *ipso facto*, from their obligation of mutual recognition.[5]

This chapter explores these two sides of mutual trust in criminal matters. Section II explores the institutional developments that have accompanied the EU legislature's work on judicial cooperation in criminal matters. EU legislative activity in this area can be divided into two stages: first, the establishment of an obligation of mutual recognition; second, the adoption of common minimum standards in order to strengthen mutual trust and, consequently, facilitate the mutual recognition of criminal judgments. Section III examines how the Court has interpreted the concept of mutual trust in order to strike a balance between the rigour of mutual recognition and the protection of fundamental rights.

II. BUILDING MUTUAL TRUST THROUGH THE ADOPTION OF COMMON MINIMUM STANDARDS

In order to underline the relationship between the implementation of mutual recognition, on the one hand, and the adoption by the EU legislature of common minimum standards, on the

[4] *Opinion 2/13 (Accession of the European Union to the ECHR)*, ECLI:EU:C:2014:2454, para 191.
[5] Joined Cases C-404/15 and C-659/15 PPU *Aranyosi and Căldăraru*, ECLI:EU:C:2016:198.

other, it is useful to briefly retrace the institutional development of cooperation in criminal matters since the Treaty of Maastricht.[6]

Following the entry into force of the Treaty of Maastricht on 1 November 1993, Article K.3(2) of the Treaty on European Union (TEU) gave the Council the power to adopt common positions or actions, and to establish conventions, in the fields of justice and home affairs, which included judicial cooperation in criminal matters (Article K.1(7) TEU).

When the Treaty of Amsterdam entered into force on 1 May 1999, the provisions on police and judicial cooperation in criminal matters were brought together in Title VI of the EU Treaty. In addition to common positions and conventions, Article 34(2) of the EU Treaty provided for the Council, acting unanimously, to adopt framework decisions for the purpose of approximating the laws and regulations of the Member States and to adopt decisions for any other purpose consistent with the objectives of Title VI.

At this stage, the rule for decision-making within the Council remained unanimity. Furthermore, the possibility of introducing mutual recognition to facilitate cooperation in criminal matters was not mentioned either in the Treaty of Maastricht or in the Treaty of Amsterdam (adopted on 2 October 1997). At its meeting in Cardiff on 15 and 16 June 1998, the European Council 'underline[d] the importance of effective judicial cooperation in the fight against cross-border crime' and formally asked the Council 'to identify the scope for greater mutual recognition of decisions of each others' courts'.[7] Eighteen months later, at its meeting in Tampere on 15 and 16 October 1999, the European Council 'endorse[d] the principle of mutual recognition which […] should become *the cornerstone of judicial co-operation* in both civil and criminal matters within the Union' (emphasis added).[8]

The EAW Framework Decision, adopted on 13 June 2002, was the 'first concrete measure in the field of criminal law implementing the principle of mutual recognition', in the words of its Recital 6, in accordance with the policy orientation set out by the Tampere European Council. Furthermore, between the adoption of the EAW Framework Decision on 13 June 2002 and the entry into force of the Treaty of Lisbon on 1 December 2009, the Council adopted no fewer than eight other Framework Decisions introducing mutual recognition obligations in criminal matters:

- Council Framework Decision 2003/577/JHA of 22 July 2003 on the execution in the European Union of orders freezing property or evidence;[9]
- Council Framework Decision 2005/214/JHA of 24 February 2005 on the application of the principle of mutual recognition to financial penalties;[10]
- Council Framework Decision 2006/783/JHA of 6 October 2006 on the application of the principle of mutual recognition to confiscation orders;[11]
- Council Framework Decision 2008/675/JHA of 24 July 2008 on taking account of convictions in the Member States of the European Union in the course of new criminal proceedings;[12]

[6] For a detailed overview of this evolution, see K Lenaerts, 'The Contribution of the European Court of Justice to the Area of Freedom, Security and Justice' (2010) 59 *International & Comparative Law Quarterly* 255.

[7] Conclusions of the Presidency of the European Council (Cardiff, 15–16 June 1998), para 39.

[8] Conclusions of the Presidency of the European Council (Tampere, 15–16 October 1999), para 33.

[9] [2003] OJ L196/45.

[10] [2005] OJ L76/16.

[11] [2006] OJ L328/59.

[12] [2008] OJ L220/32.

- Council Framework Decision 2008/909/JHA of 27 November 2008 on the application of the principle of mutual recognition to judgments in criminal matters imposing custodial sentences or measures involving deprivation of liberty for the purpose of their enforcement in the European Union;[13]
- Council Framework Decision 2008/947/JHA of 27 November 2008 on the application of the principle of mutual recognition to judgments and probation decisions for the purpose of supervising probation measures and alternative sanctions;[14]
- Council Framework Decision 2008/978/JHA of 18 December 2008 on the European Evidence Warrant for obtaining objects, documents and data for use in proceedings in criminal matters,[15] and
- Council Framework Decision 2009/829/JHA of 23 October 2009 on the application, between Member States of the European Union, of the principle of mutual recognition to decisions on supervision measures as an alternative to provisional detention.[16]

The final stage in this institutional development came with the adoption of the Treaty of Lisbon on 13 December 2007. The Treaty of Lisbon made three significant changes to judicial cooperation in criminal matters. First, Article 82(1) of the Treaty on the Functioning of the European Union (TFEU) explicitly stated, for the first time in primary law, that 'judicial cooperation in criminal matters in the Union shall be based on the principle of mutual recognition of judgments and judicial decisions'. Second, the Treaty of Lisbon abolished – in accordance with the transitional arrangements set out in Protocol 36 – the specific instruments provided for in this area by the Treaty of Amsterdam, such as the Framework Decision, in favour of the traditional instruments of the 'Community method' (in particular, the Directive). Third, qualified majority voting became the rule within the Council, in accordance with the provisions of Articles 82–84 TFEU.

How should these latest changes be interpreted? Following the somewhat rushed adoption of the EAW Framework Decision, a number of experts criticised the implementation of mutual recognition in an area characterised by a great diversity of national laws.[17] Indeed, there was a broad consensus that the adoption of common standards of criminal justice would promote acceptance of the obligation to recognise the criminal judgments of other Member States.

The state of EU law, as it emerged from the Treaty of Amsterdam, posed two problems in this respect. First, unanimity was still the rule within the Council, which made the adoption of common standards difficult. Second, framework decisions, such as the EAW Framework Decision, were deprived of direct effect by virtue of Article 34(2)(b) of the EU Treaty. Granted, the Court held in the *Pupino* case,[18] that national law had to be interpreted in conformity with framework decisions. In *Popławski I*,[19] the Court made it clear that national judges are required to interpret their national law as far as possible in the light of the text and purpose of the EAW Framework Decision in order to achieve the result sought by it. However, as

[13] [2008] OJ L327/27.
[14] [2008] OJ L337/102.
[15] [2008] OJ L350/72.
[16] [2009] OJ L294/20.
[17] By way of illustration, see S Peers, 'Mutual Recognition and Criminal Law in the European Union: Has the Council Got it Wrong?' (2004) 41 *Common Market Law Review* 5.
[18] Case C-105/03 *Pupino*, ECLI:EU:C:2005:386, paras 38 and 43.
[19] Case C-579/15 *Popławski*, ECLI:EU:C:2017:503, paras 31–36.

repeated by the Court on numerous occasions, this interpretative obligation is limited by general principles of law and cannot serve as the basis for a *contra legem* interpretation of national law.[20] Further, in *Popławski II*,[21] the Court stressed that the obligation to set aside provisions of national law that are contrary to EU law, arising from the principle of primacy, applies only to provisions of EU law that have direct effect. Consequently, a national court is *not* required, under EU law, to disapply a provision of national law which is contrary to a provision of EU law if the latter has no direct effect.

The changes introduced by the Treaty of Lisbon have remedied these two problems. First, the transition to qualified majority voting (Articles 82–84 TFEU) facilitates the adoption of common minimum rules at EU level. Second, the suppression of the framework decision as an instrument of EU law, and the use of directives, imply that EU provisions on cooperation in criminal matters can now have direct effect provided that they are 'sufficiently clear, precise and unconditional'.[22]

These two legal developments (qualified majority voting and direct effect) paved the way for the adoption of common standards of criminal justice, to be respected in all Member States, with a view to facilitating mutual recognition. The wording of Article 82(2) TFEU is particularly revealing: '*to the extent necessary to facilitate the mutual recognition* of judgments and judicial decisions' (emphasis added), the Council and the Parliament may adopt directives laying down minimum rules concerning, inter alia, mutual admissibility of evidence between Member States, the rights of individuals in criminal procedure, and the rights of victims of crime.

Following the entry into force of the Treaty of Lisbon, the Council formally acknowledged the need to strengthen mutual trust by adopting common minimum standards. Indeed, in its 'Roadmap for strengthening procedural rights of suspected or accused persons in criminal proceedings', published on 30 November 2009, it noted that 'mutual recognition presupposes that the competent authorities of the Member States trust the criminal justice systems of the other Member States' and that:

> for the purpose of enhancing mutual trust within the European Union, it is important that, complementary to the [European Convention on Human Rights], there exist European Union standards for the protection of procedural rights which are properly implemented and applied in the Member States.[23]

In the wake of this 'Roadmap', six directives providing for common minimum standards on procedural rights were adopted on the basis of Article 82(2)(b) TFEU:

- Directive 2010/64/EU of the European Parliament and of the Council of 20 October 2010 on the right to interpretation and translation in criminal proceedings;[24]
- Directive 2012/13/EU of the European Parliament and of the Council of 22 May 2012 on the right to information in criminal proceedings;[25]

[20] See, among many others, *Pupino* (n 18), paras 44–47; *Popławski* (n 19), paras 32–33; and Joined Cases C-38/21, C-47/21 and C-232/21 *BMW Bank and Others*, ECLI:EU:C:2023:1014, para 222.

[21] Case C-573/17 *Popławski*, ECLI:EU:C:2019:530, paras 58–68.

[22] See, among many others, *Popławski* (n 21), para 64; Cases C-569/20 *Spetsializirana prokuratura (Procès d'un accusé en fuite)*, ECLI:EU:C:2022:401, para 28; and C-242/22 PPU *TL (Absence d'interprète et de traduction)*, ECLI:EU:C:2022:611, paras 49–51.

[23] Council Resolution of 30 November 2009 on a Roadmap for strengthening procedural rights of suspected or accused persons in criminal proceedings [2009] OJ C295/1.

[24] [2010] OJ L280/1.

[25] [2012] OJ L142/1.

- Directive 2013/48/EU of the European Parliament and of the Council of 22 October 2013 on the right of access to a lawyer in criminal proceedings and to proceedings relating to the European arrest warrant, the right to inform a third party immediately on deprivation of liberty and the right of persons deprived of their liberty to communicate with third parties and with consular authorities;[26]
- Directive (EU) 2016/343 of the European Parliament and of the Council of 9 March 2016 strengthening certain aspects of the presumption of innocence and the right to be heard in criminal proceedings;[27]
- Directive (EU) 2016/800 of the European Parliament and of the Council of 11 May 2016 on procedural safeguards for children who are suspects or accused in criminal proceedings;[28] and
- Directive (EU) 2016/1919 of the European Parliament and of the Council of 26 October 2016 on legal aid for suspects and accused persons in criminal proceedings and for persons whose surrender is requested in European arrest warrant proceedings.[29]

It is interesting to note that these directives share several recitals which explicitly establish a link between common minimum standards, mutual trust and mutual recognition.[30] For example, Recitals 3, 4, 7 and 12 of Directive 2010/64 read as follows:

> (3) The implementation of the principle of mutual recognition of decisions in criminal matters presupposes that Member States have trust in each other's criminal justice systems. […]
>
> (4) Mutual recognition of decisions in criminal matters can operate effectively only in a spirit of trust in which not only judicial authorities but all actors in the criminal process consider decisions of the judicial authorities of other Member States as equivalent to their own, implying not only trust in the adequacy of other Member States' rules, but also trust that those rules are correctly applied. […]
>
> (7) Strengthening mutual trust requires a more consistent implementation of the rights and guarantees set out in Article 6 of the ECHR. It also requires, by means of this Directive and other measures, further development within the Union of the minimum standards set out in the ECHR and the Charter. […]
>
> (12) [This Directive] lays down common minimum rules to be applied in the fields of interpretation and translation in criminal proceedings with a view to enhancing mutual trust among Member States.

By adopting, between October 2010 and October 2016, several directives establishing minimum standards for the conduct of criminal proceedings, the EU legislature has concretely undertaken to strengthen mutual trust between Member States regarding the operation of their respective criminal justice systems. In three judgments handed down in December 2019, the Court observed that:

> the field of judicial cooperation in criminal matters has gradually acquired legal instruments whose coordinated application is intended to strengthen the confidence of Member States in their respective

[26] [2013] OJ L294/1.
[27] [2016] OJ L65/1.
[28] [2016] OJ L132/1.
[29] [2016] OJ L297/1.
[30] Recitals 3, 4, 7, 9 and 12 of Directive 2010/64; Recitals 3, 4, 10 and 14 of Directive 2012/13; Recitals 4, 6 and 8 of Directive 2013/48; Recitals 4 and 10 of Directive 2016/343; Recitals 2, 3 and 67 of Directive 2016/800; Recitals 2, 3 and 30 of Directive 2016/1919.

national legal orders with a view to ensuring that judgments in criminal matters are recognised and enforced within the European Union.[31]

III. INTERPRETING MUTUAL TRUST TO STRIKE A BALANCE BETWEEN THE OBLIGATION OF MUTUAL RECOGNITION AND THE PROTECTION OF FUNDAMENTAL RIGHTS

To a certain extent, the introduction of mutual recognition in criminal matters and the protection of fundamental rights pursue conflicting objectives, and this tension is at the heart of the Court's case law on the EAW Framework Decision.

On the one hand, the main objective of the EAW Framework Decision is to facilitate and accelerate cross-border cooperation in criminal matters with a view to contributing to the attainment of the objective set for the EU of becoming an area of freedom, security and justice (AFSJ).[32] Indeed, classical extradition procedures are notoriously slow and uncertain as to their outcome. According to Recital 5 of the EAW Framework Decision, the introduction of a new simplified system of surrender of sentenced or suspected persons for the purposes of execution or prosecution of criminal sentences makes it possible to remove the complexity and potential for delay inherent in the present extradition procedures. In plain language: the EAW mechanism aims to *combat impunity* within the EU, in situations where the requested person is present in the territory of a Member State other than that in which he or she has allegedly committed an offence.[33]

On the other hand, the most extensive protection of fundamental rights would require the authorities of the executing State to verify whether the treatment of the person concerned in the issuing State is compatible with fundamental rights standards applicable to criminal proceedings, as may be the case in the context of classical extradition procedures.[34] However, a systematic verification, by the authorities of the executing State, of the reality of each and every fundamental right breach alleged by the person concerned would lead to delays and complications incompatible with the objective of simplification and expediency pursued by the EAW Framework Decision.

Preserving the effectiveness of the mutual recognition mechanism established by the EAW Framework Decision *while* guaranteeing the protection of fundamental rights: this is the fundamental tension that the Court must address in the context of disputes on the execution of EAWs. The starting point for the Court's reasoning, when it examines a concrete manifestation of this tension, is always the same: *mutual trust*.

[31] Cases C-566/19 PPU *Parquet général du Grand-Duché de Luxembourg (Procureurs de Lyon et Tours)*, ECLI:EU:C:2019:1077, para 43; C-625/19 PPU *Openbaar Ministerie (Swedish Prosecution Service)*, ECLI:EU:C:2019:1078, para 34; and C-627/19 PPU *Openbaar Ministerie (Public Prosecutor, Brussels)*, ECLI:EU:C:2019:1079, para 22.

[32] Cases C-699/21 *EDL (Ground for refusal based on illness)*, ECLI:EU:C:2023:295, para 32; and C-261/22 *GN (Grounds for refusal based on the best interests of the child)*, ECLI:EU:C:2023:1017, para 35.

[33] Cases C-551/18 PPU *IK (Enforcement of an additional sentence)*, ECLI:EU:C:2018:991, para 39; and Joined Cases C-354/20 PPU and C-412/20 PPU *Openbaar Ministerie (Independence of the issuing judicial authority)*, ECLI:EU:C:2020.1033, para 62.

[34] By way of illustration, Art 3 of the European Convention on Extradition (Paris, 13 December 1957) provides that 'extradition shall not be granted if the offence in respect of which it is requested is regarded by the requested Party as a political offence', or 'if the requested Party has substantial grounds for believing that a request for extradition for an ordinary criminal offence has been made for the purpose of prosecuting or punishing a person on account of his race, religion, nationality or political opinion, or that that person's position may be prejudiced for any of these reasons'.

Indeed, mutual trust is a distinguishing and constitutional feature of the EU, as clearly explained in *Opinion 2/13* on the Accession of the EU to the ECHR.[35] The EU legal structure is based on the fundamental premise that each Member State shares with all the other Member States, and recognises that they share with it, a set of common values on which the EU is founded, as stated in Article 2 TEU. That premise implies and justifies the existence of *mutual trust* between the Member States that those values will be recognised (paragraph 168). At the heart of that legal structure are the fundamental rights recognised by the Charter, which Member States are required to respect when they are implementing EU law (paragraphs 169 and 171). Accordingly, the principle of *mutual trust* requires, particularly with regard to the AFSJ, each of those States, save in exceptional circumstances, to consider all the other Member States to be complying with EU law and particularly with the fundamental rights recognised by EU law (paragraph 191). Thus, when implementing EU law, the Member States may, under EU law, be required to presume that fundamental rights have been observed by the other Member States, so that not only may they not demand a higher level of national protection of fundamental rights from another Member State than that provided by EU law, but, save in exceptional cases, they may not check whether that other Member State has actually, in a specific case, observed the fundamental rights guaranteed by the EU (paragraph 192).

The importance of these few paragraphs cannot be overstated: indeed, they form the very foundation of the Court's approach to the *limited* possibility of refusing to execute an EAW on the grounds of a breach of fundamental rights in the issuing State. Since every Member State is required, under EU law, to comply with the fundamental rights recognised by EU law, they should indeed presume, within the scope of EU law, that fundamental rights have been observed by the other Member States. This presumption of compliance is reflected in the text of the EAW Framework Decision itself. Indeed, the EU legislature has not provided an explicit ground for non-execution based on a breach of fundamental rights. Rather, Article 1(3) states, in general terms, that this framework decision 'shall not have the effect of modifying the obligation to respect fundamental rights and fundamental legal principles as laid down in Article 6 TEU'.

In practice, the contours of mutual trust determine the area in which Member States may invoke a breach of fundamental rights as a reason for not complying with their obligation to recognise the criminal judgments of other Member States. Three periods can usefully be distinguished in the Court's case law in that regard. In the first period, the Court emphasised the need for a strict interpretation of the grounds for non-execution, so as to preserve the effectiveness of the EAW mechanism. During the second period, which began with the *Aranyosi and Căldăraru* case,[36] the Court was called upon to specify the restrictive conditions under which a breach of fundamental rights could lead to a refusal to execute an EAW. In a nutshell, the Court held that systemic or generalised deficiencies in the issuing State are not sufficient: the person concerned must also be exposed to an individual risk of his or her fundamental rights being infringed. In the third period, made up of more recent cases, the Court examined the opposite question, namely whether the fact that the person concerned is exposed to an individual risk of violation of his or her fundamental rights is sufficient to justify refusal to execute an EAW.

[35] *Opinion 2/13 (Accession of the European Union to the ECHR)* (n 4).
[36] *Aranyosi and Căldăraru* (n 5).

A. First Period: The Strict Interpretation of the Grounds for Non-Execution

Radu is one of the first cases before the Court in which a breach of a fundamental right has been invoked to justify non-execution of an EAW.[37] The Court was asked whether the executing judicial authorities can refuse to execute an EAW issued for the purposes of conducting a criminal prosecution on the ground that the issuing judicial authorities did not hear the requested person before that arrest warrant was issued (paragraph 31). The answer is no. The Court highlighted that Member States may refuse to execute an EAW only in the cases of mandatory non-execution (Article 3) and optional non-execution (Articles 4 and 4a) listed in the EAW Framework Decision, which do not cover this scenario (paragraphs 36–38). Moreover, an obligation for the issuing judicial authorities to hear the requested person before an EAW is issued would lead to the failure of the very system of surrender in so far as such an arrest warrant must have a certain element of surprise (paragraph 40). In any event, the EAW Framework Decision guarantees the right to be heard in the executing Member State, in such as way as to not compromise the effectiveness of the EAW system (paragraphs 41–42).

Mention must also be made of the seminal *Melloni* case.[38] Mr Melloni had been sentenced in absentia in Italy to ten years' imprisonment for fraudulent bankruptcy. He objected to his surrender by the Spanish authorities to the Italian authorities on the grounds that it was impossible under Italian law to obtain a review of his conviction in absentia, whereas the right to obtain such a review derived from the right to a fair trial as guaranteed by the Spanish Constitution. The Court emphasised that Article 4a(1) *exhaustively* governs the non-execution of an EAW in the event of a conviction in absentia. Since Mr Melloni fell within one of the four cases in which enforcement cannot be refused, the Spanish authorities could not make enforcement of the EAW conditional on the possibility of obtaining a review in Italy (paragraphs 40–44).

Moreover, the Spanish authorities could not rely on Article 53 of the Charter to apply their higher constitutional standard of fundamental rights. Indeed, where the EU legislature has harmonised a legal issue exhaustively (the enforcement of EAWs in the event of a conviction in absentia), and without infringing the Charter, allowing a Member State to apply its own national standards would compromise the primacy, unity and effectiveness of EU law (paragraphs 55–60). Accordingly, allowing a Member State to avail itself of Article 53 of the Charter to make the surrender of a person convicted in absentia conditional upon the conviction being open to review in the issuing Member State, a possibility not provided for under EAW Framework Decision, would undermine the principles of mutual trust and recognition which that decision purports to uphold and would, therefore, compromise the efficacy of that framework decision (paragraphs 61–63).

The cases from the first period have several features in common. The fundamental rights issues raised were governed by the provisions of the EAW Framework Decision. The Court confined itself to the grounds for non-execution set out in that Framework Decision, which must be construed strictly.[39] The overall result strengthened the mutual recognition obligation, promoting the effectiveness of the EAW mechanism. The second period would be very different indeed.

[37] Case C-396/11 *Radu*, ECLI:EU:C:2013:39.
[38] Case C-399/11 *Melloni*, ECLI:EU:C:2013:107.
[39] *Popławski* (n 19), para 19.

B. Second Period: Can Systemic or Generalised Deficiencies in the Protection of Fundamental Rights Justify Non-Execution of an EAW?

The second and third period cases raised fundamental rights issues that were not explicitly governed by the EAW Framework Decision. As a result, the Court was faced with the difficult task of establishing a new exception to the mutual recognition obligation, in order to guarantee the protection of fundamental rights, without compromising the overall effectiveness of the EAW mechanism.

Aranyosi and Căldăraru was the landmark judgment in this area.[40] The case concerned the execution in Germany of EAWs issued by the Hungarian authorities for Mr Aranyosi, a Hungarian national, and by the Romanian authorities for Mr Căldăraru, a Romanian national. The German referring court wondered whether it could, or even should, refuse to enforce the EAWs because of the risk that Mr Aranyosi and Mr Căldăraru would be subjected to conditions of detention in breach of Article 3 of the ECHR. The referring court pointed out, in that regard, that the European Court of Human Rights had condemned Hungary and Romania on account of overcrowding in their prisons. While recalling that mutual trust in principle precludes the executing State from verifying respect for fundamental rights in the issuing State (paragraphs 77–80), the Court accepted that certain limitations may be placed on mutual recognition and mutual trust 'in exceptional circumstances' (paragraph 82). Indeed, as is stated in Article 1(3) thereof, the EAW Framework Decision cannot alter the obligation to respect fundamental rights as enshrined in, inter alia, the Charter (paragraph 83). The prohibition of inhuman or degrading treatment or punishment, provided for in Article 4 of the Charter, is absolute and can justify refusal to execute an EAW (paragraphs 84–87).

However, in order to preserve the effectiveness of the EAW mechanism, such limitations to mutual recognition would have to pass a two-stage test. First, the executing judicial authority must establish, on the basis of reliable information, that the conditions of detention in the issuing Member State suffer from deficiencies that either are systemic or generalised or affect certain groups of persons or certain places of detention (paragraph 89). Yet such a finding is not sufficient, on its own, to justify non-execution of an EAW. Second, the executing judicial authority must also determine whether, in the particular circumstances of the case, there are substantial grounds to believe that, following the surrender of that person to the issuing Member State, he or she will run a real risk of being subject in that Member State to inhuman or degrading treatment (paragraphs 91–94).

The two-stage test was soon to be applied to other allegations of fundamental rights violations in the issuing State. The question asked to the Court in Case C-216/18 PPU *Minister for Justice and Equality (Deficiencies in the system of justice)*[41] was whether the executing authority could refuse to execute an EAW on the basis of reliable information about systemic or generalised deficiencies affecting the independence of the judicial system of the issuing Member State, namely Poland. The Court held that a real risk of breach of the fundamental right to an independent tribunal and, therefore, of the fundamental right to a fair trial as laid down in the second paragraph of Article 47 of the Charter, is capable of justifying refusal to execute an EAW on the basis of Article 1(3) of the EAW Framework Decision (paragraphs 47–59). However, the executing authority must apply the two-step test established in *Aranyosi and Căldăraru* in this scenario as well. Thus, this authority must first appraise, on

[40] *Aranyosi and Căldăraru* (n 5).
[41] Case C-216/18 PPU *Minister for Justice and Equality (Deficiencies in the system of justice)*, ECLI:EU:C:2018:586.

the basis of reliable information, the existence of systemic or generalised deficiencies liable to compromise the independence of the judiciary in the issuing Member State; and then assess whether, following his surrender, there is a real risk that the requested person will suffer a breach of his fundamental right to a fair trial (paragraphs 60–68).

As is apparent from Recital 10 of the EAW Framework Decision, it is only if the European Council were to adopt a decision determining, as provided for in Article 7(2) TEU, that there is a serious and persistent breach in the issuing Member State of the principles set out in Article 2 TEU, such as those inherent in the rule of law, and the Council were then to suspend the EAW Framework Decision in respect of that Member State that the executing judicial authority would be required to refuse *automatically* to execute any EAW issued by it. In the absence of such decisions, the executing authority must carry out a specific assessment of whether the individual concerned runs a real risk that the essence of his fundamental right to a fair trial will be affected (paragraphs 70–73). In other words, systemic or generalised deficiencies are not sufficient to justify non-execution of an EAW.

The applicability of the two-step test (systemic or generalised deficiencies on the one hand, individual risk on the other), in the event of an alleged violation of the fundamental right to a fair trial in the issuing State, has been confirmed in Joined Cases C-354/20 PPU and C-412/20 PPU *Openbaar Ministerie (Independence of the issuing judicial authority)*[42] and in Joined Cases C-562/21 PPU and C-563/21 PPU *Openbaar Ministerie (Tribunal established by law in the issuing Member State)*.[43] In both judgments, the Court clearly set out the rationale underlying the two-step test: the objective of combating impunity precludes an interpretation of Article 1(3) of the EAW Framework Decision according to which the existence of or increase in systemic or generalised deficiencies so far as concerns the independence of the judiciary in a Member State is sufficient, in itself, to justify a refusal to execute an EAW issued by a judicial authority of that Member State.[44]

C. Third Period: Can an Individual Risk of Fundamental Rights Violation Justify Non-Execution of an EAW?

In the third period, the Court was called upon to examine the question opposite to that examined in the second period, namely: is it sufficient, to justify refusal to execute an EAW, that the person concerned be exposed to an individual risk of his or her fundamental rights being infinged? Three judgments handed down in 2023 addressed this issue.

In *Puig Gordi and Others*,[45] the Spanish Supreme Court had issued EAWs against Mr Puig Gordi, among others. However, the Belgian judicial authorities, considering that the Spanish Supreme Court was not competent to hear the criminal proceedings against Mr Puig Gordi and therefore to issue this EAW, refused to enforce it (paragraphs 13–16). Following that refusal, the Spanish Supreme Court referred a number of questions to the Court for a preliminary ruling, seeking in particular to determine whether the authorities of the executing State could refuse to execute an EAW where there was a dispute as to the jurisdiction of the

[42] *Openbaar Ministerie (Independence of the issuing judicial authority)* (n 33), paras 51–58.

[43] Joined Cases C-562/21 PPU and C-563/21 PPU *Openbaar Ministerie (Tribunal established by law in the issuing Member State)*, ECLI:EU:C:2022:100 (paras 50–66).

[44] *Openbaar Ministerie (Independence of the issuing judicial authority)* (n 33), paras 62–64; and *Openbaar Ministerie (Tribunal established by law in the issuing Member State)* (n 43), para 62.

[45] Case C-158/21 *Puig Gordi and Others*, ECLI:EU:C:2023:57.

issuing judicial authority. The Court began by recalling that the executing judicial authority is required to assess whether, if the person concerned is surrendered to the issuing Member State, that person runs a real risk of infringement of his or her fundamental right to a fair trial before a 'tribunal previously established by law', enshrined in the second paragraph of Article 47 of the Charter (paragraph 98). The jurisdiction of a court to hear a case, under the relevant national rules, is indeed part of the requirement to have a 'tribunal established by law' (paragraph 99).

However, to this end, the executing authority must apply the two-step test set out in *Aranyosi and Căldăraru* and confirmed in *Minister for Justice and Equality (Deficiencies in the system of justice)*: first, it must assess the existence of systemic or generalised deficiencies in the operation of the judicial system of the issuing Member State, concerning the requirement for a tribunal established by law; second, it must find, in the light of all the relevant circumstances of the specific case, that the court called upon to try the person concerned in the issuing Member State manifestly lacks jurisdiction for that purpose (paragraphs 101–108).

Interestingly, the Court clarified that the mere presence of an individual risk of infringement of the right to a fair trial within the meaning of the second paragraph of Article 47 of the Charter, without finding the presence of systemic or generalised deficiencies in the operation of the judicial system of the issuing State, was *not* sufficient to justify a refusal to execute. Indeed, in the absence of such deficiencies, the executing authority is obliged, by virtue of the principle of mutual trust, to presume that the judicial system of the issuing State offers effective remedies guaranteeing the person concerned the right to a fair trial (paragraphs 111–14).

The judgment in *GN*[46] further confirmed the applicability of the two-step test, in relation to other fundamental rights: the right to family life (Article 7 of the Charter) and the rights of the child (Article 24 of the Charter). Italian authorities had refused to enforce an EAW issued by the Belgian authorities against GN, who had been sentenced in Belgium to five years' imprisonment for human trafficking and aiding illegal immigration. GN was the mother of a young child and was pregnant with a second child. The reason for non-execution was that the Belgian authorities had not provided assurances that a detention regime comparable to that in Italy existed in Belgium, which protected both the mother's right not to be deprived of her relationship with her children and the children's right to maternal and family assistance.

The Court held that, under Article 1(3) of the EAW Framework Decision, a risk of breach of the fundamental rights enshrined in Articles 7 and 24 of the Charter may exceptionally justify non-execution of an EAW (paragraph 43). To that end, the executing authority must, first, ascertain the existence of systemic or general deficiencies in the conditions of detention of mothers of young children or of care for such children in the issuing Member State. Second, it must verify that, given their personal situation, the person targeted by the EAW and/or his or her children run a real risk of having their fundamental rights violated (paragraphs 43–48). If necessary, the executing judicial authority must, pursuant to Article 15(2) of the EAW Framework Decision, request from the issuing judicial authority all relevant information on the conditions under which that person will be detained and the children taken into care. However, the executing authority cannot request information on the so-called second step when the existence of systemic or generalised deficiencies has not been established (paragraphs 49–50). In other words, the Court implicitly confirmed that the mere existence of an individual risk, with regard to fundamental rights, is *not* sufficient to justifiy non-execution of an EAW.

[46] *GN (Grounds for refusal based on the best interests of the child)* (n 32).

The only exception to the two-step test was established in the *EDL* case.[47] EDL was suspected of having committed, on Croatian territory, the offence of possession of narcotics for the purpose of distribution and sale. Before the Milan Court of Appeal, he opposed his surrender to the Croatian authorities, alleging psychiatric problems. On the basis of a psychiatrist's assessment, that court considered that the execution of the EAW would lead to a deterioration in EDL's general state of health, the effects of which could be exceptionally serious, or even to an increased risk of suicide. In its preliminary ruling, the Court highlighted that the EAW Framework Decision does not provide for non-execution of an EAW on the ground that the person concerned suffers from serious, chronic and potentially irreversible illnesses. Indeed, having regard to the principle of mutual trust, there is a presumption that the care and treatment provided in the Member States for the management of such illnesses will be adequate, whether in prisons or in the context of alternative arrangements (paragraph 35).

However, the executing authority may be required to make use of the possibility provided for in Article 23(4) of the EAW Framework Decision and temporarily postpone surrender if it would expose the person to a real risk of inhuman or degrading treatment within the meaning of Article 4 of the Charter, either as a result of or, in certain circumstances, *regardless of the level of quality of the care available in the issuing Member State* (paragraph 39). The last consideration is of crucial importance in understanding why the Court did not impose a requirement of systemic or generalised deficiencies in the provision of health care in the issuing State. Indeed, the very act of surrendering a seriously ill person may, in itself, materialise a risk of inhuman or degrading treatment, irrespective of the quality of care in the issuing State. In such a scenario, refusal to execute the EAW does not undermine mutual trust as it is unrelated to the issuing State: this is why the executing authority is not required to check for systemic or generalised deficiencies in that State (the so-called first step). Consequently, refusal to execute an EAW may, exceptionally, be justified by a mere individual risk of inhuman or degrading treatment within the meaning of Article 4 of the Charter, in circumstances where the surrender of a seriously ill person is manifestly likely to seriously endanger his or her health (paragraphs 52–55).

IV. CONCLUSION

If mutual trust is classically conceived as a pre-condition for the proper functioning of mutual recognition, one may say, by way of conclusion, that the implementation of mutual recognition through the EAW Framework Decision has had the effect of strengthening mutual trust. The adoption of EU directives setting common minimum standards on procedural rights and the clarification in the court's jurisprudence of the 'exceptional circumstances' which may justify non-recognition of a judgment of a court of another Member State, provides greater assurance for courts deciding on the surrender of an individual, that his or her fundamental rights will be respected in that other Member State.

[47] *EDL (Ground for refusal based on illness)* (n 32).

3

Mutual Trust in Judicial Cooperation in Criminal Matters

KÜLLIKE JÜRIMÄE*

I. INTRODUCTION

JUDICIAL COOPERATION IN criminal matters has been built on the principle of mutual trust, and is reflected in the principle of mutual recognition of judgments and judicial decisions. Over time, the level of trust and its requirements have been constantly developed in the case law of the European Court of Justice (ECJ).[1]

EU law and the structured network of principles resulting from it is based on the fundamental premise that each Member State shares with all the others the set of common values on which the EU is founded, as stated in Article 2 of the Treaty on European Union (TEU). That implies and justifies the existence of mutual trust between the Member States that those values will be recognised and that the law of the EU that implements them will be respected.[2] Mutual trust and mutual recognition of judgments, which is the result of the harmonisation of certain aspects of national criminal laws, are intrinsically linked. Indeed, the principle of mutual recognition of judgments and judicial decisions means that there is mutual trust that every Member State accepts the application of the criminal law in force in another Member State, even if the application of its own national law would lead to a different solution.[3]

In consequence, when implementing EU law, the Member States are required to presume that fundamental rights are observed by the other Member States. More specifically, mutual trust imposes two negative obligations on them. First, a Member State may not demand a higher level of national protection of fundamental rights from another Member State than that provided by EU law as interpreted by the ECJ. Second, save in exceptional circumstances, a Member State is not entitled to control whether the other relevant Member State respects the fundamental rights guaranteed by the EU in a specific case.

It can be argued that following the principal of mutual trust is likely to lead to a levelling down of the protection of fundamental rights in the EU and so undermine the common values on which it is based. However, it could be justified by the imperatives of effectiveness and unity of EU law.

* Judge at the European Court of Justice. The views expressed in this chapter are strictly personal.

[1] See S Prechal, 'Mutual Trust before the Court of Justice of the European Union' (2017) *European Papers* 75, 76.

[2] *Opinion C-2/13 (Accession of the European Union to the ECHR)*, ECLI:EU:C:240:2454, para 168.

[3] Cases C-367/16 *Piotrowski*, ECLI:EU:C:2018:27, para 52; and C-281/22 *GK and Others (Parquet européen)*, ECLI:EU:C:2023:18, para 57.

In its case law, the ECJ has struck a balance between these two considerations, and has clarified the scope of the principle of mutual trust and its consequences, particularly in terms of the dialogue between the competent authorities of the Member States. The case law on Council Framework Decision 2002/584/JHA of 13 June 2002 on the European arrest warrant and the surrender procedures between Member States (hereafter the EAW Framework Decision)[4] is particularly eloquent in this regard. On the basis of this case law, I will argue that the principle of mutual trust is not only seen as a foundation of the European Arrest Warrant (EAW) system (section III) but is also used as a guiding light for European judicial cooperation (section IV). Before doing so, however, it is worth briefly explaining the origin of this principle in the then Community law and how it became a solid keystone of judicial cooperation in criminal matters (section II).

II. THE ORIGIN OF THE PRINCIPLE OF MUTUAL TRUST

The principle of mutual trust was mentioned for the first time in the 1977 judgment in the *Bauhuis* case on the interpretation of the directive on animal health problems affecting intra-Community trade.[5] In this case, the ECJ ruled that Member States should place trust in each other in so far as it concerns the guarantees provided by the inspections carried out by the exporting Member State. According to the Court, mutual trust constitutes a basic element of the system introduced by the directive, without which it would have no purpose.[6]

The idea of 'mutual trust', initially developed by the ECJ in the context of trade policy, was introduced into the criminal justice discourse of the EU more than two decades later. In 1999, the Tampere European Council declared that the principle of mutual recognition 'should become a "cornerstone" of judicial cooperation in both civil and criminal matters within Union'.[7]

Later on, the Commission clarified that the only way to make mutual recognition possible is through mutual trust. The Commission underlined that it consists 'not only [in] trust in the adequacy of one's partner's rules, but also [in] trust that these rules are correctly applied'.[8]

In 2001, the initial programme to implement mutual recognition was established and made an important contribution to the trust discourse by introducing the presumption of trust.[9] It stated that:

> Implementation of the principle of mutual recognition of decisions in criminal matters presupposes that Member States have trust in each other's criminal justice systems. That trust is grounded, in particular, on their shared commitment to the principles of freedom, democracy and respect for human rights, fundamental freedoms and the rule of law.[10]

Two other programmes were then adopted by the Council to take account of the developments in the Area of Freedom, Security and Justice (AFSJ). The so-called Hague Programme

[4] [2002] OJ L190/1 as amended by Council Framework Decision 2009/299/JHA [2009] OJ L81/24.

[5] Council Directive 64/433/EEC [1963–64] OJ Spec Ed 164.

[6] Case 47/76 *Bauhuis*, ECLI:EU:C:1977:6.

[7] Conclusions of the Presidency of the European Council (Tampere, Finland, 15–16 October 1999), para 33.

[8] Commission, 'Mutual Recognition of Final Decisions in Criminal Matters' COM (2000) 495 final, para 3.1 'Mutual Recognition'.

[9] See A Willems, 'Mutual Trust as a Term of Art in EU Criminal Law: Revealing its Hybrid Character' (2016) *European Journal of Legal Studies* 211, 216.

[10] Council of the European Union, 'Programme of measures to implement the principle of mutual recognition of decisions in criminal matters' (Programme) [2001] OJ C12/10, p 1.

highlighted that 'strengthening mutual confidence requires an explicit effort to improve mutual understanding among judicial authorities and different legal systems'.[11] The so-called Stockholm Programme indicated that this understanding would be 'one of the main challenges for the future'.[12]

On the basis of the Conclusions of the Tampere European Council and the initial programme of measures, the EU legislature adopted the EAW Framework Decision.[13]

Even if the ECJ made use of the principle of mutual trust in the area of criminal matters for the first time[14] in the context of the Convention implementing the Schengen Agreement,[15] it is above all the EAW Framework Decision that gave, and still gives, the ECJ the opportunity to develop its case law on the principle of mutual trust. In particular, its recent case law has focused on the impact of respect for fundamental rights in the execution of EAWs.

III. THE ECJ'S CASE LAW ON THE EAW FRAMEWORK DECISION

In a number of cases,[16] the ECJ was asked whether and under which conditions the executing judicial authority can refuse to execute an (EAW), besides the exceptions provided for in Articles 3, 4 and 4(a) of the EAW Framework Decision.

A. The Duty to Execute an EAW and its Limited Exceptions

In these judgments, the ECJ invariably begins its reasoning by building on the principle of mutual trust. It notes that both the principle of mutual trust between Member States and the principle of mutual recognition, which is itself based on the mutual trust between the latter, are of cardinal importance in EU law given that they allow an area without any borders to be created and maintained.[17]

The very purpose of the EAW Framework Decision was to replace the multilateral system of extradition that had existed since 1957 with a system of surrender of convicted or suspected persons between judicial authorities with the intention of enforcing judgments or conducting

[11] Council of the European Union, 'The Hague Programme: strengthening freedom, security and justice in the European Union' [2005] OJ C53/01, point 3.2 Confidence-building and mutual trust, p 11.

[12] Council of the European Union, 'The Stockholm Programme – An open and secure Europe serving and protecting citizens' [2010] OJ C115/1, point 1.2.1 Mutual Trust, p 5.

[13] Several other instruments have since been adopted to meet these challenges (see Section IV below).

[14] In Joined Cases C-187/01 and C-385/01 *Gözütok and Brügge*, ECLI:EU:C:2003:87, para 33, the Court stated that the application of principle of *ne bis idem*, enshrined at Art 54 of this Convention, necessarily presupposes the existence of the mutual trust of the Member States in their criminal justice systems and that each of them recognises the criminal law in force in the other Member States even when the outcome would be different if its own national law were applied.

[15] The Schengen acquis – Convention implementing the Schengen Agreement of 14 June 1985 between the Governments of the States of the Benelux Economic Union, the Federal Republic of Germany and the French Republic on the gradual abolition of checks at their common borders [2000] OJ L239/19.

[16] Joined Cases C-404 and C-659/15 PPU *Aranyosi and Căldăraru*, ECLI:EU:C:2016:198; Cases C-220/18 PPU *Generalstaatsanwaltschaft (Conditions of detention in Hungary)*, ECLI:EU:C2018:589; C-216/18 PPU *Minister for Justice and Equality (Deficiencies in the system of justice)*, ECLI:EU:C:2018:586; C-128/18 *Dorobantu*, ECLI:EU:C:2019:857; Joined Cases C-428 and C-429/21 PPU *Openbaar Ministerie (Right to be heard by the executing judicial authority)*, ECLI:EU:C:2021:876; C-354 and C-412/20 PPU *Openbaar Ministerie (Tribunal established by law in the issuing Member State)*, ECLI:EU:C:2020:1033; Cases C-158/21 *Puig Gordi and Others*, ECLI:EU:C:2023:57; and C-699/21 *EDL (Ground for refusal based on illness)*, ECLI:EU:C:2023:295.

[17] *EDL (Ground for refusal based on illness)* (n 16), para 30 and case law cited.

prosecutions within the territory of the EU.[18] This simplified and more effective system aimed at facilitating and accelerating judicial cooperation with a view to contributing to the attainment of the objective set for the EU of becoming an AFSJ. Such system was based on the high level of trust between Member States.[19]

Building on this foundation, the ECJ observed that Member States are required, according to Article 1(2) of the EAW Framework Decision, to execute any EAW on the basis of the principle of mutual recognition and in accordance with the provisions of that framework decision.[20] It follows, first, that the executing authorities may refuse to execute an EAW only on the grounds stemming from the EAW Framework Decision as interpreted by the Court.[21] Second, while the execution of an EAW is the rule, refusal to execute such a warrant is an exception that must be interpreted strictly.[22]

Therefore, in principle, the executing judicial authority cannot refuse to execute an EAW on grounds other than those explicitly provided for by the Framework Decision. According to the Court, in order to ensure the full application of the principles of mutual trust and mutual recognition, it is primarily for each Member State to ensure that the requirements inherent in fundamental rights are safeguarded. In other words, the executing judicial authority has to assume that the fundamental rights of the person concerned have been or will be respected in the Member State of the issuing judicial authority.

Nevertheless, even in the context of judicial cooperation, mutual trust does not mean blind trust.[23] It is now settled case law that, in exceptional circumstances, executing judicial authorities can depart from the obligation to execute an EAW.

B. The Refusal to Execute an EAW on the Basis of Fundamental Rights

As stated in Article 1(3) thereof, the EAW Framework Decision was not to have the effect of modifying the obligation to respect fundamental rights as enshrined in the Charter and fundamental legal principles as set down in Articles 2 and 6 TEU.[24]

However, this does not mean that any evidence of a risk that the person concerned will suffer a limitation of any fundamental right protected by the Charter in the issuing Member State can justify the executing judicial authority's refusal to execute the EAW.

To date, the ECJ has recognised, under very strict conditions, the possibility of a refusal only if such a risk concerns the rights enshrined in Article 4,[25] in Article 47,[26] and recently in Article 7 and in Article 24(2) and (3)[27] of the Charter.

Concerning Article 4 of the Charter, the prohibition on inhuman or degrading treatment or punishment is absolute and closely linked to respect for human dignity. The ECJ

[18] *Minister for Justice and Equality (Deficiencies in the system of justice)* (n 16), para 39.

[19] ibid, para 40. See also *EDL (Ground for refusal based on illness)* (n 16), para 32 and case law cited.

[20] *EDL (Ground for refusal based on illness)* (n 16), para 33 and the case law cited.

[21] ibid, para 34.

[22] ibid.

[23] See Prechal (n 1) 76.

[24] See *Aranyosi and Căldăraru* (n 16), para 83; *Minister for Justice and Equality (Deficiencies in the system of justice)* (n 16), para 45; *Generalstaatsanwaltschaft (Conditions of detention in Hungary)* (n 16), para 58.

[25] *Aranyosi and Căldăraru* (n 16); *Generalstaatsanwaltschaft (Conditions of detention in Hungary)* (n 16); and *Dorobantu* (n 16).

[26] *Minister for Justice and Equality (Deficiencies in the system of justice)* (n 16); *Openbaar Ministerie (Independence of the issuing judicial authority)* (n 16); *Openbaar Ministerie (Tribunal established by law in the issuing Member State)* (n 16); and *Puig Gordi and Others* (n 16).

[27] Case C-261/22 *GN (Motif de refus fondé sur l'intérêt supérieur de l'enfant)*, ECLI:EU:C:2023:1017.

acknowledged that the right guaranteed by this article admits no derogation and concluded that the executing judicial authority is bound to assess the existence of a risk of such treatment or punishment when it is called upon to decide on the execution of an EAW and when it is in possession of evidence of such risk.[28]

Regarding Article 47 of the Charter, the ECJ followed a similar approach. Indeed, the requirement of judicial independence forms part of the essence of the fundamental right to a fair trial. This right is of cardinal importance as a guarantee that all the rights which individuals derive from EU law will be protected and that the values common to the Member States set out in Article 2 TEU, in particular the rule of law, will be safeguarded.[29]

When the executing judicial authority has evidence that there is a risk that the person concerned will suffer a violation of the fundamental rights he or she derives from Article 4 or Article 47 of the Charter if this person is surrendered to the issuing Member State, this judicial authority cannot automatically refuse to surrender the person concerned. According to the case law of the ECJ, it must carry out a two-step examination.

First, the executing judicial authority must rely on objective, reliable, specific and properly updated information that demonstrates that the identified risk relates to deficiencies in the issuing Member State which are systemic, generalised or which may affect certain groups of people.[30]

Second, this judicial authority must carry out a specific and precise verification to determine whether the deficiencies identified in the first step of the examination may specifically affect the person concerned if he or she is surrendered. In other words, it must be verified whether there are substantial grounds for believing that this person runs a real and individual risk of having his or her fundamental right breached.[31]

In principle, if these two steps are not fulfilled, the executing judicial authority cannot refuse the execution of the EAW.

The same methodology was followed regarding the risk of violating the right to privacy and the best interests of children, in the case of children living with their mother, who was the subject of an EAW.[32]

C. The Possibility of Suspension under Article 23 of the EAW Framework Decision

In the recent case *EDL (Ground for refusal based on illness)*, the ECJ was called upon to determine whether it was possible to derogate from this two-step examination in the presence of an individual risk of violation of fundamental rights intrinsic to the person concerned, independent of any possible systemic or generalised deficiency in the issuing Member State.

In the main proceedings, the person concerned by an EAW suffered from a psychotic disorder with a significant risk of suicide in the event of imprisonment. Under these circumstances, the surrender of that person risked endangering his life or health. By relying on Articles 3, 4 and 35 of the Charter, related, in substance, to health protection, the Italian Constitutional

[28] *Aranyosi and Căldăraru* (n 16), para 85; and *EDL (Ground for refusal based on illness)* (n 16), para 38 and the case law cited.

[29] *Minister for Justice and Equality (Deficiencies in the system of justice)* (n 16), para 48.

[30] *Aranyosi and Căldăraru* (n 16), para 89; *Openbaar Ministerie (Tribunal established by law in the issuing Member State)* (n 16), para 50; and *Puig Gordi and Others* (n 16), para 102.

[31] *Aranyosi and Căldăraru* (n 16), para 92; *Openbaar Ministerie (Tribunal established by law in the issuing Member State)* (n 16), para 53; and *Puig Gordi and Others* (n 16), para 106.

[32] *GN (Motif de refus fondé sur l'intérêt supérieur de l'enfant)* (n 27).

Court asked the ECJ, essentially, if the executing judicial authority must refuse to surrender such person if this risk cannot be ruled out.

In its judgment, the ECJ made clear that the executing judicial authority cannot, in principle, refuse to surrender the person concerned even though this person suffers from serious, chronic and potentially irreversible illnesses. Considering the principle of mutual trust, the ECJ recalled that there is a presumption that the care and treatment provided in the issuing Member State will be adequate.[33]

However, that does not mean that the executing judicial authority must systematically ignore indications that the life or health of the person concerned may be endangered in the event of surrender. In this respect, the ECJ ruled that, in exceptional circumstances, the surrender can be temporarily postponed pursuant to Article 23(4) of the EAW Framework Decision.[34] In particular, it must be done when it cannot be ruled out that the surrender of the person concerned, who is seriously ill, may expose this person to a real risk of inhuman or degrading treatment within the meaning of Article 4 of the Charter, regardless of the level of quality of the care available in the issuing Member State.

The difficulty here is that Article 23(4) of the EAW Framework Decision only provides for a suspension limited in time. For that reason, the ECJ clarified that, in exceptional circumstances, when that risk cannot be eliminated within a reasonable period, the executing judicial authority cannot give effect to the EAW and must refuse the surrender.[35]

D. The Obligation to Maintain Dialogue

It could be argued that in this specific situation or when the two-step examination leads to a refusal to execute the EAW, mutual trust between the issuing Member State and the executing Member State lessens. This is, in my view, a misguided conclusion. On the contrary, the principle of mutual trust, read in conjunction with the principle of loyal cooperation, does indeed remain at the heart of the Court's reasoning. It constitutes the guiding light of judicial cooperation between the judicial authorities concerned. In recent cases, the ECJ has made it clear that even when the surrender represents a risk of breach of the fundamental rights of the person concerned, the judicial authorities involved have an obligation to maintain dialogue and rely on the information exchanged.

This obligation to engage in dialogue, based on Article 15 of the EAW Framework Decision, is illustrated by the judgment of 31 January 2023 in *Puig Gordi and Others*.[36] Here, the ECJ recalled that the issuing and executing judicial authorities must make full use of the instruments of dialogue provided for in the EAW Framework Decision,[37] in order to foster the mutual trust on which judicial cooperation is based.[38] More specifically, that obligation means that the executing judicial authority must request the issuing judicial authority to furnish, as a matter of urgency, all supplementary information that it deems necessary.[39] This judicial authority is obliged[40] to answer and the executing judicial authority is obliged

[33] *EDL (Ground for refusal based on illness)* (n 16), para 35.
[34] ibid, para 36.
[35] ibid, paras 51–53.
[36] *Puig Gordi and Others* (n 16).
[37] See Arts 8(1) and 15 of the EAW Framework Decision.
[38] *Puig Gordi and Others* (n 16), para 132.
[39] *Openbaar Ministerie (Tribunal established by law in the issuing Member State)* (n 16), para 84.
[40] ibid, para 85.

to take into consideration this information in its general assessment of the two-step examination.

Recently, in *GN (Motif de refus fondé sur l'intérêt supérieur de l'enfant)*, the ECJ clarified that the information which the executing judicial authority is entitled to request may concern both the first and the second stage of the examination which that authority must carry out. However, that authority may not request information from the issuing judicial authority concerning solely the second stage of that examination where it considers that there are no systemic or generalised deficiencies or deficiencies affecting an objectively identifiable group of persons to which the person concerned belongs.[41]

The obligation to participate in this dialogue in good faith was particularly emphasised by the ECJ in this case. In fact, the executing authority had questioned the Antwerp public prosecutor's office (Belgium), the issuing authority, among others, about the conditions of detention of mothers of young children in Belgium. The public prosecutor's office merely replied that the Belgian Ministry of Justice should be contacted.

In that context, the ECJ ruled that:

> the issuing judicial authority is obliged to provide the executing judicial authority with the additional information requested, failing which it will disregard the principle of loyal cooperation. In order, in particular, to ensure that the operation of the European arrest warrant is not paralysed, the duty of sincere cooperation, enshrined in the first subparagraph of Article 4(3) TEU, must govern the dialogue between the executing and issuing judicial authorities. [Consequently, i]f the issuing judicial authority does not respond satisfactorily to the request for additional information made by the executing judicial authority, the latter must then make an overall assessment of all the information at its disposal in the context of each of the two stages.[42]

The ECJ took a similar stance in *EDL (Ground for refusal based on illness)*. It stated that prior to temporarily postponing the execution of the EAW, the executing judicial authority must ask the issuing judicial authority to provide it with all relevant information that could lead to ruling out the risk of breaching Article 4 of the Charter.[43] If such safeguards are provided by the issuing judicial authority, the EAW must be executed. Undoubtedly, the dialogue is still based on the premise that the issuing Member State is responsible for ensuring the full respect of fundamental rights.

It follows from this case law that this dialogue between judicial authorities is the ultimate expression of mutual trust, as a safeguard to maintain the AFSJ.

IV. THE PRINCIPLE OF MUTUAL TRUST AS A GUIDING LIGHT FOR EUROPEAN JUDICIAL COOPERATION

The EAW Framework Decision is not the only act of EU law that implements the principle of mutual trust in criminal matters. The importance of this principle in this context has been highlighted by other instruments of EU law, two examples of which follow.

The first is Council Framework Decision 2008/909/JHA of 27 November 2008 on the application of the principle of mutual recognition to judgments in criminal matters imposing custodial sentences or measures involving deprivation of liberty for the purpose of their

[41] *GN (Motif de refus fondé sur l'intérêt supérieur de l'enfant)* (n 27), para 50.
[42] ibid, paras 52–54.
[43] *EDL (Ground for refusal based on illness)* (n 16), para 47.

enforcement in the European Union.[44] In this regard, in a recent case, a German court asked the ECJ whether it could refuse to declare a custodial sentence imposed on MD in Poland to be enforceable in Germany, on account of the breach of the second paragraph of Article 47 of the Charter and of Article 2 TEU by Poland. In that context, it was unsure whether, for the purpose of the recognition and enforcement in Germany of the custodial sentence imposed on M.D. in Poland, it should make its own decision as to whether the Polish judicial system was deficient and whether the fundamental right to a fair trial of the person concerned was infringed or alternatively is it for the ECJ to do so, in order to avoid divergences between the Member States of the EU. In addition, that German court considered that it is not clear that the approach adopted by the ECJ in its judgment of 25 July 2018, *Minister for Justice and Equality (Deficiencies in the system of justice)*,[45] in relation to the EAW Framework Decision can also be applied to Framework Decision 2008/909.

In its answer, the ECJ stated that:

> like [the EAW Framework Decision], Framework Decision 2008/909 gives concrete expression, in criminal matters, to the principles of mutual trust and mutual recognition which require, particularly with regard to the [AFSJ], that each Member State, save in exceptional circumstances, consider the other Member States to be complying with EU law and particularly with the fundamental rights recognised by EU law.[46]

Article 8 of Framework Decision 2008/909 provides, therefore, that the executing authority is, in principle, required to grant the request seeking recognition of a judgment and enforcement of a custodial sentence or measure involving deprivation of liberty handed down in another Member State which has been forwarded in accordance with Articles 4 and 5 of the aforesaid Framework Decision. That authority may, in principle, refuse to give effect to such request only on the grounds of non-recognition and non-enforcement exhaustively listed in Article 9 of Framework Decision 2008/909.

Nevertheless, the ECJ admitted that it recognised, in its case law on the EAW, that additional limitations of the principles of mutual recognition and mutual trust can be made in exceptional circumstances.[47] In the same way as the EAW Framework Decision, Article 3(4) of Framework Decision 2008/909 provides that the latter is not to have the effect of modifying the obligation to respect fundamental rights and fundamental legal principles as enshrined in Article 6 TEU. Furthermore, Recital 13 of that Framework Decision states that the latter respects fundamental rights and observes the principles recognised by Article 6 TEU and reflected by the Charter.

The ECJ ruled that, like the EAW Framework Decision, Framework Decision 2008/909 must be interpreted as meaning that the competent authority of the executing Member State may, in exceptional circumstances, refuse to recognise and enforce a criminal conviction handed down in the issuing Member State where there is evidence of systemic or generalised deficiencies that are liable to affect the independence of the judiciary in that Member State and thereby undermine the essence of the fundamental right of the person concerned to a fair trial.[48] In this regard, the competent authority of the executing Member State must follow the same two-step examination as in the context of the EAW Framework Decision.[49]

[44] [2009] OJ L81/24.
[45] *Minister for Justice and Equality (Deficiencies in the system of justice)* (n 16).
[46] Case C-819/21 *MD*, ECLI:EU:C: 2023:841, para 19.
[47] ibid, para 21.
[48] ibid, para 27.
[49] ibid, paras 28–30.

Indeed, as the ECJ stressed, allowing that authority to suspend, on its own initiative, the mechanism laid down in Framework Decision 2008/909 by refusing, in principle, to give effect to all the requests seeking recognition of judgments and enforcement of criminal sentences from the Member State affected by those deficiencies, would call into question the principles of mutual trust and mutual recognition which underpin that Framework Decision.[50]

The second example concerns Council Regulation (EU) 2017/1939 of 12 October 2017 implementing enhanced cooperation on the establishment of the European Public Prosecutor's Office.[51] In the very first judgment on the interpretation of this regulation, the ECJ clarified that the abovementioned regulation established a fundamental distinction between, on the one hand, the justification and adoption of a delegated investigation measure by a handling European Delegated Prosecutor and, on the other hand, its enforcement in another Member State by an assisting European Delegated Prosecutor. It pointed out that this distinction reflects 'the logic underlying the system of judicial cooperation in criminal matters between the Member States, which is based on the principles of trust and mutual recognition'.[52]

The ECJ based this finding on various EU instruments on judicial cooperation in criminal matters. First, it highlighted in particular that the principle of mutual recognition, which implies that there is mutual trust between Member States, also finds expression in Article 1(2) of Directive 2014/41. This article provides that the Member States are to execute a European Investigation Order (EIO) on the basis of that principle and in accordance with the provisions of that directive.[53] Second, the system of judicial cooperation provided for by the mechanism of the EIO[54] is also based, like that established by the EAW, on a division of competences between the issuing judicial authority and the executing judicial authority. Under this division, it is the responsibility of the issuing judicial authority to check compliance with the substantive conditions necessary for issuing an EIO, without this assessment being subsequently reviewed by the executing judicial authority, in accordance with the principle of mutual recognition.[55]

The ECJ consequently deduced that if a cross-border investigation measure ordered by a handling European Delegated Prosecutor is subject, in the executing Member State, to judicial authorisation,[56] that judicial authorisation cannot be made subject to an examination of the factors relating to the justification and adoption of the delegated investigation measure concerned. Indeed, such an examination would lead, in practice, to a less effective system than that established by legal instruments such as the EIO and the EAW, which would thus undermine the objective pursued by the establishment of the European Public Prosecutor's Office.[57] The review relating to the judicial authorisation required under the law of the Member State of the assisting European Delegated Prosecutor may relate only to matters connected with that enforcement.[58]

[50] ibid, para 34.

[51] [2017] OJ L283/1.

[52] *GK and Others (Parquet européen)* (n 3), para 55.

[53] ibid, para 62.

[54] Directive 2014/41/EU of the European Parliament and of the Council of 3 April 2014 regarding the European Investigation Order in criminal matters [2014] OJ L130/1.

[55] *GK and Others (Parquet européen)* (n 3), para 63.

[56] Under the first subparagraph of Art 31(3) of Council Regulation (EU) 2017/1939 of 12 October 2017.

[57] *GK and Others (Parquet européen)* (n 3), para 68.

[58] ibid, para 72.

When interpreting different EU legislative acts adopted in the field of judicial cooperation in criminal matters, the ECJ has clarified to what extent those legislative instruments share the same objective and have in common the need for mutual trust between the Member States and, in particular, the authorities involved in judicial cooperation.

V. CONCLUSION

First mentioned in the late 1970s in connection with the free movement of goods, the idea of mutual trust was taken up again by the European Council just over 20 years later as the necessary foundation for future judicial cooperation in civil and criminal matters. Used by the EU legislature in a number of legislative instruments, it constitutes an integral part of the ECJ's interpretation of these instruments. However, it is clear from the examples presented here that the ECJ tends to interpret the various legislative acts adopted for judicial cooperation in criminal matters, and which share the same objective, in the light of the EAW – the yardstick of mutual trust. It remains to be seen whether the Member States, including their courts, go along with this.

4

Defining a Notion of Judicial Authority in the Context of the Area of Freedom, Security and Justice

IRMANTAS JARUKAITIS*

I. INTRODUCTION

Legal notions are the primary building elements of each legal system. Legal rules and other legal standards are formed and take shape by combining various legal notions in different ways. EU law is not an exception in that regard. However, it is special in the sense that it presupposes the existence of national legal systems of EU Member States and is intertwined with them in different ways. This is especially true when EU law does not seek full harmonisation (or does not exercise its exclusive competence), but rather coordinates national legal systems or harmonises them only to a certain extent in order to achieve the objectives of EU law. In these types of situations, one of the relevant questions is the relationship between these building elements belonging to different legal systems. To be more precise, in order to interpret certain rules established by EU legal acts, one has to answer the question, are they based on legal notions established by national or EU law? There is no doubt that this question is a question of EU law. Only after answering this question may one proceed with a proper interpretation of these notions and give them a particular meaning.

A notion of 'judicial authority', which, as we will see, is one of the central notions of EU law in the Area of Freedom, Security and Justice (AFSJ), is a good example of this. Thus, the aim of this chapter is to provide a concise analysis of the jurisprudence of the European Court of Justice (ECJ), developing this notion in the context of the AFSJ in order to see its evolution, and challenges inherent to the need to reconcile the effectiveness and uniformity of EU law with the autonomy and diversity of national legal systems, including their institutional setup.

II. EU PRIMARY LAW AND KEY ASPECTS OF THE NOTION OF JUDICIAL AUTHORITY

Article 3(2) of the Treaty on European Union (TEU) explicitly indicates that the establishment of the AFSJ is one of the main objectives of the EU. Looking at Article 3 TEU, the Lisbon Treaty visually gave the AFSJ even more weight than the establishment of the internal market, which

* Judge of the European Court of Justice, Associated Professor in the Faculty of Law at Vilnius University.

for a long time was considered to be at the heart of the European integration process. By the conclusions of its meeting in Tampere in 1999, the European Council had put forward the principle of mutual recognition as the cornerstone of judicial co-operation in both civil and criminal matters within the Union.[1] It was a sign of a fundamental paradigm shift[2] – a departure from a sovereignty-based classic *political* approach to international cooperation in criminal matters and its replacement by *judicial* cooperation based on the principles of mutual trust and mutual recognition resulting from a high level of confidence between the Member States. Needless to say, this kind of trust and recognition is based on the fundamental premise that each Member State shares with all the other Member States, and recognises that they share with it, a set of common values on which the EU is founded, as stated in Article 2 TEU. That premise implies and justifies the existence of mutual trust between the Member States that those values will be recognised, and therefore that the EU law that implements them will be respected.[3]

Within the context of the AFSJ, Article 67(3) of the Treaty on the Functioning of the European Union (TFEU) directly envisages the adoption of measures for coordination and cooperation between police and *judicial authorities* and other competent authorities, the mutual recognition of judgments in criminal matters and the approximation of criminal laws. At the same time, Article 82(1) TFEU stipulates that judicial cooperation in criminal matters in the EU is based on the principle of mutual recognition of *judgments and judicial decisions* and also provides for the approximation of national laws of the Member States in certain areas of criminal law. Further, the terminology of the TFEU becomes more complex because it also speaks about the 'judiciary' and 'judicial staff' (Article 82(1)(c) TFEU) and the cooperation between 'judicial or *equivalent authorities*' of the Member States in relation to proceedings in criminal matters and the enforcement of decisions (Article 82(1)(d) TFEU).

Thus, one may wonder what is the exact meaning of the notion of 'judicial authority', which, alongside the notion of 'judicial decision', holds a central place because it is used horizontally in the context of the AFSJ? This question is pertinent and important given the fact that the EU does not have a material competence to regulate the organisation of judicial systems of the Member States, and the ECJ is very clear on that point.[4] On the other hand, in this type of situation, in order to ensure a uniform application of EU law and the principle of equality, it is not unusual for EU law to follow a functional approach and to develop autonomous notions depending on its needs.[5]

[1] Conclusions of the Presidency of the European Council (Tampere, Finland, 15–16 October 1999).

[2] See, for example, Opinion of AG Ruiz-Jarabo Colomer in Case C-303/05 *Advocaten voor de Wereld VZW*, ECLI:EU:C:2006:552, paras 38–47, where he mentions completely different perceptions of national courts, legislatures, and academics of the European arrest warrant (EAW) system once it was introduced. Attention should be also drawn to point 5 of the Preamble of the European Arrest Warrant Framework Decision (Council Framework Decision 2002/584/JHA of 13 June 2002 on the European arrest warrant and the surrender procedures between Member States [2002] OJ L190/1 (EAW Framework Decision)), which explicitly indicates that the objective set for the Union to become an AFSJ leads to *abolishing* extradition between Member States and replacing it with a *system of surrender between judicial authorities*.

[3] See, for example, Cases C-284/16 *Achmea*, ECLI:EU:C:2018:158, para 34; C-156/21 *Hungary v European Parliament and Council*, ECLI:EU:C:2022:97, paras 125 and 129; and C-157/21 *Poland v European Parliament and Council*, ECLI:EU:C:2022:98, paras 143 and 149.

[4] See, for example, Case C-430/21 *RS*, ECLI:EU:C:2022:99, para 38. However, while exercising their competence in this field Member States have the obligation to respect the values of Art 2 TEU (among them the principle of the rule of law) and Art 19 TEU establishing the obligation to provide remedies sufficient to ensure effective legal protection in the fields covered by EU law. Additionally, depending on the context, the principle of procedural autonomy might also be relevant: see, for example, Case C-497/20 *Randstad Italia SpA*, ECLI:EU:C:2021:1037, paras 58–63.

[5] One of the examples being the notion of a 'court or tribunal' in Art 267 TFEU, which is broader than a notion of 'court' under national legal systems. See, for example, Case C-274/14 *Banco Sandander*, ECLI:EU:C:2020:17, para 51. In the context of the EAW Framework Decision see, for example, Case C-294/16 PPU, *JZ*, ECLI:EU:C:2016:610, para 37.

Given the aforementioned context, it is not surprising that secondary EU legislation does not provide for a detailed answer to that question. At the same time, different approaches to this issue can be observed in different pieces of EU legislation. While the EAW Framework Decision simply refers to the 'issuing judicial authority' and the 'executing judicial authority' without defining them,[6] other EU legal acts – for example the European Investigation Order Directive[7] and the E-evidence Regulation[8] – speak more broadly about an 'issuing authority' and explicitly mention a *public prosecutor* alongside a judge, a court and an investigating judge and distinguish them from 'any other *competent authority*' (emphasis added) which acts in its capacity as an investigating authority in criminal proceedings.[9] Additionally, attention should be drawn to the references to national law in the aforementioned provisions of EU legislation. Therefore, the first question that needs to be answered is whether the notion of judicial authority is an autonomous concept of the EU law? The answer is relevant first of all from an institutional point of view, because if the answer is 'yes' then it would be up to the ECJ to disclose its precise meaning as part of EU law, while a negative answer would mean that it rests in domain of national legislatures and national courts.

The ECJ answered this question affirmatively in the *Poltorak*[10] and *Kovalkovas*[11] judgments and explained that the reference to national laws was meant only to designate the judicial authority *with the competence to issue the EAW* but could not be read as implying the definition of the notion of judicial authority in itself. Further, the ECJ explicitly provided that the notion of judicial authority is not limited to judges or courts of a Member State, but (echoing the idea of *equivalent authorities* in Article 82 TFEU) *may* extend to the authorities required to participate in administering justice in the legal system concerned.[12] However, the ECJ excluded police services and ministries of justice from the scope of this notion, based on the usual meaning of the term 'judiciary', the provisions of the TEU and the principle of separation of powers.[13] The *Poltorak* and *Kovalkovas* judgments allow for drawing some conclusions. First, by deciding that the notion of judicial authority is an autonomous notion of the EU law, it reserved the right of authentic interpretation of that notion for itself. Second, one may say that the assessment was more institutional than substantial.[14] This may be explained by the fact that the preliminary questions posed by national courts in the *Poltorak* and *Kovalkovas* cases had a straightforward institutional character and the answer to them was relatively obvious.[15] Still, the references in those judgments to the principle of separation

[6] Art 6(1) and (2) of the EAW Framework Decision.

[7] Directive 2014/41/EU of the European Parliament and of the Council of 3 April 2014 regarding the European Investigation Order in criminal matters [2014] OJ L130/1 (EIO Directive).

[8] Regulation (EU) 2023/1543 of the European Parliament and of the Council of 12 July 2023 on European Production Orders and European Preservation Orders for electronic evidence in criminal proceedings and for the execution of custodial sentences following criminal proceedings [2023] OJ L191/118 (E-evidence Regulation).

[9] Art 2(c) of the EIO Directive; Art 4 of the E-evidence Regulation.

[10] Case C-452/16 PPU *Poltorak*, ECLI:EU:C:2016:858, paras 30–32.

[11] Case C-477/16 PPU, *Kovalkovas*, ECLI:EU:C:2016:861, paras 31–33.

[12] Attention should be drawn to the fact that the question of whether a *national* arrest warrant issued by police, but confirmed by public prosecutor's office, is a judicial decision within the meaning of Art 8(1)(c) of the EAW Framework Decision, was dealt with by the ECJ in its *Özçelik* judgment, adopted at the same time as *Poltorak* and *Kovalkovas* judgments: Case C-453/16 PPU *Özçelik*, ECLI:EU:C:2016:860. Although the issue of the independence of a public prosecutor is not dealt with by the judgment, the AG explicitly mentioned this aspect in his Opinion: Opinion of AG Campos Sánchez-Bordona in Case C-453/16 PPU *Ozçelik*, ECLI:EU:C:2016:783, para 57.

[13] *Poltorak* (n 10), paras 33–46.

[14] See also the Opinion of the AG Campos Sánchez-Bordona in Case C-452/16 PPU *Poltorak*, ECLI:EU:C:2016:782.

[15] In *Poltorak*, one of the preliminary questions was very straightforward: is the Swedish police board covered by the term 'judicial authority', within the meaning of Art 6(1) of the EAW Framework Decision, whereas in *Kovalkovas* the same question was posed with regard to the Ministry of Justice of the Republic of Lithuania.

of powers, distinguishing the 'administration of justice' from functions of the executive and mentioning the guarantees attached to the judicial supervision inevitably lead to the question: what is the *nature* of judicial functions in this particular context and what *substantial criteria* must be satisfied in order to be qualified a judicial authority?

The opportunity to develop its jurisprudence and to answer this question arose in 2019 when ECJ had to deal with a string of preliminary references, submitted by the Irish Supreme Court and the High Court (dealt with before the Grand Chamber of the ECJ)[16] and later by the Higher Regional Court of Berlin,[17] the Court of Appeal of Luxembourg[18] and the District Court of Amsterdam.[19] The ECJ had to answer questions, whether at all and under what conditions public prosecutors' offices might be treated as 'issuing judicial authorities' within the meaning of Article 6 of the EAW Framework Decision. Litigants in the main proceedings claimed that the respective prosecutor's offices of the issuing Member States were not independent from the executive. In its judgments the ECJ developed criteria defining a required level of independence of a judicial authority and also gave some guidance (of course, subject to the ultimate verification by national courts) in each case depending on the particular institutional setup of an issuing Member State.

First, the ECJ pointed to a close connection between the principles of mutual recognition and mutual trust, which are implemented by the EAW system in order to develop the AFSJ, and to the consequence that the execution of an EAW is a rule, while the refusal to execute it is intended to be an exception.[20] After recalling that the notion of a judicial authority is an autonomous notion of EU law, the ECJ pointed out that, taking into account the procedural autonomy of the Member States, the purposes pursued by the EAW Framework Decision and its provisions, this notion is wider and is capable of including not only judges or courts of the Member States, but also other authorities participating in the administration of criminal justice. Thus, a public prosecutor's office, must, *in principle*, be regarded as participating in the administration of justice in the relevant Member State.[21] Nevertheless, despite the fact that an EAW must be issued on the basis of a national arrest warrant (issued by a judge or a court), an issuing judicial authority must act independently in the exercise of its functions when adopting a decision to issue an EAW, because the latter may involve a restriction of the right to liberty protected by Article 6 of the Charter of Fundamental Rights of the European Union (Charter).[22] This in fact means that there is a requirement of two-level protection. Thus, in order to be qualified as a judicial authority, an authority which participates in the administration of justice but is not a judge or a court has to be itself capable of exercising its functions objectively in order to take into account all exculpatory and incriminatory evidence before it without being exposed to the risk of direct or indirect external influence in a specific case, particularly from the executive.[23]

While analysing these arguments put forward by the ECJ, attention first of all has to be drawn to the fact that Advocate General Campos Sánchez-Bordona had a different opinion about the answers to be given in the above-mentioned cases than the Grand Chamber

[16] Joined Cases C-508/18 and C-82/19 PPU *OG and PI*, ECLI:EU:C:2019:456; and Case C-509/18 *PF*, ECLI:EU:C:2019:457.

[17] Case C-489/19 PPU *NJ*, ECLI:EU:C:2019:849.

[18] Joined Cases C-566/19 and C-626/19 PPU *JR and YC*, ECLI:EU:C:2019:1077.

[19] Cases C-625/19 PPU *XD*, ECLI:EU:C:2019:1078; and C-627/19 PPU *ZB*, ECLI:EU:C:2019:1079.

[20] *OG and PI* (n 16), paras 43–46; and *PF* (n 16), paras 22–25.

[21] *OG and PI* (n 16), paras 48–60; and *PF* (n 16), paras 27–39.

[22] *OG and PI* (n 16), paras 66, 68 and 72; and *PF* (n 16), paras 44–46 and 50.

[23] *OG and PI* (n 16), paras 69–71 and 73–74; and *PF* (n 16), paras 47–49 and 51–52.

of the ECJ.[24] Although acknowledging that public prosecutors participate in the administration of justice, the Advocate General drew a clear line between the role of a prosecutor ordering or approving a national arrest warrant for a *limited time*, before a detained person must be released or brought to a court, and the need to ensure a second level of protection in the context of an issue of an EAW, where the deprivation of liberty may last much longer.[25] Besides, he pointed to different degrees of independence enjoyed by prosecutors and judges and the fact that in a State governed by the rule of law, effective judicial protection is ensured by judges and courts, not other State authorities.[26] Further, although acknowledging the possibility of a challenge to an EAW issued by a public prosecutor's office before a court of an issuing Member State, the Advocate General ruled out such a possibility because of the practical difficulties for the requested person to exercise his defence rights and for the efficient functioning of the EAW system.[27] Finally, in his Opinion in the *PF* case, the Advocate General added an argument related to the *travaux préparatoires* of the EAW Framework Decision.[28] For all these reasons, the Advocate General in reality put an equals sign between the notion of judicial authority and that of the judicial branch, and concluded that a public prosecutor's office may not be treated as an issuing judicial authority within the meaning of Article 6(1) of the EAW Framework Decision.

As explained above, the ECJ took a different approach by emphasising that, in situations in which an authority participating in the administration of justice is not a judge or a court, national law should provide for the possibility of challenging a decision issuing an EAW, including its proportionality, before a court in proceedings which meets the requirements inherent in effective judicial protection.[29] Thus, for the Court, this type of a 'layered' protection (independence from the executive provided to public prosecutor's office coupled with the right to challenge an EAW before a national court) in the course of the issuing of an EAW suffices to ensure effective protection of the rights of a requested person.

Attention should be also drawn to the fact that both the references of national courts and the answers provided by the ECJ place the emphasis on the independence of a judicial authority from the *executive* and the need to consider the organisational structure of a public prosecutor's office. This is not surprising, since when developing the criteria of independence in this particular context, one must look at it from the point of view of the functioning of the EAW system and its direct objective in a particular criminal case – detention and further surrender of a person for the purposes of a criminal prosecution or the execution of a judgment.[30]

[24] See the Opinion of AG Campos Sánchez-Bordon in Joined Cases C-508/18 and C-82/19 PPU *OG and PI*, ECLI:EU:C:2019:337; and in Case C-509/18 *PF*, ECLI:EU:C:2019:338.

[25] Opinion of AG Campos Sánchez-Bordona in *OG and PI* (n 24), paras 36–37 and 54–59. The AG also pointed out the fact that under German law the German Public Prosecutor's office had no right to issue 'even' a national arrest warrant, this power being limited exclusively to national courts: para 76 of the Opinion.

[26] ibid, paras 66–67.

[27] ibid, paras 72–75.

[28] Opinion of AG Campos Sánchez-Bordona in Case C-509/18 *PF* (n 24), paras 36–45.

[29] *OG and PI* (n 16), para 75; and *PF* (n 16), para 53.

[30] Thus, in *JR and YC* (n 18), para 54, the ECJ makes a distinction between *general policy* instructions and the possibility of specific instructions in an individual case. Besides, in *JR and YC*, para 56, the ECJ explicitly indicated that the requirement of independence does not prohibit any internal instructions, which may be given to public prosecutors *by their hierarchical superiors, who are themselves public prosecutors*, based on the hierarchical relationship underpinning the functioning of the public prosecutor's office. This context, and the 'narrow' field of application of the Framework Decision, is in contrast with a much wider array of challenges that might arise in the context of performed judicial functions, the organisation of judiciary and judicial independence both externally (see, for example, Case C-896/19 *Repubblika*, ECLI: EU:C:2021:311, para 54 which emphasises that the independence of the judiciary must in particular be ensured in relation to the legislature and the executive) and internally (see, for example,

This logic also explains a distinction the ECJ makes between an EAW issued in order to surrender a person for the purposes of a *criminal prosecution* and an EAW issued for the purposes of the *execution of a judgment*.[31] In the first scenario, where there has not been a final judgment and the presumption of innocence is relevant, the higher level of protection is required. In contrast, the second situation concerns a person who has already been convicted by a judgment of a court. Thus, a surrender is sought only to enforce a decision adopted by a judge or a court.[32]

III. FURTHER DEVELOPMENTS IN THE ECJ CASE LAW

On a more practical level, the ECJ practice, developed so far, reveals that while the public prosecutors' offices of Belgium,[33] France,[34] Lithuania[35] and Sweden[36] seemed to fulfil the requirement of independence from the executive in the eyes of the Court, this was not the case with their Austrian[37] and German counterparts.[38] Furthermore, in 2020 the ECJ had

Cases C-554/21 *Financijska agencija v HANN-INVEST*, C-622/21 *MINERAL-SEKULINE*; and C-727/21 *UDRAGA KHL MEDVEŠČAK ZAGREB*, in which national courts inquire as to what extent internal court mechanisms designed to ensure the uniformity of court practice are compatible with the independence of judiciary (cases pending before the ECJ at the time of writing).

[31] Art 1(1) of the EAW Framework Decision provides that the EAW is a judicial decision issued by a Member State with a view to the arrest and surrender by another Member State of a requested person, *for the purposes of conducting a criminal prosecution or executing a custodial sentence or detention order*.

[32] The ECJ clearly distinguished these two scenarios in *ZB* (n 19), in which, in contrast to other cases that reached the ECJ, the preliminary question was posed in the context of an EAW issued for the purposes of *enforcing a judgment* by which a person was sentenced to prison. See *ZB* (n 19), paras 29–38.

[33] ibid, paras 26–28, indicating that Belgian public prosecutors enjoy the independence guaranties required by the abovementioned jurisprudence of the ECJ.

[34] See, as abovementioned, *JR and YC* (n 18), paras 54–56. The ECJ underlined that under the applicable legislation in France a public prosecutor's office has the obligation to carry out its duties objectively, free from any instruction in a specific case from the executive. The Minister for Justice may issue *only general instructions* concerning criminal justice *policy* to public prosecutors. Those general instructions cannot have the effect of preventing a public prosecutor from exercising his discretion as to the proportionality of issuing an EAW in a particular case. It should be noted that before the reforms undertaken in 2013, the French Minister of Justice had the right to issue written instructions to the prosecutors in individual cases: E Vergès, 'Politique pénale et action publique: la difficile conciliation du modèle français de ministère public et des standards européens' (2013) *Revue de Science Criminelle et de Droit Pénal Comparé* 605, 605–606.

[35] See *PF* (n 16), paras 54–56, where the ECJ, among other aspects, explicitly mentioned the independence guarantees of Lithuanian public prosecutors established by the Lithuanian Constitution. In addition, the Ruling of the Constitutional Court of the Republic of Lithuania of 13 May 2004, which confirms such reading of Lithuanian law, should be mentioned: https://lrkt.lt/en/court-acts/search/170/ta1268/content, accessed 22 February 2024. Still the ECJ noted that its case file was not informative enough to conclude that Lithuanian legislation provided for the effective judicial review of decisions of the Prosecutor General of Lithuania: thus, this question was left for the verification of the referring court: see *PF* (n 16), para 56.

[36] See *XD* (n 19), para 20, where the national court clearly indicated that it had no doubts as regards the independence of the Swedish public prosecutor's office, but had some doubts as regards the effectiveness of judicial review of a decision to issue an EAW. The ECJ ruled that Swedish regulation, while not providing for a separate judicial remedy, is nevertheless in line with the requirement of effective judicial review, because a decision of the national court ordering provisional detention of the person concerned must also assess the proportionality of other possible measures, including an issue of an EAW. See *XD* (n 19), paras 46–53.

[37] See *NJ* (n 17), paras 40–48. On the one hand, the ECJ indicated that under Austrian law the public prosecutor's office is subordinate to the Federal Minister of Justice. On the other hand, the Austrian regulation in its entirety was regarded as compatible with the EAW Framework Decision, because each EAW, issued by a public prosecutor's office, *needs to be systematically and ex officio endorsed by an Austrian court and produces legal effects only after that endorsement*. Thus, any external instruction would be irrelevant, because an Austrian court adopts an autonomous judicial decision giving the final form to the EAW.

[38] See *OG and PI* (n 16), paras 76–88. The ECJ underlined that according to both the information set out in the orders for reference as well as that provided by the German Government, the Minister of Justice had 'external' powers

the opportunity to develop its jurisprudence as regards the implementation of Article 6 of the EAW Framework Decision in the Netherlands.[39]

Given the aforementioned jurisprudence of the ECJ, it should be underlined that it may not be read as *requiring* the Member States to ensure some sort of independence of public prosecutor's offices, because the EAW Framework Decision simply does not establish such a requirement. This requirement of independence is only a prerequisite for an institution to be accepted as a judicial authority within the meaning of Article 6 of the EAW Framework Decision. The aforementioned examples of national regulations show that the Member States may have recourse to different legal solutions when designating national authorities as judicial authorities.[40]

The reception of ECJ practice by legal commentators was mixed, with the main discussion revolving around the issue of whether the notion of judicial authority should cover public prosecutors or not in the context of their independence. Some of the commentators were more favourable to the approach of Advocate General Campos Sánchez-Bordona, reserving the notion of judicial authority only to judges and courts. Some considered that it would be a difficult task for the executing judicial authority to evaluate the requisite level of independence of public prosecutor's office in the issuing Member State, while others referred to the need to ensure the consistency with the ECJ practice developed in other fields.[41] There were also those who argued that the ECJ was right not to follow this approach,[42] or suggested broader reforms envisaging more harmonisation in the field of the AFSJ in order to ensure more adequate level of fundamental rights protection within the EU.[43]

In the light of the ECJ jurisprudence discussed so far, it should be said that after concluding that the notion of judicial authority is an autonomous concept of EU law, the ECJ proceeded with the interpretation of the concept that would respond to the needs of the

to issue instructions, allowing him to have a direct influence on a decision to issue or not issue an EAW. Some commentators provided recent practical examples of use of these powers: see, for example, T Niedernhuber, 'How Much Independence is Necessary to Issue a European Arrest Warrant' (2020) *European Criminal Law Review* 19.

[39] Case C-510/19 *Openbaar Ministerie and YU and ZV v AZ*, ECLI:EU:C:2020:953, paras 67–69. In contrast to the aforementioned cases, this case concerned the notion of '*executing* judicial authority' within the meaning of Art 6(2) of the EAW Framework Decision. The ECJ ruled that its jurisprudence interpreting the notion of 'issuing judicial authority' is transferrable to the interpretation of the notion of 'executing judicial authority', because the status and the nature of the judicial authorities referred to in Art 6(1) and (2) of the EAW Framework Decision are identical, although those authorities exercise separate functions (see paras 41–55 of the judgment). Further, given the fact that Dutch public prosecutors may be subject to instructions in specific cases from the Dutch Ministry of Justice, the ECJ concluded that it cannot be held that the public prosecutor concerned satisfies the necessary conditions to be characterised as 'executing judicial authority' within the meaning of the EAW Framework Decision.

[40] The immediate effect of the *OG and PI* judgment was that instead of a public prosecutor's offices, German courts started issuing EAWs and different options of reform were considered: see, for example, Niedernhuber (n 38), 18–19. It seems that after long discussions an option granting more independence to public prosecutors' offices in order to qualify as a judicial authority is favoured: https://www.bildungsserver.de/onlineressource.html?onlineressourcen_id=62906, accessed 29 February 2024.

[41] For example, AH Ochnio, 'Why is a Redefinition of the Autonomous Concept of an "Issuing Judicial Authority" in the European Arrest Warrant Proceedings Needed?' (2020) *European Papers* 1305; M Böse, 'The European Arrest Warrant and the Independence of Public Prosecutors: *OG & PI, PF, JR & YC*' (2020) 57 *Common Market Law Review* 1268; T Harkin, 'The Case Law of the Court of Justice of the European Union on '"Judicial Authority" and issuing European Arrest Warrants' (2021) 12 *New Journal of European Criminal Law* 508.

[42] For example, C Heimrich, 'European Arrest Warrants and the Independence of the Issuing Judicial Authority – How Much Independence Is Required? (Case Note on Joined Cases C-508/18 and C-82/19 PPU *OG and PI*)' (2019) 10 *New Journal of European Criminal Law* 396; L Mancano 'You'll Never Work Alone: A Systemic Assessment of the European Arrest Warrant and Judicial Independence' (2021) 58 *Common Market Law Review* 713.

[43] P Bárd et al, 'The Judicialisation of the European Arrest Warrant Rule of Law and Fundamental Rights as Preconditions for Merited Mutual Trust', https://cdn.ceps.eu/wp-content/uploads/2023/08/Judicialisation-of-the-European-Arrest-Warrant-STREAM-Report.pdf, accessed 22 February 2024.

effective functioning of the EAW system and the effective protection of fundamental rights of the requested person.[44] This, on the one hand, led to numerous interpretations of that notion as covering not only judges and courts, but also public prosecutors' offices of the Member States. However, in the latter case, the ECJ established two additional requirements: first, that the authority participates in the administration of justice in the Member States; and, second, that the authority acts independently, without being exposed to the risk of direct or indirect external instructions from the executive in individual cases. Such a definition of the notion leaves some flexibility to the Member States when it comes to their institutional set-up.

The aforementioned functional approach regarding the interpretation of the EAW Framework Decision is even more visible and may be compared with the situations when it comes to the interpretation of other pieces of EU legislation in the field of the AFSJ. Provisions of the EIO Directive and their interpretation is a good example of such an approach. In its *Staatsanwaltschaft Wien/A and Others* judgment,[45] while interpreting the notions of 'judicial authority' and 'issuing authority' within the meaning of Article 1(1) and Article 2(c) of the EIO Directive, the ECJ drew attention to different wording, context, *purposes* and *consequences* stemming from the issue of an EAW and an EIO.[46] These differences allowed the ECJ to come to the conclusion that the notion of 'judicial authority' under the EIO Directive should be interpreted differently from that used in the EAW Framework Decision and that the notion of judicial authority within the meaning of the EIO Directive covers public prosecutors' offices of the Member States even *in the absence of the independence guarantees* required by the ECJ's jurisprudence on the EAW Framework Decision.[47]

Finally, it should be noted that the ECJ line of jurisprudence interpreting the notion of judicial authority employed by the EAW Framework Decision should be distinguished from situations related to systemic challenges to the rule of law in some EU Member States. In this type of case the ECJ does not interpret the notion of judicial authority within the meaning of Article 6 of the EAW Framework Decision, but rather provides an interpretation of the whole EAW Framework Decision in light of the Charter and refers to systemic or generalised deficiencies concerning the independence of *the judiciary in the issuing Member State*. This is so because the ECJ has to take into account a whole range of different considerations that are at stake and to strike a balance between them. Needless to say, in this type of situation the 'test' of *judicial* independence or rather situations, in which the execution of the issued EAW may be refused, is different.[48]

[44] At the same time, it should be emphasised that the Court clearly indicated that the availability of judicial review of a decision taken by an authority other than a court to issue an EAW is not a condition for classification of that authority as an issuing judicial authority within the meaning of Art 6(1) of the EAW Framework Decision; see *XD* (n 19), para 30.

[45] Case C-584/19 *Staatsanwaltschaft Wien/A and Others*, ECLI:EU:C:2020:1002.

[46] ibid, paras 49–73.

[47] ibid, para 75. Besides, recent references of national courts regarding the interpretation of the EIO Directive show that the question of interpretation of the notion of 'issuing authority' within the meaning of that directive may touch upon certain complex questions related to the functioning of the EIO: see Case C-670/22 *Staatsanwaltschaft Berlin (EncroChat)*, pending.

[48] Case C-216/18 PPU *Minister for Justice and Equality (Deficiencies in the system of justice)*, ECLI:EU:C:2018:586; Joined Cases C-354/20 PPU and C-412/20 PPU *L and P v Openbaar Ministerie (Independence of the issuing judicial authority)*, ECLI:EU:C:2020:1033; and Joined Cases C-562/21 PPU and C-563/21 PPU *X and Y v Openbaar Ministerie*, ECLI:EU:C:2022:100.

IV. CONCLUSION

Each legal notion has a functional character and domain of application. In addition, it should be 'workable' in a sense that it should have a clear meaning and utility in order to 'convey a message' and to structure legal regulation in specific situations predetermined by the legislature. It should be also distinguishable from other legal notions in order not to create confusion. In this context, a development of notions of EU law, which operates together with national legal systems, adds another layer of complexity because of the necessity to take into account the existing national regulation and to complement it.

The notion of judicial authority in the area of the AFSJ is a good example of such an exercise. Developed in a particular context, it must respond to several considerations, including the need to ensure effective functioning of the cooperation established by the EU legislation without compromising the protection of fundamental rights, as well as the institutional set-ups within the Member States. Seen from this perspective, the notion of judicial authority responds to the aforementioned needs, because it is employed in well-defined legal domains and contains clearly-defined criteria, distinguishing it from other related notions of EU law (for example, the notion of 'court or tribunal' within the meaning of Article 267 TFEU[49]). The absence of later references from national courts once the notion was clarified in a string of cases in 2019–2020 would seem to suggest that its content is clear and operational. Certainly, one may discuss the overall coherence of the jurisprudence of the ECJ, developing different legal tests and differing degrees of independence of institutions participating in the administration of justice (including courts) in the context of different domains of EU law. However, that is a discussion that goes far beyond the scope of this chapter.

[49] Regarding the notion of 'court or tribunal' as an autonomous concept of EU law, one may note the existence of a certain paradox. On the one hand, the jurisprudence of the ECJ establishes a clear set of criteria to allow the evaluation of whether a national institution is a court within the meaning of Art 267 TFEU. On the other hand, the results of such verification may be paradoxical (from the point of view of national law) in the sense that an institution that is not considered to be a court from the point of view of national law, may be treated as such from the point of view of Art 267 TFEU (see, for example, Case C-387/16 *Nidera*, ECLI:EU:C:2018:121), but an institution that is considered to be a court from the point of view of national law, may be considered as not fulfilling those criteria from the point of view of Art 267 TFEU (see, for example, Cases C-132/20 *Getin Noble*, ECLI:EU:C:2022:235; and C-718/21 *Krajowa Rada Sądownictwa*, ECLI:EU:C:2023:1015). Still, this is entirely consistent and logical, because, first, such a result is predetermined by the application of the same set of criteria; and second, the result responds to the true function of the notion (namely, to define whether the precondition of 'true' judicial dialogue is met).

5

The Case Law on Effective Remedy under the Dublin III Regulation: The Gradual Construction of a Fragile Mosaic

JESPER SVENNINGSEN AND YANN LAURANS*

I. INTRODUCTION

SINCE JANUARY 2006, when Judge Bay Larsen joined the European Court of Justice (ECJ), President Skouris and later President Lenaerts have designated him to act as Rapporteur in many important cases falling within the Area of Freedom, Security and Justice. In the course of his illustrious career at the ECJ, Judge Bay Larsen has risen to become Vice-President, and it is to celebrate the work of Vice-President Bay Larsen that we contribute this essay on how the case law on effective remedy under the Dublin III Regulation has been shaped.

Unlike in the General Court, in the ECJ, the President designates directly a judge to act as rapporteur in each case.[1] With this important prerogative, the President of the ECJ uses case management to ensure a high degree of coherence and foreseeability in new areas of law.

Whereas the line of continuity from the Dublin Convention[2] through to the Dublin II Regulation[3] was clear, the Dublin III Regulation[4] introduced a broad restructuring of the Dublin system, seeking both to streamline it and to grant new rights to the persons concerned. The remedies made available to those persons constitute the cornerstone of that system.

Article 27(1) of that Regulation is the essential foundation for any discussion on the scope of the right of appeal of persons subject to that system:

> The applicant or another person as referred to in Article 18(1)(c) or (d) shall have the right to an effective remedy, in the form of an appeal or a review, in fact and in law, against a transfer decision, before a court or tribunal.

* Respectively, Judge at the General Court and Legal Secretary in the Chambers of Vice-President Bay Larsen. All opinions expressed herein are personal.

[1] See Art 14(1) of the Rules of Procedure of the Court of Justice.

[2] Convention determining the State responsible for examining applications for asylum lodged in one of the Member States of the European Communities [1997] OJ C254/1.

[3] Council Regulation (EC) No 343/2003 of 18 February 2003 establishing the criteria and mechanisms for determining the Member State responsible for examining an asylum application lodged in one of the Member States by a third-country national [2003] OJ L50/1.

[4] Regulation (EU) No 604/2013 of the European Parliament and of the Council of 26 June 2013 establishing the criteria and mechanisms for determining the Member State responsible for examining an application for international protection lodged in one of the Member States by a third-country national or a stateless person [2013] OJ L180/31.

The other paragraphs of Article 27 of the Dublin III regulation supplement that rule, but are limited to regulating certain ancillary aspects of the right of appeal, such as the possible suspension of the transfer decision or legal assistance. The minimalist nature of the rule laid down in Article 27(1) should be noted. Not only is the nature of the appeal or review ambiguous,[5] but no clarification is given as to the actual detailed rules of the appeal, review or subject matter of the review by the competent court.

In addition, the frequency of secondary movements of applicants for international protection in the EU resulting in disputes relating to transfer decisions has given rise to an abundance of litigation. Hence it is not surprising that the ECJ has had many questions referred for preliminary rulings on the scope of the right of appeal provided for in the Dublin III Regulation. Those many references have led the ECJ to deliver almost 20 judgments over the course of a decade, several of which have been decided by the Grand Chamber. In order to present the case law resulting from those judgments, we would like to borrow a favourite image often alluded to by Judge Bay Larsen, that of a *mosaic*. In our view, that image is entirely apt here. Although none of the judgments delivered by the ECJ in relation to the appeal or review provided for by the Dublin III Regulation can claim to have developed a 'general conception' of that appeal or review, if one steps back for a moment to take a look at the image as a whole, it becomes possible to discern the many pieces of that appeal or review which, added gradually over time, have made the overall legal picture what it is today. It is this mosaic, to which Judge Bay Larsen has made a significant contribution, that we would like to examine in this essay.

From that point of view, it must be pointed out that, as is appropriate for a work of that kind, that mosaic is deployed in two dimensions. On the one hand, the most intense debate before the ECJ has concerned the definition of the actual scope of an appeal against a transfer decision. More specifically, it has been about determining which elements, of form and/or substance, may be subject to judicial review. On the other hand, it is possible to distinguish in that mosaic various pieces which, when assembled, delineate the form of an effective remedy against transfer decisions.

II. THE EXTENSION OF THE SCOPE OF THE APPEAL UNDER THE DUBLIN SYSTEM

As its name suggests, the Dublin III Regulation does not construct an *ex nihilo* system but reforms a pre-existing one. From the time of the Dublin II Regulation, it was established that persons had the option of relying on certain fundamental rights when bringing an appeal against a transfer decision. That principle has not only been confirmed, but significantly strengthened, in the context of the application of the Dublin III Regulation. However, the latter regulation did not merely strengthen the protection of fundamental rights; it led to a significant broadening of the scope of the appeal against transfer decisions, essentially making it possible to challenge all kinds of misapplication of that regulation.

[5] In particular, the difference between the 'appeal' and 'revision' referred to in that provision is not self-evident, particularly since it is apparent from the provision that revision must be carried out, in fact and in law, by a court or tribunal.

A. The Growing Place of Fundamental Rights

In order to properly understand the developments brought about by the Dublin III Regulation, it is useful to recall the approach taken by the ECJ towards the appeal against the transfer decision under the Dublin II Regulation, as embodied primarily in *Abdullahi*.[6]

In that case, the ECJ was asked whether an asylum seeker, in an appeal against a transfer decision, could challenge the application by the competent authorities of a criterion for determining the Member State responsible for examining his application, namely the irregular crossing of an external border of the EU. Basing itself on the overall scheme of the Dublin II Regulation, in particular its largely inter-State nature, the ECJ ruled out such a possibility. It expressly stated, however, that in such a situation the person concerned could rely on the existence of systemic deficiencies in the asylum procedure and in the conditions for the reception of asylum seekers in the Member State responsible, which constitute substantial grounds for believing that the person concerned would face a real risk of being subjected to inhuman or degrading treatment. Here, therefore, it was the risk of a serious breach of the Charter of Fundamental Rights of the European Union (the Charter), in the form already recognised by the ECJ in *NS and Others*,[7] which opened up the possibility of effectively challenging the transfer decision.

The possibility of relying on such an infringement of fundamental rights was not called into question when the Dublin III Regulation was adopted. Moreover, not allowing such a ground of review would have been inconsistent, since the exclusion of any possibility of transfer in the event of 'systemic deficiencies', which was not provided for by the Dublin II Regulation, was codified by the EU legislature in Article 3(2) of the Dublin III Regulation.

Under the Dublin III Regulation, however, the possibility of relying on fundamental rights in support of an appeal or review brought against a transfer decision is not limited solely to cases of 'systemic deficiencies', which were referred to in the operative part of the *Abdullahi* judgment. Thus, when asked about the compatibility with EU law of a transfer decision which was incompatible with Article 4 of the Charter, without, however, reaching the threshold of 'systemic deficiencies', the ECJ stated unambiguously that a purely individual risk of infringement of Article 4 was sufficient to rule out any possibility of validly adopting a transfer decision. That point was first established in *CK*,[8] with regard to the risk of a serious deterioration in the health of a person suffering from psychiatric disorders. It was then solemnly confirmed in *Jawo*,[9] in respect of the risk of exposure to extreme poverty. In that regard, it should be noted that, unlike *Abdullahi*, the judgments in *CK* and *Jawo* do not concern the scope of the appeal or review under the Dublin system. However, if the ECJ had not considered that the infringements of Article 4 of the Charter at issue could be relied on, it would probably not have answered the questions referred,[10] which makes it possible to rely on the

[6] Case C-394/12 *Abdullahi v Bundesasylamt*, ECLI:EU:C:2013:813.

[7] Joined Cases C-411/10 and C-493/10 *NS and Others v Secretary of State for the Home Department*, ECLI:EU:C:2011:865.

[8] Case C-578/16 PPU *CK and Others v Republika Slovenija*, ECLI:EU:C:2017:127.

[9] Case C-163/17 *Jawo v Bundesrepublik Deutschland*, ECLI:EU:C:2019:218.

[10] Indeed, this is precisely the approach taken in *Abdullahi*. Thus, after finding that the person concerned could not rely on the incorrect application of Art 10 of the Dublin II Regulation, the ECJ considered that it was not necessary to answer the questions relating to the interpretation of that provision which had been referred to it by the referring court.

latter two judgments in order to find that the possibility of relying on fundamental rights was strengthened following the adoption of the Dublin III Regulation.

Other judgments of the ECJ illustrate the importance attached to the right to private and family life, guaranteed by Article 7 of the Charter, and to the best interests of the child, enshrined in Article 24 of the Charter, in the determination of persons' procedural rights under the Dublin III Regulation.

In *H and R*, the ECJ held that,[11] in a situation in which an applicant for international protection was not, in principle, authorised to rely on a misapplication of a criterion for determining the Member State responsible, she was nevertheless entitled to rely on an infringement of Articles 8–10 of the Dublin III Regulation, because the responsibility criterion set out in those articles is intended to contribute to the protection of the best interests of the child and the family life of the persons concerned. Therefore, an applicant for international protection may not only rely directly on the fundamental rights guaranteed by the Charter, but also indirectly on the relationship between those fundamental rights and certain provisions of secondary law in order to obtain the right to rely on those provisions in the context of an appeal or review brought against a transfer decision.

Then, in *I and S v Staatssecretaris van Justitie en Veiligheid (Refusal to take charge of an unaccompanied Egyptian minor)*,[12] the ECJ adopted a particularly ambitious – and to date unique – approach, with the aim of offering applicants for international protection a real opportunity to defend their right to private and family life. In that case, an unaccompanied minor had lodged an application for international protection in Greece. Since the minor had indicated that he had an uncle who was legally resident in the Netherlands, the Greek authorities had requested the Netherlands authorities to take charge of the minor. After those authorities had refused to take him in charge, the same minor had brought an action before a Netherlands court against that refusal to take charge. This particular constellation placed the minor concerned in a delicate situation. On the one hand, the decision of the Netherlands authorities necessarily precluded his transfer to the Netherlands, irrespective of whether or not the reasons underlying that decision were consistent with EU law. On the other hand, it is clear from the wording of Article 27(1) of the Dublin III Regulation that the EU legislature provided for an appeal only against the transfer decision and not against other intermediate or preparatory decisions.

Faced with that tension, the ECJ, relying largely on Articles 7, 24 and 47 of the Charter, held that an applicant for international protection in such a situation must have the right to bring an appeal or review against a decision refusing to take charge made by a Member State other than that which conducts the process of determining the Member State responsible. It is worth emphasising the highly constructed nature of this outcome. While the Dublin III Regulation offers, prima facie, protection only in order to avoid an abusive transfer to a Member State other than that in which an application for international protection has been made, in this case the ECJ accepted protection with a view to obtaining a transfer, even though the Member State to which the application for international protection had been made was prepared to examine it. The need to provide applicants for international protection with judicial protection enabling them to rely on the rights that they derive from the Charter is thus regarded as justifying a complete transformation of the structure of the remedies available

[11] Joined Cases C-582/17 and C-583/17 *Staatssecretaris van Veiligheid en Justitie v H and R*, ECLI:EU:C:2019:280.
[12] Case C-19/21 *I and S v Staatssecretaris van Justitie en Veiligheid (Refusal to take charge of an unaccompanied Egyptian minor)*, ECLI:EU:C:2022:605.

to applicants for international protection. The question could even be asked whether such an appeal alters somewhat the purpose of the Dublin system by making it a possible vehicle for family reunification on the initiative of applicants for international protection.

While the judgments cited above show that the application of the Dublin III Regulation by the ECJ has ensured enhanced protection of fundamental rights in comparison with the solutions adopted under the Dublin II Regulation, this must be viewed more as a strengthening of an already established trend than a change in the logic underlying the right to bring an appeal or review. Nevertheless, an analysis of the ECJ's case law makes it possible to discern such a change in the possibility of relying on provisions other than those which have as their object the protection of fundamental rights.

B. General Monitoring of the Correct Application of the Dublin III Regulation

As observed above, it follows from the judgment in *Abdullahi* that the right of appeal available under the Dublin II Regulation did not allow the persons concerned to challenge the mechanism at the heart of the take charge procedure, namely the application of the criteria for determining the Member State responsible for examining an asylum application.

In situations where an infringement of fundamental rights is not successfully invoked, the discussion of the lawfulness of a transfer decision taken at the end of a take charge procedure inevitably turns towards determining the Member State responsible. Consequently, it is not surprising that, shortly after the entry into force of the Dublin III Regulation, the ECJ was asked, by the courts of various Member States, about the continuation of the '*Abdullahi* scheme' following the reform of the Dublin system brought about by that regulation.

The ECJ answered those questions in *Ghezelbash*[13] and *Karim*.[14] The importance of those judgments justifies careful consideration of their reasoning. After recalling the approach taken in *Abdullahi*, the ECJ emphasised that, as regards the scope of the rights granted to the applicant for international protection, the Dublin III Regulation differs, in essential respects, from the Dublin II Regulation. It then turned to the wording of Article 27(1) of the Dublin III Regulation, as well as Recital 19 thereof, which states, inter alia, that the appeal against transfer decisions should cover both the examination of the application of that regulation (a concept which covers the application of the criteria for determining responsibility) and the legal and factual situation in the Member State to which the applicant is transferred. The ECJ also noted the general reform of the Dublin system brought about by the Dublin III Regulation, as embodied in particular in the grant of a series of new rights, including procedural rights, to the persons concerned. It inferred therefrom that the EU legislature did not confine itself to establishing organisational rules governing only relations between the Member States, with a view to determining the Member State responsible, but decided to involve applicants for international protection in that process, obliging the Member States to inform them of the criteria for determining responsibility and to give them the opportunity to provide information enabling the correct application of those criteria, and by guaranteeing them a genuine right to an effective remedy against any transfer decision taken at the end of the process. The ECJ also held that a 'broad' right of appeal is compatible with the objectives pursued by the Dublin III Regulation. It observed, in particular, that it is already

[13] Case C-63/15 *Ghezelbash v Staatssecretaris van Veiligheid en Justitie*, ECLI:EU:C:2016:409.
[14] Case C-155/15 *Karim v Migrationsverket*, ECLI:EU:C:2016:410.

apparent from the case law that the EU legislature did not intend that the judicial protection enjoyed by asylum seekers should be sacrificed to the requirement of expedition in processing applications for international protection. Lastly, the ECJ implicitly recalled the importance of the discussions concerning the determination of the Member State responsible, pointing out that the Common European Asylum System is limited to a minimum harmonisation of the standards governing international protection, meaning that significant differences remain between the Member States.

On the basis of all those factors, the ECJ held that the right of appeal provided for by the Dublin III Regulation is of a different nature than that offered by the Dublin II Regulation, in so far as it is not limited to permitting the protection of certain fundamental rights, but allows any misapplication of the criteria for determining responsibility to be challenged.[15] This outcome obviously has far-reaching practical consequences, in that it increases the possibilities for challenging transfer decisions. Moreover, in the ECJ's view, it will result in requests for a preliminary ruling intended to clarify the scope of the various criteria for responsibility.[16]

Once it became possible to rely on the 'substantive' rules set out in the Dublin III Regulation, the question still remained as to whether it was permissible for the persons concerned to rely on the breach of formal or procedural rules in order to challenge a transfer decision. This issue is of considerable practical importance. As the ECJ has observed on several occasions,[17] the application of that regulation is governed by a series of mandatory time limits in place at all stages of the take charge and take back procedures. Those time limits are, moreover, often decisive because they are relatively brief, and non-compliance normally entails a transfer of responsibility to the 'delaying' Member State. It follows that, in a context where take charge or take back requests are most often addressed to a Member State of first entry or first application, a fact easily established, the persons concerned are very often led to rely on the expiry of a time limit during the procedure.

If such an argument could not succeed within the framework defined by *Abdullahi*, there was doubt as to the treatment to be given to it in the light of the interpretation of the Dublin III Regulation adopted in *Ghezelbash* and *Karim*. That doubt was resolved in *Mengesteab*[18] and *Shiri*.[19] In those judgments, the ECJ held unambiguously that the review of the application of the Dublin III Regulation which could be carried out in the context of an appeal against a transfer decision concerned all the rules laid down by that Regulation, including the rules imposing a procedural time limit. In that regard, it relied, in essence, on the fact that, although the provisions laying down mandatory time limits are intended to regulate the take charge and take back procedures, they also contribute, in the same way as the criteria for determining responsibility, to determining the Member State responsible. The ECJ inferred therefrom that those provisions precluded the adoption of a transfer decision relating to the 'wrong' Member State after the expiry of a mandatory time limit.

An examination of the scope of the appeal against transfer decisions seems to indicate that the ECJ considered that the EU legislature had radically altered the nature of that appeal or

[15] Although *Ghezelbash v Staatssecretaris van Veiligheid en Justitie* (n 13) concerned a specific criterion for determining responsibility, it is apparent from the judgment in Case C-490/16 *AS v Republica Slovenlja*, ECLI:EU:C:2017:585 that the approach set out in that first judgment may also apply to other criteria for determining responsibility.

[16] See, for a notable example, Case C-646/16 *Jafari v Bundesamt für Fremdenwesen und Asyl*, ECLI:EU:C:2017:586.

[17] See, inter alia, Joined Cases C-47/17 and C-48/17 *X and X v Staatssecretaris van Veilighed en Justitie*, ECLI:EU:C:2018:900.

[18] Case C-670/16 *Mengesteab v Bundesrepublik Deutschland*, ECLI:EU:C:2017:587.

[19] Case C-201/16 *Shiri v Bundesamt für Fremdenwesen und Asyl*, ECLI:EU:C:2017:805.

review when adopting the Dublin III Regulation. A shift had occurred from a limited recourse to exceptional cases of systemic violation of fundamental rights to a remedy that may be employed against any misapplication of the rules of the Dublin system. The person concerned by a transfer decision no longer appears to be an individual affected by inter-State arrangements binding on him or her, but a stakeholder in a system in which he or she can assert his or her rights. That revolution is embodied, in particular, in the unambiguous rejection of the argument that the fact that the Member States concerned agree on the transfer is sufficient to justify that transfer, irrespective of the complaints raised by the person concerned.[20] Such a redefinition of the scope of the appeal or review is essential, but is not sufficient in itself, since the effectiveness of the appeal or review can only be assessed in the light of all those detailed rules, on which the ECJ has also been called upon to rule on several occasions over the last decade.

III. THE EFFECTIVENESS OF THE REMEDY AGAINST TRANSFER DECISIONS

In the light of the concept of an appeal developed in cases concerning the scope of appeals against transfer decisions, it is not surprising that the ECJ, when asked for a preliminary ruling relating to the detailed rules of those remedies, concentrated on ensuring their effectiveness. That said, that concern obviously does not mean that the effectiveness of such remedies entails an unlimited extension of the procedural rights of applicants for international protection. A certain number of cases set out the boundaries of that extension.

A. Guarantees of the Effectiveness of the Remedy

Various questions relating to the effectiveness of appeals against transfer decisions have been referred to the ECJ.

In the first place, on several occasions, the ECJ has been asked which date the national court had to take into account when assessing the validity of a transfer decision. This issue might appear, at first sight, to relate to a rather marginal aspect of the appeal procedure under the Dublin system. However, in practice, it carries significant importance. Thus, one of the main procedural time limits for the application of the Dublin III Regulation is the transfer period laid down in Article 29(1). It is apparent from that provision that the Member States have, in principle, six months in which to effect the transfer, calculated either from the date of acceptance by the requested Member State or, in the case of an appeal with suspensive effect, from the date of the final decision on the appeal. However, the actual implementation of the transfer is often delicate, not only because it is necessary to detain the person concerned, but also because implementation involves the cooperation of the Member State responsible, which is not guaranteed, since that Member State may well become responsible merely because it has not responded to the requests sent to it. Under Article 29(2) of the Dublin III Regulation, failure to comply with the transfer time limit entails transfer of responsibility to the Member State which was supposed to carry out the transfer. The conditions under which the effectiveness of that rule can be ensured are therefore of indisputable importance for persons who are the subject of a transfer decision.

[20] See, inter alia, *Mengesteab v Bundesrepublik Deutschland* (n 18), paras 59–60.

In addition, the importance of events subsequent to the order for reference was confirmed by the ECJ's rejection, in *Hasan*,[21] of the argument that implementing the transfer would render the determination of the Member State responsible for examining the application for international protection definitive. It follows that not only events which occurred between the adoption of a transfer decision and its implementation may be relevant, but also those which occur after that implementation.

In that context, it would obviously have been simple to ensure the application of the rules relating to the consequences of the transfer decision by obliging the national courts to rule on an appeal brought against that decision by taking into account facts subsequent to that decision. However, the existence of divergent national traditions of judicial review of administrative decisions gives rise to difficulties. Whereas, in some Member States, the courts responsible for such a review may rely on facts which occurred at any time, other Member States require that the review be based solely on the facts which existed when the administration took its decision.

Faced with that problem, the ECJ held that applicants for international protection must have an effective remedy enabling them to rely on facts which are decisive for the correct application of the Dublin III Regulation, even if they post-date the transfer decision.[22] As regards the practical consequences of that principle, the ECJ proceeded in two stages. First, when questioned by courts whose national procedural rules generally allow facts subsequent to the transfer decision to be taken into account, the ECJ was able, without major difficulties, to find that such legislation guaranteed an effective remedy against the transfer decision.[23] Second, the ECJ had to rule on national rules which preclude such taking into account in an action for annulment brought against a transfer decision. On that occasion, the ECJ stated that Member States are not required to organise their system of legal remedies in such a way as to guarantee such consideration in the context of the examination of the action by which the lawfulness of the transfer decision may be called into question. The detailed rules governing the effective remedy guaranteeing such consideration are ultimately a matter for the procedural autonomy of the Member States, subject to the principle of effectiveness, which precludes that action from being brought only in exceptional circumstances.[24] Member States may therefore opt for a system comprising several complementary actions, provided that it is sufficiently effective.

Second, as a transfer decision is fundamentally a removal decision, the guarantee of the effectiveness of an appeal against such a decision may require, at the very least, a suspension of its effects pending the decision to be taken on the appeal. This matter is regulated in Article 27(3) of the Dublin III Regulation, which offers Member States three specific options to define the conditions under which an appeal must be granted suspensive effect. The very detailed nature of the provision may explain why the ECJ has not often been called upon to clarify the obligations of the Member States in this regard. Nevertheless, in the judgment in *Staatssecretaris van Justitie en Veiligheid (Suspension of the time limit for transfer on appeal)*,[25] it had the opportunity to determine the scheme applicable, at the appellate level, to

[21] Case C-360/16 *Bundesrepublik Deutschland v Hasan*, ECLI:EU:C:2018:35.

[22] See, inter alia, ibid, para 31.

[23] See *Shiri v Bundesamt für Fremdenwesen und Asyl* (n 19); and *Bundesrepublik Deutschland v Hasan* (n 21).

[24] See Case C-194/19 *HA v État belge (Elements subsequent to the transfer decision)*, ECLI/EU:C:2021:270; and Joined Cases C-323/21, C-324/21 and C-325/21 *B and F v Staatssecretaris van Justitie en Veiligheid (Transfer deadline – Plurality of applications)*, ECLI:EU:C:2023:4.

[25] Case C-556/21 *EN, SS, and JY v Staatssecretaris van Justitie en Veiligheid (Suspension of the time limit for transfer on appeal)*, ECLI:EU:C:2023:272.

an action having suspensive effect at first instance. In essence, the ECJ held that the Member States were not required to give suspensive effect to the appeal procedure, although they had the power to do so, in which case they could apply the entire system provided for in the Dublin III Regulation. Once again, as long as a sufficient degree of effectiveness of the remedy is achieved, procedural autonomy has a significant place.

The ECJ has, moreover, been confronted with two types of situations in which a Member State which does not wish to implement a transfer decision immediately, or has not been able to do so, relies on the suspensive nature of an appeal or review in order to avoid the expiry of the transfer period.[26]

First, in *Staatssecretaris van Justitie en Veiligheid (Transfer Period – Trafficking in human beings)*,[27] the ECJ ruled on a practice of the Dutch authorities of suspending the implementation of a transfer decision pending the outcome of an administrative appeal brought against a decision refusing to grant a residence permit to a victim of trafficking in human beings. On the one hand, it considered that it is open to Member States to postpone the implementation of a transfer decision in such a situation. On the other hand, since, in particular, the Member States are not required to do so and in the light of the principle of expeditious processing of applications for international protection, the ECJ held that the appeal could not be regarded as suspensive under Article 27(3) of the Dublin III Regulation and that the transfer period therefore continued to run if the implementation of a transfer decision was suspended on such a ground.

Second, in the judgments in *Khir Amayry*[28] and *Bundesrepublik Deutschland (Administrative suspension of the transfer decision)*,[29] the ECJ established a form of equivalence between the suspension resulting directly from a legal appeal or review, provided for in Article 27(3) of the Dublin III Regulation, and the suspension resulting from an administrative decision pending the outcome of an appeal, allowed under Article 27(4) of that Regulation. Those two types of suspension were, in particular, considered to be such as to justify postponing the calculation of the transfer period. That interpretation, which preserves, inter alia, the interests of the Member State intending to carry out the transfer, is logically to encourage the exercise of the option laid down in Article 27(4) and thus to facilitate the suspension of the effects of a transfer decision. However, it follows from the judgment in *Bundesrepublik Deutschland (Administrative suspension of the transfer decision)* that that approach may be taken only where there is a direct link between such a suspension and the bringing of an action against the transfer decision. The ECJ pointed out, in particular, that a suspension ordered on account of the COVID-19 pandemic was not such as to justify a suspension of that order.

Third, the concern of preserving the effectiveness of appeals against transfer decisions may also be taken into consideration by the ECJ when interpreting provisions of the Dublin III Regulation which have only an indirect connection with the exercise of such remedies. By way of illustration, reference is made to the judgment in *Hassan*.[30] In that judgment, the

[26] It should be borne in mind that, under Art 29(1) of the Dublin III Regulation, if the suspensive nature of the appeal were to be regarded as established, that would mean that the transfer period does not begin to run until the final decision on the appeal.

[27] Case C-338/21 *Staatssecretaris van Justitie en Veiligheid v SS, NZ and SS (Transfer deadline – Trafficking in human beings)*, ECLI:EU:C:2023:269.

[28] Case C-60/16 *Khir Amayry v Migrationsverket*, ECLI:EU:C:2017:675.

[29] Joined Cases C-245/21 and C-248/21 *Bundesrepublik Deutschland v MA, PB and LE (Administrative suspension of the transfer decision)*, ECLI:EU:C:2022:709.

[30] Case C-647/16 *Bundesrepublik v Hassan*, ECLI:EU:C:2018:368.

ECJ emphasised that a transfer decision could not be adopted before the requested Member State had agreed to take charge or to take back. Among the considerations put forward in support of that interpretation of the Dublin III Regulation, the ECJ relied in particular on the fact that, once the transfer had been accepted in principle, the transfer decision had to be notified to the person concerned in order to ensure that that person was fully informed of all the reasons underpinning that decision so as to enable him, if appropriate, to challenge that decision before the court with jurisdiction and to request that its enforcement be suspended.

B. The Limits on the Appeals and Remedies under the Dublin System

Ensuring the effectiveness of appeals and remedies against transfer decisions is obviously not incompatible with the placing of certain limits on the procedural rights of the persons concerned. Those limits may already result, to a certain extent, from the principle that certain detailed rules governing those remedies fall within the procedural autonomy of the Member States, in so far as that principle leaves the Member States a margin of discretion in defining those detailed rules. Without purporting to be exhaustive, it is possible to cite at least two notable judgments.

In the first place, in *H*[31] the ECJ found that there was a significant limitation on the remedies available to persons who have been the subject of a take back procedure for challenging a transfer decision. Although that limitation is technical in nature, it remains of great practical importance. In order to understand the nature of the limitation, it is helpful to recall that the Dublin III Regulation distinguishes the take charge procedure from the take back procedure.

When asked about the possibility of a person who has been the subject of a take back procedure relying on the fact that the Member State to which he should be transferred is not the Member State designated by the criteria for determining the Member State responsible, the ECJ reiterated the approach taken in *Ghezelbash*, under which an appeal or review against a transfer decision may relate, in general, to the correct application of the Dublin III Regulation. It stated, however, that the person concerned may not rely effectively, in support of an appeal or review, on provisions of that Regulation which, in so far as they did not apply in the situation, were not binding on the competent authorities. The ECJ notes that, although the criteria for determining the Member State responsible are central to the take charge procedure, the same is not true of the take back procedure. Whilst that procedure is intended to refer the person concerned to the Member State of first application with a view to completing the process of determining the Member State responsible, it does not assume that the responsibility of the Member State of first application will be retained at the end of that process. Conversely, when that procedure is aimed at a Member State which has begun the examination of the substance of the application for international protection, it implies that that Member State has already accepted its responsibility for examining that application and is not intended to enable the decision taken in that regard to be re-examined *a posteriori*.

Those findings, together with the consideration of various contextual and teleological factors, led the ECJ to hold that a person who has been the subject of a take back procedure

[31] *Staatssecretaris van Veiligheid en Justitie v H and R* (n 11).

may not, in principle, rely on the fact that the Member State to which he should be transferred is not the Member State designated by the criteria for determining the Member State responsible. Although that principle is covered by an exception, referred to above, justified by the desire to guarantee the effectiveness of the right to private and family life, the fact remains that the judgment in *H* clearly limits the remedies available to persons who have been the subject of a take back procedure. The scope of the outcome in that case is all the more significant since, in the context of the current operation of the Dublin system, the vast majority of the procedures carried out on the basis of that Regulation are take back procedures.

In the second place, although the ECJ accepted, in *Staatssecretaris van Justitie en Veiligheid (Refusal to take charge of an unaccompanied Egyptian minor)*, that certain acts preparatory to a transfer decision could be challenged, it would be wrong to infer therefrom that all such acts were recognised as having comparable status. Thus, in *MA and Others*,[32] the ECJ held that EU law does not require a remedy to be made available against the decision not to use the option set out in the 'sovereignty clause' in Article 17(1) of the Dublin III Regulation. That clause allows a Member State to examine an application for international protection even where such an examination is not its responsibility. It is therefore clear that an applicant for international protection who has lodged his or her application with a Member State other than the Member State responsible may have an interest in the activation of that clause. The ECJ has, however, refused to infer the existence of a right of appeal against a decision not to make use of that clause, relying both on the wording of the Dublin III Regulation and on the fact that such a decision will adversely affect the person concerned only if the Member State in question ultimately adopts a transfer decision, in which case that person may bring an action against that decision.

IV. CONCLUSION

As the above analysis shows, there have been a number of noteworthy judgments relating directly or indirectly to the right of appeal under the Dublin system, covering a wide variety of issues. However, it would be an overstatement to consider that all of those judgments contribute to sketching a judicial picture of how that right of appeal is to be interpreted. With a few exceptions, the judgments focused primarily on the provisions contained in the Dublin III Regulation and on the choices made by the EU legislature. Thus, the significant extension of the right of appeal under the Dublin III Regulation is not the result of a 'constitutional' interpretation by the ECJ based essentially on Article 47 of the Charter, but rather of a 'legislative' interpretation resulting directly from the overall reform of the Dublin system entailed by the adoption of that Regulation.

The closely formulated inclusion of the main elements of that case law in the text of the Dublin III Regulation places its future very logically in the hands of the EU legislature. Given the practical importance of the relatively low effectiveness of transfer decisions and the time limits inherent in bringing an appeal or review, it is not surprising that the scope of, and detailed rules for, the right to appeal against transfer decisions have been discussed in the negotiations on the New Pact on Migration and Asylum. Successive steps have allowed a mosaic to be pieced together gradually, influenced significantly by the work of Vice-President Bay Larsen.

[32] Case C-661/17 *MA and Others v The International Protection Appeals Tribunal and Others*, ECLI:EU:C:2019:53.

6

Judicial Review of Acts of the European Public Prosecutor's Office: The Limits of Effective Judicial Protection of European Prosecution

KATELIN LIGETI*

I. INTRODUCTION

Lars Bay Larsen is a pioneer and a true proponent of European criminal law, who paved the way of this young discipline to its present-day relevance. Today, European criminal law assumes a decisive role in criminal justice science and Lars Bay Larsen inspired and encouraged many scholars to devote their research to issues of European criminal law. This chapter deals with the European Public Prosecutors Office, a topic to which Lars Bay Larsen himself has made outstanding contributions.

On 1 June 2021, more than 20 years after it was first envisioned by the authors of the *Corpus Juris*[1] and thanks to the European Commission's sustained advocacy of and support for the criminal law protection of the European Union (EU)'s financial interests, the European Public Prosecutor's Office (EPPO) began operation.[2] The EPPO brings a seminal change to EU criminal justice: instead of working through cooperation across national judicial authorities, the EPPO exercises genuine European powers of investigation and prosecution in the

* Professor at the University of Luxembourg, Dean of the Faculty of Law, Economics and Finance.

[1] M Delmas Marty and JAE Vervaele (eds), *The Implementation of the Corpus Juris in the Member States*, vol 1 (Intersentia, 2000).

[2] Council Regulation (EU) 2017/1939 of 12 October 2017 implementing enhanced cooperation on the establishment of the European Public Prosecutor's Office [2017] OJ L283/1 (EPPO Regulation). The EPPO started its operations with 22 Member States of the EU participating in the enhanced cooperation. Only Denmark, Ireland, Hungary, Poland, and Sweden were outside the EPPO. After a few years of troublesome relations between the EPPO and Poland, Poland joined the EPPO in February 2024 (Commission Decision (EU) 2024/807 of 29 February 2024 confirming the participation of Poland in the enhanced cooperation on the establishment of the European Public Prosecutor's Office [2024] C/2024/1444, OJ L 2024/807, 29.02.2024). According to the Commission Decision confirming the participation of Poland in the EPPO, the EPPO will commence its operational activities in Poland once the European Prosecutor from Poland has been appointed. To ensure the efficiency of the EPPO's activities, the Commission decided that the EPPO Regulation will apply retrospectively in Poland to any offence within the competence of the EPPO committed after 1 June 2021, ie after the EPPO started its operations. Therefore, at the time of writing 23 Member States of the EU participate in the EPPO. Denmark and Ireland have an opt-out from the AFSJ, whereas Sweden has also announced its interest in joining the EPPO.

Area of Freedom, Security and Justice (AFSJ) to fight offences affecting the financial interests of the EU.

The lengthy and difficult negotiations leading to the EPPO's establishment revealed the tensions that accompany vertical criminal-justice integration in the EU. The EPPO as established is a hybrid agency in a threefold sense. First, the EPPO is in charge only of investigation and prosecution; adjudication is left to national courts.[3] The European prosecution system is therefore not completed by a European criminal court.[4] Second, the EPPO has a hybrid structure in which one highly complex centralised level is coupled with one that is decentralised.[5] Whereas the decision to prosecute is taken at the central level, the decentralised level is in charge of investigation. The central office is based in Luxembourg,[6] and comprises the European Chief Prosecutor[7] and two Deputies,[8] the College[9] (composed of one European Prosecutor from each participating Member State),[10] 15 Permanent Chambers,[11] and the Administrative Director.[12] The Permanent Chambers decide whether to prosecute before a national court or to consider a referral of the case, dismissal, or application of a simplified prosecution procedure.[13] The central level is completed by a decentralised structure of European Delegated Prosecutors (EDPs) operating in the Member States. The EDP handling a case leads the investigation on behalf of the EPPO on his/her own and either undertakes the appropriate investigative measures directly or instructs the national authorities to do so.[14] Third, the EPPO's activities are governed by a hybrid legislative framework comprising a set of European rules which are completed by national law and various European and national soft-law provisions.[15] The EPPO Regulation itself provides for a complex interaction between EU law and national law in the operations of the EPPO. Article 5(3) of the EPPO Regulation states that national law will apply to the extent that a matter is not regulated by the Regulation, while a number of provisions in the EPPO Regulation refer expressly to the application of national law, in particular regarding EPPO investigations; these include provisions on the conduct of investigations,[16]

[3] Art 86(1) of Treaty on the Functioning of the European Union (TFEU).

[4] See on this point V Mitsilegas and F Giuffrida, 'Judicial Review of EPPO Acts and Decisions' in K Ligeti et al (eds), *The European Public Prosecutor's Office at Launch* (Wolters Kluwer CEDAM, 2020) 128–29.

[5] K Ligeti, 'The European Public Prosecutor's Office' in V Mitsilegas et al (eds), *Research Handbook on EU Criminal Law*, 2nd edn (Edward Elgar, forthcoming).

[6] EPPO Regulation, Arts 8(3) and 106.

[7] Appointed by the Council and the European Parliament for a non-renewable term of seven years. EPPO Regulation, Art 14(1).

[8] The two Deputies are appointed from amongst the European Prosecutors 'to assist the European Chief Prosecutor in the discharge of his/her duties and to act as replacement when he/she is absent or is prevented from attending to those duties': EPPO Regulation, Art 11(2).

[9] The College is composed of the European Chief Prosecutor and one European Prosecutor per participating Member State. The role of the College is essentially managerial: it is responsible for the general oversight of the EPPO and has no power to take operational decisions in individual cases: EPPO Regulation, Art 9.

[10] Appointed by the Council for a non-renewable term of six years with the possibility to extend the mandate for a maximum of three years at the end of the six-year period: EPPO Regulation, Art 16(3).

[11] Their number was determined by the Decision on the Permanent Chambers, College Decision 015/2020: EPPO Regulation, Art 10.

[12] The Administrative Director is entrusted with the daily management of the EPPO for both administrative and budgetary purposes: EPPO Regulation, Art 19.

[13] EPPO Regulation, Art 35(1). Art 36(3) and (4) of the EPPO Regulation provides that the Permanent Chamber can also decide to bring the case to prosecution in a different Member State than the one of the handling EDP or to combine several cases.

[14] EPPO Regulation, Art 28(1). EPPO Regulation, Art 28(4) allows, in exceptional cases and with the approval of the competent Permanent Chamber, the supervising European Prosecutor to conduct the investigations under the conditions mentioned in the provision.

[15] For a critical analysis of the EPPO's legal framework see L De Matteis, 'The EPPO's Legislative Framework: Navigating through EU Law, National Law and Soft Law' (2023) 14 *New Journal of European Criminal Law* 6.

[16] EPPO Regulation, Art 28(1).

rules on investigative measures,[17] rules on cross-border investigations,[18] enforcement,[19] and pre-trial arrest.[20] The EPPO therefore applies both national law and European law during its activities and – as expressed in Article 5(1) of the EPPO Regulation – it ensures respect for the rights enshrined in the Charter of Fundamental Rights of the European Union (the Charter). The interaction between the applicable European and national rules is complicated by European and national soft-law provisions defining the details of the EPPO's workings and operations.

The complexity of this hybrid system of European prosecution is not without friction. It was already the subject of much scholarly writing during the negotiations, voicing concerns mainly about the shortcomings and contradictions of the EPPO's legislative framework and its appropriateness to ensure effective criminal enforcement of crimes against the EU budget as well as effective judicial protection of individuals subject to EPPO proceedings.[21]

This contribution will focus on the jurisdiction of the European Court of Justice (ECJ) to hold the EPPO judicially accountable. It examines the system of ex post judicial review in relation to the decisions taken by the EPPO during the investigation and prosecution phase. This implies that aspects of ex ante judicial authorisation are thus not dealt with here.[22] This focus is inextricably linked with the second aspect this contribution seeks to explore, namely the impact of the establishment of the EPPO on the right to effective judicial protection laid down in Article 47 of the Charter. To answer these questions, Section II presents the rules on judicial review in the EPPO Regulation, followed by an analysis in Section III of the impact of these rules on the position of the individual. This chapter concludes with some remarks on the ECJ's limited control over the EPPO.

II. RULES ON JUDICIAL REVIEW IN THE EPPO REGULATION

Established as a 'body of the Union',[23] one would expect that the EPPO's procedural acts and failures to act would be subject to judicial review before the ECJ in accordance with EU law.[24] Instead, the rules on judicial review formulated in Article 42(1) of the EPPO Regulation provide for a derogatory system that largely exempts the EPPO's acts from scrutiny by the ECJ. Save for a limited number of scenarios, Article 42(1) of the EPPO Regulation confers on national courts the competence to exercise judicial review of those EPPO procedural acts intended to produce legal effects vis-à-vis third parties and failures to adopt such acts.

Limiting the jurisdiction of the ECJ to review acts of the EPPO goes back to the initial Commission Proposal to establish the EPPO,[25] which declared in its Article 36 that, in the

[17] EPPO Regulation, Art 30(2) and (3).

[18] EPPO Regulation, Art 31.

[19] EPPO Regulation, Art 32.

[20] EPPO Regulation, Art 33.

[21] Ligeti (n 5).

[22] The ECJ has repeatedly emphasised the important relationship of ex ante and ex post review and stipulated standards for ex post review if ex ante review is not granted. On this topic see K Ligeti and G Robinson, 'Composite Enforcement and Comprehensive Judicial Protection' in M Luchtman et al (eds), *EU Enforcement Authorities: Punitive Law Enforcement in a Composite Legal Order* (Hart Publishing, 2021) 70–71.

[23] EPPO Regulation, Art 3(1).

[24] HH Herrnfeld, 'Article 42: Judicial Review' in HH Herrnfeld et al (eds), *European Public Prosecutor's Office: Article-by-Article Commentary* (Nomos/Beck/Hart Publishing, 2021) 402.

[25] Commission, 'Proposal for a Council Regulation on the establishment of the European Public Prosecutor's Office' COM (2013) 534 final. See on this point K Ligeti and A Weyemberg, 'The European Public Prosecutor's Office: Certain Constitutional Issues' in L Herkelens et al (eds), *The European Public Prosecutor's Office: An Extended Arm or a Two-Headed Dragon?* (TMC Asser Press, 2015) 53.

performance of its functions, the EPPO shall be considered a national authority. This fiction implied that the Union courts would have no jurisdiction over the activities of the EPPO, either under Article 263 (action for annulment) or pursuant to Article 265 (action against a failure to act) or Article 268 (action for damages) TFEU.[26] Furthermore, even the possibility of seeking a preliminary ruling under Article 267 TFEU was curtailed by Article 36 of the Commission Proposal. Accordingly, provisions of national law rendered applicable by the Regulation (eg the national rules which become relevant for the execution of an investigative measure) could not be considered provisions of Union law for the purposes of Article 267 TFEU (preliminary reference).[27]

By excluding legal redress before EU courts, the Commission Proposal departed from the principle of EU law according to which EU courts control the legality of the actions of EU bodies and national courts exert control over the actions of national authorities.[28] The Commission Proposal justified this departure by evoking the special nature and different position of the EPPO compared to other EU bodies and agencies. It further argued that the investigative and prosecutorial acts of the EPPO are closely linked to the trial stage, which takes place before national courts, and its effects would, therefore, be felt mainly within the legal orders of the Member States.[29] Finally, the Commission felt that giving national courts the competence to review the procedural acts of the EPPO was needed to respect the principle of subsidiarity.[30]

Assimilating the EPPO to a national authority for the purposes of judicial review received criticism from the outset.[31] It was difficult to see how a national court could control the legality of the central decisions of the EPPO in a coherent fashion.[32] The lack of judicial protection by the Union courts was most striking in relation to the choice of forum. According to Article 27(4) of the Commission Proposal, the EPPO would choose the forum for the trial stage by considering the criteria listed in that article, namely, the place where the offence (or the majority thereof) was committed, the place of habitual residence of the offender, the place where the evidence is located, or where the 'direct' victims have their habitual residence. The EPPO had to consider these criteria 'bearing in mind the proper administration of justice'.[33] The lack of judicial review available against this specific decision created not only a certain risk of forum shopping[34] but also presented a serious barrier to judicial protection.

[26] Explanatory Memorandum to the Commission Proposal (n 25).

[27] Meij rightly points out that 'Such an effort to restrict the preliminary jurisdiction of the Court, doing away with classic approaches to coherency of EU law and practical possibilities to achieve consistency of EPPO action, introduces in the legislative process a certain arbitrariness which does not correspond to prevailing perceptions of the EU legal order as based on the rule of law'. See A Meij, 'Some Explorations into the EPPO's Administrative Structure and Judicial Review' in Herkelens et al (n 25), 101 on this point.

[28] See Case 314/85 *Foto Frost v Hauptzollamt Lübeck-Ost*, ECLI:EU:C:1987:452; and Case 294/83 *Les Verts v European Parliament*, ECLI:EU:C:1986:166, especially para 23.

[29] See Explanatory Memorandum to the Commission Proposal (n 25), 7.

[30] See Explanatory Memorandum to the Commission Proposal (n 25), para 3.2. It has been pointed out that the Commission wrongly referred to the subsidiarity principle; this should be applied to assessing the legitimacy of establishing the EPPO itself, rather than to the question of judicial review, which is a meta-question. For a critical review of the Commission's Proposal see Mitsilegas and Giuffrida (n 4), 119–20.

[31] For example, see Meij (n 27) for demands of the European Parliament.

[32] In the Commission Proposal the EPPO was not only equipped with central decision-making powers in relation to prosecution (see Commission Proposal, Arts 16(1), 27(2), 28(1) and 29(1)) but could also undertake investigations directly (see Commission Proposal, Art 18(6)).

[33] Commission Proposal (n 25), Art 27(4).

[34] See Resolution of the European Parliament of 12 March 2014 (A7-0234/2014), point 5(i). See also Meijers Committee, Note to the LIBE Committee of the European Parliament (25 September 2013), available at www.commissie-meijers.nl, accessed 29 February 2024; and Opinion of the Fundamental Rights Agency (4 February 2014), http://fra.europa.eu, accessed 29 February 2024.

These concerns notwithstanding, in the adopted text of the EPPO Regulation the participating Member States decided to follow the Commission's initial reasoning and agreed only minor improvements to the ECJ's jurisdiction to hold the EPPO judicially accountable. Article 42(1) of the EPPO Regulation confers on national courts the competence to exercise judicial review of procedural acts by the EPPO which are intended to produce legal effects vis-à-vis third parties and failures to adopt such acts. Pursuant to Article 42(2) of the EPPO Regulation the ECJ is competent only to give preliminary rulings in accordance with Article 267 TFEU. The preliminary rulings shall concern: (a) the validity of procedural acts of the EPPO, insofar as such a question of validity is raised directly on the basis of Union law;[35] (b) the interpretation or validity of Union law;[36] and (c) the interpretation of Articles 22 and 25 of the Regulation 'in relation to any conflict of competence between the EPPO and the competent national authorities'.[37] Article 42(2) reflects the fact that 'judicial review of the validity of acts of a Union institution falls within the exclusive competence of Union courts'.[38] In other words, Union courts are competent for judicial review on the basis of Union law whereas review on the basis of national law falls within the exclusive competence of national courts.

The same mechanism applies to the action of annulment under Article 263(4) TFEU. Article 42(3) of the EPPO Regulation stipulates that 'the decisions of the EPPO to dismiss a case' can be subject to an action of annulment insofar as 'they are contested directly on the basis of Union law'. In particular, the ECJ will be competent on matters falling under the scope of Article 42(8) of the EPPO Regulation; mainly, it shall review acts related to the protection of personal data, public access to documents, and the dismissal of EDPs.[39]

Compared to the rules initially proposed by the Commission, the adopted Regulation slightly extends the ECJ's Article 267 TFEU jurisdiction and opens possibilities – albeit limited – to request a preliminary ruling from the ECJ. The ECJ's jurisdiction based on Article 263 TFEU remains, however, significantly curtailed and EPPO acts performed at the decentralised level of the office remain outside European judicial control.

To justify the derogatory rules on judicial review of the EPPO and the resulting division of competence between national courts (Article 42(1)) and the ECJ (Article 42(2)–(8)), the EPPO Regulation refers to Article 86(3) TFEU. Article 86(3) TFEU allows the EPPO Regulation to determine 'the rules applicable to the judicial review of procedural measures' taken by the EPPO 'in the performance of its functions'. It is, however, questionable whether the possibility allowed in Article 86(3) TFEU empowers EU lawmakers not only to develop the competence of the ECJ in relation to the judicial control of the EPPO, but to actually create an exemption from the general rule. Leading experts doubt the compatibility of this derogatory regime with primary EU law.[40]

[35] EPPO Regulation, Art 42(2)(a).

[36] EPPO Regulation, Art 42(2)(b).

[37] EPPO Regulation, Art 42(2)(c).

[38] M Böse, 'Judicial Control of the European Public Prosecutor's Office' in T Rafaraci and R Belfiore (eds), *EU Criminal Justice: Fundamental Rights, Transnational Proceedings and the European Public Prosecutor's Office* (Springer, 2019) 195.

[39] Pursuant to EPPO Regulation, Art 42(4)–(6), the ECJ will also maintain its jurisdiction for compensation claims (Art 268 TFEU), staff-related matters (Art 270 TFEU), and arbitration clauses in contracts concluded by the EPPO (Art 272 TFEU), although this could also imply national law and rules of procedure that could grant jurisdiction to national courts.

[40] For the respective discussions during the negotiation of the EPPO Regulation see Herrnfeld (n 24), 403. Mitsilegas argues that the possibility allowed by Art 86(3) TFEU as well as other similar Treaty provisions does not mean that rules of secondary EU law can substantially limit judicial review by the ECJ: see V Mitsilegas, 'European Prosecution between Cooperation and Integration: The European Public Prosecutor's Office and the Rule of Law' (2021) 28 *Maastricht Journal of European and Comparative* Law 245, 260.

As expressed in Recitals 86, 87, and 97, the EPPO Regulation justifies the limited review of the EPPO at EU level on five main grounds. The first is the EPPO's hybrid nature, 'the tasks and structure of the EPPO, which is different from that of all other bodies and agencies of the Union [... requiring] special rules regarding judicial review'.[41] The second relates to the strong link between the operations of the EPPO and the legal orders of the Member States: whilst being an EU body, the EPPO is de facto integrated in the national legal systems of the participating Member States The EPPO exercises the functions of the prosecutor in the competent courts of the Member States and it applies both EU law and national law throughout its operations, with the latter, in principle, falling outside ECJ jurisdiction.[42] Recital 87 explicitly mentions the EPPO's strong link to national legal system. The EPPO's 'acts will be carried out by national law enforcement authorities acting under the instructions of the EPPO'; it therefore is appropriate to subject those procedural acts to judicial review by the competent national court. The third and the fourth grounds are much more practical and relate to reasons such as national courts' easier access to case files and a desire not to overburden the ECJ.[43] The fifth and last is the need to maintain consistency. Since national courts are competent for providing ex ante judicial authorisation for EPPO investigative measures, it is coherent also to entrust national courts with the ex post judicial review of those investigative measures.[44]

III. INDIVIDUALS' FUNDAMENTAL RIGHTS IN EPPO PROCEEDINGS: CAUGHT BETWEEN A VARIABLE GEOMETRY OF JUDICIAL CONTROL AND THE NEED FOR EFFECTIVE JUDICIAL PROTECTION

The limitations introduced by the EPPO Regulation to the jurisdiction of the ECJ are questionable not only for their compatibility with primary EU law, but also in terms of their constitutionality: it is doubtful if they provide effective judicial protection to individuals subject to EPPO proceedings. The right to effective judicial protection, enshrined in Article 47 of the Charter, is an essential component of the rule of law within any legal system. Within the EU legal system, Article 47 provides that everyone whose rights and freedoms guaranteed by EU law are violated has the right to a fair and public hearing and an effective remedy within a reasonable time by an independent and impartial tribunal previously established by law.

The EU legal order, marked by the shared administration of EU institutions and national authorities, requires the principle of effective judicial protection to be realised at both national and EU level. Article 19(1) of the Treaty on the European Union (TEU) thus provides that Member States shall ensure that remedies sufficient to ensure effective legal protection in the fields covered by Union law are available. At EU level, the TFEU provides several routes for the review of the legality of acts of bodies, offices, or agencies of the EU intended to produce legal

[41] EPPO Regulation, Recital 86.

[42] This follows from Art 19 TEU. See Case C-50/00 P *Unión de Pequeños Agricultores v Council*, ECLI:EU:C:2002:462, para 43; and Case C-62/14 *Gauweiler and Others*, ECLI:EU:C:2015:400, para 28. The Court has, however, jurisdiction in specific cases where the national law refers to the content of a provision of Union law (see eg Case C-28/95 *Leur-Bloem*, ECLI:EU:C:1997:369, paras 25 and 27) or where the Court must provide all points of interpretation necessary for the national court to assess the compatibility with fundamental rights of national law implementing Union law (see Art 51 of the Charter as interpreted by the ECJ in Case C-617/10 *Åkerberg Fransson*, ECLI:EU:C:2013:105, para 19). See also the interpretation by the Court of 'implementing Union law' in Case C-198/13 *Julian Hernández and Others*, ECLI:EU:C:2014:2055.

[43] Herrnfeld (n 24), 406.

[44] ibid, 406.

effects vis-à-vis third parties. The most important of these routes are actions for annulment launched against such acts[45] and references for a preliminary ruling[46] concerning the interpretation and validity of such acts under EU law.

From the very beginning, Article 42 of the EPPO Regulation provoked questions as to both the persuasiveness and constitutionality of its underlying choice. Many scholars see the division of power to review certain EPPO acts between national courts and the ECJ as incompatible not only with the Treaty but also with the right to effective judicial protection.[47]

Excluding European judicial review of the activities of the EPPO's decentralised level and subjecting EPPO procedural acts intrusive to fundamental rights to review by national courts in accordance with national procedural law de facto leads to a variable geometry of judicial control on the ground. Since national legal systems differ considerably as to the possibility and extent of judicial control over prosecutors' investigative acts in the pretrial phase, the reference to the applicable national rules risks substantially weakening the judicial review of the EPPO's investigative acts to the direct (and often irreparable) detriment of the fundamental rights of those impacted by EPPO proceedings.

Article 42(1) of the EPPO Regulation leaves it to national law to define those who are entitled to request a review as well as the modalities of such review (time limits, relevant procedures). Since Article 42(1) of the EPPO Regulation does not contain any details on the nature or extent of the review by national courts, the decision of the national court is not limited to declaring that a certain procedural act of the EPPO violated the applicable national standards; the national court may remedy the violation at hand by, for instance, granting the suspect access to the case file where the EPPO previously denied it. Furthermore, the review is not limited to the legality of the act, but it could extend to the modalities of its execution (eg the expediency of an investigative measure undertaken by the EDP). When reviewing the EPPO's procedural acts, as stated in Recital 88 of the EPPO Regulation, the national courts shall apply the EPPO Regulation and, to the extent the matter is not dealt with in the EPPO Regulation, national law.

The EPPO Regulation gives a very broad margin to national courts in ensuring adequate judicial control over the activities of the decentralised level of the EPPO. From the perspective of persons whose fundamental rights are impacted by EPPO investigations, the broad reliance on national law and national courts may appear arbitrary, especially in cases where a certain act is open to judicial review in one Member State but not in others. For instance, the decision to initiate an investigation is not open to review in all Member States. Based on Recital 88(1) of the EPPO Regulation, Member States are responsible for ensuring effective

[45] Art 263(1) TFEU.

[46] Art 267(1)(b) TFEU.

[47] For instance, Böse argues that 'the treaty framework of judicial protection does not prohibit Union courts from interpreting and applying national law, but even may require them to do so'. According to Böse, '[a]s far as Union law refers to and, thereby, incorporates national law, the Courts of the Union must take the latter into account when assessing the legality of a measure adopted by a Union institution'. In support of this view, Böse refers to AG Mengozzi's statement according to which 'it is perfectly normal that the Courts of the European Union should interpret the applicable national law, where appropriate having regard also to the relevant national case-law'. In these situations, especially concerning Arts 268, 270 and 272 TFEU in the aforementioned proceedings, AG Mengozzi affirms that 'not to allow the interpretation of national law made by EU bodies to be reviewed could even [...] undermine the right to effective legal protection, which constitutes a general principle of EU law and is now also enshrined in the Charter of Fundamental Rights'. See Opinion of AG Mengozzi in Case C-401/09 P *Evropaïki Dynamiki*, ECLI:EU:C:2011:31, paras 35, 70 and 75. In this regard, Böse argues that 'if decisions of the EPPO are – at least in part – based upon national law, judicial review of these decisions by Union courts must consequently extend to compliance with the relevant national law': Böse (n 38), 198. See also Mitsilegas (n 40), 259–62.

remedies against the EPPO's procedural acts. The exact scope of this obligation is, however, not further defined and leaves open whether it extends to requiring Member States to ensure judicial review of the activities of the EPPO if such review is not given under the relevant provisions of national law. It follows from established ECJ case law that judicial review must always be provided for if persons' fundamental rights are impacted.[48] If, however, the EPPO's decision does not directly impact the suspect's or other persons' fundamental rights and national law does not provide for the possibility of seeking review against such type of decision, national differences will persist.[49] For instance, an EPPO decision to appoint an expert or to reimburse witness costs are decisions that are not intended to produce legal effects vis-à-vis third persons and if seeking judicial remedy against such acts is not possible under national law, EU law currently does not create an obligation to allow remedy to be sought.

The only aspect where harmonisation of divergent national rules on judicial review seems possible, relates to the definition of the EPPO's 'procedural acts' subject to judicial review. Article 42(1) of the EPPO Regulation does not specify what is meant by 'procedural acts'.[50] Based on established ECJ case law one might expect that this term should receive uniform interpretation as an autonomous concept of EU law.

> [I]t follows from the need for a uniform application of EU law, and from the principle of equality, that the terms of a provision of EU law, which makes no express reference to the law of the Member States for the purpose of determining its meaning and scope, must normally be given an autonomous and uniform interpretation throughout the European Union, which must take into account the context of that provision and the purpose of the legislation in question.[51]

Defining the EPPO's 'procedural acts' as an autonomous concept of EU law[52] could ensure at least minimum convergence of the range of EPPO acts that can be subject to judicial review. It will not resolve, however, the larger challenge of fragmented and uneven treatment of individuals' fundamental rights in EPPO proceedings.

The adopted text of the EPPO Regulation also retained the Commission's initial approach to judicial control of the EPPO's choice of forum. Recital 87 of the EPPO Regulation specifically mentions that;

> [p]rocedural acts that relate to the choice of the Member State whose courts will be competent to hear the prosecution, which is to be determined on the basis of the criteria laid down in this Regulation, are intended to produce legal effects vis-à-vis third parties and should therefore be subject to judicial review by national courts, at the latest at the trial stage.

Pursuant to Article 26(4) of the EPPO Regulation, the Permanent Chamber, taking into account the criteria laid down in the EPPO Regulation,[53] can reallocate the case during

[48] Case C-402/05 P *Kadi*, ECLI:EU:C:2008:461, para 282 ff.

[49] Herrnfeld argues that the EPPO's decision to initiate an investigation (EPPO Regulation, Art 26) or to exercise its right of evocation (EPPO Regulation, Art 27) would not qualify as procedural acts against which EU law would require Member States to provide for possibilities to seek judicial review: Herrnfeld (n 24), 422.

[50] The competence for the judicial review of the administrative decisions of the EPPO lies with the ECJ (EPPO Regulation, Art 42(8)).

[51] Cases C-108/16 PPU *Dworzecki*, ECLI:EU:C:2016:346, para 28; Case C-494/14 *Axa Belgium* ECLI:EU:C:2015:692, para 21; C-66/08 *Kozłowski*, ECLI:EU:C:2008:437, para 42. On the role of the ECJ in developing autonomous concepts see V Mitsilegas, 'Autonomous Concepts, Diversity Management and Mutual Trust in Europe's Area of Criminal Justice' (2020) 57 *Common Market Law Review* 45.

[52] Herrnfeld (n 24), 409.

[53] Namely, in order of priority: (a) the place of the suspect's or accused person's habitual residence; (b) the nationality of the suspect or accused person; and (c) the place where the main financial damage occurred.

the investigation[54] or decide to bring the case to prosecution in a Member State other than that where the investigation took place. Excluding judicial review at the European level of the Permanent Chamber's decision to allocate or reallocate the case during the investigation or the prosecution has primordial consequences for suspects and other persons impacted by the proceedings of the EPPO. National courts exercising review over the EPPO's decision to allocate or reallocate the case will be called to essentially assess 'an EU body's application of a set of operating criteria under EU law'.[55] If, in the course of the review, the national court encounters difficulties in interpreting and applying the criteria set out in the EPPO Regulation, it can refer the case for clarification to the ECJ via the preliminary reference procedure. National courts enjoy, however, discretion in judging whether the case needs to be referred to the ECJ:[56] such a ruling must be deemed essential by the national court in order to reach judgment, and is mandatory only in cases pending before a court or tribunal against whose decisions there is no judicial remedy under national law.[57] If no preliminary reference is sought, the remedies available to persons whose fundamental rights are impacted by the EPPO's forum choice are limited to appeals offered under the respective national law.[58] It is doubtful whether this limitation of the ECJ's jurisdiction is reconcilable with the right to an effective judicial review, including the respect for the principles of legality (including foreseeability) and equality before the law.[59]

Although Article 42(2) of the EPPO Regulation opens the possibility for national courts and tribunals in certain cases to request a preliminary ruling from the ECJ, this avenue of judicial control risks being ineffective without substantial amendments to Member States' national criminal procedural laws. For instance, Article 25(6) of the EPPO Regulation stipulates that if both national authorities and the EPPO claim jurisdiction to investigate a case, 'the national authorities competent to decide on the attribution of competences concerning prosecution at national level shall decide who is to be competent for the investigation of the case'. Since in most of the Member States the competent national authority is the prosecution service, the eligibility criteria of Article 267 TFEU for requesting a preliminary ruling are not met. In turn, this may lead to a paucity of requests for a preliminary ruling on the validity of decisions on conflicts of competence.

IV. CONCLUSION

The new and unprecedented hybrid nature of the EPPO entails a complex interplay between national law and EU law, on the one hand, and national authorities and the EPPO, on the other, which restricts the ECJ's control over the EPPO. The ECJ's limited possibility to hold the EPPO judicially accountable not only weakens judicial review of the EPPO's procedural acts but – as Mitsilegas noted – 'undermines effective judicial protection and the role of the defence, by

[54] EPPO Regulation, Art 26 stipulates that the investigation is initiated and handled by an EDP from the Member State where the criminal activity is focused or, in case of several interlinked offences falling within the scope of competences of the EPPO, by the EDP of the Member State where the 'bulk of the offences has been committed'.

[55] A Zivic et al, 'Who's Afraid of EU Primary Law? Judicial Review of the EPPO's Decision on Forum Choice' (2022) 13 *New Journal of European Criminal Law* 398, 411.

[56] Research shows that even courts of last instance enjoy a de facto discretion.

[57] Respectively TFEU, Art 267(3) and (4).

[58] Zivic et al (n 55), 412–13.

[59] See Mitsilegas and Giuffrida (n 4), 132–33 with further references.

leaving key EPPO decisions [such as the initiation of an investigation, and decisions on forum choice] without a sufficient level of judicial scrutiny and accountability'.[60]

National courts' ability to submit requests to the ECJ for preliminary rulings on the interpretation of the EPPO Regulation is incremental and slow and cannot counterbalance current shortcomings. The EPPO Regulation reduces the ECJ's ability to provide for common concepts and principles and to check whether fundamental rights are properly implemented. As a result, the protection of fundamental rights is handled in a fragmented and uneven way in the AFSJ.

With the benefit of more years of practice and more developed jurisprudence, the system of judicial review of the EPPO Regulation ought to provide fertile ground for in-depth analysis. Following from the right to a fair trial, individuals have a fundamental right to know which prosecuting authority (national or European) is in charge of their case, what law is applicable, and which remedies are available.[61] It remains to be seen whether the presumption that EPPO decisions are national decisions as far as remedies are concerned will survive a potential assessment by the ECJ and even by the European Court of Human Rights.

[60] Mitsilegas (n 40), 261–62.

[61] K Ligeti and A Marletta, 'EU Criminal Justice Actors: Accountability and Judicial Review vis-à-vis the EU Citizen' (2016) 7 *New Journal of European Criminal Law* 175.

7

A Laboratory of Constitutional Development: Domestic Differentiation and the Effective Application of EU Law in the Area of Freedom, Security and Justice

THEODORE KONSTADINIDES, ANTOINE MASSON AND JULIEN STERCK*

I. INTRODUCTION

UNITED IN DIVERSITY: this motto, often cited to describe the EU as a 'union' founded upon the constitutive relationship between different cultures, identities and traditions, also finds expression in EU law itself. Indeed, while EU law aims to bring the legal systems of Member States into line with each other, it takes domestic differentiations into account in order to ensure that polyphony is inherent to its effective application.[1] Accordingly, domestic differentiation consists of the possibility for Member States to gain explicit recognition of certain specific political, cultural, legal or even geographical characteristics. In this sense, differentiation differs from pluralism, in that the latter merely deals with the way in which legal systems can coexist, whereas differentiation is concerned with enabling the distinctive features of each Member State to be accommodated within EU law as their common legal order.

In the 'united in diversity' context, the Area of Freedom, Security, and Justice (AFSJ) represents a remarkable instance of what can be described as a 'laboratory of constitutional development' within the EU's legal architecture. Given the nature of the policies that fall under the AFSJ title, it is an area where EU institutions have increasingly sought to address the challenge of bridging the gap between the often abstract precepts of EU law and the complex realities that exist within the Member States. The fact that EU law is based on a system of selective enforcement is textually visible in the context of the AFSJ, as exemplified by the opt-in

* Theodore Konstadinides, Professor of Law at the Essex Law School, University of Essex; Antoine Masson, Legal Secretary at the European Court of Justice, associate lecturer at the ESSEC Business School (Paris), the executive director of the Law & Management research network and director of a law book series; Julien Sterck, Legal Secretary at the European Court of Justice. All views expressed herein are personal to the authors.

[1] On the differentiation between Member States in the EU, see, for instance, A Angelaki, *La différenciation entre les États membres de l'Union européenne* (Bruylant, 2020).

and opt-out mechanisms at play. Still, the AFSJ is an ever-ambitious area of EU law. It is not, therefore, limited to the mere coordination of competing claims to national exceptions to a common framework. In the AFSJ, differentiations also result, maybe more than in any other field of EU law, from the increased possibility of tailoring the application of EU provisions according to domestic concerns. It can be argued that such form of differentiation is actually internal to the AFSJ. It derives from the implementation by Member States of provisions designed to that effect in the various relevant legal instruments.

The AFSJ offers accordingly a focused lens through which to scrutinise how domestic differentiations are taken into account for the effective application of EU law.[2] While it is challenging to comprehensively address all facets of the AFSJ, this chapter primarily seeks to highlight the role that domestic differentiation has within its framework and the Union's ethos of unity in diversity focusing on criminal and asylum law. This is particularly important in the context of developing policies that both address the aftermath of recent security and migration crises and aim at enhancing citizens' protection of their freedom, security and justice. The discussion in this chapter demonstrates that, despite numerous challenges and crises threatening the EU legal order, the AFSJ still holds strong in reinforcing the idea that the Union's strength lies in its ability to unite diversity within the Member States under a common legal framework.

II. DOMESTIC DIFFERENTIATION: A CORE ELEMENT OF THE AFSJ

In EU primary legislation, the concept of domestic differentiation is first and foremost visible in the Union's commitment to the principles of subsidiarity and proportionality, enshrined in Article 4(1) of the Treaty on European Union (TEU) and Protocol (No 2) on the application of the principles of subsidiarity and proportionality. However, these provisions do not provide much insight about the nature or limits of domestic differentiation as a concept. What we do learn from the first few articles of the TEU is that differentiation is a dynamic concept, interpreted through the interplay of the notion of constitutional identity and the principle of conferral, enshrined in Article 4(2) TEU and Article 5 TEU respectively, which serve as interpretative signposts within EU law.

In particular, the principle of conferral plays a central role in demarcating the scope and limits of powers conferred by the Member States on the Union. This principle serves as a jurisprudential bulwark that ensures a proper allocation of competences between the European and the domestic spheres. It lays the groundwork for a tailored divergence in policy implementation, enabling Member States to pursue national objectives without encroaching upon the Union's collective objectives. Complementary to the principle of conferral is the concept of constitutional identity, which has a special place in the EU's constitutional development. This concept serves as a facilitator for Member States to see their constitutional specificities taken into account in the process of integration within the broader EU framework. Far from being a mere juridical construct, constitutional identity incorporates a host of diverse constitutional traditions, legal specificities, and societal values. In this context, respectful disagreement is not only permissible but is indeed envisioned within the vertical constitutional design of the Union. Both conferral and constitutional identity find concrete expression in specific areas of

[2] On the different forms differentiation can take in EU law, see B de Witte, 'Variable Geometry and Differentiation as Structural Features of the EU Legal Order' in A Ott et al (eds), *Between Flexibility and Disintegration: the Trajectory of Differentiation in EU Law* (Edward Elgar, 2017) 9.

the AFSJ, an area that covers matters at the very core of national identity and sovereignty, and which, therefore, are essentially of a sensitive nature.

Differentiation within the AFSJ, in a precursor form, commenced during the adoption of the Schengen Agreement in 1985 developed outside the Treaty framework.[3] The Maastricht Treaty established a clear distinction in policies now governed by the AFSJ by establishing the Justice and Home Affairs (JHA) pillar within the TEU. As such, these policies adopted a unique governance model while remaining within a supranational institutional framework. Later, the Amsterdam Treaty modified how AFSJ law applied territorially. It transitioned the separation between Schengen and non-Schengen countries to an internal variance within the EU's legal order. Consequently, differentiation within the AFSJ legal framework started to align closely with the positions of certain 'differentiated' Member States such as Denmark, Ireland, and the UK.

The Treaty of Amsterdam's incremental expression of differentiation dynamics within the Union's constitutional order was further strengthened in the Lisbon Treaty. When it comes to the AFSJ in particular, differentiation was embedded in Article 67(1) of the Treaty on the Functioning of the European Union (TFEU), which affirms that the EU 'shall constitute an area of freedom, security and justice with respect for fundamental rights and the different legal systems and traditions of the Member States'.[4] This reference to domestic differentiations regarding the AFJS widened the scope for intergovernmental opt-out regimes to become inherent to the AFSJ, including sensitive areas such as criminal law, providing a mechanism to address the unique interests and considerations of individual Member States, while still preserving the broader consistency and effectiveness of EU law.[5] The opt-out and opt-in arrangements that were applicable to the UK (before Brexit), Ireland and Denmark[6] underline that the AFSJ is inherently multifaceted, conceived with both spatial and structural differentiation in mind.[7] But even though opt-outs offer flexibility, they can also pose challenges to the uniform application of EU law. While the UK and Ireland's opt-out approach differs from Denmark's, the associated Protocols permitting them to be exempt from AFSJ-related EU laws impacted both substance and procedure.[8] At the same time, Member States participating in the AFSJ moved forward with establishing a distinct set of EU rules for areas that are traditionally viewed as sensitive and closely tied to national sovereignty, such as internal security, asylum and judicial cooperation in criminal matters.[9]

[3] Agreement between the Governments of the States of the Benelux Economic Union, the Federal Republic of Germany and the French Republic on the gradual abolition of checks at their common borders [2000] OJ L239/13.

[4] See, for instance, Case C-583/22 PPU *MV (Formation of a cumulative sentence)*, ECLI:EU:C:2023:5, para 65. In this respect, it is interesting that the differentiation admitted in the AFJS appears to be broader than that referred to in Art 4(2) TEU, the latter referring to the Member States' 'national identities, inherent in their fundamental structures, political and constitutional'.

[5] Opt-outs are provisions that allow specific Member States to abstain from participating in particular policy areas. These arrangements, negotiated individually, ensure that they are not bound by common decisions in those areas, thus preventing potential policy gridlocks at the EU level.

[6] Protocol (No 19) on the Schengen *acquis* integrated into the framework of the European Union, Protocol (No 20) on the application of certain aspects of Article 26 of the Treaty on the Functioning of the European Union to the United Kingdom and to Ireland, Protocol (No 21) on the position of the United Kingdom and Ireland in respect of the area of freedom, security and justice and Protocol (No 36) on transitional provisions.

[7] See, for instance, M Garcia et al, 'L'Espace de liberté sécurité justice: un droit à géographie variable' (2023) *Revue trimestrielle de droit européen* 828 and J Bauchy et al, 'L'Espace de liberté sécurité justice: un droit à géométrie variable' (2023) *Revue trimestrielle de droit européen* 839.

[8] S Peers, 'In a World of their Own? Justice and Home Affairs Opt-Outs and the Treaty of Lisbon' (2008) 10 *Cambridge Yearbook of European Legal Studies* 383.

[9] These areas have been described as 'high policies' as they touch on the core sovereignty of Member States: F Tekin, *The Area of Freedom, Security and Justice: Brexit does not Mean Brexit* (Jacques Delors Institut Berlin, 2017) 6, www.delorscentre.eu/fileadmin/user_upload/201709013_Brexit-and-the-AFSJ_Tekin.pdf, accessed 22 February 2024.

In more recent years, greater consideration has been given, not so much to the possibility of being exempted from the application of EU legislation in the AFSJ, but rather to accommodating domestic sensitivities in the very application of its provisions. In this regard, judicial cooperation in criminal matters has become the prime example of the differentiating dynamics at play in the AFSJ. The legislation surrounding the European arrest warrant (EAW) became an important testing area of differentiation due to criminal law's strong link to national sovereignty. Accordingly, the procedural discretion afforded to Member States by Article 4 of the EAW Framework Decision allows them to adapt the optional grounds for refusal of extradition to fit their domestic legal cultures.[10] Whether it be the legal concept of dual criminality or the complexities surrounding the priority of domestic prosecutions, the EAW provisions illustrate the subtleties of how domestic differentiation is endorsed across the Union's legal landscape. Article 1(3) of the EAW Framework Decision also provides that it shall not have the effect of modifying the obligation to respect fundamental rights and fundamental legal principles as enshrined in Article 6 TEU. While this is true, refusal to execute an EAW is intended to be an exception which must be interpreted strictly. As will be discussed in the next section, EU institutions, and especially the European Court of Justice (ECJ), have held firm in their position that refusal to execute an EAW is an exception to the principle of mutual recognition and as such it must be interpreted strictly.

Asylum law also exhibits the differentiation dynamics engaged in the AFSJ. First, it shows that, in the intricate landscape of partial harmonisation, EU law recognises the key role that is still played by national sovereignty.[11] For example, while Directive 2011/95[12] defines the standards to be met in order to qualify for refugee status or subsidiary protection statuses, Article 2(h) of that Directive states that Member States are not precluded from granting a right of asylum under their national law, even when the person concerned does not meet the conditions set under EU law.[13] Moreover, EU law does not merely seek to organise harmonious relationships with these national systems. It also embraces them as integral to its legal system. For example, by virtue of its Article 3(1), Directive 2003/109, which grants certain rights to third-country nationals who are long-term residents, applies – under certain conditions – to third-country nationals with residence permits issued on grounds other than those provided for by EU law.[14] Second, asylum law shows that differentiation might result from the numerous options set out in EU law instruments, such as the possibility for Member States to determine

[10] Council Framework Decision 2002/584/JHA of 13 June 2002 on the European arrest warrant and the surrender procedures between Member States [2002] OJ L190/1, as amended by Council Framework Decision 2009/299/JHA of 26 February 2009 [2009] OJ L81/24 (EAW Framework Decision).

[11] This is a form of differentiation that is mostly ignored in the ECJ's case law insofar as it lies outside EU law, leading to some unfortunate formulations. See, in this regard, Opinion of AG Hogan in *Opinion 1/19 (Istanbul Convention)*, ECLI:EU:C:2021:198, para 107.

[12] Directive 2011/95/EU of the European Parliament and of the Council of 13 December 2011 on standards for the qualification of third-country nationals or stateless persons as beneficiaries of international protection, for a uniform status for refugees or for persons eligible for subsidiary protection, and for the content of the protection granted [2011] OJ L337/9.

[13] One typical example is what is known in French law as 'constitutional asylum', which has its origins in the Preamble to the French Constitution that states that any man persecuted for his actions in favour of liberty has the right of asylum on the territory of the French Republic. However, this protection is granted under conditions that differ from those in force in EU law.

[14] Council Directive 2003/109/EC of 25 November 2003 concerning the status of third-country nationals who are long-term residents [2004] OJ L16/44. Admittedly, by virtue of Art 3(2)(c) of that Directive, the question could arise as to whether beneficiaries of constitutional asylum can rely on this instrument. However, this is undoubtedly the case for those who were granted a residence permit as third-country national salaried workers, an area that is still largely the responsibility of the Member States; or a residence permit as a family member of a national of a Member State who has not travelled to another Member State.

the scope of certain categories at the implementation level or of conferring rights beyond those provided for by the relevant EU law provisions. For example, under Articles 36–39 of the revised Asylum Procedures Directive (APD),[15] Member States have a margin of discretion regarding the designation of 'safe countries', be it 'safe countries of origin', 'safe third countries', or 'European safe third countries'. This gives Member States certain leeway to adjust their asylum processes according to their geopolitical interests and human rights obligations. However, this flexibility can also draw criticism for adding complexity to an already complex system. For instance, it can be argued that the EU, in its efforts to streamline and unify its asylum system, is inadvertently legitimising inconsistency in the handling of asylum applications in the Member States. The variation in national asylum processes carries important consequences for the protection of the right to asylum, as observed by the Commission more than a decade ago, leading to a considerable number of initial asylum decisions being reversed on appeal in the Member States.[16]

Still, the conditions of application of EU law in the AFSJ in the context of asylum are largely entrusted to the procedural autonomy of the Member States. For example, with regard to the APD, the ECJ found that the conditions for the respect for the rights of the defence of the person concerned where that person's right of access to their file is restricted pursuant to the second subparagraph of its Article 23(1),[17] as well as the introduction of a second level of jurisdiction against decisions rejecting an application for international protection and against return decisions,[18] fall within the procedural autonomy of Member States.

As the above examples illustrate, domestic differentiation is not a peripheral concept but rather a foundational construct that is embedded within the DNA of EU constitutional law and finds a specific expression in the AFSJ. It facilitates a complex interaction of legal doctrines and principles, calibrated to balance the duality of preserving national sovereignty whilst fostering an ever-closer Union. The operationalisation of differentiation, as seen through the wide range of EU policies and legislation, serves as a testament to the EU's overarching ambition: to harmonise national governance models while at the same time preserving the idiosyncratic constitutional identities that comprise its core. While differentiation may sometimes contribute to disparities and tensions within the Union, potentially hindering the ideals of integration, cohesion and stability that it consistently aims to preserve, allowing for differentiation is crucial to the effectiveness of EU law and the AFSJ as a whole.

III. THE SCOPE OF DOMESTIC DIFFERENTIATION IN THE AFSJ: BALANCING 'DIVERSIFYING' AND BEING 'DIFFERENT'

The question of differentiation in the AFSJ exhibits a certain form of paradox, since differentiation might endanger the uniform application of EU law, but it is also a condition for the effective enforcement of EU law in this field. In striking the correct balance, the principle of effectiveness plays a central role. It provides that differentiation is endorsed when it

[15] Directive 2013/32/EU of the European Parliament and of the Council of 26 June 2013 on common procedures for granting and withdrawing international protection [2013] OJ L180/60.

[16] Report from the Commission to the European Parliament and the Council on the application of Directive 2005/85/EC on minimum standards on procedures in Member States for granting and withdrawing refugee status COM (2010) 465 final.

[17] Case C-159/21 *Országos Idegenrendészeti Főigazgatóság and Others*, ECLI:EU:C:2022:708, para 43.

[18] Case C-180/17 *Staatssecretaris van Veiligheid en Justitie (Suspensory effect of the appeal)*, ECLI:EU:C:2018:775, para 34.

corresponds to a variation that is expressed within the AFSJ and contributes to its realisation. At the same time, effectiveness places a limit to the expression of differences that would jeopardise the AFSJ common framework.

A. Differentiation as Effectiveness Enhancement: The Role of Mutual Recognition in the AFSJ

As established, the AFSJ is primarily concerned with regulating areas that are integral to the sovereign functions of Member States. These areas include unique elements specific to each one of them, leading to distinct considerations that are manifest in legal proceedings before the ECJ. Both the relevant legislation and the ECJ's interpretation are consistent in their message that the AFSJ functions in an environment where the successful implementation of EU legal instruments depends on both acknowledging diversity among Member States and fostering mutual recognition and trust between them. Most importantly, the ECJ has set the conditions for accommodating diversity within the limits allowed by the applicable EU legislation where such accommodation contributes to the greater effectiveness of EU law.

An illustrative example of this balance between differentiation and effectiveness can be found in the realm of judicial cooperation in criminal matters, particularly emphasised in Recital 6 of the EAW Framework Decision, where mutual recognition is deemed the cornerstone of judicial cooperation in criminal matters. Mutual recognition essentially implies that the effectiveness of mechanisms built upon this principle hinges on the acceptance of differing positions among the involved national authorities. Specifically, it requires the judicial authority in *Member State A* responsible for executing the EAW to enforce the decision of the requesting judicial authority in *Member State B*, even if that decision was made based on distinct substantive criteria and procedures not identical, but yet consistent with the legal order and principles of the enforcing authority in *Member State A*.

The ECJ has been steadfast in safeguarding the differentiation/mutual recognition rationale as manifested in the relevant EU legislation. Notably, each of the grounds that permit or require the executing judicial authority to refuse to execute an EAW, as relied upon in the ECJ's jurisprudence, originates from the EAW Framework Decision. These grounds have a narrowly defined scope, permitting the refusal to execute an EAW only in exceptional circumstances.[19] For instance, the ECJ has determined that it falls within the competence of the judicial authorities in the issuing Member State to evaluate their jurisdiction to issue a warrant, and such jurisdiction cannot be subject to review by the executing judicial authority. Consequently, as long as the conditions outlined in the EAW Framework Decision are adhered to, executing judicial authorities are obliged to acknowledge and accept that the legal systems of their counterparts may exhibit variances, and that their protection represents a deliberate choice by the Union's legislature.[20] This aspect is crucial for ensuring the proper functioning of the simplified and effective system for the surrender of persons convicted or suspected of committing criminal offences, as established by the EAW Framework Decision.[21] It implies that Member States interact in a spirit of sincere cooperation, which includes respecting the distinct characteristics and unique specificities of their partners.

[19] Case C-158/21 *Puig Gordi and Others*, ECLI:EU:C:2023:57, paras 73–74.
[20] See, to that effect, ibid, paras 85–87.
[21] See, to that effect, ibid, paras 76 and 116.

As highlighted in the preceding section, EU asylum law is also rich with differentiation examples where national variations are allowed to cater to domestic needs and, in doing so, to ensure the effective application of EU law. In this regard, the balance between differentiation and mutual recognition evidenced in Article 67(1) TFEU as a general provision of the AFSJ, finds, when it comes to asylum policies, specific expression in Article 78(3) TFEU, which provides for the possibility to adopt, '[i]n the event of one or more Member States being confronted by an emergency situation characterised by a sudden inflow of nationals of third countries, [...] provisional measures for the benefit of the Member State(s) concerned.' On this legal basis, the Council adopted, in particular, Decision 2015/1601, which promotes the principle of solidarity and equitable distribution of duty amongst Member States.[22] In particular, as reflected in its Recitals 3 and 4, this Decision introduced provisional measures in the area of international protection securing the commitment of all EU Member States to take into account the position of Italy and Greece as frontline Member States in the context of the so-called migrant crisis and to share the migration burden with them. Not all Member States were content with this plan. Indicatively, Slovakia and Hungary launched a legal challenge against Decision 2015/1601, which was dismissed by the ECJ in a judgment that reinforced the binding nature of the principle of solidarity among EU Member States. This judgment shows that, when necessary, the legal duty of solidarity imposed on Member States can be interpreted as recognising the need for a differentiated approach being taken to a minority of Member States. As the ECJ explained, the fact that some Member States, such as Greece and Italy, could not effectively manage their asylum systems – due to an overwhelming surge in migrant arrivals in 2015, which was putting immense strain on those systems – needed to be accounted for.[23]

The judgment in *Slovakia and Hungary v Council* raises considerable interest, as it implicitly demonstrates the ECJ's approach to two uses of differentiation. On the one hand, it showcases the importance of considering domestic differences arising out of necessity to ensure the successful implementation of EU law within the AFSJ (effectiveness-driven differentiation). On the other hand, it rejects the argument that the mandatory relocation quotas, as set by Decision (EU) 2015/1601, are not fair for countries which are largely ethnically uniform and culturally and linguistically distinct from the incoming migrants (exemption-driven differentiation).[24] The ECJ emphasised that, while domestic differences are acknowledged, they cannot be used as reasons to deviate from the overarching aims of EU law.

Additionally, the principle of mutual recognition can extend beyond the stipulations of the relevant EU legislation, accommodating a broader range of national constitutional specificities and requirements. For example, the ECJ ruled that aside from the guarantees included in the EAW Framework Decision, Member States could provide for a right of appeal with suspensive effect against decisions regarding an EAW. This is permitted even if it was not originally anticipated in the EAW Framework Decision, so far as the final decision is made within the time constraints set out in the EAW Framework Decision.[25] In reaching this conclusion, the ECJ emphasised the obligation to respect fundamental rights as laid down in national law and pointed to Recital 12 of the EAW Framework Decision to stress that this

[22] Council Decision (EU) 2015/1601 of 22 September 2015 establishing provisional measures in the area of international protection for the benefit of Italy and Greece [2015] OJ L248/80.

[23] See Joined Cases C-643/15 and C-647/15 *Slovakia and Hungary v Council*, ECLI:EU:C:2017:631, in particular, paras 126, 128 and 235.

[24] ibid, in particular, paras 302–304. On this aspect of the ECJ's judgment, see J Sigla, 'Differentiation in the EU Migration Policy: The "Fractured" Values of the EU' (2020) 7 *European Papers* 909, 921–22.

[25] Case C-168/13 PPU *F*, ECLI:EU:C:2013:358, paras 51 and 75.

legal instrument does not prevent Member States from applying their constitutional standards, including those ensuring the right to a fair trial.[26] By advocating for a solution where constitutional standards are integrated harmoniously within the enforcement of the EAW Framework Decision, the ECJ arrived at a conclusion that bolstered the effective application of EU law in the AFSJ. Had national constitutional standards been perceived as clashing with the membership commitment to uphold EU law, the efficacy of EU law application in the AFSJ might have been impaired.

Therefore, it can be argued that to ensure the effective application of EU law within the AFSJ, there is a necessity for legal flexibility allowing for differentiation. This may initially appear contradictory to the treaties' ethos and the objective of uniform application of EU law. Yet, in areas such as extradition, asylum, and immigration, the application of EU law in individual Member States is influenced by various pertinent policy and geopolitical challenges. International developments often have varying effects across Member States, which are typically managed within the scope of their domestic policy frameworks. Concurrently, maintaining the unity, and integrity of the Union's constitutional framework remains crucial for the evolution of EU law and its ability, through accommodation of varying degrees of differentiation among Member States, to ensure its effective application in the AFSJ.

B. Effectiveness as a Constraint on Differentiation: The Role of Autonomy in the AFSJ

While Member States often exercise a considerable margin of appreciation in applying EU law, domestic variation reaches its limit when it threatens the effective implementation of EU legislation. This balancing act is particularly critical in the AFSJ due to its structure, which is founded on mutual recognition, and where procedural autonomy is given a particular importance, and also due to its sensitivity, given its close ties to national sovereignty.

Procedural autonomy is crucial, especially in areas such as judicial cooperation, where inherent independence is a key feature. At the same time, the ECJ's case law is concerned with ensuring that national procedural autonomy is exercised in a manner compatible with fundamental rights or general principles of EU law, whether it be in relation to the imposition of criminal penalties, judicial cooperation in criminal matters,[27] asylum and immigration,[28] or judicial cooperation in civil matters.[29] An example that sheds light on this aspect is the judgment in the *G ST T* case,[30] which illustrates the permissible degree of autonomy afforded to national law in relation to trademark infringements as criminal offences. The ECJ concluded that domestic legislation prescribing a minimum five-year prison sentence for trademark infringements was in breach of EU law. While the ECJ recognised that Member States have the discretion to define the severity and nature of penalties for such offences in the absence of specific EU legislation, these national punitive measures must align with the principle of proportionality under EU law which, in this instance, prevented the application of such uniform minimum sentence for all cases of unauthorised commercial trademark use.

[26] ibid, paras 48 and 53.

[27] See, for instance, Case C-242/22 PPU *TL (Absence of an interpreter and of translation)*, ECLI:EU:C:2022:611, paras 75–84.

[28] See, for instance, Case C-338/21 *Staatssecretaris van Justitie en Veiligheid (Transfer time limit – Trafficking in human beings)*, ECLI:EU:C:2023:269, paras 40–48.

[29] See, for instance, Case C-18/21 *Uniqa Versicherungen* ECLI:EU:C:2022:682, paras 36–39.

[30] Case C-655/21 *G ST T (Proportionnalité de la peine en cas de contrefaçon)*, ECLI:EU:C:2023:791.

The above judgment aside, from a substantive perspective, the way in which the imperative regarding the effective implementation of EU law is promoted by the ECJ differs according to whether the differentiation is linked to the use of retained competences or whether it is expressly provided for by EU law. In the first instance, it is only required that national differentiation is not to be confused with regimes provided under EU law. For instance, the national protection which Member States have discretion to grant to refugees must not be confused with the refugee status provided under EU law.[31] However, in the second instance, since national differentiation is encapsulated into EU law, it must comply not only with the minimum conditions laid down, the general principle of EU law and the Charter, but also with the general scheme and objectives pursued by the instrument authorising such differentiation. Differentiation must also be suitable for achieving the objectives of the EU legal instrument which justifies taking account of national particularities and must not go beyond what is necessary to attain them.[32] For instance, Article 3 of Directive 2011/95 provides for the ability of Member States to introduce or retain more favourable standards for determining who qualifies as a refugee or as a person eligible for subsidiary protection, and for determining the content of international protection, in so far as those standards are compatible with the Directive. Therefore, the ECJ pointed out, Member States can neither grant refugee status and subsidiary protection statuses to third-country nationals in situations which have no connection with the rationale of international protection,[33] nor grant them to persons expressly excluded from these statuses.[34]

Indeed, the recognition of a degree of autonomy enjoyed by Member States acknowledges that the AFSJ, being intricately linked to national sovereignty, often necessitates a heightened consideration of national specificities. However, the ECJ has consistently ruled that such recognition of domestic singularities must not impede the effective implementation of EU law. Regarding fundamental rights, since the *Melloni* case, the ECJ has articulated that within the AFSJ also, while national authorities and courts are permitted to uphold their own standards for the protection of fundamental rights, this latitude is contingent upon ensuring that the primacy, unity, and effectiveness of EU law are not compromised.[35]

Even when invoking justifications such as public policy, public security, or national security in line with national needs – which may differ across Member States and change over time – there are limits within the context of the Union, particularly when these grounds are used as justifications to deviate from established obligations under EU law in the AFSJ. While the ECJ acknowledges that Member States have the autonomy to define what constitutes these justifications in accordance with their varying national requirements and changing times, it also highlights that such justifications must be construed narrowly. This means that their interpretation cannot be left solely to the discretion of individual Member States without oversight from EU institutions.[36]

The *Tsakouridis* case provides an illustrative example, involving the expulsion of a Greek national from Germany following his involvement in narcotics trafficking as part of an

[31] See Joined Cases C-57/09 and C-101/09 *Bundesrepublik Deutschland v B and D*, ECLI:EU:C:2010:661, paras 117–19.

[32] See, for instance, Case C-519/18 *Bevándorlási és Menekültügyi Hivatal (Family reunification – Sister of a refugee)*, ECLI:EU:C:2019:1070, paras 62 and 65–66.

[33] See Case C-652/16 *Ahmedbekova*, ECLI:EU:C:2018:801, para 71.

[34] Case C-91/20 *Bundesrepublik Deutschland (Maintaining family unity)*, ECLI:EU:C:2021:898, para 46.

[35] See Cases C-399/11 *Melloni*, ECLI:EU:C:2013:107, para 60; and, more recently, C-612/15 *Kolev and Others*, ECLI:EU:C:2018:392, para 75.

[36] See, for instance, Case C-18/19 *Stadt Frankfurt am Main*, ECLI:EU:C:2020:511, para 42.

organised group.[37] In this instance, the ECJ determined that Member States cannot expel EU citizens on public security grounds without thoroughly examining each specific case. For the justification of 'imperative grounds of public security' to be valid, a significant degree of severity is therefore required. In this case, Germany argued that involvement in organised narcotics trafficking could potentially pose a serious threat to the public's safety, justifying expulsion. However, the ECJ emphasised that any expulsion must be based on a genuine and present threat. This means that expulsion orders cannot be solely grounded on past criminal convictions or for the purpose of general prevention. The ruling demonstrates that while Member States are entitled to differentiate on national security grounds, such actions must be proportionate, targeted, and consistent with EU law, ensuring that they are not applied excessively or without proper justification.

The concept of autonomy in the field of judicial cooperation becomes particularly important when considering how the ECJ has delineated the balance between protecting fundamental rights and values, with the necessary differentiation it brings, and the assurance of effective implementation of EU law in the AFSJ. Article 1(3) of the EAW Framework Decision clearly states that this decision should not alter the obligation to respect fundamental rights and legal principles as enshrined in Article 6 TEU. This is particularly relevant when there is substantial reason to believe that such surrender of suspects might lead to a breach of their fundamental rights. The ECJ's jurisprudence has offered guidance to Member States on the conditions under which execution of an EAW can be refused, ensuring that while facilitating the cooperation necessary for the EAW to be operable, Member States also uphold the fundamental rights guaranteed by EU law.

In this context, the ECJ's approach in *LM* has been central with regard to the limits that EU law imposes on the EAW system, in particular when it comes to the formalisation of the two-step test that may justify, in exceptional circumstances, that an executing judicial authority refrains from giving effect to an EAW.[38] Regarding such possibility, beyond the grounds of refusal explicitly outlined in the EAW Framework Decision, the first step is to establish – through objective, reliable, specific, and duly updated evidence – the existence of systemic or generalised deficiencies in the respect for fundamental rights. Yet, the ECJ clarified in its judgment that such deficiencies (in this case pertaining to the independence of the judiciary in Poland) are not sufficient in themselves to amount to a real risk that a suspect's right to a fair trial is infringed. Should this first step be fulfilled, a second step requires an assessment, specifically and precisely, of whether there are substantial grounds for believing that the person concerned 'will run a real risk of breach of his or her fundamental rights',[39] providing thereby an aid to a national court making an individual assessment and setting the refusal of surrender threshold high.

In contrast to earlier decisions like *Melloni*, the ECJ's recognition of fundamental rights as a ground of EU law for non-execution of an EAW as formalised in *LM* is a welcome

[37] Case C-145/09 *Land Baden-Württemberg v Panagiotis Tsakouridis*, ECLI:EU:C:2010:708.

[38] Case C-216/18 PPU *Minister for Justice and Equality (Deficiencies in the system of justice)*, ECLI:EU:C:2018:586. For previous case law on this two-step test, see, in particular, Joined Cases C-404/15 and C-659/15 PPU *Aranyosi and Căldăraru*, ECLI:EU:C:2016:198. For a recent application of this two-step test see the judgment in C-261/22 *GN (Ground for refusal based on the best interests of the child)*, ECLI:EU:C:2023:1017. In this case, the ECJ applied the two-step test in relation in particular to Art 24(2) of the Charter, whilst AG Ćapeta advocated that executing an EAW against a mother with young children should be denied as soon as it is in the child's best interest: see Opinion of AG Ćapeta in Case C-261/22 *GN (Ground for refusal based on the best interests of the child)*, ECLI:EU:C:2023:582.

[39] *Minister for Justice and Equality (Deficiencies in the system of justice)* (n 38), paras 61 and 68.

development. The ECJ appears to be addressing the absence of a specific EU legal provision that prevents the refusal of extradition due to breaches of fundamental rights by the issuing authorities, thereby aligning with several Member States where a breach of fundamental rights is a clear reason to refuse extradition as per their national laws. Historically, this void often compelled executing courts to hand over criminal suspects, even if there were concerns about the preservation of the suspect's rights by the issuing Member State. Through bottom-up scrutiny, national courts are invited to partake in monitoring the observance of fundamental rights and rule of law commitments in their counterparts in specific cases.[40] Yet, by subjecting the refusal to execute an EAW to such scrutiny in the light of proof of a significant systemic issue, such empowerment is exercised in balance with considerations for the effectiveness of EU law, which rests on the concomitant commitment to mutual recognition that is the cornerstone of the EAW mechanism.[41] The Court, in its interpretation in *LM*, was cautious in order to avoid constitutional pitfalls while discreetly confronting challenges from Member States that showed signs of democratic erosion.

The reach of such development is even more revealing when considered in the light of the new focus given to Article 2 TEU, which provides that '[t]he Union is founded on the values of respect for human dignity, freedom, democracy, equality, the rule of law and respect for human rights, including the rights of persons belonging to minorities'. The Court indicated, in particular, that EU law is based on the fundamental premise that each Member State shares with all the other Member States these common values on which the Union is founded.[42] This provides the foundations of the mutual trust among Member States in the recognition of these values. It follows that the relationships between issuing and executing authorities of an EAW rest on the assumption that, in principle, the latter can be confident in the ability of the former to protect and uphold fundamental rights. Yet, it enables executing authorities to take into account exceptional circumstances where the conditions of such trust need to be protected where there are robust grounds to consider that the issuing Member State stands out in that the said presumption of respect for fundamental rights can be questioned. In this sense mutual trust, and the principle of mutual recognition upon which it is based, are paramount to the effective functioning of the AFSJ's framework.

IV. CONCLUSION

EU membership is an exercise in self-restraint. Domestic singularities need to be counterbalanced against the decision to join the Union and the effectiveness application of EU law that this decision implies. This is clearly reflected in the context of the AFSJ's development. Yet, self-restraint should not overshadow one of the most innovative aspects revealed by the normative dynamics in this field: the AFSJ stands as a unique laboratory for constitutional evolution within the EU as, perhaps more than any other field, it is enriched by and showcases what can be achieved by measured and integration-friendly differentiation, driven by

[40] However, a protection of fundamental rights, for instance against any inhuman or degrading treatment enshrined in Art 4 of the Charter, is still possible outside the framework of the systemic deficiencies test: see Case C-578/16 *CK v Slovenia*, ECLI:EU:C:2017:127.

[41] In this regard, it is important to note that the ECJ has stressed the importance of domestic authorities engaging in a dialogue, notably on the basis of Art 15 of the EAW Framework Decision; see, for instance, Case C-220/18 PPU *Generalstaatsanwaltschaft (Conditions of detention in Hungary)*, ECLI:EU:C:2018:589, paras 108–16.

[42] *Minister for Justice and Equality (Deficiencies in the system of justice)* (n 38), paras 35–36.

flexibility and dialogue in effectively applying AFSJ instruments, while respecting the specific nuances and exceptions crucial to the preservation of national sovereignty.

Looking ahead, the concept of solidarity, which (in addition to differentiation) is recognised in Article 67(1) TFEU as an inherent part of the AFSJ, and in Article 67(2) TFEU in relation to forging a common asylum, immigration and external border control policy,[43] might take a key role in determining the AFSJ's future. Balancing the Union's regional and global security goals against the legal boundaries of the AFSJ, both institutionally and substantively, presents a challenging solidarity dilemma. The effort to align diverse national practices with the EU's collective objectives is bound to face difficulties in the aftermath of the numerous crises that the EU has faced in recent years and in the light of new ones which may further test the allegiance of Member States to their counterparts and the European project more broadly.

As the EU's ambition to unite in diversity continues to evolve, the AFSJ will undoubtedly remain an essential area for exploring the dynamic interplay of fundamental constitutional principles and national differentiation as an expression of national identity and sovereignty specificities within the Union's adaptable yet integration-driven legal framework.

[43] For reference to this consideration in the ECJ's case law, see Case C-483/20 *Commissaire General aux réfugiés et aux apatrides (Unité familiale – Protection déjà accordée)*, ECLI:EU:C:2022:103, para 28.

8

Opt-Outs in the Area of Freedom, Security and Justice: The Danish Example

CHRISTIAN THORNING*

I. INTRODUCTION

FOR MORE THAN 30 years, Denmark has held a special position within the Area of Freedom, Security and Justice (AFSJ) cooperation. In fact, not only is the position special but it is also unique, for no other Member State shares it.

This chapter offers an overview of the main characteristics of 'the Danish example'. First, an account is provided of the legal construction of the Danish position, including how it has developed as a consequence of the immense evolution of the AFSJ cooperation since the Maastricht Treaty. Second, a sketch of the legal effects is presented, including a brief discussion of the mitigating measures that have come into existence in relation to certain specific outcomes of the opt-out. Third, 'the Irish example', which formerly also included the position of the United Kingdom (UK), is discussed with a view to comparing it to the Danish position. Fourth, a separate section is dedicated to cases on which the European Court of Justice (ECJ) has addressed aspects of the Danish AFSJ position. Fifth and finally, conclusions are drawn, including some considerations on 'the Danish example' as a potential template for future developments of EU law within AFSJ.

The approach adopted in this chapter is legal-doctrinal and not normative.[1]

II. THE LEGAL CONSTRUCTION OF THE DANISH OPT-OUT

On 2 June 1992, the Danish electorate rejected the Maastricht Treaty in a popular referendum that was binding pursuant to the Danish Constitution. Consequently, Denmark was in no position to ratify the Treaty and the fate of the foreseen establishment of a European Union looked grim. A consolidated political effort, combined with legal imagination, enabled the European Council, already at its meeting in Edinburgh in December 1992, to agree on a tailor-made solution that would break the stalemate.

* Danish Ambassador to the Republic of Iraq, former Principal Agent for the Danish Government before the Court of Justice of the European Union.

[1] The chapter draws on certain elements comprehensively addressed in C Thorning, *The Danish EU Opt-Outs: Their Legal Significance, Past and Present* (Hart Publishing, forthcoming).

The legal construction of that solution was a novelty; so too was its content. Denmark was permitted a special position on certain aspects within four specific areas of EU cooperation: Union citizenship; the Euro; defence cooperation; and finally on what was then called Justice and Home Affairs (JHA), now the AFSJ.

The solution did not appear out of the blue. Prior to the meeting in Edinburgh, homework had been done, not least on the part of Denmark. As a follow-up to the negative outcome of the June 1992 referendum, a large majority of the Danish political parties – including the ones forming the government – had joined forces in formulating the specific Danish political concerns regarding the new treaty. Moreover, a sketch of a legally binding solution to accommodate the main concerns was also provided. In Denmark this is popularly known as 'the National Compromise'.[2]

This Danish memorandum formed the background for the comprehensive solution agreed by the European leaders in Edinburgh. The solution is found in Part B of the Presidency Conclusion.[3] At its centrepiece stands a decision by which the said special Danish position is instituted;[4] section D of the decision regulates the position on 'Justice and Home Affairs' (now the AFSJ).

The decision, known as 'the Edinburgh Decision', is one adopted by the Heads of State and Government and thus not by the European Council. From a Danish point of view, the Edinburgh Decision was clearly seen as an instrument binding under international law. This was explicitly stated by the Danish Government on several occasions, including in the explanatory notes to the Danish Bill on the subsequent ratification of the Maastricht Treaty.[5] The status as 'a treaty' was deliberately emphasised by way of ensuring its deposit in the registry for treaties at the United Nations headquarters in New York.[6] It follows implicitly that the Edinburgh Decision was viewed as not forming part of EU law.

It was indeed a novelty that particular issues relating to the EU treaties were solved by way of a legal instrument binding the parties, the EU Member States, under international law but not at the same time an instrument forming part of EU law. The construction sparked a debate among scholars, including on the question of whether the Edinburgh Decision nonetheless did have a legal impact directly under EU law, notably vis-à-vis the question of jurisdiction of the ECJ.[7] It was the Danish viewpoint that the Edinburgh Decision was subject to the jurisdiction of the International Court of Justice (ICJ) in The Hague, although Denmark also argued that the Edinburgh Decision would, where appropriate, be included when interpreting and applying the Maastricht Treaty.[8] The issue of judicial competence of the ICJ never materialised, since the course of events of the subsequent European integration process made this issue less pertinent.

Before the aspect of the European integration process is explored, a look is taken at the content of the special position on AFSJ as instituted by the Edinburgh Decision. As it happens,

[2] See eg N Petersen, 'Denmark and the European Union 1985–96. A Two-level Analysis' (1996) 31 *Cooperation and Conflict* 185.

[3] Denmark and the Treaty on European Union [1992] OJ C348/1.

[4] Annex I of the conclusions.

[5] Folketingstidende, saml. 1992–93 – L177.

[6] Decision constituting an agreement concerning certain problems raised by Denmark on the Treaty on European Union (Edinburgh, 12 December 1992).

[7] See for example D Curtin and R van Ooik, 'Denmark and the Edinburgh Summit: Maastricht without Tears: A Legal Analysis' in D O'Keeffe and PM Twomey (eds), *Legal Issues of the Maastricht Treaty* (Wiley Chancery, 1994); D Howarth, 'The Compromise on Denmark and the Treaty on European Union: A Legal and Political Analysis' (1994–1995) 18 *Journal of European Integration* 57.

[8] The explanatory notes to the Danish ratification bill L177, Folketingstidende saml. 1992–93, column 6705.

the position was not special at all at the time of the Edinburgh Decision. Section D of the Decision takes the following wording 'Denmark will participate fully in cooperation on Justice and Home Affairs on the basis of the provisions of Title VI of the Treaty on European Union'.

This provision clearly does not constitute an opt-out per se; rather, it is a statement of an obvious legal position of any Member State given that the entire cooperation within the field was indeed based on the cited Title of the Treaty on European Union (TEU). However, there was a point to it all.

At the time, Title VI of TEU, which provided the legal base for the cooperation on AFSJ (then JHA), formed the 3rd pillar of the Union structure established by the Maastricht Treaty. The character of that pillar was intergovernmental, as opposed to the supranational character of the ordinary 'communitarian' cooperation within the 1st pillar. The point of Section D of the Edinburgh Decision was thus legally to fix the Danish participation on AFSJ solely at the intergovernmental level.

The Danish position became special as a consequence of the subsequent treaty change via the Amsterdam Treaty that entered into force in 1999. At the prior intergovernmental conference (IGC), it was a firm position of Denmark to maintain its legal position as laid out in the Edinburgh Decision. Given the fact that the Amsterdam Treaty transferred roughly half of the AFSJ cooperation on asylum, migration, border control and judicial cooperation in civil matters from the 3rd to the 1st pillar,[9] a proper Danish opt-out on AFSJ had to be established within EU law to avoid compromising the Danish position. At the same time, Denmark honoured a commitment given in Edinburgh, which was not to prevent a closer cooperation between the other Member States on matters covered by the special Danish position.[10] In other words, the so-called 'pillar jump' undertaken by the Amsterdam Treaty within AFSJ was acceptable to Denmark even though it meant that Denmark henceforth could no longer be part of the affected parts of the AFSJ.

While also addressing issues relating to upholding the Danish opt-out on defence cooperation as regulated by the Edinburgh Decision Section C, a comprehensive solution was found by way of introducing the 'Protocol on the Position of Denmark'. The new protocol regulated both opt-outs as part of EU primary law.[11]

Some ten years later, the Lisbon Treaty completed what had begun in Amsterdam by transferring the remaining part of the AFSJ, ie cooperation within police and judicial cooperation in criminal matters from their prior intergovernmental nature to the supranational cooperation. By doing so, the Lisbon Treaty terminated the 3rd pillar altogether.[12] In the IGC held prior to the conclusion of the Lisbon Treaty, the negotiation position of the Danish Government had once again been to ensure the continuation of the special Danish position, including the opt-out on AFSJ. Consequently, the necessary adaptations of the opt-out provisions within the protocol were agreed, on the basis of which Denmark accepted the treaty changes; although this meant that the scope of the AFSJ opt-out now covered the entire area of cooperation.[13]

[9] A new Title IV within the then-Treaty establishing the European Community (TEC).

[10] Fifth (final) Recital of the Edinburgh Decision, Denmark and the Treaty on European Union [1992] OJ C348/1.

[11] Protocol No 5 on the Position of Denmark annexed to the Treaty establishing the European Community and to the Treaty on European Union, *cf* Treaty of Amsterdam amending the Treaty on European Union, the Treaties establishing the European Communities and certain related acts [1997] OJ C340/1. In its current version, it is Protocol No 22 on the Position of Denmark [2012] OJ C326/299.

[12] The Nice Treaty had introduced certain changes to the decision-making procedures also within AFSJ, however this had no consequence for the Danish opt-out as the Nice Treaty had left the police and judicial cooperation in criminal matters within the 3rd pillar.

[13] There is one modification to this, as certain aspects of visa policy fall outside the scope of the opt-out; *cf* Art 6 of the current Protocol on the Position of Denmark. This is due to the fact that the Maastricht Treaty regulated the said

III. THE LEGAL IMPACT OF THE DANISH AFSJ OPT-OUT

The current Protocol on the Position of Denmark as last updated by the Lisbon Treaty contains in Parts I and III the specific provisions on the Danish position within the AFSJ.[14] Essentially the opt-out means that Denmark does not take part in the adoption of, nor is Denmark bound by, any measures pursuant to the AFSJ title of the Treaty on the Functioning of the European Union (TFEU), including international agreements concluded by the Union pursuant to that title as well as rulings of the ECJ on measures pursuant to the same Title V. Denmark does not contribute financially to the concerned measures.[15] Also, Denmark is not bound by any of the AFSJ treaty provisions themselves.

The opt-out is not applicable in relation to policy documents such as declarations and council conclusions etc. It relates to legal measures only. The exclusion of Denmark from the AFSJ *acquis* is a predefined and automatic legal effect that requires no action on the side of Denmark or anyone else. It is a pure, unavoidable and predefined 'opt-out'.

IV. MITIGATING MEASURES

Acknowledging the original definition by the Edinburgh Decision,[16] it is clear that even though the opt-out is unconditional, it relates to the form of cooperation (supranational cooperation) but not to a legally binding cooperation on AFSJ matters per se, as long as it is done on an intergovernmental level. This legal fact creates the possibilities of special legal constructions with a view to mitigating the effects of the opt-outs that leave Denmark outside the AFSJ cooperation.[17]

The prominent example of such a mitigating solution is the so-called 'Schengen Technicality' that forms an integral part of Protocol 22.[18] Denmark was a party to the intergovernmental Schengen cooperation that existed prior to its incorporation into the EU Treaties by the Amsterdam Treaty. The Schengen rules determined to have a legal basis in the 1st pillar part of the AFSJ cooperation[19] would by default fall within the scope of the opt-out, thus leaving Denmark outside. That was considered an unfortunate outcome.

The established solution to mitigate this outcome prescribes that:

> Denmark shall decide within a period of six months after the Council has decided on a proposal or initiative to build upon the Schengen *acquis* covered by [the AFSJ part of Protocol 22] whether it will implement this measure in its national law.[20]

visa issues as part of the ordinary 'communitarian' cooperation outside of the intergovernmental 3rd pillar to which the Edinburgh Decision, Section D, referred.

[14] Protocol No 22 on the Position of Denmark is annexed to the TEU and the TFEU. Part II contains the provisions on the Danish defence opt-out, which the Danish electorate in a referendum in June 2022 voted no longer to uphold. That decision was in line with the provisions given in Part IV of the Protocol on a right for Denmark – at any time – to decide that it 'no longer wishes to avail itself of all or part of this Protocol'. Part IV also regulates for an option for Denmark to change the position on AFSJ. This aspect is explained below in relation to the discussion of 'the Irish case'.

[15] With the exemption of ordinary administrative costs of the institutions.

[16] The Edinburgh Decision is still in force.

[17] Denmark cannot by unilateral alignment of national laws obtain the effect of mutual recognition that EU law may provide and neither can Denmark empower EU institutions to exercise authority.

[18] Protocol No 22 on the Position of Denmark, Art 4. The term 'Schengen Technicality' is unofficial, but it is in use, eg in the explanatory notes to Bill L29 of 12 November 2015 on changing the Danish position vis-à-vis the AFSJ opt-out. On that Bill see further below the section on 'the Irish example'.

[19] The then Title IV of the TEC.

[20] Protocol No 22 on the Position of Denmark, Art 4(1).

If Denmark makes that choice, a legally binding agreement is constituted between Denmark and the other EU Member States that are bound by the adopted Schengen measure, ie which are 'Schengen members'.[21] The construction respects the nature of the Danish opt-out, given that Denmark does not become part of the said legal measures, which consequently do not become binding on Denmark as EU law. Thus, it is not the measures themselves but their content that Denmark becomes legally bound by, and that binding effect takes place on an intergovernmental level between Denmark and the other EU Schengen States. The Schengen Technicality is applicable to all Schengen measures, including the Regulation establishing the European Border and Coast Guard Agency (FRONTEX).[22] Denmark thus participates in FRONTEX alongside the other Member States but on an intergovernmental level.

The difference in practical life between a supranational and an intergovernmental legal obligation is probably marginal. However, legally it implies that the infringement procedures of the European Commission and ECJ are not applicable.[23]

The Schengen Technicality does not leave Denmark in a particularly favourable position given that Denmark will face 'appropriate measures' if Denmark decides not to implement in its national law a Schengen measure adopted by others.[24] Ultimately, this implies that Denmark would no longer be seen as a Schengen State. It is telling that, to date, Denmark has implemented all Schengen measures pursuant to the Schengen Technicality. Consequently, the scope of 'appropriate measures' has not been tested.

The question of whether an AFSJ measure builds upon the Schengen *acquis* is ultimately an issue on which the ECJ must rule.[25] The ECJ has had the opportunity to clarify that it is a matter based on 'objective factors which are amenable to judicial review, including in particular the aim and the content of the act'.[26] More specifically, the ECJ has stated that:

> […] when classifying a measure as falling within an area of the Schengen *acquis* or as a development of that *acquis*, the need for coherence of that *acquis*, and the need – where that *acquis* evolves – to maintain that coherence, must be taken into account.[27]

Besides the treaty-based Schengen Technicality, ad hoc solutions have come about in relation to a few specific AFSJ measures. Unlike the case of Schengen, such solutions have solely depended on the goodwill of the EU, as Denmark has no right to such arrangements.

[21] ibid.

[22] Regulation (EU) 2019/1896 of the European Parliament and of the Council of 13 November 2019 on the European Border and Coast Guard and repealing Regulations (EU) No 1052/2013 and (EU) 2016/162 [2019] OJ L295/1. The position of Denmark is referred to in Recital 125 as follows: 'In accordance with Articles 1 and 2 of Protocol No 22 on the position of Denmark annexed to the TEU and to the TFEU, Denmark is not taking part in the adoption of this Regulation and is not bound by it, or subject to its application. Given that this Regulation builds upon the Schengen acquis, Denmark shall, in accordance with Article 4 of that Protocol, decide within a period of six months after the Council has decided on this Regulation whether it will implement it in its national law.'

[23] Vedsted-Hansen rightly argues that the EU Charter most likely is also not applicable, in J Vedsted-Hansen, 'Det retlige forbehold og personers mobilitet' in BE Olsen and KE Sørensen (eds), *EU-retten i Danmark* (Jurist- og Økonomforbundets Forlag, 2018) 128.

[24] The decision to implement a Schengen measure does not cover future changes, recasts etc. A new and separate decision of Denmark pursuant to the Schengen Technicality would then be necessary.

[25] See in particular Cases C-77/05 *United Kingdom of Great Britain and Northern Ireland v Council of the European Union*, ECLI:EU:C:2007:803; and C-482/08 *United Kingdom of Great Britain and Northern Ireland v Council of the European Union*, ECLI:EU:C:2010:631.

[26] C-77/05 *United Kingdom of Great Britain and Northern Ireland v Council of the European Union* (n 25), para 79.

[27] C-482/08 *United Kingdom of Great Britain and Northern Ireland v Council of the European Union* (n 25), para 48.

In the aftermath of the entering into force of the Amsterdam Treaty, three agreements were entered into between the EU and Denmark on Danish association to a total of four AFSJ measures.[28] The Commission has made it clear that such agreements are of an exceptional nature and that 'the participation of Denmark in the Community [EU] regime would have to be fully in the interests of the Community [Union]'.[29] The Commission refers to the agreements as 'Parallel Agreements', which is a term alien to the treaties. What is clear is that the agreements are concluded on the legal basis of the treaties on the conclusion of EU agreements with a third country. Despite its Member State status, Denmark is nonetheless treated as a third country.

Following the entry into force of the Lisbon Treaty, the legal foundations of the EU's law enforcement agency (Europol) and the agency on judicial cooperation in criminal matters (Eurojust) were reformed. The prior intergovernmental measures, on which the agencies were established, were repealed and replaced by new legislative acts adopted pursuant to the relevant provisions of the treaties, the consequence of which was that they fell within the scope of the opt-out.[30] Acknowledging this as an exceptional, unfortunate situation, cooperation agreements were negotiated and ultimately adopted directly between Denmark and the two agencies, respectively. The one on Europol entered into force in 2017,[31] and the one on Eurojust in 2019.[32] Again, the approach is that Denmark is treated as if it were a third country. Denmark does not enjoy the full rights of the two agencies as other EU Member States do.

Finally, with regard to the European Asylum Support Office,[33] which built itself on prior intergovernmental cooperation among Member States that included Denmark, the solution to somewhat accommodate the excluded Denmark was found by way of granting Denmark observer status. That was done through a provision of the Regulation establishing the Office.[34]

[28] Council Regulation (EC) No 1348/2000 of 29 May 2000 on the service in the Member States of judicial and extrajudicial documents in civil or commercial matters [2000] OJ L160/37; Council Regulation (EC) No 44/2001 of 22 December 2000 on jurisdiction and the recognition and enforcement of judgments in civil and commercial matters [2001] OJ L12/1; Council Regulation (EC) No 343/2003 of 18 February 2003 establishing the criteria and mechanisms for determining the Member State responsible for examining an asylum application lodged in one of the Member States by a third-country national [2000] OJ L50/1; and Council Regulation (EC) No 2725/2000 of 11 December 2000 concerning the establishment of 'Eurodac' for the comparison of fingerprints for the effective application of the Dublin Convention [2000] OJ L316/1 (popularly referred to as 'Dublin' and 'Eurodac').

[29] Commission, 'Proposal for a Council Decision concerning the signing of the Agreement between the European Community and the Kingdom of Denmark extending to Denmark the provisions of Council Regulation (EC) No 1348/2000 on the service in the Member States of judicial and extrajudicial documents in civil or commercial matters' COM (2005) 146 final.

[30] Regulation (EU) 2016/794 of the European Parliament and of the Council of 11 May 2016 on the European Union Agency for Law Enforcement Cooperation (Europol) and replacing and repealing Council Decisions 2009/371/JHA, 2009/934/JHA, 2009/935/JHA, 2009/936/JHA and 2009/968/JHA [2016] OJ L135/53; and Regulation (EU) 2018/1727 of the European Parliament and of the Council of 14 November 2018 on the European Union Agency for Criminal Justice Cooperation (Eurojust), and replacing and repealing Council Decision 2002/187/JHA [2018] OJ L295/138.

[31] Agreement on Operational and Strategic Cooperation between the Kingdom of Denmark and the European Police Office (Valetta, 29 February 2017).

[32] Agreement on Criminal Justice Cooperation between Eurojust and the Kingdom of Denmark (Luxembourg, 7 October 2019).

[33] The current regulation is Regulation (EU) 2021/2303 of the European Parliament and of the Council of 15 December 2021 on the European Union Agency for Asylum and repealing Regulation (EU) No 439/2010 [2021] OJ L468/1.

[34] Regulation (EU) No 439/2010 of the European Parliament and of the Council of 19 May 2010 establishing a European Asylum Support Office [2010] OJ L132/11, Recital 23 and Art 48.

V. THE IRISH EXAMPLE

The effect of the special Danish position on AFSJ is one of a proper opt-out from a defined part of EU cooperation. It offers no room for policy choices or discretion. This stands in contrast to the position enjoyed by Ireland, a position that Ireland formerly shared with the UK.

Like the Danish position, 'the Irish example' is also treaty based; it is laid out in Protocol No 21.[35] The starting point is the same as in the Danish case, ie Ireland does not participate in and does not become bound by the AFSJ measures. However, Protocol 21 permits Ireland a right to exercise a political choice to repeal these effects on a case-by-case basis. Ireland may thus choose to become part of an AFSJ measure, which includes all its legal effects under EU law. Ireland may do so either at the proposal stage or at the later stage when the measure is adopted by the other Member States. Put in a nutshell: Ireland may choose 'to opt-in'.

While at first glance the Danish Schengen Technicality may appear to be similar to the Irish 'opt-in', legally that is not the case. Neither are any of the few other examples of ad hoc association of Denmark to AFSJ legal measures. They cannot equal an opt-in, as that would circumvent the provision of the Edinburgh Decision that Denmark only participates in the AFSJ cooperation on an intergovernmental level. If that has to change, a specific legal basis must be provided and, importantly, the change from the opt-out to the opt-in model would require confirmation in a Danish referendum.[36]

The Lisbon Treaty did in fact provide Denmark with the option to make such a change. It was done by inserting a legal basis to this effect in the last part IV of Protocol No 22.[37] If Denmark chose to avail itself of this new option, the opt-out provisions of the Protocol would simply be replaced by a set of provisions entailed in an annex to the same protocol. These provisions mirror the ones of 'the Irish example' also known as the provisions of Protocol 21 with the necessary adaptations, notably with a view to catering for the fact that Denmark is a full Schengen State, whereas Ireland is not.

On 3 December 2015, a referendum was held in Denmark on an adopted bill by the Danish Parliament on the effect of converting the Danish opt-out to the opt-in model.[38] The bill was rejected by 53.1 per cent no-votes to 46.9 per cent yes-votes, with the consequence that the Danish AFSJ opt-out has remained unchanged.

VI. THE DANISH AFSJ OPT-OUT BEFORE THE ECJ

No Member State actively participates in all cases before the ECJ. An exercise of identifying particular interests and subsequently balancing those findings against the litigation resources available takes place.[39] The opt-out does not exclude Denmark from its right, pursuant to the treaties, to participate in cases before the ECJ on AFSJ matters. However, given that

[35] Protocol No 21 on the Position of the United Kingdom and Ireland in respect of the Area of Freedom, Security and Justice [2016] OJ C202/295.

[36] On the complex issue of Danish referenda see eg the legal comments to Art 20 of the Danish Constitution in JP Christensen et al, *Grundloven med kommentarer* (Jurist- og Økonomforbundets Forlag, 2015).

[37] Protocol No 22 on the Position of Denmark, Art 8. The provision to abolish the entire opt-out is maintained in Art 7.

[38] Bill L29 of 8 October 2015, 'Forslag til lov om omdannelse af retsforbeholdet til en tilvalgsordning', Folketingstidende, saml 2015–16, L29.

[39] C Thorning, 'Varetagelse af danske interesser ved EU-Domstolen' in Olsen and Sørensen (eds) (n 23), 207.

Denmark does not participate in the adoption of EU law within the AFSJ field and the fact that Denmark is not bound by it either, as a rule of thumb Denmark does not prioritise participation in AFSJ cases before the ECJ.

That rule comes with a modification that relates to Schengen matters, which Denmark, as mentioned above, is a party to – albeit on a special legal footing. Therefore, Denmark does have a direct legal interest in the interpretation of the underlying EU law on Schengen matters, and Denmark therefore does participate in cases before the ECJ on these matters. The same is the case in relation to the EU regulations forming the basis for the Parallel Agreements and the other special arrangements as mentioned above. In such cases it is not the special Danish position that is an issue of interest but the interpretation of the EU law concerned.

There is yet another category of AFSJ cases that constitutes an exemption from the mentioned rule of thumb. This relates to instances where the ECJ itself has raised questions on the interpretation and understanding of the Danish AFSJ opt-out. That has occurred in certain cases dealing with the extent and character of external competences within AFSJ. The AFSJ opt-out explicitly states that no provision, measure or decision pursuant to Title V of Part Three of TFEU shall in any way affect the competences, rights and obligations of Denmark.[40] The ECJ has wondered whether the opposite holds true, ie whether the special Danish position impacts the character of the Union's external competence.

One such example occurred in *Opinion 1/13*.[41] The ECJ asked *ex officio* whether parties saw any possible impact of the Danish opt-out on the issue of exclusive Union competence derived from the ERTA doctrine.[42] Alongside the Commission, The European Parliament, The Council and a few Member States, Denmark argued before the ECJ that its special position had no bearing on the assessment of the nature of the external competence that the EU might have in the field under review. Denmark held that 'were the ECJ to be of the position [which it was] that an exclusive external EU competence existed, it would have bearings on the legal position of the Member States, with the exception of Denmark'.[43] In its *Opinion*, the ECJ made no reference to the issue. The silence of the ECJ on the matter, which the ECJ itself had raised, may be interpreted as the ECJ being content with the concordant observations of the parties.

The special Danish position also appeared as an issue in relation to *Opinion 1/03*.[44] More specifically the question was whether the Parallel Agreement between the EU and Denmark on Regulation 44/2001 (Brussels I) had any bearing on the nature and scope of the EU's external competence. The answer was in the negative.[45] In *Opinion 1/19* on the Istanbul Convention, the ECJ clarified that the application of the Danish AFSJ in relation to the underlying

[40] Protocol No 22, Art 2.

[41] *Opinion 1/13 (Accession of third States to the Hague Convention)*, ECLI:EU:C:2014:2303.

[42] Question of the ECJ of 17 March 2014 for written answer: 'The Danish Government, as well as the other parties, are requested to clarify – in light of Opinion 1/03 of 7 February 2006 (Rec. p-I-1145) – the possible impact on the present case of the fact that, in accordance with Protocol No 22 on the position of Denmark, annexed to the EU and FEU Treaties, this Member State is not participating in the adoption of measures in the area of freedom, security and justice and therefore that it did not participate in the adoption of Regulation No 2201/2003 and it is not bound by it' (unofficial translation from French).

[43] C Thorning, 'The ERTA Doctrine Post-Lisbon: Opinion 1/13 (*Convention of the Civil Aspects of International Child Abduction)*' in RA Wessel and G Butler (eds), *EU External Relation Law: The Cases in Context* (Hart Publishing, 2022) 753.

[44] *Opinion 1/13 Lugano Convention of the Civil Aspects of International Child Abduction*, ECLI:EU:C:2006:81.

[45] See Thorning (n 43), fn 37.

EU law measures did not give rise to any particular legal difficulties when determining the competence issue.[46]

More generally, the ECJ has clarified the fundamental question of the applicability of Protocol 22 on Denmark and equally Protocol 21 on Ireland (and formerly the UK) by stating that 'it is the legal basis for a measure [...] which determines the protocols to be applied, and not vice versa'.[47] This of course means that measures with a legal basis outside of Title V of Part Three of the TFEU fall outside the Danish opt-out. A recent prominent testimony to this is the UK Withdrawal Agreement[48] and the EU's Trade and Cooperation Agreement with the UK,[49] as confirmed by the ECJ.[50]

VII. CONCLUSION

The Danish example is, legally speaking, both simple and complex at the same time. It is simple because the dedicated protocol to the treaties clearly defines from which part of EU law Denmark is excluded; yet it is complex because the nature of the special Danish position opens up the possibility for cooperation arrangements outside the special status that Denmark enjoys within EU law. The latter may be perceived as confusing and, for some, the carefully drafted mitigating measures even as 'perverse'.[51]

The position is certainly unique. Common to the mitigating measures – including the three Parallel Agreements – is a legal construction whereby Denmark, from the side of the EU, is treated as if Denmark were a third country, although Denmark is not. The Danish opt-out does not – as a legal consequence – change Denmark's status as a Member State.

It falls beyond the scope of this chapter to make assessments of whether the opt-out model of Denmark is desirable or not. It can be observed, however, that it has proved long-lasting. Its legal construction has developed, however, only as a consequence of the evolution of European integration within AFSJ. Interestingly, no propagation of 'the Danish example' has occurred. The intensity of the European integration process within AFSJ that took place soon after the Maastricht Treaty probably explains why that is so. Whereas the Edinburgh Decision is characterised by regulating a special position that relates to future integration, it becomes far more complicated to institute differentiation to an integration process that already has happened.[52] An attempt to solve a stalemate situation by way of using the model of an intergovernmental decision was made in 2016 to cater for the then-British concerns.[53] However, the British request

[46] *Opinion 1/19 (Istanbul Convention)*, ECLI:EU:C:2021:198, para 313. See also ibid, para 142. On the other hand, the situation pursuant to Protocol No 21 on Ireland was more complex: see ibid, paras 321–27.

[47] Case C-137/12 *European Commission v Council of the European Union*, ECLI:EU:C:2013:675, para 74.

[48] Agreement on the withdrawal of the United Kingdom of Great Britain and Northern Ireland from the European Union and the European Atomic Energy Community [2020] OJ L29/7.

[49] Trade and Cooperation Agreement between the European Union and the European Atomic Energy Community, of the one part, and the United Kingdom of Great Britain and Northern Ireland, of the other part [2021] OJ L149/10.

[50] Case C-479/21 PPU *Governor of Cloverhill Prison and Others*, ECLI:EU:C:2021:929.

[51] J Shaw, 'The Treaty of Amsterdam: Challenges of Flexibility and Legitimacy' (1998) 4 *European Law Journal* 77.

[52] See F Schimmelfennig, 'Overcoming Crisis in the European Union. The Limits of Differentiated Integration' in M Dawson and M Jachtenfuchs (eds), *Autonomy without Collapse in a Better European Union* (Oxford University Press, 2022) 49.

[53] 'Decision of the Heads of State and Government, meeting within the European Council, concerning a New Settlement for the United Kingdom within the European Union', Annex 1 of the Conclusions of the European Council of 18 and 19 February 2016, *cf* 'A New Settlement for the United Kingdom within the European Union' [2016] OJ C691/1.

remained to repatriate powers to the national level, which the 2016 decision – just like the Edinburgh Decision – fell short of. The model failed its purpose and ultimately the UK left the Union altogether.

On a different level, yet still noteworthy, the attempt in 2015 to convert the Danish opt-out into the opt-in model also failed. The Danish electorate insisted on keeping the intergovernmental cooperation as the only form of cooperation that may involve the participation of Denmark. The Danish position has thus remained unchanged since the days of the Maastricht Treaty.

It is doubtful, at best, whether the Danish example could serve as a template for the future. It is more likely that it will retain its unique status until the day when the Danish electorate decides that it is time to change, or possibly even to abolish, the Danish position.

Part II

The Driving Principles of the Area of Freedom, Security and Justice

9

The Fight against Impunity in the Case Law of the European Court of Justice

CONSTANTINOS LYCOURGOS*

I. INTRODUCTION

IMPUNITY REFERS TO the absence of effective punishment for the breach of a norm, and the fight against impunity requires effective law enforcement. Although this fight is necessary irrespective of the kind of legal norm that is being breached,[1] its importance is proportional to the seriousness of the norms involved, which makes criminal offences particularly sensitive. In theory, a comprehensive fight against impunity can only be conceived worldwide. Indeed, this is one of the objectives set out in secondary legislation adopted in the context of the EU's external action,[2] including certain regimes of restrictive measures.[3]

However, free movement within the area of freedom, security and justice (AFSJ) presents specific challenges, since, in the absence of appropriate adjustments, it could allow easy evasion of criminal punishment by individuals suspected or convicted of offences, simply using their right to free movement. Thus, the construction of this area of EU law and policy has been unavoidably characterised by measures aiming to fight against impunity, as well as by the increasing interaction of EU law with national criminal law. The AFSJ aims, inter alia, to prevent criminals from finding ways to exploit differences in the judicial systems of Member States, as stated at the Tampere European Council in 1999.[4] Hence, Articles 3(2) Treaty on

* Judge at the European Court of Justice. All views expressed herein are personal to the author. The author would like to thank Mr Emanuel Castellarin, Legal Secretary at the European Court of Justice, for his assistance in the preparation of this chapter.

[1] Regarding a situation where there could be a systemic risk that acts constituting infringements of EU competition rules may go unpunished, see Case C-308/19 *Whiteland Import Export*, ECLI:EU:C:2021:47, paras 56–57 and 65. Regarding the interpretation of some provisions of Regulation (EU, Euratom) No 883/2013 of the European Parliament and of the Council of 11 September 2013 concerning investigations conducted by the European Anti-Fraud Office (OLAF) [2013] OJ L248/1, in the light of the aim of avoiding the impunity of perpetrators of unlawful activities discovered during such an investigation, see Case C-130/19 *Court of Auditors v Pinxten*, ECLI:EU:C:2021:782, paras 152–53. For an overall account in EU law, see V Mitsilegas, 'Conceptualising Impunity in the Law of the European Union' in L Marin and S Montaldo (eds), *The Fight against Impunity in EU Law* (Hart Publishing, 2020) 15.

[2] eg see Case C-263/14 *Parliament v Council*, ECLI:EU:C:2016:435, paras 49–50, on the Agreement between the European Union and the United Republic of Tanzania on the conditions of transfer of suspected pirates and associated seized property from the European Union-led Naval Force to the United Republic of Tanzania (Brussels, 1 April 2014) [2014] OJ L108/3.

[3] eg see, for a summary of Council conclusions of 6 March 2017 on the Democratic Republic of the Congo, Case C-242/21 P *Boshab v Council*, ECLI:EU:C:2022:375, para 16.

[4] Conclusions of the Presidency of the European Council (Tampere, Finland, 15–16 October 1999), para 5.

European Union (TEU) and 67(3) Treaty on the Functioning of the European Union (TFEU) include preventing and combating crime among the objectives of the AFSJ.

The objective of preventing the risk that persons who have committed an offence might enjoy impunity is to be seen in that context, as observed for the first time explicitly in *Spasic* (2014).[5] Furthermore, it must be considered a legitimate objective in EU law, as first stated, regarding extradition, in *Petruhhin* (2016).[6] Starting from *Popławski I* (2017),[7] Framework Decision 2002/584/JHA on the European arrest warrant (the EAW Framework Decision)[8] has also explicitly been interpreted in this light. Moreover, since *Taricco* (2015),[9] the European Court of Justice (ECJ) has attached significant consequences to the fight against impunity in relation to the Union's financial interests. Lars Bay Larsen significantly influenced the development of this growing body of case law. Since he became a Judge at the Court of Justice in 2006, not only has he sat in most of those cases, but he was also the reporting judge in other relevant EAW cases referred to below, in particular *X*, *Puig Gordi* and *Sofiyska gradska prokuratura and Others (Successive arrest warrants)*.

This short analysis of the fight against impunity as it appears in the ECJ's case law will not go into the case law relating to extradition,[10] which concerns the functioning of the AFSJ only in a way that is incidental to the examination of the rights of Union citizens. Nor will it touch upon the case law relating to the Union's financial interests,[11] given that the impunity that the relevant EU law seeks to avoid does not concern ordinary national criminal penalties, but the breach of EU norms which are of direct relevance for the Union's own interests. On the contrary, this contribution will focus on the interaction between the fight against impunity and mutual recognition, a principle to which Lars Bay Larsen devoted several of his writings.[12] As he leaves the Court of Justice, it is appropriate to take stock of the case law of the ECJ in two fields: the *ne bis in idem* principle set out in the Convention implementing the Schengen Agreement (CISA),[13] and the EAW.

In this context, the fight against impunity essentially consists of allowing the punishment throughout the AFSJ of offences established under national law, according to the intensity with which each Member State punishes those offences. The aim is to enable the Member State

[5] Case C-129/14 PPU *Spasic*, ECLI:EU:C:2014:586, paras 61–65.

[6] Case C-182/15 *Petruhhin*, ECLI:EU:C:2016:630, para 37.

[7] Case C-579/15 *Popławski I*, ECLI:EU:C:2017:503. See also Case C-203/20 *AB and Others (Revocation of an Amnesty)*, ECLI:EU:C:2021:1016, para 58.

[8] Council Framework Decision 2002/584/JHA of 13 June 2002 on the European arrest warrant and the surrender procedures between Member States [2002] OJ L190/1.

[9] Case C-105/14 *Taricco*, ECLI:EU:C:2015:555.

[10] *Petruhhin* (n 6); Cases C-191/16 *Pisciotti*, ECLI:EU:C:2018:222; C-897/19 PPU *Ruska Federacija*, ECLI:EU:C:2020:262; C-398/19 *Generalstaatsanwaltschaft Berlin (Extradition to Ukraine)*, ECLI:EU:C:2020:1032; and C-237/21 *Generalstaatsanwaltschaft München (Request for extradition to Bosnia and Herzegovina)*, ECLI:EU:C:2022:1017.

[11] *Taricco* (n 9); Cases C-42/17 *MAS and MB (Taricco II)*, ECLI:EU:C:2017:936; C-524/15 *Menci*, ECLI:EU:C:2018:197; C-574/15 *Scialdone*, ECLI:EU:C:2018:295; C-612/15 *Kolev*, ECLI:EU:C:2018:392; C-310/16 *Dzivev and Others*, ECLI:EU:C:2019:30; C-357/19 *Euro Box Promotion*, ECLI:EU:C:2021:1034; and C-107/23 *Lin*, ECLI:EU:C:2023:606.

[12] See, in particular, L Bay Larsen, 'Some Reflections on Mutual Recognition in the Area of Freedom, Security and Justice' in P Cardonnel et al (eds), *Constitutionalising the EU Judicial System: Essays in Honour of Pernilla Lindh* (Hart Publishing, 2012) 139; 'Afterword(s) on Mutual Recognition and the Respect for Fundamental Rights Revisited – Following the Judgment in *Aranyosi and Căldăraru*' in C Brière and A Weyembergh (eds), *The Needed Balances in EU Criminal Law: Past, Present and Future* (Hart Publishing, 2018) 433.

[13] Convention implementing the Schengen Agreement of 14 June 1985 between the Governments of the States of the Benelux Economic Union, the Federal Republic of Germany and the French Republic on the gradual abolition of checks at their common borders (Schengen, 19 June 1990) [2000] OJ L239/19. This convention came into force on 26 March 1995.

that intends to impose a penalty to ensure that this penalty is actually imposed and enforced. Thus, EU law aims to create the conditions for the enforcement of penalties provided for by the Member States, irrespective of the Union's own interests and of the degree of harmonisation achieved by the EU legislator. This does not mean, however, that EU law is indifferent to the seriousness of the offence involved. Indeed, for offences that are considered to be the most serious and worthy of punishment, the Union legislator has provided that the enforcement in a Member State of decisions adopted by another Member State be carried out without verification of double criminality.[14]

The cases in which the ECJ has dealt with the aforementioned legal instruments demonstrate an overall coherence, characterised by the quest for effective law enforcement while ensuring respect for fundamental rights. This objective is achieved through two complementary approaches. As regards the CISA, the ECJ has been cautious to avoid an overly broad interpretation of the *ne bis in idem* requirement, thus limiting the effects in a given Member State of judicial decisions adopted in another Member State. In this field, the fight against impunity is pursued through a certain restraint on mutual recognition (Section II). On the other hand, as regards the EAW system, the ECJ supports the aim of combating impunity by construing widely the requirement for mutual recognition, as a practical expression of mutual trust (Section III).

II. TRANSNATIONAL *NE BIS IN IDEM*: CURTAILING MUTUAL RECOGNITION TO FIGHT IMPUNITY

Article 54 of the CISA states that a person whose trial has been finally disposed of in one Contracting Party may not be prosecuted in another Contracting Party for the same acts provided that, if a penalty has been imposed, it has been enforced, is actually in the process of being enforced or can no longer be enforced under the laws of the sentencing Contracting Party. At the same time, the respect of the *ne bis in idem* principle is also a fundamental right protected by Article 50 of the Charter. While Article 54 CISA subjects the application of the *ne bis in idem* principle to the so-called 'execution condition', Article 50 of the Charter does not. The ECJ consistently considers the objective of combating impunity as a criterion for determining the practical implications of transnational *ne bis in idem* against this background.

A. The Scope of Article 54 CISA

The ECJ has sought guidance on the scope of Article 54 of the CISA on the objective of fighting against impunity, in the light of Article 3(2) TEU.[15] The influence of this objective is particularly visible in the definition of the '*bis*' condition. It is well established that Article 54 of the CISA may not be applied to a decision terminating criminal proceedings

[14] See in particular Art 2(2) of the EAW Framework Decision and, regarding the enforcement of sentences following a European arrest warrant, Art 25 of Council Framework Decision 2008/909/JHA of 27 November 2008, on the application of the principle of mutual recognition to judgments in criminal matters imposing custodial sentences or measures involving deprivation of liberty for the purpose of their enforcement in the European Union [2008] OJ L327/27.

[15] Case C-469/03 *Miraglia*, ECLI:EU:C:2005:156, para 34, regarding the fourth indent of the (then) first subparagraph of Art 2 TEU; and Case C-486/14 *Kossowski*, ECLI:EU:C:2016:483, para 46.

without a determination as to the merits of the case, since such a decision cannot constitute a decision 'finally disposing' of the case against that person.[16] Applying the *ne bis in idem* principle to such decisions would make it harder or impossible to penalise unlawful conduct in the Member States concerned, which would clearly run counter to the very purpose of Article 3(2) TEU.[17]

Similarly, the objective of fighting impunity has shed light on the execution condition enshrined in Article 54 CISA. The ECJ has observed that the purpose underlying this condition, which is to avoid a person remaining unpunished, is very different from the purpose of detention on remand pending trial, which is a preventive measure.[18] Also on this basis, the ECJ has considered that the execution condition is not fulfilled where the person concerned only spent a short time in police custody and/or was being held on remand pending trial.[19] The ECJ reached the same conclusion as regards a situation where only one part of the sentence had been enforced, namely where the sentence imposed consisted of both a fine and a custodial sentence but only the fine had been paid.[20]

B. Article 54 CISA and Article 50 of the Charter

The ECJ has also relied on the objective of fighting against impunity to conclude that Article 54 CISA is compatible with Article 50 of the Charter. In *Spasic*, to assess the compliance of Article 54 CISA with the first sentence of Article 52(1) of the Charter, the ECJ initially observed that the execution condition laid down in Article 54 CISA does not call into question the *ne bis in idem* principle as such. Indeed, this provision is intended to avoid a situation in which a person definitively convicted and sentenced in one Contracting State ultimately remains unpunished if that State does not execute the sentence.[21] Then, the ECJ found that the execution condition is proportionate. First, it is appropriate for attaining the objective pursued, as it avoids the risk that the person concerned would enjoy impunity by leaving the State in which that person was sentenced. Second, it is necessary to achieve this objective, given that instruments of mutual assistance set by EU legislation, primarily Framework Decision 2008/909, cannot ensure that persons definitively convicted and sentenced in the EU will not enjoy impunity if the State which imposed the first sentence does not execute the penalties imposed. Finally, in the system established by Article 54 CISA, a person could only be prosecuted for the same acts in another Member State in cases where the system currently provided by EU law was not sufficient to prevent the impunity of persons definitively convicted and sentenced in the EU.[22]

This case law paved the way for the use of Article 54 CISA, in the light of the objective of fighting against impunity, as a general source of inspiration when dealing with transnational

[16] *Miraglia* (n 15), paras 30 and 33–34, regarding a situation where the sole ground for the decision not to pursue the prosecution was that criminal proceedings had been initiated in another Member State against the same defendant and in respect of the same acts. *Kossowski* (n 15), paras 42 and 48–49, regarding a situation where the sole ground for that decision was that the accused had refused to give a statement and the victim and a hearsay witness were living in another Member State, so that it had not been possible to verify their statements.

[17] *Miraglia* (n 15), para 34; and *Kossowski* (n 15), para 49.

[18] Case C-288/05 *Kretzinger*, ECLI:EU:C:2007:441, para 51.

[19] ibid, para 52.

[20] *Spasic* (n 5), paras 77 and 85.

[21] ibid, para 58. Admittedly, this provision also seeks to ensure legal certainty through respect for decisions of public bodies which have become final: ibid, para 77; and Case C-665/20 PPU X *(European arrest warrant – Ne bis in idem)*, ECLI:EU:C:2021:339, para 99.

[22] *Spasic* (n 5), paras 64–73.

ne bis in idem in the AFSJ. Thus, the ECJ found guidance in its previous case law on the scope of Article 54 CISA when determining the scope of Article 50 of the Charter. The ECJ ruled that the '*bis*' condition of the *ne bis in idem* principle is not met, including under the Charter, when the merits of the case have not been determined.[23] This observation has potential implications for several AFSJ instruments, in particular the EAW Framework Decision. Thus, the ECJ has judged that Article 50 of the Charter does not preclude the issue of an EAW against a person who was subject to a criminal prosecution that was initially discontinued by a final judicial decision adopted on the basis of an amnesty, and resumed following the adoption of a law revoking that amnesty and setting aside that judicial decision, in the case where that decision was adopted before any determination as to the criminal liability of the person concerned.[24]

The use of the objective of fighting against impunity as a tool to ensure the consistent application of Article 54 CISA and Article 50 of the Charter is also noticeable with respect to the effects of Interpol red notices. Until such time as it has been established that the *ne bis in idem* principle applies, the provisional arrest of a person who is the subject of an Interpol red notice is not precluded. Indeed, such a provisional arrest may be necessary to prevent the impunity of that person. On the contrary, when the *ne bis in idem* principle applies, the trial of that person in respect of the acts covered by the red notice has already been finally disposed of. Therefore, the prevention of impunity would not justify the restriction of that person's freedom of movement under Article 21 TFEU, caused by a provisional arrest.[25]

Overall, the ECJ's case law shows a tendency to take account of the negative effect that an excessively broad interpretation of the *ne bis in idem* principle could have on the effectiveness of criminal penalties in the transnational context of the AFSJ. Mutual recognition should be limited to decisions of a Member State which, unlike those which risk causing a situation of impunity, reflect the exhaustion of the mechanisms implemented by the judicial system of that Member State to ensure that a punishment is not (or no longer) necessary. Allowing mutual recognition of decisions that do not 'finally dispose' of the merits of the case or ignoring the execution condition of Article 54 CISA would amount to preventing, through the unjustified inaction of one Member State, the attainment of another Member State's legitimate objective of punishing criminal offences. This would ultimately jeopardise the objective of fighting crime at the AFSJ level. On the contrary, the full effectiveness of a Member State's decisions in criminal matters sometimes requires action by another Member State, as in the EAW system.

III. THE EAW SYSTEM: FIGHTING AGAINST IMPUNITY THROUGH MUTUAL RECOGNITION

Although not explicitly mentioned in the EAW Framework Decision, the objective of avoiding that fugitives take advantage of differences in the judicial system of Member States, formerly pursued by extradition procedures, is at the heart of the EAW.[26] It is quite obvious that the

[23] *AB and Others (Revocation of an Amnesty)* (n 7), para 56.
[24] ibid, para 61.
[25] Case C-505/19 *Bundesrepublik Deutschland (Interpol red notice)*, ECLI:EU:C:2021:376, paras 86–88 and 91.
[26] On the specificity of the situation of an accused person subject to an EAW who is in a Member State different from the Member State in which he or she has allegedly committed a criminal offence, compared to an accused person who has remained in the latter Member State, see Case C-105/21 *Spetsializirana prokuratura (Information on the national arrest decision)*, ECLI:EU:C:2022:511, paras 62 and 64.

impunity of the requested person would be incompatible with this objective,[27] pursued both by the EAW Framework Decision[28] and by Article 3(2) TEU.[29] On the basis of Article 1(1) of the EAW Framework Decision, the ECJ has stated on several occasions that the objective of the mechanism of the EAW is also, through the surrender of the requested persons, to combat impunity.[30] This observation has significant practical implications.

A. The Interpretation of Specific Provisions of the EAW Framework Decision

The ECJ has considered the fight against impunity as a relevant objective in interpreting specific provisions of the EAW Framework Decision.[31] In particular, Article 4 (Grounds for optional non-execution of an EAW) leaves the executing judicial authorities a margin of appreciation. The ECJ's case law aims to ensure that the exercise of this margin of appreciation does not undermine the overall functioning of the EAW system.

The ECJ insisted on the objective of ensuring the effectiveness of the surrender procedure in *Procureur général près la cour d'appel d'Angers*. This objective implies that the condition of double criminality set out in Articles 2(4) and 4(1) of the EAW Framework Decision does not require there to be an exact match between the constituent elements of the offence as defined in the law of the issuing Member State and those of the offence as provided for in the law of the executing Member State, as well as between the legal interests protected under the laws of those two Member States. This observation contributes to the conclusion that the executing judicial authority may not refuse to execute an EAW issued for the purpose of enforcing a custodial sentence where that sentence was imposed on the requested person in the issuing Member State for the commission of a single offence consisting of multiple acts, only some of which constitute a criminal offence in the executing Member State.[32]

In *X (European arrest warrant – Ne bis in idem)*, the ECJ had to interpret Article 4(5) of the EAW Framework Decision. This ground for optional non-execution, which applies where the requested person has been finally judged by a third State in respect of the same acts, is subject to the condition that, where there has been a sentence, the sentence has been served, is currently being served or may no longer be executed under the law of the sentencing country. The ECJ ruled that in such case the executing judicial authority, in exercising its margin of discretion, must strike a balance between preventing impunity and combating crime with ensuring legal certainty for the individual, as both objectives are relevant for the implementation of that provision.[33]

[27] On this objective of avoiding impunity, see the explicit reference in Art 25 of Framework Decision 2008/909/JHA (n 14), which concerns the enforcement of sentences following an EAW.

[28] *Popławski I* (n 7), para 23; Cases C-514/17 *Sut*, ECLI:EU:C:2018:1016, para 47; C-573/17 *Popławski II*, ECLI:EU:C:2019:530, para 82; and C-488/19 *JR (Arrest warrant – Conviction in a third State, Member of the EEA)*, ECLI:EU:C:2021:206, para 72.

[29] *Petruhhin* (n 6), paras 36 and 37; and *Popławski II* (n 28), para 82.

[30] See, inter alia, Case C-551/18 PPU *IK (Execution of an additional sentence)*, ECLI:EU:C:2018:991, para 39. See also Case C-314/18 *SF (European arrest warrant – Guarantee of return to the executing State)*, ECLI:EU:C:2020:191, para 47.

[31] Regarding Arts 12 and 24 of the EAW Framework Decision, see Case C-492/22 PPU *CJ (Decision to postpone surrender due to criminal prosecution)*, ECLI:EU:C:2022:964, paras 70 and 74. Regarding Art 27, see Case C-142/22 *Minister for Justice and Equality (Request for consent – Effects of the original European arrest warrant)*, ECLI:EU:C:2023:544, paras 45 and 51.

[32] Case C-168/21 *Procureur général près la cour d'appel d'Angers*, ECLI:EU:C:2022:558, paras 45, 47 and 61.

[33] *X (European arrest warrant – Ne bis in idem)* (n 21), paras 99, 103 and 104.

In *Popławski I*, the ECJ was confronted with the legislation of a Member State, which implemented Article 4(6) of the EAW Framework Decision[34] by providing that the judicial authorities of that Member State were systematically obliged to refuse to execute an EAW where a person requested for the execution of a custodial sentence resided in that State. Such authorities had no margin of discretion in this regard and that Member State did not, in the case at issue, actually undertake to execute the custodial sentence pronounced against the requested person. The ECJ considered that such legislation created a risk of impunity of the person concerned, and therefore could not be regarded as compatible with that Framework Decision.[35] In *Popławski II*, the ECJ clarified that the relevant domestic legislation of the executing State must be interpreted, to the greatest extent possible, in such a way that its application makes it possible to avoid impunity. Thus, the effectiveness of the EAW Framework Decision could be preserved in spite of its lack of direct effect. In the case at hand, the ECJ concluded that such an interpretation required that the refusal to execute the EAW at issue would be subject to the guarantee that the custodial sentence of the requested person would actually be enforced in the executing Member State.[36]

In *Sut*, the ECJ held that, when a person who is the subject of an EAW issued for the purposes of enforcing a custodial sentence resides in the executing Member State, the executing judicial authority may invoke Article 4(6) of the EAW Framework Decision for reasons related to the social rehabilitation of that person. The fact that the offence which provides the basis for the warrant is, under the national law of the executing Member State, punishable by fine only, does not, as such, prevent such an outcome. However, the ECJ also stated that the conditions provided by the EU legislature for the application of this ground of refusal aim at avoiding any risk of the requested person going unpunished.[37] Thus, the execution of the warrant may only be refused if, in accordance with the national law of the executing Member State, the actual enforcement in that Member State of the custodial sentence imposed on the requested person is possible[38] and, indeed, the said sentence is enforced.

A similar reminder of the need to effectively ensure the enforcement of custodial sentences can be found in *JR*, regarding Article 4(7)(b). This provision covers offences committed outside the territory of the issuing Member State, when the law of the executing Member State does not allow prosecution for the same offences when committed outside its territory. The ECJ noted, in that respect, that the prevention of impunity would be jeopardised if the executing State could, on the basis of the said provision, refuse to surrender the requested person in a situation where the courts of the issuing Member State have recognised and agreed to enforce a judgment delivered by a court of another State whereby a custodial sentence was imposed on that person for an offence committed in the territory of the latter State. Such an interpretation would discourage Member States from requesting the recognition of judgments and encourage the competent authorities of the State enforcing a recognised judgment to limit the use of conditional release instruments, as such conditional release could enable the sentenced person to avoid execution of the remainder of the sentence by moving to another Member State.[39]

[34] The said Art 4(6) allows the executing judicial authority to refuse to execute an EAW 'if the European arrest warrant has been issued for the purposes of execution of a custodial sentence or detention order, where the requested person is staying in, or is a national or a resident of the executing Member State and that State undertakes to execute the sentence or detention order in accordance with its domestic law'.

[35] *Popławski I* (n 7), para 23.

[36] *Popławski II* (n 28), paras 85 and 104–107.

[37] *Sut* (n 28), para 47; and *Popławski II* (n 28), para 103.

[38] *Sut* (n 28), para 49.

[39] *JR* (n 28), paras 73 and 76.

Overall, it appears that the fight against impunity is consistently used to ensure that the Member States' wish to limit EAW execution in conformity with Article 4 of the EAW Framework Decision does not frustrate the principle of mutual recognition enshrined in Article 1(2).

B. Issues not Explicitly Addressed by the EAW Framework Decision

The ECJ has also found inspiration in the objective of fighting against impunity when dealing with issues that no provision of the EAW Framework Decision addresses specifically. This is shown by the case law regarding the issuance of several successive EAWs against the same person and for the same acts. In *Puig Gordi*, the ECJ noted that this practice is not excluded by any provision of the EAW Framework Decision, including where the execution of a first EAW concerning that person has been refused, and that it may prove necessary in some cases.[40] The same reasoning was followed regarding the Agreement on the surrender procedure between the EU, on the one hand, and Iceland and Norway, on the other, as that agreement seeks, inter alia, to fight against the impunity of requested persons. This purpose would be defeated by a systematic prohibition on issuing a new arrest warrant in the event of refusal to execute a first arrest warrant.[41]

The observation that the fight against impunity is an overarching objective of the EAW Framework Decision also has consequences beyond the EAW system, which allow consistency with other legal mechanisms. On the one hand, this is a common objective of the EAW and of extradition to third countries. However, where national or international rules binding on the requested Member State protect nationals of that Member State from extradition to a third country, allowing unconditionally such extradition of Union citizens present on the territory of the said Member State would result in unequal treatment, which would give rise to a restriction of freedom of movement, within the meaning of Article 21 TFEU.[42] Hence, the exchange of information with the Member State of which the person requested for extradition is a national must be given priority over extradition, in order, where relevant, to afford the authorities of that Member State the opportunity to issue an EAW for the purposes of prosecution of that person. This solution is less restrictive than extradition for the freedom of movement of a Union citizen,[43] given that it allows that citizen, where an EAW is issued, to be prosecuted in its Member State of origin and, thus, to enjoy equal treatment with nationals of the requested Member State. Ultimately, however, as impunity cannot be the result of the procedure, extradition must be granted if an EAW is not issued.

On the other hand, the procedures laid down by the EAW Framework Decision and by the Dublin III Regulation are autonomous. Therefore, the ECJ has ruled that the fact that a person's entry into the territory of the requesting Member State as the result of the surrender of that person under an EAW cannot, as such, preclude a take back request. Indeed, the

[40] Case C-158/21 *Puig Gordi and Others*, ECLI:EU:C:2023:57, paras 140–41.

[41] Case C-71/21 *Sofiyska gradska prokuratura and Others (Successive arrest warrants)*, ECLI:EU:C:2023:668, paras 34–36.

[42] See *Petruhhin* (n 6), paras 32–33; *Pisciotti* (n 10), paras 44–45; *Ruska Federacija* (n 10), paras 55–56 (regarding Art 4 of the EEA Agreement); and *Extradition to Ukraine* (n 10), paras 39–40. For further clarifications, see in particular *Pisciotti* (n 10), para 54; *Extradition to Ukraine* (n 10), paras 44 and 53.

[43] *Petruhhin* (n 6), paras 48 and 49; *Pisciotti* (n 10), para 51; *Ruska Federacija* (n 10), para 70; *Extradition to Ukraine* (n 10), para 43.

opposite approach could deter Member States from requesting the surrender of an applicant for international protection for criminal prosecution, which could promote impunity.[44]

C. The EAW Framework Decision, Fight against Impunity and Fundamental Rights

Despite the above considerations, EU law does not unconditionally accept the enforcement objectives of the issuing Member State. Although these objectives are legitimate, they need to be pursued in compliance with fundamental rights, even when this implies a lesser degree of effectiveness of criminal penalties. Indeed, there can be some tension between mutual recognition and the protection of fundamental rights in a transnational context. For example, the ECJ clarified that the issuance of several successive EAWs against the same person and for the same acts only complies with the EAW Framework Decision provided that the execution of a new EAW does not result in an infringement of Article 1(3) and provided that the issuing of the latter warrant is proportionate.[45]

In some circumstances, respect for fundamental rights requires that an EAW not be executed. In that regard, the ECJ set the so-called 'two-stage test', whereby the requested person may not be surrendered if two cumulative conditions are met. First, the executing judicial authority must establish whether there are systemic or generalised deficiencies in the issuing Member State. At the second stage, and only if the existence of such deficiencies is established, it must be shown that, as a result of those deficiencies, there are substantial grounds for believing that the requested person will run a real risk of breach of his or her fundamental rights. The fight against impunity features prominently among the considerations that shape the conditions of application of the 'two-stage test'.

This test was first set out in *Aranyosi and Căldăraru* with respect to the risk of inhuman or degrading treatment as a result of detention conditions in the issuing Member State.[46] However, in the case law that followed, the ECJ clarified that an obligation on the part of the executing judicial authorities to assess the conditions of detention in all the prisons in which the individual concerned might be detained in the issuing Member State would be clearly excessive and impossible to reconcile with the time limits prescribed in Article 17 of the EAW Framework Decision. Such an assessment could in fact substantially delay that individual's surrender and, accordingly, render the operation of the EAW system wholly ineffective, which would result in a risk of impunity for the requested person.[47]

In this respect, it must be noted that the very existence of the first stage of the test can be explained by considerations pertaining to the protection of the EAW system, which allows requested persons to be moved from one Member State to another and, thus, fight against impunity. Indeed, securing the protection of fundamental rights must not necessarily be a task undertaken by any judicial authority to which a fundamental rights argument is presented. Responsibility for securing respect for fundamental rights lies primarily with the authorities of the issuing Member State. The principle of mutual trust establishes a presumption that this obligation is respected and requires the authorities of the requested Member State to rely

[44] Case C-213/17 *X*, ECLI:EU:C:2018:538, paras 58–59.

[45] *Puig Gordi* (n 40), para 146; and *Sofiyska gradska prokuratura and Others (Successive arrest warrants)* (n 41), para 43.

[46] Joined Cases C-404/15 and C-659/15 PPU *Aranyosi and Căldăraru*, ECLI:EU:C:2016:198, paras 88–94 and 104.

[47] Case C-220/18 PPU *Generalstaatsanwaltschaft (Conditions of detention in Hungary)*, ECLI:EU:C:2018:589, paras 84 and 85; and Case C-128/18 *Dorobantu*, ECLI:EU:C:2019:857, para 65.

on the fact that the issuing Member State will indeed comply with it. On this basis, the ECJ requires that an EAW be executed without investigating the individual risk of breach of the fundamental rights of the person concerned if there is insufficient objective, reliable, specific and properly updated evidence showing that there are systemic or generalised deficiencies in the requesting Member State. This reasoning consistently underpins the ECJ's case law.

In *LM*, the 'two-stage test' was extended to the risk of breach of the fundamental right to a fair trial because of deficiencies concerning the independence of the issuing Member State's judiciary.[48] In this context, the 'impunity argument' played a crucial role in justifying the second stage of the test. To reject the thesis that the finding of systemic and generalised deficiencies concerning the independence of the issuing Member State's judiciary should suffice to justify non-execution of an EAW, in *Openbaar Ministerie* the ECJ observed that the objective of fighting against impunity precludes such an interpretation of Article 1(3) of the EAW Framework Decision.[49] Such an interpretation would entail a high risk of impunity for fugitives, even if there is no evidence, relating to the personal situation of those individuals, to suggest that they would run a real risk of their fundamental right to a fair trial being breached in case of surrender.

The ECJ refrained from applying the 'two-stage test' regarding the execution of an EAW for the first time in *EDL*, regarding a situation where the execution of an EAW entailed a real risk of a significant reduction in the requested person's life expectancy or of a rapid, significant and irreversible deterioration in his state of health. In this context, the need to fight against the impunity of fugitives led the ECJ to underline the exceptional nature of the circumstances in which this test may be set aside. Indeed, it is difficult to envisage systemic or generalised deficiencies with regard to the specific situation of an individual unsuited to prison life, for whom the execution of any arrest warrant would have exceptionally serious effects, or even an increased risk of suicide.[50] The ECJ also insisted on the need for interaction between the authorities of the issuing Member State and those of the executing Member State aimed at ensuring compliance with fundamental rights while preventing impunity. Thus, the reminder of the objective of fighting impunity was made in conjunction with the duty of sincere cooperation and with the duty to make full use of the instruments provided for in the EAW Framework Decision in order to foster mutual trust. These considerations led to making non-execution of an EAW conditional upon specific procedural requirements. The executing judicial authority may temporarily postpone the surrender of the requested person on the basis of Article 23(4) of the EAW Framework Decision, read in conjunction with Article 4 of the Charter. In this case, however, it must ask the issuing judicial authority to provide it with all the information necessary to rule out the risk to the requested person's life or health referred to in the said provision of the EAW Framework Decision. If the issuing judicial authority provides such safeguards, the EAW must be executed.[51]

This case shows that the 'two-stage test' must be adapted to unforeseen circumstances, so that the fight against impunity cannot be the only objective of the EAW system. In this context, cooperation mechanisms among Member States provided for in the EAW Framework Decision, and arguably in other AFSJ instruments, must be taken into account to reconcile,

[48] Case C-216/18 PPU *Minister for Justice and Equality (Deficiencies in the system of justice)*, ECLI:EU:C:2018:586, para 79.

[49] Case C-354/20 PPU and C-412/20 PPU *Openbaar Ministerie (Independence of the issuing judicial authority)*, ECLI:EU:C:2020:1033, paras 62–64.

[50] Case C-699/21 *EDL (Ground for refusal based on illness)*, ECLI:EU:C:2023:295, paras 10–11.

[51] ibid, paras 43–48.

to the maximum possible extent, respect for fundamental rights and avoiding impunity. To a certain extent, this outcome can be achieved going beyond the alternative between unconditional execution and mere refusal of execution of an EAW. However, it is difficult to transpose the reasoning of *EDL* to situations that are certainly delicate but not exceptional. For relatively common situations, simply taking account of individual circumstances, irrespective of systemic or generalised deficiencies in the issuing Member State, would risk making the enforcement of criminal penalties unpredictable. The 'two-stage test' therefore remains appropriate to avoid a real risk of impunity. Thus, in *GN*, the ECJ held that this test is applicable where the executing judicial authority considers refusing to surrender the person who is the subject of an EAW on the grounds that that person is the mother of young children living with her.[52]

IV. CONCLUSION

The fight against impunity as an objective of EU law is not systematically mentioned in cases on criminal matters in the AFSJ. This objective is certainly not the only driving force of the ECJ's case law in this area. In any event, it cannot override the requirement for respect for fundamental rights as guaranteed by the Charter. Nonetheless, insofar as EU law allows legitimate differences in the judicial systems of Member States, the concrete assessment of fundamental rights must necessarily take into account the overall functioning of the AFSJ. This is confirmed by the conceptual role played by the fight against impunity in the interpretation of Article 50 of the Charter and in the application of the 'two-stage test' with regard to the EAW.

Overall, in less than a decade, the 'impunity argument' has become a recurrent and sometimes decisive feature of an increasing number of judgments relating to this field of EU law. It is also not excluded that the case law on the fight against impunity in the AFSJ may become relevant in other areas.[53] By construing, depending on the legal act involved, widely or narrowly the obligation for mutual recognition of national decisions, the ECJ aims at maximising opportunities for the enforcement of criminal penalties. Case law ensures that mutual recognition effectively serves Member States' enforcement requirements, to fill the gaps that interaction between national legal systems might leave in terms of the fight against crime and to avoid any 'safe haven' for suspected or convicted persons.

[52] Case C-261/22 *GN (Grounds for non-execution relating to the best interest of the child)*, ECLI:EU:C:2023:1017.

[53] In *La Quadrature du Net I*, the ECJ stated that, in order to perform the proportionality assessment of restrictions to the scope of the rights covered by Directive 2002/58 on privacy and electronic communications, account must be taken of the fact that, where an offence is committed online, the IP address might be the only means of investigation enabling the person to whom that address was assigned at the time of the commission of the offence to be identified: Joined Cases C-511/18, C-512/18 and C-520/18 *La Quadrature du Net and Others*, ECLI:EU:C:2020:791, para 154.

10

Article 6 of the Charter in the Area of Freedom, Security and Justice: On Some Aspects of the EU Case Law on the Fundamental Right to Liberty and Security

DIMITRIOS GRATSIAS*

I. INTRODUCTION

WHILE THE FUNDAMENTAL right to liberty and security might well be among the most well-established human rights,[1] at first glance Article 6 of the Charter of Fundamental Rights of the European Union (Charter) does not seem to occupy a prominent place in the case law of the European Court of Justice (ECJ).[2]

Indeed, laconically phrased,[3] Article 6 of the Charter tends to be overshadowed by extended references to the corresponding and much more detailed Article 5 of the European Convention on Human Rights (ECHR) and the very extensive case law of the European Court of Human Rights (ECtHR) pertaining to that provision.[4] It is also in many cases coupled with the right to

* Judge at the European Court of Justice, Member of the Council of State (Supreme Administrative Court) of Greece. Any opinion expressed in this contribution is personal.

[1] See N Piçarra, 'Some Notes on the Fundamental Right to Liberty and Security of Person in the EU Legal Order' in K Lenaerts et al (eds), *Building the European Union – Liber Amicorum in Honour of José Luís da Cruz Vilaça* (Hart Publishing, 2021) 87; F Rossi Dal Poso, 'Diritto alla libertà e alla sicurezza' in R Mastroianni et al (eds), *Carta dei Diritti Fondamentali dell'Unione Europea* (Giuffrè Editore, 2017) 96; D Wilsher, 'Article 6' in S Peers et al (eds), *The EU Charter of Fundamental Rights: A Commentary* (Hart Publishing, 2021) 148; M Nowak, 'Article 6. Right to Liberty and Security' in *Commentary of the Charter of Fundamental Rights of the European Union* (EU Network of Independent Experts on Fundamental Rights, 2006) 67, https://sites.uclouvain.be/cridho/documents/Download.Rep/NetworkCommentaryFinal.pdf, accessed 25 February 2024.

[2] See, for example, JN Stefanelli and E Guild, 'The Right to Liberty in the Field of Migration, Asylum and Borders' in S Iglesias Sánchez and M González Pascual (eds), *Fundamental Rights in the Area of Freedom, Security and Justice* (Cambridge University Press, 2021) 118.

[3] For an overview of the evolution of the drafting of Art 6 and the Charter in general, see M Steiert and N Coghlan (eds), *The Charter of Fundamental Rights of the European Union: The 'Travaux Préparatoires' and Selected Documents* (European University Institute, 2020), https://hdl.handle.net/1814/68959, accessed 25 February 2024.

[4] See, for example, Cases C-601/15 PPU *N*, ECLI:EU:C:2016:84, paras 77–82; C-528/15 *Al Chodor*, ECLI:EU:C:2017:213, paras 37–38; C-519/20 *Landkreis Gifhorn*, ECLI:EU:C:2022:178, paras 42–43; and C-105/21 *Spetsializirana prokuratura (Information on the national arrest decision)*, ECLI:EU:C:2022:511, paras 55–57, where the referring court was, in essence, seeking clarification of a previous judgment of the ECJ, comparing it to ECtHR case law; C-608/21 *Politseyski organ pri 02 RU SDVR*, ECLI:EU:C:2023:426, paras 55, 56, 66–67, where Art 6 of the Charter is only mentioned in the preliminary part of the judgment. See also the Opinions of AG Campos Sánchez-Bordona

a fair trial guaranteed by Article 47 of the Charter.[5] Moreover, despite its scope being to ensure protection against State arbitrariness in general,[6] it is its procedural aspect that is mostly emphasised,[7] while debate seems to persist in the relevant literature concerning the possibility of identifying an independent right to personal security enshrined in Article 6.[8]

Nevertheless, in recent years, the right to liberty and security is becoming inevitably more and more relevant, as, notably in the Area of Freedom, Security and Justice (AFSJ), the scope of EU law extends into the fields of immigration, asylum, and even criminal law and as the relevant secondary law that Member States are called to implement proliferates.[9]

In this respect, the ECJ has, on the one hand, interpreted a number of acts of secondary law in the light of Article 6 of the Charter and examined the validity of such acts in the light of this provision (Section II). On the other hand, and in that context, the ECJ has identified, in Article 6, the source of some important procedural guarantees (Section III). The following pages will briefly focus on these two aspects.

II. A REFERENCE FOR THE VALIDITY AND THE INTERPRETATION OF ACTS OF SECONDARY EUROPEAN LAW

According to settled case law, an examination of the validity of secondary EU law must, in principle, be undertaken solely in the light of provisions of primary law and, notably, of the

in Case C-453/16 PPU *Özçelik*, ECLI:EU:C:2016:783, paras 48 and 55; and of AG Pitruzzella in Case C-653/19 PPU *Spetsializirana prokuratura*, ECLI:EU:C:2019:983, paras 42–48.

[5] A joint reference to Arts 6 and 47 of the Charter seems not to be necessary when there is a direct reference to Art 5(4) ECHR, as the right for everyone who is deprived of his liberty by arrest or detention to take proceedings, 'by which the lawfulness of [their] detention shall be decided speedily by a court and [their] release ordered if the detention is not lawful', is specifically laid out in the latter provision: see, for example, the judgment in *Politseyski organ pri 02 RU SDVR* (n 4), notably para 66.

[6] See, for example, *Al Chodor* (n 4), para 39, where the ECJ affirms that 'the execution of a measure depriving a person of liberty is to be in keeping with the objective of protecting the individual from arbitrariness [which] means, in particular, that there can be no element of bad faith or deception on the part of the authorities'. More recently, see Case C-241/21 *Politsei- ja Piirivalveamet (Detention – Risk of committing a criminal offence)*, ECLI:EU:C:2022:753, para 49 and case law cited. See also Piçarra (n 1), 87 and Wilsher (n 1), 127.

[7] As has been noted, the right to personal liberty 'does not strive toward the ideal of a society without prisons, but merely represents a procedural guarantee', as it is not 'the deprivation of personal liberty in and of itself that is disapproved of but rather arbitrary arrest and detention': Nowak (n 1), 67.

[8] According to Nowak, the right to personal security does not seem to be attributed any independent significance beyond personal liberty in the ECtHR's case law. More specifically, he points out that, despite controversial discussions during the drafting, in the 1999 European Convention, of Art 6 of the Charter, it was, 'decided to maintain the term in the restrictive understanding of the Strasbourg case-law'. See Nowak (n 1), 68–69. The ECJ's case law seems to identify, however, within Art 6 of the Charter, two distinct rights, that is to say a right to liberty *and* a right to security, see Joined Cases C-293/12 and C-594/12 *Digital Rights Ireland and Others*, ECLI:EU:C:2014:238, para 42; Joined Cases C-511/18, C-512/18 and C-520/18 *La Quadrature du Net and Others*, ECLI:EU:C:2020:791, para 123; *Opinion 1/15 (EU-Canada PNR Agreement)*, ECLI:EU:C:2017:592, para 149; and, in the context of the AFSJ, *N* (n 4), paras 47 and 52, where reference is made to *rights* laid down in Art 6 of the Charter, of which the *right to liberty* is laid down in that provision. See also Opinion of AG Pitruzzella in Case C-817/19 *Ligue des droits humains*, ECLI:EU:C:2022:65, para 67; as well as of AG Wathelet in Case C-310/18 PPU *Milev*, ECLI:EU:C:2018:645, para 60, where, by reference to the case law of the ECtHR, there is specific mention of the fact that Art 5 ECHR 'protects the *physical* security of the individual' (emphasis added). AG Campos Sánchez-Bordona, for his part, draws a clear line between *public security* and *security* in the sense of Art 5 ECHR: the latter 'protects personal security, in the sense of a guarantee of the right to physical freedom from arbitrary arrest or detention [...]': Opinion of AG Campos Sánchez-Bordona in Joined Cases C-511/18 and C-512/18 *La Quadrature du Net and Others*, ECLI:EU:C:2020:6, paras 97–100 and case law cited. For a discussion of this particular question, see also T Lock, 'Article 6 CFR' in M Kellerbauer et al (eds), *The EU Treaties and the Charter of Fundamental Rights* (Oxford University Press, 2019) 2111, 2111–12 and Rossi Dal Poso (n 1), 97 and 103 ff.

[9] Wilsher (n 1), notably 149.

fundamental rights guaranteed by the Charter. However, as mentioned above, it is rather common for the ECJ to refer to Article 5 ECHR and to the ECtHR case law in cases related to Article 6 of the Charter: according to the Explanations relating to Article 6 of the Charter and the requirement of homogeneity,[10] the rights laid down in Article 6 correspond to those guaranteed by Article 5 of the ECHR and the limitations which can legitimately be imposed on the exercise of those rights may not exceed those permitted by the ECHR.[11] As the ECJ has explained, for the purpose of interpreting Article 6 of the Charter, account must be taken of Article 5 of the ECHR as the minimum threshold of protection.[12]

Notably, the right to liberty is to be respected when EU institutions take action in the field of judicial cooperation in criminal matters,[13] provided for in Articles 82–86 of the Treaty on the Functioning of the European Union (TFEU). Amongst the acts of secondary law in this field, Framework Decision 2002/584/JHA on the European arrest warrant (the EAW Framework Decision)[14] has been, as expected, extensively interpreted by the ECJ in relation with Article 6 of the Charter, as the issuing of a European arrest warrant (EAW) is 'capable of impinging on the right to liberty of the person concerned'.[15]

Thus, the ECJ has had occasion to interpret the EAW system in light of Article 6, notably with regard to, on the one hand, the conditions which have to be fulfilled for detention to be justified for the purpose of the execution of such a warrant,[16] and on the other, the definition of the EAW issuing authorities.[17] The ECJ has also interpreted the notion of 'detention' within the meaning of the EAW Framework Decision as an autonomous concept of EU law.[18] In this regard, the Court assessed the nature of varying restrictive measures, and gave guidance concerning the duration of detention in view of the execution of such an EAW,[19] in relation

[10] See, for example, Opinions of AG Kokott in Case C-17/10 *Toshiba Corporation and Others*, ECLI:EU:C:2011:552, para 120; and of AG Pikamäe in Case C-608/21 *Politseyski organ pri 02 RU SDVR*, ECLI:EU:C:2023:23, para 37.

[11] See *N* (n 4), paras 46–47; and Case C-294/16 PPU *JZ*, ECLI:EU:C:2016:610, para 50 and case law cited. See also C Guillain and D Ribant, 'Article 6. Droit à la liberté et à la sûreté' in F Picod et al (eds), *Charte des droits fondamentaux de l'Union européenne – Commentaire article par article* (Bruylant, 2019) 133, 150, 163 and 182. As has been underlined, this 'homogeneity' means that only the specific grounds of detention laid out in Art 5 ECHR can be tolerated in the context of Art 6 of the Charter. See Rossi Dal Poso (n 1) 100.

[12] *Landkreis Gifhorn* (n 4), para 42 and case law cited.

[13] On this particular field, see L Mancano, 'The Right to Liberty and Security in EU Criminal Law' in I Sánchez and G Pascual (eds), *Fundamental Rights in the EU Area of Freedom, Security and Justice* (Cambridge University Press, 2021) 272. Unsurprisingly, the right to liberty is not as relevant when it comes to the field of judicial cooperation in civil matters (see Art 81 TFEU). However, in Case C-92/12 PPU *Health Service Executive*, ECLI:EU:C:2012:255, the referring court, the High Court of Ireland, sought guidance regarding the interpretation of Council Regulation (EC) No 2201/2003 of 27 November 2003 concerning jurisdiction and the recognition and enforcement of judgments in matrimonial matters and the matters of parental responsibility, repealing Regulation (EC) No 1347/2000 [2003] OJ L338/1. The case concerned a child of Irish nationality with a history of mental challenges and the judgment placing them in a secure care institution situated in England. Such a judgment, in the words of the ECJ, 'concerns the fundamental right to liberty recognised in Article 6 [of the Charter] as possessed by "everyone", and, consequently, also by a "child"' (para 111).

[14] Council Framework Decision 2002/584/JHA of 13 June 2002 on the European arrest warrant and the surrender procedures between Member States [2002] OJ L190/1.

[15] Case C-489/19 PPU *NJ (Public Prosecutor's Office, Vienna)*, ECLI:EU:C:2019:849, para 35 and case law cited.

[16] Case C-237/15 PPU *Lanigan*, ECLI:EU:C:2015:474. See, in detail, Guillain and Ribant (n 11), 157 ff and Mancano (n 13), 277–78 and 280.

[17] See Case C-509/18 *PF (Prosecutor General of Lithuania)*, ECLI:EU:C:2019:457; Joined Cases C-508/18 and C-82/19 PPU *OG and PI (Public Prosecutor's Offices, Lübeck and Zwickau)*, ECLI:EU:C:2019:456; as well as *NJ (Public Prosecutor's Office, Vienna)* (n 15).

[18] See judgment in *JZ* (n 11), para 37.

[19] ibid, notably para 57, where, in interpreting Art 26 of the EAW Framework Decision, the ECJ affirmed that 'measures such as a nine-hour night-time curfew, in conjunction with the monitoring of the person concerned by means of an electronic tag, an obligation to report to a police station at fixed times on a daily basis or several times a week, and a ban on applying for foreign travel documents, are not, in principle, having regard to the type, duration, effects and

to a provision of national law according to which the maximum period of detention of the requested person is suspended while the executing judicial authority considers whether to refer a question for a preliminary ruling.[20]

The ECJ has also examined, in the light of Article 6 of the Charter, the validity of the EAW Framework Decision. Taking also into account Article 47 of the Charter,[21] the ECJ has considered that there is no infringement of those two provisions despite the fact that, according to that Framework Decision, the information communicated to persons arrested for the purposes of the execution of a EAW is limited and those persons are not informed about the remedies available in the issuing Member State and are not given access to the materials of the case until after their surrender.[22]

Finally, it follows from the case law on the EAW mechanism that while maintaining its relevance in a procedural context, the scope of application of Article 6 of the Charter finds its limits whenever the *material conditions* of detention are concerned. These fall under the scope of Article 4 of the Charter, enshrining the prohibition on torture and inhuman or degrading treatment or punishment.[23]

Apart from EAW-related cases, in the field of judicial cooperation in criminal matters, Article 6 of the Charter has been a reference when the ECJ was called upon to interpret acts of secondary law aiming to establish minimum standards in criminal proceedings, concerning the right to information in criminal proceedings,[24] the right of access to a lawyer in criminal proceedings as well as other rights granted to individuals upon deprivation of liberty,[25] as well

manner of implementation of all those measures, so restrictive as to give rise to a deprivation of liberty comparable to that arising from imprisonment and thus to be classified as "detention"'.

[20] Case C-492/18 PPU *TC*, ECLI:EU:C:2019:108, para 77.

[21] As has been noted (n 5), in the ECJ's case law, Art 6 of the Charter tends to be invoked together with Art 47 of the Charter, as the former does not include specific procedural provisions. See, for example, Case C-396/11 PPU *Radu*, ECLI:EU:C:2013:39, paras 30–31. In that case, the ECJ found that, despite the referring court mentioning Art 6, the arguments submitted by Mr Radu concerning the alleged infringement of the latter and of Art 5 ECHR were 'indissociable from his arguments relating to the infringement of his rights of defence'. In Case C-414/20 PPU *MM*, ECLI:EU:C:2021:4, paras 79–80, without referring to Art 6 of the Charter, the ECJ ruled that neither the EAW Framework Decision nor Art 47 of the Charter require a national court to release a person who is the subject of a pre-trial detention measure if it finds that the EAW that led to that person's surrender is invalid, in the absence of harmonisation of the conditions under which a pre-trial detention measure may be issued and maintained in respect of a person who is the subject of a criminal prosecution.

[22] Case C-649/19 *Spetsializirana prokuratura (Letter of rights)*, ECLI:EU:C:2021:75, paras 64, and 80–81. It should be noted that the ECJ took into consideration the fact that persons that are the subjects of a EAW issued for the purposes of criminal prosecution acquire, from the moment of their surrender, the status of 'accused person' within the meaning of Directive 2012/13/EU of the European Parliament and of the Council of 22 May 2012 on the right to information in criminal proceedings [2012] OJ L142/1, and therefore enjoy all the rights associated with that status so that they can prepare their defence and safeguard the fairness of the proceedings (para 77). Following this judgment, the referring court issued another request for a preliminary ruling, considering that the first judgment had not removed all of its doubts. The ECJ had occasion to reaffirm its approach in the judgment in *Spetsializirana prokuratura (Information on the national arrest decision)* (n 4).

[23] See, notably, Joined Cases C-404/15 and C-659/15 PPU, *Aranyosi and Căldăraru*, ECLI:EU:C:2016:198, where the referring court asked the ECJ, in substance, whether the EAW Framework Decision is to be interpreted as meaning that a request for surrender for the purposes of prosecution is inadmissible where there are strong indications that detention conditions in the issuing Member State infringe the fundamental rights of the requested person. The ECJ reformulated the question, considering that it concerned detention conditions incompatible with Art 4 of the Charter (para 74), while referencing Art 6 thereof in relation to the procedure for the execution of an EAW. Compare with Case C-220/18 PPU *Generalstaatsanwaltschaft (Conditions of detention in Hungary)*, ECLI:EU:C:2018:589.

[24] Directive 2012/13 (n 22).

[25] Directive 2013/48/EU of the European Parliament and of the Council of 22 October 2013 on the right of access to a lawyer in criminal proceedings and in European arrest warrant proceedings, and on the right to have a third party informed upon deprivation of liberty and to communicate with third persons and with consular authorities while deprived of liberty [2013] OJ L294/1.

as the presumption of innocence and the right to be present at the trial.[26] In this context, referring to Article 6 of the Charter, the ECJ has found, for example, that the relevant directives on the right to information and the right of access to a lawyer must be interpreted as applying to judicial proceedings which authorise, on therapeutic and safety grounds, the committal to a psychiatric hospital of persons who have committed acts which represent a danger to society in a state of insanity and that those persons must be informed as soon as possible of their rights from the moment they become suspects of acts that would justify the restriction of their liberty.[27] Further, the ECJ has underlined the limits of the scope of application of EU law in criminal matters and, thus, of the Charter and of Article 6 thereof, in a case concerning detention on remand pending trial.[28]

The right to liberty has, moreover, proven to be particularly relevant as far as secondary law acts governing the situation of third-country nationals are concerned,[29] such as those relevant to the Dublin system,[30] to international protection and the reception of applicants thereof[31] or the procedures for returning illegally staying third country nationals.[32]

In this context, the ECJ has, for instance, provided guidance on the time limits of detention of applicants of international protection pending their transfer from one Member State to another according to the Dublin system rules when there is a significant risk of absconding,[33] establishing criteria underlying the reasons for believing that such applicants may abscond[34] and the grounds justifying detention of an illegally staying third-country national pending their return.[35] It has also, in the light of Article 6 of the Charter, not only interpreted secondary

[26] Directive (EU) 2016/343 of the European Parliament and of the Council of 9 March 2016 on the strengthening of certain aspects of the presumption of innocence and of the right to be present at the trial in criminal proceedings [2016] OJ L65/1.

[27] Case C-467/18 *Rayonna prokuratura Lom*, ECLI:EU:C:2019:765, para 54. See also Wilsher (n 1), 133.

[28] See *Spetsializirana prokuratura* (n 4), notably para 40 and Opinion of AG Pitruzzella in the same case (n 4), paras 42–48. The latter explains, in para 48 of his Opinion, that 'Directive 2016/343 was not intended to put into effect the right to liberty, as enshrined in Article 6 [of the Charter] and Article 5 [ECHR], but only to harmonise *certain* aspects of the presumption of innocence'. On pre-trial detention, see also *Milev* (n 8) and Mancano (n 13), 283–84.

[29] For the role of the right to liberty in this field even before the ECJ started explicitly referencing Art 6 of the Charter, see Stefanelli and Guild (n 2), 105, which refers notably to Case C-357/09 PPU *Kadzoev* ECLI:EU:C:2009:741.

[30] Regulation (EU) No 604/2013 of the European Parliament and of the Council of 26 June 2013 establishing the criteria and mechanisms for determining the Member State responsible for examining an application for international protection lodged in one of the Member States by a third-country national or stateless person [2013] OJ L180/31.

[31] Directives 2011/95/EU of the European Parliament and of the Council of 13 December 2011 on standards for the qualification of third country nationals or stateless persons as beneficiaries of international protection, for a uniform status for refugees or for persons eligible for subsidiary protection, and for the content of the protection granted [2011] OJ L337/9; 2013/32/EU of the European Parliament and of the Council of 26 June 2013 on common procedures for granting and withdrawing international protection [2013] OJ L180/60; and 2013/33/EU of the European Parliament and of the Council of 26 of June 2013 laying down standards for the reception of applicants for international protection [2013] OJ L180/96. See S Bartolini and T Bombois, 'Immigration Detention Before the CJEU: the Interrelationship Between the Return Directive and the Recast Reception Conditions Directive and their Impact on the Rights of Third Country Nationals' (2016) 6 *European Human Rights Law Review* 518.

[32] Directive 2008/115/EC of the European Parliament and of the Council of 16 December 2008 on common standards and procedures in Member States for returning illegally staying third-country nationals [2008] OJ L348/98.

[33] See Case C-60/16 *Khir Amayry*, ECLI:EU:C:2017:675, para 49, where the ECJ ruled that, although such detention, based on Art 28 of Regulation No 604/2013, can be justified in light of Art 6 of the Charter for a duration of up to six weeks as long as it is necessary for the purposes of the transfer procedure, it cannot be justified if maintained for longer periods (3 or 12 months) during which the transfer could be reasonably carried out (para 49).

[34] Judgment in *Al Chodor* (n 4), paras 40–47.

[35] See judgment in *Politsei- ja Piirivalveamet (Detention – Risk of committing a criminal offence)* (n 6), para 55, where the ECJ, having referenced Art 6 of the Charter (see paras 44–50), affirmed that the relevant provision of Directive 2008/115 must be interpreted as not permitting a Member State to order the detention of an illegally staying third-country national solely on the basis of a general criterion based on the risk that the effective enforcement of the removal would be compromised, without satisfying one of the specific grounds for detention provided for and clearly defined by the legislation implementing that provision in national law.

clauses governing detention of applicants for international protection,[36] notably when such detention is required for reasons of protection of national security or public order,[37] but also examined and confirmed the validity of certain aspects of that legislation.[38]

III. A SOURCE OF SPECIFIC PROCEDURAL GUARANTEES

An overview of the relevant ECJ case law also reveals the importance of Article 6's procedural component. This is not surprising, given the right to liberty's original conception as a guarantee of due process of law.[39]

Procedural guarantees have been laid out by the ECJ, for example, with regard to detention for the purposes of executing an EAW. The ECJ has held that detention in this context can only be justified as long as it has been carried out in a sufficiently diligent manner and in so far as its duration is not excessive; it has also specifically identified a procedural role for the executing judicial authority. The latter is required:

> to carry out a concrete review of the situation at issue, taking account of all the relevant factors with a view to evaluating the justification for the duration of the procedure, including the possible failure to act on the part of the authorities of the Member State concerned and any contribution of the requested person to that duration.[40]

[36] See, for example, Case C-36/20 PPU *Ministerio Fiscal (Authority likely to receive an application for international protection)*, ECLI:EU:C:2020:495, para 105 and the case law cited, where upon interpretation of Art 8(3) of Directive 2013/33, which sets out an exclusive list of the various grounds potentially justifying detention of applicants for international protection, the ECJ reaffirmed that, in view of the importance of the right to liberty and the gravity of the interference with that right that detention represents, limitations on its exercise must apply only in so far as is strictly necessary. The ECJ went on to find that the ground for detention put forward in the main proceedings to justify one of the concerned party's detention, namely the fact that it was not possible to find him a place in a humanitarian reception centre, did not correspond to any of the six grounds for detention referred to in said provision (para 106), making it contrary to the requirements of the aforementioned Directive (para 107).

[37] See Case C-72/22 PPU *Valstybės sienos apsaugos tarnyba and Others*, ECLI:EU:C:2022:505, notably paras 89 and 91, where the ECJ found that placing or keeping an applicant in detention under point (e) of the first subparagraph of Art 8(3) of Directive 2013/33 is only justified on the ground of a threat to national security or public order 'if the applicant's individual conduct presents a genuine, present and sufficiently serious threat affecting a fundamental interest of society or the internal or external security of the Member State concerned', while the illegal nature of the presence of that applicant cannot, in itself, be regarded as demonstrating the existence of such a threat.

[38] See Case C-18/16 *K*, ECLI:EU:C:2017:680, where the ECJ examined the validity of points (a) and (b) of the first subparagraph of Art 8 of Directive 2013/33, allowing for the detention of such applicants, respectively, in order to determine or verify their identity or nationality and when such detention is necessary to determine the elements on which their application is based. The ECJ ruled that a limitation of the right to liberty in these terms does not affect the essence of the right to liberty (para 35) and proceeded to examine the proportionality of the interference with said right (paras 37–49), taking into account the relevant case law of the ECtHR (paras 50–53), to finally conclude that the examination of those provisions disclosed nothing capable of affecting their validity in the light of Arts 6 and 51 of the Charter (para 54). See also *N* (n 4), para 52 ff, on the validity of Art 8(3)(e) of Directive 2013/33, where the ECJ stated that it follows from the wording and context of the provision examined that the limitation in question is subject to compliance with a series of conditions, whose aim is to create a strictly circumscribed framework in which such a measure may be used (para 57), stressing notably the fact that the strict circumscription of the competent national authorities' power to detain an applicant on the basis of the examined provision is also ensured by the interpretation given by the ECJ to the concepts of 'national security' and 'public order' found in other directives but applying in the case of Directive 2013/33 (paras 64–67). On this judgment, see Bartolini and Bombois (n 31), 521; and Guillain and Ribant (n 11), 174 ff.

[39] See Wilsher (n 1), 123.

[40] Judgment in case *Lanigan* (n 16), paras 58–59. It is to be noted that the ECJ has also underlined that, where the requested person's custody comes to an end, notably in view of its duration, the executing judicial authority is required to attach to their release 'any measures it deems necessary so as to prevent [them] from absconding and to ensure that the material conditions necessary for [their] effective surrender remain fulfilled for as long as no final

Concerning the dual level of protection required for the issuing of an EAW,[41] the ECJ also held that such a warrant could be issued by the public prosecutor of a Member State, despite the risk of the latter being subject to directions or instructions from the executive, provided that the warrants in question are subject to endorsement by a court, reviewing:

> independently and objectively, having access to the entire criminal file to which any directions or instructions [...] from the executive are added, the conditions of issue and the proportionality of those arrest warrants, thus adopting an autonomous decision which gives them their final form.[42]

Also regarding judicial review, the ECJ ruled that Directives 2012/13 and 2013/48 preclude national legislation which provides for judicial proceedings authorising, on therapeutic and safety grounds, the committal to a psychiatric hospital of persons who, in a state of insanity, have committed acts representing a danger to society, in so far as that legislation does not enable the competent court to verify that the procedural rights covered by those directives were respected in proceedings prior to those before that court, which were not subject to such judicial review.[43]

Specific procedural guarantees can also be found in the case law concerning third-country nationals. Interpreting Directive 2008/115 in light of Articles 6 and 47 of the Charter, the ECJ ruled that any decision adopted by a competent authority, upon expiry of the maximum period allowed for the initial detention of a third-country national, on the further course to take concerning the detention must be in the form of a written measure that includes the reasons in fact and in law for that decision.[44] The ECJ has also explained, citing ECtHR case law, that failure to fix a maximum duration of the detention of an applicant for international protection respects their right to liberty, as enshrined in Article 6 of the Charter, only in so far as the applicant enjoys, as required by the relevant provisions of Directive 2013/33, effective procedural safeguards that allow their detention to be ended as soon as it ceases to be necessary or proportionate in the light of the objective pursued and that when such a detention is not limited in time, the competent authority must act with appropriate due diligence.[45]

decision on the execution of the [EAW] has been taken' (para 63). See also, for the particular case of consecutive failed surrender attempts, Case C-640/15 *Vilkas*, ECLI:EU:C:2017:39, notably para 43; concerning extension of the time limits laid down in EAW Framework Decision, Case C-804/21 PPU *C and CD (Legal obstacles to the execution of a decision on surrender)*, ECLI:EU:C:2022:307, with no explicit reference to Art 6 of the Charter; see, also, for the particular case of surrender being postponed for the purpose of a criminal prosecution against the requested person in the executing Member State, Case C-492/22 PPU *CJ (Decision to postpone surrender due to criminal prosecution)*, ECLI:EU:C:2022:964), notably para 82.

[41] This 'dual level of protection' refers to the benefit of procedural safeguards and fundamental rights that a requested person must enjoy at the first stage of the relevant proceedings, that is when a national decision, such as a national arrest warrant, is adopted by the issuing Member State, in addition to the judicial protection provided at the second level of those proceedings, at which a EAW is issued: see judgment in *NJ (Public Prosecutor's Office, Vienna)* (n 15), paras 33–34.

[42] ibid para 49. Compare with the issuing of a European investigation order within the sense of Directive 2014/41/EU of the European Parliament and of the Council of 3 April 2014 regarding the European Investigation Order in criminal matters [2014] OJ L130/1 and see Case C-584/19 *Staatsanwaltschaft Wien (Falsified transfer orders)*, ECLI:EU:C:2020:1002, para 73, where the ECJ stated that, despite the fact that such an order may, in principle, cover any investigative measure for the purposes, inter alia, of criminal proceedings and that some of those measures may be intrusive in so far as they entail an interference in particular with the right to privacy or the right to property of the person concerned, such an order, 'unlike a [EAW], is not such as to interfere with the right to liberty of the person concerned, enshrined in Article 6 [of the Charter]'.

[43] *Rayonna prokuratura Lom* (n 27), para 63.

[44] Case C-146/14 PPU *Mahdi*, ECLI:EU:C:2014:1320, para 52. See also Bartolini and Bombois (n 31), 524.

[45] Joined Cases C-924/19 PPU and C-925/19 PPU *Országos Idegenrendészeti Főigazgatóság Dél-alföldi Regionális Igazgatóság*, ECLI:EU:C:2020:367, para 264.

The coupling of Articles 6 and 47 of the Charter, and, on some occasions, the sole reference to the latter,[46] might give the impression that higher importance is attributed to the right to effective judicial protection. However, the following example is striking as to the importance of the right to liberty in the construction of the ECJ's reasoning and the link between the two fundamental rights guaranteed by the Charter. In a case concerning the interpretation of various provisions of Regulation No 604/2013 and of Directives 2008/115 and 2013/33, 'in view of the importance of the right to liberty, the gravity of the interference with that right which the detention of persons *on grounds other than the prosecution or punishment of criminal offences* represents and of the requirement, highlighted by the common rules laid down by the EU legislature, on a high level of judicial protection', the ECJ ruled that where the conditions governing the lawfulness of detention were not or are no longer satisfied:

> the competent judicial authority must take into consideration all the elements, in particular the facts, brought to its knowledge [...] and [...] raise, where appropriate, the failure to comply with a condition governing lawfulness arising from EU law, *even if that failure has not been raised by the person concerned*.[47] (emphasis added)

If this judgment certainly reveals a distinction between measures restrictive of the right to liberty decided in a criminal law context and those decided in a context involving rights of third country nationals,[48] it cannot be denied that, in this instance, the ECJ nuanced its traditional case law according to which EU law does not, in principle, require national courts to raise of their own motion pleas alleging infringement of provisions of that law. However, as it is emphasised in paragraph 91 of the judgment, this case law refers more specifically to instances 'where examinations of those pleas would oblige [national courts] to go beyond the ambit of the dispute defined by the parties themselves by relying on facts and circumstances other than those on which the party with an interest in application of those provisions has based its claim'.[49] The ECJ explained this difference in approach by referring to '[t]he strict circumscription [...] of detention and the continuation of a detention measure [leading] to a situation which is not similar in every respect to administrative proceedings, in which the initiative and delimitation of the dispute lie with the parties'.[50] Taking into account the significant importance of the right to liberty and the fact that litigation involving third-country nationals

[46] See Wilsher (n 1), 119, referring to the judgment in joined cases *Országos Idegenrendészeti Főigazgatóság Dél-alföldi Regionális Igazgatóság* (n 45).

[47] Joined Cases C-704/20 and C-39/21 *Staatssecretaris van Justitie en Veiligheid and X (Ex officio review of detention)*, ECLI:EU:C:2022:858, para 88; see F Gazin, 'Immigration – Examen d'office de la légalité d'une rétention' (2023) *1 Europe comm*. 9. See also judgment in *Landkreis Gifhorn* (n 4), paras 64–65, where the ECJ held that, where a court is called upon to order, on the basis of national legislation implementing Directive 2008/115, that the detention of a third-country national for the purpose of their removal is to be carried out in a prison facility or that such detention is to be extended, the court must be in a position to ensure that its decision is preceded by an examination of the compatibility of such legislation with EU law. The court must therefore be able to take into account 'both the facts stated and the evidence adduced by the administrative authority requesting detention [...] and any observations that may be submitted by the third country national. Furthermore, it must be able to consider *any other element that is relevant for its decision should it so deem necessary*' (emphasis added).

[48] As has been pointed out, detention under both Directive 2013/33 and Directive 2008/115 is not punitive in nature. See Bartolini and Bombois (n 31), 520. However, it can be complex to distinguish between prosecution and detention in a criminal law context and in the context of these Directives when a legal order establishes an 'offence of illegal staying'. In that regard, see Case C-329/11 *Achughbabian*, ECLI:EU:C:2011:807.

[49] Judgment in *Staatssecretaris van Justitie en Veiligheid and X (Ex officio review of detention)* (n 47), para 91; the ECJ cites, more specifically, Joined Cases C-430/93 and C-431/93, *van Schijndel and van Veen*, ECLI:EU:C:1995:441, paras 21–22; Case C-225/05 *van der Weerd and Others*, ECLI:EU:C:2007:318, paras 35–36; and Case C-927/19 *Klaipėdos regiono atliekų tvarkymo centras*, ECLI:EU:C:2021:700, para 145.

[50] *Staatssecretaris van Justitie en Veiligheid and X (Ex officio review of detention)* (n 47), para 92.

may not be the only type of litigation in which the initiative and delimitation of the dispute does not lie with the parties, one should not entirely exclude an extension of this case law in the future.[51]

IV. CONCLUSION

While by no means exhaustive, this contribution has sought to demonstrate how the relevance of Article 6 of the Charter in the ECJ's case law is expanding and how the Court of Justice 'develops its own autonomous approach' on the matter,[52] sometimes even stepping beyond the ECtHR's case law,[53] especially as the scope of EU law is expanding in areas previously reserved to the Member States' legal orders, providing for additional safeguards against State arbitrariness. In a rapidly changing world, where technology is already redefining law enforcement and public security, it will become increasingly important to cherish and develop the standards of protection of the individual that follow from that case law, a challenge that the ECJ must and will rise to meet.

[51] Compare, however, Case C-660/21 *KB and FS (Raising ex officio of an infringement in criminal proceedings)*, ECLI:EU:C:2023:498, para 49, keeping in mind that no specific mention of Art 6 of the Charter is made in this judgment by the Court; and Opinion of AG Pikamäe in the case, ECLI/EU:C:2023:52, paras 76–78, where he expresses the opinion that the judgment in *Staatssecretaris van Justitie en Veiligheid and X (Ex officio review of detention)* (n 47) seems to have been 'dictated by a specific normative context'.

[52] See Guillain and Ribant (n 11), 174 and Wilsher (n 1), 126 and 149.

[53] See, concerning mandatory time limits in the context of Directive 2008/115, Bartolini and Bombois (n 31), 528 and Mancano (n 13), 279; concerning the obligation of Member States to consider alternatives before resorting to detention as well as the detention of migrants in specialised facilities, Stefanelli and Guild (n 2), 117. See, however, the remarks made by Guillain and Ribant (n 11), 172 ff.

11

The Principle of Democracy in EU Law

INETA ZIEMELE*

I. INTRODUCTION

ARTICLE 2 IN the introductory title of the TEU lists 'democracy' among the values of the European Union (EU), which are common to all Member States. Since the entry into force of the Lisbon Treaty and the Charter of Fundamental Rights of the European Union (the Charter), Article 2 has further inspired important developments in EU law and institutional practices. The Treaty on European Union (TEU) in Article 6(1) provided that the EU is founded, inter alia, on the principle of democracy and therefore the principle has been part of the EU's legal order; nevertheless the agreement on democracy as a value adds to it a new dimension for the purposes of the Union's outlook. It may well be that these developments are, at least in part, a further response to the earlier criticisms under the label of 'democratic deficit' advanced with regard to the functioning of the European Community (Union).[1] At the same time, evolution of European integration processes, which address the issues pertinent to a more democratic outlook of the EU's functioning, appears to be a rather natural course of events in the community which shares a number of values and principles. Democracy is part of the common constitutional traditions of the Member States and as such, it was waiting for the necessary legislative and institutional steps and solutions to acquire its expression as a matter of EU law. This chapter, drawing on the recent case law of the European Court of Justice (ECJ), outlines and explains the application of the principle of democracy as one of the general principles of the EU law.[2]

II. THE EU TREATIES

Article 2, to the extent that it refers to democracy as a foundational value of the EU, is further concretised in Title II TEU. That Title contains several provisions disclosing the content of democracy (Articles 9–12 TEU) for the purposes of the functioning of the Union. In fact,

* Judge at the European Court of Justice. The views expressed in this chapter are strictly personal. I am grateful to Ms Inese Freimane-Deksne of the European University Institute for the research assistance provided for the purposes of the chapter.

[1] There is a wealth of doctrinal writings on the issue. See eg A Follesdal and S Xih, 'Why There is a Democratic Deficit in the EU: A Response to Majone and Moravcsik' (2006) 44 *Journal of Common Market Studies* 533.

[2] See further K Lenaerts, 'The Principle of Democracy in the Case Law of the European Court of Justice' (2013) 62 *International and Comparative Law Quarterly* 271.

the very title refers to democratic principles in plural indicating that the value of democracy covers and refers to several legal principles that are essential for a more democratic outlook of the legal system. Article 14(3) TEU embeds the representative character of the EU democracy, providing that the Members of the European Parliament are elected by direct universal suffrage in a free and secret ballot, as indeed Article 10(1) TEU has determined. Article 13(2) TEU includes the principle of institutional balance. Article 15 of the Treaty on the Functioning of the European Union (TFEU) includes the principle of transparency, providing for the right of access to documents of the EU institutions (paragraph 3 of Article 15 TFEU) and of their decision-making processes (paragraphs 1 and 2 of Article 15 TFEU).

Furthermore, the Charter, forming part of primary EU law following the entry into force of the Lisbon Treaty, in Recital 2 of the Preamble states that '[...] *the Union* is founded on the indivisible, universal values of human dignity, freedom, equality and solidarity; it *is based on the principles of democracy* and the rule of law [...]' (emphasis added). The Preamble proceeds to state in Recital 3 that 'the Union contributes to the preservation and to the development of these common values while respecting the diversity of the cultures and traditions of the peoples of Europe as well as the national identities of the Member States and the organization of their public authorities at national, regional and local levels [...]'. The right to stand as a candidate at elections guaranteed in Article 39(2) of the Charter reciprocates the principle of direct universal suffrage in a free and secret ballot enshrined in Article 14(3) TEU. Likewise, by virtue of Article 42 of the Charter, the right of access to documents is granted the status of a fundamental right in the EU law. Article 41 embodies the principle of good governance of the Union as part of fundamental rights in the Charter and an expression of the principle of democracy. Moreover, other rights provided for by the Charter, such as freedom of thought, conscience and religion (Article 10), freedom of expression and information (Article 11), freedom of assembly and association (Article 12), are expressions of the principle of democracy and will certainly make an impact in the application of the EU law.[3]

The EU has evolved into a common legal and economic space, which is based on common values, and democracy is one of its pillars. From this derives a certain vision for legislative processes and developments of legislation. It is true that the inter-governmental process has not lost its pertinence within the EU, but the principle of democracy has been internalised within the functioning of the EU institutions so that the question can also be asked what impact this principle has on inter-governmental EU processes. The purpose of this chapter is to show the principles of democracy enshrined in Title II TEU in action as disclosed by recent case law.

III. THE CASE LAW OF THE ECJ

The ECJ has examined the impact of the general principle of democracy in EU law in several different legal and factual constellations. The principle has had a bearing on election rights in the EU. It evidently affects the assessment of the scope and extent of citizens' initiatives under the EU law. It is also a paradigm for the examination of the relationship between Member States, between the EU institutions, and between the Member States and the EU. Finally, it

[3] In 2021, the Commission brought infringement proceedings against Poland and the Czech Republic based on the alleged violation of Art 22 TFEU because EU citizens who are not nationals of these States are not entitled to become members of the political parties in those States. The case is still pending at the time of writing.

is relevant in the cases in which EU legal acts face a challenge based on the arguments on the particular constitutional structure of a Member State referred to in Article 4(2) TEU.

A. Right to Stand as a Candidate to the European Parliament

In *Junqueras Vies*,[4] the Supreme Court of Spain referred to the Court a number of preliminary questions relating to the interpretation of Article 9 of Protocol No 7 on the Privileges and Immunities of the European Union. Those questions arose in the context of an action brought by a politician elected to the European Parliament in the elections of 26 May 2019 against an order refusing to grant him a special authorisation to leave prison. This person was placed in detention prior to the elections, in the context of criminal proceedings brought against him for his participation in the organisation of the referendum on self-determination held on 1 October 2017 in the autonomous community of Catalonia. Following the referral to the ECJ, the Supreme Court of Spain sentenced him to a 13-year term of imprisonment and, for that same period, to a 13-year disqualification from holding any public office or exercising any public function. The case gave an opportunity to clarify the personal, temporal and material scope of the immunities enjoyed by Members of the European Parliament.

The Court held that a person who is elected to the European Parliament acquires the status of a Member of Parliament as a result of and from the time of the declaration of the election results, which means that he/she enjoys the immunities guaranteed by Article 9 of the Protocol. In that regard, the Court noted that the electoral procedure and the declaration of the results are, in principle, governed by the law of the Member States. However, the election of Members of the European Parliament by direct universal suffrage in a free and secret ballot constitutes an *expression of the constitutional principle of representative democracy* provided for in Article 10(1) TEU as a concrete form of the value of democracy referred to in Article 2 TEU.[5] In this context, EU law defines the scope of the principle of democracy. The immunity as regards travel granted to every Member of the European Parliament entails lifting any measure of provisional detention imposed prior to the declaration of that Member's election, in order to allow that person to travel to and take part in the inaugural session of the European Parliament. The Court pointed out that the immunities are intended to ensure the proper functioning and independence of the European Parliament. In that context, the immunity as regards travel serves to ensure the right to stand as a candidate at elections, guaranteed in Article 39(2) of the EU Charter of Fundamental Rights. The right provided for in the Charter echoes and guarantees the principle of direct universal suffrage in a free and secret ballot enshrined in Article 14(3) TEU. The ECJ identifies two main objectives of the functioning of immunity in relation to the Members of the Parliament. First, that the composition of the European Parliament 'must reflect faithfully and completely the free expression of choices made by the citizens of the European Union' and, second, that the 'European Parliament must be protected, in the exercise of its tasks, against hindrances or risks to its proper operation'.[6] The case is particularly important for the independent functioning of democratically elected EU institution and serves as a protection against any possible abuse of the work of the EU.

[4] Case C-502/19 *Junqueras Vies*, ECLI:EU:C:2019:1115.
[5] ibid, para 63 and the case law cited.
[6] ibid, para 83.

B. Separation of Powers

The principle of democracy applies also in inter-institutional relations. In *Council v Commission* a question was asked about the limits of the Commission's power to withdraw its proposals within the legislative process in the Union.[7] The case concerned a proposal made by the Commission for a framework regulation laying down general provisions for macro-financial assistance (MFA) to third countries. The Commission had suggested granting assistance by way of implementing acts. The Parliament and the Council in particular objected to this approach as, in their view, there would be insufficient political and democratic scrutiny of the decision-making processes. As a result, they proposed to amend the proposal, introducing the use of the ordinary legislative procedure for the adoption of each decision granting MFA. The Commission considered that such an alteration would distort its original proposal and give rise to significant constitutional problems. Therefore it decided to withdraw the proposal. The Council initiated proceedings against the Commission under Article 263 TFEU, seeking annulment of the latter's decision. The Council argued that the Commission had infringed the principle of institutional balance and the principle of sincere cooperation under Article 13(2) TEU as well as the obligation to state reasons under Article 296(2) TFEU. It has to be noted that the Council and the Federal Republic of Germany in the proceedings argued that the principle of democracy, as provided for in Article 10(1) and (2) TEU, sets the limit to the attribution of such a discretion to the Commission.[8] In their submissions, the Parliament as well as the Council argued that their members are accountable to national parliaments and that therefore they guarantee the democratic legitimacy of legislative processes. The Commission disagreed with such an understanding of the principle of democracy in the EU institutional setting, insisting on its own democratic legitimacy. In the context of the relevance of the principle of democracy within the EU's architecture, this debate cannot be underestimated. It is clear that all three institutions – ie the Council, the Parliament and the Commission – consider their democratic legitimacy to be an important characteristic that they ought to have.

The Court held that the Commission has the power, as long as the Council has not acted, to alter its proposal or even withdraw it. At the same time, this power cannot confer upon the Commission a right of veto in the conduct of the legislative process. If the Commission decides to withdraw its proposal, it must state to the Parliament and the Council the reasons for the withdrawal. The withdrawal by the Commission of a legislative proposal cannot be regarded as an infringement of the principle of institutional balance or the principle of sincere cooperation under Article 13(2) TEU.[9] It has to be pointed out that the ECJ considered arguments with regard to the infringement of the principle of democracy, provided for in Article 10(1) and (2) TEU, as unfounded. It pointed out that:

> […] it is apparent from Article 17(2) TEU, read in conjunction with Articles 289 TFEU and 293 TFEU, that the Commission has the power not only to submit a legislative proposal but also, provided that the Council has not yet acted, to alter its proposal or even, if need be, withdraw it. Since that power of the Commission to withdraw a proposal is inseparable from the right of initiative with which that institution is vested and its exercise is circumscribed by the provisions of the abovementioned articles of the TFEU, there can be no question, in this instance, of an infringement of that principle.[10]

[7] Case C-409/13 *Council v Commission*, ECLI:EU:C:2015:217.
[8] ibid, para 37.
[9] ibid, paras 74–76.
[10] ibid, para 96.

At the same time, the Court also pronounced on the principle of sincere cooperation, laid down in Article 13(2) TEU, considering that the actions of the Commission of abruptly withdrawing its legislative proposal are not evidence of the violation of this principle. It can be derived from the reasoning of the Court that the principle of sincere cooperation among EU institutions – which is crucial in any setting where the principle of separation of powers underlies the functioning of a system – indeed assists in maintaining a proper balance among the institutions and thus of the proper functioning of democracy therein.

C. EU Citizens and Legislative Process

There is no question that the democratic functioning of the EU depends on the involvement of EU citizens in these processes. Therefore *Puppinck v Commission* remains a particularly important case and probably not the last word of the ECJ in this context.[11] In this case, the appeal was brought by the organisers of the European Citizens' Initiative (ECI) against the judgment of the General Court whereby that court had dismissed their action for the annulment of the communication from the Commission in relation to the ECI. In accordance with Article 11(4) TEU and Regulation No 211/2011, not less than one million EU citizens who come from at least one quarter of Member States may take the initiative of inviting the Commission to propose to the EU legislature the adoption of a legal act for the purpose of implementing the Treaties. Before they can begin the collection of the required number of signatures, the organisers of the ECI must register it with the Commission, which has to examine in particular its subject matter and its objectives. The applicants registered their ECI with the Commission. The objective of that ECI was to prohibit and put an end to the financing, by the EU, of activities that involve the destruction of human embryos, including the direct or indirect funding of abortion. After its registration, the ECI 'One of us' collected the signatures required, and was then formally submitted to the Commission. The Commission stated in a communication that it did not intend to take any action in response to that ECI.

The Court held that the General Court did not err in upholding the decision of the Commission not to submit a proposal for legislation in response to the ECI 'One of us'. The power of legislative initiative conferred on the Commission is one of the expressions of the principle of institutional balance. The Court also emphasised that the fact that the Commission is not obliged to take any action in response to an ECI does not mean that such an initiative is deprived of effectiveness. The ECI mechanism constitutes one of the instruments of participatory democracy, which complemented, on the adoption of the Treaty of Lisbon, the system of representative democracy. 'The right to undertake an ECI constitutes, as does, in particular, the right to petition the Parliament, an instrument concerning the right of citizens to participate in the democratic life of the Union, provided for in Article 10(3) TEU […].'[12] However, it shall fit within the pre-existing institutional balance and its added value resides not in certainty of outcome, but in the possibilities that it creates for the EU citizens to initiate debate on policy issues within the EU institutions. The ECI is intended to confer on Union citizens a right comparable to the Parliament and the Council, which right does not undermine the Commission's power of legislative initiative.[13]

[11] Case C-418/18 P *Puppinck v Commission*, ECLI:EU:C:2019:1113.
[12] ibid, para 54.
[13] ibid, para 61.

The *Council v Commission* and *Puppinck v Commission* cases carve out a careful balance of a legislative process within the EU and reflect the multifaceted character of the principle of democracy within this architecture.

D. Compliance with Common EU Values

To this day, the so-called conditionality judgments in cases *Hungary v Parliament and Council* and *Poland v Parliament and Council* represent the most important interpretation of Article 2 TEU.[14] On 16 December 2020, the Parliament and the Council adopted Regulation 2020/2092, which establishes a general regime of conditionality for the protection of the Union budget in the case of breaches of the principle of the rule of law in a Member State. In order to attain that objective, the regulation allows the Council, on a proposal from the Commission, to adopt protective measures such as the suspension of payments to be made from the Union budget or the suspension of the approval of one or more programmes to be paid from that budget. Hungary and Poland each brought an action before the ECJ for the annulment of that regulation considering that it amounted to sentencing the Member States, which the EU Treaties do not permit and therefore the EU legislature had exceeded the powers conferred on it by the Treaties. The only mechanism in this context available to the EU is provided for in Article 7 TEU.

The Court dismissed the actions brought by Hungary and Poland and established that this mechanism has been adopted on an appropriate legal basis and respects the limits of the powers conferred on the EU. In the judgments, the Court emphasised that the compliance by the Member States with the common values under Article 2 TEU on which the EU is founded and, 'under Article 49 TEU, respect for those values is a prerequisite for the accession to the European Union of any European State applying to become a member of the European Union'.[15] Once the State becomes a Member of the EU, the premise that the values of Article 2 are common 'implies and justifies the existence of mutual trust between the Member States that those values will be recognised and, therefore, that the EU law that implements them will be respected […]' and thus 'the laws and practices of Member States *should continue to comply with the common values* on which the European Union is founded'.[16] The ECJ considered it particularly important to emphasise that: 'Compliance with those values cannot be reduced to an obligation which a candidate State must meet in order to accede to the European Union and which it may disregard after its accession.'[17] Since that compliance is a condition for the enjoyment of all the rights deriving from the application of the Treaties to a Member State, the EU must be able to defend those values, within the limits of its powers. In point 127 of the *Hungary v Parliament and Council* case, the Court set out two fundamental concepts. First, it built on *Van Gen den Loos*, which articulated the European Union (Communities then) as a new kind of legal order, and explained that today it is *a new legal order based on common values* expressed in Article 2 TEU and that it is the common values that form the very identity of that new legal order.

[14] Cases C-156/21 *Hungary v Parliament and Council*, ECLI:EU:C:2022:97; and C-157/21 *Poland v Parliament and Council*, ECLI:EU:C:2022:98.

[15] *Hungary v Parliament and Council* (n 14), para 124.

[16] ibid, para 125.

[17] ibid, para 126.

Second, the Court articulates a kind of *principle of self-defending democracy* for the purposes of the EU law. The passage reads as follows:

> The values contained in Article 2 TEU have been identified and are shared by the Member States. They define the very identity of the European Union as a common legal order. Thus, the European Union must be able to defend those values, within the limits of its powers as laid down by the Treaties.

Additionally, in *Poland v Parliament and Council*, the Court explicitly referred to the value of 'democracy' under Article 2 TEU in the context of the voting procedure under Article 16(4) TEU, establishing that this provision seeks to ensure that the Council's decisions are sufficiently representative of both the Member States and the population of the EU. Moreover, the judgments, in response to the arguments of Hungary and Poland as to confidentiality of the opinion of the Council's Legal Service concerning the initial proposal, which led to the adoption of the contested Regulation, emphasise the application of the principle of openness and the overriding public interest in the transparency of the legislative procedure in a democratic system.[18]

The ECJ's reasoning in the *Wightman and Others v Secretary of State for Exiting the European Union* case is in harmony with the role attributed to the principle of democracy in the context of the membership conditions in the Union.[19] The case concerned the UK's withdrawal from the EU. The request for a preliminary ruling had been submitted to the Court by the Court of Session, Inner House, First Division (Scotland), in judicial review proceedings brought by members of the UK Parliament, the Scottish Parliament and the European Parliament, to determine whether and how the notification referred to in Article 50 TEU could be revoked before expiry of the two-year period provided for in paragraph 3 of that provision, with the effect that such revocation would result in the UK remaining in the EU.

The Court concluded that the notification referred to in Article 50 TEU can be revoked unilaterally after the Member State has taken the revocation decision, *in accordance with its constitutional requirements and following a democratic process*. The ECJ, following the classical method of interpretation, explained that the wording of Article 50 TEU is instructed by the applicable context. In this regard, the Court referred to Article 2 TEU and Article 49 TEU, underlying the essentially democratic nature of the accession process and membership in the EU. From this follows that the States have freely and voluntarily committed themselves to the values that they have in common.[20] The Court concluded that: 'In those circumstances, given that a State cannot be forced to accede to the European Union against its will, neither can it be forced to withdraw from the European Union against its will.'[21] In other words, the withdrawal process too is guided by the principle of democracy, especially, as argued in this case, since the will of the people concerned might change during that process and that has to be taken into account.

E. National Identity

Undoubtedly, the cases in which the Member States raise their objections to a particular application of the treaty provisions and the EU's secondary legislation based on their national identity

[18] ibid, paras 55–59.
[19] Case C-621/18 *Wightman and Others v Secretary of State for Exiting the European Union*, ECLI:EU:C:2018:999.
[20] ibid, para 63.
[21] ibid, para 65.

provide for an interesting constellation for the application of the principle of democracy due to the fact that in the EU Member States their identity embraces the principle of democracy as well. The question therefore arises whether there could be a different understanding of democracy at national and European levels in relation to the competences conferred upon the Union.[22]

In the *Commission v Germany* case, the Commission brought the infringement proceedings under Article 258 TFEU against the Federal Republic of Germany. Germany allegedly had failed to transpose correctly the relevant provisions of Directive 2009/72 (concerning common rules for the internal market in electricity) and of Directive 2009/73 (concerning common rules for the internal market in natural gas). The Commission argued that paragraph 24 of the Energy Industry Act confers on the Federal Government powers to fix transmission and distribution tariffs, and to determine the conditions for balancing services, even though, according to the provisions of the directives, such powers lie exclusively with national regulatory authorities.[23] Germany argued, inter alia, that the conferral of powers on independent national authorities is possible only if the EU legislature has first adopted sufficiently precise provisions on such authorities. Where the relevant EU law does not provide for clear and precise tasks, it is for the Member States to regulate the matter. Moreover, such a legal opinion also arises from democratic principles and the rule of law, which form part of the fundamental political and constitutional structures of the Federal Republic of Germany, which, in accordance with Article 4(2) TEU, the EU must respect.

The Court upheld, in its entirety, the action for failure to fulfil obligations brought by the Commission against Germany and provided an important clarification of the functioning of the principle of democracy as it concerns the arguments of the parties. The ECJ explained, inter alia, that (1) the principle of democracy must be taken into account when interpreting acts of secondary law, and (2) the principle of democracy does not preclude the existence of independent public authorities outside the classical hierarchically organised public administration of a State, and that their compliance with the law is ensured through judicial review by national courts and not by political institutions.[24] The Court emphasised that the EU legislative procedure, in which the directives were adopted, fully reflects the principle of representative democracy, as provide in Article 10(1) TEU, which article concretises the value of democracy referred to in Article 2 TEU.[25] The interpretation of the principle of democracy within the confines of this case reflects and corresponds to a democratic functioning of any public administration in a democratic State.

IV. CONCLUSION

The general legal principle of democracy in its many aspects is imperative to the functioning of the EU and the interpretation and application of EU law. It emanates from the value of democracy enshrined in Article 2 TEU and is part of a constitutional foundation of the Union. The manner in which the principle affects concretely the scope and content of the EU

[22] More on this question and the harmonious approach to diversity in unity, see *EUnited in diversity: between common constitutional traditions and national identities*. Conference proceedings. International Conference, Riga, Latvia, 2–3 September 2021.

[23] Case C-718/18 *Commission v Germany*, ECLI:EU:C:2021:662.

[24] ibid, paras 126 and 128.

[25] ibid, paras 124–25.

law provisions, as the case may be, is explained by the Court of Justice. It is important that in all areas of EU law the question is asked whether the legislative process and its end result have complied with the principle of democracy, as set out in the treaties and the Charter. In this task, national courts have an important role to play through the preliminary reference procedure in asking the relevant questions. It should be emphasised that the most notable contribution to the implementation of the general principle of democracy in the EU law is the legally binding Charter. European constitutional traditions exemplify that democracy, rule of law and human rights are the three inter-linked pillars for the conceptualisation of our societies and human interaction therein. The EU and the legal order that it is founded upon can meet the expectations of the European societies, when the area of freedom, security and justice, as well as the common internal market, function in accordance with these three inter-linked pillars. As provided for in Article 51(1) of the Charter, fundamental rights apply where Member States implement EU law as well as in relation to the EU institutions. It is to be expected that, as we continue to develop the Union, more and more its democratic functioning will be tested based on the examination of the application of the EU treaties and the secondary legislation in light of the fundamental rights provided for in the Charter and the general principles of the Union law, including and especially the principle of democracy.

12

The Principle of Solidarity and the Area of Freedom, Security and Justice

ULLA NEERGAARD*

I. INTRODUCTION[1]

> [S]olidarity ... is something that cannot be enforced – either it's there, or it isn't. I remember when during a debate on relocation at a European Council summit, it was suggested that, in our conclusions, we include the term 'the obligation of solidarity'. I protested, saying this was an obvious oxymoron ...[2]

WITH THESE FEW words, President of the European Council, Donald Tusk, in his farewell speech at the College of Europe in 2019 managed to express how both the substance and legal status of European solidarity have remained controversial and complex.[3] However, shortly after, the COVID-19 pandemic burst out, and when that had more or less finally calmed down, a war started raging in Europe with other large implications in its wake. By now, Europe is thus often referred to as being in the middle of a pluri-crisis, where the current dominant narrative has become to enumerate the many simultaneous crises that are occurring. In particular, this includes the, often interrelated, crises related to energy, climate and sustainability, defence and security, the economy and – in the context of this chapter – most importantly migration and refugees.

Due to the scale and gravity of the unprecedented problems, unsurprisingly the debate on solidarity in the European Union (EU) has thus reignited, gaining renewed political and academic attention as well as an increasing presence in the case law of the European Court of Justice (ECJ). In the more specific context of the Area of Freedom, Security and Justice (AFSJ), solidarity is also constantly being debated and it seems, in that regard of

* Professor of EU Law at the University of Copenhagen, Denmark.

[1] The chapter builds on reflections, which were first presented by its author at a lecture held together with Sybe de Vries entitled 'European Solidarities: Evolution and Multi-Dimensional Facets in Times of Emergence of a Pluri-crisis' (held at the XX Jean Monnet Seminar on 'The Challenges of Solidarity Resurfacing in the EU', 25–28 April 2023 at the Inter-University Centre, Dubrovnik, Croatia). Those reflections have to some degree also been presented in 'The Political, Economic and Social Physiognomy of the European Union', in A Kornezov (ed), *XXX FIDE Congress Publications*, Volume IV (Ciela Norma, forthcoming).

[2] 'Keynote speech by President Donald Tusk at the opening ceremony of the 2019/2020 academic year at the College of Europe', available at coleurope.eu/sites/default/files/speech-files/speech_donald_tusk.pdf?download=1, accessed 25 February 2024.

[3] See R Bieber, 'Book Review: Transnational Solidarity: Concept, Challenges and Opportunities, edited by Helle Krunke, Hanne Petersen and Ian Manners' (2022) 59 *Common Market Law Review* 262.

importance, that solidarity is given a prominent role in the central Treaty provisions (in Title V of the Treaty on the Functioning of the European Union (TFEU)) themselves. Thus, Article 67(2) TFEU (in Chapter 1 regarding 'General provisions') prescribes a 'common policy on asylum, immigration and external border control, based on solidarity between Member States, which is fair towards third-country nationals'. Also, Article 80 TFEU (in Chapter 2 regarding 'Policies on border checks, asylum and immigration') stipulates that '[t]he policies of the Union set out in this Chapter and their implementation shall be governed by the principle of solidarity and fair sharing of responsibility, including its financial implications, between the Member States'.[4] Despite solidarity thus being so specifically linked to the AFSJ, solidarity in that context appears just as controversial and complex as elsewhere in EU law.

The aim of this chapter is, with that background, to examine 'AFSJ solidarity'. Yet, the chapter does not seek to provide an exhaustive discussion of the multiple matters at stake, nor will it, for instance, advocate specific changes and reforms (and in that context plead for more or less solidarity in the area) or come up with exact definitions. It will more modestly strive to establish some fundamental understanding of European solidarity in newer times, which can be of relevance in the present context of the AFSJ. Although referring to works by authors from other disciplines, the approach taken is primarily EU law oriented, whilst bearing in mind that EU law scholars, in comparison to researchers in political theory, philosophy, social theory and sociology, have been rather slow to respond in-depth to the meaning and importance of solidarity in EU law.[5]

The chapter will first touch upon the core of the foundations of the concept 'solidarity' in EU law (Section II). Then the focus will turn to different categories of manifestations of European solidarity, which may possibly be identified (Section III), and, in general terms, subsequently relate these to solidarity in the AFSJ (Section IV). Finally, it will conclude by summarising the findings as well as by raising a few other, more general, points of concern (Section V).

II. FOUNDATIONS

EU law constitutes an important framework for translating solidarity values into legal concepts and realities.[6] In other words, EU law can provide an architectural design within which solidarity could be promoted.[7] Such an architectural design can legally shape many different kinds of solidarity mechanisms, organised on the basis of principles and norms. The design, including the degree of intensity of the presence of solidarity, can change over time.

[4] L Mastroianni, 'Solidarity in EU Immigration and Asylum Law: A Corpus Linguistic Analysis' in E Kassoti and N Idriz (eds), *The Principle of Solidarity. International and EU Law Perspectives* (Asser Press, 2023) 192, points out that Art 67(2) TFEU is framed in a way of protecting the state and requires cooperation not between the state and the individual but between the state and the EU. The author explains regarding Art 80 TFEU, at 193, that the purpose of applying the principle of solidarity not only in emergency situations, but also in day-to-day policymaking, is emphasised.

[5] A Biondi et al, 'Introduction: European Solidarity – What Now?' in A Biondi et al (eds), *Solidarity in EU Law. Legal Principle in the Making* (Edward Elgar, 2018) 7.

[6] P Van Cleynenbreugel, 'Typologies of Solidarities in EU Law: A Non-Shifting Landscape in the Wake of Economic Crises' in Biondi et al (eds) (n 5), 17.

[7] ibid, 18.

As is well known, the European Union emerged from the ashes of the Second World War, and is an experiment that is exceptional in its width and its collective basis.[8] The famous Schuman declaration of 9 May 1950, which is considered to be the first truly political manifesto of European integration, is a clear result of that.[9] As may be recalled, the declaration states that: 'Europe will not be made all at once, or according to a single plan. It will be built through concrete achievements which first create a de facto solidarity.'[10] Solidarity has thus always been considered to be closely aligned to a process of integration. In terms of development, a significant increase in the express use of solidarity and the importance accorded to it in the Treaties, case law, etc, over the years is evident. This is not at all surprising, given the close connection between integration and solidarity.

As a brick laid down in the building of a European identity, solidarity has many notable attributes, because in Europe it has such a very long history, which begins much, much earlier than the establishment of the EU or the European Economic Community (EEC). In fact, it predates the EEC by at least a couple of thousand years. Thus, at the conceptual level, it is genuinely something that is shared among Europeans, and this is reflected in the second sentence of Article 2 in the Treaty on the European Union (TEU).

Despite its long existence, it is in no way an easy task to define solidarity, because over time it has had various meanings and has been conceptualised in many different ways. Even today, it remains indeterminate. Abat I Ninet has pointed at a number of reasons why it is not easy to define solidarity as such. These include:

> [...] the complexity and forms of solidarity (horizontal, vertical, organic, mechanical), the lack of a precise legal definition, the effects of the process of juridification to the normative definition of the principle of solidarity, the link solidarity has with other principles and values (loyalty, cooperation, cohesion, subsidiarity), and its material implications for internal and external policies.[11]

The roots of European solidarity may (in part) be traced, for instance, in religion; and in the laws of nation states. A certain understanding of solidarity may also be established by reference to the word's etymology, as well as through different political movements throughout history. Even today, solidarity can at times serve as a political catchword. The campaigns led by young people to save the climate for future generations – which have given the concept new vitality – is one such example.[12] Concurrently, solidarity now has been analysed and discussed theoretically in many different academic disciplines, besides law, for at least a century. The power of the word probably stems from its many different roots, which engender flexibility, durability and emotional intensity.[13]

Nevertheless, both the substance and legal status of European solidarity have remained controversial and complex. Therefore, solidarity remains an EU legal conundrum and is likely to stay that way for a long time.

[8] N Karagiannis, 'Chains of Solidarity. Violence and Debt' in H Krunke et al (eds), *Transnational Solidarity. Concept, Challenges and Opportunities* (Cambridge University Press, 2020) 64.

[9] Biondi et al (n 5), 2.

[10] See eg 'Roberts Schuman: Architect of the European Integration Project' https://european-union.europa.eu/principles-countries-history/history-eu/eu-pioneers/robert-schuman_en, accessed 25 February 2024.

[11] A Abat i Ninet, 'Transnational Claims in the European Union and the Founding Principle of Solidarity' in Krunke et al (eds) (n 8), 208.

[12] S-E Liedman, 'Solidarity: A Short History from the Concept's Beginnings to the Present Situation' in Krunke et al (eds) (n 8), 11.

[13] ibid, 14.

III. MANIFESTATIONS

Garben has recently pleaded for '[…] a stronger legal obligation on Member States to fully commit to both acts of reciprocity-based solidarity (cooperation and redistribution), and that this should take place in a specifically dignity-oriented way […]'.[14] In the same direction, Advocate General Sharpston, as she then was, said:

> Solidarity is the lifeblood of the European project. Through their participation in that project and their citizenship of European Union, Member States and their nationals have obligations as well as benefits, duties as well as rights. Sharing in the European 'demos' is not a matter of looking through the Treaties and the secondary legislation to see what one can claim. It also requires one to shoulder collective responsibilities and (yes) burdens to further the common good. Respecting the 'rules of the club' and playing one's proper part in solidarity with fellow Europeans cannot be based on a penny-pinching cost-benefit analysis along the lines (familiar, alas, from Brexiteer rhetoric) of 'what precisely does the EU cost me per week and what exactly do I personally get out of it?' Such self-centredness is a betrayal of the founding fathers' vision for a peaceful and prosperous continent. It is the antithesis of being a loyal Member State and being worthy, as an individual, of shared European citizenship. If the European project is to prosper and go forward, we must all do better than that.[15]

Others might rather plead for as little commitment as possible.

Anyhow, solidarity in the context of EU law has so far – in simplified terms – mainly manifested in two general ways. These may be observed to exist often side by side.[16] Each displays different 'degrees of intensity' and can, in principle, be viewed as related to a given level of development of the EU as to its 'maturity'; the assumption implicitly being that the EU may increasingly move in the direction of resembling the organisation and institutionalisation of solidarity in complex national societies. Also, the interest here is primarily – but not exclusively – on solidarity between Member States, as most often organised through the EU-institutional framework. According to Schiek, this kind of solidarity may at the same time then include indirect solidarity between the citizens.[17] The interest thus primarily lies in an EU-internal perspective rather than also an external perspective. At the same time, outside the scope of interest, for example, is the altruistic solidarity between EU citizens exercised at a completely personal level without any severe legal organisation involved; or solidarity within a given Member State organised legally between the state in question and its citizens (except where that is a necessary prerequisite for the EU-transnational solidarity which is the main focus).

Against that background, the first manifestation that may be identified is characterised by not being underpinned by many commitments, as it is mainly concerned with cooperation and harmonisation. In other words, this type of solidarity is concerned with the most common kind of EU action aiming at deepening European integration. Here, importantly, there is no significant transfer of resources or burden-sharing taking place. Therefore, although solidarity exists, it is not, after all, connected with a high degree of obligations.

[14] S Garben, 'Dignity- and Reciprocity-Based Solidarity as the Normative Framework of the EU's Constitutional Settlement' in A-C Hartzén et al (eds), *Law, Solidarity and the Limits of Social Europe. Constitutional Tensions for EU Integration* (Edward Elgar, 2022) 180–81.

[15] See Opinion of AG Sharpston in Joined Cases C-715/17, C-719/17 and C-719/17 *European Commission v Republic of Poland, Republic of Hungary, and Czech Republic*, ECLI:EU:C:2019:917, paras 253–54.

[16] See in that respect eg D Schiek, 'Solidarity in the Case Law of the European Court of Justice Opportunities Missed?' in Krunke et al (eds) (n 8), 254 and 263.

[17] ibid, 263.

The second manifestation to be identified includes more obligations than the first. It would require redistribution at some level. Here, a more intense supranational, positive regulatory action to the detriment of national political and redistributive competences takes place. This manifestation of solidarity is likely to be reciprocity-based so that regulatory redistribution of advantages and disadvantages across Member States occur.[18] The EU citizenship entitlements for individuals, social security entitlements and labour conditions across the Member States, possibilities for a common European research and development framework, a European industrial policy and an enhancement programme for peripheral regions in Member States are examples of such actions.[19]

However, a third manifestation of solidarity might also be identified. This manifestation of European solidarity could be viewed as including EU action at a very sophisticated level. It thus reflects the idea that the EU has 'matured' to the extent that it has moved, or will move, towards having at least most elements of the idea of a 'transfer union' as put forward by the Nobel-prize winning economist, Stiglitz.[20] It could, in other words, be seen as genuinely based on an expanded version of the original Roman civil law concept, '*obligatio in solidum*'. However, that is now in an EU-constitutionalised form, requiring Member States, in principle, to be responsible in an – imagined – similar manner.

Stiglitz understands the term 'transfer union' as the Member States transferring resources to each other, even temporarily, in a time of need.[21] An example would be the recovery package provided in the wake of the COVID-19 crisis. In principle, such a manifestation of solidarity would, in other words, imply an obligation on all Member States to be held responsible in any given case. Solidarity could thereby become solidarity among strangers, helping others in need, and hence not necessarily reciprocity-based.[22] It would be one for all; all for one.[23]

These three simplified categories serve to paint a generalised picture with a broad brush. It is indicated that the first category is seen as the least committing category (and mainly anchored around cooperation/harmonisation and not necessarily connected with transfers of resources). The second is with respect to commitment, situated somewhere in between the first and the third categories (and mainly anchored around redistribution and most likely reciprocity-based). Finally, the third category is understood as being the most committing (and mainly anchored around resource transferring not necessarily being reciprocity-based). The first category can thus more specifically be viewed as including the most common kind of EU action, whereas the second category indicates a certain increased level of intensity as to commitment in comparison with the first category.[24] Finally, the third category is viewed as

[18] See in that direction Van Cleynenbreugel (n 6), 21.

[19] ibid.

[20] See J Stiglitz, *The Euro and Its Threat to the Future of Europe* (Penguin Random House, 2016) 22.

[21] ibid, where Stiglitz more precisely explains: 'When a group of countries shares a common currency, success requires more than just good institutions. For reforms to work, decisions have to be made, and those decisions will reflect the understandings and values of the decision-makers. There have to be common understandings and values of the decision-makers of what makes for a successful economy and a minimal level of 'solidarity', or social cohesion, where countries that are in a strong position help those that are in need. Today, there is no such understanding, no real sense of social cohesion. Germany says repeatedly that the Eurozone is not a 'transfer union' – that is, an economic grouping in which one country transfers resources to another, even temporarily in a time of need.'

[22] H Brunkhorst, 'Democratic Solidarity between Global Crisis and Cosmopolitan Hope' in Krunke et al (eds) (n 8), 43.

[23] ibid.

[24] In that regard, see eg C Lahusen, 'Civic Solidarity in Transnational Spaces. Organisation and Institutionalisation of Solidarity within the European Union' in Krunke et al (eds) (n 8), 310, who explains: '[S]ocial science research has insisted on the assumption that solidarity in complex societies is organised and institutionalised by means of redistributive policies and measures, and is thus basically institutionalised in the form of the modern welfare state

including EU action at a more sophisticated level in relation to solidarity, thereby reflecting that the EU has 'matured' so much that it has moved towards having elements of a 'transfer union', ie a kind of an EU-constitutionalised '*obligatio in solidum*' principle.

IV. DIRECTIONS

When Europe faces migration and asylum crises, Member States are expected as an expression of solidarity to help each other by financial and other means, thus alleviating the burden of the most pressured Member States, ie sharing the burden and responsibility collectively.[25] Against that background, it may be of relevance to consider whether the EU is moving towards establishing a so-called 'transfer union', ie a kind of an EU-constitutionalised '*obligatio in solidum*' in the the AFSJ, thus creating a special 'AFSJ solidarity'. For the present purposes, the following analysis is limited to a few, yet essential, examples of judgments rendered by the ECJ.

In that regard, it is of interest that, in generalised terms, solidarity in EU law seems to continuously manifest itself as stronger and stronger in character. This point of view may, in particular, be supported by reference to the *Opal* case (about a gas pipeline in relation to rules on third-party access and tariffs). Here, the Grand Chamber of the ECJ – as the preliminary culmination of a long line of cases embracing the concept of solidarity – in the summer of 2021 stipulated that:

> [T]he principle of solidarity underpins the entire legal system of the European Union [...] and it is closely linked to the principle of sincere cooperation, laid down in Article 4(3) TEU, pursuant to which the European Union and the Member States are, in full mutual respect, to assist each other in carrying out tasks which flow from the Treaties. In that regard, the Court has held, inter alia, that that principle not only obliges the Member States to take all the measures necessary to guarantee the application and effectiveness of EU law but also imposes on the EU institutions mutual duties to cooperate in good faith with the Member States [...].[26]

In that context, the allegedly abstract nature of the principle of solidarity, often said to be a mere political concept, is – at least with respect to what is referred to as 'energy solidarity' – opposed, as the ECJ also stated that:

> [T]here is nothing that would permit the inference that the principle of solidarity referred to in Article 194(1) TFEU cannot, as such, produce binding legal effects on the Member States and institutions of the European Union. On the contrary, as the Advocate General noted in points 76 and 77 of his Opinion, that principle, as is apparent from the wording and structure of that provision, forms the basis of all of the objectives of the European Union's energy policy, serving as the thread that brings them together and gives them coherence.[27]

In addition, the ECJ stressed that acts adopted by the EU institutions, including by the Commission under that policy, must be interpreted, and their legality assessed, in the light of the principle of 'energy solidarity'.[28] Furthermore, that principle, like general principles of EU

[...] Conversely to traditional charity and care, as provided by the family, church, neighbourhood or nobility, solidarity is a legally codified right, thus implying enforceable obligations and entitlements on the side of recipients and contributors.'

[25] I Goldner Lang, 'The EU Financial and Migration Crises: Two Crises – Many Facets of EU Solidarity' in Biondi et al (eds) (n 5), 133.

[26] Case C-848/19 P *Federal Republic of Germany v European Commission*, ECLI:EU:C:2021:598, para 41.

[27] ibid, paras 42–43.

[28] ibid, para 44.

law, is seen as constituting a criterion for assessing the legality of measures adopted by the EU institutions.[29] Also, it becomes clear that the principle entails rights and obligations both for the EU and for the Member States. The EU is bound by an obligation of solidarity towards the Member States, and the Member States are bound by an obligation of solidarity between themselves and with regard to the common interest of the EU and the policies pursued by it.[30]

Importantly, the ECJ in the *Opal* case also emphasised:

> As regards the allegedly abstract nature of the principle of solidarity, invoked by the Federal Republic of Germany in order to argue that it cannot be used in the context of judicial review of the legality of Commission acts, it must be pointed out that the Court, as the Advocate General noted in point 69 of his Opinion, expressly referred to the principle of solidarity mentioned in Article 80 TFEU in coming to the conclusion that, in essence, Member States had failed to fulfil certain of their obligations under EU law on border controls, asylum and immigration (judgments of 6 September 2017, *Slovakia and Hungary v Council*, C-643/15 and C-647/15, EU:C:2017:631, paragraph 291, and of 2 April 2020, *Commission v Poland, Hungary and Czech Republic (Temporary mechanism for the relocation of applicants for international protection)*, C-715/17, C-718/17 and C-719/17, EU:C:2020:257, paragraphs 80 and 181).[31]

The ECJ has now, in the *Opal* case, clearly ruled that the principle of solidarity entails rights and obligations both for the EU and for the Member States.[32] This could, in all likelihood be seen to be in contrast to the statement of Tusk referred to above. In this context, reference should also be made to the principle of sincere cooperation enshrined in Article 4(3) TEU, which is often referred to by the ECJ as a kind of almost magic amplifier of solidarity.[33] Also, it has become clear that the principle of solidarity may – at least for the time being – be viewed as consisting of sub-categories of a general principle of solidarity, as the *Opal* judgment was mainly concerned with 'energy solidarity'. Thus, depending on the context at issue, it may be conceptually useful and correct to refer to solidarities (in the plural).[34] Other sub-categories of a general principle of solidarity, such as 'AFSJ solidarity' – perhaps with a different understanding – may thus exist in parallel.[35]

In fact, the subject area in which the ECJ has made notable use of the concept of solidarity as a key component, is in the interpretation of the abovementioned Article 80 TFEU relating to the policies of immigration, asylum and border control.[36] As explained by Advocate General

[29] ibid, para 45.

[30] ibid, para 49.

[31] ibid, para 42.

[32] ibid, para 49.

[33] The ECJ has in that regard stated in Case C-514/19 *Union des industries de la protection des plantes*, ECLI:EU:C:2020:803, para 49, that: '[U]nder the principle of sincere cooperation enshrined in Article 4(3) TEU, the European Union and the Member States must, in full mutual respect, assist each other in carrying out tasks which arise from the Treaties. In that regard, the ECJ has held, inter alia, that that principle not only obliges the Member States to take all the measures necessary to guarantee the application and effectiveness of EU law but also imposes on the EU institutions mutual duties to cooperate in good faith with the Member States (judgments of 4 September 2014, *Spain v Commission*, C-192/13 P, EU:C:2014:2156, paragraph 87, and of 19 December 2019, *Amoena*, C-677/18, EU:C:2019:1142, paragraph 55).'

[34] See in that regard, Bieber (n 3), 264; N Karagiannis (ed), *European Solidarity* (Liverpool University Press, 2007) 1–12; and, in particular, the title of R Coman et al (eds), *Les solidarités européennes: Entre enjeux, tensions et reconfigurations* (Bruylant, 2019).

[35] See eg Opinion of AG Sánchez-Bordana in Case C-848/19 P *Federal Republic of Germany v European Commission*, ECLI:EU:C:2021:218, para 97, where it is said that where 'the Treaties have sought to emphasise the purely political component of solidarity, they have done so expressly. This can be seen in the specific provisions on the common foreign and security policy, among which Article 24(2) and (3) TEU refers to the "mutual political solidarity" of the Member States.'

[36] ibid, para 68.

Campos Sánchez-Bordana, the ECJ has explicitly invoked the principle of solidarity in cases where it has had to adjudicate on the distribution between the Member States of quotas of applicants for international protection.[37] In that regard, he has pointed out that – after stating that, in accordance with Article 80 TFEU, the principle of solidarity governs the Union's asylum policy – the ECJ has relied on that principle in order to draw appropriate legal consequences, including the upholding of actions brought by the Commission against Member States, which had failed to fulfil their obligations in that regard.[38] The cases of particular interest in relation to 'AFSJ solidarity' are two that were also highlighted by the ECJ in the *Opal* case.[39] In the first of these, namely *Slovak Republic and Hungary v Council*, the ECJ crucially stated that:

> When one or more Member States are faced with an emergency situation within the meaning of Article 78(3) TFEU, the burdens entailed by the provisional measures adopted under that provision for the benefit of that or those Member States must, as a rule, be divided between all the other Member States, in accordance with the principle of solidarity and fair sharing of responsibility between the Member States, since, in accordance with Article 80 TFEU, that principle governs EU asylum policy.[40]

Furthermore, the ECJ decided that:

> If, as the Republic of Poland maintains, the mechanism provided for in Article 5(7) of the contested decision were ineffective because it requires Member States to check large numbers of persons in a short time, such practical difficulties are not inherent in the mechanism and must, should they arise, be resolved in the spirit of cooperation and mutual trust between the authorities of the Member States that are beneficiaries of relocation and those of the Member States of relocation. That spirit of cooperation and mutual trust must prevail when the relocation procedure provided for in Article 5 of the contested decision is implemented.[41]

Advocate General Sharpston, as she then was, has therefore understood the case – and in particular the latter of the two quoted premises – as meaning that in:

> [...] what was clearly an emergency situation, it was the responsibility of *both* the frontline Member States *and* the potential Member States of relocation to make that mechanism work adequately, so that relocation could take place in sufficient numbers to relieve the intolerable pressure on the front-line Member States.[42]

She added that that is what solidarity is about.

As to the second of the two central judgments referred to by the ECJ in the *Opal* case, namely *Commission v Poland, Hungary and Czech Republic*, regarding the temporary mechanism for the relocation of applicants for international protection, it was in line with the above and stipulated:

> As already pointed out in paragraph 80 of the present judgment, the burdens entailed by the provisional measures provided for in Decisions 2015/1523 and 2015/1601, since they were adopted under Article 78(3) TFEU for the purpose of helping the Hellenic Republic and the Italian Republic to better cope with an emergency situation characterised by a sudden influx of third-country nationals on their territory, must, in principle, be divided between all the other Member States, in accordance

[37] ibid, para 69.

[38] ibid.

[39] *Federal Republic of Germany v European Commission* (n 26), para 42.

[40] Joined Cases C-643/15 and C-647/15 *Slovak Republic and Hungary v Council of the European Union*, ECLI:EU:C:2017:631, para 291.

[41] ibid, para 309.

[42] Opinion of AG Sharpston in *European Commission v Republic of Poland and Others* (n 15), para 234.

> with the principle of solidarity and fair sharing of responsibility between the Member States, which, in accordance with Article 80 TFEU, governs the Union's asylum policy.[43]

Thus, on that basis, it may with some right – as claimed by the Advocate General Campos Sánchez-Bordana – be held that, even though the principle of solidarity is multifaceted and deployed at different levels, its importance in primary law as a value and an objective in the process of European integration is such that it may be regarded as significant enough to create legal consequences.[44] As also emphasised by him:

> Central to the approach thus taken by the Court is a particular conception of the normative value of the Treaties: their provisions serve the same purpose as any provision having constitutional status and it falls to the body required to interpret them (ultimately, the Court of Justice) to determine the prescriptiveness of their content. It is true that the variety of forms in which the principle of solidarity manifests itself makes it difficult for that principle to be applied in the same way and to the same extent in all areas of EU competence. I would emphasise, however, that there is no reason not to regard solidarity, in some of those areas of competence, as having the capacity to operate as a 'guiding principle' for the actions of the European Union in those fields, in which cases this has an impact on its effects in law. This is true of the principle of solidarity in the context of asylum policy and must, by analogy, also be true in the context of energy policy.[45]

This makes it very clear that 'AFSJ solidarity' has by now manifested itself in continuously stronger ways and, significantly, it now contains elements of at least the first two of the above-mentioned kinds of manifestations, and possibly also the third.

This development may at the same time be seen as reflected in the 'New Pact on Migration and Asylum' of the EU, which has been called historic. It intends to create a set of regulations and policies to create a fairer, efficient, and more sustainable migration and asylum process for the EU, and seeks to establish a common approach to migration and asylum that is based on solidarity, responsibility, and respect for human rights.[46] It includes the so-called 'Solidarity Declaration', which aims to provide a voluntary, simple and predictable solidarity mechanism designed to support the Member States most affected in the Mediterranean as well as other Member States under pressure, including on the Western Atlantic route, by offering relocations, financial contributions and other measures of support.[47]

[43] Joined Cases C-715/17, C-718/17 and C-719/17 *Commission v Poland, Hungary and Czech Republic*, ECLI:EU:C:2020:257, para 181. Also see ibid, para 80, in which it is stated: 'It is important to recall that the burdens entailed by the provisional measures provided for in Decisions 2015/1523 and 2015/1601, since they were adopted under Art 78(3) TFEU for the purpose of helping the Hellenic Republic and the Italian Republic to better cope with an emergency situation characterised by a sudden influx of third-country nationals on their territory, must, in principle, be divided between all the other Member States, in accordance with the principle of solidarity and fair sharing of responsibility between the Member States, since, in accordance with Article 80 TFEU, that principle governs the Union's asylum policy (see, to that effect, judgment of 6 September 2017, *Slovakia and Hungary v Council*, C-643/15 and C-647/15, EU:C:2017:631, paragraph 291).'

[44] Opinion of AG Sánchez-Bordana in *Federal Republic of Germany v European Commission* (n 35), para 70.

[45] ibid, paras 71–73.

[46] See further https://home-affairs.ec.europa.eu/policies/migration-and-asylum/new-pact-migration-and-asylum_en, accessed 25 February 2024. Also see eg H Gray, 'Solidarity in European Union Law. More an Abstract Ideal than a Substantive Principle?' in F Tava and N Quénivet (eds), *European Solidarity. Interdisciplinary Perspectives* (ECPR Press, 2023) 77; and E Karageorgiou, 'Why the European Commission's Pragmatic Approach to Asylum Is Not Enough: Re-imagining Solidarity as a New Form of Conducting Regional Politics' in Kassoti and Idriz (eds) (n 4), 163.

[47] See further eg Commission, 'Migration and Asylum: Commission Welcomes Today's Progress in the Council on the New Pact of Migration and Asylum' https://ec.europa.eu/commission/presscorner/detail/en/ip_22_3970, accessed 25 February 2024; and Commission, 'Effective Solidarity' https://commission.europa.eu/strategy-and-policy/priorities-2019-2024/promoting-our-european-way-life/migration-and-asylum/new-pact-migration-and-asylum/effective-solidarity_en, accessed 25 February 2024.

V. CONCLUSION

In closing, the above analysis has provided a general background understanding of solidarity in EU law by taking a contextual and slightly evolutionary perspective, thereby demonstrating that although the concept is controversial and complex, it is no longer merely a political concept, but rather is moving towards becoming more and more committing. This seems to especially hold true with regard to 'AFSJ solidarity'.

However, although it appears that big steps have been taken in recent times, the challenges as to solidarity in dimensions related to the 'AFSJ' are far from being overcome, and one may wonder whether they ever could be.[48] Some would claim that the prospects of further institutionalising 'AFSJ solidarity' within the EU are dependent on obtaining sufficient public support from EU citizens.[49] They would also say that such a development is unlikely, for the simple reason that Europe lacks the requisite relative homogeneity, and that such homogeneity would depend on viewing others as good people and – equally important – as likeminded on matters such as reciprocity and fairness.[50] Some would remain antagonistic to the further strengthening of 'AFSJ solidarity', not finding it desirable at all. On the contrary, others would support such a development.[51] In any event, the conceptual framework and the degree of intensity sought – according to which such discussions may take place – would gain from solidarity in EU law being further defined, as an initial step.

[48] See eg J Bengoetxea, 'The Solidarity Constitution in the EU: Refugees and Asylum as Litmus Test' in Hartzén et al (eds) (n 14), 117.

[49] Lahusen (n 24), 310.

[50] A Somek, 'Postnational European Democracy Aristotelian Caveats' in Krunke et al (n 8), 250–51.

[51] Van Cleynenbreugel (n 6), 21.

13

Ne Bis in Idem *and EU Law:* *A Critical View of Recent Judgments*

STEVE PEERS*

I. INTRODUCTION

For nearly 30 years, since the Schengen Convention began to be applied in 1995, there have been a set of rules on the application of the *ne bis in idem* (double jeopardy) in transnational cases across EU Member States – eventually extending to all EU Member States and beyond, to include the Schengen associated countries.[1] This has subsequently been complemented by the Charter of Fundamental Rights, eventually binding, which includes also a cross-border double jeopardy rule in its Article 50, alongside a more traditional ban on double jeopardy within a single jurisdiction.[2] But the role of the Schengen rules remains central, and moreover unique – as national constitutions and international human rights instruments set out only a national version of the rule, and other attempts at international harmonisation have attracted few ratifications.[3]

With the integration of the Schengen *acquis* into the EU legal order in 1999, including a limited form of jurisdiction for the European Court of Justice (ECJ), replaced by the normal jurisdiction of the Court after the Treaty of Lisbon came into force, the ECJ began to play a key role in the interpretation of the rules. While the volume of its case law on *ne bis in idem* has now been dwarfed by the volume of its case law on the European arrest warrant, it still remains the second biggest chunk of case law on criminal law and policing matters, and has addressed a lot of important issues arising from the rules.

Although the case law raises a number of issues, this chapter focuses on those that might be said to broach key tensions as regards the concept of the area of freedom, security and justice. First of all, who is covered by this freedom? Second, does it extend even to extradition

* Professor of Law at Royal Holloway, University of London, UK.

[1] On these rules, see B van Bockel (ed), *Ne Bis in Idem in EU Law* (Cambridge University Press, 2016); E Sharpston and J Maria Fernandez-Martin, 'Some Reflections on Schengen Free Movement Rights and the Principle of *Ne Bis in Idem*' (2008) 10 *Cambridge Yearbook of European Legal Studies* 413; and S Peers, 'Double Jeopardy and EU Law: Time for a Change?' (2006) 8 *European Journal of Law Reform* 199.

[2] See the analysis of Art 50 by J Tomkin in T Hervey et al (eds), *The EU Charter of Fundamental Rights: A Commentary*, 2nd edn (Hart Publishing, 2021) 1505.

[3] Council of Europe Convention on the transfer of criminal proceedings (ETS 73), Arts 35–37; Council of Europe Convention on the international validity of criminal judgments (ETS 70) Arts 53–55. See also Art 9 of the Council of Europe Convention on extradition (ETS 24), as revised by Art 2 of the First Protocol to that Convention (ETS 86); these provisions are more widely ratified but more limited in scope.

to non-EU countries? Third, how much should Member States be permitted to derogate from the double jeopardy rule, given that it is also classified as a fundamental right?

The Schengen double jeopardy rules play an important role in transnational criminal proceedings because, unlike in the areas of civil law or asylum applications, neither the EU nor any other body has set out rules allocating jurisdiction or choice of law as regards criminal prosecutions.[4] While both EU and international law require Member States to assert their jurisdiction over various specific criminal offences in various ways, there is no rule determining which jurisdiction applies if – as will often be the consequence of the jurisdiction rules, because they usually permit or even require extraterritorial jurisdiction – more than one State could prosecute. There is an EU Framework Decision on conflict of jurisdiction, but it does not allocate jurisdiction as such;[5] neither does the proposed Regulation on transfer of proceedings.[6] So while the civil law cases on irreconcilable judgments play a subsidiary role, because there are jurisdiction rules which play the primary role, in the area of criminal law it is the rules on double jeopardy which play the primary role, due to the absence of rules allocating jurisdiction.

II. TEXT OF THE RULES

The *ne bis in idem* rules are set out in Articles 54–58 of the Schengen Convention, which is roughly based on a prior European Political Cooperation Convention that did not come into force, itself roughly based on prior Council of Europe Conventions that attracted few ratifications.

First of all, Article 54 of the Schengen Convention sets out the main rule, which applies subject to a prior sentence having been enforced, or being enforced, unless it can no longer be enforced (the 'enforcement condition'):

> A person whose trial has been finally disposed of in one Contracting Party may not be prosecuted in another Contracting Party for the same acts provided that, if a penalty has been imposed, it has been enforced, is actually in the process of being enforced or can no longer be enforced under the laws of the sentencing Contracting Party.

Exceptions to the rule appear in Article 55 of the Convention:

> 1. A Contracting Party may, when ratifying, accepting or approving this Convention, declare that it is not bound by Article 54 in one or more of the following cases:
>   (a) where the acts to which the foreign judgment relates took place in whole or in part in its own territory; in the latter case, however, this exception shall not apply if the acts took place in part in the territory of the Contracting Party where the judgment was delivered;
>   (b) where the acts to which the foreign judgment relates constitute an offence against national security or other equally essential interests of that Contracting Party;
>   (c) where the acts to which the foreign judgment relates were committed by officials of that Contracting Party in violation of the duties of their office.

[4] On cooperation in civil matters, see S Peers, *EU Justice and Home Affairs Law*, vol 2, 5th edn (Oxford University Press, 2023) ch 8. The issues of jurisdiction and choice of law are inextricably linked for criminal law and asylum law, but not for civil law.

[5] Council Framework Decision 2009/948/JHA of 30 November 2009 on prevention and settlement of conflicts of exercise of jurisdiction in criminal proceedings [2009] OJ L328/42.

[6] Proposal for a Regulation for a Regulation of the European Parliament and of the Council on the transfer of proceedings in criminal matters COM (2023) 185 final.

2. A Contracting Party which has made a declaration regarding the exception referred to in paragraph 1(b) shall specify the categories of offences to which this exception may apply.
3. A Contracting Party may at any time withdraw a declaration relating to one or more of the exceptions referred to in paragraph 1.
4. The exceptions which were the subject of a declaration under paragraph 1 shall not apply where the Contracting Party concerned has, in connection with the same acts, requested the other Contracting Party to bring the prosecution or has granted extradition of the person concerned.

The Commission has reported that a number of Member States have invoked the first two exceptions, but none have invoked the third exception.[7] These declarations have not been published, although two of them appear in ECJ judgments.[8] It appears from the judgments, though, that the Commission's reporting on the declarations is not fully accurate;[9] it is hard to check because the declarations do not seem to have been published. For its part, the Council also refers to declarations by Norway (as a Schengen associate), France and Italy (which were not notified as required), and the issue of whether newer Member States can make declarations.[10] In Italy and Greece, national courts have ruled that declarations are invalid.[11]

Next, Article 56 of the Schengen Convention provides for deduction of penalties in the event of multiple prosecutions, while Article 57 provides for cooperation between Member States. Finally, Article 58 provides for the possibility of more generous national rules on *ne bis in idem*.

There was a specific *ne bis in idem* rule in the Convention on the Protection of the EU's Financial Interests,[12] but this has now been replaced (for most Member States) by a Directive which has no special double jeopardy rule.[13] There is still a distinct rule in the Convention on corruption,[14] although the Commission has proposed also replacing this with a Directive (again with no special double jeopardy rule).[15] The relevant provisions are nearly (but not quite) identical; there is no case law on the relationship between the general and specific rules.

[7] Commission staff working document – Annex to the Green Paper on conflicts of jurisdiction and the principle of ne bis in idem in criminal proceedings COM (2005) 696 final, p 47 and n 97, which states that Austria, Denmark, Greece, and Finland invoked both Art 55(1)(a) and (b) of the Schengen Convention, while Germany, Sweden, and the UK (pre-Brexit) invoked only its Art 55(1)(a).

[8] Case C-486/14 *Kossowski*, ECLI:EU:C:2016:483, para 7, which sets out the German declaration as regards Art 55(1)(a); and Case C-365/21 *MR*, ECLI:EU:C:2023:236, para 10, which sets out the German declaration as regards Art 55(1)(b) of the Schengen Convention.

[9] Germany has made a declaration as regards both Art 55(1)(a) and Art 55(1)(b) of the Schengen Convention.

[10] See Note from the Council Presidency to the Article 36 Committee, 'Declarations by Member States pursuant to Article 55 of the Schengen Convention' Brussels 1 June 2006, 10061/06 (COPEN 61, COMIX 514, p 2).

[11] Opinion of AG Szpunar in Case C-365/21 *MR*, ECLI:EU:C:2022:823, paras 29–30. At n 31, the Opinion states that Switzerland and Liechtenstein also made declarations.

[12] Council Act of 26 July 1995 drawing up the Convention on the protection of the European Communities' financial interests [1995] OJ C316/48, Art 7.

[13] Directive (EU) 2017/1371 of the European Parliament and of the Council of 5 July 2017 on the fight against fraud to the Union's financial interests by means of criminal law [2017] OJ L198/29. Denmark is still bound by the Convention, but not the Directive.

[14] Council Act of 26 May 1997 drawing up, on the basis of Article K.3(2)(c) of the Treaty on European Union, the Convention on the fight against corruption involving officials of the European Communities or officials of Member States of the European Union [1997] OJ C195/1, Art 10.

[15] Proposal for a Directive of the European Parliament and of the Council on combating corruption, replacing Council Framework Decision 2003/568/JHA and the Convention on the fight against corruption involving officials of the European Communities or officials of Member States of the European Union and amending Directive (EU) 2017/1371 of the European Parliament and of the Council COM (2023) 234 final.

III. INTERPRETATION

As already noted, there is a significant body of ECJ case law on the interpretation of the Schengen double jeopardy rules.[16] In general, the case law has stressed the link between Article 54 of the Convention and free movement, stating that the objective of the rule 'is to ensure that no one is prosecuted on the same facts in several Member States on account of his having exercised his right to freedom of movement'.[17] In this context, free movement entails that a person who has served a sentence if found guilty of an offence, or been acquitted, 'may travel within the Schengen territory without fear of prosecution in another Member State on the basis that the legal system of that Member State treats the act concerned as a separate offence'.[18] As with other areas of justice and home affairs cooperation, this takes place on the basis of mutual trust, without underlying harmonisation of criminal law being necessary.[19] But conversely, the ECJ has stressed that the double jeopardy rules also form an aspect of the Treaty's criminal law objectives.[20]

A. Personal Scope of the Double Jeopardy Rule

The link with free movement might seem to suggest that the protection of the double jeopardy principle can only be invoked by those who enjoy free movement: EU citizens, nationals of EEA EFTA countries and Switzerland, and accompanying family members. However, from the outset the ECJ assumed in practice that non-EU citizens could also invoke the rule.[21]

Subsequently, in the *HF* judgment, the ECJ was asked to address the point explicitly. The case concerned a Serbian citizen who was the subject of extradition proceedings in Germany on the basis of an extradition request from the US; he had already been prosecuted and convicted for the same acts in Slovenia.[22] The ECJ confirmed that non-EU nationals do indeed fall within the scope of Article 54 of the Schengen Convention. First of all, Article 54 refers to a 'person', making no distinction on the basis of nationality. Second, Article 50 of the Charter, the double jeopardy provision, made no such distinction either; nor was it placed in the 'citizens' rights' provisions of the Charter. As for the objectives of the Schengen rules, they aimed not only to facilitate free movement but also legal certainty, and they applied to non-EU citizens because

[16] Joined Cases C-187/01 and C-385/01 *Gözütok and Brügge*, ECLI:EU:C:2003:87; Cases C-469/03 *Miraglia*, ECLI:EU:C:2005:156; C-436/04 *van Esbroek*, ECLI:C:2006:165; C-467/04 *Gasparini*, ECLI:EU:C:2006:610; C-150/05 *Van Straaten*, ECLI:EU:C:2006:614; C-288/05 *Kretzinger*, ECLI:EU:C:2007:441; C-367/05 *Kraaijenbrink*, ECLI:EU:C:2007:444; C-297/07 *Bourquain*, ECLI: EU:C:2008:708; C-491/07 *Turansky*, ECLI:EU:C:2008:768; C-129/14 PPU *Spasic*, ECLI:EU:C:2014:586; C-398/12 *M*, ECLI:EU:C:2014:1057; *Kossowski* (n 8); C-234/17 *XC*, ECLI:EU:C:2018:853; C-505/19 *WS*, ECLI:EU:C:2021:376; C-435/22 PPU *HF*, ECLI:EU:C:2022:852; *MR* (n 8); C-726/21 *GR*, ECLI:EU:C:2023:764; C-27/22 *Volkswagen*, ECLI:EU:C:2023:663; C-147/22 *S*, ECLI:EU:C:2023:790; and C-164/22 *Juan*, ECLI:EU:C:2023:684. See also, as regards the *ne bis in idem* exception to the European arrest warrant, Case C-268/17 *AY*, ECLI:EU:C:2018:602.

[17] Case law starting with *Gözütok and Brügge* (n 16), para 38.

[18] Case law beginning with *van Esbroek* (n 16), para 34.

[19] Case law beginning with *Gözütok and Brügge* (n 16), para 32 and *van Esbroek* (n 16), para 29.

[20] See, for instance, *Spasic* (n 16), paras 61–62, referring to Art 3(2) TEU and Art 67(3) TFEU.

[21] *Gözütok* concerned a Turkish citizen, while *Spasic* (n 16) concerned a Serbian citizen. It is striking that the ECJ did not examine the point even though in its *Gözütok and Brügge* (n 16) judgment it made extensive reference to the link between free movement and the Schengen double jeopardy rules. The Opinions of the Advocates General in those cases do not consider the point either, see Opinion of AG Ruiz-Jarabo Colomer in Case C-187/01 *Gözütok and Brügge*, ECLI:EU:C:2002:516; and Opinion of AG Jääskinen in Case C-129/14 PPU *Spasic*, ECLI:EU:C:2014:739.

[22] *HF* (n 16), paras 71–94. On the non-EU origin of the extradition request, see the discussion below.

they related to *travel* within the Schengen area without fear of multiple prosecutions for the same acts.

In fact, in the ECJ's view, it was not even relevant whether the non-EU citizen was lawfully resident; the only requirement in Article 54 was that the trial was finally disposed of, subject to the enforcement condition. No other provision of the Schengen Convention made such a link with lawful residence or free movement either; the double jeopardy rule is in a different part of the Convention than the provisions dealing with immigration issues. It was sufficient that the objective of *legal certainty* was being furthered. Doubts about whether the first conviction in another Member State had taken full account of the facts had to be dismissed too, in light of the principle of mutual trust.

On the face of it, this approach, stressing legal certainty as a parallel objective of the rules – sometimes the main objective, depending on the circumstances of the case – seems clear enough. But it was undermined by another ECJ judgment just a few months later.[23] In *Volkswagen*, the ECJ stated that the Schengen rules did *not* apply, because the aim of the Schengen provisions was to secure travel within the Schengen area without multiple prosecutions for the same acts, and the 'possibility of travelling freely is not at issue in the case in the main proceedings, given that it concerns two undertakings established in Germany and in Italy respectively'. Although the ECJ did apply Article 50 of the Charter to the facts of the case, the application of the Charter provision is not identical to the application of the Schengen double jeopardy rules. The ECJ did not address the parallel objective of legal certainty or acknowledge that its recent *HF* judgment (which it referred to in the *Volkswagen* judgment as a precedent on the point) had qualified the relevance of the objective of ensuring freedom to travel within the Schengen area to the interpretation of the Schengen double jeopardy rules.

With great respect, this ruling is unconvincing and inconsistent with the *HF* judgment. Applying the reasoning in *HF*, the Schengen Convention double jeopardy rules do not limit themselves to natural persons; nor does the Charter provision; and the objective of legal certainty is obviously met by also applying the Schengen rules to legal persons. And in any event, EU law more generally also aims to facilitate activities across borders by legal persons, not only natural persons. Therefore, even the link made between the double jeopardy rules and travelling within the EU should, by analogy, be relevant to legal persons.

B. Territorial Scope of the Double Jeopardy Rule

A second key development in recent case law is the extension of the territorial scope of the Schengen rules to include proceedings even in non-Member States; this can be seen in the *WS* and *HF* judgments.[24] Both cases concerned the issue of an Interpol 'red notice' by the US, with a view to potential extradition. *WS* related to a German citizen regarding allegations of corruption. The German authorities had investigated WS in respect of the same acts, and discontinued proceedings after WS paid a sum of money in accordance with national criminal law. Interpol then added a flag on the red notice at the request of the German authorities, to indicate that those authorities considered that the *ne bis in idem* principle applied in light of the fact that the proceedings in Germany had been concluded. However, WS sought the

[23] *Volkswagen* (n 16).
[24] *WS* (n 16); and *HF* (n 16).

further remedy of instructing the national authorities to take steps to get the notice removed altogether, on the grounds that other EU and Schengen States might arrest him if he travelled outside Germany.

In the ECJ's view, the ban on further prosecutions for the same acts after a final judgment in a Member State, as set out in Article 54 of the Convention, prevented not only a second prosecution by a Member State, but also assistance with a non-EU State's prosecution by means of provisional arrest. Although provisional arrest to give effect to the red notice was in principle a justified restriction on free movement, it was not, or was no longer, justified once the authorities were aware that the *ne bis in idem* principle would be infringed.

The ECJ rejected the obvious argument that this interpretation in effect extended the Schengen rules to non-EU (and non-Schengen) countries. It accepted that non-EU countries (other than the Schengen associates) are not bound by the double jeopardy rules; nevertheless assisting a non-EU country with its prosecution was, in the context of criminal proceedings, a measure by a Member State which restricted free movement. There was no conflict with international law in this case, because Interpol rules deferred to national law and international treaties in the event of any conflict.

Subsequently, the *HF* case raised further issues as regards extradition requests from non-EU countries. As noted above, the case concerned an extradition request from the US for a non-EU citizen being processed by a second Member State, even though a first Member State had already prosecuted the person concerned for the same acts. The ECJ confirmed that Article 54 of the Convention could apply to fully-fledged extradition requests, given that it already applied to red notices, which were a provisional form of such requests. It then confirmed that Article 54 protected non-EU citizens, even if they were not lawful residents, as further discussed above.

The ECJ also supplied strong remedies for breach of the Schengen rules. While the German/US extradition treaty did not provide for refusing extradition due to a *ne bis in idem* impact of a judgment in another State, Member States' powers had to be exercised in accordance with EU law. Here, the primacy of EU law and the direct effect of Article 50 of the Charter and Article 54 of the Convention could be invoked against the extradition rule in the national court. Nor was the Germany/US extradition treaty sheltered by the protection for pre-membership treaties with non-EU countries set out in Article 351 of the Treaty on the Functioning of the European Union (TFEU), since that extradition treaty post-dated German membership of what has since become the EU; it was irrelevant that the EU's competence over criminal matters was developed long after Germany was a founding member of the then-EEC.

With respect, the ECJ's analysis in these cases as regards the territorial scope of the rules is unconvincing – for exactly the same reason that its analysis of the *personal* scope is *convincing*. (In the *HF* judgment, the two issues unavoidably overlap.) The strongest argument for the broad personal scope of the rules is textual, because neither the Convention rule nor the Charter provision limit themselves to EU citizens, as the ECJ rightly pointed out in *HF*. On the other hand, applying the same rule of interpretation, the Schengen rules *do* have a limited *territorial* scope, to persons being 'prosecuted in another Contracting Party'. Although, in both these cases, coercive action is being taken against a person within a Member State's criminal justice system, this is not pursuant to any prosecution *by a Member State*. The prosecution is (or was, or will be) by a *non*-Member State.

However, there are other lines of argument that might justify some EU law scrutiny over these cases on a different basis. A line of judgments by the ECJ has asserted that extradition of EU citizens outside the EU can have an effect on free movement, and therefore falls within the scope of EU law.[25] This case law relates to citizens of one Member State being extradited by a second Member State to a non-EU country, and so logically could be extended to cover cases like *WS*, which concerned the impact of a red notice issued by a non-EU country in the event that the EU citizen concerned travelled to other Member States. This interpretation also has its limits, though this case law to date provides for consultation with the Member State of nationality before extradition to a non-EU country to see if that Member State wants to prosecute its citizen or enforce a sentence against them, not a right to resist extradition on double jeopardy grounds as such. However, an extension of the case law to refuse extradition in circumstances like *WS* would be logical, and more soundly reasoned than pretending that prosecutions planned in the US are prosecutions by a Member State.

The logic of this argument, as regards extradition to non-EU countries, cannot apply to non-EU citizens, other than those with free movement arrangements with the EU. But where the EU has an extradition arrangement with a non-EU country – as it does with the US (as well as Norway, Iceland and the UK, and to a limited extent Switzerland and Liechtenstein as regards the extradition rules in the Schengen Convention), it could reasonably be argued that Member States' application of those rules falls within the scope of the Charter, because they are *implementing EU law* (see Article 51 of the Charter), given that the double jeopardy rule in Article 50 of the Charter, unlike the Schengen provision, does not explicitly limit itself to prosecutions by EU Member States (or a Schengen state). This interpretation also has its limits, though: it would not apply to non-EU citizens facing extradition to a non-EU country which does not have an extradition arrangement with the EU – unless the EU ever decides to adopt general legislation regulating extradition to non-EU countries.

IV. CONDITIONS AND DEROGATIONS

Like most rights, the right against double jeopardy in the Schengen rules is not unlimited. A second prosecution for the same facts is possible either where the enforcement condition set out in Article 54 of the Convention has not been met, or where the derogations from the rule set out in Article 55 of the Convention apply.

The ECJ has been asked to rule on the validity of both the enforcement condition and the derogations, given that they both limit a fundamental right set out in the Charter. First of all, as regards Article 54, the ECJ upheld the validity of the enforcement condition in the *Spasic* judgment. In the ECJ's view, applying the rules for limiting rights set out in Article 52 of the Charter, the enforcement condition was 'provided for by law',[26] since it was set out in the text of Article 54 of the Convention. Next, the condition did not infringe the 'essence' of the right, given that it 'does not call into question the *ne bis in idem* principle as such', but rather aimed to 'avoid a situation' where the person concerned 'ultimately remains unpunished'.[27] In other words, even if the person concerned was being *prosecuted* twice for the same acts, in practice they were still only being *punished* once for them. The condition also aimed to avoid impunity for criminal offences – so met an 'objective of general interest', as required by the Charter.

Given its objective of avoiding impunity, the enforcement condition, in the ECJ's view, was appropriate, proportionate and necessary to attain its end, because the ECJ concluded

[25] Starting with Case C-182/15 *Petruhhin*, ECLI:EU:C:2016:630.
[26] *Spasic* (n 16), para 56.
[27] ibid, paras 56–57.

that various mutual recognition and cooperation measures provided for by EU law would not necessarily prevent impunity, due to the conditions and limits applicable to them. In any event, where those mutual recognition measures did work, the enforcement condition would be unnecessary; it would only come into play where they were not working.

In the light of this focus on avoiding impunity for committing criminal offences, one might have expected the ECJ to take a more critical view of the derogations in Article 55 of the Convention, which apply even if a sentence imposed in the first Member State *has* been (or *is* being, or can no longer be) enforced. In other words, they allow not only a second prosecution, but also a second *punishment* – or another prosecution following a first acquittal. If someone is being or was punished already, they obviously were not benefiting from any impunity; and if they were acquitted, then the issue of impunity does not arise in the first place.

Nevertheless, the ECJ upheld the validity of at least one of the Article 55 derogations: Article 55(1)(b), concerning national security or other equally essential interests of a Member State, in the *MR* judgment.[28] In this case, Germany had adopted a declaration referring to organised crime as an essential interest for the purposes of Article 55(1)(b), and a non-EU citizen was being prosecuted by Germany for alleged investment fraud that fell within the scope of the derogation, having been convicted and served time already in Austria for (arguably) the same acts.

In the ECJ's view, again analysing the compatibility of the rule with the Charter, it was first of all 'provided for by law' in Article 55 of the Convention. The ECJ did not examine whether the German notification also met that requirement as such, although later on in the judgment it insisted on clarity and precision of the national declaration in other contexts. As for the 'essence' of the right, the ECJ referred to its case law on Article 50 of the Charter (not the Schengen rules as such) that the essence of Article 50 of the Charter was respected where a limitation 'does no more than allow for further proceedings and penalties in respect of the same acts in pursuit of a distinct objective'.[29] Applying that test, the ECJ referred to its case law on the 'national security' provision of Article 4(2) of the Treaty on European Union (TEU), which

> corresponds to the primary interest in protecting the essential functions of the State and the fundamental interests of society, by the prevention and punishment of activities capable of seriously destabilising the fundamental constitutional, political, economic or social structures of a country and, in particular, of directly threatening society, the population or the State itself.[30]

So the offences concerned:

> […] must not only be particularly serious but they must affect that Member State itself. The same applies to offences against the other interests of the Member State, as referred to in that provision. Since they must be essential to that Member State in the same way as its security is, those other interests must have a similar importance and, therefore, be just as integral to that Member State.[31]

Therefore, the Article 55(1)(b) derogation provides for a 'distinct objective', since it allows 'that Member State to punish offences which affect the Member State itself and, in so doing, to pursue objectives that necessarily differ from those for which the person prosecuted has already been tried in another Member State'.[32]

[28] *MR* (n 8).
[29] Referring to Case C-117/20 *bpost*, ECLI:EU:C:2022:202, para 43.
[30] *MR* (n 8), para 55. The ECJ referred to case law including Joined Cases C-511/18, C-512/18 and C-520/18 *La Quadrature du Net and Others*, ECLI:EU:C:2020:791, para 135.
[31] *MR* (n 8), para 56.
[32] ibid, para 57.

Second, punishment of harm to security or equally essential interests of a Member State met an objective of general interest. As for proportionality, that entailed balancing the extent of infringement of the right against the public interest being pursued; that test was satisfied here given the seriousness of the crime. The principle of necessity was satisfied by the requirement to adopt a precise declaration of the scope of the derogation, and the requirement under Article 56 of the Convention to deduct time served arising from those acts in the first Member State.

The ECJ also assessed whether a declaration under Article 55(1)(b) could cover financial crime. Although the exception:

> primarily covers offences – such as espionage, treason or serious harm to the functioning of public authorities – which, by their very nature, relate to the security or other equally essential interests of the Member State concerned … it does not follow from this that the scope of that exception is necessarily limited to such offences.[33]
>
> Indeed, it cannot be ruled out that a prosecution for offences whose constituent elements do not specifically include harm to the security or other equally essential interests of the Member State may be equally capable of falling within that exception where, in the light of the circumstances in which the offence was committed, it can be duly established that the prosecution in respect of the acts in question is intended to punish harm to that security or to those other equally essential interests.[34]

The ECJ then qualified its position by noting that the acts in question must 'particularly seriously affect the Member State concerned itself', and that 'not every criminal organisation necessarily and in itself harms the security or other equally essential interests of the Member State concerned', from which it follows that the exception could only apply to organised crime where its actions could create such harm, 'due to the elements that distinguish them'.[35] While it could not be ruled out that purely financial crimes could meet the threshold to apply Article 55(1)(b):

> in order for the actions of that criminal organisation to be considered to amount to such harm, those offences must, irrespective of the actual intention of that organisation and over and above the breaches of public order which every offence entails, affect the Member State itself.[36]

Since it appeared that the organised crime in this case did not damage the German state itself, the derogation was probably not applicable – although the final decision on this was left to the national court.

It is striking that in this case the ECJ disagreed with its Advocate General,[37] who argued that the derogation was invalid because: the declarations were not 'provided for by law', given the uncertainties as to which declarations were valid and the failure to publish them at EU level,[38] and the prospect of derogations under *any* head of Article 55 of the Convention breached the 'essence' of the Article 50 Charter right, given the double punishment and the development of the mutual trust principle within the EU.

Unlike the Advocate General's Opinion, the ECJ's judgment in *MR* only addressed the validity of one of the three possibilities for derogation set out in Article 55 of the Convention – leaving aside Article 55(1)(a) (where the acts took place in whole or part on the second Member

[33] ibid, paras 75–76.
[34] ibid, para 76.
[35] ibid, paras 77–78.
[36] ibid, para 81.
[37] Opinion of AG Szpunar in *MR* (n 11).
[38] ibid, paras 41–51.

State's territory, if they did not take place in part in the territory of the first Member State) and 55(1)(c) (where the acts were committed by the second Member State's official 'in violation of the duties of their office').[39] In light of the judgment in *MR*, are those possible derogations also valid?

The ECJ passed up a previous opportunity to answer this question as regards Article 55(1)(a) in *Kossowski*, ruling instead that the point was irrelevant because the case did not concern a final judgment in the first place.[40] However, the Advocate General's Opinion in that case argued that Article 55(1)(a) was invalid, because it was no longer relevant in light of the concept of mutual trust that the EU had developed.[41]

Implicitly the ECJ's judgment in *MR* rejected the argument that the development of the mutual trust principle renders the derogations invalid – at least as far as Article 55(1)(b) is concerned. Arguably the point could still be raised as regards the validity of Article 55(1)(a) or (c). Explicitly, the ECJ has rejected the argument that the derogations are not 'provided by law', despite the persuasive points made in the *MR* Opinion that the national declarations should be published and the overall legal framework for the derogations is a dog's dinner. The *MR* judgment states that the national declarations must instead be examined as part of the assessment of proportionality, concluding that they are a safeguard that helps to ensure the necessity of the second prosecution.[42] With great respect, the judgment is unconvincing on this point. The structure and wording of Article 52(1) of the Charter suggests that proportionality and the 'provided by law' requirements are distinct rules; the ECJ's case law (in line with, for instance, the European Court of Human Rights case law on Article 8 European Convention on Human Rights) treats them as different requirements;[43] and the argument does not survive detailed scrutiny on its own terms: one could easily imagine a national declaration that was highly precise, yet hugely disproportionate.

Accepting the ECJ's weak reasoning on the 'provided by law' point as a given, though, what does this mean going forward? The next issue to consider is the 'essence of the right' point, where the ECJ rules that a 'distinct objective' can justify 'further proceedings and penalties',[44] and this does not infringe the essence of the right. With great respect again, this is also highly unconvincing. The essence of the right is not to be tried twice; what does the objective of the Member State have to do with that? Again, the logic of this reasoning ignores the structure of Article 52(1) of the Charter, which refers to the public interest objectives of interference with a right and the 'essence' of the right separately. In fact, it mixes up the rationale of these separate parts of Article 52(1): the 'essence' rule is there to protect the rights of the individual, not the interests of the State.

Again, accepting this weak reasoning as a given, it does not necessarily follow that the derogation in Article 55(1)(a) meets this threshold, for the ECJ's definition of the 'distinct objective' being served relates to offences which affect the Member State itself distinctly. It might be argued that an offence affects a Member State distinctly merely because it took place on its

[39] It should be noted that the derogations listed in Art 55 are exhaustive, see *Gözütok and Brügge* (n 16), para 44.

[40] *Kossowski* (n 8), para 55. Conversely, in *MR* (n 8), paras 33–44, the ECJ answered the derogations question despite hinting strongly to the national court that the acts committed in Austria and (allegedly) Germany were not the 'same acts' – even though the national court had not asked about that point.

[41] Opinion of AG Bot in Case C-486/14 *Kossowski*, ECLI:EU:C:2015:812, paras 32–68. AG Bot did not discuss whether the options for derogations in Art 55(1)(b) and (c) of the Schengen Convention were valid.

[42] *MR* (n 8), paras 51 and 63.

[43] See S Peers and S Prechal 'Article 52 – Scope and Interpretation of Rights and Principles' in Hervey et al (eds) (n 2), 1617.

[44] *Kossowski* (n 8), para 52.

territory; but that interpretation would flip the *ne bis in idem* rule on its head, allowing for multiple prosecutions in a vast number of cases, given that territorial jurisdiction is the basic jurisdictional rule in criminal law and is likely to be a frequent basis for asserting the possibility of a second prosecution. Such an approach would not respect the ECJ's usual approach of interpreting exceptions from rules (particularly those linked to human rights) narrowly.

On the other hand, it might reasonably be argued that the Article 55(1)(c) derogation meets this threshold, because a violation of duties by a national official has a distinct impact on the Member State that employs them as an official, as compared to a Member State where they do not have that legal status.

Finally, as regards proportionality, the *MR* judgment also refers to the seriousness of the crimes involved as a justification for the derogation. This is a valid argument as regards national security or equally essential interests, and there is a decent argument that crimes of corruption, covered by Article 55(1)(c) of the Convention, are also quite serious. However, when it comes to Article 55(1)(a), it is implausible to argue that crimes are serious merely because they took place on the territory of a Member State.

It follows that even accepting the ECJ's flawed reasoning in the *MR* judgment, there is a strong argument that the derogation in Article 55(1)(a) of the Convention is nevertheless invalid for breaching the essence of the Article 50 Charter right and the principle of proportionality. Conversely, there is a rather better argument that the derogation in Article 55(1)(c) of the Convention is valid.

V. CONCLUSION

As noted above, the ECJ's judgments on *ne bis in idem* have addressed many issues and attracted much controversy; due to the limited space here it was not possible to discuss the case law on defining final judgments or the same acts, for instance. But at least the case law on those issues confines itself to the wording of the Schengen rule, rather than asserting implausibly that it covers prosecutions to take place in non-EU countries – or that it does *not* cover prosecutions taking place *in* Member States, but against legal persons. There is an ongoing inconsistency in the reasoning around some key issues: free movement of people is a central feature in interpreting the rules until it comes to applying them to a non-EU citizen (who does not even enjoy freedom of travel within Schengen, due to unlawful residence); but then it becomes a central feature again when not applying the Schengen rules to legal persons.

While an argument could certainly be made for the EU to legislate on the issue of extradition from the EU to non-EU countries, with a view to facilitating judicial cooperation with those countries while reconciling it with human rights concerns, constructing the law in this field in the meantime based on judicial interventions (both as regard *ne bis in idem* and the citizenship case law) has been awkward.

Finally, the derogations from the *ne bis in idem* rule amount to a' childhood illness' of the law in this field that should no longer be happening: the childhood of EU justice and home affairs law ended long ago. But the ECJ has failed to take advantage of two opportunities to cure that illness. Hopefully, the diagnoses of Advocates General have paved the way for a legislative or judicial rethink of the meaning of, and need for, these derogations.

14

Reflections on a Structural Element of EU Law on Migration: The Principle of Non-Refoulement *in Light of the European Court of Justice's Case Law*

YANN LAURANS AND CHIARA MARIA RICCI*

I. INTRODUCTION

DURING HIS TENURE at the Court of Justice of the European Union, Mr Bay Larsen, as well as exercising his judicial functions, has actively participated in the dissemination of the case law of the EU Courts and in the analysis of developments in the area of freedom, security and justice (AFSJ). Among the various subjects he has touched upon, one that stands out in light of that case law is the clarification of the complex relationship between the Common European Asylum System (CEAS) and international law.[1] The present contribution will look into a specific aspect of this relationship by focusing on a particular principle derived from international law: the principle of *non-refoulement*.

The malleability of that principle, combined with its importance, has provoked debates and controversy as to its scope and its precise foundations.[2] However, it seems undisputed that the principle of *non-refoulement* has its origin in international treaty law[3] and, in one form or another, is guaranteed, inter alia, by the Geneva Convention,[4] the Convention against

* Yann Laurans and Chiara Maria Ricci are Legal Secretaries in the Chambers of Vice-President Bay Larsen. All opinions expressed herein are personal to the authors.

[1] L Bay Larsen, 'Quelques remarques sur les relations entre le droit international et le régime d'asile européen commun' *La Cour de justice de l'Union européenne sous la présidence de Vassilios Skouris (2003–2015): Liber amicorum Vassilios Skouris* (Bruylant, 2015); and 'Entre autonomie et cohérence: les développements des relations entre le régime d'asile européen commun et le droit international depuis 2015' in D Petrlík et al (eds), *Évolution des rapports entre les ordres juridiques de l'Union européenne, international et nationaux Liber amicorum Jiří Malenovský* (Bruylant, 2020).

[2] See, for example, I Goldner Lang and B Nagy, 'External Border Control Techniques in the EU as a Challenge for the Principle of Non-Refoulement' (2021) 17 *European Constitutional Law Review* 444.

[3] See, in particular, J Mink, 'EU Asylum Law and Human Rights Protection: Revisiting the Principle of Non-Refoulement and the Prohibition of Torture and Other Forms of Ill-treatment' (2012) 14 *European Journal of Migration and Law* 119, 131–32; and H Raspail, 'Le principe de non-refoulement en situation d'afflux massif" (2018) *Revue trimestrielle des droits de l'Homme* 613, 619–20.

[4] Convention Relating to the Status of Refugees (Geneva, 28 July 1951) (Geneva Convention).

Torture,[5] and the European Convention on Human Rights (ECHR). Furthermore, it has been increasingly argued that the principle of *non-refoulement* has progressively acquired a customary value in international law.[6] Turning to the expression of that principle in EU law, it should be noted that it is expressly mentioned in Article 78 of the Treaty on the Functioning of the European Union (TFEU), as that provision provides that the Union shall develop a common policy on asylum, subsidiary protection and temporary protection with a view, inter alia, to 'ensuring compliance with the principle of non-refoulement'. That entrenchment is partly indirect, in so far as it sets an objective for the EU legislature, but it nevertheless shows the centrality of that principle for EU policy on international protection. It is also supplemented by Article 18 and Article 19(2) of the Charter of Fundamental Rights of the European Union (the Charter). The first of these provisions implicitly refers to the principle of *non-refoulement*, by requiring compliance with the Geneva Convention, which specifically enshrines that principle. The second prohibits the removal, expulsion or extradition of a person to a State where there is a serious risk that he or she would be subjected to the death penalty, torture or other inhuman or degrading treatment or punishment. It is therefore unsurprising that the European Court of Justice (ECJ) referred to these two provisions of the Charter in order to state that the principle of *non-refoulement* is guaranteed as a fundamental right in EU law.[7]

Nevertheless, this essential statement did not lead the ECJ to define, in one or more key judgments, a series of elements which, when combined, would make it possible to determine the field of application and the scope of the principle of *non-refoulement* in EU law. However, it would be wrong to infer from that finding that that principle only plays a marginal role in the ECJ's case law. Not only is it regularly quoted by the ECJ, but it can also be argued that the 'logic of *non-refoulement*' implicitly underpins, more generally, the approach taken by the ECJ in relation to the reception and the international protection of third-country nationals. In this context, the present contribution seeks to take stock of the current position of the principle of *non-refoulement* in the ECJ's case law, over eight years after it was formally endorsed by the ECJ.[8] This contribution will therefore focus on the view developed in this regard by the ECJ, without seeking to anticipate possible future developments in areas which the ECJ has not yet addressed. In particular, this chapter will not address the complex issue relating to the scope of the principle of *non-refoulement* in the area of border control, which still largely appears to be *terra incognita* for the ECJ.

In this contribution, we shall first focus on the solutions adopted by the ECJ in what is, to date, the main area of application of the principle of *non-refoulement*, namely the application of the Returns Directive (Section II).[9] Second, we will consider the extent to which, beyond that Directive alone, that principle can be regarded as underpinning the CEAS (Section III).

II. THE RETURNS DIRECTIVE, THE MAIN AREA OF APPLICATION OF THE PRINCIPLE OF *NON-REFOULEMENT*

Since the Returns Directive is the central act harmonising the return and removal policies implemented by the Member States, it was to be expected that its application would raise

[5] Convention against Torture and Other Cruel, Inhuman or Degrading Treatment or Punishment (adopted 10 December 1984, entered into force 26 June 1987) 1465 UNTS 85.

[6] See, in particular, R Mungianu, *Frontex and Non-Refignement, The International Responsibility of the EU* (Cambridge University Press, 2016) 99–103.

[7] Cases C-373/13 *T*, ECLI:EU:C:2015:413, para 65; and C-181/16 *Gnandi*, ECLI:EU:C:2018:465, para 53.

[8] This chapter is based on the ECJ's case law as it stands at the end of 2023.

[9] Directive 2008/115/EC of the European Parliament and of the Council of 16 December 2008 on common standards and procedures in Member States for returning illegally established status [2008] OJ L348/188.

questions as to the place to be granted to the principle of *non-refoulement*. Gradually, the ECJ's case law has provided guidance on both the scope of that principle (A) and the cases in which it limits the prerogatives of the Member States (B).

A. The Scope of the Principle of *Non-Refoulement* in the Context of the Procedures Laid Down in the Returns Directive

Although primary EU law includes a general enshrinement of the principle of *non-refoulement*, one of its most important concrete expressions can be found in the Returns Directive. In that respect, Article 5 of that Directive lays down a crosscutting rule under which Member States must, when implementing that Directive, respect the principle of *non-refoulement*. Moreover, in order to ensure full protection, Article 4(4)(b) of that Directive imposes the same obligation as regards third-country nationals who would be excluded from its scope of application because they are subject to a refusal of entry.

In the light of the relatively general wording of Article 5 of the Returns Directive, which does not specify the practical implications entailed by the compliance with the principle of *non-refoulement*, the ECJ has been called upon to provide clarification in that regard. It is rather obvious that a person cannot be expelled to a country in which his or her return would infringe the principle of *non-refoulement*, since Article 9 of the Returns Directive expressly requires removal to be postponed in such a case. However, as the Returns Directive distinguishes between the adoption of a return decision, referred to in Article 6 thereof, and removal, which is the subject of Article 8 thereof, the precise consequences of applying the principle of *non-refoulement* on each of those two successive stages of the return procedure could legitimately appear to be relatively uncertain. The ECJ's case law relating to that issue originally harboured certain tensions. On the one hand, in the *CPAS de Seraing* judgment, the ECJ highlighted that, since a return decision necessarily imposes an obligation to return to a third country, that decision must be suspended where there is a risk of breach of the principle of *non-refoulement*, without the potential suspension of a future removal decision providing sufficient protection for the rights of the person concerned.[10] On the other hand, in the *Westerwaldkreis* judgment, the ECJ held that the Returns Directive prohibits tolerating the existence of an intermediate status of third-country nationals staying illegally on the territory of a Member State but in respect of whom no valid return decision subsists, including where the principle of *non-refoulement* excludes any prospect of removal.[11]

The lack of guarantee offered against the adoption of a return decision, which appeared to be put forward in the *Westerwaldkreis* judgment, was regarded by some authors as creating a deficiency in the protection arising from the principle of *non-refoulement*.[12] However, in the *Staatssecretaris van Justitie en Veiligheid (Removal – Medicinal cannabis)* judgment, the ECJ overcame that difficulty by holding that Article 5 of the Returns Directive constitutes a general rule which is binding on the competent national authority at all stages of the return procedure and by inferring that the article precludes a third-country national from being the subject of a return decision where that decision concerns, as the receiving country, a country in respect of which an enforced return would be incompatible with the principle of *non-refoulement*.[13]

[10] Case C-402/19 *CPAS Seraing*, ECLI:EU:C:2020:759, paras 44–45.

[11] Case C-546/19 *Westerwaldkreis*, ECLI:EU:C:2021:432, paras 57–59.

[12] I Majcher, *The European Union Returns Directive and Its Compatibility with International Human Rights Law, Analysis of Return Decision, Entry Ban, Detention, and Removal* (Brill Nijhoff, 2020) 113.

[13] Case C-69/21 *Staatssecretaris van Justitie en Veiligheid (Removal – Medicinal cannabis)*, ECLI:EU:C:2022:913, paras 55–56.

That solution was applied, inter alia, to a situation in which the competent national authority had already found such an obstacle to an enforced return and had, nevertheless, adopted a return decision.[14] Where such a finding has not yet been made, the acknowledged scope of the principle of *non-refoulement* requires that authority to rule out, before the adoption of a return decision, any serious doubts as to the risk of breach of that principle in the event of an enforced return.[15]

Beyond delimiting the cases in which a return decision may be adopted, the ECJ has also addressed certain indirect effects of the principle of *non-refoulement*, by providing indications as to the status to be granted to a third-country national whose enforced return to his or her country of origin is excluded by virtue of that principle. It appears, above all, that that status is primarily a matter of national law. Indeed, the ECJ has repeatedly held that the Returns Directive is not designed to determine the consequences of the illegal stay of third-country nationals in respect of whom no return decisions to a third country can be issued, on the territory of a Member State, including where that impossibility stems from the principle of *non-refoulement*.[16] That finding means, in particular, that EU law does not in any way oblige the Member States to issue a residence entitlement or a residence permit to a third-country national who cannot lawfully be removed.

Nevertheless, where a person who is the subject of a return decision cannot temporarily be expelled, the Returns Directive requires certain minimum safeguards to be provided. Admittedly, the Commission's ambitious proposal,[17] which required some of the rights guaranteed to long-term residents to be respected, was not taken up by the EU legislature. However, Article 14 of the Returns Directive requires Member States to take into account certain principles, including family unity and emergency health care, during periods for which removal has been postponed in accordance with Article 9 of that Directive. The ECJ provided some guidance as to the scope of the safeguards provided by Article 14 of the Returns Directive, in cases where the principle of *non-refoulement* required such a postponement. It first held, in the *Abdida* judgment, that the basic needs of a third-country national whose removal is postponed must be met, in order to ensure that emergency health care and essential treatment of illness can effectively be provided.[18] It then found that the benefit of the guarantees provided for in Article 14 of that Directive extend to a parent of such a third-country national, where the latter is placed in a situation of dependence on that parent, in order to ensure an effective possibility not to be forced to return where this is precluded by the principle of *non-refoulement*.[19]

On another level, the ECJ has inferred certain procedural requirements from the principle of *non-refoulement*. More specifically, even if the Returns Directive does not directly require that an appeal brought against a return decision be given suspensive effect, the ECJ found that an automatic suspensive effect had to be recognised, where the return decision may expose the person concerned to a real risk of being subjected to inhuman or degrading treatment.[20]

[14] Case C-663/21 *Bundesamt für Fremdenwesen und Asyl (Refugee who has committed a serious crime)*, ECLI:EU:C:2023:540, para 51.

[15] *Staatssecretaris van Justitie en Veiligheid (Removal – Medicinal cannabis)* (n 13), para 80.

[16] Cases C-673/19 *M and Others (Transfer to a Member State)*, ECLI:EU:C:2021:127, para 44; and *Staatssecretaris van Justitie en Veiligheid (Removal – Medicinal cannabis)* (n 13), para 84.

[17] Proposal for a Directive of the European Parliament and of the Council on common standards and procedures in Member States for returning illegally staying third-country nationals COM (2018) 634 final.

[18] Case C-562/13 *Abdida*, ECLI:EU:C:2014:2453, para 63.

[19] Case C-402/19 *CPAS Seraing*, ECLI:EU:C:2020:759, para 50.

[20] *Gnandi* (n 7), para 56; and Case C-175/17 *Belastingdienst/Toeslagen (suspensory effect of the appeal)*, ECLI:EU:C:2018:776, para 33.

Nonetheless, the ECJ did not consider that such a risk would require that there be two levels of jurisdiction when challenging return decisions.[21]

B. Cases in which the Principle of *Non-Refoulement* is to be Applied within the Framework of the Returns Directive

In the light of the extended effects of the principle of *non-refoulement* in the context of return procedures, the identification of the cases in which the applicability of that principle is established, under EU law, is quite important.

The ECJ's case law on this issue was originally developed on the basis of Article 19(2) of the Charter. In the *Abdida* judgment, for the first time, the ECJ held that Member States may not, in accordance with Article 5 of the Returns Directive taken in conjunction with Article 19(2) of the Charter, remove a third-country national to a State where there is a risk that he or she would be subjected to inhuman or degrading treatment.[22] That solution was subsequently repeated systematically.[23] Its importance has also been emphasised by stressing that the prohibition on inhuman or degrading treatment is absolute, in so far as it is closely linked to respect for human dignity, the subject of Article 1 of the Charter.[24] More specifically, as Article 19(2) of the Charter constitutes the 'exterior side' of that prohibition, its 'interior side' being set out in Article 4 of the Charter, the ECJ relied extensively on the case law of the European Court of Human Rights (ECtHR) relating to Article 3 of the ECHR in order to clarify the scope of the principle of *non-refoulement*. The ECJ thereby aimed to ensure that it will not be possible to remove a third-country national in a situation where his or her removal would be excluded under the case law of the Strasbourg Court.[25] This 'transposition' in Luxembourg of the solutions adopted in Strasbourg was notably used with respect to the limits placed on the removal of third-country nationals exposed to a serious deterioration in their state of health, situations which have been examined by the ECJ in a series of judgments. It does not seem relevant, for the purpose of this contribution, to address the different stages of the development of that case law, the latest stage of which to date being expressed in the *Staatssecretaris van Justitie en Veiligheid (Removal – Medicinal cannabis)* judgment.[26] It should nevertheless be noted that the importance of that case law arguably stems from the fact that EU legislation does not, in principle, provide specific protection against such a risk, which may also explain why the question of compliance with the prohibition of inhuman or degrading treatment is raised, in that type of situation, at the stage of the return procedure.

On a different note, although Article 19(2) of the Charter has a prominent position in the conduct of return procedures, it is not the only provision of the Charter that can prevent the adoption of a return decision or a removal. In this respect, it is worth noting that such an effect has been recognised in Article 7 of the Charter, which protects the right to private and family life.[27] It should be stressed that this solution has not been expressly linked to the principle of

[21] *Belastingdienst/Toeslagen (suspensory effect of the appeal)* (n 20), para 34.

[22] *Abdida* (n 18), para 48.

[23] *Gnandi* (n 7), para 56; and *Staatssecretaris van Justitie en Veiligheid (Removal – Medicinal cannabis)* (n 13), para 57.

[24] *Staatssecretaris van Justitie en Veiligheid (Removal – Medicinal cannabis)* (n 13), para 57.

[25] Case C-353/16 *MP (Subsidiary protection of a person previously a victim of torture)*, ECLI:EU:C:2018:276, paras 37–46.

[26] *Staatssecretaris van Justitie en Veiligheid (Removal – Medicinal cannabis)* (n 13), para 66.

[27] ibid, para 92.

non-refoulement and that the wording of Article 5 of the Returns Directive appears to treat differently that principle and family life. In any case, besides the direct limits on forced return, the ECJ held that a return decision could not be adopted without taking into account the relevant details of the third-country national concerned,[28] which means, inter alia, that he or she must be heard on that subject.[29]

Furthermore, Article 18 of the Charter, which guarantees the right to asylum, is also one of the grounds on which the application of the principle of *non-refoulement* in EU law is based.[30] In the light of the close link between the Geneva Convention and the entrenchment of the principle of *non-refoulement* in the international legal order, such an effect given to Article 18 appears, at first sight, to be logical. However, the practical consequences of taking Article 18 of the Charter into account in addition to Article 19(2) of the Charter seem to be relatively limited in most cases, as the ECJ has, in practice, mostly assessed only the existence of a risk of inhuman or degrading treatment. It should nevertheless be noted that the *M and Others (Transfer to a Member State)* judgment differs in that regard from the cases mentioned so far. Indeed, in the case which gave rise to that judgment, the application of the principle of *non-refoulement* was not based on an assessment of a risk of inhuman or degrading treatment, but on the fact that the third-country nationals concerned enjoyed refugee status in a Member State other than the one in which they were staying illegally.[31] Even if, in that judgment, the ECJ relied both on Articles 18 and 19 of the Charter, a closer connection can be found here with the first of these provisions, given the specific role granted to the refugee status.

As the latter example shows, the application of the principle of *non-refoulement* can sometimes rely on refugee status, without, however, entirely depending on the granting of that status. The links between that principle and the CEAS are not, however, limited to that finding and must be analysed in more detail in the second part of this contribution.

III. THE CEAS, A REGIME UNDERPINNED BY THE PRINCIPLE OF *NON-REFOULEMENT*

Even if the ECJ has essentially referred to the principle of *non-refoulement* in cases relating to the application of the Returns Directive, this principle is also of particular importance in the context of the CEAS. Arguably, the choices made by the EU legislature led the ECJ to implicitly incorporate that principle into the logic of granting international protection (A). That principle also appears, at various stages, to be a complement to the international protection procedure (B).

A. The Principle of *Non-Refoulement* and the Granting of International Protection

The necessary link between the principle of *non-refoulement* and the grant of international protection, as provided for by EU law, is expressed in Article 21 of the Qualification Directive.[32]

[28] Case C-82/16 *KA and Others (Family reunification in Belgium)*, ECLI:EU:C:2018:308, para 104.

[29] Case C-808/18 *Commission v Hungary (Reception of applicants for international protection)*, ECLI:EU:C:2020:1029, para 250.

[30] *Staatssecretaris van Justitie en Veiligheid (Removal – Medicinal cannabis)* (n 13), para 55.

[31] *M and Others (Transfer to a Member State)* (n 16), para 40.

[32] Directive 2011/95/EU of the European Parliament and of the Council of 13 December 2011 on standards for the qualification of third country nationals or citizens as beneficiaries of international protection, for a uniform status for refugees or for persons eligible for subsidiary protection, and for the content of the protection granted (recast) [2011] OJ L337/9.

This provision requires Member States to respect the principle of *non-refoulement* in accordance with their international obligations. The general obligation set out in Article 21(1) of that Directive can be construed as contributing to the implementation, in positive law, of the rights conferred on every person by EU law with a view to ensuring lasting protection for him or her against persecution,[33] thus confirming the intrinsic link between international protection and the principle of *non-refoulement*. Beyond that reminder of the general international obligations of the Member States, the link between that article and the Geneva Convention is evidenced by the fact that the derogations from the principle of *non-refoulement* set out in Article 21(2) of the Qualification Directive correspond to those provided for in Article 33(2) of the Geneva Convention. The existence of a 'correspondence' between these two provisions was also expressly stated by the ECJ.[34] The ECJ further specified that, where the derogations provided for in Article 21(2) of the Qualification Directive apply, Member States have discretion in determining whether or not to *refoule* a refugee.[35]

Although it follows from the foregoing that international protection implies, unless a derogation applies, the benefit of *non-refoulement*, the relationship between the grant of that protection and the principle of *non-refoulement* can also be inverted. Indeed, it follows from the definition of the concepts of 'refugee' and 'person eligible for subsidiary protection', set out in Article 2(d) and (f) of the Qualification Directive, that the grant of international protection is subject to establishing that a return of the person concerned to his or her country of origin would expose him or her to a serious risk of persecution or serious harm. In other words, it is because a third-country national is unable to return to his or her country of origin, since he or she cannot be returned without suffering serious interference with his or her fundamental rights, that he or she must be granted international protection. Similarly, the concepts allowing derogation from the 'ordinary' application of the rules governing international protection, such as those of a safe third country or first country of asylum, are precisely based on the fact that the person concerned may be removed without fear to a third country. The ECJ noted, in that respect, that the possibility of regarding a third country as a 'first country of asylum', within the meaning of points (a) and (b) of the first paragraph of Article 35 of the Procedures Directive,[36] presupposes that the person concerned enjoys sufficient protection in that country, including benefiting from the principle of *non-refoulement*.[37] The benefit of that principle is therefore regarded, once again, as being at the heart of the status of beneficiary of international protection.

In those circumstances, the specific assessment of the merits of an application for international protection follows an approach which is related, even sometimes largely similar, to that taken by the ECJ in the cases in which the application of the principle of *non-refoulement* in the context of the Returns Directive was at issue. Admittedly, the ECJ's case law relating to that assessment cannot be analysed in detail here, as such an analysis would go far beyond the subject-matter of the present contribution. Yet, mentioning the first cases which have provided the basis for the interpretation of the Qualification Directive may allow us to illustrate the underlying role of the principle of *non-refoulement* in the examination of applications for international protection. In this context, it is thus worth mentioning the *Y and Z* judgment, in

[33] *T* (n 7), para 68.

[34] Joined Cases C-391/16, C-77/17 and C-78/17 *M and Others (Revocation of refugee status)*, ECLI:EU:C:2019:403, para 94.

[35] *T* (n 7), para 43.

[36] Directive 2013/32/EU of the European Parliament and of the Council of 26 June 2013 on common procedures for granting and implementing international protection (recast) [2013] OJ L180/60.

[37] Case C-585/16 *Alheto*, ECLI:EU:C:2018:584, para 138.

which the ECJ held that the existence of persecution on grounds of religion could not result from a potentially justifiable limitation of religious freedom, but presupposed an interference whose gravity is equivalent to that of an infringement of the basic human rights from which no derogation can be made,[38] in other words, an infringement justifying the application of the principle of *non-refoulement*. The logic developed, with respect to Article 15(b) of the Qualification Directive, in the *Elgafaji* and *M'Bodj* judgments arguably demonstrates even more clearly the existing link between granting international protection and the principle of *non-refoulement*. In those judgments, the ECJ stressed that the serious harm referred to in Article 15(b) of the Qualification Directive corresponds, in essence, to cases of infringement of Article 3 of the ECHR.[39] Furthermore, the ECJ referred to a requirement to interpret that first provision in a manner consistent with Article 19(2) of the Charter, namely one of the main expressions of the principle of *non-refoulement* in EU law.[40]

However, such proximity should not be mistaken for complete confusion of the rationales of international protection and *non-refoulement*. The *M'Bodj* judgment clearly illustrates the difference between those two rationales by stressing the decisive role of the behaviour of the actors of persecution when the grant of international protection is at stake. In that judgment, after referring to the case law of the ECtHR preventing, in exceptional cases, the removal of a seriously ill third-country national to his or her country of origin, the ECJ found that such a third-country national should necessarily be granted subsidiary protection. Indeed, the ECJ considered that such protection presupposed that the applicant would be intentionally deprived of health care and that it could not therefore be the result of the mere absence of appropriate treatment in the country of origin.[41] That idea was subsequently repeated and clarified, notably in the *MP (Subsidiary protection of a person previously a victim of torture)* judgment, taking into account the effect of the Convention against Torture.[42] Drawing such a fine distinction between the grant of international protection and the full application of the principle of *non-refoulement* may explain why that principle can also be regarded as a sort of 'complement', adding, in certain cases, to the mechanisms specific to the international protection procedure.

B. The Principle of *Non-Refoulement* as a Complement to the International Protection Procedure

The complexity of the relationship between the principle of *non-refoulement* and the international protection procedure implies that that principle is not only integrated, to a certain extent, into that procedure, but may also interact with it by imposing additional obligations or checks on the competent authorities. Two scenarios may be mentioned in that regard.

First, as it results from the foregoing considerations that the scope of international protection is sometimes narrower than the principle of *non-refoulement*, that principle may logically apply to persons who do not or no longer benefit from international protection. These may include persons who have not applied for international protection, who are excluded from that

[38] Joined Cases C-71/11 and C-99/11 *Y and Z*, ECLI:EU:C:2012:518, paras 59–61 and 65.
[39] Cases C-465/07 *Elgafaji*, ECLI:EU:C:2009:94, para 28; and C-542/13 *M'Bodj*, ECLI:EU:C:2014:2452, para 38.
[40] *M'Bodj* (n 39), para 38.
[41] ibid, para 41.
[42] *MP (Subsidiary protection of a person previously a victim of torture)* (n 25), paras 55 and 57.

protection, applicants whose application has been rejected, or refugees whose protection has been revoked on grounds of public policy or national security.[43]

This approach of 'supplementary' application of the principle of *non-refoulement* was followed by the ECJ in the *Abdida* judgment, where it found for the first time that a situation such as that in the main proceedings fell outside of the scope of the Qualification Directive and then that an examination based on Article 5 of the Returns Directive taken in conjunction with Article 19(2) of the Charter had to be carried out.[44] This approach was subsequently confirmed, again with regard to seriously ill third-country nationals, in the *MP (Subsidiary protection of a person previously a victim of torture)* judgment, taking into account the effect of the Convention against Torture.[45] It was then developed and systematised in the *M (Revocation of refugee status)* judgment, where the ECJ was specifically asked to rule on the compatibility of procedures for the revocation of international protection with the principle of *non-refoulement*. In this judgment, the ECJ stressed, on the basis of Articles 4 and 19 of the Charter, that the protection afforded by EU law was broader than that resulting from the Geneva Convention, in so far as, even in the event of revocation of refugee status, the Charter precludes, in absolute terms, the *refoulement* of a third-country national where such *refoulement* would expose him or her to the risk of infringement of his fundamental rights enshrined in those provisions.[46] The scope of the principle of *non-refoulement* under EU law thus goes beyond the rights of refugees under international law and consequently requires additional protection where that protection is not afforded within the procedures governing the grant of international protection.

Second, the proposed overview would not be complete without mentioning the specific case of protection against infringements of fundamental rights that might result from a transfer based on the Dublin III Regulation.[47] Admittedly, in the *Slovakia v Council* judgment, the ECJ rejected an argument based on the application of the principle of *non-refoulement*, holding that the transfer, in the context of a relocation operation, of an applicant for international protection from one Member State to another for the purpose of ensuring that his application is examined within a reasonable time cannot be regarded as *refoulement* to a third State.[48] It should nevertheless be noted that the ECJ has established, in a largely praetorian manner, safeguards intended to prevent the transfer of a third-country national to another Member State from exposing him or her to serious infringements of fundamental rights.

The first judgment following that line of case law is the well-known *NS* judgment, in which the ECJ, drawing inspiration in part from the ECtHR, held that the competent authorities of a Member State cannot transfer an applicant for international protection to another Member State where they cannot be unaware that systemic deficiencies in the asylum procedure and in the reception conditions of asylum seekers in that Member State amount to substantial grounds for believing that the asylum seeker would face a real risk of being subjected to inhuman or

[43] For an analysis of the various possible scenarios, see H Raspail, 'En droit de l'asile et droits de l'homme: une zone grise du droit européen' (2020) *Journal de droit européen* 156.

[44] *Abdida* (n 18), paras 33 and 48.

[45] *MP (Subsidiary protection of a person previously a victim of torture)* (n 25), para 44.

[46] *M and Others (Revocation of refugee status)* (n 34), paras 94–95.

[47] Regulation (EU) No 604/2013 of the European Parliament and of the Council of 26 June 2013 establishing the envisages and engineering for determining the Member State responsibility for Examination an application for international protection in one of the Member States by a third country national or a government person (recast) [2013] OJ L180/31.

[48] Cases C-643/15 and C-647/15 *Slovakia and Hungary v Council*, ECLI:EU:C:2017:631, para 342.

degrading treatment within the meaning of Article 4 of the Charter.[49] That judgment may have given rise to some doubts as to the applicable regime where such a risk does not stem from systemic deficiencies. Such doubts were nevertheless dispelled in the *CK* judgment, which excluded the transfer of a seriously ill applicant for international protection,[50] and, above all, in the *Jawo* judgment, in which the ECJ relied on the absolute nature of the prohibition on inhuman or degrading treatment in order to rule out the possibility of transferring an applicant for international protection in the event of a risk, even in the absence of systemic flaws.[51]

In this respect, it should be pointed out that here the ECJ relied on Article 4 of the Charter, rather than on Article 19(2) thereof, thus distancing itself from its case law on the principle of *non-refoulement*. Even if the relevant foundations within the framework of the Dublin III Regulation are therefore somewhat original, the approach followed appears to be largely similar, thus ensuring compliance of the Dublin system with international law.[52] It should nevertheless be noted that the reasoning followed here by the ECJ falls within a different context, in so far as it could rely on the case law on the principle of mutual trust, which was developed, more generally, within the AFSJ.[53] It should also be recalled that protection against the risk of inhuman or degrading treatment, whether or not it arises from systemic flaws, also applies in the context of the execution of European arrest warrants.[54]

IV. CONCLUSION

It follows from the examination of the relevant case law of the ECJ that the application of the principle of *non-refoulement* under EU law is based primarily on the Charter, but may rely, at least in part, on EU legislation. The future of that case law will therefore have to be observed carefully, in the light of the significant ongoing reform of the EU rules on international protection, particularly since it is intended, inter alia, to regulate the entry into the territory of the EU of applicants for international protection and to facilitate the return of unsuccessful applicants. In those circumstances, although Mr Bay Larsen played a leading role in the application of the acts relating to international protection of the first and second generations, there is little doubt that issues related to the application of the third generation acts will keep his successors busy.

[49] Joined Cases C-411/10 and C-493/10 *NS and Others*, ECLI:EU:C:2011:865, para 106.

[50] Case C-578/16 PPU *CK and Others*, ECLI:EU:C:2017:127, para 96.

[51] Case C-163/17 *Jawo*, ECLI:EU:C:2019:218, para 87.

[52] On the application of the principle of *non-refoulement* to transfer between Member States, see R Garrett and N Barrett, 'Dublin III in Practice: Synthesizing a Framework for European Non-Refoulement Cases at the Human Rights Committee' (2021) 13 *Journal of Human Rights Practice* 250.

[53] *Opinion 2/13 (Accession of the European Union to the ECHR)*, ECLI:EU:C:2014:2454, para 191.

[54] Joined Cases C-404/15 and C-659/15 PPU *Aranyosi and Căldăraru*, ECLI:EU:C:2016:198; and Case C-699/21 *EDL (Ground for refusal based on addiction)*, ECLI:EU:C:2023:295.

15

Subsidiary Protection in EU Law: Some Reflections on its Specific Features

TATIANA CASSAGNABÈRE AND ANNA GRASSO*

I. INTRODUCTION

OUR COMMON HUMANITY requires that every person shall have the right to seek to be safe. The essential need to protect people from being persecuted for reasons of race, religion, nationality, membership of a social group or political opinion, was enshrined in the Geneva Convention Relating to the Status of Refugees of 28 July 1951 (Geneva Convention),[1] which constitutes the cornerstone of the international legal regime for the protection of refugees,[2] and provides a common normative framework for all States for the granting of asylum.

Over time, the concept of international protection has been enriched and developed with a view to offering alternative protection to people facing risks that hardly fulfil the criteria of individual persecution set out in this Convention. Therefore, the EU Member States agreed on a common policy on the protection to be afforded to those persons. In that context, the Tampere Conclusions (October 1999) have provided the political orientation for the Union's strategy in the field of international protection, emphasising the need to address this protection in an integrated way.

Anchored on this political orientation, a Common European Asylum System (CEAS) was adopted. It provides common procedures on international protection for EU Member States in order to offer a uniform status to both applicants and beneficiaries of international protection. It notably created, alongside refugee status, a new category of protection, ie 'subsidiary protection'.

Among the legislative instruments adopted in the context of the European harmonisation of asylum law, the 'Qualification Directive'[3] defines common standards for the qualification

* Tatiana Cassagnabère and Anna Grasso are Legal Secretaries in the Chambers of Vice-President Bay Larsen.

[1] Convention relating to the Status of Refugees (Geneva, 28 July 1951).

[2] Recital 3 of Council Directive 2004/83/EC of 29 April 2004 on minimum standards for the qualification and status of third-country nationals or stateless persons as refugees or as persons who otherwise need international protection and the content of the protection granted (Qualification Directive) [2004] OJ L304/12, and *corrigendum* [2005] OJ L204/24 (Directive 2004/83).

[3] Directive 2004/83 was amended by Directive 2011/95/EU of the European Parliament and of the Council of 13 December 2011 on standards for the qualification of third-country nationals or stateless persons as beneficiaries

of third-country nationals as refugees or as beneficiaries of subsidiary protection, and the content of each form of status. This Directive was the first piece of EU legislation to establish a single minimum[4] legal status that is binding for most of the EU Member States in order to protect persons in need of protection other than refugees. Indeed, a person eligible for subsidiary protection is, by definition, one 'who does not qualify as a refugee'.[5] Furthermore, those Member States are allowed to introduce or retain more favourable standards, subject to the condition that they are in accordance with the Qualification Directive.[6]

The European Court of Justice (ECJ) was seized of a large number of cases concerning CEAS in order to bring clarification relating in particular to the access conditions and the extent of subsidiary protection under the Qualification Directive. Judge Bay Larsen was the reporting judge in the very first of those cases,[7] as well as many others that followed.

Since the seminal *Salahadin Abdulla* case, the Court ruled that in connection with the concept of 'international protection' Directive 2004/83 governs two distinct systems of protection: refugee status and subsidiary protection status.[8] Indeed, the Court underlined the difference between the two forms of protection afforded by the Geneva Convention and Qualification Directive respectively.[9]

Subsidiary protection is complementary and additional to the refugee protection enshrined in the Geneva Convention.[10] From a procedural perspective, this implies that an application for subsidiary protection must not be examined before the competent authority has concluded that the applicant for international protection does not qualify for refugee status.[11] The ECJ also ruled that, within the system of Directive 2004/83, the possible cessation of refugee status occurs 'without prejudice to the right of the person concerned to request the granting of subsidiary protection status'.[12]

On the threshold of a likely major reform of the CEAS, it might be worth focusing on the legislative and jurisprudential developments relating to subsidiary protection in order to highlight its features by pointing out the interaction with European human rights law and international humanitarian law, with regard to its access requirements (Section II) and the influence of the content of refugees status on the content of the subsidiary protection (Section III).

II. QUALIFICATION FOR SUBSIDIARY PROTECTION: ACCESS REQUIREMENTS AND THE RELATIONSHIP WITH THE INTERNATIONAL LAW

The minimum requirements for granting subsidiary protection laid down in the Qualification Directive must add to the protection of refugees under the Geneva Convention through the

of international protection, for a uniform status for refugees or for persons eligible for subsidiary protection, and for the content of the protection granted [2011] OJ L337/9 (Directive 2011/95), in order to reflect the objective of Art 78(1) and (2)(a) and (b) of the Treaty on the Functioning of the European Union (TFEU) which requires that the EU develop a common policy on asylum with a 'uniform status' for refugees and other persons in need of international protection. In this chapter, 'qualification directive' means indistinctly Directives 2004/83 and 2011/95.

[4] Art 3 and Recital 14 of Directive 2004/83.

[5] Art 2(f) of Directive 2011/95.

[6] Art 3 and Recital 14 of Directive 2004/83.

[7] Case C-133/06 *Parliament v Council*, ECLI:EU:C:2008:257.

[8] Cases C-175/08, C-176/08, C-178/08 and C-179/08 *Salahadin Abdulla and Others*, ECLI:EU:C:2010:105, para 78.

[9] Case C-364/11 *Abed El Karem El Kott and Others*, ECLI:EU:C:2012:826, paras 66–67.

[10] Recitals 5 and 24 of Directive 2004/83; and Case C-465/07 *Elgafaji*, ECLI:EU:C:2009:94, para 33.

[11] Case C-604/12 *HN*, ECLI:EU:C:2014:302, para 35.

[12] *Salahadin Abdulla and Others* (n 8), para 80.

identification of persons genuinely in need of international protection and through such persons being offered an appropriate status. In this context, analysis of the ECJ's case law relating to subsidiary protection reveals a certain approximation between the regime of this protection and the standards of international law, in particular with those enshrined in the European Convention for the Protection of Human Rights and Fundamental Freedoms,[13] though without erasing the specificities of this protection (A).[14] This analysis may also reveal a certain autonomy between the subsidiary protection regime and the standards of international law, in particular international humanitarian law (B).

A. The Subsidiary Protection Criteria and the Interaction with the European Convention on Human Rights

The Qualification Directive requires EU Member States to guarantee subsidiary protection to a third-country national or a stateless person eligible for subsidiary protection.[15] That national cannot be considered a refugee, but substantial grounds have to be shown to prove that, if returned to his or her country of origin, he or she would face a real risk of suffering serious harm.[16] Subsidiary protection status ceases once the circumstances that motivated it no longer exist.[17]

The Qualification Directive establishes a counterpart to refugee's 'persecution' in the definition of persons eligible for subsidiary protection which is the criterion of 'serious harm'. Article 15 of the Qualification Directive defines the acts that amount to serious harm as required by the definition of persons eligible for subsidiary protection. Three forms of serious harm are set out in this provision: (a) death penalty or execution; (b) torture or inhuman or degrading treatment or punishment of an applicant in the country of origin; (c) serious and individual threat to a civilian's life or person by reason of indiscriminate violence in situations of international or internal armed conflict.

In *Elgafaji*, the ECJ initiated a certain approximation with the regime established by the European Convention on Human Rights (ECHR). The ECJ emphasised that the three types of serious harm defined in Article 15 constitute the qualification for subsidiary protection where substantial grounds have been shown for believing that the applicant faces a real risk of such harm if returned to the relevant country of origin.[18] In that respect, the ECJ ruled that while the fundamental right guaranteed under Article 3 of the ECHR forms part of the general principles of EU law, observance of which is ensured by the ECJ, and while the case law of the European Court of Human Rights (ECtHR) is taken into consideration in interpreting the scope of that right in the European legal order, Article 15(b) was the provision in Directive 2004/83 corresponding, in essence, to Article 3 of the ECHR.[19] Indeed, Article 15(b) of the Qualification Directive establishes a right to subsidiary protection for people

[13] The European Convention for the Protection of Human Rights and Fundamental Freedoms, signed at Rome, 4 November 1950 (ECHR).

[14] L Bay Larsen, 'Quelques remarques sur les relations entre le droit international et le régime d'asile européen commun' in A Tizzano et al (eds), *La Cour de justice de l'Union européenne sous la présidence de Vassilios Skouris (2003–2015): Liber amicorum Vassilios Skouris* (Bruylant, 2015) 73.

[15] Art 18 of the Qualification Directive.

[16] Art 2(e) of Directive 2004/83 and Art 2(f) of Directive 2011/95.

[17] Art 16 of the Qualification Directive.

[18] *Elgafaji* (n 10), para 31.

[19] ibid, para 28.

at risk of 'torture, inhuman or degrading treatment or punishment', reflecting the *non-refoulement* principle which derives from Article 3 of the ECHR.

As for Article 15(c) of Directive 2004/83, the ECJ considered that it should be seen as distinct in scope and content from Article 15(b). Thus, the former has its own distinct area of application, its content 'is different from Article 3 of the ECHR, and its interpretation must, therefore, be carried out independently, although with due regard for fundamental rights' as guaranteed under the ECHR.[20]

The terms 'death penalty', 'execution' and 'torture or inhuman or degrading treatment or punishment of an applicant in the country of origin', used in Articles 15(a) and 15(b) of the Qualification Directive, cover situations in which the applicant for subsidiary protection is specifically exposed to the risk of a particular type of harm. By contrast, the harm defined in Article 15(c) of the Qualification Directive consists of a 'serious and individual threat to a civilian's life or person' and thus covers a more general risk of harm.[21]

The term 'individual' has to be understood as covering harm to civilians irrespective of their identity, where the degree of indiscriminate violence characterising the armed conflict taking place reaches such a high level that substantial grounds are shown for believing that a civilian, returned to the relevant country or to the relevant region, would, solely on account of his presence on the territory of that country or region, face a real risk of being subject to the serious threat referred to in this provision of the Qualification Directive.[22]

It is worth noting that the interpretation of Article 15 of Directive 2011/95, the wording of which coincides with that of Article 15 of Directive 2004/83, was later developed by the ECJ.[23] It pointed out the need to take into account all the relevant circumstances of the individual case, relating both to the individual position of the applicant and personal circumstances and to the general situation in the country of origin, in order to identify persons genuinely in need of subsidiary protection. In that respect, the ECJ recalled that it follows from this provision that both the circumstances relating to the general situation in the country of origin, particularly the general level of violence and insecurity in that country, and those relating to the individual position and personal circumstances of the applicant, are capable of constituting factors relevant to the assessment of any application for subsidiary protection, within the meaning of Article 15, which is the subject of such an assessment.[24] Furthermore, even if an application for international protection made under Article 15(c) of Directive 2011/95 does not rely on factors specific to the applicant's circumstances, such an application must be subject to an individual assessment, in respect of which a whole series of factors must be taken into account, as part of a comprehensive appraisal of all the relevant circumstances of the individual case.[25]

As to the question of whether Article 15(c) of Directive 2011/95 must be interpreted as meaning that in order to assess whether there is a real risk of suffering a type of serious harm as defined in that provision, the competent national authority must be able to take account of factors relating to the individual position and personal circumstances of the applicant other than the mere fact of coming from an area of a given country where 'the most extreme cases

[20] ibid, para 28.

[21] ibid, paras 32–33.

[22] ibid, para 35.

[23] Cases C-901/19 *Bundesrepublik Deutschland (Concept of 'serious and individual threat')*, ECLI:EU:C:2021:472; and C-125/22 *Staatssecretaris van Justitie en Veiligheid (Concept of serious harm)*, ECLI:EU:C:2023:843.

[24] *Staatssecretaris van Justitie en Veiligheid (Concept of serious harm)* (n 23), para 43.

[25] *Bundesrepublik Deutschland (Concept of 'serious and individual threat')* (n 23), paras 40–41; and *Staatssecretaris van Justitie en Veiligheid (Concept of serious harm)* (n 23), para 50.

of general violence', within the meaning of the *NA v the United Kingdom* judgment of the ECtHR,[26] occur, the ECJ answered positively. Once again, the ECJ stressed, the specificity of the subsidiary protection vis-à-vis the one afforded by the ECHR, as it ruled that while being fully compatible with the case law of the ECtHR relating to Article 3 ECHR, the interpretation of Article 15(c) of Directive 2011/95 by the ECJ provides applicants for international protection more extensive protection than that offered by the said Article 3.[27]

Such an approach, that aims to limit the approximation between the subsidiary protection regime and the standards laid down in the ECHR, has already been noted in the *M'Bodj* judgment,[28] concerning the interpretation of Article 15(b) of the Qualification Directive which defines serious harm as the torture or inhuman or degrading treatment or punishment of a third-country national in his country of origin. The autonomy of the CEAS vis-à-vis the protection established by the ECHR has notably been expressed by the observation according to which protection against expulsion under this Convention does not mean that a person should be granted leave to reside in a Member State by way of subsidiary protection under Directive 2004/83.[29]

The ECJ emphasised that Article 15(b) of the Qualification Directive is applicable only to the inhuman or degrading treatment of an applicant in his country of origin so that subsidiary protection should be granted only in those cases. However, the risk of deterioration in the health of a third-country national suffering from a serious illness as a result of the absence of appropriate treatment in the country of origin is not sufficient to warrant that person being granted subsidiary protection unless that third-country national is intentionally deprived of health care. Thus, the ECJ concluded that the requirement to interpret Article 15(b) of Directive 2004/83 in a manner consistent with Article 19(2) of the Charter of Fundamental Rights of the European Union (the Charter), to the effect that no person may be returned to a State in which there is a serious risk that that person will be subjected to inhuman and degrading treatment and, having due regard to Article 3 of the ECHR, to which Article 15(b), in essence, corresponds, is not such as to call that interpretation into question.[30]

This autonomy of the CEAS vis-à-vis the protection established by the ECHR was also confirmed in the *MP* case,[31] in which the ECJ ruled that the fact that Article 3 of the ECHR precludes, in very exceptional cases, a third-country national suffering from a serious illness being removed to a country in which appropriate treatment is not available, does not mean that that person should be granted leave to reside in a Member State by way of subsidiary protection under the Qualification Directive.

B. The Distinction between the Subsidiary Protection Regime and International Humanitarian Law

The *Diakité*[32] case offers an example of the relationship between international humanitarian law and subsidiary protection. In this case, the ECJ distinguished the interpretation of

[26] *NA v the United Kingdom* App no 25904/07, ECLI:CE:ECHR:2024:0123JUD002465019, para 115.
[27] *Staatssecretaris van Justitie en Veiligheid (Concept of serious harm)* (n 23), para 66.
[28] Case C-542/13 *M'Bodj*, ECLI:EU:C:2014:2452.
[29] L Bay Larsen, 'Entre autonomie et cohérence: les développements des relations entre le régime d'asile européen commun et le droit international depuis 2015' in D Petrlík et al (eds), *Évolution des rapports entre les ordres juridiques de l'Union européenne, international et nationaux: Liber amicorum Jiří Malenovský* (Bruylant, 2020) 169.
[30] *M'Bodj* (n 28), paras 36 and 38.
[31] Case C-353/16 *MP*, ECLI:EU:C:2018:276, para 46.
[32] Case C-285/12 *Diakité*, ECLI:EU:C:2014:39.

Article 15(c) of Directive 2004/83 from what follows from humanitarian law and thereby affirmed the autonomy of the EU protection system.

Under this provision, in the context of an internal armed conflict, the ECJ was called upon to specify whether, in order to determine if a third-country national or a stateless person is eligible for subsidiary protection, Article 15(c) should be interpreted regarding international humanitarian law or autonomously.

The ECJ pointed out that international humanitarian law and the subsidiary protection regime introduced by the Qualification Directive pursue different aims and establish quite distinct protection mechanisms.[33] In this regard, the ECJ stated that the type of harm specified in Article 15(c) of this Directive consists of a serious and individual threat to a civilian's life or person by reason of indiscriminate violence in situations of international or internal armed conflict. In this context, the EU legislature has used the phrase 'international or internal armed conflict', as opposed to the concepts on which international humanitarian law is based (international humanitarian law distinguishes between 'international armed conflict' and 'armed conflict not of an international character').[34]

The ECJ emphasised that the EU legislature wished to grant subsidiary protection not only to persons affected by 'international armed conflicts' and by 'armed conflict not of an international character', as defined in international humanitarian law, but also to persons affected by internal armed conflicts, provided that such conflict involves indiscriminate violence.[35]

As indicated above, the reason for this distinction from what follows from international humanitarian law is the different aims pursued; while the rules under international humanitarian law are designed, inter alia, to provide protection for civilian populations in a conflict zone by restricting the effects of war on persons and property, it does not – by contrast with Article 2(e) of Directive 2004/83 read in conjunction with Article 15(c) of this Directive – provide for international protection to be granted to certain civilians who are outside both the conflict zone and the territory of the conflicting parties. As a consequence, the definitions of 'armed conflict' provided in international humanitarian law are not designed to identify situations in which such international protection would be necessary and would thus have to be granted by the competent authorities of the Member States.[36]

The ECJ concluded that it is not possible, without disregarding those two distinct areas, to make eligibility for subsidiary protection reliant upon a finding that the conditions for applying international humanitarian law have been met. Accordingly, the ECJ ruled that under this provision, in order to assess whether an internal armed conflict exists, it is not necessary for that conflict to be categorised as a certain type of conflict under international humanitarian law.[37]

It appears that the ECJ protects the autonomy of the CEAS by refusing to apply the criteria's characteristic of international regimes 'out of touch' with the protection of persons facing a real risk of suffering serious harm as defined in Article 15 of the Qualification Directive. However, it is more a question of difference of content than of formal value which leads to ensuring those regimes a much more limited relevance.[38]

[33] ibid, para 24.
[34] ibid, para 20.
[35] ibid, para 21.
[36] ibid, para 23.
[37] ibid, para 35.
[38] Bay Larsen (n 14), 78.

III. RAPPROCHEMENT BETWEEN THE CONTENT OF RIGHTS AND BENEFITS GRANTED BY SUBSIDIARY PROTECTION AND REFUGEES STATUS

The degree of approximation of the content of subsidiary protection with that of refugee status may be sought both in the comparison of the rights and benefits granted to the two statuses by the Qualification Directive (A) and in the links between such rights and benefits and those enshrined in the Geneva Convention (B).

A. The Partial Alignment of Rights and Benefits Granted to the Beneficiaries of Subsidiary Protection with those of Refugees under the Qualification Directive

An analysis of the text of the Qualification Directive shows that, when it was recast, the content of the rights guaranteed to refugees and beneficiaries of subsidiary protection underwent significant changes, unlike the conditions for granting status. In addition to the augmentation of certain guarantees, those amendments are broadly characterised by a reduction in the differences between the two categories of beneficiaries of international protection. Certain disadvantages for beneficiaries of subsidiary protection under Directive 2004/83 have been abandoned in the recast. An upward alignment of the rights guaranteed to beneficiaries of subsidiary protection is therefore sought in that Directive.

That process is explained by the intention of the EU legislature to ensure, in principle, the same rights and benefits for both categories of beneficiaries of international protection. Several elements recall this desire for equal treatment between these two categories in the Preamble of Directive 2011/95[39] and, as previously, in Article 20(2) of this Directive, which emphasises that unless otherwise specified, the application of Chapter VII on the content of international protection should be understood for both categories. Those legislative indications found very explicit resonance in the *Alo and Osso* case,[40] in which the ECJ unambiguously stated that the content of international protection is the same for the two categories within the meaning of the Qualification Directive, since only express indications may derogate from that principle.

As regards the rights and advantages granted to those categories, their content is set out in Chapter VII of the Qualification Directive. That chapter essentially imposes obligations on the Member States relating to the minimum guarantees and advantages to be granted in respect of international protection.

On the one hand, a common set of rights, mainly of a social and economic nature, is laid down identically for both categories of beneficiaries of that protection. No distinction is expressly drawn between those two categories as regards freedom of movement within the territory of the Member State,[41] access to information,[42] employment,[43] education,[44] procedures for the recognition of qualifications,[45] healthcare,[46] protection for unaccompanied

[39] Recital 39 of Directive 2011/95.
[40] Joined Cases C-443/14 and C-444/14 *Alo and Osso*, ECLI:EU:C:2016:127.
[41] Art 33 of Directive 2011/95.
[42] ibid, Art 22.
[43] ibid, Art 26.
[44] ibid, Art 27.
[45] ibid, Art 28.
[46] ibid, Art 30.

minors,[47] accommodation[48] and integration facilities.[49] It should be noted that a higher standard has been granted concerning access to employment, health care and integration facilities, for which every differentiation of regime from that of refugees has been abandoned. For these rights and benefits a full approximation of refugee status and subsidiary protection in relation to Directive 2004/83 can thus be seen. It results in an increase, in essence, of the level of protection granted by Directive 2011/95 to beneficiaries of subsidiary protection status as compared with that provided for by Directive 2004/83. As stated above, that level of protection may moreover be increased by the Member States, which remain free to provide a higher protection than that required under EU law.

On the other hand, significant differences persist in the treatment of the two categories of beneficiaries of international protection. The reasons for that are not explicitly set out in the Qualification Directive, although Recital 39 of Directive 2011/95 indicates that 'derogations [...] are necessary and objectively justified'.

Two of those differences should be noted. The first concerns the duration of the residence permit to be issued to those categories.[50] This is an essential aspect of international protection status since it relates to the very presence of the beneficiary and his or her family members[51] in the territory of a Member State. While refugees are eligible for a renewable period of residence of three years, beneficiaries of subsidiary protection may benefit from one year, renewable for at least two years. Moreover, even if the prescriptiveness of this indication is doubtful, as far as it is included just in Recital 40 of Directive 2011/95, it seems to be indicated as a possible precondition for certain social and economic advantages to be granted.[52]

The second difference concerns the scope of the social benefits to which a beneficiary of subsidiary protection may aspire. Social security support for beneficiaries of subsidiary protection remains potentially lower than the one awarded to refugees. While there is a principle of equality between persons protected under the two statuses and nationals as regards the 'necessary social assistance', including the actual amount of benefits granted,[53] Member States still have the right to limit such assistance solely to 'core benefits' in the case of beneficiaries of subsidiary protection.[54]

A third provision may be highlighted, in the context of that examination, because of its somewhat ambiguous scope *rationae personae*. This is Article 21(2) of the Qualification Directive, which admits the possibility, in some strict circumstances,[55] to *refoule* 'a refugee, whether formally recognised or not'.

The principle of *non-refoulement* is of major importance. In fact, it is one of the objectives of the common policy on asylum, subsidiary protection and temporary protection, as set out

[47] ibid, Art 31.

[48] ibid, Art 32.

[49] ibid, Art 34.

[50] ibid, Art 24.

[51] See, in that regard, ibid Art 23(1) and (2) of Directive 2011/95 and Case C-768/19 *Bundesrepublik Deutschland (Family member)*, ECLI:ECLI.EU:C:2021:709.

[52] Recital 40 of Directive 2011/95.

[53] Case C-713/17 *Ayubi*, ECLI:ECLI:EU:C:2018:929, para 20.

[54] Art 29(2) of Directive 2011/95. Recital 45 of this Directive refers to 'the grant of assistance in the form of a minimum income, assistance in the event of illness, pregnancy and parental assistance'.

[55] The restriction of the principle of *non-refoulement* applies only where there are serious reasons for considering that the person concerned is a danger to the security of the State or, if convicted of particularly serious crimes, constitutes a danger to the community of that State. These situations repeat those provided for in Art 33(2) of the Geneva Convention.

in Article 78(1) TFEU. It is an international obligation[56] that is now enshrined in Article 19 of the Charter and reaffirmed in Article 21(1) of the Qualification Directive. This provision states, without distinction between the two categories of beneficiaries of international protection, that 'Member States shall respect the principle of *non-refoulement* in accordance with their international obligations'.

Although the standards concerning the extent to which human rights are binding on the EU or its Member States present the principle of *non-refoulement* as absolute,[57] conditional situations of *refoulement* are envisaged by Article 21(2) of the Qualification Directive. As already mentioned, this provision refers only to 'a refugee, whether formally recognised or not'. Indeed, it does not refer explicitly to beneficiaries of subsidiary protection and thus casts doubt on their inclusion within its scope *rationae personae*. The successive paragraph,[58] by also referring only to refugees, increases uncertainty as to this scope.

That being said, it can also be observed that Article 21 of the Qualification Directive falls within the framework of Chapter VII. In this regard, the ECJ has already emphasised that notably Article 21(2) of Directive 2004/83 is part of this chapter, the purpose of which is to define the benefits which both candidates for refugee or subsidiary protection status whose claims have been upheld, may enjoy.[59]

In any event, the current application of Article 21(2) of the Qualification Directive is limited by the very wording of this provision which makes *refoulement* subject to the absence of prohibitions to that effect by the international obligations of the Member States. Those obligations and EU law have been considered by Advocate General Wathelet as 'now largely offset[ting] the exception to the principle of *non-refoulement*'.[60]

In the *M* case, the ECJ interpreted this provision, notably analysing its relationship with Article 4 of the Charter protecting the same right of Article 3 ECHR, which, in its turn, overlaps at least to the extent set out in section II.A of this chapter, with the conditions for granting subsidiary protection.[61]

The ECJ noted that Article 33(2) of the Geneva Convention denies the refugee the benefit, in the circumstances referred to also in Article 21(2) of Directive 2011/95, of the principle of *non-refoulement* to a country 'where his life or freedom would be threatened'.[62] However, Article 21(2) of Directive 2011/95 must be interpreted and applied, following the ECJ's reasoning, 'in a way that observes the rights guaranteed by the Charter, in particular Article 4 and Article 19(2)'. Consequently, Member States cannot remove, expel or extradite a 'foreign national', irrespective of his conduct, where there are substantial grounds for believing that he will face a genuine risk, in the country of destination, of being subjected to treatment prohibited by these provisions.[63] In this way, the ECJ specified, in terms that seem to have a quite general application scope, the limits existing in the Charter on the possibility to *refoule*.

[56] Art 33(1) of the Geneva Convention; Art 3 of the Convention against Torture and Other Cruel, Inhuman or Degrading Treatment or Punishment (New York, 10 December 1984); and Art 7 of the International Covenant on Civil and Political Rights (New York, 16 December 1966).

[57] Art 19 of the Charter and *MSS v Belgium and Greece*, App no 30696/96 (ECtHR, 21 January 2011).

[58] Art 21(3) of Directive 2011/95 leaves Member States free to refuse to grant a residence permit to a refugee to whom the exceptions to the principle of *non-refoulement* listed in Art 21(2) applies.

[59] Case C-373/13 *T*, ECLI:EU:C:2015:413, para 68.

[60] Opinion of Wathelet AG in Joined Cases C-391/16, C-77/17 and C-78/17 *M (Revocation of refugee status)*, ECLI:EU:C:2018:486, para 57.

[61] See, in that regard, *Sufi and Elmi v United Kingdom* App no 8319/07 and 11449/07 (ECtHR, 28 June 2011), para 226.

[62] Case C-391/16 *M (Revocation of refugee status)*, ECLI:EU:C:2019:403, para 94.

[63] ibid, para 94.

Regardless of the precise scope of Article 21(2) of the Qualification Directive, a partial alignment between certain rights and benefits granted to refugees and beneficiaries of subsidiary protection can be noted in this secondary law act. This situation paved the way for a rapprochement between EU subsidiary protection status and international refugee status.

B. The Influence of the Geneva Convention on the Content of Subsidiary Protection

It has been noted that the recognition of links between subsidiary protection and the protection conferred by the Geneva Convention is not self-evident.[64] The relationship between the CEAS and the Geneva Convention has been defined as being of a systemic nature.[65] This specific relationship is also present in primary law with regard to subsidiary protection, since Article 78 TFEU requires asylum and subsidiary protection policy to comply with the Geneva Convention. In secondary law, Article 78 appears to be reflected, also as regards subsidiary protection, in Article 20(1) of the Qualification Directive, which opens the chapter on the content of international protection by stating that 'this Chapter is without prejudice to the rights laid down in the Geneva Convention'.

However, the provisions on the content of subsidiary protection do not specifically refer to provisions of the Geneva Convention and it does not provide a specific right applicable to subsidiary protection. Thus, unsurprisingly, the ECJ clearly stated that, in principle, that Convention is relevant only as regards refugee status.[66]

Following that logic, recognition of the cardinal role of the Geneva Convention for the interpretation of the Qualification Directive was initially acknowledged by the ECJ with regard to the provisions relating to refugee status.[67] In practice, this means that, in the event of equivalence of the safeguards provided by that Directive and the Geneva Convention, the ECJ interprets the provisions together, sometimes indistinctly.[68]

In the *Alo and Osso* case, the extension of that logic led to the ECJ accepting the application of the safeguards provided by the Geneva Convention to subsidiary protection status. Not being able to rely on explicit and specific links between the Convention and the subsidiary protection, the ECJ, in order to take this step, relied on the assumption that the regimes established by the Qualification Directive are equal for beneficiaries of subsidiary protection and for refugees.

By reasoning in that way, since the rights conferred on refugees must be read in accordance with the Geneva Convention, they will also benefit, by 'transitivity', beneficiaries of subsidiary protection. That reasoning represents the variation of two considerations previously upheld by the ECJ: on the one hand, the lower limit that the Geneva Convention constitutes for the rights and benefits conferred to refugees by the Qualification Directive, and on the other hand, the identity of principle between that status and subsidiary protection status. In doing so, the ECJ has taken into account the content of Article 26 of the Geneva Convention in order to

[64] Bay Larsen (n 29), 176.
[65] Bay Larsen (n 14), 75.
[66] *Alo and Osso* (n 40), para 31.
[67] *Abed El Karem El Kott* (n 9), para 43.
[68] *Salahadin Abdulla* (n 8), paras 57 and 65; and Joined Cases C-57/09 and C-101/09 *B and D*, ECLI:EU:C:2010:661, para 86.

determine the scope of the right to freedom of movement guaranteed to beneficiaries of international protection by Article 33 of the Qualification Directive.

In essence, the ECJ appears to have 'imported' a requirement explicitly provided only by the Geneva Convention to the EU subsidiary protection regime.

In *Ahmed*,[69] the ECJ extended that logic of 'transitivity import' to cases which do no concern the content of subsidiary protection status but the grounds for exclusion from it. Subsequently, in the *Bilali* case,[70] the ECJ applied the abovementioned logic to causes of loss of subsidiary protection status. In those cases, the provisions of the Qualification Directive relating to subsidiary protection were only 'similar' to those applicable to refugees under the Qualification Directive and the Geneva Convention.[71] In addition, especially[72] in *Bilali*, the ECJ accepts the 'particular relevance' of documents issued by the United Nations High Commissioner for Refugees for the purposes of interpreting the provisions relating to subsidiary protection,[73] as it had been able to do, in the same way, for those relating to refugees.[74]

It can therefore be seen that the ECJ, in some circumstances, interprets the provisions concerning subsidiary protection in the light of the Geneva Convention. However, it may be noted that that solution is based fully and solely on a choice made by the EU legislature at the level of secondary legislation. Conversely, it may be considered that EU legislature, unlike the national legislatures, could take the initiative of withdrawing that choice, notably by introducing an 'indication' contrary to the equal treatment of the two categories of beneficiaries of international protection. In that case, that right would remain in force only for refugee status as established by the Geneva Convention.

IV. CONCLUSION

This brief examination of the status of subsidiary protection allows one to consider that the exogenous normative influence to which this protection is subject does not entirely remove its specificity.

It appears that a certain distance may be observed between subsidiary protection and the rules of international law when a distinction may be drawn between the aims of those rules and those relating to subsidiary protection. That analysis of the purpose is not to be found in the ECJ's reasoning when it comes to clarifying the content of subsidiary protection in relation to refugee status. The trend towards a rapprochement of the two regimes is based on a transitivity logic due to equality or similarity between the rules on the content of subsidiary protection and the protection conferred to refugees.

Although genuine, this equality is no less partial. Significant distinctions exist between the two statuses of protection. In addition, as the case law of the ECJ shows, that trend is reversible and is based on the will of the EU legislature. In that regard, after the political agreement reached in December 2023, the New Pact on Migration and Asylum will most likely soon be

[69] Case C-369/17 *Ahmed*, ECLI:EU:C:2018:713.
[70] Case C-720/17 *Bilali*, ECLI:EU:C:2019:448, para 56.
[71] ibid, para 56 and *Ahmed* (n 70), paras 43–50.
[72] In *Ahmed* (n 70), para 57, this recognition was much more moderate.
[73] *Bilali* (n 71), paras 57–58.
[74] Case C-528/11 *Halaf*, ECLI:EU:C:2013:342, para 44.

adopted. Among the various legislative acts whose reform is recommended, the Qualification Directive will probably be subject to some changes.

Although a revolution is not foreseen concerning the criteria for granting subsidiary protection and the content of this protection, an analysis – including a systemic one – of the new regime will undoubtedly make it possible to determine whether and, if so, to what extent the relationship between subsidiary protection, international standards and refugee status will change.

Part III

The Dynamics at Work in the Area of Freedom, Security and Justice

16

The Transfer of Asylum Seekers to Non-EU 'Safe' Countries under Scrutiny from the European Court of Justice

JAN PASSER AND PIERRE SCHMITT*

I. INTRODUCTION

THE 1990S WITNESSED a surge in asylum applications within Europe, partly related to the collapse of the Soviet Union and the conflicts in the former Yugoslavia. This situation led the Members of the European Communities to agree upon a new system of cooperation in this field, attributing the responsibility for asylum applications mainly to the Member State in which the asylum seeker entered first.[1] In 2015, the European continent experienced the arrival of approximately one million migrants and refugees fleeing conflicts in Syria, Afghanistan and Iraq, which is known as the European refugee crisis.[2] EU Member States decided on a crisis relocation mechanism and a quota system for asylum seekers. More recently, another wave of asylum seekers from Ukraine reached Europe.

Member States have not always adopted a consistent approach towards these migrations flows, sometimes fiercely protecting their borders, other times welcoming asylum seekers with open arms.[3] Even if one could argue that the absorption capacity of European societies has certain limits, it is important to remember that such variations may not exclusively rely upon national politics, but they have to obey the general framework of asylum rules in international and EU law. In this regard, two fundamental principles should be recalled: first, the right of asylum serves, in substance, to offer protection to people fleeing persecution or serious harm in their own country. It seems consequently legitimate to consider that this right does not extend to any country of choice, but rather that at least one country should be accessible, in which such protection could be guaranteed. Second, international protection does not aim at

* Jan Passer is a Judge at the European Court of Justice and Pierre Schmitt is Legal Secretary at the European Court of Justice. All opinions expressed herein are personal to the authors. The authors would like to thank Ondřej Kadlec for his helpful comments on an earlier version of this contribution.

[1] Convention determining the State responsible for examining applications for asylum lodged in one of the Member States of the European Communities (Dublin Convention) [1997] OJ C254/1.

[2] European Commission, *The EU and the Migration Crisis* (2017), https://op.europa.eu/en/publication-detail/-/publication/e9465e4f-b2e4-11e7-837e-01aa75ed71a1, accessed 3 March 2024.

[3] See for instance, on Germany, N Zaun and A Ripoll Servent, 'One Step Forward, Two Steps Back: the Ambiguous Role of Germany in EU Asylum Policies' (2021) 43 *Journal of European Integration* 157.

circumventing immigration laws or automatically legalising stays in any country of choice of the asylum seeker.

European Member States have sought in recent years to establish mechanisms allowing for the transfer of the responsibility for asylum seekers to non-EU third countries.[4] These mechanisms include the concepts of 'safe country of origin', 'safe third country', the 'European safe third country' and the 'internal protection'. In particular, 'safe countries of origin' have to be distinguished from 'safe third countries', which serve as transit for asylum seekers where the latter can be returned under certain circumstances, including the necessity of a connection between the transit country and the asylum seeker. The 'European safe third country' refers to third countries which observe particularly high human rights and refugee protection standards and for which EU Member States should be allowed not to examine, or not to examine fully, applications for international protection regarding applicants. Finally, the concept of 'internal protection' does not refer to a State in its entirety but rather a safe region or a safe place within the country of origin.

As will be further examined in this contribution, these mechanisms allow both a more rapid processing of applications and a more efficient decision-making, sometimes leading to the inadmissibility of the application, sometimes leading to a presumption of safety for the applicant. Yet, scholars[5] have criticised these concepts for being detrimental to the rights of refugees and certain NGOs[6] qualify these concepts as denials of the right of asylum mainly because 'nobody can guarantee that a country is safe for all its citizens' and the 'presumption in the examination of asylum seekers' applications breach the principle of equality before the law and make the procedure fundamentally biased'. In addition, concerns have been raised about the assessment of the concept of 'safety', which cannot, according to the United Nations High Commissioner for Refugees (UNHCR), be answered in a general way, but only on an individual basis.[7] Finally, NGOs fear that geopolitical interests may prevail over the rights of asylum seekers given that more expeditious procedures that would not fulfil the procedural guarantees required by the Geneva Convention.

National jurisdictions act as 'primary guardians'[8] as far the implementation of safe country concepts is concerned at national level. Some of them, confronted with questions relating to the interpretation of these concepts, have issued requests for preliminary rulings at the European Court of Justice (ECJ). This contribution aims to present and briefly discuss these concepts in the light of the latter's case law.

[4] M Giuffré et al, 'On "Safety" and EU Externalization of Borders' (2022) 24 *European Journal of Migration and Law* 570, 574. Nationals of EU Member States may also apply for refugee status in another EU Member Sate. Such applications are governed by Protocol (No 24) on asylum for nationals of Member States of the European Union (also known as the Aznar Protocol) [2008] OJ L115/305, following which Member States shall be regarded as constituting safe countries of origin in respect of each other for all legal and practical purposes in relation to asylum matters.

[5] See for instance BN Osso, 'Unpacking the Safe Third Country Concept in the European Union: B/orders, Legal Spaces, and Asylum in the Shadow of Externalization' (2023) 20 *International Journal of Refugee Law* 1, 18; and S Peers, *EU Justice and Home Affairs Law*, 5th edn (Oxford University Press, 2023) 297 ff.

[6] European Association for the Defence of Human Rights, *International Federation for Human Rights and EuroMed Rights, 'Safe' Countries: A Denial of the Right of Asylum* (2016) https://euromedrights.org/wp-content/uploads/2016/10/AnalysePaysSurs-FINAL-EN-12052016_final.pdf, accessed 1 February 2024, 3.

[7] UN High Commissioner for Refugees, UNHCR Provisional Comments on the Proposal for a Council Directive on Minimum Standards on Procedures in Member States for Granting and Withdrawing Refugee Status Council Document 14203/04, Asile 64, of 9 November 2004 (2005) 37, available at http://www.unhcr.org/refworld/docid/42492b302.html.

[8] European Union Agency for Asylum, *Applying the Concept of Safe Countries in the Asylum Procedure* (2022) 16, available at https://euaa.europa.eu/sites/default/files/publications/2022-12/2022_safe_country_concept_asylum_procedure_EN.pdf, accessed 22 April 2024.

II. THE SAFE COUNTRY OF ORIGIN

International protection is only needed if national protection is not available. This is the so-called principle of 'surrogacy', which Andreas Zimmermann and Claudia Mahler qualify as a 'basic principle of refugee law'.[9] This principle has been translated into the European legislation through the concept of 'safe country of origin'.

Pursuant to Article 36 of Directive 2013/32,[10] a third country designated as a safe country of origin in accordance with that Directive may, after an individual examination of the application, be regarded as safe for a particular applicant who is either a national of that country or a stateless person who was formerly habitually residing there, unless this applicant submits any serious grounds for considering the country not to be safe in his or her particular circumstances. The notion of 'safe country of origin' is defined in Annex I of Directive 2013/32 as follows:

> a country is considered as a safe country of origin where, on the basis of the legal situation, the application of the law within a democratic system and the general political circumstances, it can be shown that there is generally and consistently no persecution as defined in Article 9 of Directive 2011/95/EU,[11] no torture or inhuman or degrading treatment or punishment and no threat by reason of indiscriminate violence in situations of international or internal armed conflict.

The designation of a safe country of origin is regulated at the national level by each Member State, following the criteria listed in Annex I of Directive 2013/32. Currently, 22 EU+[12] countries have established lists of safe countries of origin.[13] As an exception, EU+ countries may exclude geographical areas or profiles within safe countries of origin. For instance, LGBTQI applicants from Georgia may apply for international protection in the Netherlands, or Moldovan asylum seekers from Transnistria may apply in the Czech Republic and in Switzerland. Except for EU candidate or potential candidate countries, which feature on most national lists of safe countries of origin, the latter largely differ as to the countries included. Such differences are probably linked to diverse asylum flows.[14]

Pursuant to Article 37 of Directive 2013/32, Member States shall regularly review the situation in third countries designated as safe countries of origin. This assessment shall be based on a range of sources of information, including in particular information from other Member States, the European Asylum Support Office (EASO), UNHCR, the Council of Europe and other relevant international organisations. Moreover, 'Member States shall notify to the Commission the countries that are designated as safe countries of origin'.

It must be noted that that concept is not included, as such, in the grounds of inadmissibility laid down in Article 33 of Directive 2013/32.[15] Yet, the EU Member States can apply the accelerated procedure if the applicant is from a safe country of origin pursuant to Article 31(8)(b).

[9] A Zimmermann and C Mahler, 'Article 1A(2)' in A Zimmermann et al (eds), *The 1951 Convention Relating to the Status of Refugees and its 1967 Protocol – A Commentary* (Oxford University Press, 2011) 448.

[10] Directive 2013/32/EU of the European Parliament and of the Council of 26 June 2013 on common procedures for granting and withdrawing international protection [2013] OJ L180/60.

[11] Directive 2011/95/EU of the European Parliament and of the Council of 13 December 2011 on standards for the qualification of third-country nationals or stateless persons as beneficiaries of international protection, for a uniform status for refugees or for persons eligible for subsidiary protection, and for the content of the protection granted [2011] OJ L337/9.

[12] EU+ refers to the 27 EU Member States plus Iceland, Liechtenstein, Norway and Switzerland.

[13] *Applying the Concept of Safe Countries in the Asylum Procedure* (n 8), 6.

[14] EASO, *Safe country of origin' concept in EU+ countries* (2021) 9, available at https://euaa.europa.eu/sites/default/files/publications/EASO-situational_update-safe_country_of_origin-2021.pdf, accessed 22 April 2024.

[15] Case C-585/16 *Alheto*, ECLI:EU:C:2018:584, para 123.

So far, the concept of safe country of origin has merely been interpreted by the ECJ in one case, C-404/17,[16] in which the Court was seized by a Swedish jurisdiction of a request for preliminary ruling. This case concerned an application for asylum made by a Serbian national, which was rejected as manifestly unfounded following a reasoning similar to that provided for in Articles 36 and 37 of Directive 2013/32. Yet, Swedish authorities had not adopted provisions designating safe countries of origin, nor provided that the fact of coming from a safe country of origin is liable to lead to a rejection of the application as manifestly unfounded. In its judgment, the ECJ held that an application for international protection may not be regarded as manifestly unfounded in a situation in which the applicant stems from a safe country of origin if the Member State in which the application was lodged has not adopted rules implementing the concept of safe country of origin. In particular, a Member State cannot rely on the rebuttable presumption laid down by the provisions of Directive 2013/32 relating to procedures based on the concept of safe country of origin, without also having fully implemented those rules with regard to the laws, regulations and administrative provisions which it is for the Member State to take.[17] This ruling also confirms that the list of 'manifestly unfounded' grounds is an exhaustive one.[18]

In addition, a request for preliminary ruling was launched by the Czech Regional Court in Brno in relation to the concept of 'safe country of origin' with territorial exceptions.[19] The facts underlying the national dispute related to an applicant for international protection in the Czech Republic originating from Moldova. He notably claimed to be afraid of the Russian war in Ukraine and its possible escalation towards Moldova. In its request for preliminary ruling, the referring court also explained that during the judicial proceedings, the Moldovan Parliament had extended a state of emergency and Moldova has withdrawn its obligations from European Convention on Human Rights (ECHR) under its Article 15. The Ministry of Interior has however found the application inadmissible because the Czech Republic considers Moldova a safe country of origin with the exception of Transnistria. The referring court notably asked the ECJ about the concept of safe country of origin, and if one country can actually be considered as safe when: (1) that country withdraws from its obligations under the ECHR in the event of a threat; and (2) a Member State designates a country as safe only in part of its territory, not as a whole. The case is currently pending.

One should keep in mind that the concept of 'safe country of origin' seeks to allow a preservation of resources of Member States in situations where asylum seekers come from safe countries but seek to circumvent asylum rules. Yet, its scope of application needs to be verified by national and European jurisdictions in order to avoid any misuse of the concept and to guarantee procedural guardrails for asylum seekers.

[16] Case C-404/17 *A*, ECLI:EU:C:2018:588. One should mention that a Czech Regional Court also raised a request for a preliminary ruling concerning the concept of 'safe country of origin' in 2022. In particular, the Czech Court asked, in essence, whether the principle of non-refoulement precludes the adoption of a return decision as regards a third-country national staying illegally on the territory of a Member State where that national submits that he or she will be exposed in his or her country of origin to threats to his or her life from individuals and whether it is permissible for that Member State to have recourse to the concept of a 'safe country of origin'. However, in its judgment in Case C-257/22 *Ministerstvo vnitra České republiky, Odbor azylové a migrační politiky (Champ d'application de la directive retour)*, ECLI:EU:C:2023:852, the ECJ held that it was not necessary to reply to the part of the question relating to this concept because a third-country national cannot be subject to a return decision if he/she applied for international protection and a first-instance decision on that application had not yet been delivered.

[17] *A* (n 16) para 31.

[18] Peers (n 5), 290.

[19] Case C-406/22 *Ministerstvo vnitra České republiky, Odbor azylové a migrační politiky*, pending.

III. INTERNAL PROTECTION

Following the same logic as the one underlying the principle of 'safe country of origin', if there is at least a part of the territory of this country where a national protection is available, there is no need to offer international protection. This concept of 'internal protection' also refers to the country of origin of the applicant for international protection, not in its entirety, but rather a safe region or a safe place within that country in which the asylum seeker can safely relocate.

According to Article 8 of Directive 2011/95, Member States may determine that an applicant is not in need of international protection if in a part of the country of origin, he or she has no well-founded fear of being persecuted or is not at real risk of suffering serious harm or has access to protection against persecution or serious harm, and he or she can safely and legally travel to and gain admittance to that part of the country and can reasonably be expected to settle there. Recital 27 of the Directive further clarifies that:

> [w]here the State or agents of the State are the actors of persecution or serious harm, there should be a presumption that effective protection is not available to the applicant. When the applicant is an unaccompanied minor, the availability of appropriate care and custodial arrangements, which are in the best interest of the unaccompanied minor, should form part of the assessment as to whether that protection is effectively available.

According to Article 8(2) of the Directive, in their examination Member States shall have regard to the general circumstances prevailing in that part of the country and to the personal circumstances of the applicant at the time of taking the decision on the application.

The ECJ has only indirectly addressed this issue in a few cases, as in its judgment in Case C-901/19, where it held that:

> the elements to be taken into account in assessing whether there is a real risk of serious harm, within the meaning of Article 15(c) of Directive 2011/95 may also include the intensity of the armed confrontations, the level of organisation of the armed forces involved, and the duration of the conflict (see, to that effect, judgment of 30 January 2014, *Diakité*, C-285/12, EU:C:2014:39, paragraph 35), as well as other elements such as the geographical scope of the situation of indiscriminate violence, the actual destination of the applicant in the event that he or she is returned to the relevant country or region and potentially intentional attacks against civilians carried out by the parties to the conflict.[20]

Apart from these considerations, the Court has yet to address the meaning of the criteria underlying the concept of internal protection, as to the reasonableness for the applicant to settle in a part of the country of origin or the personal circumstances of the applicant.[21]

IV. THE SAFE THIRD COUNTRY

For asylum seekers who may not receive protection within their country of origin, or at least within part of its territory, as well as for States who refuse to grant protection to asylum

[20] Case C-901/19 *Bundesrepublik Deutschland (Concept of 'serious and individual threat')*, ECLI:EU:C:2021:472, para 43. See also Case C-465/07 *Elgafaji*, ECLI:EU:C:2009:94, para 40, in which the ECJ held that 'in the individual assessment of an application for subsidiary protection [...] the following may be taken into account [...] the geographical scope of the situation of indiscriminate violence and the actual destination of the applicant in the event that he is returned'.

[21] European Union Agency for Asylum, *Qualification for International Protection. Judicial Analysis*, 2nd edn (2023) 151 and 154, available at https://euaa.europa.eu/publications/judicial-analysis-qualification-international-protection-second-edition, accessed 3 March 2024.

seekers, it may be legitimate to take into consideration a third country with which this person has a connection and which would be able to provide protection to that person.

As mentioned in Article 3(3) of the Dublin III Regulation,[22] 'any Member State shall retain the right to send an applicant to a safe third country, subject to the rules and safeguards laid down in Directive 2013/32/EU'. This provision explicitly refers to 'any Member State' and not the 'Member State which is responsible for examining the asylum application'. Hence, any Member State can make use of the safe third country option, provided that the conditions of Directive 2013/32 are met. Moreover, the fact that a Member State has accepted that it is responsible for examining an application for international protection does not prevent it from subsequently sending the applicant to a safe third country.[23]

Pursuant to Article 33(1) of Directive 2013/32, Member States are not required to examine whether the applicant qualifies for international protection in accordance with Directive 2011/95 where an application is considered inadmissible. The aim of this article is to relax the obligation of the Member State responsible for examining an application for international protection by defining the cases in which such an application is considered to be inadmissible.[24] Article 33(2) of Directive 2013/32 sets out an exhaustive[25] list of situations in which the Member States may consider an application for international protection to be inadmissible. Inter alia, Article 33(2)(c) states that Member States may consider an application for international protection as inadmissible if a country which is not a Member State is considered as a safe third country for the applicant, pursuant to Article 38 of Directive 2013/32.

Article 38(1)–(4) enumerates the minimum standards for a third State to qualify as safe by Member States. In short, a safe third country is a non-EU State in which life and liberty are not threatened on account of race, religion, nationality, membership of a particular social group or political opinion, there is no risk of serious harm, the principle of non-refoulement is respected, there is no risk of removal in contravention of the prohibition of torture and cruel, inhuman or degrading treatment and the person concerned has the possibility to request refugee status and, if found to be a refugee, to receive protection in accordance with the Geneva Convention.

This particular wording 'in accordance with the Geneva Convention' seems to imply that the third country does not necessarily have to have ratified the Geneva Convention to be able to qualify as a safe third country. One may wonder, in this regard, how the situation of Turkey, which has ratified the Geneva Convention, but retained a geographical limitation following which it does not recognise refugees from States outside Europe, should be assessed. This issue was raised by applicants in a recent request for preliminary ruling brought before the ECJ in Case C-134/23, but the referring Court rejected their argument in its request, considering that Turkey respects the principle of non-refoulement and offers adequate protection of certain fundamental rights, including the right of access to health care and the labour market. As a result, the referring Court did not take this issue into consideration in its questions. The case is currently pending.

The application of the concept of 'safe third country' is subject to rules laid down in national law. This includes the rules on the connection between the applicant for international

[22] Regulation (EU) No 604/2013 of the European Parliament and of the Council of 26 June 2013 establishing the criteria and mechanisms for determining the Member State responsible for examining an application for international protection lodged in one of the Member States by a third-country national or a stateless person [2013] OJ L180/31.

[23] Case C-695/15 PPU *Mirza*, ECLI:EU:C:2016:188, paras 42–46.

[24] ibid, para 43.

[25] Case C-297/17, C-318/17, C-319/17 and C-438/17 *Ibrahim and Others*, ECLI:EU:C:2019:219, para 76 and *Mirza* (n 23), para 43. The ECJ found, in substance, that the exhaustive feature of the list set out in Art 33(2) of Directive 2013/32 is based on both the wording of that article and its purpose.

protection and the third country concerned that it would be reasonable to return that person to that country. It also covers the methodology by which the competent authorities satisfy themselves that the concept of 'safe third country' may be applied to a particular country or to a particular applicant. This methodology shall include case-by-case consideration of the safety of the country for a particular applicant and/or national designation of countries considered to be generally safe. Pursuant to Recital 46 of Directive 2013/32:

> where Member States apply safe country concepts on a case-by-case basis or designate countries as safe by adopting lists to that effect, they should take into account, inter alia, the guidelines and operating manuals and the information on countries of origin and activities, including EASO Country of Origin Information report methodology, [...] as well as relevant UNHCR guidelines.

These conditions are cumulative,[26] which implies that the ground of inadmissibility cannot be applied where one of those conditions has not been satisfied. Therefore, it is only where national legislation which has the effect of dismissing an application for international protection as inadmissible satisfies all of these conditions that such legislation could constitute an application of the ground of inadmissibility laid down in Article 33(2)(c) of that Directive.[27]

Noticeably, the concept of 'effective protection' is absent in this framework. In 2003, the Commission defined this concept as requiring, as a minimum:

> physical security, a guarantee against refoulement, access to UNHCR asylum procedures or national procedures with sufficient safeguards, where this is required to access effective protection or durable solutions, and social-economic well being, including, as a minimum, access to primary healthcare and primary education, as well as access to the labour market, or access to means of subsistence sufficient to maintain an adequate standard of living.[28]

Compared to this extensive perception, the criteria defined in Directive 2013/32 mainly relate to the issue of safety. Consequently, it seems that Member States may apply less stringent protection standards in the European system of safe third countries.[29]

Nonetheless, the Member State authorities have to conduct a case-by-case examination of the country's safety in general as well as for a particular applicant. This includes a personal interview in accordance with the guarantees laid down in Article 15 of Directive 2013/32.[30] A full and *ex nunc* examination of the facts and points of law has to be carried out, which implies that:

> in the event that the court or tribunal hearing an appeal plans to examine a ground of inadmissibility which has not been examined by the determining authority, it must conduct a hearing of the applicant in order to allow that individual to express his or her point of view in person concerning the applicability of that ground to his or her particular circumstances.[31]

If the criteria are met and if there is a connection between the applicant and the third country, the Member State may determine the third country safe for this applicant. In addition, Article 39(2)(b) allows Member States to designate third countries as 'generally safe'. Nevertheless, even in this case, an applicant may rebut the presumption of safety in his or her particular situation.

[26] Case C-564/18 *Bevándorlási és Menekültügyi Hivatal (Tompa)*, ECLI:EU:C:2020:218, para 40; and *Alheto* (n 15), para 121.

[27] *Bevándorlási és Menekültügyi Hivatal (Tompa)* (n 26), para 41.

[28] European Commission, 'Towards a more accessible, equitable, and managed international protection regime' (Communication) COM (2003) 315 final, 6.

[29] Osso (n 5), 17.

[30] Case C-517/17 *Addis*, ECLI:EU:C:2020:579, para 74.

[31] *Alheto* (n 15), para 130.

This procedure has been subject to judicial debate at national level, which led to several requests for preliminary rulings at the ECJ, concerning the compliance of national legislation with the principles described above. In particular, the requirement of a connection with a safe third country has been subject to contestation before Hungarian courts. In this context, Case C-564/18 concerned a Syrian national of Kurdish ethnicity, who applied for international protection in Hungary after having transited in the Republic of Serbia, which qualifies as a safe third country pursuant to Hungarian legislation. Hungarian authorities rejected the application as inadmissible and ordered the applicant to return to Serbian territory. This decision was challenged before a national court, which raised two questions to the ECJ. In its judgment, the latter found, first, that the condition laid down in Article 38(1) of Directive 2013/32 was not satisfied because the application of the ground of inadmissibility in Hungarian legislation did not require the compliance of the third country with the principle of non-refoulement. Second, the ECJ clarified that the transit by an applicant for international protection through the third country concerned cannot alone constitute a 'connection' within the meaning of Article 38(2)(a) of Directive 2013/32.[32] These findings were reiterated in another judgment, delivered by the Grand Chamber in Cases C-924/19 PPU and C-925/19 PPU.[33]

In these judgments, the ECJ has interpreted the concept of 'safe third country' in a narrow way, rejecting the argument of Hungary following which a transit through a non-EU country could be considered as constitutive of a connection with that country.[34]

In a subsequent case, concerning actions for failure to fulfil obligations under Article 8(2), Article 12(1)(c), Article 22(1) and Article 33(2) of Directive 2013/32 brought against Hungary, the Court reported the doubts expressed by Hungary 'whether Article 33 of Directive 2013/32 is capable of striking an adequate balance between the overload of systems for processing asylum applications caused by unjustified applications and the legitimate interests of asylum seekers genuinely in need of international protection'.[35] Hungary argued that its legislation was:

> intended to suppress abuse by providing that [...] an application lodged by a person who has transited, where applicable over a long period of time, through a State in which he or she has not been persecuted and does not risk being persecuted is, in principle, inadmissible, even if that person has not applied for international protection in that State.[36]

Nevertheless, the Court, sitting as the Grand Chamber, upheld for the most part the Commission's action. It notably held that the national legislation could not be regarded as applying one of the grounds of inadmissibility in respect of a safe third country, provided for in Article 33(2)(c) of that Directive,[37] and could not, therefore – contrary to what Hungary claimed – be regarded as a correct transposition of that provision.

Another case, which is still pending, concerns the question of whether Turkey can be classified as generally safe for certain categories of applicants for international protection where, although it has made a legal commitment to permit readmission to its territory, it is clear that it has refused readmission for a long period of time (in this case, more than 20 months)

[32] *Bevándorlási és Menekültügyi Hivatal (Tompa)* (n 26).
[33] Case C-924/19 PPU and C-925/19 PPU *Országos Idegenrendészeti Főigazgatóság Dél-alföldi Regionális Igazgatóság*, ECLI:EU:C:2020:367.
[34] Peers (n 5), 291.
[35] Case C-821/19 *Commission v Hungary (Criminalisation of assistance to asylum seekers)*, ECLI:EU:C:2021:930, para 29.
[36] ibid, para 30.
[37] ibid, para 41 and *Bevándorlási és Menekültügyi Hivatal (Tompa)* (n 26), para 51.

and the possibility of its changing its position in the near future does not appear to have been investigated. As explained by the referring Court, the Greek Council of State, this temporary measure is notably related to the COVID-19 pandemic.[38]

Hence, even if certain aspects of the EU regulatory framework of safe third countries may be considered as vague or not sufficiently clearly defined, the case law developed so far by the ECJ has focused on guaranteeing procedural safeguards to asylum seekers and avoiding too large an interpretation of the concepts of 'connection' and consequently of 'safe third country'.

V. THE EUROPEAN SAFE THIRD COUNTRY

Finally, one should mention the concept of 'European safe third countries', even if it remains subject to intense debates and is largely unapplied in practice.

Initially, Article 29(1) and (2) of Directive 2005/85[39] was meant to provide for a 'Minimum common list of third countries regarded as safe countries of origin'. Following the procedure described in that provision, the Council could, acting by a qualified majority on a proposal from the Commission and after consultation of the European Parliament, adopt a minimum common list of third countries which shall be regarded by Member States as safe countries of origin. However, the Court of Justice held that, by making the future adoption of common lists of safe countries subject to mere consultation of the Parliament instead of the co-decision procedure, the Council exceeded the powers conferred on it by the Treaty in relation to asylum.[40] Hence, the provision was annulled.

The procedure was reviewed in Directive 2013/32 in order to give Member States the responsibility to establish such a list. According to its Recital 45:

> with respect to certain European third countries, which observe particularly high human rights and refugee protection standards, Member States should be allowed to not carry out, or not to carry out full examination of, applications for international protection regarding applicants who enter their territory from such European third countries.

Article 39 of Directive 2013/32 establishes this regime, which has been qualified as a 'less stringent regime for rejecting applications from applicants from European safe third countries if those applicants […] have entered illegally into the territory of a Member State'.[41] Three cumulative conditions are laid down in this provision in order for a country to be able to fall within this category: such third country is required to have ratified and to observe the provisions of the Geneva Convention without any geographical limitation; to have in place an asylum procedure prescribed by law; and to have ratified and to observe the ECHR, including the standards relating to effective remedies. If these conditions are met, EU Member States may refrain from conducting a full examination of the application and send the applicant to the concerned third State. Yet, Member States shall lay down in national law the modalities for implementing this procedure.

Under the migratory pressure in the Mediterranean, the subject came back on the table of EU legislators in 2015.[42] The Commission issued a proposal aiming to establish such a list based on

[38] Case C-134/23 *Elliniko Symvoulio gia tous Prosfyges*, pending.

[39] Council Directive 2005/85/EC of 1 December 2005 on minimum standards on procedures in Member States for granting and withdrawing refugee status [2005] OJ L326/13.

[40] Case C-133/06 *Parliament v Council*, ECLI:EU:C:2008:257, para 61 ff.

[41] Opinion of AG Kokott in Case C-695/15 PPU *Mirza*, ECLI:EU:C:2016:146, para 54.

[42] Commission, 'Proposal for a Regulation of the European Parliament and of the Council establishing an EU common list of safe countries of origin for the purposes of Directive 2013/32/EU of the European Parliament and of

the common criteria set out in Directive 2013/32 in order to facilitate the use by Member States of this procedure and reduce existing divergences between Member States' national lists of safe countries of origin. In its proposal, the Commission came to the conclusion that Albania, Bosnia and Herzegovina, the former Yugoslav Republic of Macedonia, Kosovo, Montenegro, Serbia and Turkey were safe countries of origin to be included in the EU common list of safe countries. At that time, the nationals of these seven countries counted for approximately 17 per cent of the total number of applications lodged in the EU.[43] Yet, while the co-legislators agreed on the approach, they could not decide which countries should be on that list. Finally, the Commission withdrew its proposal for an EU list of safe countries on 21 June 2020.[44]

In practice, this concept, which allows EU Member State to avoid any examination of the application for international protection, received little consideration, given that it is not defined in law in 24 EU+ countries and not applied in practice in three additional EU+ countries.[45]

VI. CONCLUSION

The expansion of concepts such as 'the safe country of origin', 'the safe third country', 'the European safe third country' and 'internal protection' may allow more efficient and expedited procedures for national authorities. These mechanisms allow a wide margin of discretion to Member States, which in turn may lead to a decrease of rights of asylum seekers.

As this contribution revealed, the jurisprudence of the ECJ is still developing on these mechanisms. National jurisdictions seem to act as primary guardians of the system. Nevertheless, the judgments delivered so far by the ECJ in this field, even if they are not yet abundant, seem to favour a narrow interpretation of these concepts.[46]

As far as the concept of 'safe country of origin' is concerned, the unique judgment of the ECJ confirms both the necessity of a national regulation implementing the European legislation, as well as the exhaustive feature of the list of 'manifestly unfounded' situations. The ECJ issued a more extensive jurisprudence on the concept of 'safe third country', focusing on the compliance of national legislation with procedural safeguards, such as the requirement of a personal interview and interpreting the concept of 'safe third country' in a narrow way, considering that transit through a non-EU country could not solely constitute a sufficient connection with that country.[47] Noticeably, much of the case law concerns a single Member State, Hungary. Finally, the concept of 'European safe third country' is only rarely applied and the one of 'internal protection' has not yet been directly examined by the ECJ. Yet, numerous interesting cases are currently pending, which will give the opportunity to the ECJ to further examine these concepts.

the Council on common procedures for granting and withdrawing international protection, and amending Directive 2013/32/EU' COM (2015) 452 final.

[43] European Parliament, *Briefing, Safe Countries of Origin: Proposed Common EU List* (2017) 7, available at https://www.europarl.europa.eu/RegData/etudes/BRIE/2015/569008/EPRS_BRI(2015)569008_EN.pdf, accessed 3 March 2024.

[44] European Parliament, 'European List of Safe Countries of Origin', in *Legislative Train 12.2023, 17 Civil Liberties, Justice and Home Affairs – LIBE*, available at https://www.europarl.europa.eu/legislative-train/package-strong-asylum-policy/file-european-list-of-safe-countries-of-origin, accessed 3 March 2024.

[45] *Applying the Concept of Safe Countries in the Asylum Procedure* (n 8), 16.

[46] European Council on Refugees and Exiles, *Policy Note 08 – Debunking the 'Safe Third Country' Myth* (2017) 3, available at https://www.ecre.org/wp-content/uploads/2017/11/Policy-Note-08.pdf, accessed 3 March 2024.

[47] Peers (n 5), 291.

17

Schengen and Internal Border Control

KARSTEN ENGSIG SØRENSEN*

I. INTRODUCTION

REMOVING INTERNAL BORDER control would appear to be a key project in developing an internal market with free movement of, inter alia, persons and goods. In particular, in the 1980s and 1990s the internal market project did ensure that formalities for crossing borders for both goods and persons were relaxed, but it proved impossible completely to do away with internal border control. Therefore, the Schengen Agreement, which had its background in a collaboration among some Member States, was created to accomplish this important step. Later in 1999, the Schengen rules were integrated in the Area of Freedom, Security and Justice (AFSJ) framework in Part Three, Title V, Chapter 2 in the Treaty on the Functioning of the European Union (TFEU).

Initially, the Schengen rules' effort to remove internal border control seemed very successful. But a little more than ten years ago, some Member States began to reintroduce border controls for longer periods and eventually – from 2015 – this became more widespread. This has triggered a crisis for the Schengen rules, and so far, it has proven difficult to solve it.

This chapter will explore why and how the removal of internal border control ended up as part of the AFSJ. Subsequently it will examine why the project has run into trouble in recent years, and what has been done to rectify this situation.

II. INTERNAL BORDER CONTROL AND FREE MOVEMENT OF PERSONS

Creating an internal market with free movement of goods, persons, services and capital would logically also include the removal of internal border control. This seems to be confirmed by Article 26(2) TFEU, which states that the internal market should be an area without internal frontiers where free movement can take place. When formulating the plans for the establishment of an internal market in 1985, the Commission also pointed out that free movement requires the removal of border control. In its White Paper, border controls were identified as one of the most obvious examples of physical hindrances to the internal market, and it was suggested 'to do away with internal frontier controls in their entirety'.[1] Of course, free

* Professor at the Department of Law, Aarhus University, Denmark.

[1] White Paper from the Commission to the European Council: Completing the internal market COM (85) 310 final, paras 11 and 27.

movement can take place even if there is border control, but such control will take time and will constitute an obstacle. Consequently, border control imposes a cost on free movement,[2] and additionally it has great symbolic importance. Thus, the Commission suggested that physical barriers such as border controls 'to the ordinary citizen are obvious manifestation of the continued division of the Community'.[3]

In the years after the White Paper was published, the European Union (EU) legislators managed to remove most of the barriers imposed on goods at internal borders. The cornerstone for doing so was the establishment of the Common Customs Tariff which, when implemented in 1968, marked the birth of the customs union. As the external border controls were harmonised, the argument for maintaining internal border controls diminished. In 1979, the European Court of Justice (ECJ) stated that customs controls had lost their raison d'être as regards intra-community trade, other than where they were necessary for implementing the exceptions to free movement in what is now Article 36 TFEU.[4] In 1983 the first rules were adopted for the simplification of internal border controls.[5] These rules were further developed in 1985 with the introduction of a single document for use throughout the EU.[6]

Free movement of persons was also made easier, but it proved hard to abandon border control entirely. The first important step towards the realisation of free movement of persons was the adoption of Council Directive 68/360/EEC[7] and Directive 73/148/EEC[8] on the abolition of restrictions on movement and residence within the Community for workers and persons with regard to establishment and the provision of services. These rules established that persons have a right to leave a Member State upon production of a valid identity card or passport, and that other Member States must allow persons to enter their territory upon production of a valid identity card or passport. These rules prevent Member States imposing any other formalities, such as requiring visas. The ECJ has made it clear that additional formalities, such as asking about the purpose and duration of a visit or about financial means, are not acceptable.[9] However, the rules do not prevent the imposition of border controls, as identity cards and passports may be controlled. These rules were subsequently supplanted to Directive 2004/38/EC,[10] which also clearly stated that the right of entry and exit is 'without prejudice to

[2] See the estimates made by the Commission in its communication entitled 'Back to Schengen – A Roadmap', COM (2016) 120 final, 3–4 covering cost for transport, tourism, public administration and commuters and adding up to as much as €18 billion per year.

[3] White Paper Completing the internal market (n 1), para 24.

[4] See Case 159/78 *Commission v Italy*, ECLI:EU:C:1979:243, para 7. The ECJ also referred to tax collection, transit control and the collection of statistics as considerations that could justify customs controls, but these areas have been harmonised since this decision, so only Art 36 exceptions are now relevant.

[5] Council Directive 83/643/EEC of 1 December 1983 on the facilitation of physical inspections and administrative formalities in respect of the carriage of goods between Member States [1983] OJ L359/8.

[6] Council Regulation 678/85/EEC of 18 February 1985 simplifying formalities in trade in goods within the Community [1985] OJ L79/1.

[7] Council Directive 68/360/EEC of 15 October 1968 on the abolition of restrictions on movement and residence within the Community for workers of Member States and their families [1968] OJ L257/13.

[8] Council Directive 73/148/EEC of 21 May 1973 on the abolition of restrictions on movement and residence within the Community for nationals of Member States with regard to establishment and the provision of services [1973] OJ L172/14.

[9] See Case C-68/89 *Commission v Netherlands*, ECLI:EU:C:1991:226. See also Case C-321/87 *Commission v Belgium*, ECLI:EU:C:1989:176, according to which the requirement to show residence permits in addition to passports or identity cards was not accepted.

[10] Directive 2004/38/EC of the European Parliament and of the Council of 29 April 2004 on the right of citizens of the Union and their family members to move and reside freely within the territory of the Member States amending Regulation (EEC) No 1612/68 and repealing Directives 64/221/EEC, 68/360/EEC, 72/194/EEC, 73/148/EEC, 75/34/EEC, 75/35/EEC, 90/364/EEC, 90/365/EEC and 93/96/EEC [2004] OJ L158/77.

the provisions on travel documents applicable to national border controls'. The Member States were thus reluctant to give up their rights as nation States to control their borders.[11]

With the entry into force of the Single European Act, Article 7a in the Treaty Establishing the European Community (TEC (now Article 26(2) TFEU)) was introduced. A Dutch citizen sought to rely on this provision in Case C-378/97, *Wijsenbeek*, as he refused to show his passport when arriving in Rotterdam on a flight from Strasbourg. In its ruling the ECJ denied that the provision meant that there was an obligation for the Member States to do away with internal border controls when the deadline then listed in Article 7a TEC (31 December 1992) expired.[12] However, the ECJ did open up for the possibility that the situation could be different with harmonised rules 'governing the crossing of the external borders of the Community, immigration, the grant of visas, asylum and the exchange of information on those questions'.[13] Wijsenbeek had also relied on Article 8a TEC (now Article 21 TFEU), which grants union citizens the right to exercise free movement. Here the ECJ also held that as long as the rules on the external border have not been harmonised, union citizens exercising their right of free movement need to establish their nationality of a Member State to be allowed to exercise this right, and consequently internal border controls are acceptable.[14] Even if the ECJ did allow for internal border controls, it stressed that penalties for not observing a duty to submit to an internal border control should be proportional.[15]

Since the judgment in this case was rendered all the way back in 1999, much work has since been carried out to create such common rules for external border control, which raises the question whether Article 26(2) TFEU now has the effect of restricting the use of internal border control under the free movement rules.[16]

The issue resurfaced in Joined Cases C-368/20 and C-369/20, *NW v Landespolizeidirektion Steiermark*. In the first of the two joined cases, the referring court asked both whether the Austrian border control infringed the Schengen Borders Code (Code)[17] and, if that was not the case, whether it infringed Article 21 TFEU and Article 45 of the Charter. Since the ECJ did find that the control infringed the Code (more on this below), there was no need to address the second question.[18]

Advocate General Øe did, however, address the issue briefly in his Opinion on the case delivered on 6 October 2021. He suggested that the right to move freely was not an unrestricted right, since according to Article 21 TFEU it may only be exercised 'subject to the limitations and conditions laid down in the Treaties and by the measures adopted to give them effect'. It is therefore not an unconditional right, as it can be restricted if justified and done proportionately.[19] He argued that to the extent that temporary border control is introduced in accordance with Article 25 of the Code, there was a justification, and it must be regarded as

[11] Described as the 'crown jewel' of national sovereignty by K Lenaerts, 'The Contribution of the European Court of Justice in the Area of Freedom, Security and Justice' (2010) 59 *International and Comparative Law Quarterly* 255, 256.

[12] See Case C-378/97 *Wijsenbeek*, ECLI:EU:C:1999:439, para 40.

[13] ibid, para 40.

[14] ibid, para 42.

[15] ibid, para 44.

[16] See for instance S Salomon and JJ Rijpma, 'A Europe Without Internal Frontiers: Challenging the Reintroduction of Border Controls in the Schengen Area in Light of Union Citizenship' (2023) 24 *German Law Journal* 281.

[17] The most recent version is Regulation (EU) No 2016/399 of the European Parliament and of the Council of 9 March 2016 on a Union Code on the rules governing the movement of persons across borders (Schengen Borders Code), with later amendments [2016] OJ L77/1.

[18] See Joined Cases C-368/20 and C-369/20 *NW v Landespolizeidirection*, ECLI:EU:C:2022:298, para 95.

[19] See Opinion of AG Saugmandsgaard Øe in Joined Cases C-368/20 and C-369/20 *NW v Landespolizeidirection*, ECLI:EU:C:2021:821, para 80.

proportionate. Therefore, the assessment under Article 21 TFEU and Article 45 of the Charter is not likely to add to the assessment under Article 25 of the Code. Consequently, the free movement rights do not provide for a stricter regime on reintroducing internal border control than already provided by the Schengen rules.

Since the ECJ had already in its *Wijsenbeek* judgment accepted that lifting internal border control is linked to the harmonisation of external border control, it does seem logical that the Schengen regime should regulate both aspects. Internal border control should only be lifted, as long as it is aligned with the operation of the external border control. If the free movement rights were to impose a duty to lift internal border control altogether – also in relation to those Member States that are not Schengen members – it would jeopardise the working of the Schengen rules regulating external border control.

Even though the free movement rights are not likely to affect the exercise of the identity check that is carried out on persons at the internal border (other than the question of penalties), it should be recalled that there are many other aspects that still need to be assessed under these rights. During the COVID-19 pandemic many Member States not only introduced internal border control, but also implemented restrictions on entry and exit. Such restrictions go beyond the checks that are part of border controls and therefore can be examined under Article 21 TFEU, etc.[20]

III. THE SCHENGEN BORDERS CODE AND THE REMOVAL OF INTERNAL BORDER CONTROL

Since it proved difficult to complete the removal of border controls under the EU regime, France and Germany in 1984 entered into an agreement to ease border controls between the two countries. When this cooperation was expanded with the addition of the Benelux countries in 1985, the Schengen Agreement became a reality. This was followed by the Schengen Convention in 1990, implementing the 1985 Schengen Agreement.[21] Later, further States joined the cooperation,[22] and the Schengen rules were incorporated in the EU regime by the entry into force of the Amsterdam Treaty in 1999. The rules are now included in Part Three, Title V, Chapter 2 TFEU.

Today, the most important rules of the Schengen cooperation are in the Code. This contains rules requiring participating States to remove internal border controls, see Articles 22–24. It also includes rules on the introduction of temporary internal border controls, that will be addressed in Section IV below.

[20] The ECJ addressed this issue in Case C-128/22 *Nordic Info BV*, ECLI:EU:C:2023:951. For an analysis of the different problems raised by the Member States' reaction to the COVID-19 pandemic see, inter alia, D Thym and J Bornemann, 'Schengen and Free Movement Law during the First Phase of the COVID-19 Pandemic: Of Symbolism, Law and Politics' (2020) 5 *European Papers* 1143, L Schumacker, 'Proportionality of Internal Border Controls: From the COVID-19 Pandemic to the 2021 Proposal' (2022) 18 *Croatian Yearbook of European Law & Policy* 151, and U Neergaard et al, 'Closure of Borders in the Three Nordic EU Member States During Covid-19 Pandemic' in K Hyltén-Cavalius and J Paju (eds), *Free Movement of Persons in the Nordic States* (Hart Publishing, 2023). See also the 2022 report published by the European Court of Auditors entitled, 'Free Movement in the EU during the COVID-19 Pandemic. Limited Scrutiny of Internal Border Controls, and Uncoordinated Actions by Member States'.

[21] Convention implementing the Schengen Agreement of 14 June 1985 between the Governments of the States of the Benelux Economic Union, the Federal Republic of Germany and the French Republic on the gradual abolition of checks at their common borders [2000] OJ L239/19.

[22] Ireland and Cyprus do not participate, and Denmark only does so under Protocol (No 22) on the Position of Denmark. Bulgaria and Romania do not apply the whole Schengen regime yet. Finally, Iceland, Liechtenstein, Norway and Switzerland are non-Member States that participate.

The main provision for the removal of internal border controls is Article 22 of the Code which states: 'Internal borders may be crossed at any point without a border check on persons, irrespective of their nationality, being carried out.'

According to Article 2(11) of the Code, 'border checks' mean checks carried out at border crossing points to ensure that persons – including their means of transport and the objects in their possession – may be authorised to enter the territory of the Member States or to leave it.

According to the *travaux preparatoires* for what is now Article 22 of the Code, the provision aims to remove any control. Crossing an internal border between two Member States to which the Schengen rules apply must thus not be treated any differently than a journey between regions, provinces, counties or other administrative areas within a Member State.[23]

At an earlier stage the Commission took the position that Article 22 also requires the participating States to do away with border surveillance.[24] This, however, was challenged by the Netherlands when in August 2012 it introduced a surveillance system called @migo-Boras.[25] Since then, the Commission has accepted that such surveillance may be part of the exercise of police power that Article 23 authorises.[26]

Article 23 of the Code makes it clear that giving up border controls does not mean giving up all forms of control, as Schengen Member States still have the possibility of carrying out controls other than at their borders. There is a risk that controls made just behind the border may be used to keep a de facto border control. This is particularly true for police controls, and Article 23(a) addresses this issue by only allowing for the exercise of police controls if the exercise of those controls does not have an effect equivalent to border checks. The provision sets out some criteria indicating that police actions are not equivalent to the border checks,[27] and the ECJ has used these criteria when analysing whether police controls infringe the Code. In these cases, the police have often been granted extra powers for checks performed in border areas. That, however, is not in itself sufficient to make it equivalent to border control, as it is foreseen that special powers may be granted in such areas.[28] The ECJ is assessing whether the police have been granted such powers that it allows them to perform checks that are equivalent to border control. If that is the case, then the possibility that the police could use that power to conduct checks equivalent to border control is enough, and there is no need to examine whether the police in fact have made use of the extensive power granted to them. Thus, it is necessary for States to restrict the use of police power so as to guide the police not to use it in such a way.[29] But apart from examining the powers granted, it will also be relevant to assess the

[23] Proposal for a Council Regulation establishing a Community Code on the rules governing the movement of persons across borders COM (2004) 391 final, 31.

[24] Report of the Commission on the application of Title III (Internal Borders) of Regulation (EC) No 562/2006 (Schengen Borders Code) COM (2010) 554 final, 3.

[25] A Rettman, 'Netherlands Defends Border Control Project' (3 January 2012), available at euobserver.com, accessed 3 March 2024. The Commission did address the Netherlands on a potential infringement of the Code, the free movement rights and the data protection regime in November 2011, see Biannual report on the functioning of the Schengen area 1 November 2011–30 April 2012, COM (2012) 230 final, 6.

[26] See Commission Recommendation (EU) 2017/820 on proportionate police checks and police cooperation in the Schengen area, para 1(d), [2017] OJ L122/79.

[27] These criteria are not exhaustive: see the Opinion of AG Mazák in Joined Cases C-188/10 and C-189/10 *Melki and Abdeli*, ECLI:EU:C:2010:319 and COM (2010) 554 (n 24), 3. It has since been confirmed by the ECJ in Case C-278/12 PPU *Adil*, ECLI:EU:C:2012:508, para 65.

[28] See *Adil* (n 27), para 73.

[29] The line of argument has been the reason for setting aside police legislation in Joined Cases C-188/10 and C-189/10 *Melki and Abdeli*, ECLI:EU:C:2010:363 and partly in Case C-9/16 *A*, ECLI:EU:C:2017:483. In *Adil* (n 27) and Case C-554/10 *FU*, ECLI:EU:C:2014:56, the ECJ accepted the power granted to the Dutch and German police as being sufficiently restricted.

purpose of initiating controls. If the goal is to encounter a serious threat, this may indicate that it is not a de facto border control.[30] Finally, the ECJ has held that Article 23 also prohibits a State from requiring that coach transport undertakings providing cross-border services within the Schengen area must check the passports of those passengers travelling into the country.[31]

Under Article 24 of the Code, Member States have to remove 'all obstacles to fluid traffic flow at road crossing-points at internal borders, in particular any speed limits not exclusively based on road-safety considerations'. This provision seems to suggest that the Member States should remove customs posts etc that have previously been used for controls, but Article 24 also states that Member States must be prepared to provide for facilities for checks if internal border controls are reintroduced. The Commission has expressed the view that the wording of Article 22 must mean that it is permitted to retain a permanent infrastructure, as long as this does not impede the flow of traffic.[32]

IV. TEMPORARY REINTRODUCTION OF BORDER CONTROL

The main Achilles heel of the regulation outlined above has been the rule allowing Member States to reintroduce temporary border control, and thereby allowing several Member States to make extensive use of this possibility, whereby the term 'temporary' sometimes seems misplaced. In the following, the Schengen rules regulating such reintroductions will therefore be briefly outlined followed by an overview of the use of the possibility, and the effort made to reduce extensive use thereof by some States.

A. The Rules

Articles 25–35 of the Code allow for the reintroduction of internal border control in three different situations and according to different procedures, requirements, and conditions. In all cases there should be a serious threat to public policy or internal security.

Articles 25–27 regulate foreseeable threats to public policy or internal security. If such a serious threat emerges, States can 'exceptionally' reintroduce border control, as long as its scope and duration is proportional. Such controls can be introduced for up to 30 days. If the threat persists, the period can be prolonged by renewable periods of 30 days, up to a maximum of six months. The State concerned must notify the Commission and the other Schengen Member States at least four weeks before taking action, unless the circumstances giving rise to the measures arise within a shorter timeframe. The Commission is supposed to issue an opinion after consulting the other Member States.

It is normally these rules that have been used when reintroducing border control, but the Code also allows for reintroduction in other situations. Under Article 28, a Schengen Member State can introduce immediate border controls at internal borders if there is a serious threat to public policy or internal security. This option may be used where the threat is not foreseeable but immediate. This measure must only be used in exceptional cases and is limited to up to ten days. If the serious threat to public policy or internal security persists, the period may be

[30] Thus, the ECJ seems to accept the police control conducted by Belgium as part of its effort to control travellers in and out of Belgium during the first month of the COVID-19 pandemic: see *Nordic Info BV* (n 20), paras 118–22.
[31] See Joined Cases C-412/17 and C-474/17 *Touring Tours and Travel GmbH* Cases, ECLI:EU:C:2018:1005.
[32] COM (2010) 554 (n 24), 11.

prolonged by renewable periods of 20 days, up to a maximum of two months. Article 29 of the Code allows a State to introduce temporary border checks at internal borders when there are persistent serious deficiencies in the external border management of another Schengen Member State, as demonstrated during a Schengen evaluation. This period could be prolonged up to three times, if the exceptional circumstances persist, up to a limit of maximum two years.

B. Their Use

Since the very beginning, there were examples where Schengen Member States used the option to introduce temporary border control for short periods to cope with major events such as conferences, sport events or similar. But with time, States have started to make reintroductions of a different nature. This was the case in April 2011 when France reintroduced temporary border controls on its border with Italy. The background to this was that the Italian authorities had issued temporary residence permits for the humanitarian protection of a number of immigrants from North Africa who had arrived in Italy before 5 April 2011. This granted them the right to move freely within the Schengen territory. In response to the Italian measures, France introduced internal border controls between the two countries which resulted, inter alia, in the French authorities blocking a train from Italy.[33] There was some doubt as to whether the temporary border controls introduced by France infringed the Code, but the Commission reached the conclusion that there had been no formal infringement of the rules.[34]

This was only the first time the migration crisis triggered the reintroduction of border controls. Thus, the civil war in Syria and the resulting migration to Europe resulted in several States introducing temporary border control to cope with the large number of migrants. The Council adopted a decision on 12 May 2016 to recommend temporary border control under Article 29 of the Code, and this recommendation was prolonged until November 2017.[35] Nevertheless, a number of States continued their reintroduced border control after that date.

The next crisis to trigger the wide reintroduction of border control was the COVID-19 pandemic. No fewer than 17 States reintroduced border control when the pandemic broke out in March 2020, but many States – though not all – removed it again the same year. The Code did not allow for the reintroduction of border control due to reasons of public health, as it only mentions threat to public policy or internal security. This omission of public health was intended, and therefore raises some doubts as to whether the reintroduction during the COVID-19 period was legal. However, the ECJ has recently confirmed that a serious and widespread risk, such as that caused by the COVID-19 pandemic, can amount to a serious threat to public policy or internal security.[36]

From spring 2022, the war in Ukraine has also been the cause of reintroductions of border controls.

As a result of the above, Austria, Denmark, France, Germany, Norway and Sweden have managed to keep some form of internal border control since 2016. In recent years, when

[33] For an account of what happened see S Carrera et al, 'A Race against Solidarity. The Schengen Regime and the Franco-Italian Affair' (2011) *CEPS Paper in Liberty and Security in Europe* No 1 1.

[34] See the Commission statement of 25 July 2011, Memo/11/538. In Carrera et al (n 33), the authors conclude that France presumably did not fulfil the conditions for reintroduction of border controls on its border with Italy in April 2011.

[35] The first of these decisions was Council implementing decision (EU) 2016/894 setting out a recommendation for temporary internal border control in exceptional circumstances putting the overall functioning of the Schengen area at risk [2016] OJ L151/8.

[36] *Nordic Info BV* (n 20), paras 124–27.

Denmark has not used migration and COVID-19 as the (main) cause for the reintroduction, other threats have been given as the reasons: terrorist threats; organised crime threats; foreign intelligence threats; and most recently threats caused by Quran burnings. Normally an extension for another six months is based on several threats, and many threats continue to reappear in subsequent requests for extensions. Also, just as is the case with other States, it appears that the threats that are listed are not always actual threats, such as the migration threat in 2015–16 and the COVID-19 threat in 2020, but risks of threat that may materialise.[37]

With this practice it appeared very easy for the Schengen Member States to reintroduce border control and keep it for longer periods. As a consequence, the effort to remove internal border control seemed to be in jeopardy, and there was a need to curb the liberal use of reintroduction of border control.

C. The Response

Following the events at the Franco-Italian border in April 2011, both France and Italy asked for a review of the rules on the reintroduction of internal border controls, and the European Council called for a mechanism to be introduced to respond to exceptional circumstances that put the overall functioning of the Schengen cooperation at risk, but without jeopardising the principle of the free movement of persons.[38]

The Commission responded to this request in a proposal of 16 September 2011.[39] The proposal contained two elements.[40] First, it was proposed to introduce strengthened monitoring and evaluation mechanisms for border controls by introducing both announced and unannounced visits. The second element of the Commission's proposal was that a Member State which wants to reintroduce border controls will have to submit a request to the Commission at least six weeks in advance of when the need to reintroduce border controls is foreseeable. If the need to reintroduce border controls is not foreseeable six weeks before controls need to be reintroduced, then the need should be notified as soon as possible. The Commission will then decide on a request after the Member States and the European Parliament have been informed. If necessary, Member States may always introduce immediate measures, but only for a limited period not exceeding five days.[41] The reason for this change

[37] See also J Pettersson Fürst, 'Defensive Integration through Cooperative Re-Bordering? How Member States Use Internal Border Controls in Schengen' (2024) 31 *Journal of European Public Policy* 478 and for an evaluation of the Danish requests see AK Mangold and A Kompatscher, 'Foreneligheden af permanent kontrol ved den tysk-danske grænse mod EU-lovgivning', report prepared for R Andreasen Member of European Parliament, dated 22 December 2022, available at www.ft.dk, accessed 3 March 2024.

[38] See European Council of 23–24 June 2011, EUCO 23/11 of 24 June 2011.

[39] The proposal consists of a package including a proposal for a new regulation, a proposed amendment to the Code and one communication, see COM (2011) 559, 560 and 561. While the Commission based its proposal on Art 77(2) TFEU, which requires co-decision with the European Parliament (ordinary legislative procedure), a considerable number of Member States as well as the Council Legal Service argued that the correct legal basis should be Art 70 TFEU. This article enables the Council, on a proposal from the Commission, to adopt arrangements on mutual evaluations by qualified majority. The ordinary legislative procedure would not apply.

[40] The Commission has also stated that it will continue to work on guidelines to ensure the coherent implementation of the Schengen rules. It said that this could include guidelines on issuing travel documents and residence permits, which seems to be a reaction to one of the problems raised in the Franco-Italian case.

[41] See Art 25 of the Commission's Proposal for a Regulation of the European Parliament and of the Council amending Regulation (EC) No 562/2006 in order to provide for common rules on the temporary reintroduction of border control at internal borders in exceptional circumstances, COM (2011) 560 final. The Commission mentions terrorist attacks and other major criminal incidents as examples of situations in which urgent measures could be necessary; see Annex 2 of the communication of the Commission entitled 'Schengen governance – strengthening the area without internal border control' COM (2011) 561 final.

was that the Commission felt that only a decision taken at Union level will allow all European interests to be taken into account.[42]

The latter part of the proposal would have been a radical reform, delegating it to the Commission to decide on the introduction of temporary border controls. Not surprisingly this part of the proposal was not adopted and apart from a minor change to what is now Article 23, the rules outlined above were not changed.[43]

Another attempt to change the rules on reintroduction of border controls was made in 2017. The backdrop of the proposal was the increased use of temporary border control since September 2015 due to migration.[44] The proposal aimed to set a maximum period of two years for the duration of temporary border controls, if they can be attributed to the same grounds, and if commensurate exceptional national measures are taken within the territory to address the threat. The proposal also introduced further procedural measures to ensure that the use of internal border checks remains exceptional and proportionate, thus encouraging Member States to use police checks and cooperation instead of internal border controls. The EU legislator was not able to reach agreement on this proposal either and it was eventually withdrawn. A new attempt to legislate was made by the Commission in 2021, see below.

Since it had proved difficult to recalibrate the system though reform, it might be expected that the focus of the Commission would be on making sure that the existing rules were used correctly. But even though the Commission did react to the many reintroductions and has frequently warned that the ambition of removing the internal border control was in danger, it did not go further than that.[45] Thus, the Commission did not use the power granted in Article 27(4) of the Code to issue an opinion that it has concern about the necessity or proportionality of the control reintroduced, nor did it make use of the possibility to start consultation. Also, the Commission did not begin any infringement procedures against States that had reintroduced border controls. The fact that the Commission did not react with any of these 'official' steps is likely to be seen as an acceptance of the legality of the reintroductions that have taken place.[46]

In the end, it was a private individual who allowed the ECJ to interpret the existing rules in a way that paved the way for better enforcement. The backdrop to Joined Cases C-368/20 and C-369/20, *NW v Landespolizeidirektion Steiermark*, was that NW was charged twice in 2019 when entering Austria at two different crossing points not being willing to show his passport despite the fact that Austria since 2015 had reintroduced border controls. NW challenged the legality of these border controls, and the issue was referred to the ECJ as preliminary questions.[47] In its judgment the ECJ stressed that the rules allowing the reintroduction of border control were an exception to Article 22 of the Code that provided for the removal of internal

[42] See Commission Communication (n 41), 5.

[43] The result of the reform is Regulation (EU) No 1051/2013 of the European Parliament and of the Council of 22 October 2013 amending Regulation (EC) No 562/2006 in order to provide for common rules on the temporary reintroduction of border control at internal borders in exceptional circumstances [2013] OJ L295/1. See the analysis of the reform by G Cornelisse, 'What's Wrong with Schengen? Border Disputes and the Nature of Integration in an Area without Internal Borders' (2014) 51 *Common Market Law Review* 741.

[44] Commission, 'Proposal for a Regulation of the European Parliament and of the Council amending Regulation (EU) 2016/399 as regards the rules applicable to the temporary reintroduction of border control at internal borders' COM (2017) 571 final.

[45] Apparently, the Commission preferred a political angle rather than a judicial one: see S Salomon and JJ Rijpma, 'The Promise of Free Movement in the Schengen Area – The Decision of the Court of Justice in Landespolizeidirektion Steiermark (NW)' (2023) 48 *European Law Review* 124, 134.

[46] Thus, the lack of reaction from the Commission has been interpreted by the Danish Minister of Justice as an acceptance of the Danish reintroductions: see the answer to question no 751 dated 6 June 2023.

[47] Curiously a Dane was inspired by NW to try to provoke a case concerning Danish border control. When he declined to show his passport when entering Denmark via the Danish-German border in 2023, he was not charged or

border control. An exception needs to be interpreted strictly.[48] In this case it meant that Article 25(4) only allows the Sates to extend the temporary border control for a maximum period of six months. If there are new elements to the threat originally identified as the reason for the reintroduction, then States may be allowed to extend the border control up to six months, but not beyond that. The same is true if there is a reappraisal of the necessity or proportionality of the border control established.[49] According to the ECJ, the EU legislator has considered that a period of six months is sufficient for a State to adopt alternative measures to meet the identified threat.[50] If, on the other hand, there is a new threat to public policy or internal security, that threat may allow the State to reintroduce internal border control – again up to six month if the threat evolves.[51]

The ECJ hereby made it clear that it is only possible to extend the border control beyond six months if there is a new threat. Since some States have invoked the same threat repeatedly as a reason for extending their border control, this clarification of the correct application of the Code would potentially end the ever-continuing renewal of temporary border control. However, that did not happen.

Taking Denmark as an example, the Member State chose to reintroduce temporary border control for another six months just a few weeks after the ECJ had handed down its judgment in *NW v Landespolizeidirektion Steiermark*. In a letter dated 13 April 2022 to the Commission, the Danish government mainly pointed to the new threats caused by the war in Ukraine. This letter, however, was sent before the ECJ handed down its judgment, and therefore logically the Danish government could not take it into account. Again, on 14 October 2022, the Danish government wrote to the Commission to announce that it would continue the border control for another six months. The main reason was the war in Ukraine (the same threat), but it also mentions that the war has increased the number of criminal groups crossing the border and terrorist threats against Denmark. Furthermore, the letter from the Danish government mentions other threats; migration along the Mediterranean routes, Swedish criminal networks and the return of persons who years ago travelled from Denmark to Syria/Iraq to join militant Islamist groups and may now return. Again, in spring and autumn 2023, Denmark notified the Commission that it would prolong the temporary border control, relying mainly on the same threats, although both times also relying on threats due to Quran burnings.[52]

An assessment from the Ministry of Immigration and Integration dated 27 May 2022 noted that it was unclear what the ECJ would characterise as a 'new threat', but the ministry assumed that the migration problems that would follow from the war in Ukraine were such a new threat.[53] Thus, the assumption was that this migration crisis presented a new crisis compared to the migration crises that triggered the reintroduction in 2016 and the following years. It may be argued that the migration crisis is the same threat, as the migrants enter Denmark through the same channels, and therefore they should be coped with in the same way. After having temporary border control for this reason for a period, Denmark should have developed techniques to cope with such a crisis. If this is the case, then migration may not be sufficient to justify an extension of the border control. Surely, migration caused by the war in Ukraine cannot be a new threat both in spring 2022 and autumn 2022.

fined. Instead, he was invited to a 'constructive, friendly conversation' with the police. He must have been frustrated. The story is reported in JyskeVestkysten, 10 September 2023 by AL Rickert.

[48] *NW v Landespolizeidirection* (n 18), para 64.

[49] ibid, para 66. Also the ECJ made it clear that States cannot rely on Art 72 TFEU to prolong the reintroduction beyond what is allowed in the Code: ibid, para 90.

[50] ibid, para 77.

[51] ibid, para 71.

[52] See letters addressed to Commissioner Johansson dated 14 April 2023 and 13 October 2023.

[53] The assessment is available at www.ft.dk, accessed 3 March 2024.

It is difficult to make an assessment of the legality of the Danish extensions, because Denmark continuously invokes several reasons for reintroducing temporary border controls. Even though some of them have been used before, it may not have been used in the last request for a renewal. Does this make it a new threat? Also, the Danish government, from time to time, includes new reasons, such as migration caused by the war in Ukraine and the problems caused by Quran burnings. Such new reasons may justify the reintroduction of the temporary border control, but is this the case only if they are serious enough to justify their reintroduction, or should the other reasons put forward by the Danish government be taken into account? These questions are not univocally answered by the ruling of the ECJ.

It would seem that the judgment in *NW v Landespolizeidirektion Steiermark* made little impression on the Danish government. The fact that the Commission has not given an opinion according to Article 27(4) of the Code seems to have allowed the Danish government to believe that nothing has changed. However, in August 2023 it was announced in the Danish news that the Commission had started to investigate Danish border control and had requested consultation.[54] The result of these consultations is not known, but they apparently took place before the most recent notification of a renewal. Thus, it seems as if the consultation did not have much impact.

V. CONCLUSION: THE WAY FORWARD

The Danish example is not unique, as other Schengen Member States have also kept their temporary border controls after April 2022.[55] So at this point it is not clear that the judgment in *NW v Landespolizeidirektion Steiermark* will change the behaviour of the States (or the Commission). This might be remedied, if the ECJ in a subsequent ruling could clarify what constitutes a new threat.[56] However, since Member States often find several reasons for introducing border control, pointing to different reasons at different times, and as long as the Commission is not challenging the Member States, a more precise definition is not likely to change the current situation. Therefore, it is likely that a reform of the Schengen Borders Code is needed to change the current situation. The Commission launched such a reform in 2021 suggesting a number of changes to the existing rules regarding reintroductions of internal border controls.[57] The proposal allows for the reintroduction for a period longer than six months but at the same time strengthens the procedure and condition for extending the border control. So even though the rules are relaxed somewhat, it could still mean a strengthened regime if the Member States accept that they must comply more strictly with the new rules.

[54] See LS Andersen and S Gjerding 'EU-Kommissionen indleder undersøgelse af dansk grænsekontrol' (2023) in *Information*. It appears that the Commission is committed to make such consultations with all States that reintroduce border controls: see Commission, 'State of Schengen report 2023' (Communication) COM (2023) 274 final.

[55] In a report from 2023 it is concluded that the six Member States that have kept internal border controls in place since 2015 have acted unlawfully. About their recent notifications it says: 'In their latest Notifications, these same Member States have artificially repackaged and provided further information in a failed attempt to justify the novelty of the grounds behind the prolongation of internal border checks. The Study shows, however, that these are not new grounds and that they continue to use the same grounds as before.' See the study requested by the LIBE committee of the European Parliament entitled, 'An Assessment of the State of the EU Schengen Area and its External Borders. A Merited Trust Model to Uphold Schengen Legitimacy' (2023), 11.

[56] The judgment does set out some criteria for what constitutes a new threat, but these criteria most likely need to be spelled out in more detail, see also Salomon and Rijpma (n 45), 129.

[57] See Commission, 'Proposal for a Regulation of the European Parliament and of the Council amending Regulation (EU) 2016/399 on a Union Code on the rules governing the movement of persons across borders' COM (2021) 891 final.

18

EU Citizenship and Nationality – A Question of Competence

HENRIK SAUGMANDSGAARD ØE AND PHILIP RENNEMO-HENRIKSEN*

I. INTRODUCTION

From a European Union (EU) perspective, EU citizenship (or Union citizenship) is arguably the most important status for nationals of the EU Member States. EU citizenship grants the rights on which nationals of the EU Member States can rely under EU law, including the Charter of Fundamental Rights of the European Union (the Charter).[1]

Even though EU citizenship is not covered by the area of freedom, security and justice (AFSJ) provisions, the denial or relinquishment of Union citizenship will cause the person concerned to be treated as a third-country national under the provisions of the AFSJ, which in fact can have, for example, possible asylum or immigration implications. Equally, this area of law encompasses some of the same legal assessments as the AFSJ areas, including in particular the assessment of the principle of proportionality.[2] It is in this light that our contribution should be read in relation to the AFSJ.

Pursuant to Article 20 in the Treaty on the Functioning of the European Union (TFEU), EU citizenship is conditional on nationality of a Member State and EU citizenship is not to replace national citizenship. However, the latter part was not always the wording of the provision.

EU citizenship was introduced by Article 8 of the Maastricht Treaty and caused quite a stir in Denmark. In fact, on 2 June 1992, Denmark by referendum rejected the Maastricht Treaty and, consequently, the treaty could not enter into force. In December 1992, the European Council in Edinburgh decided[3] that Denmark should be allowed four legal reservations.[4] One of the legal reservations relates to EU citizenship,[5] according to which the EU citizenship in no

* Respectively Gorrissen Federspiel, former Advocate General at the European Court of Justice and Assistant Attorney at Gorrissen Federspiel, External Lecturer at the University of Copenhagen.

[1] For another Liber Amicorum contribution on Union citizenship, see K Lenaerts, 'Union Citizenship and the Principle of Non-discrimination on Ground of Nationality' in *Festskrift til Claus Gulmann* (Forlaget Thomsen A/S, 2006) 289.

[2] See eg Opinion of AG Szpunar in Case C-118/20 *Wiener Landesregierung (Révocation d'une assurance de naturalisation*, ECLI:EU:C:2021:530, para 86 where he states that 'the principle of proportionality lies at the heart of EU law'.

[3] European Council in Edinburgh, 11–12 December 1992, Part B, Annex 1.

[4] See additionally, C Thorning, 'De danske forbehold' in U Neergaard and KE Sørensen (eds), *Danmark og EU gennem 50 år – en milepæl* (Djøf Forlag, 2023).

[5] The additional three under the decision related to 'Economic and Monetary Union', 'Defence Policy', and 'Justice and Home Affairs'.

way takes the place of the national citizenship, and the question whether a person possesses national citizenship is entirely settled by national law.[6] Following this decision, a new referendum was held in Denmark on 18 May 1993, where the Maastricht Treaty was accepted and then entered into force on 1 November 1993.

The Danish take on EU citizenship was seemingly shared by the other Member States. In any case, the wording '[c]itizenship of the Union shall complement and not replace national citizenship' was added to the Amsterdam Treaty and is still part of the TFEU wording. Consequently, one might question the extent of Denmark's legal reservation on EU citizenship. The point on national citizenship being entirely settled by national law is still part of Denmark's legal reservation.

The case law of the European Court of Justice (ECJ) shows that national citizenship being entirely settled by national law is not just the case for Denmark, but for all EU Member States. Further, the case law shows that whilst it is for the laws of the Member State to determine whether a national is to acquire or lose citizenship to that Member State, when the loss of the national citizenship also entails the loss of EU citizenship and the attached rights, the laws of the Member State must comply with EU law, including the principle of proportionality.

The importance of proportionality in this context has been established by a number of judgments by the ECJ in which Lars Bay Larsen took part. It is in honour of Vice-President Bay Larsen that in the following pages we discuss the importance of the principle of proportionality in relation to the loss of EU citizenship. The principle will be discussed in the light of these judgments, starting in Section II with the *Rottman* case,[7] which established that when the loss of national citizenship entails the loss of EU citizenship, the regulation on the loss of the national citizenship must be in accordance with EU law, including the principle of proportionality. In Section III, the implications of the *Ruiz Zambrano*[8] case are discussed, taking a closer look at the 'genuine enjoyment of the rights' attached to Union citizenship and the persons involved in this assessment. Section IV concerns the *Tjebbes and Others* case[9] and discusses the requirements that the Member States must fulfil in order for their national regulations to be in accordance with EU law. In Section V, the focus is on the *Wiener Landesregierung* case,[10] where the ECJ established that national measures were contrary to the principle of proportionality. The ECJ's recent judgment of 5 September 2023 is mentioned in Section VI;[11] that case concerned the Danish Law on Nationality's compliance with EU law and the principle of proportionality. Lastly, in Section VII, we give an example of the importance of the rights attached to EU citizenship.

II. NATIONAL REGULATION OF CITIZENSHIP AND ITS RELATIONSHIP WITH EU LAW

When discussing proportionality and the deprivation of EU citizenship, the *Rottman* case[12] is a natural starting point. In 1998, an Austrian national, Dr Rottman, applied for German citizenship and was issued the naturalisation document in February 1999. In accordance with Austrian law, this caused him to lose his Austrian nationality.

[6] European Council in Edinburgh (n 3), Annex 1, Section A 'Citizenship'.

[7] Case C-135/08 *Rottman*, ECLI:EU:C:2010:104.

[8] Case C-34/09 *Ruiz Zambrano*, ECLI:EU:C:2011:124.

[9] Case C-221/17 *Tjebbes and Others*, ECLI:EU:C:2019:189.

[10] Case C-118/20 *Wiener Landesregierung (Révocation d'une assurance de naturalisation)*, ECLI:EU:C:2022:34.

[11] Case C-689/21 *Udlændinge- og Integrationsministeriet (Perte de la nationalité danoise)*, ECLI:EU:C:2023:626.

[12] See also G De Groot et al, 'Decision of 2 March 2010, Case C-135/08, *Janko Rottman v. Freistaat Bayern* – Case Note II – The Consequences of the Rottman Judgment on Member State Autonomy – The European Court of Justice's Avant-Gardism in Nationality Matters' (2011) 7 *European Constitutional Law Review* 150.

During the German naturalisation process, Dr Rottman failed to mention that serious fraud proceedings had been brought against him in Austria. Consequently, the Freistaat Bayern withdrew Dr Rottman's naturalisation with retroactive effect on the grounds that Dr Rottman had obtained German nationality by deception.

The second instance court held that this decision was compatible with German law. Upon appeal, the referring court, the Bundesverwaltungsgericht (German federal administrative court), also found that the withdrawal of the naturalisation was in accordance with German law. The court also noted that because the withdrawal would make Dr Rottman stateless, with the result that he would lose his EU citizenship, the withdrawal had to be compatible with EU law as stated in the *Mecheletti and Others* case.[13] Under these circumstances, the Bundesverwaltungsgericht asked the ECJ, whether the withdrawal of the naturalisation under the events in the case was contrary to EU law and in particular Article 20 TFEU, inasmuch as the withdrawal deprived the person of the status of a citizen of the Union and the benefits of the rights attached thereto.

In the case, the German and Austrian Governments had argued that the rules on the acquisition and loss of nationality fall within the competence of the Member States and that because Dr Rottman at the time of the withdrawal of the naturalisation was a German national, it was purely an internal situation, meaning that EU law was not applicable.

The ECJ acknowledged that it is in fact for each Member State to lay down the conditions for the acquisition and loss of nationality.[14] However, when situations that are within the competence of Member States are also covered by EU law, the national rules must have due regard to the latter.[15]

When an EU citizen has his or her naturalisation withdrawn and this causes that person to potentially lose the status conferred by Article 20 TFEU and the attached rights, such situation falls, 'by reason of its nature and its consequences, within the ambit of European Union law'.[16] Furthermore, the 'citizenship of the Union is intended to be the fundamental status of nationals of the Member States'.[17]

Consequently, national decisions, such as withdrawing naturalisation in a situation like this, are amenable to judicial review from an EU law perspective,[18] although it is legitimate for a Member State to protect 'the special relationship of solidarity and good faith between it and its nationals and also the reciprocity of rights and duties, which form the bedrock of the bond of nationality'.[19]

Ultimately, the ECJ concluded that the decision to withdraw Dr Rottman's naturalisation was subject to EU law and to examination of the proportionality of the decision in the light of national law[20] whilst taking into account:

> [...] the consequences that the decision entails for the person concerned and, if relevant, for the members of his family with regard to the loss of the rights enjoyed by every citizen of the Union. In this respect it is necessary to establish, in particular, whether that loss is justified in relation to the gravity of the offence committed by that person, to the lapse of time between the naturalisation decision and the withdrawal decision and to whether it is possible for that person to recover his original nationality.[21]

[13] Case C-369/90 *Micheletti and Others v Delegación del Gobierno en Cantabria*, ECLI:EU:C:1992:295.
[14] *Rottman* (n 7), para 39.
[15] ibid, para 41.
[16] ibid, para 42.
[17] ibid, para 43.
[18] ibid, para 48.
[19] ibid, para 51.
[20] ibid, para 55.
[21] ibid, para 56.

The case showed that although it is up to the respective Member States to create regulations on the acquisition and loss of nationality, the regulation must be compatible with EU law, including the principle of proportionality, when a decision of revoking a person's national citizenship results in that person losing his or her Union citizenship.

In its judgment of 8 March 2011,[22] the ECJ found that Article 20 TFEU precludes a Member State from refusing a third-country national a right of residence in – and a work permit to – that Member State insofar as that person's children, who are EU citizens and dependent upon their parent, are deprived of the genuine enjoyment of their rights attached to the status of EU citizenship.[23]

III. PROTECTING THE GENUINE ENJOYMENT OF THE RIGHTS ATTACHED TO EU CITIZENSHIP

Due to civil war in Colombia, Mr and Mrs Zambrano had moved to Belgium in 1999 with their three-year-old son, in possession of a visa issued by the Belgian embassy in Bogotá, Colombia.

In 2000, they both applied for asylum in Belgium and were both refused. In the years to come, Mr and Mrs Zambrano fought to take up residence and receive work permits in Belgium, all of which were refused. Throughout this time, Mrs Zambrano had given birth to two children, Diego and Jessica, who acquired Belgian nationality pursuant to the Belgian Nationality Code.[24]

Ultimately, Mr Zambrano brought the refusal to take up residence, which stated that he was required to hold a work permit, in front of the Tribunal du travail de Bruxelles (Employment Tribunal, Brussels, Belgium), arguing, inter alia, that he enjoyed a derived right of residence, as recognised in the *Zhu and Chen* case,[25] for his minor children who were Belgian nationals and that he therefore was exempt from the obligation to hold a work permit. The Tribunal du travail de Bruxelles then brought this question in front of the ECJ.

All the governments which submitted observation in the case and the European Commission argued that because the children who were Belgian nationals resided in Belgium and had never left the Member State, the situation did not come within the situations envisaged by the freedoms of movement and residence guaranteed under EU law and that EU law consequently did not apply.[26]

The ECJ, however, stated that Article 20 TFEU confers the status of citizen of the Union on every person holding the nationality of a Member State and that the children who were Belgian nationals 'undeniably' enjoyed that status[27] and that EU citizenship is intended to be the fundamental status of nationals of the Member State.[28]

[22] *Ruiz Zambrano* (n 8).

[23] See also C Barnard, 'Free Movement of Natural Persons and Citizenship of the Union' in C Barnard and S Peers (eds), *European Union Law*, 3rd edn (Oxford University Press, 2017) 397.

[24] Moniteur belge, 12 July 1984, page 10095, in the version applicable at the time of the facts in the main proceedings of the case, the Belgian Nationality Code.

[25] Case C-200/02 *Zhu and* Chen, ECLI:EU:C:2004:639.

[26] *Ruiz Zambrano* (n 8), para 37.

[27] ibid, para 40.

[28] ibid, para 41.

Referring to the *Rottman* case on the preclusion of national measures that have the effect of depriving citizens of their Union citizenship,[29] the ECJ found it had to be assumed that such a refusal:

> [...] would lead to a situation where those children, citizens of the Union, would have to leave the territory of the Union in order to accompany their parents. Similarly, if a work permit were not granted to such a person, he would risk not having sufficient resources to provide for himself and his family, which would also result in the children, citizens of the Union, having to leave the territory of the Union. In those circumstances, those citizens of the Union would, in fact, be unable to exercise the substance of the rights conferred on them by virtue of their status as citizens of the Union.[30]

Consequently, the ECJ found that Article 20 TFEU precluded a Member State from refusing a third-country national a right of residence in – and a work permit for – that Member State insofar as that person's children, who are EU citizens and dependent upon their parent, are deprived of the genuine enjoyment of their rights attached to the status of EU citizenship.

In its judgment of 12 March 2019,[31] the ECJ elaborated upon the importance of proportionality with respect to Union citizenship.

IV. A CLOSER LOOK AT THE CONTENT OF THE PRINCIPLE OF PROPORTIONALITY

In *Tjebbes and Others*,[32] four women (Ms Tjebbes, Ms Koopman, Ms Saleh Abady, and Ms Duboux) had for different reasons held dual citizenships, Netherlands nationality being one of the citizenships and a non-EU country being the other.

Common to three of the women was that when their Netherlands passports expired, the Netherlands authorities decided not to examine their passport applications, as the authorities believed that the women had lost Netherlands nationality pursuant to Article 15(1)(c) of the Netherlands Law on Nationality.[33] Under this provision, adults lose their Netherlands nationality if they also hold a foreign nationality and if they have their principal residence for an uninterrupted period of 10 years outside the Netherlands and the EU.

The fourth woman, Ms Duboux, had never held a Netherlands passport, but, being a minor, she was entered into her mother's passport, as her mother held dual nationality, including Netherlands nationality. Once her mother lost her Netherlands nationality under Article 15(1)(c), Ms Duboux was also deprived of her Netherlands nationality under Article 16(1)(d) of the Netherlands Law on Nationality, pursuant to which minors lose Netherlands nationality if either of their parents lose their Netherlands nationality pursuant to, inter alia, Article 15(1)(c).

The women filed complaints to different district courts in the Netherlands and later lodged appeals before the Raad van State (Council of State, Netherlands).

The question posed to the ECJ was whether Article 20 TFEU, based on the principle of proportionality, and in the light of, inter alia, Article 7 of the Charter, must be interpreted as precluding legislation such as that at issue, where the loss of Netherlands nationality without an individual examination would cause loss of Union citizenship and the attached rights.

[29] ibid, para 42.
[30] ibid, para 44.
[31] *Tjebbes and Others* (n 9).
[32] For a critical review see K Swider, 'Legitimizing Precarity of EU Citizenship: Tjebbes' (2020) 57 *Common Market Law Review* 1163, 1163–82.
[33] Rijkswet op het Nederlanderschap of 19 December 1984, Nederlands Law on Nationality.

In answering the question, the ECJ referenced its conclusions from the *Rottman* case, stating that the matter of the case had to have due regard to EU law,[34] and then went on to address the circumstances in the case.

It was apparent that the Netherlands legislation sought to introduce a system to avoid the undesirable consequences of one person having multiple nationalities.[35] The ECJ stated that it was legitimate to wish to protect a 'genuine link' between the persons and the Netherlands and 'to wish to protect the unity of nationality within the same family'.[36] EU law does not preclude, in principle, the loss of nationality to the Member State when the Member State prescribes for reasons of public interest the loss of its nationality.[37]

However, the loss of nationality must be proportionate under EU law 'so far as concerns the consequences of that loss for the situation of the person concerned and, if relevant, for that of the members of his or her family, from the point of view of EU law'.[38]

For this decision, the ECJ stated that the loss of nationality would be incompatible with the principle of proportionality '... if the relevant national rules did not permit at any time *an individual examination* of the consequences of that loss for the persons concerned from the point of view of EU law' (emphasis added).[39]

The ECJ further stated that:

> [...] the competent national authorities and courts must be in a position to examine, as an ancillary issue, the consequences of the loss of that nationality and, where appropriate, to have the person concerned recover his or her nationality *ex tunc* in the context of an application by that person for a travel document or any other document showing his or her nationality.[40]

Such examination requires an individual assessment of the situation of the person concerned and that of his or her family of whether the consequences of losing the nationality, and thus Union citizenship, are proportionate to the objective pursued by the national legislation. Furthermore, those consequences cannot be hypothetical or merely a possibility.[41]

As part of this examination of proportionality, the loss of nationality must also be consistent with Article 7 of the Charter, which has to be read in junction with Article 24(2) of the Charter regarding the obligation to take into consideration the best interests of the child.[42]

Following the loss of Netherlands nationality and Union citizenship, the person in question would, inter alia, be exposed to limitations when exercising his or her right to move and reside freely within the territory of the Member States,[43] as manifested, inter alia, in Articles 20 and 21 TFEU.[44]

In light of the circumstances of the case, the ECJ concluded that Article 20 TFEU, read in light of Articles 7 and 24 of the Charter, does not preclude national regulation under which persons by losing their nationality to a Member State also lose their Union citizenship and associated rights, as long as the national regulation has due regard to the principle of proportionality by basing the loss of that nationality on an *individual examination* of the

[34] As described in section III above and *Tjebbes and Others* (n 9), paras 30–33.
[35] *Tjebbes and Others* (n 9), para 34.
[36] ibid, para 35.
[37] ibid, para 39.
[38] ibid, para 40, where the ECJ referenced the *Rottman* case (n 7), paras 55–56.
[39] *Tjebbes and Others* Case (n 9), para 41.
[40] ibid, para 42.
[41] ibid, para 44.
[42] ibid, para 45.
[43] ibid, para 46.
[44] ibid, para 46.

consequences of the persons and their families. Furthermore, the persons concerned must be in a position to recover their nationality *ex tunc* in the context of an application by those persons for a travel document or any other document showing their nationality where applicable.[45]

In its judgment of 18 January 2022,[46] the ECJ later confirmed this state of law whilst stating that the national regulation in question was contrary to the principle of proportionality.

V. PROPORTIONALITY: FINDING THE RIGHT BALANCE

On 15 December 2008, JY, at the time an Estonian national, applied for Austrian citizenship. On 11 March 2014, she received an assurance from the Niederösterreichische Landesregierung (Government of the Province of Lower Austria, Austria) that she would be granted Austrian nationality if she could prove, within two years, that she had relinquished her citizenship of the Republic of Estonia.

JY moved to Vienna and relinquished her Estonian citizenship on 27 August 2015. Consequently, she became stateless.

By decision of 6 July 2017, the Wiener Landesregierung (Government of the Province of Vienna, Austria) revoked the assurance and rejected JY's application for Austrian nationality.

This decision was justified on the grounds that JY had committed two serious administrative offences by failing to display a vehicle inspection disc and by driving a motor vehicle while under the influence of alcohol. Additionally, she had committed eight administrative offences before receiving the assurance, between 2007 and 2013. As such, the Wiener Landesregierung no longer found that JY satisfied the conditions for grant of nationality as laid down in the StbG[47] because she jeopardised road safety and specifically jeopardised the safety of other road users.

The questions brought before the ECJ were twofold: (i) did the situation at hand fall within the scope of EU law; and, in the affirmative, (ii) was the situation compatible with the principle of proportionality?

In answering the first question, the ECJ divided the procedural actions of the Austrian authorities in this case into two steps: (i) JY had to relinquish her Estonian citizenship; and (ii) the Austrian authorities' decision to revoke the assurance. Here, it was only step (ii) which entailed the loss of Union citizenship,[48] because JY's decision to relinquish her citizenship had not been voluntary,[49] since it was a requirement for obtaining Austrian nationality.[50]

Emphasising the fundamental status of EU citizenship for nationals of the Member States,[51] the ECJ found that the procedure as a whole affected the status conferred by Article 20 TFEU, 'since it may result in a person in a situation such as that of JY being deprived of all the rights attaching to that status …'[52]

Overall, the situation at hand, by reason of its nature and its consequences, fell within the scope of EU law.[53]

[45] ibid, para 48.

[46] *Wiener Landesregierung (Révocation d'une assurance de naturalisation)* (n 10).

[47] Bundesgesetz über die österreichische Staatsbürgerschaft 1985 (BGBl. Nr 311/1985), 1985 Austrian Law on Citizenship.

[48] *Wiener Landesregierung (Révocation d'une assurance de naturalisation)* (n 10), paras 31–32.

[49] ibid, para 36.

[50] ibid, paras 34–35.

[51] ibid, para 38.

[52] ibid, para 40.

[53] ibid, para 44.

Turning to the question whether the actions of the Austrian authorities were proportionate, the importance of Union citizenship and the attached rights was stressed and that even a temporary loss of that status means that the person in question is indefinitely prevented from enjoying these rights.[54]

Austria had an obligation to ensure the effectiveness of Article 20 TFEU, because Estonia had already relinquished JY's citizenship to that Member State,[55] and so the decision of revocation had to be coherent with the principle of proportionality.[56]

Upon analysing the proportionality of the decision of revocation, the ECJ stated that:

> In this respect it is necessary to establish, in particular, whether that decision is justified in relation to the gravity of the offence committed by that person and to whether it is possible for that person to recover his or her original nationality …[57]

Furthermore, the decision had to be consistent with Article 7 of the Charter.[58]

The eight administrative offences were dismissed, as these were known to the Austrian authorities when the assurance was given.[59] Regarding the two serious administrative offences, the decision of revocation was based on the protection of 'public order and road safety'.[60]

Whilst the concepts of public policy and public security can justify the loss of Union citizenship under Article 20 TFEU, these concepts must be interpreted strictly.[61] As for public policy, this presupposes an existence of 'a genuine, present and sufficiently serious threat affecting one of the fundamental interests of society' and public security covers, inter alia, 'a threat to the functioning of institutions and essential public services and the survival of the population'.[62]

Consequently, JY had not, by having committed traffic offences, posed such threats to public policy and public security as these concepts have been interpreted under EU law, which may have justified her loss of Union citizenship.[63] The ECJ concluded that the decision to revoke JY's Austrian nationality, which had the effect of her losing her Union citizenship, was not proportionate to the gravity of the offences committed by her.[64]

With the above case law in mind, we will now turn to a judgment of 5 September 2023,[65] where the ECJ was faced once again with a question related to Article 20 TFEU and Union citizenship, this time with Danish law at the centre.[66]

VI. CASE C-689/21 *UDLÆNDINGE- OG INTEGRATIONSMINISTERIET (PERTE DE LA NATIONALITÉ DANOISE)*

A woman, X, was born in the US and held dual citizenship, both US and Danish, despite never having resided in Denmark except for a brief period of 44 weeks. On 17 November 2014, she

[54] ibid, paras 45–48.
[55] Which the ECJ stated that it should not have done until the new nationality had been acquired: ibid, para 50.
[56] ibid, para 51.
[57] ibid, para 60.
[58] ibid, para 61.
[59] ibid, para 65.
[60] ibid, para 66.
[61] ibid, para 68.
[62] ibid, para 69.
[63] ibid, paras 70–71.
[64] ibid, para 73.
[65] *Udlændinge- og Integrationsministeriet (Perte de la nationalité danoise)* (n 11).
[66] See also J Farcy, 'Arrêt "Udlændinge- og Integrationsministeriet": la perte automatique de la nationalité d'un État membre pour défaut de lien effectif remise en cause par le principe de la proportionnalité' (2023) *Journal de droit européen* 453.

applied to retain her Danish nationality after her 22nd birthday. X had been a part of the Danish basketball team in 2015 and had in 2005 spent three to four weeks in France.

Section 8(1) of the Danish Law on Nationality[67] requires such retaining applications to be submitted before the applicant turns 22, unless the person thus becomes stateless. Consequently, the Danish Ministry of Immigration and Integration informed her by decision that she had lost her Danish nationality, as she also held US citizenship and that it was not possible to apply the derogation, since her application to retain Danish nationality had been made after she had turned 22. Subsequently, she brought an action before the Københavns Byret (District Court, Copenhagen, Denmark) for annulment of this decision. The action was referred to the Østre Landsret (High Court of Eastern Denmark, Denmark).

The question before the ECJ was whether this legislation was compatible with Article 20 TFEU, read in the light of Article 7 of the Charter. Focus was on the fact that X was born outside of Denmark and had never been resident there nor demonstrated a genuine link with Denmark. Consequently, she would lose the nationality of Denmark at the age of 22, which would entail the loss of her Union citizenship and the attached rights.

The ECJ referenced the above case law, emphasising that the matter at hand was within the ambit of EU law[68] and that it was legitimate for Denmark to wish to protect the special relationship of solidarity and good faith between it and its nationals[69] and that absence of a genuine link between X and Denmark entails the loss of nationality.[70]

According to the *travaux préparatoires* of the Danish Law on Nationality,[71] the purpose of section 8(1) of the Law is to 'prevent Danish nationality being handed down from generation to generation to persons established abroad who have no knowledge of or link with the Kingdom of Denmark'.[72]

In principle, such legislation is not precluded, but due to the importance of Union citizenship and the rights attached thereto, regard had to be made to the principle of proportionality 'so far as concerns the consequences of that loss for the situation of the person concerned and, if relevant, for that of the members of his or her family, from the point of view of EU law'.[73]

Referencing the *Tjebbes and Others* case, the ECJ stated that absence of an individual examination would be inconsistent with the principle of proportionality,[74] but that there was no time limit for this examination, meaning that it is for the Member States to lay down procedural rules which ensure that the rights attached to Union citizenship are safeguarded.[75] However, the limitation must be reasonable in the interests of legal certainty, so that the 'periods are not liable to make it in practice impossible or excessively difficult to exercise the rights conferred by EU law …'.[76]

[67] Consolidated Danish Law on Nationality No 1656 of 23 December 2022.

[68] *Udlændinge- og Integrationsministeriet (Perte de la nationalité danoise)* (n 11), para 30.

[69] ibid, para 31.

[70] ibid, para 32.

[71] The Østre Landsret referred to section 2.2.2 of the explanatory memorandum to Bill No L 138 of 28 January 2004, concerning section 8 of the Law on Nationality (Opinion of AG Szpunar in Case C-689/21 *Udlændinge- og Integrationsministeriet (Perte de la nationalité danoise)*, ECLI:EU:C:2023:53). However, the *travaux préparatoires* does not state this as firmly as it is referenced in the case, but instead focuses on the person's social cohesion or connectedness (in Danish: 'samhørighed') with Denmark.

[72] *Udlændinge- og Integrationsministeriet (Perte de la nationalité danoise)* (n 11), para 34.

[73] ibid, para 38 with references to the *Rottman* case (n 7), paras 55–56; and *Tjebbes and Others* (n 9), para 40.

[74] *Udlændinge- og Integrationsministeriet (Perte de la nationalité danoise)* (n 11), para 39.

[75] ibid, para 40.

[76] ibid, para 42.

Consequently, a Member State may require that an application for the maintenance or recovery of nationality is submitted 'within a reasonable period'.[77] Under Danish law, the examination is made only if the national submits the application after the person has turned 21 but before the person's 22nd birthday.[78]

The ECJ found that because a genuine link to Denmark must be demonstrated at the time of the person's 22nd birthday, that person must be able to raise such matters after his or her 22nd birthday.[79] Consequently, the person must have a reasonable period of time to make the request for an examination of the proportionality of the consequences of that loss and, where appropriate, the retention or recovery *ex tunc* of that nationality. In the words of the ECJ: 'That period must then extend, for a reasonable length of time, beyond the date on which that person reaches that age'.[80] The relevant date for the purposes of the examination is that on which the person concerned reaches the age of 22.[81]

The ECJ then concluded that Article 20 TFEU, read in the light of Article 7 of the Charter, did not preclude legislation such as the Danish, provided:

> that the persons concerned are given the opportunity to lodge, within a reasonable period, an application for the retention or recovery of the nationality, which enables the competent authorities to examine the proportionality of the consequences of the loss of that nationality from the point of view of EU law and, where appropriate, to allow the retention or recovery *ex tunc* of that nationality.[82]

VII. CONCLUSION: ON THE PRINCIPLE OF PROPORTIONALITY IN THE LIGHT OF THE CASE LAW OF THE ECJ AND THE IMPORTANCE OF THE RIGHTS ATTACHED TO EU CITIZENSHIP

As is evident from the case law reviewed, the principle of proportionality is of utmost importance when it comes to national legislation on the loss of national citizenship when this entails deprivation of EU citizenship.

The principle of proportionality is manifested in both Article 5(4) TFEU and Article 52 of the Charter. According to the latter provision, limitations on the exercise of the rights and freedoms recognised by the Charter may be made only 'if they are necessary and genuinely meet objectives of general interest recognised by the Union or the need to protect the rights and freedoms of others'.[83]

Placing this principle in the context of EU citizenship, the case law of the ECJ shows that at least three considerations must be borne in mind when making the review of whether national regulation is proportionate:[84] (i) the individual examination of the consequences of losing citizenship of the EU for the persons concerned and their families; (ii) the requirement that those consequences be consistent with the fundamental rights guaranteed by the Charter; and (iii) where appropriate, the obligation to have the person concerned recover his or her nationality *ex tunc*.

[77] ibid, para 43.
[78] ibid, para 46.
[79] ibid, para 49.
[80] ibid, para 50.
[81] ibid, para 56.
[82] ibid, para 59.
[83] Art 52(1) of the Charter.
[84] Opinion of AG Szpunar in Case C-689/21 *Udlændinge- og Integrationsministeriet (Perte de la nationalité danoise)* (n 71), para 46.

Looking at the *Udlændinge- og Integrationsministeriet* case, there was no individual examination if the person had submitted his or her application after the age of 22. According to Advocate General Spzunar, such deprivation of nationality is 'arbitrary and inconsistent'.[85] He further argued that the examination must be possible when an application has been submitted after the person has turned 22.[86] As noted above, the ECJ agreed and stated that this period must extend for a reasonable length of time beyond the date on which that person reaches the age of 22[87] and that the relevant date of the examination is when the person concerned turns 22.[88]

This raises the natural follow-up question of what constitutes a reasonable length of time. What if the person, at the age of 50, decided to apply for the retention or recovery of the nationality without having lived in Denmark at all since turning 22? If the examination of proportionality had to be made at this point, it would perhaps be proportionate to decline the application as, at the least, the person had spent the past 28 years without the rights attached to EU citizenship and so the consequences of losing these rights would perhaps not be considered detrimental to the person. However, the relevant date for this examination is when the person turns 22. One might wonder whether this means that the outcome of the individual examination will be the same[89] no matter when the person applies, as the relevant date for the examination is static, and that the only deciding factor is whether the person has applied within a reasonable period of time.

This point is raised due to the importance of EU citizenship and its attached rights. As just one example, EU citizenship grants the right to move and reside freely within the territory of the Member States under Articles 20(2)(a) and 21 TFEU. This right is expressed in Directive 2004/38,[90] which has Union citizenship at its core, as seen in the first recitals of the Directive and in particular the third, which reads that 'Union citizenship should be the fundamental status of nationals of the Member States when they exercise their right of free movement and residence …'

Directive 2004/38 and EU citizenship were the subjects of the judgment of 15 July 2021 in *A (Soins de santé publics)*.[91] A, an Italian citizen, was married to a Latvian national, and moved in January 2016 from Italy to Latvia to reside with his wife and their two infant children. Upon arriving in Latvia, he applied to the Latvian National Health Service to be affiliated with the Latvian social security system. In February 2016, his request was denied, and this decision was upheld by the Ministry of Health. The basis for refusal was that A did not fall into any of the categories of individuals eligible for state-financed medical care in Latvia, as he was neither employed nor self-employed in the country.

A pursued the matter by ultimately bringing the case before the Augstākā tiesa (Senāts) (Supreme Court of Latvia). Here, guidance was sought from the ECJ regarding the conformity with EU law of the Latvian authorities' rejection of A's request, particularly in the areas of citizenship and social security.

[85] ibid, para 83.

[86] ibid, para 87.

[87] *Udlændinge- og Integrationsministeriet (Perte de la nationalité danoise)* (n 11), para 50.

[88] ibid, para 56.

[89] Provided that the person applying is able to provide the necessary documentation from this age.

[90] Consolidated version of Directive 2004/38/EC of the European Parliament and of the Council of 29 April 2004 on the right of citizens of the Union and their family members to move and reside freely within the territory of the Member States amending Regulation (EEC) No 1612/68 and repealing Directives 64/221/EEC, 68/360/EEC, 72/194/EEC, 73/148/EEC, 75/34/EEC, 75/35/EEC, 90/364/EEC, 90/365/EEC and 93/96/EEC [2004] OJ L158/77.

[91] Case C-535/19 *A (Soins de santé publics)*, ECLI:EU:C:2021:595. See also J Carlier and P Van Malleghem, 'Libre circulation des personnes dans l'Union européenne' (2022) *Journal de droit européen* 172.

One of the questions before the ECJ was whether Article 11(3)(e) of Regulation No 883/2004[92] and Article 7(1)(b) of Directive 2004/38 preclude national legislation which excludes from the right to be affiliated to the public sickness insurance system of the host Member State, in order to obtain medical care financed by that State, economically inactive Union citizens who are nationals of another Member State and who fall, by virtue of Article 11(3)(e) of that regulation, within the scope of the legislation of the host Member State and who are exercising their right of residence in the territory of that State under Article 7(1)(b) of that directive. Article 7(1)(b) reads as follows:

> (1) All Union citizens shall have the right of residence on the territory of another Member State for a period of longer than three months if they: [...]
>
> (b) have sufficient resources for themselves and their family members not to become a burden on the social assistance system of the host Member State during their period of residence and have comprehensive sickness insurance cover in the host Member State; [...].

In answering this question, the ECJ found that the host Member State (Latvia) had to ensure that A had comprehensive sickness insurance in Latvia as to not become a burden on the social assistance system.[93] However, emphasising that a requirement of doing so free of charge would render this condition of not becoming a burden on the social assistance system 'redundant',[94] the ECJ referenced Advocate General Saugmandsgaard Øe, stating that the host Member State may make the affiliation to its public sickness insurance system of an economically inactive Union citizen subject to certain conditions, such as taxation, as long as these conditions observed the principle of proportionality.[95]

The result of this case is just one example of the benefits of the rights associated with EU citizenship and its importance to an EU citizen. Article 7(1)(b) of Directive 2004/38 only applies to EU citizens and so, if A had lost his Italian nationality before acquiring Latvian citizenship,[96] and thus lost his EU citizenship, he would not have been able to invoke Article 7(1)(b) of Directive 2004/38.

Consequently, the importance of EU citizenship to Union citizens cannot be understated and neither can the observation of the principle of proportionality for Member States in circumstances where the loss of citizenship of a Member State will entail the loss of EU citizenship and the attached rights. In its recent judgment of 5 September 2023, the ECJ once again manifested that EU citizenship is 'destined to be the fundamental status of nationals of the Member States'.[97]

[92] Consolidated version of Regulation (EC) No 883/2004 of the European Parliament and of the Council of 29 April 2004 on the coordination of social security systems [2004] OJ L166/1.

[93] *A (Soins de santé publics)* (n 91), paras 50–51.

[94] ibid, para 56.

[95] ibid, para 59 and Opinion of AG Saugmandsgaard Øe in Case C-535/19 *A (Soins de santé publics)*, ECLI:EU:C:2021:114, para 124.

[96] As were the circumstances in the *Wiener Landesregierung (Révocation d'une assurance de naturalisation)* case (n 10).

[97] *Udlændinge- og Integrationsministeriet (Perte de la nationalité danoise)* (n 11), para 29.

19

The Interaction between Directive 2003/86 and the Charter of Fundamental Rights of the European Union in the Family Reunification of a Third-Country National

LUCIA SERENA ROSSI*

I. INTRODUCTION

JUDGE LARS BAY Larsen has a considerable expertise on the topic of immigration in EU law. During his time at the Court of Justice, he has been judge rapporteur of several notable cases, including C-257/17, C 380/17, C-484/17, and C-381/18, and a member of the bench in C-706/18, all cited in this chapter.

This contribution will examine how the European Court of Justice (ECJ) interprets Directive 2003/86,[1] which sets forth a basic legal framework for family reunification between third-country nationals in Member States of the European Union (EU) in the light of the values of the Charter of Fundamental Rights of the European Union (the Charter). An examination of the case law shows how, under the influence of the Charter, the ECJ recognises a broad concept of family and yet follows a strict interpretation of the conditions set out by that Directive.

Sections II, III, and IV consider how the ECJ has treated the concept of family and its components within the meaning of the Directive; Sections V, VI, VII, and VIII examine the ECJ's treatment of what conditions the Directive allows Member States to impose; brief conclusions will follow in order to put the ECJ's case law in a broader context.

II. AN EXPANDED CONCEPT OF 'FAMILY'

Articles 7 and 24 of the Charter have become increasingly important in the ECJ's case law on family reunification concerning Directive 2003/86.[2] The primary outcome of this influence has been an expanded definition of 'family' for the purposes of reunification.[3]

* Judge at the European Court of Justice, Professor of EU Law at the University of Bologna, Italy. All opinions hereby expressed are personal and do not bind the institution in any way.

[1] Council Directive 2003/86/EC of 22 September 2003 on the right to family reunification [2003] OJ L251/12.

[2] E Frasca and J-Y Carlier, 'The Best Interests of the Child in ECJ Asylum and Migration Case Law: Towards a Safeguard Principle for the Genuine Enjoyment of the Substance of Children's Rights?' (2023) 60 *Common Market Law Review* 345, 368 and 379; K Hyltén-Cavallius, 'Who Cares? Caregivers' Derived Residence Rights from Children in EU Free Movement Law' (2020) 57 *Common Market Law Review* 399, 417–18.

[3] Case C-356/11 *O and Others v Maahanmuuttovirasto*, ECLI:EU:C:2012:776, paras 55 and 65 ('the nuclear family referred to in Recital 9 [...] was conceived broadly by the European Union legislature').

In *O and Others*, the definition of nuclear family, meaning spouses and children, was extended beyond blood ties. The ECJ considered two families where a non-EU citizen applicant had an EU citizen child in a first marriage; they brought those children into a second marriage with another non-EU citizen and gained custody over non-EU citizen children; then the applicants sought family reunification for their non-EU citizen spouses and children.[4] The case therefore presented the ECJ with a combined *Zambrano*-Directive 2003/86 problem: on the one hand, the citizen rights of the first-marriage children had to be guaranteed; on the other, the application for reunification directly and fundamentally concerned two non-citizens.[5]

The ECJ's answer was twofold: first, it acknowledged the reality of complex families – some of which would inevitably end up in immigration litigation, the applicants – by broadly interpreting the definition of family.[6] In applying Directive 2003/86, this was justified by reading the extensive subparagraphs of Article 4(1) together with the recitals to imply the European legislature's intentionally broad conception of family.[7]

Second, it demanded a factual, circumstantiated, case-by-case assessment by national courts, especially insofar as the values of the Charter or optional derogations in Directive 2003/86 were implicated; in other words, families may be complex not only in the relationships between members, but also in the nexus of the legal rights involved, demanding that the referring national judge take an individualised approach.[8] The ECJ therefore struck a balance, similar to that struck by the European Court of Human Rights (ECtHR) in its case law,[9] between the Charter's fundamental rights and the national margins of discretion, showing the way to incorporate the values of the Charter's Articles 7 and 24 into family reunification law.[10] In later cases, the ECJ has read a case-by-case assessment requirement into Article 17 of the Directive, leading its analyses of national courts' procedures to further resemble ECtHR methodology.[11]

In *Bevándorlási*, concerning family reunification between refugee siblings, the ECJ considered Article 10(2) of the Directive, which allows States to authorise reunification with family members other than spouses and children (covered by Article 4) only 'if they are dependent on the refugee'.[12] The ECJ concluded that a 'situation of real dependence' is not defined exclusively by the sponsor's ability to provide, but is also demonstrated by the need of the family member claiming dependence.[13] The nature of this need can result from either financial or social conditions, and the dependency assessment's point of departure is the family member's ability to support themselves in the State of origin at the time of application.[14] According to the ECJ, 'all relevant circumstances' must be considered,[15] including a given decision's impact on the fundamental rights granted by the Charter.[16]

[4] ibid, paras 18–33.
[5] ibid, paras 56 and 68.
[6] ibid, paras 64–65.
[7] ibid.
[8] ibid, paras 49–54.
[9] *MA v Denmark* App no 6697/18, ECLI:CE:ECHR:2021:0709JUD000669718, paras 131–53. See also *Tuquabo-Tekle and Others v The Netherlands* App no 60665/00, ECLI:CE:ECHR:2005:1201JUD006066500, paras 42–44; and *Tanda-Muzinga v France* App no 2260/10, ECLI:CE:ECHR:2014:0710JUD000226010, paras 64–69.
[10] Frasca and Carlier (n 2), 376–78.
[11] Case C-519/18 *TB v Bevándorlási és Menekültügyi Hivatal*, ECLI:EU:C:2019:1070, para 53. See also Cases C-153/14 *Minister van Buitenlandse Zaken v K and A*, ECLI:EU:C:2015:453, para 60; and C-380/17 *K and B v Staatssecretaris van Veiligheid en Justitie*, ECLI:EU:C:2018:877, para 53.
[12] *Bevándorlási* (n 11), paras 7, 21 and 44–52.
[13] ibid, paras 46–52.
[14] ibid, para 48.
[15] ibid, para 52.
[16] ibid, paras 64–67.

The ECJ acknowledged the plain-language limits on non-nuclear family members under Article 10, but interpreted that article's requirements through a more flexible definition of dependence. Furthermore, Article 10's limits become more flexible – in other words, reunification with non-nuclear family members is rendered more permissible – in cases concerning refugees, where its interpretation is coloured by the Directive's recitals and the Charter's fundamental values. A more relaxed standard exists for refugees under Recital 8 of the Directive, which acknowledges refugees' special vulnerability and frequently diminished ability to provide for family members or to provide proof of their circumstances to national authorities.[17] This mirrors the Directive's articles addressing refugees, Articles 9–12, all of whose provisions contain mandatory or optional expansions of refugees' right to family reunification.[18] According to the ECJ, this heightens the State obligation that national procedures consider a more extensive set of circumstances of refugee non-nuclear family members, including 'age, level of education, professional and financial situation, and state of health', the sometimes great variation of individual needs, and the specific circumstances of asylum.[19] By way of comparison, the analogous ECtHR approach was concisely stated in *Tanda-Muzinga*: '[H]aving regard to the special situation in which [refugees] find themselves, it is appropriate in numerous cases to give them the benefit of the doubt when assessing the credibility of their statements and the documents submitted in support thereof'.[20] The ECJ cannot, however, ignore when a refugee has pleaded inapplicable law; as the recent case *XXX v Commissaire* has shown, the right to family reunification is not interchangeable with and has no bearing on the right to international protection, whatever the similarity in circumstances.[21]

Another recent case, *Landeshauptmann von Wien*, was in certain aspects similar to *Bevándorlási*. A refugee minor sought family reunification with his seriously disabled adult sister and their parents, on whom the sister totally depended. In the course of the proceedings he attained majority and was no longer permitted to reunify with his siblings under Austrian national law implementing the Directive.[22] The applicants claimed that, under Directive Article 10(3)(a), the sponsor's parents must be admitted, and Articles 7 and 24 of the Charter and the principle of effectiveness of rights (*effet utile*) also required admission of the sponsor's sister.[23] Advocate General Collins considered this a *contra legem* interpretation of Article 10 and advised against it.[24] Both Article 10 and Recital 10 lay out the national margins of discretion regarding which non-nuclear family members nations may decline to admit.[25] However, in order to ensure an adequate assessment of all interests at play, as well as to determine all applicable rights under Union law, Advocate General Collins did consider it necessary to take into account all the applications simultaneously, and in light of one another.[26]

The ECJ took notice of the applicants' exceptionally grave circumstances, notably the sister's extremely serious medical condition, requiring constant care that only her parents

[17] ibid, paras 50–51. See *Tanda-Muzinga v France* (n 9), paras 58, 69, 75–76 and 78–79; *Senigo Longue and Others v France* App no 19113/09, ECLI:CE:ECHR:2014:0710JUD001911309, paras 66–75.

[18] Directive 2003/86, Arts 9–12.

[19] *Bevándorlási* (n 11), para 75.

[20] *Tanda-Muzinga v France* (n 9), para 69.

[21] Cases C-374/22, *XXX v Commissaire général aux réfugiés et aux apatrides*, ECLI:EU:C:2023:902, paras 17–18 and 20–22; and C-614/22 *XXX v Commissaire général aux réfugiés et aux apatrides*, ECLI:EU:C:2023:903, paras 17–18 and 20–22.

[22] Opinion of AG Collins in Case C-560/20, *CR, GF, TY v Landeshauptmann von Wien*, ECLI:EU:C:2023:375, paras 9–14.

[23] ibid, para 31.

[24] ibid, para 32.

[25] ibid, para 33 and fn 45.

[26] ibid, paras 41–42.

could provide.[27] The ECJ resolved the case on the basis of *effet utile*: though the sister had no right to family reunification herself, her exceptional medical circumstances required, without alternative, that her parents stay with her. As a result, in order to ensure the effectiveness of the unaccompanied refugee minor's rights stemming from Article 10(3)(a), national authorities were required to issue an entry permit for the sister in this individual case.[28]

III. THE CONCEPT OF EFFECTIVE FAMILY LIFE (ARTICLE 16 OF THE DIRECTIVE)

The expansive definition of 'family' is subject to the important condition in Article 16(1)(b) of Directive 2003/86 which allows States to reject family reunification applications if 'the sponsor and his/her family member(s) do not or no longer live in a real marital or family relationship'.

What does this mean, practically? The ECJ has provided an answer in *Bundesrepublik Deutschland v SW and Others*[29] when it defined 'family' by reading the Directive's recitals in conjunction with Articles 7 and 24 of the Charter.[30] In the case of the applicant's nuclear family member, the ECJ characterised the family relationship as necessarily 'real' but not automatically 'close'.[31] According to the ECJ, neither cohabitation nor reciprocal economic support is necessary; the reality of the family members' relationship turns rather on their intentions to occasionally see each other and maintain regular contact.[32] While a State cannot require financial support as a dispositive element in assessing 'real' or effective family life, the ECJ did imply that it could be a weighty circumstantial evidence where, for example, a family member had the means to visit or financially support another family member in need, but chose not to.[33]

The ECJ had the immediate opportunity to apply this standard in *Bundesrepublik Deutschland v XC*. The minor applicant's father sought asylum in Germany eight months before the applicant reached majority, and the father was granted refugee status seven months after the applicant reached majority.[34] Articles 4(1) and 10(3) of Directive 2003/86, however, explicitly require minority status of a sponsor's children.[35] Though the ECJ noted that a family reunification request could only be valid after recognition of refugee status, making the applicant's request theoretically impossible, even these procedural limits managed to flex under the values of the Charter and the recitals of the Directive.[36] National courts must consider the totality of family circumstances together with the time of the sponsor's application, and may – or in certain circumstances must – derogate from the requirement of majority if it would accord with the Charter's values and the goals of the Directive.[37]

Within that assessment, the effectiveness of XC's family life would have to be considered during the eight-month period between her father's application and her attainment of

[27] Case C-432/20 *Landeshauptmann von Wien*, ECLI:EU:C:2022:39, paras 54–55.

[28] ibid, paras 51 and 55–58.

[29] Case C-273/20 *Bundesrepublik Deutschland v SW and Others*, ECLI:EU:C:2022:617, para 56.

[30] ibid, paras 58–61. See also G Pizzolante, 'Il Riconoscimento nell'Ordinamento di Destinazione degli *Status* Familiari Costituiti all'Estero per Motivi di Ricongiungimento' 2020 *Freedom, Security & Justice: European Legal Studies* 118, http://www.fsjeurostudies.eu/files/FSJ.2020.II.PIZZOLANTE.5.pdf, accessed 3 March 2024.

[31] *Bundesrepublik Deutschland v SW* (n 29), para 62.

[32] ibid, paras 65–67. See also M Borraccetti and F Ferri, 'Direttiva 2003/86 e Ricongiungimento con Figlio Rifugiato: Rilievo dell'Età del Figlio e Qualificazione del Rapporto di Vita Familiare Effettiva tra gli Interessati' (2022) *Diritto, Immigrazione e Cittadinanza* 317, 320–21.

[33] *Bundesrepublik Deutschland v SW* (n 29), paras 63–68.

[34] Case C-279/20 *Bundesrepublik Deutschland v XC*, ECLI:EU:C:2022:618, paras 15–17.

[35] ibid, paras 3–10.

[36] ibid, paras 38–51.

[37] ibid, paras 52–54.

majority.[38] Due to the situation in their country of origin, Syria, and her father's status as a refugee, no actual contact had been possible, though XC's own status and resources were not clear.[39] The ECJ held to its demand that national courts make a case-by-case assessment. While the legal parent-child link was not by itself sufficient and did not create a presumption of real family life, a lack of material, concrete financial support or in-person contact could not exclude it; rather, under the right, individual circumstances, intent alone could be enough to demonstrate existence of real family life.[40]

In *X v Belgische Staat*, the ECJ was confronted with the question of whether there is still effective family life between parents and a minor daughter who has married.[41] As an unaccompanied refugee minor, the situation of the applicant's daughter triggered Article 24 of the Charter, imposing on the ECJ the need to consider the best interests of the child, and Recital 8 of the Directive, demanding special concern for refugees.[42] This combination overpowered the national margin of discretion under Article 4(2)(a) of the Directive, as well as the provisions of the Dublin III Regulation.[43] The married status of X's daughter could not be treated as having automatically severed her family life with her mother; therefore X, living in Lebanon, could be sponsored by her daughter who was already living in Belgium.[44]

IV. AGE REQUIREMENTS

In *Noorzia*, the goal of protecting children from forced marriages, certainly compatible with the best interests of the child principle, was used to preserve wide national margins of discretion, so that the Austrian immigration services were allowed to deny family reunification.[45] Here, the sponsor, over the age of majority, sought reunification with her spouse, who had achieved majority during the application process but was still a minor when he first submitted his application.[46]

Article 4(1)(a) of the Directive allows spousal reunification, but this right is qualified by the public policy objectives of subparagraphs 4 and 5.[47] States may, within their margin of discretion and according to their own political and cultural context, set a minimum age for both the sponsor and spouse, up to the age of 21.[48] Favouring these margins as well as the principles of equal treatment and legal certainty, the ECJ held that this age limit referred to age at the time of application, rather than age when the spouses can join each other.[49] The ECJ in this instance declined to follow Advocate General Mengozzi's conclusions that the Charter's Article 7 guarantee of a right to respect for family life, in this case between minor spouses, outweighed the Austrian margin of discretion to interpret the Directive. Instead, the ECJ gave more weight to the principles of equal treatment and legal certainty supporting the national argument that spouses' ages be considered at the time of application, rather than at the time national authorities render their decision.[50]

[38] ibid, para 64.
[39] ibid, paras 17, 61 and 64–65.
[40] ibid, paras 63–69.
[41] Case C-230/21 *X v Belgische Staat*, ECLI:EU:C:2022:887, paras 12–24.
[42] ibid, paras 41 and 47–48.
[43] ibid, paras 28, 39, 42 and 48–49.
[44] ibid, paras 18–23 and 49.
[45] Case C-338/13 *Marjan Noorzia v Bundesministerin für Inneres*, ECLI:EU:C:2014:2092, paras 12, 15–19.
[46] ibid, paras 7–10.
[47] Directive 2003/86/EC, Art 4(1)(a) and Art4(4)–(5).
[48] *Noorzia* (n 45), paras 14–16.
[49] ibid, paras 17–19.
[50] ibid, paras 16–18. See Opinion of AG Mengozzi in Case C-338/13 *Noorzia*, ECLI:EU:C:2014:288.

The ECJ affirmed its position on submission dates in *A and S* and *État belge*. In *A and S*, the sponsor arrived in the Netherlands as an unaccompanied minor and was granted a five-year residence permit for asylum; she applied for her parents' and siblings' reunification there, and while the sponsor's application was pending, she attained majority.[51] While the wording of Article 4(2)(a) seemed to leave Member States a comparable margin of discretion as in *Noorzia*, the applicable law differed from *Noorzia* in that this provision was expressly qualified by Article 10(3).[52] Furthermore, the principles of equal treatment and legal certainty supported counting time from the submission date,[53] and the objectives of the Directive reflected in Recitals 2, 4 and 8, as well as the values of the Charter, made acceptance of the sponsor's family all the more pressing.[54]

In *État belge*, the ECJ considered the date of submission relative to Article 4(1) of the Directive, which generally obligates States to grant family reunification for spouses and descending minor children.[55] The case concerned a refugee father, whose minor children residing abroad attained majority during the lengthy appeals process against rejection of their initial reunification application.[56] The ECJ resolved this question by restating the *Noorzia* and *A and S* principles of equal treatment, legal certainty, the objectives of the Directive, and the values of the Charter.[57] However, it also found Article 47 of the Charter, regarding the right to real and effective legal remedy, implicated in an appeals process that could be dismissed for mootness.[58] Given the great disparity of appellate processing times across Member States, the doctrine of considering the minor's age and qualities from the time of application further strengthened the overarching goal of avoiding discriminatory treatment of applicants in different countries.[59]

As previously noted, the ECJ tries to ensure its case law results in a workable and clear set of procedural rules for Member States, rather than a confusing, 'à la carte' labyrinth of exceptions.[60]

V. CONDITIONS REGARDING INTEGRATION TO THE MEMBER STATE

The necessity for national authorities and judges to conduct case-by-case assessments has emerged as a powerful theme over recent years as Articles 7 and 24 of the Charter have been increasingly absorbed into family reunification case law.[61] For example, the best interests of the child can sometimes be interpreted to go against family reunification as much as support it, notably in cases of split families where it may better serve the child's interests to stay with a parent outside the Union who is better able to protect or provide for the child.[62] Another good

[51] Case C-550/16 *A and S v Staatssecretaris van Veiligheid en Justitie*, ECLI:EU:C:2018:248, paras 20–28.
[52] ibid, paras 46–47.
[53] ibid, paras 56–64.
[54] ibid, paras 4, 32 and 58. See also J Silga, 'Le droit au regroupement familial des réfugiés mineurs non Accompagnés devenus majeurs: l'Affaire A et S, entre progrès incontestable et portée relative' (2018) *European Papers* 1027, 1034–36.
[55] Joined Cases C-133/19, C-136/19 and C-137/19 *BMM and Others v État belge*, ECLI:EU:C:2020:577, para 24.
[56] ibid, paras 13–22.
[57] ibid, paras 29–47.
[58] ibid, paras 48–58.
[59] ibid, paras 40–43.
[60] Frasca and Carlier (n 2), 374–75.
[61] ibid, 351, 383–86.
[62] ibid, 356–61 and 382–83. See also *SN and MBN v Switzerland* App no 12937/20, ECLI:CE:ECHR:2021:1123JUD001293720, paras 104–20; *Jeunesse v Netherlands* App no 12738/10, ECLI:CE:ECHR:2014:1003JUD001273810, paras 117–19.

example of the ECJ's unfavourable view on hard-and-fast rules or blanket exclusions can be found in its case law on civic integration examinations.[63]

In *K and A*, the ECJ acknowledged Member States' interest in requiring integration examinations but held them subject to the general legal principle of proportionality: they cannot 'exceed what is necessary' to achieve their valid aims.[64] By invoking this principle, the ECJ demonstrated its sensitivity to the fact that these examinations can be a 'disguised mechanism of immigration selection and control […] mainly operating as a tool of exclusion'.[65]

Importantly, the principle of proportionality generally requires case-by-case examinations, but it cannot result in an excessive burden for national judges.[66] According to the ECJ, national tests imposing minimum levels of civic integration and basic knowledge of the State's language might be permissible.[67] Under the principle of proportionality, however, these tests must not: (1) make family reunification 'impossible or excessively difficult'; (2) limit consideration of special circumstances preventing the applicant taking the exam; or (3) present such a high cost (whether through course fees or examination fees) that they would practically exclude immigrants of diminished circumstances.[68] The ECJ affirmed this standard without variation in two 2018 cases, *C and A* and *K*.[69] However, in a third 2018 case, *K and B*, the ECJ implied that refugee status might amount to the special circumstances necessitating an exception to mandatory passage, by stating that *K and A*'s interpretation of Article 17 as requiring case-by-case assessments must be qualified by Recital 8's objective of 'special attention' and 'more favourable conditions' for refugees.[70]

VI. ECONOMIC RESOURCES (ARTICLE 7 OF DIRECTIVE 2003/86)

Article 7's allowance of State requirements of economic resources is another element which might be used to exclude a large number of family reunification cases, given the frequent economic motivation for immigration. Article 7(1)(c) allows a State to limit family reunification on the basis of the stability, regularity, and sufficiency of their economic resources, and, within a qualitative assessment, to consider circumstantial factors such as reliance on the State welfare system, the national minimum wage, and the number of family members.

In *Chakroun*, the ECJ considered what part the State's welfare system and minimum wage should come into play in the analysis of individual situations.[71] States cannot use the mere fact of reliance on a welfare system, or income below a certain threshold (even below minimum wage) as automatic exclusionary factors.[72] These can only be 'reference[s]' in a circumstantial

[63] D Vitiello, 'In Search of the Legal Boundaries of an "Open Society". The Case of Immigrant Integration in the EU' (2022) *Freedom, Security & Justice: European Legal Studies* 162–64 http://www.fsjeurostudies.eu/files/FSJ.2.2022.8.VITIELLO.pdf, accessed 3 March 2024. See also M Bottero, 'Integration (of Immigrants) in the European Union: A Controversial Concept' (2022) 24 *European Journal of Migration Law* 516, 532–35.

[64] *K and A* (n 11), paras 53–56.

[65] Bottero (n 63), 533.

[66] *K and A* (n 11), paras 60 and 71. On the Court's balance between proportionality and national obligations, see P Dąbrowska-Kłosińska, 'The Right to Family Reunion vs Integration Conditions for Third-Country Nationals' (2018) 20 *European Journal of Migration Law* 251, 275–82 and 285.

[67] *K and A* (n 11), para 71.

[68] ibid.

[69] Cases C-257/17 *C and A v Staatssecretaris van Veiligheid en Justitie*, ECLI:EU:C:2018:876, paras 54–65; and C-484/17 *K v Staatssecretaris van Veiligheid en Justitie*, ECLI:EU:C:2018:878, paras 20–24.

[70] *K and B* (n 11), para 53; Directive 2003/86, Recital 8, Art 17.

[71] Case C-578/08 *Rhimou Chakroun v Minister van Buitenlandse Zaken*, ECLI:EU:2010:117, paras 46–47.

[72] ibid, paras 48–52.

evaluation, as the 'extent of needs can vary greatly depending on the individuals'.[73] Thus, the limitations on the right to family reunification found in Articles 7 and 10 are interpreted narrowly in light of the recitals of the Directive, the Charter, and ECtHR case law.[74] The ECJ considered the Directives' objective as promoting family reunification, and therefore exercise of this right – as it may be considered a right held even by non-citizens[75] – is 'the general rule'.[76]

In *Khachab* the ECJ reaffirmed the narrow construction of limitations on the right to family reunification found in *Chakroun*, this time by considering the regularity of the applicant's employment.[77] National authorities and courts may assess the applicant's resources not only at the time of application, but also prospectively, such as the ability to retain employment or for resources to last, as well as throughout the application process and when considering applications for renewal of residence permits.[78] This standard should not be seen so much as widening or curtailing the national margins of discretion or the rights of immigrants, as it should be seen as a widening of the procedural boundaries and scope of assessment, for such an analysis could be a double-edged sword, which could let certain immigrants in and shut others out, depending on their circumstances.[79]

In *Landeshauptmann von Wien*, the ECJ considered national discretion to impose Directive Article 7 requirements on a refugee minor's sister, pursuant to the third paragraph of Article 12(1).[80] The ECJ concluded in light of Article 10(3)(a) that the European legislator had envisaged a separate regime specifically for unaccompanied refugee minors due to their heightened vulnerability, and therefore admittance of both parents was mandatory, that is, outside the bounds of national discretion.[81] Underlining Articles 7 and 24 of the Charter, the ECJ also held that it was practically impossible that refugee parents not accompanying their minor child could have or furnish proof of Directive Article 7's conditions, and that these requirements would negate the effectiveness of the minor sponsor's Article 10(3)(a) family reunification rights.[82] The ECJ therefore declined to follow Advocate General Collins' conclusion that the Member State could impose Article 7 requirements on the sponsor's sister, concentrating instead on the special circumstances and best interests of the sponsor, whose importance the Advocate General had also noted.[83]

VII. PUBLIC ORDER

A critical question concerning national margins of discretion is how to handle those situations where family reunification could pose a threat to public order, in the opinion of the authorities. This sometimes results in exceptions to an otherwise valid right to family reunification – though such exceptions are not without limits.

[73] ibid, paras 45–52.
[74] ibid, para 44; Case C-558/14 *Mimoun Khachab v Subdelegación del Gobierno en Álava*, ECLI:EU:C:2016:285, para 25.
[75] Directive 2003/86, Recitals 3, 6 and 11; C Oviedo Moreno, 'Assessing Stable and Regular Resources for Family Reunification in Spain' (2021) 12 *Tildschrift Voor Asiel & Migrantenrecht* 355, 358.
[76] *Chakroun* (n 71), para 43.
[77] *Khachab* (n 74), paras 16–18, 25–29.
[78] ibid, paras 32–38.
[79] Oviedo Moreno (n 75), 357–58; *Khachab* (n 74), paras 39–48.
[80] *Landeshauptmann von Wien* (n 27), paras 62–70.
[81] ibid, paras 73–75.
[82] ibid, paras 76–80.
[83] Opinion of AG Collins in Case C-560/20, *Landeshauptmann von Wien*, ECLI:EU:C:2023:375, paras 41–43.

In *YZ and Others*, the Netherlands government alleged fraudulent immigration by the sponsor, resulting in illegal secondary immigration by way of family reunification by his wife and minor child.[84] While the ECJ confirmed that, under Article 16(2)(a), Member States have 'a priori' discretion not to recognise family members' derived right of residence in cases of fraud, Article 17 requires a 'case-by-case [...] balanced and reasonable assessment of all the interests in play' before States can exercise that discretion.[85] This includes an assessment of the gravity of the infraction, for while prevention of fraud is a general principle of EU law, the wife and child were not personally responsible and had no knowledge of the fraud.[86] Therefore, the ECJ limits national margins of discretion concerning public order where States might not have sufficient procedural safeguards to ensure proportional responses to a given offence.[87]

Drug trafficking and drunk driving are offences which pose a tangible threat to public order, and which the ECJ has held to allow rejection, non-renewal, or deportation in family reunification cases, in similar terms to what has been decided by the ECtHR.[88] In *GS and VG*, the Netherlands invoked Article 6(1)–(2) of the Directive, which allows rejection or non-renewal for reasons of 'public policy, public security or public health'.[89] The ECJ found that 'a serious crime, which tends to indicate that the mere existence of such a conviction could suffice to establish that there is a threat to public policy [...] without it being necessary to establish a genuine, present and sufficiently serious threat'.[90]

If the conviction is sufficiently serious, this can be the only factor needed for authorities to establish existence of a genuine threat.[91] But the public policy exception is still subject to the principle of proportionality and a case-by-case assessment of all interests in play, which in practice means national procedures cannot be simply automatic, summary, or excessively formalistic.[92] As such, in *A v Migrationsverket*, the ECJ interpreted the Convention implementing the Schengen Agreement as not requiring automatic refusal of family reunification in the case of the applicant's suspected identity fraud and drug convictions, signalled in the Schengen Information System.[93] Rather, States also have the discretion to admit criminally convicted applicants, after balancing the interests of the Member State where the convictions occurred with the humanitarian interests of the applicant.[94]

VIII. PROCEDURAL CONDITIONS

The requirement of case-by-case assessments, motivated by Article 17 of the Directive, the principle of proportionality, and the Charter's values, informs other procedural conditions

[84] Case C-557/17 *Staatssecretaris van Veiligheid en Justitie v YZ and Others*, ECLI:EU:C:2019:203, paras 24–28.

[85] ibid, paras 47–48 and 50–51.

[86] ibid, paras 55–56 and 62.

[87] Opinion of AG Mengozzi in Case C-557/17 *YZ and Others*, ECLI:EU:C:2018:820, paras 30–33.

[88] Joined Cases C-381/18 and C-382/18 *GS and VG v Staatssecretaris van Justitie en Veiligheid*, ECLI:EU:C:2019:1072, para 70; *Veljkovic-Jukic v Switzerland* App no 59534/14, ECLI:CE:ECHR:2020:0721JUD005953414, paras 5, 49 and 55–60; *KA v Switzerland* App no 62130/15, ECLI:CE:ECHR:2020:0707JUD006213015, paras 49–55.

[89] *GS and VG* (n 88), paras 50–51.

[90] ibid, para 58.

[91] ibid, paras 65–67.

[92] ibid, paras 64 and 68–70. See also K Groenendijk and T Strik, 'Directive 2003/86 on the Right to Family Reunification: A Surprising Anchor in a Sensitive Field' in E Tsourdi and P De Bruycker, *Research Handbook on EU Migration and Asylum Law* (Edward Elgar, 2022) 317–20.

[93] Case C-193/19 *A v Migrationsverket*, ECLI:EU:C:2021:168, paras 14 and 36.

[94] ibid, paras 33–35 and 38.

not left to national margins of discretion. The case of *E* concerned the inability of a sponsoring aunt and alleged guardian of a minor to provide official documentation proving the death of that minor's parents.[95] The ECJ applied its case-by-case assessment requirement to the language of Article 5(2), which necessitates State consideration of other evidence if documentary evidence is unavailable.[96] In addition to the plain language of the Directive, the ECJ's case law mandates 'account of all the relevant aspects, including the age, gender, education, background and social status of the sponsor or the family member concerned as well as specific cultural aspects'.[97] Especially where refugees are concerned, in view of Recital 8, authorities' consideration of the reliability and authenticity of documents and the sponsor's ability to cooperate must be coloured by the 'particular difficulties' the sponsor faces.[98]

Procedural requirements can also go against more open immigration policies, as in *X v Belgische Staat*.[99] There, the ECJ found that a national procedural law, requiring approval of family reunification if no action had been taken after six months, was contrary to Article 5(2)'s requirement of evidence of family relationship.[100] Even if, as X was, the applicant is a refugee or beneficiary of subsidiary protection, therefore subject to more favourable immigration policies, the Directive's plain language cannot be avoided; approval, as well as rejection, must not be automatic.[101]

On the other hand, if Member States wish to conduct too thorough an assessment, this could be disproportionate to the applicant's circumstances, particularly those of refugees abroad.[102] Such was the case in *Afrin*, where the Belgian government required Syrian refugees to risk a hazardous journey through a disputed territory to appear in person at a consular post.[103] While this requirement supported the goals of Article 5(1), the excessive difficulty undermined Directive 2003/86's objective of promoting family reunification; it was contrary to Recital 8's exhortation to consider the special circumstances of refugees and lay down more favourable conditions; and the peril of the journey was contrary to the best interests of the children.[104]

IX. CONCLUSION: FRAMING THE ECJ'S CASE LAW IN A BROADER CONTEXT

Despite the Directive's relative brevity at around only 20 articles, it has great importance for family reunification in the Union and has produced an abundant body of case law. The ECJ faces a growing problem: the proliferation of cases leads to an increase in detailed rulings; these then encourage new requests for clarification. It would probably be useful for the Commission to produce a communication on Directive 2003/86, restating the ECJ's case law. After 20 years, a simple and clear résumé of how the ECJ interprets the Directive could lead to greater legal certainty and uniform application of the Directive at the national level and, more importantly, it could also help many individuals better secure their rights under the Charter.

[95] Case C-635/17 *E v Staatssecretaris van Veiligheid en Justitie*, ECLI:EU:C:2019:192, paras 19–26.
[96] ibid, paras 60–63.
[97] ibid, para 63.
[98] ibid, paras 65–69.
[99] Case C-706/18 *X v Belgische Staat*, ECLI:EU:C:2019:993, paras 30–35.
[100] ibid.
[101] ibid, para 38.
[102] Case C-1/23 *X and Others v État belge*, ECLI:EU:C:2023:296, paras 56–58.
[103] ibid, paras 12–21.
[104] ibid, paras 43–46 and 50–52.

As seen in the previous sections, the case law concerning the Directive is very rich. Familial circumstances can vary greatly: non-citizens can be mixed with citizens (*O and Others*); family relationships may change over the course of proceedings (*Bundesrepublik Deutschland v XC* – attainment of majority; *X v Belgische Staat* – minor marriage); refugee minor children (*Bevándorlási*) or people with disabilities (*Landeshauptmann von Wien*) may be involved; the criminal history of family members (*GS and VG*) or truly dramatic conditions in the country of origin (*Afrin*) can have circumstantial impact on the families.

What emerges from this case law is that national authorities and jurisdictions must always proceed to a case-by-case assessment; furthermore, once children are implicated, the best interests of the child must take a central place in considerations by authorities and courts, and children have a right under Charter Article 24(3) to reunification and regular contact with both parents.

In this respect, the ECJ's case law has paralleled that of the ECtHR. Indeed, the second Recital of Directive 2003/86 includes ECtHR case law interpreting the European Convention on Human Rights (ECHR), as well as other European and international law, as relevant jurisprudence for interpreting its provisions.[105] As the wording of certain protected rights is identical or near-identical in both the ECHR and the Charter, interpretation of the former becomes relevant not only as interpretation of general principles of EU law (Article 6 of the Treaty on European Union), but also as interpretation of the language of the Charter, which has legal weight in EU law.

Both Courts also consider a wider range of international law, interpreting it in the European context; therefore, the ECtHR's reading of instruments such as the Convention on the Rights of the Child also becomes valuable to the ECJ.[106]

The ECJ and the ECtHR engage in a constant dialogue regarding the extent of migrant families' and children's rights, how to define the family unit, and the circumstances in which a family may be reunified.[107] However their approaches may differ.

While the Strasbourg Court can apply the Convention directly, the ECJ can only apply the Charter under its Article 51, insofar as relevant in interpreting the Directive, as well as other sources of primary or secondary EU law, or judging the validity of EU acts. However, the high degree of detail of the EU legislation allows the Luxembourg Court to use a more precise and specific approach. For this reason, the ECJ usually awards principal legal weight to the language and provisions of the Directive itself, looking to the ECtHR's case law when the Directive does not fully elaborate the fundamental rights, standards, or 'strictly defined circumstances' of national discretion.[108]

For its part, the ECtHR has generally avoided in-depth consideration of EU law in family reunification cases, as – somewhat unlike the ECJ's relationship with European human rights law – it is not competent to rule on EU law.[109] This has not prevented it both from observing the development of the latter's case law,[110] considering its practical effect on the factual

[105] Directive 2003/86, Recital 2. See also Case C-540/03 *Parliament v Council*, ECLI:EU:C:2006:429, para 38.

[106] ibid, paras 37 and 50–59.

[107] S Sarolea, 'De Strasbourg à Luxembourg, Quels Droits pour les Familles Migrantes?' (2020) 33 *Revue Quebecoise de Droit International* 439, 439–41 and 455, 464.

[108] *Parliament v Council* (n 105), paras 60–62. See also H Eklund, 'The Margin of Discretion and the Boundary Question in EU Fundamental Rights Law' (2022) 59 *Common Market Law Review* 1407, 1421–27.

[109] *Jeunesse v Netherlands* (n 62), para 110; *X and Others v Ireland* App no 23851/20 and no 24360/20, ECLI:CE:ECHR:2023:0622JUD002385120, para 92.

[110] *Jeunesse v Netherlands* (n 62), paras 71–73 and 110–12; *MA v Denmark* (n 9), paras 50 and 157; and *X and Others v Ireland* (n 109), paras 50–51 and 91–93. See also *Bosphorus Hava Yollari Turizm ve Ticaret Anonim Şirketi v Ireland* App no 45036/98, ECLI:CE:ECHR:2005:0630JUD004503698, paras 147 and 159–66.

circumstances of the parties, which must necessarily be taken into account in a human rights analysis.[111] To this end, the ECtHR has been willing to go so far as to analyse EU law and project its result on the applicant's case, such as in *X and Others v Ireland*, where '[i]t found no basis in relevant EU law for the proposition that upon granting a right to reside in such circumstances all residence-related benefits must be awarded retrospectively', and that back-dated child benefits were outside of the scope of the *Zambrano* line of case law.[112] Finally, the ECtHR will not hesitate to consider EU law, including ECJ case law, as evidence of custom among European nations as well as internationally.[113]

Another important difference between the two courts is the impact of their judgments. This is due to the principles governing the status of EU law in the legal systems of Member States and to the cooperation between the ECJ's and national judiciaries through the preliminary ruling procedure, which can be triggered by any national judge and does not require – in contrast to ECtHR procedure – exhaustion of judicial remedies. This cooperation allows the ECJ to rule before a national judgment is adopted, impacting not only the outcome of the case but the substance of the national judgment itself. The new Protocol 16, although non-binding and ratified by only some members of the ECHR, could help establish a parallel – even if probably less effective – dialogue between the Strasbourg Court and national judges.

It is evident that, in certain instances, the case law of the two Courts does not coincide, but rather runs parallel towards a similar outcome.[114] For example, the ECJ resolved *Chakroun*'s Directive 2003/86 questions primarily by looking at the relationship between the Directive's provisions themselves, with minimal reliance on the Charter or Convention and no mention of ECtHR case law.[115] In *Parliament v Council*, the Parliament sought annulment of the final subparagraph of Article 4(1) of Directive 2003/86.[116] The ECJ refused to annul the subparagraph, citing the more flexible standard of assessing State obligations relative to the best interests of the child articulated in the ECtHR case *Sen v the Netherlands*.[117]

Recent geopolitical events surrounding Europe, particularly Brexit and the conflict in Ukraine, ensure a continued stream of immigration cases and give the two courts new opportunities to either coordinate or diverge in response to novel factual circumstances. In my opinion, the best way to describe that process is cross-fertilisation.

[111] *Biao v Denmark* App no 38590/10, ECLI:CE:ECHR:2016:0524JUD003859010, paras 134–35; *X and Others v Ireland* (n 109), para 93.

[112] ibid.

[113] *MA v Denmark* (n 9), paras 157–60.

[114] Eklund (n 108), 1413–16.

[115] *Chakroun* (n 71), paras 41–52 and 59–66.

[116] *Parliament v Council* (n 105), paras 1, 15–19 and 38.

[117] ibid, paras 54–56, 61–71 and 76.

20

'Tra il dire e il fare c'è di mezzo il mare': Harmonisation of Victims' Rights in EU Criminal Law

ADAM ŁAZOWSKI*

I. INTRODUCTION

As the Italian saying employed in the title of this chapter tells us, there is a sea between what is said and what is done. This aptly summarises and describes the evolution and the enforcement by Member States of two consecutive flagship pieces of European Union (EU) legislation harmonising the rights of victims of crimes.[1] The emerging picture, indeed, offers a mixed bag. On the one hand, the EU policy and legal framework keeps on evolving to remedy identified deficiencies, to improve it, and to make this proverbial sea shrink. On the other hand, delays with transposition of EU secondary legislation, and challenges with its practical implementation, show the limits of the possible, or – at best – that the discussed EU *acquis* on victims' rights remains a work in progress. In this chapter, I should like

* Professor of EU law at the Westminster Law School, University of Westminster, Visiting Professor at the College of Europe (Natolin) and at the Ivan Franko National University of Lviv.

[1] Council Framework Decision 2001/220/JHA of 15 March 2001 on the standing of victims in criminal proceedings [2001] OJ L82/1; Directive 2012/29/EU of the European Parliament and of the Council of 25 October 2012 establishing minimum standards on the rights, support and protection of victims of crime, and replacing Council Framework Decision 2001/220/JHA [2012] OJ L315/57. Taking into account the limits of the present chapter, it is impossible to cover all EU instruments which, in one way or another, deal with victims' rights. See, inter alia, Council Directive 2004/80/EC of 29 April 2004 relating to compensation to crime victims [2004] OJ L261/15; Directive 2011/99/EU of the European Parliament and of the Council of 13 December 2011 on the European protection order [2011] OJ L338/2; Regulation (EU) No 606/2013 of the European Parliament and of the Council of 12 June 2013 on mutual recognition of protection measures in civil matters [2013] OJ L181/4; Directive 2011/36/EU of the European Parliament and of the Council of 5 April 2011 on preventing and combating trafficking in human beings and protecting its victims, and replacing Council Framework Decision 2002/629/JHA [2011] OJ L101/1; Directive 2011/93/EU of the European Parliament and of the Council of 13 December 2011 on combating the sexual abuse and sexual exploitation of children and child pornography, and replacing Council Framework Decision 2004/68/JHA [2011] OJ L335/1; Directive (EU) 2017/541 of the European Parliament and of the Council of 15 March 2017 on combating terrorism and replacing Council Framework Decision 2002/475/JHA and amending Council Decision 2005/671/JHA [2017] OJ L88/6; Directive (EU) 2019/713 of the European Parliament and of the Council of 17 April 2019 on combating fraud and counterfeiting of non-cash means of payment and replacing Council Framework Decision 2001/413/JHA [2019] OJ L123/18. For a detailed account see, inter alia, J Burchett and A Weyembergh (eds), *Stronger Victims' Rights in EU Law? Assessment and Prospects* (Hart Publishing, forthcoming); V Mitsilegas, *EU Criminal Law*, 2nd edn (Hart Publishing, 2020) 296–319; S Peers, *EU Justice and Home Affairs Law*, vol 2, 5th edn (Oxford University Press, 2023) 182–91.

to argue that this state of affairs has been neither surprising nor unexpected. Bearing in mind the idiosyncrasies of the subject area, it has been inevitable. While paper is – by definition – quite accommodating and thus, figuratively speaking, anything can be written into the law, an effective system guaranteeing victims' rights requires non-legislative measures, and frequently also a societal change. Both beg for financial appropriations and, above all, a lot of good will. Altogether, it is not a 'quick fix' material. In this respect, there is only so much that the EU and its institutions can do.[2] Apart from anything else, they are constrained both by the principle of conferral[3] and by the principle of subsidiarity.[4] Thus, much depends on what happens (or does not) at the national level of the Member States.

The purpose of this chapter is to signpost the main milestones in development of EU *acquis* harmonising the rights of victims. These peregrinations in time start with an evaluation of the baby steps taken by the EU in early 2000s with adoption of Framework Decision 2001/220/JHA (Section II). A very disappointing experience with this legal act of the bygone era is the point of departure for an analysis of the legislation currently in force (Section III).[5] Section IV offers conclusions.

II. TESTING THE WATERS: FRAMEWORK DECISION 2001/220/JHA ON STANDING OF VICTIMS

A. The Origins

As with many legal acts forming what is now EU criminal law, the genesis of EU secondary legislation harmonising victims' rights in criminal proceedings goes back to the late 1990s.[6] This was facilitated by the entry into force of the Treaty of Amsterdam (ToA) which brought a qualitative change to the area of freedom, security and justice (AFSJ), even though some of the new solutions were half-baked and destined to suffer from inherent weaknesses.[7] The fate of Framework Decision 2001/220/JHA on standing of victims is a very good example to illustrate these phenomena. However, before that part of the story is told, a few preliminary observations are apt.

To begin with, the rights of victims appeared on the radar of EU decision-makers as early as 1999. Following the European Council Tampere Conclusions, an early needs assessment

[2] One should not forget about efforts made also by the Council of Europe. See further L Bachmaier, 'Council of Europe Instruments and the Case-law of the ECtHR: What Influence on EU Law?' in Burchett and Weyembergh (n 1).

[3] See further, inter alia, S Miettinen, 'The Evolution of Competence Distribution between the European Union and the Member States in the Criminal Field' in A Weyembergh and C Brière (eds), *The Needed Balances in EU Criminal Law. Past, Present and Future* (Hart Publishing, 2018).

[4] See further, inter alia, I Wieczorek, 'The Principle of Subsidiarity in EU Criminal Law' in Weyembergh and Brière (n 3).

[5] Commission, 'Proposal for a Directive of the European Parliament and of the Council amending Directive 2012/29/EU establishing minimum standards on the rights, support and protection of victims of crime, and replacing Council Framework Decision 2001/220/JHA' COM (2023) 424 final.

[6] It should be mentioned that victims' rights were dealt with in EEC law prior to creation of the third pillar and this was linked to free movement of persons. In *Cowan*, the Court of Justice ruled that in relation to citizens of Member States who exercise their free movement rights, domestic law 'may not make the award of State compensation for harm caused in that State to the victim of an assault resulting in physical injury subject to the condition that he hold a residence permit or be a national of a country which has entered into a reciprocal agreement with that Member State': Case 186/87 *Ian William Cowan v Trésor public*, ECLI:EU:C:1989:47. This judgment paved the way for adoption of Directive 2004/80.

[7] See further, inter alia, M Den Boer, 'An Area of Freedom, Security and Justice: Bogged Down by Compromise' in D O'Keeffe and P Twomey (eds), *Legal Issues of the Amsterdam Treaty* (Hart Publishing, 1999).

was presented by the Council and the Commission.[8] In turn, the European Commission followed with a tailor-made communication focusing on potential actions that could be taken at the EU level to create minimum standards of victim protection.[9] Fast forward, a proposal for a Framework Decision was tabled by Portugal during its rotating presidency in the EU.[10] Adoption of Framework Decision 2001/220/JHA was a speedy affair by EU standards, especially bearing in mind the unanimity requirement which was applicable in the Council and the fact that the EU was operating in unchartered waters.[11] Indeed, the discussed piece of secondary legislation was the first framework decision ever to be adopted by the EU. Thus, it was an important stepping stone in the big post-Amsterdam experiment of making cooperation in criminal matters more effective.[12] It followed a rather abysmal experience gained in the wake of entry into force of the Treaty on the European Union (TEU) on 1 November 1993.[13] If one, however, were to assume that the pace with which Framework Decision 2001/220/JHA was drafted and approved translated into full and effective transposition to the domestic laws of the Member States and their subsequent implementation, then one would be profoundly mistaken. The problem was not only in its general, yet demanding, content. Just like many EU criminal law instruments of that era, it suffered from the already mentioned deficiencies of the legal framework created by the ToA. Above all, it became a victim of lack of political will. This is addressed next.

B. Failures of Transposition and Implementation

Framework Decision 2001/220/JHA was approved on 15 March 2001, with the transposition deadline varying for different provisions. The general deadline was exactly one year from the date of publication of the Framework Decision in the Official Journal of the EU (22 March 2002).[14] Articles 5 and 6, covering – respectively – communication safeguards and specific assistance to victims had to be reflected in national law by 22 March 2004. The Member States had ample time to transpose Article 10, which dealt with penal mediation and its effects. In this respect, the deadline was 22 March 2006. The European Commission was given one year from each of these deadlines to produce assessments of transposition. This is where the first problems emerged. Not a single Member State complied with the notification requirement as per

[8] Action Plan of the Council and the Commission on how best to implement the provisions of the Treaty of Amsterdam on an area of freedom, security and justice [1999] OJ C19/1; see paras 19 and 51(c).

[9] Commission, 'Crime victims in the European Union: reflections on standards and action' (Communication) COM (1999) 349 final.

[10] Initiative of the Portuguese Republic with a view to adopting a Council Framework Decision on the standing of victims in criminal procedure [2000] OJ C243/4.

[11] As noted in the academic literature, one of the reasons why victims' rights appeared on the EU agenda and why the subject received such priority treatment was the status of 'cross-border victims': see MS Groenhuijsen and A Pemberton, 'The EU Framework Decision for Victims of Crime: Does Hard Law Make a Difference?' (2009) 17 *European Journal of Crime, Criminal Law and Criminal Justice* 43, 44. Interestingly, prior to the entry into force of the Treaty of Lisbon, the legal basis for harmonisation of victims' rights in criminal proceedings at the EU level was somewhat questionable. Yet, it did not stop the Council from adopting Framework Decision 2001/220/JHA and its legality has never been challenged: see Mitsilegas (n 1), 307.

[12] As noted by Groenhuijsen and Pemberton, it was also 'the first time that there [was a] so-called "hard-law instrument" concerning victims of crime available at the international level. […] Prior to 2001 only soft-law instruments were on offer'. See Groenhuijsen and Pemberton (n 11), 43.

[13] For a historical account see, inter alia, E Denza, *The Intergovernmental Pillars of the European Union* (Oxford University Press, 2002) 220–34.

[14] This was considered by academic commentators as 'extremely tight'. See Groenhuijsen and Pemberton (n 11), 47.

Article 18 of the Framework Decision 2001/220/JHA. Reminders produced by the Commission were ignored by some of the Member States; thus, it was not in position to prepare a timely report. In its own words, it 'would have been virtually meaningless'.[15] The Report was eventually published in early February 2004. The information was fragmented and the picture bleak. As aptly noted by Rianne Letschert and Conny Rijken, 'the implementation of the framework decision on the Standing of Victims was plagued with difficulties'.[16] Arguably, there were a number of reasons behind that.

A cursory reading of Framework Decision 2001/220/JHA could give a wrong impression that it should have been an easy legal act to give effect to. While it was a relatively short and general piece of legislation, it was also a tricky one. To begin with, being an early framework decision to materialise, it triggered a lot of questions as to the applicable methodology. The definition of framework decisions was duly provided by the Member States in Article 34 TEU, and it did resemble the definition of directives known from the then Article 249 in the Treaty Establishing the European Community.[17] But did it mean that the same transposition principles applied? In hindsight we know that this was the case, but then – back in the early 2000s – one could legitimately argue that, after all, there was a reason why these new legal instruments made available by the ToA were not simply called directives.[18] A reminder is fitting that during the intergovernmental conference the Member States were proceeding just like many people move on the dance floor: three steps forward, two steps back, and, perhaps, even a few steps sideways. Put differently, they were torn apart between the objective need to give the then third pillar of the EU more thrust and, at the same time, they were much too full of trepidation to extend what was known as the Community method to judicial and police cooperation in criminal matters. It was all too sensitive, too close to the heart of sovereignty, and too early to make police and judicial cooperation in criminal matters an area of EU law like any other.

The way Framework Decision 2001/220/JHA was drafted did not help matters. Some of its provisions were overly general, to the point of being vague, and therefore amenable to varying interpretations. As argued by Valsamis Mitsilegas, this was consequential to the attempt 'to strike a balance between Europeanisation and the respect for national diversity'.[19] Let us start by using Article 2 as an exhibit to demonstrate what this balancing act produced:

> 1. Each Member State shall ensure that victims have a real and appropriate role in its criminal legal system. It shall continue to make every effort to ensure that victims are treated with due respect for the dignity of the individual during proceedings and shall recognise the rights and legitimate interests of victims with particular reference to criminal proceedings.
> 2. Each Member State shall ensure that victims who are particularly vulnerable can benefit from specific treatment best suited to their circumstances.

[15] Report from the European Commission on the basis of Article 18 of the Council Framework Decision of 15 March 2001 on the standing of victims in criminal proceedings COM (2004) 54 final, 2.

[16] R Letschert and C Rijken, 'Rights of Victims of Crime: Tensions between an Integrated Approach and a Limited Legal Basis for Harmonisation' (2013) 4 *New Journal of European Criminal Law* 226, 229.

[17] See further on framework decisions as sources of EU law, inter alia, A Łazowski and B Kurcz, 'Two Sides of the Same Coin? Framework Decisions and Directives Compared' (2006) 25 *Yearbook of European Law* 177; M J Borgers, 'Implementing framework decisions' (2007) 44 *Common Market Law Review* 1361.

[18] A case in point may be argumentation submitted by the Italian Government in Case C-105/03 *Criminal proceedings against Maria Pupino*, ECLI:EU:C:2005:386, para 25. It was pleaded that: 'framework decisions and Community directives are completely different and separate sources of law, and that a framework decision cannot therefore place a national court under an obligation to interpret national law in conformity, such as the obligation which the Court of Justice has found in its case-law concerning Community directives'.

[19] Mitsilegas (n 1), 311.

Immediately, the first sentence should raise lawyers' eyebrows and trigger a fair question: what is a 'real and appropriate role in [a] criminal legal system'? Answering this question would have been a perfect classroom exercise with a group of eager law students, yet how should one deal with it when checking the compliance of national law, with the possibility of, potentially, writing a new set of rules and guidelines? Then comes respect for human dignity, which is protected by many national constitutions, some more powerfully than others. This can surely be seen through many sets of lenses, depending on where one is sitting.[20] Here the obligation resembles best endeavours clauses from international agreements. While they may look appealing, they are merely the obligations to act, not to achieve a particular result. Finally, paragraph 2 which – for obvious reasons – was a very welcome addition. Alas, it was so general that it would have been impossible to work out where to set benchmarks, not to mention that compliance with it would require combing of industrial proportions through chunky codes governing the criminal procedures of the Member States. A similar exercise would have to be conducted to ensure compliance with Article 3, governing safeguarding the right of victims to be heard and to supply evidence. In this respect, Article 4 looked much better and, by the same token, should have been easier to comply with. It dealt with a very desired victims' right to receive information. The main advantage was a non-exhaustive list of types of information that should have been provided to victims 'as from their first contact with law enforcement agencies'. Many other provisions that followed had the same general quality to them as the opening articles. It is interesting to note that some of them required measures that went beyond pure domestic law books. They attended to the factors mentioned earlier: the need to create victims' rights culture among the state authorities. Article 13 required promotion of involvement of victim support services, in particular provision of specially trained services as part of public service or funding for victim support organisations. The need for trainings of relevant authorities, especially members of the police and legal practitioners, was acknowledged in Article 14. Last but not least, Article 15 called for progressive creation of frameworks aiming at avoiding secondary victimisation.

Overall, Framework Decision 2001/220/JHA has proven to be a challenging legal act to transpose. When the European Commission published its second (and final) Report in 2009, the picture was again incomplete and bleak.[21] Neither Malta nor Greece submitted any information at all. Other Member States, of a now enlarged EU, provided the Commission with information about domestic measures taken to transpose and to implement the Framework Decision, yet in many cases the background material was incomplete and showed – at best – only partial compliance with obligations laid down therein. While the discussed Framework Decision was, beyond doubt, a step in the right direction, its benefits for victims were limited.

Going beyond factors related to this piece of legislation itself, one should also look for more general reasons behind this state of affairs. As already alluded to, at the meta level, the ToA – while boosting the third pillar of the EU – created a system which suffered from half-baked solutions and inherent weaknesses. One of them was a law enforcement deficiency. To begin with, the role of the European Commission in policing compliance with EU law was very limited as it was deprived of its traditional arsenal of procedural tools: the infringement procedures laid down in Articles 258 and 260 in the Treaty on the Functioning of the European Union (TFEU). Without the threat of litigation, potentially leading up to the imposition of

[20] See Case C-36/02 *Omega Spielhallen- und Automatenaufstellungs-GmbH v Oberbürgermeisterin der Bundesstadt Bonn*, ECLI:EU:C:2004:614.

[21] Report from the Commission pursuant to Article 18 of the Council Framework Decision of 15 March 2001 on the standing of victims in criminal proceedings (2001/220/JHA) COM (2009) 166 final.

financial penalties, the Member States had little incentive to comply with this, and other framework decisions, fully and in a timely fashion.[22] Furthermore, the European Court of Justice (ECJ) had only limited jurisdiction to assist the national courts in interpretation of EU criminal law, including Framework Decision 2001/220/JHA, as only judges from the Member States which recognised the jurisdiction of the ECJ could proceed with references for a preliminary ruling under Article 267 TFEU.[23] Despite this, some domestic courts did ask for help.[24] In one of those cases, the ECJ was given the opportunity to deal with enforcement of framework decisions at the national level. Paradoxically, Framework Decision 2001/220/JHA, which made only a modest impact on enhancement of the rights of victims, accidentally played a more important role than its drafters could possibly have imagined. In *Pupino*, it allowed the ECJ to give a badly needed boost to enforcement of EU criminal law.[25]

C. Along Came *Pupino*: Indirect Effect of Framework Decisions

Pupino was one of those serendipitous judicial developments, which had effects going well beyond the actual case and paved the way for a breakthrough in enforcement of post-Amsterdam third pillar legislation. It had a particular impact on application of the Framework Decision on the European arrest warrant, which soon after the expiry of the transposition period became the most used mutual recognition instrument in criminal matters.[26] *Pupino* has been addressed extensively in the academic literature, thus there is little point in rehearsing all its details.[27] Suffice to remind readers that the crux of the issue was whether provisions of Italian Criminal Procedure Code governing testimony, should have been interpreted in the light of Framework Decision 2001/220/JHA to allow for special treatment of vulnerable victims of crime. In *casu*, the victims were a group of small children who had been exposed to rather brutal teaching methods employed by their former kindergarten teacher. The matter raised in the reference for preliminary ruling, apart from the obvious issue of criminal law, was a fundamental question about constitutional principles applicable in the third pillar. On the one hand, it was clear from the then Article 34 TEU, and definition of framework decisions provided therein, that they could not produce direct effect. Yet did this also extend to other tenets governing enforcement

[22] On the mechanics of the infringement procedures see, inter alia, L Prete, *Infringement Proceedings in EU Law* (Kluwer Law International, 2017); and S Andersen, *The Enforcement of EU Law. The Role of the European Commission* (Oxford University Press, 2012).

[23] For a comprehensive overview see, inter alia, A Hinarejos, *Judicial Control in the European Union. Reforming Jurisdiction in the Intergovernmental Pillars* (Oxford University Press, 2009).

[24] See Cases C-467/05 *Criminal proceedings against Giovanni Dell'Orto*, ECLI:EU:C:2007:395; C-404/07 *György Katz v István Roland Sós*, ECLI:EU:C:2008:553; C-205/09 *Criminal proceedings against Emil Eredics and Mária Vassné Sápi*, ECLI:EU:C:2010:623; Joined Cases C-483/09 and C-1/10 *Criminal proceedings against Magatte Gueye and Valentín Salmerón Sánchez*, ECLI:EU:C:2011:583; Cases C-507/10 *Criminal proceedings against X*, ECLI:EU:C:2011:873; C-79/11 *Maurizio Giovanardi and Others*, ECLI:EU:C:2012:448. For an academic appraisal see A Łazowski, 'The Flood that Never Came. Case Law of the Court of Justice on the Victims' Rights *acquis*' in Burchett and Weyembergh (n 1).

[25] Case C-105/03 *Pupino* (n 18).

[26] Council Framework Decision 2002/584/JHA of 13 June 2002 on the European arrest warrant and the surrender procedures between Member States [2002] OJ L190/1. See further, inter alia, A Łazowski and V Mitsilegas (eds), *Coming of Age? The European Arrest Warrant at Twenty* (Hart Publishing, forthcoming).

[27] See, inter alia, M Fletcher, 'Extending "Indirect Effect" to the Third Pillar: The Significance of *Pupino*?' (2005) 30 *European Law Review* 862; E Spaventa, 'Opening Pandora's Box: Some Reflections on the Constitutional Effects of the Decision in *Pupino*' (2007) 3 *European Constitutional Law Review* 5; M Fletcher, 'Impact of the *Pupino* Decision on EU Law' in V Mitsilegas et al (eds), *The Court of Justice and European Criminal Law. Leading Cases in a Contextual Analysis* (Hart Publishing, 2019).

of EU law, for example the doctrine of indirect effect? In its answer to questions submitted by the judge in charge of preliminary enquiries at the *Tribunale di Firenze*, the ECJ famously ruled that indirect effect applied to the area in question. It, of course, came with all limits that indirect effect inherently carries. The obligation to interpret national law in the light of EU law is required only as far as it is possible and, inter alia, it may not lead to interpretation *contra legem*.[28] Furthermore, as the ECJ made clear in *Popławski II*,[29] it does not trigger the *Simmenthal* mandate requiring the domestic judges to set aside conflicting national law.[30] This can only be applicable in cases of direct effect, which – all those years later – remains precluded in relation to framework decisions which are still in force.

III. UPPING THE ANTE: DIRECTIVE 2012/29/EU ON RIGHTS OF VICTIMS

A. Introduction

The Treaty of Lisbon provided, inter alia, a major overhaul of the AFSJ.[31] As is well documented in the academic literature, the Third Pillar became a part of legal history as the general methods known from the European Communities became applicable. Three key reforms included the introduction of a new suite of competences for police and judicial cooperation in criminal matters, abolition of a separate catalogue of sources of secondary legislation for this area as well as full jurisdiction of the ECJ.[32]

One of the key issues that drafters of the Treaty of Lisbon had to address was the intertemporal and transitory issues for phasing-out of pre-Lisbon regime and phasing-in of the post-Lisbon framework. This covered, for instance, the status of framework decisions adopted before 30 November 2009.[33] As per Article 9 of Protocol 36 to the EU Founding Treaties, they would remain in force until 'repealed, annulled or amended in implementation of the Treaties'. Thus, the question was which of the framework decisions would be rolled over into directives (or, when permitted, regulations) and to what extent they would be revised. It quickly became clear that non-contentious dossiers would take the lead and – while a degree of continuation would be envisaged – proper reforms would be introduced. One of the first to be addressed was Framework Decision 2001/220/JHA. It belonged to one of the priorities laid down in the Stockholm Programme that served as beacon for navigation in the AFSJ in the

[28] See, inter alia, Case 80/86 *Criminal proceedings against Kolpinghuis Nijmegen BV*, ECLI:EU:C:1987:431. See further L Martin, 'The General Principles of European (Criminal) Law as Limitation to the Enforcement of EU Law: The Kolpinghuis Nijmegen Rule' in Mitsilegas et al (eds) (n 27); S Prechal, *Directives in EC Law*, 2nd edn (Oxford University Press, 2005) 193–210.

[29] Case C-573/17 *Criminal proceedings against Daniel Adam Popławski*, ECLI:EU:C:2019:530. For an academic appraisal of this judgment see D Miąsik and M Szwarc, 'Primacy and Direct Effect – Still Together: *Popławski II*, Case C-573/17, Criminal Proceedings against Daniel Adam Popławski' (2021) 58 *Common Market Law Review* 571.

[30] Case 106/77 *Amministrazione delle Finanze dello Stato v Simmenthal SpA*, ECLI:EU:C:1978:49. See further, inter alia, K Lenaerts and P Van Nuffel, *EU Constitutional Law* (Oxford University Press, 2021) 635–39.

[31] Treaty of Lisbon amending the Treaty on European Union and the Treaty establishing the European Community [2007] OJ C306/1.

[32] See, inter alia, C Ladenburger, 'Police and Criminal Law in the Treaty of Lisbon. A New Dimension for the Community Method' (2008) 4 *European Constitutional Law Review* 20; F Goudappel, 'Options for the Development of European Criminal Law under the Treaty of Lisbon' in M Trybus and L Rubini (eds), *The Treaty of Lisbon and the Future of European Law and Policy* (Edward Elgar, 2012); E Herlin-Karnell, 'EU Competence in Criminal Law after Lisbon' in A Biondi et al (eds), *EU Law after Lisbon* (Oxford University Press, 2012); and R Sicurella, 'EU Competence in Criminal Matters' in V Mitsilegas et al (eds), *Research Handbook on EU Criminal Law* (Edward Elgar, 2016).

[33] The Treaty of Lisbon entered into force on 1 December 2009.

period 2010–2014.[34] The European Council called the European Commission and the Member States to:

- examine how to improve legislation and practical support measures for the protection of victims and to improve the implementation of existing instruments;
- offer better support to victims in other ways, possibly through existing European networks that provide practical help, and put forward proposals to that end;
- examine the opportunity of making one comprehensive legal instrument on the protection of victims, by joining together Council Directive 2004/80/EC of 29 April 2004 relating to compensation to crime victims and Council Framework Decision 2001/220/JHA of 15 March 2001 on the standing of victims in criminal proceedings, on the basis of an evaluation of these two instruments.[35]

These desiderata, at least partly, have materialised in Directive 2012/29 on victims' rights. While Framework Decision 2001/220/JHA and Directive 2004/80/EC have not been merged, the legal regime harmonising victims' rights in criminal proceedings has been decisively strengthened.

The starting point was the Proposal of the European Commission published in 2011.[36] It was strongly endorsed by the Council in its Resolution of 10 June 2011 where it committed 'itself to examining this proposal as a matter of priority'.[37] Indeed, Directive 2012/29, just like its predecessor, was adopted relatively quickly, even though in the post-Lisbon world it required the approval of two co-legislators, the European Parliament and the Council. This time the transposition period was not only uniform for all provisions of the Directive, but also much longer: three years (16 November 2015).[38] As will be explained in the next section of this chapter, despite this, and despite the fact that the legal act in question was a classic directive, transposition and implementation have been anything but smooth.

B. Transposition and Implementation of Directive 2012/29

Directive 2012/29, when juxtaposed with Framework Decision 2001/220/JHA, presents itself as a much more comprehensive legal act. The drafters took into account the experience gained from the predecessor legislation as well as changes of circumstances resulting from the entry into force of the Lisbon Treaty, including a much more specific legal basis for adoption of victims' rights legislation.[39]

[34] The Stockholm Programme – An open and secure Europe serving and protecting citizens [2010] OJ C115/1.

[35] ibid, 10.

[36] Commission, 'Proposal for a Directive of the European Parliament and of the Council establishing minimum standards on the rights, support and protection of victims of crime' COM (2011) 275 final.

[37] Resolution of the Council of 10 June 2011 on a Roadmap for strengthening the rights and protection of victims, in particular in criminal proceedings [2011] OJ C187/1, 4.

[38] It should be noted that it applies to 26 Member States, as Denmark used one of its opt-outs and remains bound by Framework Decision 2001/220/JHA. See further on the status of Denmark, and for that matter other opt-out countries, R Adler-Nissen, *Opting Out of the European Union. Diplomacy, Sovereignty and European Integration* (Cambridge University Press, 2014) 114–46.

[39] Art 82(2) TFEU, which served as the legal basis, envisages that the EU may legislate, inter alia, on rights of victims of crime to the extent it is necessary to facilitate mutual recognition. However, two additional caveats apply. First, 'such rules shall take into account the differences between the legal traditions and systems of the Member States.' Second, only minimum harmonisation is permitted. Put differently, the Member States may opt for higher standards of protection of individuals in their national laws.

Directive 2012/29 starts with a lengthy Preamble providing a lot of useful information as to the raison d'être behind individual provisions, as well as their meaning. The victims' rights are organised in three clusters. To begin with, chapter 2 regulates the rights related to availability of information and support for victims. It deals with the right to understand and be understood (Article 3), the right to receive information from the first contact with a competent authority (Article 4), the right of victims when making a complaint (Article 5), the right to receive information about one's case (Article 6), as well as the right to interpretation and translation (Article 7).[40] The right to access victim support services and the types of assistance that shall be provided are regulated, respectively, in Articles 8 and 9 of the Directive. The rights related to participation in criminal proceedings are grouped in chapter 3. They include the right to be heard (Article 10), rights available should a decision not to prosecute be taken (Article 11), safeguarded rights in the context of restorative justice services (Article 12), rights to legal aid (Article 13) and reimbursement of expenses (Article 14), the right to the return of property (Article 15) and to compensation from the offender in the course of criminal proceedings (Article 16). Article 17 attends to the rights of victims who are residing in other Member States than countries of their nationality. One of the added values of Directive 2012/29 has been chapter 4, which is dedicated to the protection of victims as well as the rights of vulnerable victims of crime. This wide suite of rights covers the right to protection (Article 18), the right to avoid contact between victims and offenders (Article 19), the right to protection during criminal investigations (Article 20), the right to protection of privacy (Article 21), a requirement to conduct individual assessments of needs of victims (Article 22) as well as the right to protection of victims with special needs (Article 23), in particular children (Article 24). In the closing part, Directive 2012/29 requires measures to improve training for practitioners (Article 25) and provides a basic framework for cooperation between relevant authorities of the Member States (Article 26).

At least prima facie, Directive 2012/29 should have been an easier act to transpose. To begin with, its provisions are considerably more detailed than those in Framework Decision 2001/220/JHA. Furthermore, the ratio between clearly cut requirements and generally framed desiderata has definitely shifted, to the benefit of legal certainty. A reminder is fitting that, as per case law of the ECJ, non-transposed or partially transposed provisions of directives may produce direct effect after expiry of the transposition period. Furthermore, the already mentioned Simmenthal mandate applies, requiring national judges to set aside conflicting domestic rules.[41] Analysis

[40] Interestingly, around the same time, the EU proceeded with legislation touching upon similar matters but dealing with the rights of defendants. This included: Directive 2010/64/EU of the European Parliament and of the Council of 20 October 2010 on the right to interpretation and translation in criminal proceedings [2010] OJ L280/1; Directive 2012/13/EU of the European Parliament and of the Council of 22 May 2012 on the right to information in criminal proceedings [2012] OJ L142/1; Directive 2013/48/EU of the European Parliament and of the Council of 22 October 2013 on the right of access to a lawyer in criminal proceedings and in European arrest warrant proceedings, and on the right to have a third party informed upon deprivation of liberty and to communicate with third persons and with consular authorities while deprived of liberty [2013] OJ L294/1; Directive (EU) 2016/1919 of the European Parliament and of the Council of 26 October 2016 on legal aid for suspects and accused persons in criminal proceedings and for requested persons in European arrest warrant proceedings [2016] OJ L297/1; Directive (EU) 2016/343 of the European Parliament and of the Council of 9 March 2016 on the strengthening of certain aspects of the presumption of innocence and of the right to be present at the trial in criminal proceedings [2016] OJ L65/1; Directive (EU) 2016/800 of the European Parliament and of the Council of 11 May 2016 on procedural safeguards for children who are suspects or accused persons in criminal proceedings [2016] OJ L132/1. On the relationship between the rights of victims' and defendants see, inter alia, A Klip, 'On Victim's Rights and its Impact on the Rights of the Accused' (2015) 23 *European Journal of Crime, Criminal Law and Criminal Justice* 177; K Strada-Rozenberga, 'Do Victims' Rights and Defence Rights Really Have to be Eequal?' in Burchett and Weyembergh (n 1).

[41] See further, in the context of EU criminal law, inter alia, E Fronza, 'Primacy, Duty of Loyalty and Interpretation' in K Ambos and P Rackow (eds), *The Cambridge Companion to European Criminal Law* (Cambridge University Press, 2023).

of wording employed by the drafters of Directive 2012/29 demonstrates that many provisions are precise, unambiguous, and unconditional, thus destined for direct effect.[42] Interestingly, thus far, Directive 2012/29 has triggered only a handful of references for preliminary rulings from national courts.[43] This is despite the fact that the jurisdiction of the ECJ is now full and compulsory, and that it has at its disposal the Urgent Preliminary Ruling Procedure, allowing for fast-track treatment of cases dealing with AFSJ.[44]

It should also be noted that some provisions laid down in Directive 2012/29 are shy of straightforward obligations and for compliance require non-legal measures. This particularly applies to rules on victim support services,[45] and training of practitioners.

In an interesting, though not unique, move, the European Commission opted to identify the main potential challenges of transposition and implementation in advance. For that purpose, in 2013 it published a comprehensive set of guidelines in this respect.[46] Alas, as the European Commission Report demonstrates, by 2020 most Member States had failed to transpose the Directive in question fully to their national laws and to secure its implementation.[47] Bearing in mind that since the entry into force of the Treaty of Lisbon, the European Commission – wearing the hat of the guardian of the Treaties – has a full arsenal of procedural tools at its disposal, it triggered infringement proceedings against 21 Member States.[48] While none of these cases have reached the ECJ, and all but one have been closed during the administrative phase of the procedure, this created a platform for dialogue between the European Commission and the Member States. This may be explained by the fact that problems with implementation are not, in some instances, directly related to the transposition itself but rather deal with matters which require non-legislative measures that make use of infringement procedures problematic. Arguably, it all delivered satisfactory results.

Nevertheless, the results of the evaluation exercise published by the European Commission in 2022 show not only that the transposition and implementation require improvement, but also that Directive 2012/29 itself merits further work.[49] The Commission Report identified the lessons learned and potential actions,[50] which, in turn translated into proposal for revision of Directive 2012/29.[51]

[42] See further, inter alia, Prechal (n 28), 216–70.

[43] See Cases C-38/18 *Criminal procedure against Massimo Gambino and Shpetim Hyka*, ECLI:EU:C:2019:628; and C-603/19 *Criminal proceedings against TG and UF*, ECLI:EU:C:2020:774. See further Łazowski (n 24).

[44] See further S Iglesias Sánchez, 'The Urgent Preliminary Ruling Procedure and the European Arrest Warrant' in Łazowski and Mitsilegas (n 26).

[45] For an analysis of practical experience see further, inter alia, O Jubany et al, 'Problematising the Victims' Rights Directive from the Ground: The Implementation of Victim Support Services in Greece, Italy, Bulgaria, Cyprus, and Spain' (2022) 30 *European Journal of Crime, Criminal Law and Criminal Justice* 266.

[46] European Commission, 'DG Justice Guidance Document related to the transposition and implementation of Directive 2012/29/EU of the European Parliament and of the Council of 25 October 2012 establishing minimum standards on the rights, support and protection of victims of crime, and replacing Council Framework Decision 2001/220/JHA', https://commission.europa.eu/system/files/2019-02/13_12_19_3763804_guidance_victims_rights_directive_eu_en.pdf, accessed 26 February 2024.

[47] Commission, 'Report from the Commission to the European Parliament and the Council on the implementation of Directive 2012/29/EU of the European Parliament and of the Council of 25 October 2012 establishing minimum standards on the rights, support and protection of victims of crime, and replacing Council Framework Decision 2001/220/JHA' COM (2020) 188 final.

[48] ibid, 3.

[49] Commission, 'Commission Staff Working Document. Evaluation of Directive 2012/29/EU of the European Parliament and of the Council of 25 October 2012 establishing minimum standards on the rights, support and protection of victims of crime, and replacing Council Framework Decision 2001/220/JHA' SWD (2022) 179 final.

[50] ibid, 40–43. For an appraisal see, inter alia, C Chioni-Chotouman, 'The Revision of the Victims' Rights Directive: What Perspective?' in Burchett and Weyembergh (n 1). When this chapter was completed, this proposal was pending.

[51] Commission (n 5).

It should be noted that the role of the European Commission has extended beyond supervision of transposition and implementation by the Member States, and evaluation of measures taken. In 2020 the European Commission adopted a comprehensive strategy on victims' rights which led to many actions, including the setting up of Victims' Rights Platform as well as public outreach activities. The Commission opted for a holistic approach and the scope of the Strategy went beyond Directive 2012/29 as it covered also other pieces of EU *acquis* dealing with victims' rights.[52]

IV. CONCLUSION

As discussed in the introduction to this chapter, the experience with two consecutive EU legal acts harmonising the victims' rights offers a mixed bag. On the one hand, the rights of victims now have a firm position on the EU agenda. On the other hand, both Framework Decision 2001/220/JHA and Directive 2012/29 have become victims themselves: partial transposition and implementation have undermined their effectiveness. In hindsight, this should have been expected as an inevitable part of the game. Balancing EU and national competences is not easy in any area of EU law. In this respect, criminal law is marred by particular difficulties. Troubles with transposition and implementation of measures adopted under the umbrella of EU criminal law are widespread and the two discussed pieces of legislation are good examples that prove the general rule. The nature of victims' rights makes this a tricky area, both at the EU and at the national level. For the rights of victims to really make a difference, proper implementation of agreed rules is a *conditio sine qua non*. This, obviously, requires non-legal measures, which take time to materialise and to bear fruit, not to mention budgetary appropriations. And, above all, they require societal change. This is why both the discussed legal acts paid particular attention to the training of practitioners whose actions may affect victims' rights and who, good winds permitting, may make a difference. This also explains the vital importance of the setting up of centres and networks supporting victims. By any stretch of the imagination, this is not merely an academic problem. The European Commission claims that '[e]very year, an estimated 15% of Europeans or 75 million people in the European Union fall victim to crime'.[53] It is self-explanatory that efforts to shrink the sea between what is said and what is done are very much desired. But this is not only the task of the EU institutions; it is – first and foremost – a job that the Member States are in charge of. The analysis provided in this chapter demonstrates that there is room for improvement. The EU *acquis* on victims' rights is (still) a work in progress.

[52] For a list see n 1.

[53] 'Victims rights in the EU' https://commission.europa.eu/strategy-and-policy/policies/justice-and-fundamental-rights/criminal-justice/protecting-victims-rights/victims-rights-eu_en, accessed 26 February 2023.

21

Cross-Border Exchange of Evidence from the European Investigation Order to the European Production Order: A Game of Two Halves for the Protection of Fundamental Rights in Europe's Area of Criminal Justice?

VALSAMIS MITSILEGAS*

I. INTRODUCTION

THE EUROPEAN UNION (EU) legal framework on the cross-border exchange of evidence in criminal matters has been evolving constantly in the past two decades. Traditional forms of mutual legal assistance have been replaced by the application of the principle of mutual recognition as the cornerstone of judicial cooperation in criminal matters, including in the field of evidence. The application of the principle of mutual recognition in criminal law – most notably through the emblematic Framework Decision on the European arrest warrant (the EAW Framework Decision) – has raised a number of questions on the relationship between mutual recognition and mutual trust on the one hand, and the protection of fundamental rights in Europe's area of criminal justice on the other.[1]

Vice-President Bay Larsen has contributed decisively in these discussions in his capacity as a leading member of the composition of the European Court of Justice (ECJ) in cases involving mutual recognition in criminal matters (in a number of cases as judge rapporteur), as well as in his publications in the field. He has contended that the ECJ has never argued that mutual trust must also be blind trust, and hence that a balance must be struck between effective judicial cooperation and protection of fundamental rights.[2] He has also stressed that this balance

* Professor of European and Global Law and Dean of the School of Law and Social Justice at the University of Liverpool, UK. I would like to thank Clementina Salvi for her research assistance in the preparation of this chapter. The usual disclaimer applies.

[1] I have discussed this relationship in, inter alia, V Mitsilegas, 'The Symbiotic Relationship between Mutual Trust and Fundamental Rights in Europe's Area of Criminal Justice' (2015) *New Journal of European Criminal Law* 460; and more recently see V Mitsilegas, *EU Criminal Law*, 2nd edn (Hart Publishing, 2022) ch 4.

[2] L Bay Larsen, 'Afterword(s) on Mutual Recognition and the Respect for Fundamental Rights Revisited – Following the Judgment in *Aranyosi* and *Caldararu*' in C Brière and A Weyembergh (eds), *The Needed Balances in EU Criminal Law. Past, Present and Future* (Hart Publishing, 2018) 436.

necessitates a judicial dialogue between national authorities, as well as between the ECJ and the European Court of Human Rights (ECtHR).[3]

The present contribution will, against that background, examine the relationship between mutual recognition and fundamental rights in the field of cross-border exchange of evidence, by focusing on the changes brought by the post-Lisbon instrument on mutual recognition in the field of evidence, the Directive on the European Investigation Order (EIO Directive).[4] The analysis will outline the central place of fundamental rights protection in this instrument, which constitutes a mature iteration of mutual recognition, taking into account the contested nature of the protection of fundamental rights in the context of the text and the operation of the EAW Framework Decision.[5] The second part of the analysis will examine how the EU legal framework on cross-border exchange of evidence has evolved since the EIO, to regulate the exchange of digital evidence. This has been addressed by the Regulation on a European Production Order and a European Preservation Order,[6] which introduces a paradigm change to the judicial co-operation model as applied in the EIO system. The analysis will focus on the challenges that this new, privatised paradigm of cooperation poses for the protection of fundamental rights and the rule of law in Europe's area of criminal justice, and place these developments within a broader global context. The analysis will raise the question of whether recent developments in the field of cross-border exchange of evidence represent a game of two halves for the protection of fundamental rights in Europe's area of criminal justice.

II. MATURING MUTUAL RECOGNITION: THE EUROPEAN INVESTIGATION ORDER

The main legal instrument regulating the cross-border exchange of evidence in Europe's area of criminal justice is the EIO Directive. The Directive represents an age of maturity in the evolution of the application of the principle of mutual recognition in criminal matters. It was adopted after the entry into force of the Treaty of Lisbon and replaces a number of 'old' international law and EU third pillar law instruments on mutual legal assistance and judicial cooperation in criminal matters in the field.[7] The format of the instrument is a Directive (and not a Framework Decision as with the pre-Lisbon relevant instruments). The adoption of the Directive was subject to the co-decision process, resulting in the European Parliament acting as a co-legislator with the Council. The Directive maintains the key elements of the EU system of cooperation under mutual recognition based on judicialisation (cooperation between national judicial authorities)[8] and speed (execution will take place in principle within 30 days of the receipt of a request, if not earlier in urgent cases).[9] The scope of the EIO is broad, covering

[3] L Bay Larsen, 'Quelques remarques sur la place et les limites de la confiance mutuelle dans le cadre du mandat d'arrêt européen' (2018) *L'observateur de Bruxelles* n° 112, 10–15.

[4] Directive 2014/41/EU of the European Parliament and of the Council of 3 April 2014 regarding the European Investigation Order in criminal matters [2014] OJ L130/1.

[5] Council Framework Decision 2002/584/JHA of 13 June 2002 on the European arrest warrant and the surrender procedures between Member States [2002] OJ L190/1.

[6] Regulation (EU) 2023/1543 of the European Parliament and of the Council of 12 July 2023 on European Production Orders and European Preservation Orders for electronic evidence in criminal proceedings and for the execution of custodial sentences following criminal proceedings [2023] L191/118.

[7] These include the Council of Europe Convention on Mutual Legal Assistance in Criminal Matters, the Convention implementing the Schengen Agreement, the third pillar Convention on Mutual Legal Assistance in Criminal Matters, the Framework Decision on the European Evidence Warrant and the relevant provisions of Framework Decision 2003/577/JHA on the execution of freezing orders: EIO Directive, Art 34.

[8] Directive 2014/41, Art 1.

[9] ibid, Art 12(1)–(3).

all investigative measures for obtaining any type of evidence, including digital evidence,[10] in criminal proceedings within the EU. Once issued, the EIO should be accepted by the requested authority without any further formality and should be promptly executed by it in the same way that domestic investigative acts are carried out.[11] Care is taken to ensure the preservation of evidence, as according to Article 32: 'The issuing authority may issue an EIO in order to take any measure with a view to provisionally preventing the destruction, transformation, removal, transfer or disposal of an item that may be used as evidence'. Hence, the executing authority must decide and communicate the decision on the provisional measure as soon as possible and, wherever practicable, within 24 hours of receipt of the EIO.[12]

The above provisions illustrate that the EIO Directive has introduced a system aimed at efficiency in judicial cooperation in criminal matters in the field of evidence, including provisions on speed and on the preservation of evidence. At the same time, the Directive includes a number of fundamental rights safeguards, which represent a considerable degree of maturity in the application of the principle of mutual recognition in criminal matters. First, the issuing of the EIO must be necessary and proportionate for the purpose of the national criminal proceedings, taking into account the rights of the suspected or accused person.[13] Second, the investigative measure(s) indicated in the EIO could have been ordered under the same conditions in a similar domestic case.[14] Third, the executing authority may have recourse to an investigative measure other than that indicated in the EIO where the investigative measure selected by the executing authority would achieve the same result by less intrusive means than the investigative measure indicated in the EIO.[15] Fourth, the Directive introduces a number of grounds for refusal of the execution of an EIO,[16] including an explicit ground for refusal (in a direct departure from the model used in the EAW Framework Decision) on the basis of the presence of substantial grounds to believe that the execution of the investigative measure indicated in the EIO would be incompatible with the executing State's obligations in accordance with Article 6 of the Treaty on European Union (TEU) and the Charter of Fundamental Rights of the European Union (the Charter).[17] Fifth, the EIO Directive contains a detailed provision on legal remedies for affected individuals.[18] A key safeguard in this context is that Member States must ensure that legal remedies equivalent to those available in a similar domestic case are applicable to the investigative measures indicated in the EIO.[19] Moreover, both the issuing authority and the executing authority must take the appropriate measures to ensure that information is provided about the possibilities under national law for seeking the legal remedies when these become applicable and in due time to ensure that they can be exercised effectively.[20] Member States must further ensure that the time-limits for seeking a legal remedy will be the same as those that are provided for in similar domestic cases and are applied in a way that guarantees the possibility of the effective exercise of these legal remedies for the parties concerned.[21] The issuing State must take into account a successful challenge against the

[10] ibid, Art 13(4) refers to 'objects, documents, or data'.
[11] ibid, Art 9(1).
[12] ibid, Art 32(2).
[13] ibid, Art 6(1)(a).
[14] ibid, Art 6(1)(b).
[15] ibid, Art 10(3).
[16] ibid, Art 11(1).
[17] ibid, Art 11(1)(f).
[18] ibid, Art 14.
[19] ibid, Art 14(1).
[20] ibid, Art 14(3).
[21] ibid, Art 14(4).

recognition or execution of an EIO in accordance with its own national law; without prejudice to national procedural rules, Member States must ensure that in criminal proceedings in the issuing State the rights of the defence and the fairness of the proceedings are respected when assessing evidence obtained through the EIO.[22]

The importance of the fundamental rights safeguards set out by the EIO Directive, as interpreted in conformity with the Charter, was stressed by the ECJ. In the landmark case of *Gavanozov II*[23] – where Vice President Bay Larsen was the reporting judge, the ECJ affirmed the benefit of the right to an effective remedy guaranteed by Article 47 of the Charter for any person wishing to rely on the protection conferred on him on the basis of Article 14 of the EIO Directive read in conjunction with Article 24(7) EIO.[24] When Member States implement EU law, they are required to ensure compliance with the right to an effective remedy enshrined in Article 47(1) of the Charter, a provision which constitutes a reaffirmation of the principle of effective judicial protection.[25] The ECJ held that Article 6 of the EIO in conjunction with Article 47 of the Charter and Article 4(3) TEU on sincere cooperation preclude the issuing of an EIO the purpose of which is to carry out searches and seizures, as well as hearing of a witness by videoconference, where the legislation does not provide for any legal remedy against the issuing of an EIO.[26] This is a striking ruling, emphasising the significance of the protection of fundamental rights and the right to an effective remedy as an element underpinning the operation of the very principle of mutual recognition in criminal matters. The ECJ echoed in this context the Opinion of Advocate General Bobek, who stated that:

> […] whoever wishes to use the system of judicial assistance and mutual recognition under Directive 2014/41, or under any other instrument of judicial cooperation and mutual recognition for that matter, must come, metaphorically speaking, with clean hands, or rather, cannot come with hands that are knowingly dirty. The failure to observe that rule of basic hygiene, which has been repeatedly recognised and systematically emphasised, may indeed lead to that person being asked to leave the room and to come back only after having found some soap and carried out the necessary procedures.[27]

III. CHALLENGING MUTUAL RECOGNITION: THE EUROPEAN PRODUCTION ORDER

Shortly after the adoption of the EIO Directive, the European Commission began work on an alternative measure on the cross-border exchange of evidence in criminal proceedings, in the field of digital or electronic evidence. A key factor in the field of digital evidence is the fact that data are held largely by private companies, and predominantly by the global tech giants. The growing importance of the private sector in the generation and use of personal data in the digital world is key to understanding the challenges that initiatives on digital evidence pose for our understanding of criminal justice systems. The proliferation of the generation, use and processing of personal data as part of everyday life in the digital world and the central role that private companies such as telecommunications or internet companies play in the handling and exploitation of such data[28] have the potential to change law enforcement paradigms in

[22] ibid, Art 14(7).
[23] Case C-852/19 *Gavanozov II*, ECLI:EU:C:2021:902.
[24] ibid, para 32.
[25] ibid, para 28.
[26] ibid, para 56.
[27] Opinion of AG Bobek in Case C-852/19 *Gavanozov II*, ECLI:EU:C:2021:346, para 91.
[28] S Zuboff, *The Age of Surveillance Capitalism* (Profile Books, 2019).

the quest for the fight against impunity. In this process, the State is increasingly required to co-opt the private sector for law enforcement purposes. This privatisation of law enforcement through the responsibilisation of private actors was noted by criminologists some time ago,[29] and appeared prominently in EU and international law in the context of the fight against money laundering.[30] This paradigm has expanded gradually and steadily over time, with private actors being co-opted for the purposes of law enforcement in the fields of data retention, the transfer of passenger name records, and more recently of removing harmful online content.[31] Proposals on digital evidence take privatisation further by applying it in the context of criminal proceedings.

In the EU context, the European Commission tabled a proposal for a Regulation on European Production and Preservation Orders for electronic evidence in criminal matters in 2018.[32] The draft Regulation established a system compelling private service providers offering services in the EU to produce or preserve electronic evidence, regardless of the location of the data, upon receipt of orders issued by public authorities in EU Member States. According to the proposal, such orders (the European Production Order and the European Preservation Order) could be served on providers of electronic communication services, social networks, online marketplaces, other hosting service providers and providers of internet infrastructure, such as IP address and domain name registries, or on their legal representatives where they exist. The draft Regulation thus established a direct channel of communication between the issuing (public) authority and private service providers, with European Production Orders and European Preservation Orders addressed directly to a legal representative designated by the service provider.[33] The addressees should in principle comply with the orders and react swiftly: upon receipt of a European Production Order, the addressee must ensure that the requested data is transmitted directly to the issuing authority or the law enforcement authorities as indicated in the Order at the latest within 10 days of receipt. The Commission justified the system proposed in the draft Regulation on the basis of the special features of the internet and of the operations of electronic service providers, linked with the perceived need for greater speed in the gathering and transmission of electronic evidence. The second paragraph of the Explanatory Memorandum to the draft Regulation states that:

> Given the borderless nature of the internet, such services can be provided from anywhere in the world and do not necessarily require physical infrastructure, a corporate presence or staff in Member States where the services are offered or in the internal market as a whole. They also do not require a specific location for the storage of data, which is often chosen by the service provider on the basis of legitimate considerations such as data security, economies of scale and swiftness of access. As a result, in a growing number of criminal cases involving all types of crime, Member State authorities require access to data that might serve as evidence and that is stored outside their country and/or by service providers in other Member States or third countries.

[29] On the accountability strategy, see D Garland, 'The Limits of the Sovereign State: Strategies of Crime Control in Contemporary Society' (1996) 36 *British Journal of Criminology* 445.

[30] I have expanded on the privatisation of crime control in the context of anti-money laundering law in V Mitsilegas, *Money Laundering Counter-Measures in the European Union: A New Paradigm of Security Governance versus Fundamental Legal Principles* (Kluwer Law International, 2003).

[31] V Mitsilegas 'The Privatisation of Surveillance in the Digital Age' in V Mitsilegas and N Vavoula (eds), *Surveillance and Privacy in the Digital Age. European, Transatlantic and Global Perspectives* (Hart Publishing, 2021) 101.

[32] Commission, 'Proposal for a Regulation of the European Parliament and of the Council on European Production and Preservation Orders for electronic evidence in criminal matters' COM (2018) 225 final.

[33] Commission, 'Proposal for a Directive of the European Parliament and of the Council laying down harmonised rules on the appointment of legal representatives for the purpose of gathering evidence in criminal proceedings' COM (2018) 226 final.

Based on the unproven premise that digital evidence is a 'special case' along these lines, the draft Regulation introduced a paradigm change.[34] It established a system whereby cooperation takes place directly between a public authority in the issuing Member State and the private sector – departing from existing models of judicial cooperation and mutual recognition in EU law, which are based on cooperation and communication between public authorities in Member States.

This change is not without controversy and raises three main concerns in terms of the protection of fundamental rights at the EU and at the global level. The system introduced by the draft Regulation on digital evidence dispensed with the layer of judicial control and scrutiny of a request for evidence in the executing Member State. This layer of control is of paramount importance in the EU architecture of judicial cooperation in criminal matters on the basis of mutual recognition. The most mature measure of mutual recognition adopted thus far, which actually concerns the exchange of evidence – the EIO Directive – promotes speed and efficiency in judicial cooperation while providing for a number of safeguards to be taken into account by the judicial authorities of the executing Member State, including fundamental rights considerations. The proposal on digital evidence dispensed with this system, delegating fundamental rights scrutiny to the private sector. This approach leads effectively to the privatisation of mutual trust in Europe's area of criminal justice, which raises the second concern regarding the protection of fundamental rights.[35]

The Commission's proposal on digital evidence thus marked a fundamental shift in the scheme of cooperation in criminal matters in the EU, from a system of cooperation and communication between public (and mainly judicial) authorities to one of cooperation and communication between public authorities in the issuing State and private companies. The proposed system places undue responsibility on private providers to safeguard fundamental rights. Private providers do not enjoy equality with public authorities in terms of cooperation – this is evident by the very fact that they are subject to sanctions for infringements of their obligations under the Regulation. This lack of equality cannot underpin any meaningful relationship of mutual trust between public authorities and the private sector, which is placed largely in a subordinate position in terms of compliance with digital evidence requests from a public authority.[36] The draft Regulation did not include provisions on fundamental rights safeguards, but asking private companies to fully scrutinise these whilst at the same time facing the prospect of sanctions for non-compliance may prove to be a tall order.

The Commission's proposals challenged the fundamental architecture of judicial co-operation in criminal matters, by elevating the private sector into a central actor in the organisation and delivery of criminal justice. Privatisation and responsibilisation take a step further here: the private sector is not only required to cooperate with State authorities, but in doing so, it is essentially required to undertake fundamental rights assessments on each request for transfer of digital evidence to the State. It is questionable whether the private sector has the legitimacy, capacity or knowledge to undertake such assessment. The removal of a layer of judicial scrutiny of fundamental rights in judicial cooperation in criminal matters erodes fundamental rights and the rule of law and sits at odds with the growing fundamental rights safeguards introduced in the field of mutual recognition in criminal matters in the EU.

[34] See V Mitsilegas, 'The Privatisation of Mutual Trust in Europe's Area of Criminal Justice' (2018) 25 *Maastricht Journal of European and Comparative Law* 263.

[35] ibid.

[36] K Lenaerts, 'La vie après l'avis: Exploring the Principle of Mutual (yet not Blind) Trust' (2017) 54 *Common Market Law Review* 805.

The Commission proposals undermined these safeguards on the basis of unproven claims on the 'special nature' of digital evidence. From a rule of law perspective, the model of cooperation put forward by the Commission rests on mislabelling: it is not mutual recognition, and it is not judicial cooperation in criminal matters: rather, it is a scheme of public-private partnership at the borders between law enforcement and criminal justice.

It is unsurprising that the issue of fundamental rights scrutiny has arisen prominently in the negotiations to the proposal, and that at the time of writing it is one of the key stumbling blocks for agreement between the Council (which largely espoused the Commission proposal) and the European Parliament (which advocated stronger fundamental rights scrutiny standards). It took five years of negotiations for legislation to be eventually adopted in the summer of 2023.[37] The legislation has taken the form of a Regulation on a European Production and Preservation Order. The Regulation retains the model of public-private co-operation proposed by the Commission. European Production Orders and European Preservation Orders will be addressed directly to a designated establishment or to a legal representative of the service provider concerned.[38] This direct public-private cooperation model is tempered somewhat by the introduction – at the insistence of the European Parliament – of a notification procedure of the issuing of a European Production Order to the public authorities of the enforcing State.[39] The notification duty arises only in relation to Orders issued to obtain traffic data (except for data requested for the sole purpose of identifying the user) or to obtain content data[40] and even in these cases it does not arise under a series of circumstances.[41] The enforcing authority has 10 days to raise a ground for refusal[42] to execute the order; if such grounds for refusal are not raised, the addressee (the private company) must ensure that the requested data are transmitted directly to the issuing authority or the law enforcement authorities, as indicated in the Regulation, at the end of that 10-day period.[43]

The intervention of public authorities in the enforcing State is thus limited in scope and in time, and opportunities for fundamental rights scrutiny remain limited. The Regulation contains a chapter containing provisions on conflicts of law and remedies, but the provision on remedies for affected individuals[44] appears to be an afterthought – and follows in the text – to the detailed provision on conflicts of law,[45] which aims to give legal certainty to private providers in cases where EU law conflicts with the law of a third country. Fundamentally, the Regulation maintains the paradigm of direct public-private co-operation in the field of cross-border exchange of evidence, with private actors receiving requests directly from State authorities and transmitting evidence not only to judicial, but also to law enforcement authorities. For the reasons mentioned above, the Regulation has been adopted under an incorrect legal basis, Article 82(1) TFEU. The latter involves judicial co-operation between public authorities, and not public-private co-operation. The fundamental rights and public law safeguards underpinning the system of judicial co-operation and mutual recognition have been diluted.

[37] On the negotiations see T Christakis, 'From Mutual Trust to the Gordian Knot of Notifications: The EU E-Evidence Regulation and Directive' in V Franssen and S Tosza (eds), *The Cambridge Handbook of Digital Evidence in Criminal Matters* (Cambridge University Press, 2023).

[38] Regulation 2023/1543, Art 7(1).

[39] ibid, Art 8.

[40] ibid, Art 8(1).

[41] ibid, Art 8(2).

[42] ibid, as outlined in Art 12(1).

[43] ibid, Art 10(2).

[44] ibid, Art 18.

[45] ibid, Art 17.

IV. CROSS-BORDER EXCHANGE OF EVIDENCE IN A TRANSATLANTIC AND GLOBAL CONTEXT

This asymmetry between the public and the private sector in terms of cooperation in criminal matters raises a further fundamental rights concern when the European Production Order is viewed in a global context. The emergence of a privatised model of mutual trust as an EU benchmark may, in effect, lead to a race to the bottom in terms of fundamental rights protection at a global level. The European Production Order Regulation seems to be in line with the provisions in the recently adopted US Clarifying Lawful Overseas Use of Data (CLOUD) Act, which compels service providers to disclose all data in their possession regardless of the location of this data.[46] The CLOUD Act was adopted partly in response to the *Microsoft* litigation, where the requirement for the authorities of an EU Member State to approve a request for evidence by the US authorities via the MLA route was tested.[47] The CLOUD Act has three elements in common with the European Production Order Regulation: it attempts to bypass mutual legal assistance safeguards and the layers of fundamental rights scrutiny they entail; it establishes a direct link between public authorities and the private sector; and it bypasses the concept of territoriality in terms of the location of personal data. In this manner, transatlantic convergence leads to the development of a global level playing field privileging prosecutorial and law enforcement efficiency over fundamental rights concerns.[48] These efforts have not been accompanied by parallel efforts to create a global level playing field in the area of privacy and data protection, and it is only a matter of time before the limits to this new paradigm are exposed by courts, at least on this side of the Atlantic.

Attempts by the European Commission to change the internal EU paradigm of judicial cooperation in the field of digital evidence are inextricably linked with efforts to extend this paradigm at the transatlantic and global levels. In addition to the EU approach mirroring the US approach in the CLOUD Act, the Justice and Home Affairs Council has authorised the European Commission to negotiate agreements on digital evidence with the US.[49] In its Recommendation for a Council Decision, the Commission justified the opening of negotiations on the grounds that the current EU–US mutual legal assistance arrangements are too slow and that there is fragmentation in the applicable legal framework, with the transatlantic agreement aimed at complementing the internal EU digital evidence proposal by addressing conflicts of law.[50] The Agreement would aim to complement the protective standards set out in the EU–US Umbrella Agreement.[51] The adoption of the European Production Order Regulation has acted as a springboard for the reconvening of EU–US negotiations on this dossier.[52]

[46] For a background, see J Daskal, 'Unpacking the CLOUD Act' (2018) 11 *Eucrim* 220. For a critical analysis see N Singh Giuliani, 'The US Cloud Act Legislation that is Bad for Human Rights' in Mitsilegas and Vavoula (eds) (n 31), 83.

[47] For a background to the *Microsoft* saga, see CEPS, 'Access to Electronic Data by Third-Country Law Enforcement Authorities. Challenges to EU Rule of Law and Fundamental Rights' (July 2015) https://www.ceps.eu/ceps-publications/access-electronic-data-third-country-law-enforcement-authorities-challenges-eu-rule-law/#:~:text=Challenges%20to%20EU%20Rule%20of%20Law%20and%20Fundamental%20Rights&text=A%20key%20challenge%20for%20the,Legal%20Assistance%20(MLA)%20treaties, accessed 29 February 2024.

[48] V Mitsilegas, 'Conceptualising Impunity in the Law of the European Union' in S Montaldo and L Marin (eds), *The Fight Against Impunity in EU Law* (Hart Publishing, 2020) 13.

[49] Justice and Home Affairs Council adopted conclusions on 6/7 June 2019.

[50] Commission, 'Recommendation of a Council Decision authorising opening of negotiations between the EU and the US on cross-border access to electronic evidence for judicial cooperation in criminal matters' COM (2019) 70 final, 1–4.

[51] ibid, 10.

[52] Commission, 'EU–U.S. announcement on the resumption of negotiations on an EU-U.S. agreement to facilitate access to electronic evidence in criminal investigations' (2023), https://commission.europa.eu/news/eu-us-announcement-resumption-negotiations-eu-us-agreement-facilitate-access-electronic-evidence-2023-03-02_en, accessed 29 February 2024.

The role of the EU in developing a transatlantic and global level playing field regarding digital evidence is noteworthy. Unlike the development of the passenger name record (PNR) system (where the EU responded to the unilateral imposition of US domestic law requirements via the conclusion of transatlantic agreements, and then internalised this paradigm in EU law),[53] here the EU develops internal legislation first (mirroring US legislation in the field), and negotiates a transatlantic level playing field in parallel, while using its power within the Council of Europe to establish a global level playing field on digital evidence through the adoption of the Second Protocol to the Council of Europe Cyber-Crime Convention.[54] This strategy is problematic from both a fundamental rights and a rule of law perspective. From a fundamental rights perspective, it advocates a new paradigm of privatisation, which results in the transfer to the State of everyday personal data, disregarding the key EU law benchmarks of judicial authorisation and judicial independence. From a rule of law perspective, the EU is part of efforts to globalise this system, which would undermine its internal human rights benchmarks and values, which the EU is bound to apply in its external action.

The EU has opted to establish a transatlantic level playing field via the conclusion of a sectoral agreement, notwithstanding the established concerns on the adequacy of the US privacy and data protection system and its limited compatibility with EU law. At the same time, the EU has chosen to negotiate standards on digital evidence – which would have profound fundamental rights consequences – within the framework of a Council of Europe instrument whose principal aim is not to protect fundamental rights, and which is not exclusively focused on mutual legal assistance. Regional standards with a global reach will be developed by an instrument framed as a 'cybercrime' proposal; however, the exclusive framing of digital evidence as a cybercrime issue is misleading and may lead to limited scrutiny of the fundamental rights implications of the relaxation of safeguards in mutual legal assistance and to the introduction of lower standards through the back door. The EU external action in the global, digital context must not undermine the very values upon which the EU claims to be based, values which the EU must uphold and promote in its external action.

V. CONCLUSION: THE PERILS OF MISLABELLING AND THE CHALLENGE OF SAFEGUARDING FUNDAMENTAL RIGHTS IN EUROPE'S AREA OF CRIMINAL JUSTICE

The evolution of the EU legal framework on the cross-border exchange of evidence in criminal matters reveals a game of two halves with regard to the protection of fundamental rights. The first half consisted of the development of advanced, mature mutual recognition standards resulting in the adoption of the EIO Directive. This instrument contains the tools to achieve effective, speedy cooperation while at the same time taking full account of the requirement to meaningfully respect and uphold fundamental rights in Europe's area of criminal justice. Yet these fundamental rights safeguards have been diluted in the second half, through the adoption of the Regulation on the European Production Order, which represents a fundamental paradigm shift in the field. The Commission proposal on the European Production Order – largely backed by the Council – has been led by a highly securitised agenda and justified on the basis

[53] On the development of PNR standards, see V Mitsilegas, 'Immigration Control in an Era of Globalisation: Deflecting Foreigners, Weakening Citizens Strengthening the State' (2012) 19 *Indiana Journal of Global Legal Studies* 3.

[54] Second Additional Protocol to the Cybercrime Convention on enhanced co-operation and disclosure of electronic evidence (CETS No 224) – The Council of Europe Convention on Cybercrime is open to States beyond Council of Europe members.

of the scarcely substantiated claim that the digital is a 'special case' which justifies change to the existing approach to judicial cooperation and mutual legal assistance. The eventually adopted Regulation represents a profound paradigm change in the delivery of criminal justice, by dispensing to a great extent with the 'publicness' of the criminal justice process and establishing a model of criminal justice via public-private partnership, elevating the private sector as a key actor of the criminal justice system.

This paradigm change poses profound challenges to fundamental rights and the rule of law in the EU, both internally and externally. Internally, the new paradigm of privatised criminal justice challenges key benchmarks of fundamental rights scrutiny in the field of judicial co-operation in criminal matters, benchmarks which were hard-fought and which had been improving over time. This paradigm is also problematic from a rule of law perspective, as it rests on what is essentially a mislabelling of the adopted legislation: the envisaged paradigm of public-private partnership does not constitute judicial cooperation in criminal matters, or mutual recognition, as these constitute forms of interaction between public – and in the EU judicial – authorities which can guarantee effective protection of fundamental rights in the criminal justice process. The globalised dimension of this privatised paradigm poses additional challenges in terms of the external dimension of EU action. In the face of calls for a global level-playing field on digital evidence – calls not only by governments but by big global corporations which prioritise legal certainty at a global level in terms of their own legal duties – the EU is facing a key challenge of undermining its internal fundamental rights and rule of law benchmarks, benchmarks which the EU and its Member States are constitutionally obliged to uphold. By adopting the European Production Order Regulation, it appears that the interests of law enforcement and of the private sector, including the global tech companies, have taken precedence over the fundamental rights of affected individuals.

In view of these profound challenges to our understanding of criminal justice and for the protection of fundamental rights and the rule of law, the time has come to rethink the current executive orthodoxy on digital evidence and to consider seriously ways in which existing tried and tested legislation may provide solutions to the aims the digital evidence proposals are stated to claim to achieve. The stated aims of the European Production Order Regulation could have been achieved by the tried and tested EIO Directive, without the need to introduce a paradigm shift in judicial cooperation.[55] As seen above, this post-Lisbon Directive combines the objective of speed in judicial cooperation in criminal matters with a high level of fundamental rights scrutiny included in the grounds for refusal to recognise and execute an EIO. The requirement for speed dominating the European Production Order proposals and Regulation can be addressed by providing further resources for the implementation of the EIO Directive and by the digital enhancement of the EIO Directive, which is already taking place, combined with a framework of preservation of evidence in accordance with the Charter. In this manner, the publicness of judicial cooperation in criminal matters could be maintained while a speedy system of cooperation could still be achieved. In the current system, after the adoption of the European Production Order Regulation, there is a risk that the EIO Directive will become largely obsolete, at least as regards digital data. It remains to be seen how EU fundamental rights and access to justice benchmarks, as developed by the ECJ in case law such as *Gavanozov II*, will continue to be upheld in the context of the changed paradigm of the European Production Order.

[55] See also the findings in S Carrera et al, *Cross-Border Data Access in Criminal Proceedings and the Future of Digital Justice* (CEPS/QMUL Task Force, 2020).

In the field of external relations, bolstering the role of the EU and its criminal justice bodies and agencies (Eurojust, EPPO) in relations with third countries – via more centralised and digitalised mechanisms of mutual legal assistance led by the EU – will go a long way towards addressing concerns in terms of delays in the system. Crucially, in this manner the publicness and fundamental rights scrutiny elements of the system will be maintained, avoiding the risk of almost automatic, routine transfer of evidence to third States by private authorities. The watering down of the 'publicness' element in internal EU law challenges upholding EU fundamental rights in the context of transatlantic cooperation. In developing external action on cross-border exchange of evidence, the EU must strive towards maintaining the publicness of the system in terms of upholding and scrutinising meaningfully fundamental rights safeguards; it must also focus on upholding the rule of law by desisting from mislabelling cross-border exchange of evidence under broad terms such as 'cybercrime', whose meaning can be opaque and which can blur the boundaries between judicial cooperation and mutual legal assistance on the one hand, and security and surveillance on the other.

22

Data Protection in the Area of Freedom, Security and Justice

PETER GEORGE XUEREB AND BUCURA C MIHĂESCU-EVANS*

I. INTRODUCTION

THE ENTRY INTO force of the Lisbon Treaty marked a paradigm shift as regards the very objectives of the European Union (EU). Indeed, Article 3 of the Treaty on European Union (TEU), which sets out the EU's key objectives, solemnly declares in its very first paragraph, that the 'Union's aim is to promote peace, its values and the well-being of its peoples'. In addition, Article 3 attaches greater importance to the creation of an area of freedom, security and justice (AFSJ), as this aim is mentioned even before that of establishing an internal market.[1]

The entry into force of the Lisbon Treaty also decisively marked the EU's commitment to fundamental rights, by conferring binding legal force on the Charter of Fundamental Rights of the European Union (the Charter).[2] The latter, which is commonly referred to as the 'Bill of rights' of the EU,[3] explicitly emphasises, in Recital 2 of its Preamble, that the Union places the individual at the heart of its activities, by, inter alia, creating an AFSJ. In order to strengthen the protection of the individual in the light of changes in society, social progress and scientific and technological developments,[4] the Charter enshrined, amongst other things, the protection of personal data as a fundamental right in the EU legal order.[5]

Furthermore, a specific legal basis for data protection was provided for in Article 16 of the Treaty on the Functioning of the European Union (TFEU), allowing thereby for the establishment of comprehensive and coherent Union legislation on the protection of individuals with regard to the processing of their personal data and the free movement of such data.

* Peter George Xuereb, Judge at the European Court of Justice and Professor of European Union and Comparative Law, University of Malta; Bucura C Mihăescu-Evans, Legal Secretary at the European Court of Justice. All opinions expressed herein are personal to the authors and do not engage the responsibility of the CJEU.

[1] See Art 3, paras 2 and 3, TEU.

[2] According to Art 6, para 1, TEU, the Charter shall have the same legal value as the Treaties.

[3] See eg K Lenaerts and E de Smijter, 'A "Bill of Rights" for the European Union' (2001) 38 *Common Market Law Review* 273.

[4] See, in this regard, Recital 4 of the Preamble of the Charter.

[5] Art 8 of the Charter. See also, in the same vein, Art 7 of the Charter, according to which 'Everyone has the right to respect for his or her private and family life, home and communications'.

Building on these new legal possibilities, the Commission launched, as early as 2009, a review of the existing legal framework.[6] In a Communication released in 2010, it put forward its approach for modernising the EU's legal system for the protection of personal data in all areas of the Union's activities, taking into account, in particular, the challenges resulting from globalisation and new technologies, so as to continue to guarantee a high level of protection of individuals with regard to the processing of personal data in all areas of the Union's activities. According to the Commission, this would allow the EU to remain a driving force in promoting high data protection standards worldwide.[7]

In parallel, the Stockholm Programme[8] that established the legislative Roadmap in the AFSJ field for the period 2010–2014, explicitly listed, among the six main priorities, the reinforcement of data protection through a new comprehensive legal framework, as well as the incorporation of data protection into all EU policies, law enforcement, crime prevention and international relations. In the same line, the European Council conclusions of 26 and 27 June 2014, which set out the strategic agenda for legislative and operational planning within the AFSJ field for the period 2015–2020, listed among its three main priorities, the need to prevent and combat crime and terrorism, while also ensuring fundamental rights and values, including the protection of personal data. The European Council solemnly stressed in these conclusions that: 'In further developing the [AFSJ] over the [coming] years, it will be crucial to ensure the protection and promotion of fundamental rights, including data protection, whilst addressing security concerns [...] and to adopt a strong EU General Data Protection framework by 2015'.[9]

The agenda set out thereby led to the adoption, with a slight delay, on 27 April 2016, of the so-called 'EU data protection reform package',[10] made up of the General Data Protection Regulation (GDPR)[11] and the Data Protection Law Enforcement Directive (LED).[12]

These instruments, both intended to contribute to the completion of the AFSJ,[13] constitute a major step forward in establishing a comprehensive EU data protection regime within the EU. Yet, despite the herculean task that was carried out by the legislative institutions during the preparatory working of the GDPR and of the LED in order to achieve this goal, the data protection landscape is still split along multiple lines of fracture, the processing of personal data being also governed by various other layers of protection.

This chapter provides a quick overview of the various data protection instruments applicable in the EU criminal law enforcement context (Section II), before switching to a more in-depth assessment of the LED and of the first case law developments regarding the latter (Section III).

[6] For further details in this regard, see Commission, 'A comprehensive approach on personal data protection in the European Union' (Communication to the European Parliament, the Council, the Economic and Social Committee and the Committee of the Regions), COM (2010) 609 final, fnn 3 and 4.

[7] ibid, 5.

[8] The Stockholm Programme – An open and secure Europe serving and protecting citizens [2010] OJ C115/1.

[9] European Council, Conclusions, 26 and 27 June 2014, EUCO 79/14.

[10] See eg P de Hert and V Papakonstantinou, 'The New Police and Criminal Justice Data Protection Directive: A First Analysis' (2016) 7 *New Journal of European Criminal Law* 7.

[11] Regulation (EU) 2016/679 of the European Parliament and of the Council on the protection of natural persons with regard to the processing of personal data and on the free movement of such data, and repealing Directive 95/46/EC (General Data Protection Regulation) [2016] OJ L119/1.

[12] Directive (EU) 2016/680 of the European Parliament and of the Council on the protection of natural persons with regard to the processing of personal data by competent authorities for the purposes of the prevention, investigation, detection or prosecution of criminal offences or the execution of criminal penalties, and on the free movement of such data, and repealing Council Framework Decision 2008/977/JHA [2016] OJ L 119/89.

[13] See Recitals 2 and 10 of the GDPR and Recital 2 of the LED.

II. THE COMPOSITE NATURE OF THE EU DATA PROTECTION LEGAL FRAMEWORK IN THE AFSJ

If the GDPR and the LED are to be considered the main plinths of EU data protection within the AFSJ, various other legal instruments, of both sectoral and general nature, also come into play when it comes to the processing and exchange of personal data in the criminal law enforcement context.

Regarding the sectoral instruments, it should first be noted that the patchwork of data protection rules adopted under the former third pillar, such as the Council Decisions on the stepping up of cross-border cooperation, particularly in combating terrorism and cross-border crime (Prüm Decisions)[14] and Council Framework Decision 2006/960/JHA on simplifying the exchange of information and intelligence between law enforcement authorities of the Member States of the EU[15] are still applicable laws, each of them containing specific rules regarding the processing and/or exchange of personal data.[16]

According to Article 60 of the LED, the specific provisions for the protection of personal data contained in EU legal acts previously adopted in the field of judicial cooperation in criminal matters and police cooperation should remain unaffected by the entry into force of this Directive. Yet, it stems from Article 62(6) of the LED that the Commission is expected to review the various EU legal acts that regulate processing by the competent authorities for law enforcement purposes, including those acts that are referred to in Article 60, in order to assess the need to align them with this Directive and to make, where appropriate, the necessary proposals to amend those acts so as to ensure a consistent approach to the protection of personal data within the scope of the LED. In a Communication issued in 2020, entitled 'Way forward on aligning the former third pillar *acquis* with data protection rules', the Commission identified 10 EU legal acts that should be amended in order to be aligned with the LED, and set out a timetable for this work.[17]

Second, the GDPR and the LED do not replace, or cover, per se, data processing by the various EU bodies, offices and agencies that have been set up to help oversee policies in a large number of areas of the AFSJ, such as Europol, Eurojust and the EU Agency for the Operational Management of Large-Scale IT Systems in the AFSJ. The processing and exchange of data by these bodies, offices and agencies of the Union are governed by separate Regulations containing specific data protection rules that take into consideration their particular characteristics.[18]

If, in the current state of play, the data protection rules vary considerably among these various EU bodies, offices and agencies, according to their founding acts, a certain level of

[14] Council Decision 2008/615/JHA on the stepping up of cross-border cooperation, particularly in combating terrorism and cross-border crime [2008] OJ L210/1 and Council Decision 2008/616/JHA on the implementation of Decision 2008/615/JHA on the stepping up of cross-border cooperation, particularly in combating terrorism and cross-border crime [2008] OJ L210/12.

[15] [2006] OJ L386/89.

[16] For further details regarding the various sector-specific legislative instruments for police and judicial co-operation in criminal matters adopted at EU level before the entry into force of the LED, see Communication from the Commission to the European Parliament and the Council, entitled 'Overview of information management in the area of freedom, security and justice' COM (2010) 385 final.

[17] For further details in this respect, see Commission, 'Way forward on aligning the former third pillar acquis with data protection rules' (Communication to the European Parliament and the Council' COM (2020) 262 final, in particular, 5–12.

[18] See eg Chapter VI, entitled 'Data Protection Safeguards' of Regulation (EU) 2016/794 of the European Parliament and of the Council on the European Union Agency for Law Enforcement Cooperation (Europol) and replacing and repealing Council Decisions 2009/371/JHA, 2009/934/JHA, 2009/935/JHA, 2009/936/JHA and 2009/968/JHA (Europol Regulation) [2016] OJ L 135/53.

consolidation with the GDPR and, in particular, with the LED, is expected to be brought in within the coming years. Indeed, it stems from the latest piece of the EU data protection reform, ie Regulation 2018/1725 on the protection of natural persons with regard to the processing of personal data by the Union institutions, bodies, offices and agencies and on the free movement of such data[19] and in particular from Article 98 of this Regulation, read in the light of its Recitals 10–13, that the Commission is expected to conduct a review of the various legal acts which regulate the processing of operational personal data by Union bodies, offices or agencies when carrying out activities which fall within the scope of Chapter 4 or Chapter 5 of Title V of Part Three TFEU, in order to assess their consistency with the LED and, if necessary, amend their rules so as to align them with the latter.

Third, various EU databases in the AFSJ, such as those containing the passenger name record, the Schengen Information System, the EURODAC and the Visa Information System are governed by specific legal instruments, each of them containing particular provisions regarding the processing and/or exchange of personal data.[20] If these various databases have long been separated and characterised, inter alia, by the fact that access to them was limited to the purposes for which each of them had been established, a change in approach was marked by the entry into force of the 'Interoperability Regulations',[21] which aimed, in essence, to ease and improve information-sharing among the various existing databases. According to Aden, these Regulations constitute a 'paradigm shift for purpose limitation as a core element of data protection', while also 'add[ing] to the already regulatory fragmentation and (over-)complexity [of the AFSJ databases]'.[22]

Finally, various EU instruments of a general nature, such as the Directive on privacy and electronic communications[23] and the new legislative package aiming to facilitate and speed up access to electronic evidence used to investigate and prosecute criminal offences, regardless of the location of the data,[24] as well as certain international data protection instruments,[25] are also likely to come into play when it comes to the processing and exchange of personal data in the criminal law enforcement context.

[19] Regulation (EU) 2018/1725 of the European Parliament and of the Council repealing Regulation (EC) no 45/2001 and Decision 1247/2002/EC [2018] OJ L 295/39.

[20] For further details regarding these various databases, see, eg Commission Communication (n 16).

[21] Regulation (EU) 2019/817 of the European Parliament and of the Council of 20 May 2019 on establishing a framework for interoperability between EU information systems in the field of borders and visa and amending Regulations (EC) No 767/2008, (EU) 2016/399, (EU) 2017/2226, (EU) 2018/1240, (EU) 2018/1726 and (EU) 2018/1861 of the European Parliament and of the Council and Council Decisions 2004/512/EC and 2008/633/JHA [2019] OJ L135/27; and Regulation (EU) 2019/818 of the European Parliament and of the Council of 20 May 2019 on establishing a framework for interoperability between EU information systems in the field of police and judicial cooperation, asylum and migration and amending Regulations (EU) 2018/1726, (EU) 2018/1862 and (EU) 2019/816 [2019] L135/85. Each of these regulations contain specific data protection rules for the interoperability approach (see Chapter VII of each of these Regulations, entitled 'Data Protection').

[22] H Aden, 'Interoperability Between EU Policing and Migration Databases: Risks for Privacy' (2020) 26 *European Public Law* 93.

[23] Directive 2002/58/EC of the European Parliament and of the Council concerning the processing of personal data and the protection of privacy in the electronic communications sector [2002] OJ L201/37, that is applicable in the the criminal law enforcement context, when processing obligations are imposed on providers of electronic communications services (for further details in this regard, see Joined Cases C-511/18, C-512/18 and C-520/18 *La Quadrature du Net and Others*, ECLI:EU:C:2020:791, paras 95–104).

[24] Regulation (EU) 2023/1543 of the European Parliament and of the Council on European Production Orders and European Preservation Orders for electronic evidence in criminal proceedings and for the execution of custodial sentences following criminal proceedings [2023] OJ L191/118; and Directive (EU) 2023/1544 of the European Parliament and of the Council laying down harmonised rules on the designation of designated establishments and the appointment of legal representatives for the purpose of gathering electronic evidence in criminal proceedings [2023] OJ L191/181.

[25] See Council of Europe, Convention for the protection of individuals with regard to automatic processing of personal data, adopted in Strasbourg on 28 January 1981 and ratified by all the EU Member States. Also known

The assessment of the interplay of these various general and sector-specific legal acts with respect to the processing and exchange of personal data is beyond the scope of this chapter. Further clarifications and guidance in this respect will, most probably, gradually be provided by the European Court of Justice (ECJ) according to the preliminary references that may be lodged before it in the years to come.

III. THE DATA PROTECTION LAW ENFORCEMENT DIRECTIVE AS THE CORNERSTONE FOR DATA PROTECTION IN THE EU'S SECURITY POLICY

As pointed out by Advocate General Pitruzzella in his Opinions delivered in two recent data protection related cases, 'when put at the service of criminal repression, technological development reveals itself as fascinating as it is threatening with regard to fundamental rights'.[26] According to him, the balance to be struck in the:

> [current] data age between the individual and society, more particularly, between the former's protection of privacy and personal data and the latter's fundamental interests, such as those of combating terrorism and preventing crime, 'embodies one of the principal dilemmas of contemporary liberal democratic constitutionalism'.[27]

For some voices in the debate, the entry into force of the LED has shown that it was possible to achieve high privacy and data protection standards while processing personal data for law enforcement purposes in a rather flexible way. Thereby, it would be instrumental to shift the public debate from the false '*privacy vs security*' paradigm, according to which these two desiderata are not simultaneously achievable.[28]

In the same line of reasoning, the Commission stressed in a Communication issued in 2020 'On the EU Security Union Strategy', that:

> [s]ecurity and respect for fundamental rights are not conflicting aims, but consistent and complementary. [EU] values and fundamental rights must be the basis of security policies, ensuring the principles of necessity, proportionality and legality, and with the right safeguards for accountability and judicial redress, while enabling an effective response to protect individuals, particularly the most vulnerable.[29]

Furthermore, in its first report on the application and functioning of the LED, the Commission declared that the LED was the main instrument for ensuring data protection in the EU's

as 'Convention 108', this Convention is the only binding global agreement on data protection. A modernising protocol amending that Convention was drawn up in 2018. By Council Decision 2019/682 of 9 April 2019 authorising Member States to ratify, in the interest of the European Union, the Protocol amending the Council of Europe Convention for the Protection of Individuals with regard to Automatic Processing of Personal Data [2019] OJ L115/7, the EU Member States were authorised to ratify that protocol, insofar as its provisions fall within the exclusive competence of the EU. In addition, for activities coming within the area of police and judicial cooperation, all EU Member States have subscribed to the Council of Europe Recommendation No R (87) 15, which sets out the principles of Convention 108 for the police sector. This is not, however, a legally binding instrument.

[26] Opinion of AG Pitruzzella in Case C-205/21 *Ministerstvo na vatreshnite raboti (Recording of biometric and genetic data by the police)*, ECLI:EU:C:2022:507, para 1.

[27] Opinion of AG Pitruzzella in Case C-817/19 *Ligue des droits humains*, ECLI:EU:C:2022:65, para 2.

[28] See, for example, P de Hert and J Sajfert, 'Police, Privacy and Data Protection from a Comparative Legal Perspective' in M den Boer (ed), *Comparative Policing from a Legal Perspective* (Edward Elgar, 2018) 306.

[29] Communication from the Commission to the European Parliament, the European Council, the Council, the European Economic and Social Committee and the Committee of the Regions, entitled 'On the EU Security Union Strategy' COM (2020) 605 final.

security policy,[30] before arguing that an effective and genuinely secure EU could only be built on the basis of full compliance with the fundamental rights enshrined in the Charter and secondary EU legislation. According to it, '[t]he LED makes a key contribution to the EU's security policy by ensuring that the personal data of victims, witnesses and suspects of crime are duly protected'.[31]

As emerges from Recitals 10 and 11 of this Directive, as well as from Declaration No 21 annexed to the Final Act of the Intergovernmental Conference that adopted the Treaty of Lisbon to which these Recitals refer, by the adoption of the LED, the EU legislature has sought to adopt rules corresponding to the specific features which characterise the activities carried out by the competent authorities in the fields of judicial cooperation in criminal matters and police cooperation, 'because of the specific nature of these fields'. In order to take into account the latter, the need to strike a balance between individual data protection and the interests of the police and criminal justice process inspired the entire content of the LED. Indeed, on the one hand, this Directive allows limits to be placed on certain data subject rights[32] and on the information a data controller must provide to the data subject in relation to personal data that has been processed.[33] On the other hand, it contains various specific provisions aiming at addressing the risks linked to the processing of personal data in the criminal law enforcement context, by obliging the Member States, for instance, to comply with specific security requirements,[34] to enable the data protection controller to make a clear distinction between personal data of different categories of data subjects,[35] or to provide for the possibility for the data subject's rights to be exercised indirectly through the supervisory authority.[36]

It is not within the reach of the present chapter to delve into all these issues. The following sections confine themselves to addressing the following two aspects: (a) the objective and scope of application of the LED; and (b) the lawfulness of processing of personal data.

A. Objective and Scope of the LED

It stems from Article 1 of the LED, read in the light of its Recitals 2, 4, 7 and 15, that this Directive has a two-fold objective, ie on the one hand, to ensure effective cooperation in the law enforcement context by facilitating the free flow of personal data between the competent authorities[37] of the EU Member States and to contribute, thereby, to the completion of the AFSJ, as well as, on the other hand, to establish a common framework for the protection of personal data, where such data are processed by the police and judicial authorities in criminal matters, including in domestic matters.

In an unprecedented and rather ambitious way, having regard to the significant differences existing between the Member States in the fields of police and criminal justice, which historically fall within their national sovereignty, the EU legislature has extended the scope of the LED beyond that of Framework Decision 2008/977/JAI, which it repealed and replaced, and

[30] Communication from the Commission to the European Parliament and the Council, entitled 'First report on application and functioning of the Data Protection Law Enforcement Directive (EU) 2016/680 (LED)' COM (2022) 364 final, para 1.

[31] ibid, para 1.2.

[32] See, in particular, Arts 15 and 16 of the LED.

[33] Art 13 of the LED.

[34] Art 29 of the LED.

[35] Art 6 of the LED.

[36] Art 17 of the LED.

[37] Within the meaning of Art 3(7) of the LED.

which was limited to cross-border data flows.[38] Indeed, according to its Article 2(1), the LED applies, *in a general manner*, to the processing of personal data by the EU Member States' competent authorities in the criminal law enforcement context, when they carry out activities for the purposes set out in Article 1 of the Directive, namely for the purposes of the prevention, investigation, detection or prosecution of criminal offences or the execution of criminal penalties, including the safeguarding against and the prevention of threats to public security (LED purposes).

According to Article 2(1) of the LED, read in the light of its Recitals 12 to 14, the scope of the Directive is defined by two key elements, namely by the notion of 'competent authority' (personal scope) and by that of 'criminal offence' (material scope). Both these elements are to be interpreted in light of 'the purposes set out in Article 1(1)' of the LED for which personal data are processed in the criminal law enforcement context.[39]

While Article 3(7) of the LED provides for a definition of the first notion,[40] Recital 13 of the Directive merely states, as regards the second notion, that '[a] criminal offence within the meaning of this Directive should be an autonomous concept of Union law as interpreted by the [CJEU]'. In this latter respect, it stems from consistent case law that the terms of a provision of EU law which makes no express reference to the law of the Member States for the purpose of determining its meaning and scope must normally be given an autonomous and uniform interpretation throughout the EU.[41] The ECJ has already clarified in recent case law related to the interpretation of Article 10 of the GDPR, with reference being made to Recital 13 of the LED, that the notion of 'criminal offence' for the purposes of this provision of the GDPR requires an autonomous and uniform interpretation throughout the EU, having regard to the objective pursued by that provision and the context of which it forms part; the classification given by the Member State concerned to those offences is not conclusive in that regard as the classification may vary from one country to another.[42] Besides, further guidance in this respect is likely to be provided in the currently pending Cases C-178/22 *Procura della Repubblica presso il Tribunale di Bolzano and Others* and C-241/22 *DX (Accès aux données conservées par les fournisseurs à des fins contractuelles)*. As to the intrinsic aspect of both the personal and material scopes of the LED, related to the fact that the processing of personal data is to be carried out 'for the purposes set out in Article 1(1)' of this Directive (LED purposes), it should be remembered that, according to Article 2 of the GDPR, read in light of its Recital 19, the processing of personal data for all other non-LED purposes falls under the scope of the GDPR. If, for some, the latter constitutes a 'safety net' when the LED does not apply,[43] various doubts have been raised as regards the demarcation between the respective scopes of these two instruments.[44]

[38] See, to that effect, Recitals 7–9 of Council Framework Decision 2008/977/JAI on the protection of personal data processed in the framework of police and judicial cooperation in criminal matters [2008] OJ L350/60 and Recital 6 of the LED.

[39] This consideration is corroborated, in essence, by the assertion stressed by the ECJ in Case C-439/19 *Latvijas Republikas Saeima (Penalty points)*, ECLI:EU:C:2021:504, para 70, such as reminded in *Valsts ieņēmumu dienests (Processing of personal data for tax purposes)*, ECLI:EU:C:2022:124, at para 43, and by the *a contrario* interpretation of Case C-505/19 *Bundesrepublik Deutschland (Interpol red notice)*, ECLI:EU:C:2021:376, para 117.

[40] Further guidance in this respect was provided by the ECJ in *Bundesrepublik Deutschland (Interpol red notice)* (n 39), para 117; *Latvijas Republikas Saeima (Penalty points)* (n 39), paras 69–71; as well as in Case C-175/20 *Valsts ieņēmumu dienests (Processing of personal data for tax purposes)* (n 39), paras 42–44.

[41] See eg Cases C-287/98 *Linster*, ECLI:EU:C:2000:468, para 43; and C-673/17 *Planet49*, ECLI:EU:C:2019:801, para 47.

[42] See *Latvijas Republikas Saeima (Penalty points)* (n 39), paras 84–85 and case law cited.

[43] See N Purtova, 'Between the GDPR and the Police Directive: Navigating through the Maze of Information-sharing in Public-private Partnership' (2018) 8 *International Data Privacy Law* 52, 62.

[44] For further details in this regard, see eg COM (2022) 364 (n 30), fnn 42–44.

A number of clarifications in this respect have already been provided by the ECJ in *Valsts ieņēmumu dienests (Processing of personal data for tax purposes)*,[45] *Ligue des droits humains*,[46] *Inspektor v Inspektorata kam Visshia sadeben savet (Purposes of the processing of personal data – Criminal investigation)*[47] and *Ministerstvo na vatreshnite raboti (Recording of biometric and genetic data by the police)*.[48]

Furthermore, the issue of the LED's scope of application is the subject of some currently pending cases before the ECJ, where the court is invited to interpret, inter alia, whether the LED is applicable to the circumstances of a case where a competent authority unsuccessfully tried to access data on a seized phone[49] and to those of a case concerning a European Investigation Order in criminal matters issued by an EU Member State in order to obtain the transfer of evidence already in the possession of another Member State.[50]

B. Principles and Lawfulness of Processing

According to Article 3(2) of the LED, 'processing' means, for the purposes of the Directive:

> any operation or set of operations which is performed on personal data or on sets of personal data, whether or not by automated means, such as collection, recording, organisation, structuring, storage, adaptation or alteration, retrieval, consultation, use, disclosure by transmission, dissemination or otherwise making available, alignment or combination, restriction, erasure or destruction.

Under Article 4(1)(a) and (b) of the LED, headed 'Principles relating to processing of personal data', Member States must, inter alia, provide for personal data to be, first, processed lawfully and fairly, and, second, collected for specified, explicit and legitimate purposes and not processed in a manner that is incompatible with those purposes. Furthermore, Articles 9 and 10 of the LED incorporate some specific processing principles and conditions related, inter alia, to the protection of sensitive data.

According to Article 8(1) of the LED, entitled 'Lawfulness of processing', processing shall be lawful only if and to the extent that it is necessary for the performance of a task carried out by a competent authority for the purposes set out in Article 1(1) and is based on Union or Member State law.

The question of lawfulness of processing under the LED has already been raised before the ECJ in three main cases, each of them dealing with different aspects of this Directive.

In the very first case lodged under the LED,[51] the ECJ was invited to examine, amongst other issues, the lawfulness of processing personal data in the specific context of a red notice issued by the International Criminal Police Organisation (Interpol), and, more particularly, whether the data protection rules set by this Directive were to be interpreted as allowing a person to request erasure of his or her personal data appearing in such a red notice when the

[45] *Valsts ieņēmumu dienests (Processing of personal data for tax purposes)* (n 40), paras 39–47 and case law cited.

[46] Case C-817/19 *Ligue des droits humains*, ECLI:EU:C:2022:491, paras 63–84 and case law cited.

[47] Case C-180/21 *Inspektor v Inspektorata kam Visshia sadeben savet (Purposes of the processing of personal data – Criminal investigation)*, ECLI:EU:C:2022:967, paras 69–82 and case law cited.

[48] Case C-205/21 *Ministerstvo na vatreshnite raboti (Recording of biometric and genetic data by the police)*, ECLI:EU:C:2023:49, paras 61–73 and case law cited.

[49] Case C-548/21 *CG (Tentative d'accès aux données personnelles stockées sur un téléphone portable)*, pending; Opinion of AG Campos Sánchez-Bordona in Case C-548/21 *CG (Tentative d'accès aux données personnelles stockées sur un téléphone portable)*, ECLI:EU:C:2023:313.

[50] Case C-670/22 *MN (EncroChat)*, pending; Opinion of AG Ćapeta in Case C-670/22 *MN (EncroChat)* ECLI:EU:C:2023:817, in particular, paras 100–102.

[51] *Bundesrepublik Deutschland (Interpol red notice)* (n 40).

ne bis in idem principle was likely to apply. In that judgment, the ECJ clarified that the recording of personal data in a Member State's list of wanted persons constituted 'processing' falling under the LED. Additionally, it found that the processing in issue pursued a legitimate objective and that it could not be regarded as unlawful solely on the ground that the *ne bis in idem* principle might apply to the acts on which that red notice was based. As to the operation of transmission of those data by Interpol, the ECJ noted that, since that organisation was not a 'competent authority' in the meaning of Article 3(7) of that Directive, that operation could not be considered as constituting 'processing' for the purposes of the LED.[52]

In *Inspektor v Inspektorata kam Visshia sadeben savet (Purposes of the processing of personal data – Criminal investigation)*,[53] the ECJ was invited, inter alia, to decide whether the processing of personal data served a purpose other than that for which those data were collected, where the collection was carried out for the purpose of the detection and investigation of a criminal offence, in relation to which the data subject was regarded as a victim at the time of that collection, whereas the subsequent processing was carried out for the purpose of prosecuting that person at the end of the criminal investigation; the referring court also asked whether such treatment was permitted. Although these questions were formally confined to the interpretation of Article 1(1) of the LED, the ECJ extended the scope of the analysis to include Articles 4(2) and (6) thereof. While taking into account the wording of those provisions, their context, their purpose and the legislative history of the LED, the ECJ considered, in essence, that where personal data were collected for the purpose of 'detection' and 'investigation' of a criminal offence and were further processed for the purpose of 'prosecution', that collection and that processing served different purposes. As regards the lawfulness of processing, the ECJ first recalled the two requirements set out in Article 4(1) of the LED, namely that personal data must be collected for specified, explicit and legitimate purposes and not be processed in a manner incompatible with those purposes and that personal data must be adequate, relevant and not excessive in relation to the purpose for which they were processed. It then observed that Article 4(2) of that Directive, read in the light of Recital 29 thereof, allowed nevertheless the subsequent processing of personal data for a purpose other than that for which those data were collected, provided that that purpose was one of those set out in Article 1(1) and that processing satisfied the two conditions laid down in Article 4(2)(a) and (b), namely, first, that the controller must be authorised to process those personal data for such a purpose in accordance with EU or Member State law and, second, that the processing must be necessary and proportionate to that other purpose.[54]

In *Ministerstvo na vatreshnite raboti (Recording of biometric and genetic data by the police)*,[55] the ECJ was invited to take position, inter alia, on the lawfulness of the processing of sensitive data,[56] more particularly, of biometric and genetic data, while also being requested to provide guidance as to the implications of the drawing of the distinction amongst personal data of different categories of data subjects provided for in Article 6(a) of the LED. In its judgment, the ECJ explained, first of all, the conditions under which the processing of biometric and genetic data by the police authorities could be regarded as authorised by Member State law, within the meaning of the LED. It ruled, next, on the implementation of the requirement,

[52] See, in particular, ibid, paras 111, 114 and 117.

[53] *Inspektor v Inspektorata kam Visshia sadeben savet (Purposes of the processing of personal data – Criminal investigation)* (n 47).

[54] See, in particular, ibid, paras 44 and 50–51.

[55] *Ministerstvo na vatreshnite raboti (Recording of biometric and genetic data by the police)* (n 48).

[56] Further guidance in this respect is likely to be provided for in the upcoming judgment in Case C-118/22 *Direktor na Glavna direktsia 'Natsionalna politsia' pri MVR – Sofia*, currently pending before the ECJ.

set out in that Directive, concerning the processing of data of a category of persons with regard to whom there were serious grounds for believing that they were involved in a criminal offence, and on observance of the right to effective judicial protection and of the principle of the presumption of innocence where the national court having jurisdiction was permitted by national legislation to authorise the compulsory collection of those data, regarded as 'sensitive' by the EU legislature. It addressed, finally, the question whether national legislation providing for the systematic collection of those data was compatible with the provisions of the LED that relate to their processing, having regard to the principles applicable thereto.[57]

IV. CONCLUSION

This chapter highlights, in essence, that despite the underlying aim of Article 16 TFEU to establish a harmonised EU data protection regime, the data protection framework within the AFSJ is still, in the current state of play, of a 'composite' nature, the processing of personal data being divided amongst multiple layers of protection. Yet, the entry into force of the LED constitutes a major step forward in establishing a comprehensive EU data protection legal framework. Furthermore, it makes a key contribution to the EU's security policy, by ensuring that the personal data of victims, witnesses and suspects of crime are duly protected, while also taking into account the specific features which characterise the activities carried out by the competent authorities in the fields of judicial cooperation in criminal matters and police cooperation.

[57] For further details, see *Ministerstvo na vatreshnite raboti (Recording of biometric and genetic data by the police)* (n 48), para 82 ff.

23

Extradition from the EU: Gimme Shelter!

CHRISTOPHER VAJDA*

I. INTRODUCTION

IT IS A great pleasure and honour for me to be asked to contribute a chapter to the *Liber Amicorum* for Vice-President Bay Larsen.[1] He has made an immense contribution to the case law of the European Court of Justice (ECJ), particularly in the area of freedom, security and justice (AFSJ). His arrival at the ECJ in 2006 was shortly after the long-established rules on extradition were abolished within the EU by Council Framework Decision 2002/584/JHA (the EAW Framework Decision) which introduced the European Arrest Warrant (EAW).[2] In this chapter, I will examine how the ECJ has used both the rules of the Treaty on the Functioning of the European Union (TFEU) on free movement of persons and the EAW Framework Decision and EAW to create a protean code of EU law in the field of extradition to a third country. The novelty and importance of this development is illustrated by the fact that all eight cases discussed here are judgments of the Grand Chamber, delivered in the space of just over six years between 2016 and 2022.[3]

II. EXTRADITION FOR PROSECUTION: THE *PETRUHHIN* PRINCIPLE

A. The Basic Principles of Extradition

A useful description of the extradition process – now applicable only in the case of persons sought to be removed outside the EU – was given by the ECJ in *BY*:[4]

> It must be recalled that extradition is a procedure whose aim is to ensure that a person who is present in a territory other than that in which he or she has allegedly committed an offence does not go

* KC, Judge at the European Court of Justice (2012–2020). I am grateful for the assistance and comments I have been given by Csilla Fekete, a Legal Secretary at the ECJ. Any errors are wholly my own responsibility.

[1] Not everyone may know that Vice-President Bay Larsen is a Rolling Stones fan: see L Bay Larsen, 'Choices of Life and Law' (*Yale Law Journal*, 7 May 2019), https://www.theylj.co.uk/choices-of-life-and-law/, accessed 22 January 2024. 'Gimme Shelter' was released by the Rolling Stones in 1969, some three years after Lars Bay Larsen purchased his first Rolling Stones record, 'Paint it Black'.

[2] Council Framework Decision 2002/584/JHA on the European arrest warrant and the surrender procedure between Member States [2002] OJ L81/24.

[3] The first case, Case C-182/15 *Petruhhin*, ECLI:EU:C:2016:630 was decided in September 2016 and the last case, Case C-237/21 *SM v Generalstaatanwaltschaft München*, ECLI:EU:C:2022:1017 (*SM*) in December 2022.

[4] Case C-398/19 *BY v Generalstaatsanwaltschaft Berlin*, ECLI:EU:C:2020:1032 (*BY*), para 58.

unpunished. Although, in the light of the maxim *aut dedere, aut judicare* (either extradite or prosecute), the non-extradition of own nationals is generally counterbalanced by the possibility that the requested Member State may prosecute its own nationals for serious offences committed outside its territory, that Member State as a general rule has no jurisdiction to try cases concerning such offences when neither the perpetrator nor the victim of the alleged offence is a national of that Member State. Extradition thus ensures that offences committed in the territory of a State by persons who have fled that territory do not remain unpunished.

B. The *Petruhhin* Principle and its Limits

In *Petruhhin*, an Estonian national, Petruhhin, was subject of an Interpol Red Notice. He was arrested in Latvia. Russia sought to have him extradited for a drug trafficking offence. Under Latvian law, in essence, only Latvians were protected against extradition. The Latvian Supreme Court pointed out that the lack of protection for EU citizens against extradition when they have moved to a Member State other than the one of which they are nationals is contrary to the essence of the citizenship of the EU, that is to say, the right of EU citizens to protection equivalent to that of a Member State's own nationals. In contrast to the position adopted by the Advocate General,[5] the ECJ agreed that there was unequal treatment between EU citizens, which gave rise to a restriction of free movement within the meaning of Article 21 TFEU. Such unequal treatment needs justification, and the justification must satisfy the requirement of proportionality as well as that of mutual cooperation between Member States. Justification for non-extradition of a Member State's own nationals is based on the maxim *aut dedere aut judicare* (either extradite or prosecute), namely that generally a State is able to prosecute its own nationals but this does not apply to foreign nationals.

In the absence of any rules governing extradition between Latvia and Russia, the ECJ applied the principle of proportionality in the following manner:

> Consequently, in a case such as that at issue in the main proceedings, *the exchange of information with the Member State of which the person concerned is a national must be given priority* in order to afford the authorities of that Member State, in so far as they have jurisdiction, pursuant to their national law, to prosecute that person for offences committed outside national territory, the opportunity to issue a European arrest warrant for the purposes of prosecution. Article 1(1) and (2) of Framework Decision 2002/584 *does not preclude*, in such a case, the possibility for the Member State of which the alleged offender is a national of issuing a European arrest warrant with a view to the surrender of that person for the purposes of prosecution. (emphasis added)
>
> In cooperating accordingly with the Member State of which the person concerned is a national and *giving priority to that potential arrest warrant* over the extradition request, the host Member State acts in a manner which is less prejudicial to the exercise of the right to freedom of movement while avoiding, as far as possible, the risk that the offence prosecuted will remain unpunished.[6] (emphasis added)

The effect of this approach is to impose an obligation on the requested Member State (Member State A) to inform the Member State whose national is sought for extradition (Member State B)

[5] Opinion of AG Bot in Case C-182/15 *Petruhhin*, ECLI:EU:C:2016:330. AG Bot considered that the principle of equal treatment was not engaged since Latvian and non-Latvian nationals were not in the same situation, given that non-Latvians could not, unless permanently resident in Latvia, be prosecuted for crimes committed outside Latvia.

[6] *Petruhhin* (n 3), at paras 48 and 49. The Charter was also engaged as Petruhhin was exercising his rights under Art 18 and 21 TFEU, see paras 52–53. Where a request for extradition is made to a Member State from a third State, the Member State must verify that the conditions in Art 19(2) of the Charter are met.

whether it wishes to issue an EAW. If Member State B does wish to issue an EAW, Member State A must give priority to the EAW over the extradition request as this is a less prejudicial alternative to the exercise of the rights of free movement than extradition while at the same time avoiding the risk of impunity. But there is no obligation on Member State B to issue an EAW, even assuming Member State B has jurisdiction to do so. Thus, a citizen of one EU Member State who moves to another Member State still remains at risk of extradition to a third State for prosecution of an offence by the third State.[7] The author does not know whether Petruhhin was in fact prosecuted in Estonia. But there must have been a question as to whether the Estonian authorities had extra-territorial jurisdiction to do so, and if so, whether they had the available evidence.[8]

In *IN*, the ECJ was asked whether the principle in *Petruhhin* extends to European Economic Area (EEA) nationals.[9] Russia issued an international wanted persons notice for IN, a Russian national who had been granted asylum in Iceland on account of the criminal proceedings brought against him in Russia that were the subject of these extradition proceedings. Subsequently IN became an Icelandic national. He was then arrested when in Croatia. Croatia did not extradite its own nationals to Russia. The Croatian Supreme Court wished to know whether it was necessary, before considering whether the conditions for extradition of IN to Russia were satisfied, to inform Iceland so that it could, if it wished, seek the surrender of its national in order to bring proceedings to prevent the risk of impunity. There were two legal differences from *Petruhhin*. First, Articles 18 and 21 TFEU do not apply to Icelandic citizens. Second, neither does the EAW Framework Decision and hence the EAW procedure. However, the ECJ noted that Iceland had a:

> special relationship with the European Union, which goes beyond economic and commercial cooperation. It implements and applies the Schengen *acquis* ... but it is also a party to the EEA Agreement, participates in the common European asylum system and has concluded the agreement on the surrender procedure with the European Union.[10]

The first issue was whether there was a discrimination under the EEA Agreement, which required justification. The answer was yes. IN fell within the scope of EU law, as he was a beneficiary of the EEA Agreement. Article 4 of that Agreement prohibits any discrimination on grounds of nationality. National rules on extradition gave rise to unequal treatment on grounds of nationality, which required justification. This brought the ECJ on to the second issue,[11] namely whether there was an analogous obligation, pursuant to the *Petruhhin* principle, on an EU Member State to inform Iceland of that extradition request and to ask Iceland whether it wished to request the surrender of such a national pursuant to the Agreement on Surrender Procedure. Again, the answer was yes:

> Although Framework Decision 2002/584 does not apply to the Republic of Iceland, an EFTA State of which I.N. is a national, it must be recalled that that State, like the Kingdom of Norway, has concluded with the European Union the Agreement on the surrender procedure, which entered into force on 1 November 2019.

[7] This point is made very clearly in the Opinion of AG Richard de la Tour in Case C-237/21 *SM v Generalstaatanwaltschaft München*, ECLI:EU:C:2022:574, paras 41–45.

[8] See further Case C-191/16 *Pisciotti v Bundesrepublik Deutschland*, ECLI:EU:C:2018:222 and *BY* (n 4), the penultimate case discussed in this section.

[9] Case C-897/19 PPU *IN*, ECLI:EU:C:2020:262.

[10] ibid, para 44. Note the Surrender Agreement entered into force on 1 November 2019, some months after IN entered Croatia but before the Croatian Supreme Court made its reference on 28 November 2019.

[11] ibid, paras 70–76. There was also a distinct issue on the applicability of Art 19(2) of the Charter, see ibid, paras 63–69.

> As is clear from its preamble, that agreement seeks to improve judicial cooperation in criminal matters between, on the one hand, the Member States of the European Union and, on the other hand, the Republic of Iceland and the Kingdom of Norway, in so far as the current relationships among the contracting parties, characterised in particular by the fact that the Republic of Iceland and the Kingdom of Norway are part of the EEA, require close cooperation in the fight against crime.
>
> Furthermore, in the same preamble, the contracting parties to the Agreement on the surrender procedure have expressed their mutual confidence in the structure and functioning of their legal systems and their capacity to guarantee a fair trial.
>
> In addition, it must be observed that the provisions of the Agreement on the surrender procedure are very similar to the corresponding provisions of Framework Decision 2002/584.[12]

The reasoning here is more open textured than in *Petruhhin* given that the individual in question was not an EU citizen but the citizen of an EEA State. The ECJ considered that an EEA citizen benefited from the principle of non-discrimination and that the various arrangements on criminal justice, including notably the surrender agreement between Iceland and the EU, were similar enough to those under the EAW Framework Decision to lead to the same result.[13] Although the ECJ does not use the expression 'mutual trust', which is at the heart of the EAW Framework Decision, the surrender agreement refers to the parties 'mutual confidence in the structure and functioning of their legal systems and their capacity to guarantee a fair trial'. There are probably a number of third countries, for example, in no particular order other than alphabetical, such as Australia, Canada, New Zealand, the UK, the US, where it is likely that the EU has confidence in the structure and functioning of their legal systems and their capacity to guarantee a fair trial. However, nationals of those states are unlikely to benefit from *IN* as they have no right of free movement within the EU and cannot rely on the principle of non-discrimination in the same way as EEA nationals. Thus, a request for extradition by a third country to a Member State of such a national is not a restriction on any right to free movement that needs to be justified. In addition, there are no equivalent surrender agreements.

In *Pisciotti*,[14] an Italian national was arrested in Frankfurt pursuant to a request for extradition to the US pursuant to the EU–US Extradition Treaty (the EU–US Treaty) in order to face a criminal charge of having taken part in a worldwide marine hose cartel.[15] Article 16(2) of the Basic Law of Germany precludes a German national being extradited to a foreign country. By an Order dated 17 February 2014[16] the Bundesverfassungsgericht (BvfG) had summarily dismissed the argument that the prohibition of discrimination between EU citizens contained in Article 18 TFEU meant that an EU citizen was entitled to the same protection against extradition as a German citizen. It did so on the basis that such a prohibition did not apply to extradition to third States because that issue fell outside the scope of EU law.[17] It considered the matter so clear that there was no obligation to make a reference to the ECJ under Article 267(3) of the TFEU. After Pisciotti was extradited, pleaded guilty, served his sentence of imprisonment and was fined US$50,000 he brought a fresh action in Germany claiming damages for a sufficiently serious breach of EU law by Germany.

[12] ibid, paras 71–74.

[13] However, a Liechtenstein national would have been unlikely to benefit from *IN*, since there is no surrender agreement between the EU and Liechtenstein.

[14] *Pisciotti* (n 8).

[15] See Commission Decision https://ec.europa.eu/commission/presscorner/detail/en/IP_09_137, accessed 29 February 2024. Three individuals were subsequently successfully prosecuted in the UK for their participation in this cartel: see M Howe 'Executives jailed in marine hose cartel case' *The Guardian* (12 June 2008) https://www.theguardian.com/business/2008/jun/12/corporatefraud.ukcrime, accessed 29 February 2024.

[16] BVerfG, Beschluss der 2. Kammer des Zweiten Senats 2 BvQ 4/14 -, Rn 1-27.

[17] *Pisciotti* (n 8), para 26.

On this occasion, a reference was made to the ECJ.[18] The ECJ had little difficulty in finding that Pisciotti's case fell within scope of EU law as he had exercised his rights of free movement. This meant the discretion as to whether to extradite under EU–US Treaty had to be exercised in accordance with EU primary law.

Articles 18 and 21 TFEU therefore imposed an obligation on Germany to adopt a course of action which would be less prejudicial to Pisciotti's rights of free movement of persons by considering surrendering him to Italy rather than extraditing him to the US. The solution in *Petruhhin* (where there was no extradition treaty between the EU and a third country) was also applicable in the situation where there was an extradition agreement with a third country (as here), where there is no obligation to extradite a Member State's nationals.[19] The ECJ added, by reference to what had been said (or rather not said) in *Petruhhin*, that in order to safeguard the objective of preventing the risk of impunity, the EAW issued by a Member State other than the requested Member State must at least refer to the same offences, and the issuing Member State must have jurisdiction pursuant to its national law to prosecute that person for such offences even if committed outside its territory. Although the Italian authorities were kept informed by Germany of Pisciotti's situation before the US request for extradition, they did not issue an EAW.[20] Thus, there had been no breach by Germany of the *Petruhhin* principle.

The ECJ did not need to consider the location of the relevant evidence, witnesses, and the general ability of Italy to conduct a proper trial compared to the US. All the evidence and witnesses relating to the cartel offence was likely to have been in the US and to have been in English. Furthermore, even if there were a cartel offence in Italy, it is not certain that it would have been viewed with the same seriousness as in the US.[21] All these matters would fall within the discretion of the Italian authorities in deciding, even if they had jurisdiction, whether to issue an EAW for the trial to take place in Italy as opposed to the US.

The issue of available evidence did, however, raise its head in the next case, *BY*.[22] BY was a Romanian national who was arrested in Germany pursuant to an extradition request made by Ukraine under the European Convention on Extradition (ECE)[23] relating to a criminal prosecution in respect of the alleged misappropriation of funds of a Ukrainian State owned undertaking. Germany had made a declaration that extradition of German nationals would not be permitted as it was contrary to the German Basic Law. Following a request by the German court to the Romanian authorities as to whether they would bring a prosecution, the Romanian authorities replied that this depended on their being sufficient evidence of the guilt of BY. However, the relevant evidence was not part of the information that is required to accompany an extradition request under Article 12(2) of the ECE.

BY's case fell within the scope of EU law as there was unequal treatment, as between a German and Romanian national, as regards the proposed extradition of BY. The *Petruhhin* principle did not, however, go so far as obliging either the requested Member State or the Member State of which the EU national is a citizen to ask the third State requesting extradition to send them the criminal investigation file in order to enable the Member State of which that person is a national to assess the possibility that it might itself conduct a criminal prosecution.

[18] The reference was made by the Landgericht Berlin, which took a different view of the applicability of EU law than the BvfG. The reference was made on 18 March 2016, which was after the hearing in *Petruhhin* but before the delivery of the Opinion of the AG on 10 May 2016.

[19] Art 7(1) of the Germany US Extradition Treaty provides that Germany is not obliged to extradite its own nationals.

[20] *Pisciotti* (n 8), para 55 referring to para 52 of the Opinion of AG Bot in this case, ECLI:EU:C:2017:878.

[21] In fact, there is no indication that Italy had an offence in respect of individuals who engage in cartel offences.

[22] *BY* (n 4).

[23] European Convention on Extradition (Paris, 13 December 1957).

Hence, the obligation imposed by the *Petruhhin* principle on the requested Member State is limited to asking the Member State of which that person is a national whether such a State wishes to extradite him, but only on the basis of evidence available to that State. In the absence of the issue of an EAW, there is no obligation on the requested State to refuse extradition and prosecute itself even if its national law so permits.

This case highlights yet another important limitation on the *Petruhhin* principle. If the alleged crime is committed in a third State outside the jurisdiction of the national's Member State, that Member State is unlikely to have access to the evidence necessary to issue an EAW. Even if the third State has the evidence, it may not wish to hand that evidence over to a third country, namely the EU Member State whose nationality the person has, as the third State may well consider that, for a variety of reasons, including convenience of the witnesses, their protection (for example in a domestic violence, child abuse or informer case), and the language of the proceedings the prosecution should take place within its territory. If nevertheless an EAW is issued, the prosecution may be unsuccessful due to lack of evidence, whereas it may have been successful if the person had been extradited. So, unless carefully applied, the *Petruhhin* principle entails a risk of impunity. These are issues that can only properly be solved by amending the ECE and other extradition treaties

III. EXTRADITION FOR PROSECUTION: *NE BIS IN IDEM*

In *WS*, Interpol, at the request of the US, had published a red notice in respect of corruption proceedings against WS, a German national.[24] The effect of this notice was that WS should be located, detained or arrested with a view to his potential extradition to the US. WS argued that the US proceedings related to the same acts that had been the subject of German proceedings and had been settled with the German prosecutors. This meant that, as a matter of German law, no further criminal proceedings could be brought in Germany. However, he could not go to any other Member State without risking arrest. WS therefore brought an action against Germany requesting the red notice to be withdrawn. In essence, he argued that the existence of the red notice infringed the *ne bis in idem* principle found in Article 50[25] of the Charter of Fundamental Rights of the European Union (the Charter) and Article 54 of the Convention implementing the Schengen agreement (CISA).[26]

The ECJ had already decided that the *ne bis in idem* principle applies to a decision made other than in a criminal court, provided that the decision is based on the merits of the case and criminal proceedings are definitively discontinued.[27] The first main issue was therefore whether the term 'prosecuted' in Article 54 CISA covered a provisional arrest. The ECJ concluded that it did. In essence, the ECJ considered that the *ne bis in idem* principle in Article 54 CISA is intended to ensure that a person whose trial had been finally disposed of is not prosecuted

[24] Case C-505/19 *WS v Bundesrepublik Deutschland (Interpol red notice)*, ECLI:EU:C:2021:376.

[25] The article provides: 'No one shall be liable to be tried or punished again in criminal proceedings for an offence for which he or she has already been finally acquitted or convicted within the Union in accordance with the law'.

[26] The Convention implementing the Schengen Agreement of 14 June 1985 between the Governments of the States of the Benelux economic union, the Federal Republic of Germany and the French Republic on the gradual abolition of checks at their common borders [2000] OJ L239/19. Art 54, which is in Chapter 3 of CISA headed 'Application of the *ne bis in idem* principle', of Title III, provides: 'A person whose trial has been finally disposed of in one Contracting Party may not be prosecuted in another Contracting Party for the same acts provided that, if a penalty has been imposed, it has been enforced, is actually in the process of being enforced or can no longer be enforced under the laws of the sentencing Contracting Party.'

[27] See Joined Cases C-187/01 and C-385/01 *Gözütok* and *Brügge*, ECLI:EU:C:2003:87, cited at para 73 of *WS* (n 24).

for the same acts on account of his or her having exercised his or her right to free movement. However, while the principle of mutual trust requires a Contracting Party (A) to CISA to accept at face value a final decision communicated by the competent authorities of another Contracting Party (B), A must be in a position to satisfy itself, on the basis of documents provided by B, that the decision of the competent authorities in B constitutes a final decision, including a determination as to the merits of the case.

The second main issue was whether the *ne bis in idem* principle can justify a ground for refusal to extradite a person under the EU–US Treaty, even though there was no mention of that principle in that Treaty. The ECJ referred to Article 87 of the Interpol Rules, which provides that States are required to provisionally arrest a person who is the subject of a red notice only insofar as such a measure is 'permitted under national and applicable international treaties'. The ECJ took this to be a recognition in international law of the EU law *ne bis in idem* principle. So there was no conflict between international and EU law on this point.

In *HF*, a Serbian national, HF, had been remanded in custody in Germany pursuant to a red notice issued by Interpol at the request of the US, seeking to extradite him under the Germany–US Extradition Treaty in order to prosecute him for offences committed between September 2008 and December 2013.[28] The custody was challenged on the basis that it was contrary to the principle of *ne bis in idem* in Article 54 CISA (which applies across all Contracting Parties) in conjunction with Article 50 of the Charter,[29] as an earlier request made by the US to the Slovenian authorities to extradite HF had failed on the grounds that the acts prior to July 2010 were the subject of a judgment in Slovenia and that, as regards the other acts described in the extradition request which took place after June 2010, there was no suspicion of an offence.

The ECJ found that HF could rely on the *ne bis in idem* principle. The term 'prosecuted' in Article 54 CISA covered a request for extradition. Further, Article 54 CISA applies to any person, regardless of whether that person is an EU citizen (as does to Article 50 of the Charter[30]). The fact the Germany–US Extradition Treaty limited the principle of *ne bis in idem* to judgments given in Germany did not mean that principle could not apply within the EU. EU law required the German court to give full effect to those EU law provisions and to disapply any provision in the Germany–US Extradition Treaty (if it could not be read in a way that was compatible with EU law) that was incompatible with EU law, without having to wait for Germany to renegotiate that Treaty.[31]

Looking at the application of the *ne bis in idem* principle to the facts, the Court had no difficulty in rejecting the argument that the German authorities were entitled to question the outcome of the proceedings before the Slovenian court.[32] This was because the principle of mutual trust necessarily implies that Member States have mutual trust in their respective

[28] Case C-435/22 PPU *HF v Generalstaatanwaltschaft München*, ECLI:EU:C:2022:852.

[29] ibid, para 74. The text of Art 50 is set out in n 25. It is part of Chapter VI entitled 'Justice', not Chapter V entitled 'Citizens' rights'. Pursuant to Art 51(1) of the Charter it applies to Member States 'only when they are implementing Union law'. As to this, see Case C-617/10 *Åklagaren v Åkerberg Fransson*, ECLI:EU:C:2013:105. Although the ECJ did not explain what EU law Germany was implementing, it was presumably Art 54 CISA.

[30] *HF* (n 28), para 74.

[31] ibid, para 110. Although the ECJ did not cite cases such as Case C-284/16 *Slowakische Republik v Achmea*, ECLI:EU:C:2018:158 and Case C-741/19 *Republic of Moldova v Komstroy*, ECLI:EU:C:2020:655, which rely on the principle of autonomy of EU law as a legal basis for EU law overriding international law, the conclusion reached here must also rely on the principle of autonomy of EU law, as the Germany–US Treaty is part of international law (although curiously it is set out in the judgment as part of German and not international law). In addition, there was an argument based on Art 351(1) TFEU which was also rejected: see *HF* (n 28), paras 115–26.

[32] ibid, para 91.

criminal justice systems, in that each of them consents to the application of the criminal law in force in the other Member States. However, in a helpful passage, the Court examined whether the principle of *ne bis in idem* did indeed apply to bar this extradition request.[33] It first recalled that for that principle to apply, the material facts need to be identical, not merely similar. It then pointed out that there was no complete overlap in time between the offences considered by the Slovenian court and those covered by the extradition request. Finally, it also invited the referring court to consider whether the offences contained in the extradition request covered the same material acts that were the subject of proceedings in Slovenia.

Both these cases illustrate the importance of the principles of *ne bis in idem* and mutual trust within the EU. Those principles are universal in their application within the EU and therefore rightly must also apply to extradition to third countries. At the same time, the Court has been careful to safeguard the equally important principle that a person does not evade a trial and punishment for alleged criminal acts. So, in *WS* the risk of provisional arrest was a justified restriction on the right of free movement where the applicability of the *ne bis in idem principle* to the facts had not been established. In *HF*, the Court elegantly addressed the doubts by the German authorities as to the scope and correctness of the Slovenian judgment by providing guidance as to whether the acts covered by the Slovenian proceedings were indeed identical to the acts in respect of which extradition was sought by the US and hence engaged the principle of *ne bis in idem*.

IV. EXTRADITION TO SERVE A CUSTODIAL SENTENCE

Finally, I will look at two cases that deal with extradition to a third country in order to serve a custodial sentence there. In *Raugevicius*, Russia sought the extradition of Raugevicius, a Lithuanian citizen, in order that he should serve a custodial sentence in Russia for a conviction imposed by a Russian court for a drug offence.[34] Raugevicius had lived in Finland for a considerable period of time and was the father of two children of Finnish nationality, residing there. Article 1 of the ECE obliges, subject to limited exceptions, a Contracting Party to extradite a person wanted for an offence or for the purpose of carrying out a sentence. Article 6 permits a Contracting Party to refuse to extradite its own nationals. Finland had made a declaration pursuant to Article 6 of the ECE which stated that, for the purpose of the ECE, the term 'nationals' includes nationals of certain other Scandinavian States as well as aliens 'domiciled in these States'. Prompted by the judgment in *Petruhhin*, the Finnish Supreme Court asked how that judgment was to be applied in a case where extradition by a third State was sought not for the prosecution of an offence but to serve a custodial sentence.

Consistently with its established case law, the ECJ held that where an EU citizen has been living in another Member State for a considerable period of time and demonstrates a certain degree of integration into that State's society, such a person is to be treated as being in a comparable situation to nationals of that Member State. Once comparability had been established, Articles 18 and 21 TFEU require that such persons 'should benefit from the provision preventing extradition from being applied to Finnish nationals and may, under the same conditions as Finnish nationals, serve their sentences on Finnish territory'.[35] On its face this was an

[33] ibid, paras 128–35. In a reference to the ECJ the facts are a matter for the national court, but the ECJ decided here to consider the facts, 'In order to provide a reply which is as useful as possible to the referring court': ibid, para 128.

[34] Case C-247/17 *Denis Raugevicius*, ECLI:EU:C:2018:898.

[35] ibid, para 47. The operative part of the judgment was in similarly unqualified terms.

extremely wide-ranging judgment as it suggested that every EU citizen who moved to another Member State and then became integrated there would have an unqualified right to serve any custodial sentence in that Member State if a national of that Member State could do so.

As is not unknown in the ECJ's jurisprudence,[36] it sometimes requires a subsequent case to clarify or modify the scope of an earlier judgment. The subsequent case here was *SM*,[37] a reference from Germany. This was an extradition request by Bosnia and Herzegovina to Germany to extradite SM, an EU national, to serve a custodial sentence there. Unlike Finland, Germany had not made an equivalent declaration under Article 6 of the ECE concerning the extradition of non-nationals.[38] So Article 1 of the ECE imposed an unconditional international law obligation on Germany to surrender SM, a non-German national.

In his Opinion in *SM* the Advocate General explained that the *Petruhhin* principle did not give a right for an EU citizen to be treated in the same way as a national of the requested Member State but rather was limited to imposing an obligation on the requested Member State to seek to ascertain whether, within the confines of international and domestic law, there is a less restrictive alternative to extradition.[39] In the case of an extradition to serve a sentence, Articles 18 and 21 TFEU went no further than to require a Member State to seek the consent of a third country to permit a custodial sentence imposed on an EU citizen to be served in that Member State where that is possible under the Member State's national law. If, however, the third country does not consent to this, extradition is not precluded by EU law, since a prohibition on extradition would mean that the person would go unpunished. The Advocate General distinguished *Raugevicius* on the basis that, as a matter of Finnish law Raugevicius was permitted to serve his sentence in Finland provided that both Finland and Russia agreed.[40] The ECJ followed this approach, emphasising that *Raugevicius* 'did not establish an automatic and absolute right for Union citizens not to be extradited out of the territory of the European Union'.[41] The Advocate General added that Articles 18 and 21 TFEU should not be interpreted in such a way as to require a Member State:

> to amend the declaration it has made pursuant to Article 6(1)(b) of the [ECE] [...] so that nationals from other Member States who reside permanently in the territory of that Member State in all cases enjoy the same protection has that granted to its own nationals.[42]

Thus he proceeded on the basis that Articles 18 and 21 TFEU had to be interpreted in a manner that did not put Member States in breach of their international obligations under the ECE. There is not an equivalent passage in the judgment of the Court. However, since the ECJ followed the Opinion of the Advocate General, one can deduce that the ECJ also did not wish to place Germany in breach of its international obligations under the ECE.

Why, one might ask, did the ECJ accept in *SM* that international law, in the shape of the ECE, was the key provision (in the sense that EU law was not to be interpreted in an autonomous manner contrary to the ECE) but said in *HF* that the Germany–US Extradition Treaty, which was also international law, had to be disapplied in favour of EU law? Unlike the Germany–US Treaty, the ECE is a multilateral rather than bilateral Treaty and, as the

[36] For an example that will be familiar to Judge Bay Larsen, one can cite Cases C-105/14 *Taricco and Others*, ECLI:EU:C:2015:555 and C-42/17 *MAS and MB*, ECLI:EU:C:2017:936.

[37] *SM* (n 3).

[38] A point made by the AG in his Opinion: see Opinion of AG de la Tour in Case C-237/21 *SM v Generalstaatanwaltschaft München* (n 7), para 6.

[39] ibid, paras 40–46.

[40] ibid, paras 48–49.

[41] ibid, para 47.

[42] ibid, para 62.

Advocate General observed in *SM*, a declaration has to be made at the time of signature or of deposit of the instrument of ratification. Any new declaration (ie that all EU nationals are to be treated in the same way as nationals of the requested State) 'could defeat the purpose of the [ECE] [...]'.[43] However, similar considerations did not preclude the ECJ in, for example, *Komstroy* holding that EU law overrode the dispute resolution procedure in Article 26 of the multilateral Energy Charter Treaty.[44] Probably a more likely explanation is that the principle of *ne bis in idem* within the AFSJ could be said to be a core value of the EU constitutional legal order, hence within the scope of the autonomy of EU law and so can override contrary international law. By contrast, the ambit of a permitted derogation to a restriction on free movement of persons arising from the risk of extradition to a third country does not have the same core value. Put another way, the principle of *ne bis in idem* within the AFSJ was considered to be an inalienable EU law right which could not be overridden by international Treaties. The same is not true of any presumed 'right' of non-extradition. Indeed, it is likely that the ECJ considered that, in the absence of international agreement, it was a bridge too far to interpret the right to free movement as encompassing an inalienable right to serve one's sentence in the EU State in which one was resident.

V. CONCLUSION

The cases I have discussed illustrate both how the ECJ has sought to create from scratch an EU legal framework for extradition but also the inherent limitations of such an approach. The limitations arise because of the need for agreement by third countries on a number of key issues underlying extradition, such as the availability of evidence for a prosecution and consent to serve a custodial sentence within the EU. Indeed the need to have all the available evidence, both documentary and oral, before a court as well as the question of whether there is jurisdiction to try an individual in a State where the alleged crime was not committed, should, on public policy grounds, preclude the issue of an EAW in a large number of, if not in most, extradition cases. Thus, with the benefit of hindsight, one can see that the practical effects of *Petruhhin* and *Raugevicius* are likely to be quite limited in the field of extradition for prosecution and sentence respectively. Nevertheless, that does not undermine their real benefit for EEA citizens in cases where those principles can apply in specific cases without giving rise either to injustice or to a real risk of impunity.

[43] ibid, fn 45 to para 62. While the ECE was signed before the EEC Treaty entered into force on 1 January 1958, it was ratified by Germany only on 2 October 1976 and so it must be open to doubt whether it benefits from the 'grandfather' provision in Art 351(1) TFEU as an agreement predating accession: see the reasoning of the ECJ in *HF* (n 28), paras 118–27.

[44] *Komstroy* (n 31).

24

You Can't Always Get What You Want (But You'll Get What You Need): *Deconstructing Alleged Paradoxes in the Case Law on the Interface of Arbitration and the EU Legal Order*

MAREK SAFJAN*

I. INTRODUCTION

DURING THE 18 years of Lars' tenure as a Member, the European Court of Justice (ECJ) has, among a myriad of other important issues, repeatedly addressed the tricky question of whether, and to what extent, our 'Union of effective judicial protection'[1] should accommodate conflict resolution by means of arbitration. Whenever the Grand Chamber had to decide on this matter since 2006, Lars was involved. So the Court's steadfast stance in favour of the autonomy of the EU legal order, including its courts, and the guarantee of effective judicial protection within that legal order, also imparts his personal achievements in the robes of a judge at the ECJ.

In revisiting the ECJ's arbitration case law for Lars' Liber Amicorum, I shall put the virtues of autonomy and effective judicial protection in perspective with the legitimate concerns of the arbitration community, which I understand and, to some extent, even share. I nevertheless find that the criticism stemming from these concerns fails to take sufficient account of the EU prerogative to ensure the effectiveness of its system of judicial protection.

II. PARADOXES

The arbitration community and scholarship sense that the ECJ case law increasingly marginalises the role of amicable dispute settlement in the EU legal order.[2]

* Former Judge at the European Court of Justice.

[1] On this concept, see M Safjan and D Düsterhaus, 'A Union of Effective Judicial Protection. Addressing a Multi-Level Challenge through the Lens of Article 47 CFREU' (2014) 33 *Yearbook of European Law* 3.

[2] See eg S Bollée, 'L'arbitrage assujetti aux "règles fondamentales", du Règlement Bruxelles I ? Réflexions critiques sur l'arrêt London Steam-Ship, note sous CJUE 20 juin 2022' (2022) 4 *Revue de l'Arbitrage* 1525; M Combet, 'L'arbitrage confronte au droit de l'Union européenne' (2023) 664 *Revue de l'Union Européenne* 59; A Mourre, 'Is Commercial Arbitration Entering in Dangerous Waters in the European Union?' (2023) 19 *Kluwer Arbitration* 1.

This criticism essentially focuses on four issues. A first source of contention is the Court's understanding of the scope of application of the EU rules on the free movement of civil and commercial judgments as defined, first, in the Brussels Convention[3] and then in the Brussels I[4] and Brussels Ia Regulations,[5] expressly excluding *arbitration*. From early on, the meaning and practical consequences of this exemption have given rise to doubts and disputes.[6] The ECJ has not only emphasised the breadth of this exemption, but also the inadmissibility of preliminary ruling requests by arbitral tribunal.[7]

Second, certain ECJ judgments are said to hamper the effects of arbitration, such as that in the *Eco Swiss* case,[8] which found a violation of EU law (*in casu* the prohibition on unfair competition) to possibly trigger public policy clauses and lead to the annulment of an arbitral award. Similarly, the *West Tankers* judgment[9] effectively eliminated the use of the anti-suit injunction instrument, ie instructing a party to an arbitral dispute to refrain from initiating a dispute before a court, in the context of EU judicial cooperation. Blows to the significance of arbitration were also seen in the *Gazprom* judgment,[10] confirming that an anti-suit injunction cannot limit a Member State's judicial authority in determining its own jurisdiction in a case and cannot lead to depriving a party of effective judicial protection.

Third, in the *Achmea case*,[11] the ECJ excluded the possibility of EU Member States engaging in investment arbitration based on bilateral investment treaties (BITs), thus significantly reducing the importance of arbitration in business practice.

Fourth, the recent judgment in the *London Steam-Ship* case[12] is presented as a particularly telling example of the Court's arguable unfriendliness towards arbitration, since it subjects the legal effects of an arbitral decision to the objectives and general principles of the Brussels I Regulation, leading, among other things, to undermining one of the key assumptions of the New York Covention,[13] ie the exclusion of any substantive control of an arbitral decision by a judicial authority.

While understanding the fears underlying all this criticism, I am not convinced by them. Instead, I believe that the need to ensure effective judicial protection of all individuals when national courts deal with arbitral awards under EU law legitimately influences the free movement of these awards in the Area of Freedom, Security and Justice (AFSJ), but it does not obstruct it. As will be shown, a correct application of the Court's interpretation of EU law, specifically the rules on recognition and enforcement of judicial decisions, respects the binding obligations governing arbitration.

[3] Brussels Convention on jurisdiction and the enforcement of judgments in civil and commercial matters (Brussels, 27 September 1968) [1978] OJ L304/36.

[4] Council Regulation (EC) No 44/2001 of 22 December 2000 on jurisdiction and the recognition and enforcement of judgments in civil and commercial matters [2001] OJ L12/1.

[5] Regulation (EU) No 1215/2012 of the European Parliament and of the Council of 12 December 2012 on jurisdiction and the recognition and enforcement of judgments in civil and commercial matters (recast) [2012] OJ L351/1.

[6] Referring to Case C-190/89 *Marc Rich*, ECLI:EU:C:1991:319. Currently, Recital 12 of Regulation No 1215/2012 explicitly indicates that this regulation does not apply to any lawsuit or judgment concerning the recognition or enforcement of an arbitral award.

[7] See the Case C-102/81 *Nordsee*, ECLI:EU:C:1982:107, para 13 in which it is stated the 'link between the arbitration procedure in this instance and the organization of legal remedies through the courts in the Member State in question is not sufficiently close for the arbitrator to be considered as a "court of Tribunal of a Member State"'.

[8] See Case C-126/97 *Eco Swiss*, ECLI:EU:C:1999:269.

[9] See Case C-185/07 *Allianz and Generali Assicurazioni Generali v West Tankers*, ECLI:EU:C:2009:69.

[10] See Case C-536/13 *Gazprom*, ECLI:EU:C:2015:316.

[11] See Case C-284/16 *Achmea*, ECLI:EU:C:2017:699.

[12] See Case C-700/20 *London Steam-Ship Owners Mutual Insurance Association*, ECLI:EU:C:2022:488.

[13] See United Nations Convention on the Recognition and Enforcement of Foreign Arbitral Awards (New York, 10 June 1958).

It even seems that a great deal of criticism results from a misunderstanding of the basic tenets of the Court's long-standing and consistent stance in favour of the autonomy and effectiveness of judicial protection under EU law.

III. PREMISES

As a preliminary point, it is appropriate to recall the fundamental premises of the EU system of cooperative judicial protection, including the free movement of judicial decisions across the EU. This simultaneously highlights the most significant differences with regard to arbitration.

The essence of EU provisions in the field of judicial cooperation (Article 67(4) TFEU) is the principle of mutual trust and recognition among the Member States. This principle was highlighted, in particular, in *Opinion 2/13*[14] on the EU's accession to the European Convention on Human Rights, which states that it allows an area without internal borders to be created and maintained and requires each Member State, save in exceptional circumstances, to consider all the other Member States to be complying with EU law and particularly with the fundamental rights recognised by EU law.

In the EU legal order, the fundamental task of ensuring the effective application of EU law has been entrusted to the Court of Justice of the European Union and the courts and tribunals of the Member States (Article 19 TEU). A well-established line of case law, especially in recent years with regard to the protection of the rule of law,[15] emphasises, on the one hand, the importance of judicial authority for the functioning of all areas of EU law and, on the other hand, the necessary guarantees of judicial independence and impartiality.

The role and position of the independent judiciary remain closely linked to the enormously important right to effective judicial protection laid down in Article 47 of the Charter of Fundamental Rights. This directly applicable provision is of instrumental significance for the realisation of all other rights and freedoms arising from EU law. Hence it is often said that in the EU the principle of judicial protection constitutes a sort of 'umbrella principle'.[16]

These premises are fundamental for a correct understanding of the ECJ approach towards arbitration.

As regards the latter, there is no doubt about its significant role in creating an appropriate legal protection infrastructure for a number of persons, especially business entities. Arbitration is an excellent and important supplement to judicial protection in professional commercial transactions. Its advantages are the less formalised procedures, providing faster and more flexible proceedings, as well as greater specialisation in certain areas of law.

The fact that arbitration has remained outside the scope of the Brussels Convention and, subsequently, the Brussels regulation governing the free circulation of judicial decisions, and is not covered by other EU law does not change this state of affairs. There is no doubt that arbitral adjudication, due to its nature as a tool at the initiative of the parties, constitutes the realisation of the principle of party autonomy, beyond any State prerogatives and control, cannot be treated in terms comparable to the judicial system. While, as mentioned above, the factor determining the free circulation of judicial decisions is the principle of mutual trust and recognition, crucial for ensuring the proper functioning of an increasingly integrated European

[14] *Opinion 2/13 (Accession of the European Union to the ECHR)*, ECLI:EU:C:2014:2454, para 191.

[15] See eg Case C-64/16 *Associacao Sindical dos Juizes Portugueses*, ECLI:EU:C:2018:117.

[16] K Lenaerts 'La vie après l'avis. Exploring the Principle of Mutual (not Blind) Trust' (2017) 54 *Common Market Law Review* 824.

legal order, the impossibility of applying it to arbitration simultaneously constitutes the most important reason for the exclusion of arbitration from the Brussels system.

While not being a component of the autonomous EU legal order and situating itself outside its scope, arbitration nevertheless remains connected in various ways with this order and the judicial system of the Member States, especially due to the system of judicial control measures in respect of the recognition and enforcement of arbitral awards. The choice made by the EU legislature to exclude arbitration from the Brussels mechanisms is not *binary*. Existing 'points of contact' with EU law have consequences that sometimes require precise qualification and explanation.

In any case, it is certain that under the philosophy of the EU legal order, these connections and 'points of contact', specific interferences between the systems of judicial and arbitral protection cannot lead to questioning or limiting the assumptions on which the EU system is based, diminishing the realisation of the most important goals associated with the effective application of EU law by courts, including, above all, the right to judicial protection before an independent and impartial court, legal security for the parties, and free movement of judicial decisions in the EU legal space. It seems that this is the most important message to be derived from the ECJ case law on the relationship between arbitration and EU law. The process of shaping this case law therefore deserves a broader perspective, so as to better understand the connection between the aforementioned assumptions and the direction taken by this case law. Let me thus try to show that the ECJ's arguable aversion towards arbitration is nothing but a myth that does not withstand an in-depth analysis of the case law.

IV. PARALLEL AUTONOMIES AND THEIR OCCASIONAL INTERTWINEMENT

The parallelism of the two systems of legal protection – judicial and arbitral – is not fundamentally disturbed by the fact that an arbitral award is subject to simplified and limited judicial control, primarily focusing on formal-procedural aspects, in connection with the recognition or enforcement of such an award. While this control typically does not include a substantive assessment of the arbitral decision, a review of the content is not entirely excluded and may occur in certain special situations, where one of the parties requests the annulment of the arbitral award based on grounds exhaustively listed in the New York Convention itself.[17]

A. Public Policy and Fundamental Principles

Even though arbitration does not fall within the scope of EU law, the legal relationships that are the subject of the dispute between the parties in arbitral proceedings often touch upon issues covered by EU regulations, with the result that an arbitral award can influence the functioning in Member States of those legal instruments that are governed by EU law. Therefore it is obvious that it must be determined whether an arbitral award does not compromise the effective and coherent application of EU law, which is crucial for preserving the EU legal order. As the ECJ found in the *Eco Swiss* case,[18] a violation by an arbitral award of one of the fundamental

[17] See Art 5 of United Nation Convention on the Recognition and Enforcement of Foreign Arbitral Awards, regarding the annulment of an arbitral award.

[18] *Eco Swiss* (n 8). See also other judgments related to the issue of the violation of EU law in arbitration jurisprudence, eg Case C-168/05 *Mostaza Claro*, ECLI:EU:C:2006:675, para 38.

treaty provisions (*in casu* the protection of free competition) can be equivalent to a violation of national public policy. Strictly speaking, this position does not imply the application of EU law to the arbitral decision but creates an interface within the Union's legal space between the New York Convention on the one hand (the public policy clause) and fundamental provisions of EU law, on the other.[19]

Consequently, the message contained in *Eco Swiss* cannot be interpreted as hampering the functioning of arbitration in the EU by interfering with the substantive content of arbitral awards, but rather as applying a method that ensures the consistency and effectiveness of legal protection measures under EU law, taking into account the immense importance attached to the uniform interpretation of that law.[20] While the requisite nature or 'intensity' of a professed violation of EU law by an arbitral award remains open to debate, it seems that this involves provisions of particular significance for the EU legal order, ie those that, according to the *Eco Swiss* judgment, may be regarded as co-defining the content of the public policy clause.[21]

One finds a reference to significant principles of EU law in the *West Tankers* judgment[22] on the admissibility and effects of an anti-suit injunction issued by a court of a Member State due to an existing arbitration clause between the parties. According to the ECJ, a decision by a national court prohibiting a person from initiating or continuing proceedings in another Member State would prevent the court of another State from examining its own competence and deciding on this matter according to the rules of the Brussels I Regulation, which define its scope of application, thereby violating the fundamental principle of mutual trust which Member States place in each other's legal systems,[23] and the objectives of the regulation, which include unifying jurisdiction in civil and commercial matters and the free flow of judgments.[24] The ECJ further considered the use of this instrument unacceptable due to its conflict with the fundamental right of each individual to effective judicial protection, in situations where a party claims the invalidity, unenforceability, or impossibility of executing an arbitration clause.[25]

The ECJ appeared to take a more nuanced position in the *Gazprom* case[26] concerning an anti-suit injunction issued by an arbitral tribunal. It held that such a decision does not limit the right of another Member State's court to examine its own competence based on the Brussels I Regulation, as the proceeding concerning the recognition or enforcement of an arbitral award does not fall within its scope but proceeds according to national procedural law and international law (the New York Convention).[27] It is on this basis that a decision can be made as to whether an arbitral award can be recognised as valid and effective or, conversely, as invalid and ineffective. In this case, the ECJ made a clear distinction between an anti-suit injunction resulting from an arbitral award and one resulting from a judicial decision (in connection with an arbitration clause), as only in the latter case can there be a violation of the principle of mutual trust and a limitation of the party's right to judicial protection. In the first case, however, a

[19] It concerns the prohibition expressed in Art 85(1) of the Treaty establishing the European Community (now Art 101 of the Treaty on the Functioning of the European Union, TFEU). The precise stance is articulated in *Eco Swiss* (n 8), para 41.

[20] *Eco Swiss* (n 8), para 40.

[21] See, for instance, the observation by N Shelkoplyas 'European Community Law and International Arbitration: Logics that Clash' (2002) 3 *European Business Organization Law Review* 569, 590 that 'the Court will have to shape the Community ordre public, it is expected to give an unambiguous indication of the criteria which are decisive for determining the principles underlying the very heart of the Community legal foundations'.

[22] See *Allianz and Generali Assicurazioni Generali v West Tankers* (n 9).

[23] ibid, para 30.

[24] ibid, para 24.

[25] ibid, para 31.

[26] See *Gazprom* (n 10).

[27] ibid, para 36.

party to an arbitral dispute is not deprived of the possibility of judicial protection and can effectively demand before a national court a declaration of the invalidity and ineffectiveness of the arbitral award in the recognition and enforcement proceedings.[28]

Instead of expressing any 'anti-arbitration tendency' on the part of the ECJ,[29] the case law concerning anti-suit injunctions in the context of arbitration thus merely ensures respect for the foundations upon which the autonomous legal order of the EU is based. This position was clearly expressed in the *West Tankers* judgment, while the *Gazprom* judgment delineated an area not belonging to the sphere of European law, where a violation of these foundations, and thereby a weakening of the EU's legal protection system based on the guarantees of effective right to court and free movement of judgments, cannot occur. These boundaries are precisely defined and do not go beyond the necessity of protecting the indicated objectives.

This approach, fully respecting the previously established line of case law, also inspired the recent judgment in the *Starlight Shipping* case,[30] where the preliminary question concerned the recognition of a British court's judgment which issued an anti-suit injunction.[31] Similar to the *West Tankers* case, the ECJ stated that a judgment of a court of a Member State in the form of an anti-suit injunction (quasi anti-suit injunction) cannot limit the competence of another Member State's court to independently determine, based on the applicable regulations, whether it is competent to resolve the dispute brought before it. This being a matter of mutual trust,[32] a judgment of another Member State's court containing a quasi-anti-suit injunction should consequently be qualified as inconsistent with the public policy of the Member State.[33]

B. A BIT of Contextualisation – What to Make of *Achmea* and *Komstroy*

The ECJ's judgment in the *Achmea* case[34] has stirred substantial controversy as it essentially eliminates investment arbitration from the legal space of the EU by excluding the use of an international agreement (BIT), according to which an investor from a Member State may initiate proceedings against another Member State before an arbitral tribunal, whose competence the latter state has agreed to recognise.

Nevertheless, this judgment also fits very clearly into the logic underpinning the line of existing case law aimed at protecting the integrity and autonomy and respecting the fundamental assumptions of the EU legal order. According to these principles, each state shares a series of common values with all other Member States,[35] which is the source of the principle of mutual trust between Member States. The *Achmea* judgment assesses investment arbitration in Member States from the perspective of these particular characteristics and the autonomy

[28] ibid, para 38.

[29] See, for instance, J Grierson, 'Comment on *West Tankers Inc. v. RAS Riunione Adriatica di Sicurta Sp.A.(The Front Comor)*' (2009) 26 *Journal of International Arbitration* 891; R Fentiman, 'Arbitration and Antisuit Injunctions in Europe' (2009) 68 *Cambridge Law Journal* 278; see also on the *Gazprom* case, J Sundaram 'Does the Judgment of the CJEU in *Gazprom* Bring about Clarity on the Grant of Anti-suit Injunctions under the Brussels I Regulation?' (2015) 27 *Denning Law Journal* 303.

[30] See Case C-590/21 *Charles Taylor Adjusting*, ECLI:EU:C:2023:633.

[31] See ibid, para 27, where it is defined as a quasi anti-suit injunction, because it does not constitute a prohibition on initiating or conducting proceedings before a foreign court (in this case, before a Greek court), but its effect is at least to discourage the party from bringing such proceedings, among others by the sanctions provided for in the event of a party's failure to comply with this ruling.

[32] See Case C-741/19 *Republic of Moldova v Komstroy*, ECLI:EU:C:2021:655, para 39.

[33] *Charles Taylor Adjusting* (n 30), paras 35–37.

[34] *Achmea* (n 11).

[35] ibid, para 34.

of the EU legal order, indicating in this context the necessity to ensure full application of EU law in all Member States, as well as judicial protection of rights that legal entities derive from EU law.[36] The absence of a right for arbitral tribunals to refer questions for preliminary ruling cannot be compensated by the possibility of limited judicial control in terms of assessing the validity of the arbitration clause in light of the applicable law or respect for the public order clause.

At the same time, it is essential not to lose sight of the significant difference between investment arbitration and commercial arbitration; while the latter originates in the autonomy of the parties' will, the former is based on a treaty, under which Member States agree to exclude disputes that may concern the application or interpretation of EU law from the jurisdiction of their own courts, and consequently from the system of effective remedies indicated in Article 19(1) TEU. BITs thus establish a mechanism through which it is impossible to ensure decisions consistent with the principle of full effectiveness of EU law. At the same time, ruling out investment arbitration does not exclude the possibility of appointing a separate judicial body authorised to interpret and apply the provisions of an international agreement, provided that the autonomy of the Union and its legal order is preserved. In the case of BITs, the Union is not a party to the agreement, and the decisions of the arbitral tribunal may concern not only the interpretation and application of the agreement itself but also EU law.[37]

The limits for investment arbitration agreements, parties to which are Member States and entities within the scope of EU law application, are very clearly defined in direct reference to previous case law.

This approach does not, of course, eliminate investment arbitration as such and does not block the possibility for an arbitral tribunal to function in the Union based on international agreements to which the Union is a party,[38] containing investment arbitration clauses, applied in different configurations (eg Member State – investor from a third country; third country – investor from another third country), as exemplified by the *Komstroy* judgment.[39] In this case, related to the control of a decision issued by an arbitration tribunal in a dispute between entities not belonging to the Union area (Moldova and an investor from Ukraine), the ECJ, responding to the question from the Cour d'appel de Paris, considered itself competent to provide an answer to the preliminary question concerning the interpretation of a provision of an international agreement to which the Union is a party.[40] The agreement concluded by the Council constituted an integral part of the EU legal order;[41] the application of French law as *lex fori* in the main proceedings entailed the application of Union law, in respect of which the court adjudicating the case is obliged to uphold in accordance with Article 19.[42] The distinction in relation to the *Achmea* judgment is very clear; unlike the BIT type agreement, in this case an international agreement was concluded with the participation of the Union, which thus assumed responsibility for its correct interpretation and application in the scope concerning the Union, enabling the preservation of the integrity and autonomy of the Union's legal order.

[36] ibid, para 36.

[37] *Achmea* (n 11), paras 57–59.

[38] See among others on the doubts about the future perspectives of investment arbitration in EU law, A Bilanova and J Kudma, 'The End of Investment Arbitration As We Know It?' (2018) 3 *European Investment Law and Arbitration Review* 261; D Segin, 'Les accords de protection des investissements conclus entre États membres saisis par le droit de l'Union. *Achmea*, C-284/16' (2009) 1 *Revue du droit de l'Union européenne* 225.

[39] *Republic of Moldova v Komstroy* (n 32).

[40] It was about the Energy Charter Treaty (Lisbon, 17 December 1994).

[41] *Republic of Moldova v Komstroy* (n 32), para 21.

[42] ibid, para 34.

V. THE JUDGMENT IN THE *LONDON STEAM-SHIP OWNERS* CASE – A (R)EVOLUTION?

The recent judgment of the ECJ's Grand Chamber in the case of *London Steam-Ship Owners* has been presented[43] as a radical departure from the established and consolidated line of jurisprudence on issues that have already been unequivocally resolved. However, when looking at this judgment through the lens of the fundamental principles underpinning the ECJ's arbitration case law, it becomes obvious that it marks no departure from, but harmoniously continues, the established line of reasoning.

This case, initiated by preliminary questions from a British court, concerned the issue of recognising before that court a final judgment of a Spanish court (final enforcement order), the content of which was in clear contradiction with an existing arbitral decision, subsequently recognised as enforceable and incorporated (repeated in its content) by a British court judgment. The questions referred primarily asked whether a judgment of a Member State court, repeating in its content the judgment of an arbitral tribunal, could be an obstacle to recognising in that Member State a judgment issued in another Member State, if, as indicated above, these judgments cannot be reconciled, and therefore their simultaneous enforceability cannot be recognised.

The starting point for assessing the British incorporation judgment was the distinction made in the previous case law between the scope of application of the Brussels I Regulation and the concept of a judgment within the meaning of this regulation, which, in both its former and current versions, operates with a broad concept of judgment, encompassing any decision, no matter how it is defined, issued by a court of a Member State, regardless of its content.[44] The ECJ's finding in favour of a 'judgment' in essence reiterates the position taken some months before in the *H Limited* case,[45] which qualified a judgment of a Member State's court issued in contentious proceedings, containing a payment order and based on a judgment of a third-country court.[46] Two prerequisites were decisive in this case: first, it was a judgment issued as a result of contentious proceedings; and second, it emanated from a Member State court.

The approach adopted in this respect even strengthens the position of arbitration by better integrating it into the legal order of a given Member State as it treats a decision issued by arbitral tribunal and repeated by a court of a Member State, in principle, as an element of that order, which cannot be ignored in the process of recognising decisions from another Member State.

Still, despite the fact that the broad concept of a judgment as one of the elements realising the regulation's free movement of judgment objective constitutes a common point of reference, there seems to be a significant difference between the *H Limited* and *London Steam-Ship* judgments. In the latter, the ECJ introduced a distinction between the general definition of 'judgment' contained in the regulation[47] and a judgment which, although having been properly

[43] See eg Bollée (n 2); Mourre (n 2).

[44] See Art 2(a) of Regulation No 1215/2012: '"Judgment" means any judgment given by a court or tribunal of a Member State, whatever the judgment may be called, including a decree, order, decision or writ of execution, as well as a decision on the determination of costs or expenses by an officer of the court'. That definition is the equivalent of the definition admitted under Regulation No 44/2001.

[45] Case C-568/20 *H Limited*, ECLI:EU:C:2022:264, paras 24–26. See also similarly Case C-394/07, *Gambazzi*, ECLI:EU:C:2009:219. This approach is founded on the autonomous interpretation being conformed with the objectives realised by the regulation, especially to ensure a free circulation of the judgments in civil and commercial matters, see Case C-456/11 *Gothaer Allgemeine Versicherung*, ECLI:EU:C:2004:258, paras 28–29.

[46] *Republic of Moldova v Komstroy* (n 32), para 33.

[47] Art 32 of Regulation No 44/2001 and Art 2(a) of Regulation No 1215/2012.

issued by a court of a Member State in the terms of an arbitral award[48] and, thus, enjoying free movement, nevertheless fails to deploy one of its natural effects within the procedure for recognising and enforcing judicial decisions among Member States, ie to block the recognition of a foreign judgment.[49]

Prima facie, this additional distinction within the concept of 'judgment', which appears in two forms, may seem somewhat paradoxical and inconsistent with previous jurisprudence. However, is this really the case? The answer must be negative if one considers a fundamental tenet of EU law interpretation, which is to construe the autonomous concepts of this law subordinated to the fundamental objectives pursued by the regulations of which they are part. The objectives in both cases differ. In the first case, the primary goal is to ensure the free movement of judicial decisions in the legal space of the EU based on the principle of mutual trust, while in the second case, as in the proceedings in the *London Steam-Ship Owners* case, the fundamental goal is to guarantee legal security and certainty of law, essential values for any legal order, by eliminating the possibility that the content of a judgment cannot be reconciled with an already issued decision by the court of the requesting country (incorporating the content of an arbitral decision) between the same parties.

A configuration similar to that in the *London Steam-Ship Owners* case appeared earlier in the jurisprudence in the *Hoffmann* case,[50] as in this instance, a decision containing a resolution irreconcilable with a decision from another Member State concerned a field (civil status) not covered by the scope of application of the Brussels Convention. Contrary to what might be assumed at first glance, the decision in the *London Steam-Ship Owners* case does not, therefore, represent a radical departure or introduce fundamental elements that could be described as a novelty in relation to previous jurisprudence, but rather it is the logical consequence of earlier lines of case law.

A continuation of previous case law and, specifically, the need to ensure conformity with fundamental principles of EU law is also the ECJ's stance on the necessity for an arbitral tribunal's decision to respect certain fundamental principles and objectives of the regulation, without which the decision cannot be recognised as having legal effects, especially in terms of creating an obstacle to recognising a decision from another Member State (Article 34(3) of Regulation No 44/2001 or Article 45(1)(c) of Regulation No 1215/2012).[51]

This stance understandably raises doubts. It seems to contradict the rule that judgments from courts of another Member State are not subject to examination either in terms of jurisdictional competence or their substantive correctness.[52] This is a logical consequence of the principle of mutual trust between Member State judiciaries. Any other approach, opening the possibility of substantive review of a judgment of a court of another Member State and its competence to issue that judgment, would inherently lead to a fundamental weakening of the free movement of judgments in the EU's legal space.

However, one cannot lose sight of the fact that in the *London Steam-Ship Owners* case, unlike in the *Hoffmann* case, the subject of assessment was not only a court decision which, as

[48] It is worth mentioning that for a 'decision' there may be, for example, a court settlement, concluded before the court, but there are no other necessary features of a court decision (this is not the decision of the court authority, preceded by a dispute proceedings), see Case C-414/92 *Solo Kleinmotoren*, ECLI:EU:C:1994:221, paras 17–18.

[49] Art 34(3) of Regulation No 44/2001 and Art 45(1)(c) of Regulation No 1215/2012.

[50] Case 145/86 *Hoffmann*, ECLI:EU:C:1988:61, para 25.

[51] *London Steam-Ship Owners* (n 12), para 54.

[52] See Case C-533/08 *TNT Express Netherland*, ECLI:EU:C:2010:243, para 55. See also *Allianz and Generali Assicurazioni Generali v West Tankers* (n 9), para 21; and Cases C-386/17 *Liberato*, ECLI:EU:C:2019:24, paras 51 and 54; and *Charles Taylor Adjusting* (n 30).

a principle, does not fall within the scope of application of the regulation but also a decision that constitutes an integral repetition of an arbitral tribunal's ruling, against which the principle of mutual trust cannot be applied.[53] This significant difference fundamentally changes the perspective, as for this reason, minimal prerequisites that an arbitral tribunal's decision (and also a decision of a Member State's court repeating that decision) must meet to be considered as creating an obstacle to recognising a court decision from another Member State (Article 34(3) of Regulation No 44/2001 and correspondingly Article 45(1)(c) of Regulation No 1215/2012) become an instrument to counterbalance the specific 'deficit' of an arbitral tribunal's decision resulting from the non-application of the principle of mutual trust.

Let us return, however, to the criteria upon which the legal relevance of a decision confirming an arbitral tribunal's ruling depends on the examined context. Can sufficient support for this be found in the case law? It indeed seems that there is perfect continuation also in relation to this issue.

The judgment in the *London Steam-Ship Owners* case points to two prerequisites that preclude such relevance, namely the violation of the *lis pendens* principle, and the non-respect of the relative effect of the arbitration clause.

As to the first issue, it is important to emphasise the significance of the *lis pendens* principle[54] for respecting the requirements of effective judicial protection and the rights of interested parties, considering that allowing concurrent, parallel judicial proceedings on matters between the same parties and with the same cause of action, would inherently and radically weaken certainty and trust in the law, and even constitute an incentive for parties to manipulate procedural instruments. In the situation analysed in the *London Steam-Ship Owners* judgment, non-respect of the *lis pendens* principle by initiating proceedings that culminated in an arbitral tribunal's decision, repeated by a court of a Member State, deprived the victims of the insured damages of the possibility of effectively asserting their rights in that state, despite the fact that the case had already been initiated before a court of another Member State and then definitively resolved in their favour. The right to effective judicial protection is one of the fundamental rights guaranteed in the legal order of the EU, as reflected in the Charter of Fundamental Rights and defines one of the most important objectives pursued starting from the Brussels Convention, through successive regulations in this field. Additionally, referring to the abovementioned objectives finds its basis in earlier jurisprudence.[55]

From this perspective, defined by the right to effective judicial protection, we must also view the importance of the second violation indicated by the ECJ in the *London Steam-Ship Owners* judgment, namely the breach of the principle of relative effect of the arbitration clause. Respecting this principle means that it cannot lead to depriving the injured person of the possibility of bringing an effective claim for compensation for damage covered by insurance directly against the insurer, if such a right is provided in the system of the Member State to which the court issuing the decision belongs. A decision of an arbitral tribunal issued based on a prorogation clause, subsequently repeated in a judgment of the court, cannot, therefore, create an obstacle to such a possibility. However, refusal to recognise a decision issued in another Member State in favour of the injured parties based on Article 34(3) of Regulation 44/2001 (correspondingly Article 45(1)(c) of Regulation 1215/2012)[56] would inevitably deprive

[53] *London Steam-Ship Owners* (n 12), para 57.

[54] See Art 27 of Regulation No 44/2001 as well as Art 29 of Regulation No 1215/2012.

[55] See Case C-559/14 *Meroni*, ECLI:EU:C:2016:349, para 44; *TNT Express Netherland* (n 52), para 49; Case C-452/12 *Nippon Insurance*, ECLI:EU:C:2013:858, para 36; and Case C-231/16, *Merck*, ECLI:EU:C:2017:771, paras 31–32 (on the *lis pendens* principle).

[56] See Case C-368/16, *Assens Havn*, ECLI:EU:C:2017:546, paras 31 and 40.

the injured parties of such effective protection. Assigning a decisive role in such a situation to the decision of an arbitral tribunal (integrally repeated by a court of a Member State) would therefore violate one of the essential objectives of the regulation, which is the protection of the injured parties against a given insurer and would lead to consequences impossible to reconcile with effective legal (jurisdictional) protection of the rights and interests of third parties not covered by the arbitration clause.

It therefore appears that the indicated principles constitute such an important component of EU law that it is fully understandable to mandate their respect as a necessary minimum standard, applicable to the decisions of arbitral tribunals, if they are to have certain legal relevance and create an obstacle to recognising a decision from another Member State.

Finally, in order to respect all these principles, a national court called upon to enter a judgment entered in the terms of an arbitral award may find itself obliged to refer questions for preliminary ruling to the ECJ.[57]

VI. CONCLUSION: *DOWN THE ROAD A PIECE*, ARBITRATION AND THE EU LEGAL ORDER

As I have shown in this contribution, the ECJ case law on the interface between arbitration and the EU legal order has been based on the same premises for many years, the most important being their fundamental difference stemming from the fact that the principle of mutual trust and recognition cannot be applied to arbitration. The second fundamental premise of this case law is the protection of the integrity of the EU legal order, which is based on coherent and uniform interpretation and application of EU law, in accordance with the principle of primacy. The relationship between arbitration and the interconnected judicial systems of the Member States thus needs to be shaped in such a way as to ensure the right to effective judicial protection, while respecting the autonomous will of the parties and the admissibility of arbitration clauses.

Instead of making radical turns, this case law has evolved consistently by adding further clarifications and gradually removing interpretative doubts.

One could argue that the framework defined by the above-mentioned premises is too rigid and overly narrows the scope of action of arbitral tribunals in respect of the EU legal order. However, many indications suggest that arbitration, especially commercial arbitration, continues to develop dynamically in the EU, and arbitral jurisprudence remains an important component of the broader European legal space. Although it may seem a paradoxical thesis, the ECJ case law discussed in this contribution ultimately strengthens the foundations of the operation of arbitral tribunals in the EU, by removing significant doubts and clearly defining the principles to be respected.

Of course, the debate on the proper place of arbitration in the EU is not closed, and a number of important issues await resolution, either through further case law or by legislative means. One such issue remains, in my opinion, the admissibility of preliminary questions from arbitral tribunals. It has not been possible to adequately address this issue in the current chapter, as it requires a thorough and substantive debate.

[57] *London Steam-Ship Owners* (n 12), para 71. See also *Republic of Moldova v Komstroy* (n 32), para 58 and the previous case law since *Eco Swiss* (n 8).

Part IV

The Impact of the Area of Freedom, Security and Justice

25

Free Movement of Persons in EU and EEA Law: An Illustration

PER CHRISTIANSEN*

I. INTRODUCTION

THE PURPOSE OF this chapter is to illustrate the influence of the European Economic Area (EEA) Agreement[1] on the relationship between the Contracting Parties (Parties). These Parties were, at the time, the European Union (EU) and the EU States, on the one hand, and the European Free Trade Association (EFTA) States, on the other, and since 1995 also Liechtenstein, Iceland and Norway (EFTA States). The Area of Freedom, Security and Justice (AFSJ) is not regulated in the EEA Agreement. Nevertheless, Iceland and Norway have implemented relevant Schengen *acquis* according to separate agreements with the EU. This aspect will thus be of special interest in the chapter. Furthermore, the judgment of the European Court of Justice (ECJ) in *Ruska Federacija*[2] is of specific interest to the present context. The reason is that it concerned the interpretation of provisions of the Treaty on the Functioning of the European Union (TFEU) and of Council Framework Decision 2002/584/JHA on the European arrest warrant and the surrender procedures between Member States (the EAW Framework Decision).[3]

In the Preamble to the EEA Agreement, high priority is attached to the 'privileged relationship' between the Parties. This relationship is based on proximity, long-standing common values and European identity. In *Ruska Federacija* the ECJ found that the EEA Agreement creates a 'special relationship' between the Parties.

Against that background, first a very brief overview of the EEA and relevant EU law provisions on the AFSJ applicable to Iceland and Norway will be given (Section II). It should be noted that EU citizenship is not part of the EEA Agreement. Then the relationship to the EEA Agreement of AFSJ and EU citizenship is briefly described (Section III).

* Judge at EFTA Court from 2011 to 2023.

[1] Agreement on the European Economic Area – Final Act – Joint Declarations – Declarations by the Governments of the Member States of the Community and the EFTA States – Arrangements – Agreed Minutes – Declarations by one or several of the Contracting Parties of the Agreement on the European Economic Area [1994] OJ L1/3.

[2] Case C-897/19 PPU *Ruska Federacija*, ECLI:EU:C:2020:262.

[3] Council Framework Decision 2002/584/JHA of 13 June 2002 on the European arrest warrant and the surrender procedures between Member States – Statements made by certain Member States on the adoption of the Framework Decision [2002] OJ L190/1.

A central issue in *Ruska Federacija* was the relevance of the judgment in *Petruhhin*.[4] A brief account of that judgment will thus be given before attention is turned to *Ruska Federacija* (Section IV). While *Petruhhin* concerned a national of an EU State (Estonia), *Ruska Federacija* concerned an Icelandic national.

Thereafter, the EFTA Court's advisory opinion in *Jabbi* will be introduced (Section V).[5] The reason is that the case concerned an interpretation of Directive 2004/38/EC.[6] The advisory opinion does not concern the AFSJ but rather the EEA Agreement. However, the EEA Agreement is a link between *Ruska Federacija* and *Jabbi*. At issue in *Jabbi* was a judgment from the ECJ, namely the judgment in *O and B*.[7] In that case the ECJ concluded that when an EU citizen, on certain conditions, had established family life with a third-country national in another EU State, the third-country national may have a derived right as a family member upon the EU citizen's return to the home State.

Finally, I will conclude with some overall reflections (Section VI).

II. BRIEF OVERVIEW OF THE EEA AGREEMENT

According to the EEA Agreement's Preamble, the objective of the Parties is to establish:

> [...] a dynamic and homogeneous European Economic Area, based on common rules and equal conditions of competition and providing for the adequate means of enforcement including at the judicial level, and achieved on the basis of equality and reciprocity and of an overall balance of benefits, rights and obligations for the Contracting Parties

This has to be ensured by:

> [...] a uniform interpretation and application of this Agreement and those provisions of Community legislation which are substantially reproduced in this Agreement and to arrive at an equal treatment of individuals and economic operators as regards the four freedoms and the conditions of competition.

Moreover, the EEA shall 'provide for the fullest possible realisation of the free movement of goods, persons, services and capital within the whole European Economic Area'. In this context the 'role that individuals will play in the European Economic Area through the exercise of the rights conferred on them by this Agreement and through the judicial defence of these rights' is important.

To attain the EEA objective, a homogeneous area is required. The principle of homogeneity is expressed directly and indirectly in different articles of the EEA Agreement, especially in its Chapter 3. A homogeneous EEA must also be dynamic because continuous EU legislation and case law are involved in the legal progress. These developments will substantially change the EFTA States' legal systems.

Furthermore, Article 4 EEA establishes that 'any discrimination on grounds of nationality shall be prohibited'. The principle of loyalty in Article 3 EEA implies that 'all appropriate measures, whether general or particular, to ensure fulfilment of the obligations arising out of

[4] Case C-182/15 *Petruhhin*, ECLI:EU:C:2016:630.

[5] Case E-28/15 *Jabbi*, [2016] EFTA Ct Rep 575.

[6] Directive 2004/38/EC of the European Parliament and of the Council of 29 April 2004 on the right of citizens of the Union and their family members to move and reside freely within the territory of the Member States [2004] OJ L158/77.

[7] Case C-456/12 *O and B*, ECLI:EU:C:2014:135.

this Agreement' should be taken by the Parties, and they should abstain 'from any measure which could jeopardize the attainment of the objectives of this Agreement'.

Much EU law is not covered within the EEA Agreement. In some such areas legal obligations between the EU and EFTA States have been established separately, such as for example in EU's AFSJ, discussed in the next section.

For the EFTA States to have access to EU's internal market without joining the EU as Member States, an institutional separation between the EU States and the EFTA States had to be established – a so-called two-pillar structure. This structure is intended to ensure the good functioning of the EEA. The existing EU institutions responsible for the internal market legislation and dispute settlement manage in the EU pillar the EEA Agreement as part of EU law applicable to the EU States. In an EFTA pillar, the EFTA States made between themselves an agreement creating an EFTA Surveillance Authority (ESA) to monitor the EFTA States' obligations and an EFTA Court to settle disputes mainly in line with EU law.

New EU legislation on the internal market relevant for the EEA is taken into the EEA Agreement by unanimous decisions in a joint committee. The EFTA States implement EU legislation into their internal legal order according to the EEA Agreement. ESA manages its surveillance tasks in cooperation with the Commission. The EFTA Court interprets and applies EEA law in accordance with the case law of the ECJ. EEA law shall be interpreted and applied by the EFTA States as far as possible uniformly with the EU States.

A fair understanding of the objective of the EEA Agreement and the institutional construction is necessary to ensure the proper working of the EEA Agreement.

III. THE AFSJ, EU CITIZENSHIP AND THE EEA AGREEMENT

As for the AFSJ, initially the goal for Iceland and Norway was to preserve the existing Nordic Passport Union once Denmark, Sweden and Finland as EU States abolished checks on persons at internal borders in the Schengen Area. However, it soon became clear that a broader cooperation in the justice field was desirable. In 1999 the EU agreed on a cooperation with Iceland and Norway on the implementation, application and development of the Schengen *acquis* in an association agreement.[8]

A management structure was set up to involve Iceland and Norway in the decision-making process through a mixed committee. The Schengen *acquis* is developed in the EU, but Iceland and Norway are included in discussions concerning practical application, implementation and the preparation of further development of the Schengen provisions. However, if Iceland or Norway do not accept new Schengen provisions, the association agreement will be considered terminated unless the parties decide otherwise.

The parties wished to improve judicial cooperation in criminal matters and the fight against crime. They expressed their mutual confidence in the structure and functioning of their legal systems and the ability to guarantee a fair trial. Within the overall context, the EU agreed with Iceland and Norway on a surrender agreement.[9] The provisions of that agreement are very

[8] Agreement concluded by the Council of the European Union and the Republic of Iceland and the Kingdom of Norway concerning the latters' association with the implementation, application and development of the Schengen acquis – Final Act [1999] OJ L176/36.

[9] Agreement between the European Union and the Republic of Iceland and the Kingdom of Norway on the surrender procedure between the Member States of the European Union and Iceland and Norway – Declarations [2006] OJ L292/2.

similar to the corresponding provisions of the EAW Framework Decision on warrants and surrender between EU States. The parties undertook to ensure that the extradition system between them should be based on a mechanism of surrender pursuant to an arrest warrant in accordance with the terms of the surrender agreement.

As for EU citizenship, it follows from the TFEU that every person holding the nationality of an EU State shall also have EU citizenship. In the EEA context it may be noted that Directive 2004/38 was incorporated into the EEA Agreement by a decision in 2007.[10] In that decision it was stated that the provisions of the directive shall be read with adaptations. Those are especially that the EEA Agreement applies to 'nationals of the Contracting Parties … but members of their family within the meaning of the Directive possessing third-country nationality shall derive certain rights according to the Directive' and that the words 'Union citizen(s)' are replaced by the words 'national(s) of EC Member States and EFTA States'.

Moreover, the Parties agreed to the following Joint Declaration attached to the decision on the implementation:

> The concept of Union Citizenship as introduced by the Treaty of Maastricht […] has no equivalent in the EEA Agreement. The incorporation of Directive 2004/38/EC into the EEA Agreement shall be without prejudice to the evaluation of the EEA relevance of future EU legislation as well as future case law of the European Court of Justice based on the concept of Union Citizenship. The EEA Agreement does not provide a legal basis for political rights of EEA nationals.
>
> The Contracting Parties agree that immigration policy is not covered by the EEA Agreement. Residence rights for third country nationals fall outside the scope of the Agreement with the exception of rights granted by the Directive to third country nationals who are family members of an EEA national exercising his or her right to free movement under the EEA Agreement as these rights are corollary to the right of free movement of EEA nationals. The EFTA States recognise that it is of importance to EEA nationals making use of their right of free movement of persons, that their family members within the meaning of the Directive and possessing third country nationality also enjoy certain derived rights […].

IV. THE ECJ AND CASE C-897/19 PPU *RUSKA FEDERACIJA*

In this section, *Ruska Federacija* will be presented and analysed. However, it is appropriate to start with *Petruhhin*, since that case was essential in *Ruska Federacija*.

Petruhhin concerned a request from Russia for the extradition of an EU citizen – an Estonian national – arrested in Latvia. Mr Petruhhin was accused of attempted organised drug-trafficking. Latvian law did not prohibit an extradition, except in a case of a Latvian national. The national court raised the issue of whether an EU citizen, such as Mr Petruhhin, enjoyed the same protection under EU law as a Latvian national.

From the ECJ's reasoning in *Petruhhin*, I extract for my purpose that

- Mr Petruhhin used his EU right to freedom of movement to move to Latvia; his situation thus falls within the scope of the principle of non-discrimination on grounds of nationality;
- a Latvian national is protected from extradition to a third country, unlike a national of another EU State, leading to a different treatment;
- the difference represents a restriction which may be justified only on objective grounds;

[10] Decision of the EEA Joint Committee No 158/2007 of 7 December 2007 amending Annex V (Free movement of workers) and Annex VIII (Right of establishment) to the EEA Agreement [2008] OJ L124/20; and EEA Supplement to the Official Journal of the European Union [2008] No 26, p 17.

- to prevent the risk of impunity is a legitimate objective, and extradition in order to prosecute in a third country appear appropriate to the objective;
- the EAW Framework Decision, however, would be an alternative measure less prejudicial and equally effective for the purpose;
- in balancing the free movement right and the need to combat impunity, an exchange of information between the EU States must have the priority to provide for the opportunity of prosecution.

Therefore, the ECJ concluded that the EU State receiving the third country's extradition request must give the EU State of the person's nationality information about the request. The first EU State must surrender that national to the other EU State, if so requested, according to the provisions on the EAW and the surrender procedures between EU States.

In *Ruska Federacija*, Russian authorities issued an international wanted persons notice for IN's arrest through Interpol on a charge of corruption in Russia. IN had been granted asylum in Iceland and later citizenship. He travelled as a tourist to Croatia and was arrested there in a border control under the wanted persons notice. Since a Croatian national would not be extradited, the Croatian court wished to know whether *Petruhhin* would apply, considering that IN was not an EU citizen but a national of Iceland.

The ECJ concluded that *Petruhhin* did apply. It held that Iceland has a 'special relationship' with the EU, which goes beyond economic and commercial cooperation. I quote from the judgment:

> [...] the EEA Agreement reaffirms, as stated in its second recital, the special relationship [in the French version: 'les relations privilégiées'] between the European Union, its Member States and the EFTA States, which is based on proximity, long-standing common values and European identity. It is in the light of that special relationship that one of the principal objectives of the EEA Agreement must be understood, namely to provide for the fullest possible realisation of the free movement of goods, persons, services and capital within the whole EEA, so that the internal market established within the European Union is extended to the EFTA States. In that perspective, a number of provisions in the EEA Agreement are intended to ensure that the interpretation of that agreement is as uniform as possible throughout the EEA. It is for the Court, in that context, to ensure that the rules of the EEA Agreement which are identical in substance to those of the FEU Treaty are interpreted uniformly within the Member States.[11]

The ECJ added that:

> [...] not only the fact that the person concerned has the status as a national of an EFTA State, which is a party to the EEA Agreement, but also the fact that that State implements and applies the Schengen acquis, renders the situation of that person objectively comparable with that of an EU citizen to whom, in accordance with Article 3(2) TEU, the Union offers an area of freedom, security and justice without internal frontiers, in which the free movement of persons is ensured.[12]

The ECJ held that EU law, in particular Article 36 EEA (freedom to provide services), must be interpreted as meaning that when an EU State, to which a national of an EFTA State has moved, receives an extradition request from a third country, the requested EU State is obliged, before considering executing the request, to inform the other EFTA State and, should that State so request, surrender that national to it, in accordance with the provisions of the surrender agreement, provided that that EFTA State has jurisdiction to prosecute that national for offences committed outside its national territory.

[11] *Ruska Federacija* (n 2), para 50.
[12] ibid, para 58.

V. THE EFTA COURT AND CASE E-28/15 *YANKUBA JABBI*

It is appropriate to start with the ECJ's judgment in *O and B*, since that case was essential in *Jabbi*.

O and B concerned Mr O and Mr B, both third-country nationals who had married and/or cohabited with Netherlands nationals in Spain and in the Netherlands. Mr O applied for a residence document in the Netherlands as a family member of an EU citizen, but his application was rejected. Mr B had lived for several years in the Netherlands. In 2005 he was declared undesirable on Dutch territory due to a prison sentence. The parties married in 2007 and the declaration of undesirability was lifted. In 2009 his application for residence in the Netherlands was rejected. Court proceeding followed and the national court requested an interpretation from the ECJ.

From the ECJ's reasoning, attention may in particular be paid to the following essential elements:

- a derived right for a family member applies where the EU citizen has exercised free movement by establishing in another EU State;
- from a literal, systematic and teleological interpretation of Directive 2004/38, it follows that it does not establish a derived right of residence for third-country nationals who are family members of an EU citizen in the EU State of which that citizen is a national;
- the ECJ examined and found that *Singh*[13] and *Eind*[14] applied. Those cases concerned the right of a worker to return to his State of origin with a family member being a national of a third country, and the right of an economically inactive person on certain conditions to do the same;
- a derived right of residence for a third-country national in these circumstances seeks to remove an obstacle for free movement by guaranteeing that that citizen will be able to continue the family life created or strengthened in the host EU State when he returns to his EU State of origin.

The ECJ concluded that Article 21(1) TFEU gave the EU citizen's third-country national family member a derived right of residence upon conditions in Directive 2004/38 applied by analogy.

In *Jabbi*, a third-country national had married a Norwegian national while both were living in Spain. The Norwegian woman was not economically active but apparently fulfilled the EEA law conditions for her stay there. Upon her return to Norway, Mr Jabbi applied for residence in Norway as the Norwegian national's family member. That application was rejected by the Norwegian immigration authorities and Mr Jabbi started proceedings against the decision.

The Oslo District Court requested the EFTA Court's advisory opinion on the question whether Article 7(1)(b), *cf* Article 7(2), of Directive 2004/38/EC confer a derived right of residence to a third-country national who is a family member of an EEA national who, upon returning from another EEA State, is residing in the EEA State in which the EEA national is a citizen.

According to the first provision, nationals of EU States and EFTA States shall have the right of residence on the territory of another EEA State for a period of longer than three months if they have sufficient resources for themselves and their family members not to become a burden on the social assistance system of the host EEA State during their period of residence and have

[13] Case C-370/90 *Singh*, ECLI:EU:C:1992:296.
[14] Case C-291/05 *Eind*, ECLI:EU:C:2007:771.

comprehensive sickness insurance cover in the host EU State. According to the second provision a right of residence shall extend to family members who are not nationals of an EU or an EFTA State, accompanying or joining the EU citizen in the host EU State.

The essential elements of the EFTA Court's reasoning are the following:

- a shared labour market would not function adequately if migrant workers were prevented from maintaining established family life. Such a limitation would have acted as a deterrent to labour market mobility. Therefore, a worker moving to another EEA State must be able to maintain family life created in that State upon the worker's return to his State of origin;
- EU legislation and case law have extended the concept of free movement of workers, and EEA law includes also the freedom of movement of an economically inactive person, including a derived right for a third-country national family member;
- the Maastricht Treaty introduced the concept of EU citizenship, which entails certain political rights, for example some voting rights and access to the European Ombudsman. However, also the right for every EU citizen to move and reside freely within the territory of the EU State is included, subject to conditions laid down in EU law to give free movement effect;
- Article 28 EEA gives a worker freedom of movement. According to its Preamble the EEA Agreement shall provide the fullest possible realisation of the four freedoms, including the free movement of persons, within the whole of the EEA. The freedoms form part of the core of the EEA Agreement and the consideration of homogeneity therefore carries substantial weight;
- Directive 2004/38 on the right of EU citizens and their family members to move and reside freely within the territory of the EU States is incorporated into the EEA Agreement. A joint declaration was added (quoted above);
- in *O and B* the ECJ had found the authority for its conclusion in Article 21(1) TFEU, whereas application of the Directive 2004/38/EC appears, for the most part, to have been rejected. Consequently, an unequal level of protection of the right to free movement of persons within the EEA could ensue.

The EFTA Court noted that:

> [...] to assess the impact of the legal findings in O. and B. for the interpretation of EEA law, that judgment must be read in its proper legal context. That context encompasses the concept of Union citizenship. The ECJ did not base its main conclusion on the Directive. Furthermore, the case law resulting from Singh and Eind was considered applicable under Article 21(1) TFEU to family members of Union citizens upon a return to the home State. The ECJ held that such a derived right seeks to remove obstacles for leaving the home State by guaranteeing that that citizen upon return to the home State will be able to continue the family life created or strengthened in the host State [...].[15]

Jabbi should be distinguished from *O and B* to the extent that that judgment is based on EU citizenship. Therefore, it should be examined whether homogeneity in the EEA can be achieved based on an authority included in the EEA Agreement. In the Preamble to the EEA Agreement, the Parties state that their objective is to reach and maintain a uniform interpretation and application of the EEA Agreement and those provisions of EU legislation substantially reproduced in its main part and annexes and, furthermore, to arrive at an equal treatment of individuals

[15] Jabbi (n 5), para 67.

and economic operators in regards to the four freedoms. However, the same recital also states that a uniform interpretation and application of the EEA Agreement shall be achieved in full deference to the independence of the courts;

The EFTA Court then stated that:

> [w]ithout independence in its adjudication no court could claim legitimacy. Every court must exercise its jurisdiction based upon the relevant legal sources. An essential legal source for the Court is the case law of the ECJ and the General Court. That case law must nevertheless be read in its context. Normally, this does not pose particular problems because the context is the same. However, when it comes to the legal sources in this case, the ECJ has partly ruled out the application of the Directive and instead applied the concept of Union citizenship in evolution of the free movement of persons in the EU.[16]

A refusal of a derived right of residence in Norway for the third-country national family member would constitute an obstacle to the Norwegian citizen's freedom of movement under EEA law. Accordingly, EEA law requires that the family member be granted a derived right of residence in that State. The possibility for individuals exercising their right of free movement to invoke this right against their home State has been recognised in the case law of the ECJ. Moreover, economically inactive EEA nationals may enjoy their right to reside in another EEA State.

The EFTA Court underlined that a derived right exists on conditions that:

- the EEA national exercised the EEA right of free movement;
- family life was created or strengthened during genuine residence in another EEA State than the EEA national's State of origin;
- the third-country national's derived right is not a result of abuse of rights or fraud, such as marriages of convenience; and
- derived rights may be restricted based on public policy, public security or public health.

Against this background, the EFTA Court found that where an EEA national has created or strengthened family life with a third-country national during genuine residence in an EEA State other than that of which he is a national, the provisions of the directive will apply by analogy where that EEA national returns with the family member to his State of origin.

The EFTA Court upheld the interpretation in *Jabbi* in an advisory opinion to the Supreme Court of Norway.[17] However, the appeal case was withdrawn before the Supreme Court could make a decision.

VI. CONCLUSION

The rejection in *O and B* of Directive 2004/38/EC as a legal basis for a derived right of residence for a third-country national, being a family member of a national of an EU or an EFTA State, in that person's State of origin represented a challenge for the EFTA Court. It had to explain why a third-country national family member must be granted a derived right of residence in the EFTA national's State of origin based on EEA law not including a provision on free movement of persons identical to that of EU citizenship.

[16] ibid, para 71.

[17] Case E-4/19 *Campbell*, judgment of 13 May 2020.

The main reason the EFTA Court gave was the principle of homogeneity. A high degree of homogeneity based on EU law is a precondition for the good functioning of the EEA. The free movement of goods, services, persons and capital in the EU internal market are at the core of the EEA. A substantial deviation from homogeneity in the EFTA States as regards the four freedoms would involve a risk to the EEA Agreement.

In order to sustain homogeneity, interpretation and application of the EEA Agreement, it must, in principle, be dynamic to a similar extent as EU law. The free movement of persons is ensured in Article 28 EEA. Legislation and case law have played an important part in the development of the four freedoms, not least regarding the free movement of persons. Such legal developments were reflected in the EEA Agreement from the start, and subsequent developments in EU legislation and case law are comprised in EEA law, for example the judgments in *Singh* and *Eind* – which were not based on EU citizenship law.

The Parties have not included EU citizenship as such in the EEA Agreement. However, in addition to political and other rights, EU citizenship includes the right for EU citizens to move and reside freely within the territory of the EU States, subject to the limitations and conditions laid down in EU law. The free movement of persons in the EEA context correlate to the right to move and reside freely in the EU context. Considering in general the evolvement of EU law, it seems difficult to assume that the Parties intended to restrict further evolution of the free movement of persons in the EEA law on account of the introduction of the EU citizenship in EU law.

The EEA principle of loyalty might also be considered. It follows from Article 3 EEA that the Parties shall take all appropriate measures, whether general or particular, to ensure fulfilment of the obligations arising out of the EEA Agreement and abstain from any measure which could jeopardise the attainment of the objectives of the Agreement.

The EFTA Court had to make a choice whether to follow the result or the reasoning on the specific point of the directive of the ECJ in *O and B*. In *Jabbi*, the EFTA Court might have pondered the hypothesis: if EU citizenship were non-existent, could the ECJ have arrived at the same conclusion as the EFTA Court?

Considering overall the case law of the ECJ, an affirmative answer would not seem a remote possibility. The ECJ has in many cases based its reasonings on the scheme and objective of EU law provisions at the expense of the text. This may sometimes cause controversy. However, examples mostly show that national authorities in the EU States have later recognised, at least implicitly, judgments with which they disagreed at the time of the judgment.

The purpose of the derived right for the third-country family member is to enable the EEA national to exercise the right to free movement and to maintain established family life. The need to protect an EEA national's family life would seem to be at least equally strong when that national returns to the EFTA State of origin with a third-country national as a family member, as the need to protect the EEA national and such a family member moving to another EEA State.

In *Jabbi* the main issue was homogeneity within the EEA, whereas in *Ruska Federacija* it was the impact of the EEA Agreement on the relations between EU and Iceland outside of the EEA Agreement, that is, for a specific part of Schengen *acquis*. In *Ruska Federacija* the reader is reminded that the ECJ must provide a national court with an answer which will be useful and enable the national court to determine the case before it. Under that obligation, the Grand Chamber amplified the EEA Agreement. The ECJ stated that the EEA Agreement expresses the special relationship between the EU and Iceland. The common denominator is homogeneity in the internal market established within the EU and extended to the EFTA States.

The EFTA Court ensured in *Jabbi* equal treatment of a Norwegian national and an EU citizen who are in the same position (a return to the State of origin with a third-country national as a family member). In *Ruska Federacija* the ECJ held that the EEA Agreement, seen together with the relevant Schengen *acquis*, ensured equal treatment of an Icelandic national and an EU citizen in the same position in an EU State (an Icelandic national protected in the same way as an EU citizen from extradition to a third country).

The conclusions in the two cases were not inevitable. In *Jabbi* the EFTA Court could have followed Norway's submission and dismissed protection of the Norwegian national's family life in Norway with a third-country national on the ground that the ECJ had already answered the national court's specific question. In *Ruska Federacija* the ECJ could have followed Norway's submission that EU citizenship was not included in EEA law and that, therefore, an Icelandic national having used the right to free movement in an EU State should not enjoy equal protection with an EU citizen in the same position.

The Commission shall, inter alia, oversee the application of EU law under the control of the ECJ. ESA shall ensure that the EFTA States fulfil their obligations under the EEA Agreement, and the EFTA Court has the final say in case of a dispute. In *Jabbi* and *Ruska Federacija*, the Commission and ESA argued in their written submissions in favour of equal treatment. Iceland argued before the ECJ in favour of protecting the interests of the Icelandic national.

Iceland and Norway are in the same position via-à-vis the EU on the relevant legal points, and the ECJ's conclusion must apply also to a Norwegian national in a similar situation. However, in *Ruska Federacija*, Norway mainly kept to a formal approach before the ECJ, as it did in the submission before the EFTA Court in *Jabbi*. The main argument was that Article 21 TFEU has no equivalent provision in EEA law.

It may be added that in *Ruska Federacija*, Norway informed the ECJ that the Supreme Court of Norway, in *Campbell*[18] (pending at the time of the hearing at the ECJ), had asked the EFTA Court to overrule its decision in *Jabbi*. Norway took the view that *Jabbi* is inconsistent with EEA law and invited the ECJ to rule that rights based solely on Article 21 TFEU fall outside the scope of the EEA Agreement. Norway's view exposed the EEA Agreement to an amount of disharmony. However, the ECJ did not follow the Norwegian invitation.

Interpretation of legal rules must take place within an accepted methodological framework. Judicial conclusions will, to varying degrees, depend on the methods of interpretation applied. Different conclusions may result from a literal approach as compared to a teleological approach, for example.

A literal interpretation will normally be the starting point. However, a literal interpretation may meet with other concerns that must be considered. A systematic interpretation may, for example, better harmonise a specific or a broader legal field at issue. A teleological interpretation may, for example, enable a conclusion that better corresponds to the perception of an appropriate and reasonable result. Choices of interpretations must be made, which may explain why competent lawyers arrive at different but acceptable conclusions.

In judicial proceedings a court will decide. Judges, perhaps especially those with a final say, do not readily admit that they deviate from previous decisions. However, they will be able, as a rule, to adapt adverse or unfortunate developments in their court's own case law, whether explicitly or not, by arriving at a different result where a previous one has fallen short.

To interpret the legal sources in dubious disputes is more akin to *Fingerspitzengefühl* rather than to legal logics. However, whether a reasoning in a specific case has been suitable

[18] ibid.

often shows itself in the acceptance or rejection of the result by other legal professionals and national authorities involved in or related to a dispute, by a wider legal community and in some cases even by public opinion. It is a force of the rule of law, provided the principle is respected, that contending parties can leave a dispute behind and move on – after a final decision has been made in a fair trial.

A limit to EEA homogeneity must be accepted. The EFTA States are not EU Member States, but they are in a special relationship with the EU and the EU States. However, departure from the principle should in practice be made only if serious and convincing legal grounds are involved. The EFTA Court did not find that the limit to homogeneity was reached in *Jabbi*. In *Ruska Federacija* the ECJ made an interpretation that was consistent with a homogenous result in the context of the AFSJ, substantiated by the EEA Agreement. In any case, a limit of EEA homogeneity should only be drawn according to careful considerations on a case-by-case basis.

Without a broad revision of the main part of the EEA Agreement, or until an alternative arrangement to the EEA is established, tension is likely to occur from time to time between the necessity of homogeneity in the EEA and the fact that EFTA States are not EU Member States.

If my reading of the ECJ's judgment in *Ruska Federacija* is tenable, it represents a line of reasoning which is related to the reasoning of the EFTA Court in *Jabbi*. A solid foundation for the courts' reasonings leading to homogenous results must be the recognition of a relationship based on proximity, long-standing common values and European identity between the EU States and the EFTA States.

Accordingly, the concurrent perception in *Ruska Federacija* and *Jabbi* may illustrate a tacit understanding from the ECJ for separate and independent reasoning in the EFTA Court's EEA context to further the homogeneity and thus stabilise the EEA Agreement. Moreover, it may illustrate that the ECJ will endeavour to keep the EEA sound. The EFTA Court must for its part continue to make efforts as far as possible to interpret EEA law uniformly with the EU law relevant for the EEA Agreement.

26

Absent Prosecution Witnesses and Active Participation at Trial: The European Court of Justice Shapes European Fairness on Criminal Justice

SILVIA ALLEGREZZA*

I. INTRODUCTION: FROM STRASBOURG TO LUXEMBOURG: BUILDING BLOCKS OF EUROPEAN FAIRNESS ON CRIMINAL EVIDENCE

FAIR TRIAL HAS many facets. Some are preconditions of general fairness, such as independence and impartiality of the adjudicating court, or public hearing, or reasonable time. Others are intrinsic to criminal trial, as exemplified by Article 6(3) of the European Convention on Human Rights (ECHR), where the panoplies of structural components of criminal fairness are listed. Article 6(3)(d) ECHR is one of them, as it advances the defendant's demand 'to examine or have examined witnesses against him'.[1] The latter is the main pillar of the right to a fair criminal trial, so deeply attached to the entire philosophy on fact-finding in criminal adjudication, so strongly linked to the general setting of powers among the court, the prosecutor and the accused person.

The dynamic and sensitive nature of fair trial rights in general, and specifically of the right to examine prosecutorial witnesses, has been fully acknowledged by the European Court of Human Rights (ECtHR). Over the last five decades, a rich case law of the ECtHR carved the content of the right at stake, described how it can be waived, defined its limits and potential remedies.[2] The ECtHR case law fostered convergences that were able to reduce the structural differences among inquisitorial and accusatorial traditions on witnesses' cross-examination. Enforcement varies according to traditional features of each system, 'only partially described

* Associate Professor of Criminal Law and Criminal Procedure at the University of Luxembourg.

[1] '... and to obtain the attendance and examination of witnesses on his behalf under the same conditions as witnesses against him': ECHR, Art 6(3)(d).

[2] ECHR, *Guide on Article 6 of the European Convention on Human Rights. Right to a Fair Trial (Criminal Limb)*, updated 31 August 2022; S Trechsel and SJ Summers, *Human Rights in Criminal Proceedings* (Oxford University Press, 2005) 291 ff; L Bachmaier Winter, 'Transnational Criminal Proceedings, Witness Evidence and Confrontation: Lessons from the ECtHR's Case Law' (2013) 9 *Utrecht Law Review* 127; S Maffei, *The Right to Confrontation in Europe* (Europa Law Publishing, 2012); S Lonati, 'Anonymous Witness Evidence before the European Court of Human Rights: Is It Still Possible to Speak of "Fair Trial"?' (2018) 1 *European Criminal Law Review* 116, 118 ff.

by the traditional partition between accusatorial/adversarial and inquisitorial systems, currently largely outdated'.[3]

Convergences exalted by the pragmatism always adopted by the ECtHR in shaping the golden rule – 'the accused person must have an adequate and proper opportunity to challenge and question a witness against him, either when that witness makes his statement or at a later stage of proceedings' as established by Article 6(3)(d) ECHR[4] – and the related exceptions and remedies.[5] For decades, the Strasbourg court adopted a holistic approach: the rights to call and examine witnesses were not considered in isolation, but always in conjunction with Article 6(1) ECHR to evaluate the procedural fairness of the trial as a whole.[6] Preconditions for the breach of Article 6 ECHR were the lack for the defendant of a concrete opportunity to examine the witness, a valid reason for the witness's absence from trial and the fact that those statements have represented the 'sole or decisive evidence'.[7] Only after 2011, with the *revirement* intervened with the case *Al-Khawaja and Tahery*,[8] did the ECtHR exclude the lack of fairness – and consequently the breach of Article 6 ECHR – when, despite the decisive nature of the untested statements, counterbalancing measures were in place to compensate the disadvantages due to the lack of examination.[9]

This contribution recognises its limitations in offering a complete overview of such a rich case law, or in summarising the many scholarly positions. We must observe, though, how imposing the requirement to assess the fairness of the proceedings as a whole 'encouraged common law judges to engage more holistically with the effect of certain kinds of evidence',[10] while forcing civil law courts into a deeper scrutiny of the legality of evidence gathering.[11]

[3] SJ Summers, *Fair Trials: The European Criminal Procedural Tradition and the European Court of Human Rights* (Hart Publishing, 2007); for a stringent criticism of this approach, see S Field, 'Fair Trials and Procedural Tradition in Europe' (2009) 29 *Oxford Journal of Legal Studies* 365. On the cultural origins of the two traditions, see M Langer, 'The Long Shadow of the Adversarial and Inquisitorial Categories' in M Dubber and T Hörnle, *The Oxford Handbook of Criminal Law* (Oxford University Press, 2014) 273.

[4] *Lucà v Italy* App no 33354/96, ECLI:CE:ECHR:2001:0227JUD003335496, para 39.

[5] Among many, see *Al-Khawaja and Tahery v the United Kingdom* App no 26766/05 and no 22228/06, ECLI:CE:ECHR:2011:1215JUD002676605, para 118; *Hümmer v Germany* App no 26171/07, ECLI:CE:ECHR:2012:0719JUD002617107, para 38; *Lucà v Italy* (n 4), para 39; *Solakov v the former Yugoslav Republic of Macedonia* App no 47023/99, ECLI:CE:ECHR:2001:1031JUD004702399, para 57; and *Schatschaschwili v Germany* App no 9154/10, ECLI:CE:ECHR:2015:1215JUD000915410, paras 104–105. In this regard, see Trechsel and Summers (n 2), 295 and T Brooks (ed), *The Right to a Fair Trial* (Routledge, 2009).

[6] *Al-Khawaja and Tahery v the United Kingdom* (n 5), para 147; *Schatschaschwili v Germany* (n 5), paras 100–109; S Mirandola, 'The Right to Examine Witnesses in Europe: A Progressively Fading Guarantee?' in S Allegrezza and V Covolo (eds), *EU Fair Trial Rights in Criminal Justice* (Hart Publishing, forthcoming).

[7] E Widder, 'The Right to Challenge Witnesses – An Application of Strasbourg's Flexible "Sole and Decisive" Rule to Other Human Rights' (2014) 3 *Cambridge International Law Journal* 1084; JD Jackson, 'Common Law Evidence and the Common Law of Human Rights: Towards a Harmonic Convergence?' (2019) 27 *William & Mary Bill of Rights Journal* 689; *Salduz v Turkey* App no 36391/02, ECLI:CE:ECHR:2008:1127JUD003639102; *Bracci v Italy* App no 36822/02, ECLI:CE:ECHR:2005:1013JUD003682202; *Gani v Spain* App no 61800/08, ECLI:CE:ECHR:2013:0219JUD006180008; and *Karpenko v Russia* App no 5605/04, ECLI:CE:ECHR:2012:0313JUD000560504.

[8] *Al-Khawaja and Tahery v the United Kingdom* (n 5). See L Hoyano, 'What is Balanced on the Scales of Justice? In Search of the Essence of the Right to a Fair Trial' (2014) *Criminal Law Review* 4; B de Wilde, 'A Fundamental Review of the ECHR Right to Examine Witnesses in Criminal Cases' (2013) 17 *The International Journal of Evidence and Proof* 168; M Biral, 'The Right to Examine or Have Examined Witnesses as a Minimum Right for a Fair Trial' (2014) 22 *European Journal of Crime, Criminal Law, and Criminal Justice* 331; and A Balsamo, 'La Corte di Strasburgo e i testimoni assenti: gli sviluppi del "nuovo corso" avviato dalla sentenza Al-Khawaja' (2013) 53 *Cassazione Penale* 2837.

[9] *Al-Khawaja and Tahery v the United Kingdom* (n 5); *Schatschaschwili v Germany* (n 5); *Al Alo v Slovakia* App no 32084/19, ECLI:CE:ECHR:2022:0210JUD003208419.

[10] Jackson (n 7), 689.

[11] JD Jackson and SJ Summers, *The Internationalisation of Criminal Evidence: Beyond the Common Law and Civil Law Traditions* (Cambridge University Press, 2012) 30.

The procedurally neutral account of fairness,[12] promoted by the ECHR, paved the way to an increasing approximation of domestic legislations, which can accommodate both adversarial and inquisitorial traditions[13] despite their origins and persistent cultural differences.[14]

The challenge of approximation of evidence law should have been taken over by the European Union (EU) as a priority.[15] The Lisbon Treaty offered a solid legal basis for such approximation[16] and the rise of judicial cooperation instruments based on mutual recognition, such as the European arrest warrant,[17] or the European investigation order (EIO) has shown how fragile mutual trust can be in lack of harmonisation.[18] Even more urgent, it appears now that the European Public Prosecutor Office (EPPO)[19] is fully operational. The lack of common rules on evidence soon forced national courts dealing with EPPO's investigations to address the European Court of Justice (ECJ) with requests for a preliminary ruling on crucial issues such as judicial authorisation for coercive investigative measures,[20] or on the dividing line between a witness and a suspect.[21]

Unfortunately, the reluctance of Member States to work toward an EU-led harmonisation of criminal evidence has been too strong and mutual recognition without harmonisation has prevailed.[22] However, evidence administration is too crucial to be kept out of the door,

[12] S Field, 'Fair Trials and Procedural Tradition in Europe' (2009) 29 *Oxford Journal of Legal Studies* 365. As for applicability in the diverse legal systems of Contracting States within the ECHR system, and in particular in the context of both common law and continental law systems, the Court has stressed that while it is important for it to have regard to substantial differences in legal systems and procedures, including different approaches to the admissibility of evidence in criminal trials, ultimately it must apply the same standard of reviews under Articles 6 §§ 1 and 3(d) irrespective of the legal system from which a case emanates. See *Al-Khawaja and Tahery v the United Kingdom* (n 5), para 130; *Schatschaschwili v Germany* (n 5), para 108.

[13] M Delmas-Marty, *Procès pénal et droits de l'homme. Vers une conscience européenne* (Presses Universitaires de France, 1992); and M Delmas-Marty (ed), *Procédures pénales d'Europe* (Presses Universitaires de France, 1995).

[14] M Langer, 'The Long Shadow of the Adversarial and Inquisitorial Categories' in MD Dubber and T Hörnle (eds), *The Oxford Handbook of Criminal Law* (Oxford University Press, 2014) 887; and M Langer, 'In The Beginning Was Fortescue: On The Intellectual Origins of the Adversarial and Inquisitorial Systems and Common and Civil Law in Comparative Criminal Procedure' in B Ackerman et al (eds), *Liber Amicorum in Honor of Professor Damaška* (Duncker & Humblot, 2016) 347.

[15] JAE Vervaele, 'Lawful and Fair Use of Evidence from a European Human Rights Perspective' in F Giuffrida and K Ligeti (eds), *Admissibility of OLAF Final Reports as Evidence in Criminal Proceedings* (University of Luxembourg, 2019) 56.

[16] See Art 82(2) TFUE according to which 'to the extent necessary to facilitate mutual recognition of judgments and judicial decisions and police and judicial cooperation in criminal matters having a cross-border dimension, the European Parliament and the Council may, by means of directives adopted in accordance with the ordinary legislative procedure, establish minimum rules. Such rules shall take into account the differences between the legal traditions and systems of the Member States'. L Bachmaier Winter, 'Mutual Admissibility of Evidence and Electronic Evidence in the EU: A New Try for European Minimum Rules in Criminal Proceedings?' (2023) *Eucrim* 223.

[17] Council Framework Decision 2002/584 on the European Arrest Warrant and the Surrender Procedures between Member States [2002] OJ L190/1; see L Bay Larsen, 'Recent Jurisprudence of the CJEU on Judicial Independence and the Framework Decision on the European Arrest Warrant' in Eurojust, *20 years of Eurojust: EU Judicial Cooperation in the Making. A Collection of Anniversary Essays* (The Hague, 2023) 87.

[18] Directive 2014/41/EU of 3 April 2014 regarding the European Investigation Order in criminal matters [2014] OJ L130/1.

[19] Council Regulation (EU) 2017/1939 of 12 October 2017 implementing enhanced cooperation on the establishment of the European Public Prosecutor's Office [2017] OJ L283/1. In this regard, see S Allegrezza, 'A European Public Prosecutor Office to Protect the EU Financial Interests' in K Ambos and P Rackow (eds), *The Cambridge Companion to European Criminal Law* (Cambridge University Press, 2023) 413. On the admissibility of evidence, for a comparison between the EIO and the EPPO, see S Allegrezza and A Mosna, 'Cross-Border Criminal Evidence and the Future European Public Prosecutor. One Step Back on Mutual Recognition?' in L Bachmaier Winter (ed), *The European Public Prosecutor's Office. The Challenges Ahead* (Springer, 2018) 141.

[20] Case 281/22 *Österreichischer Delegierter Europäischer Staatsanwalt (Parquet européen)*, ECLI:EU:C:2023:510.

[21] Case 292/23 *EPPO*, pending.

[22] On the difficulties of harmonisation in criminal procedure, see A Weyembergh, 'L'harmonisation des procédures pénales au sein de l'Union Européenne' (2004) 26(1) *Archives de politique criminelle* 37, 38–39. More recently, on the

especially when criminal justice moved from the periphery of the EU to its very heart, as a remarkable driving force of the European integration.[23] Transnational proceedings are increasing in number. Even more pervasive is the long-term effect of the directives approved according to the so-called 'Stockholm road-map',[24] which compose, together with the Treaties and the Charter of Fundamental Rights of the European Union (the Charter), a robust framework on the rights of the suspects and the accused persons in criminal proceedings. It is undisputable that these directives have de facto 'communitarised' every single criminal case, whether transnational or merely domestic,[25] offering to European law an unprecedented occasion to shape defence rights across the Union.[26] As a consequence, political deadlock on harmonisation of evidence could not stop the attempts of national courts to introduce preliminary ruling requests on how to articulate the fairness protected by the defendant's right to be present at trial with the rules on evidence.

Given the lack of a specific legislation on admissibility or collection of testimony in criminal justice, the referring national courts have relied on several provisions of the directives on procedural safeguards for the suspect or the defendant. They indeed exalt the right to fair trial as 'one of the basic principles in democratic society'.[27] And that fairness should be *at least* equivalent to the one granted by Article 6 ECHR. It follows from Article 6(3) of the Treaty on the European Union (TEU) and Article 52(3) of the Charter that Article 47 of the Charter must be interpreted and applied consistently with Article 6 ECHR. The same happens with Article 48(2) of the Charter: it corresponds to Article 6(3) ECHR and has the same meaning and scope as the latter.[28] This is stated by the explanations relating to the Charter and confirmed by the ECJ case law on procedural safeguards. What are the effects of this correspondence on rules related to evidence administration? This question was still unanswered until very recently.[29]

impact of national differences on judicial cooperation, see EU Commission, 'Study on Cross-Border Use of Evidence in Criminal Proceedings. Final Report' (March 2023) https://op.europa.eu/en/publication-detail/-/publication/2815b94e-9165-11ed-b508-01aa75ed71a1/language-en/format-PDF/source-291553958, accessed 3 March 2024.

[23] J Öberg, 'Exit, Voice and Consensus – A Legal and Political Analysis of the Emergency Brake in EU Criminal Policy' (*European Law Blog*, 11 October 2021) https://europeanlawblog.eu/2021/10/11/exit-voice-and-consensus-a-legal-and-political-analysis-of-the-emergency-brake-in-eu-criminal-policy/, accessed 3 March 2024.

[24] Directive 2010/64/EU of the European Parliament and of the Council of 20 October 2010 on the right to interpretation and translation in criminal proceedings [2010] OJ L280/1; Directive 2012/13/EU of the European Parliament and of the Council of 22 May 2012 on the right to information in criminal proceedings [2012] OJ L142/1; Directive 2013/48/EU of the European Parliament and of the Council of 22 October 2013 on the right of access to a lawyer in criminal proceedings and in European arrest warrant proceedings, and on the right to have a third party informed upon deprivation of liberty and to communicate with third persons and with consular authorities while deprived of liberty [2013] OJ L294/1; Directive (EU) 2016/343 of the European Parliament and of the Council of 9 March 2016 on the strengthening of certain aspects of the presumption of innocence and of the right to be present at the trial in criminal proceedings [2016] OJ L65/1; Directive (EU) 2016/800 of the European Parliament and of the Council of 11 May 2016 on procedural safeguards for children who are suspects or accused persons in criminal proceedings [2016] OJ L132/1; and Directive (EU) 2016/1919 of the European Parliament and of the Council of 26 October 2016 on legal aid for suspects and accused persons in criminal proceedings and for requested persons in European arrest warrant proceedings [2016] OJ L297/1.

[25] Case C-646/17 *Moro*, ECLI:EU:C:2019:489.

[26] S Allegrezza, 'Commento all'articolo 48' in R Mastroianni et al (eds), *Carta dei Diritti Fondamentali dell'Unione Europea* (Giuffrè, 2016) 946 ff; S Allegrezza, 'Toward a European Constitutional Framework for Defence Rights' in S Allegrezza and V Covolo (eds), *Effective Defence Rights in Criminal Proceedings. A European Comparative Study on Judicial Remedies* (Wolters Kluwer – Cedam, 2018) 31–33.

[27] Directive 2016/343, Recital 33.

[28] See S Allegrezza, 'Commento all'Articolo 48' (n 26), 956.

[29] The relevance of Art 48(2) of the Charter has been confirmed by AG Collins in his Opinion in Case C-348/21 *HYA and Others*, ECLI:EU:C:2022:539, para 35 and by the ECJ in Case C-348/21 *HYA and Others*, ECLI:EU:C:2022:963, para 29.

This chapter aims to contribute to the debate about the EU approach to fairness in criminal proceedings, with a specific focus on the right to effective participation and its corollaries on evidence gathering. Relying on a recent ECJ case as a blueprint, section II will unpack the absent witness dilemma. Section III will then explain the interplay between the EU legal framework – the Treaties, the Charter and the EU directives on procedural safeguards – and the ECHR *acquis* on 'fairness as a whole'. Grounding the ECHR fair trial rights on the EU Charter forces the ECJ to assess the proportionality of those limits in light of the EU concept of proportionality. Sections IV and V will then advance critical arguments on the Union alignment with the ECtHR on criminal evidence in general, and on absent witnesses in particular, suggesting the need to develop an EU autonomous concept of fairness in criminal proceedings.

II. UNPACKING THE ECJ'S APPROACH TO THE ABSENT WITNESS' DILEMMA: THE *HYA* CASE

Even though EU law provides little – if any – guidance on evidence administration in domestic cases, it comes as no surprise that the latter found its way into the courtroom before the ECJ via the numerous provisions of the directives on procedural safeguards. In particular, in some recent cases, the ECJ has been called to assess the impact of Directive 2013/48 and the right to be present at the trial in relation to witness examination in criminal proceedings. Taking the *HYA* case as a blueprint,[30] the ECJ carefully interpreted EU directives identifying the content and level of protection as well as the conditions of potential waivers and compensation measures. What happens when the witness for the prosecution has been questioned during the pre-trial stage but they did not show up for the trial before the court, depriving the accused person of his right to examine prosecution witnesses?

Whilst the topic is difficult to penetrate, a cursory analysis highlights many differences among national systems when confronted with the aforementioned scenario: on the definition of 'witness';[31] on the authority in charge of the questioning; on the possibility to anticipate at the preliminary stage the evidence-gathering according to the rules that apply to trial; on the right of the defence to participate to the questioning; on documentation modalities; on the possibility to use those statements for a guilty verdict; and more in general on their evidentiary value. As a matter of fact, this is an area of weak legislative activity and intense judicial activism – over five hundred ECtHR decisions focus on Article 6(3)(d) ECHR – which the ECJ can no longer avoid.

In the *HYA* case,[32] a Bulgarian court was confronted with the absence of crucial witnesses from trial and with the impossibility of granting to the defendants or their lawyers the right to examine them. The defendants being accused of participating in criminal organisation for the purpose of smuggling illegal migrants into the Bulgarian territory, the witnesses were third-country nationals whose attendance at the future trial was at risk from the beginning, as they were subject to expulsion or deportation. Despite this awareness, the prosecutor did not consider it necessary to examine them in the presence of the accused persons or their lawyers. Some were questioned directly by the prosecutor, others by a judge, and all before the suspects were formally charged or assisted by a lawyer.

[30] ibid.
[31] *EPPO* (n 21).
[32] *HYA and Others* (n 29).

Once at trial, the Bulgarian court relied on how crucial these witnesses' statements were for the adjudication of the merits and attempted unsuccessfully to locate them to be summoned for the trial hearing. However, the witnesses were illegal migrants, and thus may have been deported or voluntarily left the country, or it was impossible to determine their residence. Consequently, upon request of the prosecutor, the court had no other choice but to read the previous statements collected by the prosecutor or by a judge in the absence of the accused person or their lawyer. The reading would confer full evidentiary value to adjudicate on criminal liability of the defendant, as provided for by domestic law. However, the national court has doubts on the compatibility of such a practice with Article 8(1) and Article 6(1) of Directive 2016/343, as the reading of previous statements would deprive the accused person of his right to be present at their trial and obtain an effective defence. In essence, should domestic law and practice that appear in breach of the ECHR doctrine on the right to examine prosecution witnesses prevail, or should those statements be set aside in order to protect the right of the defendant to be present at trial? In a remarkable decision,[33] anticipated by the exemplary conclusions of Advocate General Collins, the ECJ confirmed the doubts of the referring court and offered, for the first time, the Union's take on basic rules on gathering oral evidence in criminal trial.

It is of utmost importance to recall some background elements of the case, as the long-term consequences of this leading judgment will depend greatly upon the similarity of the facts with the case at stake: witnesses were examined during the pre-trial stage solely by the prosecutor but before a judge; all examinations took place without the accused persons or their lawyers being present; the defence participation would have been possible but it has been ignored; there are objective reasons for the absence of the witnesses from the trial hearing; the prosecutor asked for the statements to be read out and turned into evidence (which they would not be, without the reading); the statements of the absent witnesses appear crucial for the assessment of the guilt of the defendants.

The ECJ decision opens with a vigorous endorsement of the correspondence on content, meaning and scope between the rights recognised by Article 47 and 48(2) of the Charter with those laid down by the Convention, as established by Article 52(3) of the Charter.[34] There is an additional force in the argument, as it fills in with rich and articulated content the laconic text of Article 48(2) of the Charter. The material scope of Article 48(2) includes not only all the specific procedural safeguards listed in Article 6(3) ECHR, but also those that the Strasbourg Court has read into it as implied guarantees.[35] The opening statement is a revealing indicator of the expansive effect of the Charter as a constitutional framework of fundamental rights protection,[36] and how the ECJ can rely on its provisions when there is the need for a paradigm shift of the European integration process.

How does this constitutional framework impact the rules on criminal evidence? The answer turns around the content of the right to be present at trial as foreseen by Article 8(1) of Directive 2016/343. Although neither Article 8(1) nor any other provision of that Directive mention the right of an accused person to examine prosecution witnesses, the referring court fears that ensuring their mere presence at trial without granting the effective exercise of the rights provided by Article 6(3) ECHR would impair the very essence of that right. In resisting a reductive interpretation sustained by the Commission – according to which the Directive in

[33] ibid.

[34] ibid, paras 29–30.

[35] For instance, the right to be present at trial and the right to remain silent. See S Allegrezza, 'Toward a European Constitutional Framework for Defence Rights' (n 26).

[36] V Mitsilegas, *EU Criminal Law after Lisbon* (Hart Publishing, 2022) 5.

question provides obligations for the Member States 'without prejudice to national rules and systems on the admissibility of evidence'[37] – both the Advocate General and the ECJ agree that for the right to be present of the accused person to be effective, it should encompass all legal rights in the context of that trial for the purpose of his or her defence, including the right to question prosecution witnesses. If the defendant were to be deprived of that chance, they would only passively attend the reading,[38] their role being reduced to that of mere spectators.[39]

III. BUILDING BRIDGES BETWEEN THE CHARTER AND THE ECHR

The ECJ achieves this by purporting to confer on the defendant the right to examine or have examined witnesses against them at the judicial stage as a way to grant an effective right to participation. The reasoning proceeds as follows.

First, all the Directives, and in particular Directive 2016/343,[40] observe the fundamental rights and principles as enshrined in the Charter and in the ECHR, including fair trial, presumption of innocence and the rights of the defence. More specifically, Recital 33 of Directive 2016/343 clearly states that the right to a fair trial is one of the basic principles in a democratic society and the 'right of an accused person to be present at the trial is based on that right and should be ensured throughout the Union'. Moving from this strong normative statement, the ECJ considers a duty to interpret Articles 47 and 48 of the Charter in such a way as to 'not disregard' the guarantees of Article 6 ECHR in light of the right to effective participation confer.

To this purpose, the ECJ coherently recalls the rich case law of the ECHR on the right to participation, that implies the right to participate *effectively*.[41] According to the Strasbourg Court, effective participation in a criminal trial includes the right for the defendant to examine or have examined prosecutorial witnesses, being confronted with them in order to challenge their statements and verify their credibility. Additionally, the ECJ affirms something even stronger: a more restrictive interpretation of Article 8(1) of Directive 2016/343 – such as the one defining presence as a mere spectatorship, implying to direct power when it comes to evidence administration – would have the effect of 'depriving the fundamental right to a fair trial of its essential content'.[42]

However, no right of the Charter is absolute. Limitations are possible when: they are provided for by law; they respect the essence of the right in question; and they comply with the principle of proportionality, as established by Article 52(1) of the Charter.[43] Therefore, it is the duty of the ECJ to assess whether the national legislation at stake, allowing the reading of pre-trial untested statements and their use for the final decision, could infringe the right of the accused to be present at trial or, on the contrary, whether it is a tolerable limitation, as allowed by Article 52(1) of the Charter.

Once the ECHR fair trial rights have been grounded on the EU Charter, it comes as a natural step to identify what the exceptions are to the right to cross-examine prosecutorial

[37] Directive 2016/343 (n 24), Art 10(2).
[38] *HYA and Others* (n 29), para 37.
[39] Opinion of AG Collins in *HYA and Others* (n 29), para 43.
[40] See Directive 2016/343 (n 24), Recital 47.
[41] *Marcello Viola v Italy* App no 45106/04, ECLI:CE:ECHR:2006:1005JUD004510604; *Al-Khawaja and Tahery v the United Kingdom* (n 5), para 142.
[42] *HYA and Others* (n 29), para 45.
[43] ibid, para 50.

witnesses established by the ECtHR case law and to what extent they represent legitimate limitations in light of Article 52(1) of the Charter. In other words, the ECHR's 'fairness as a whole' penetrates the EU legal framework and becomes a proportional limitation of the Charter's right to fair trial. This the ECJ achieves by relying on the ECtHR case law to determine the essential content of the right at stake and the criteria to assess how proportional the limitations are. The result is that exceptions to the right to be present in our specific case are respectful of its essential content uniquely when untested 'statements by absent witnesses can be taken into account only in limited circumstances, for legitimate reasons and with due regard for the fairness of the criminal proceedings as a whole',[44] *id est* the alpha and the omega of the ECtHR long-standing jurisprudence on the issue at stake.

More articulated is the assessment of proportionality. The ECJ combines the elements of the autonomous proportionality test in EU law[45] – limitations should not exceed what is appropriate and necessary to pursue a legitimate aim and, when possible, priority should be given to the least onerous measures – with a direct referral to the decisions of the Strasbourg court, where proportionality ends up corresponding to the fairness of the trial as a whole. In this way, the ECJ completes the transposal into EU law of the ECHR principles, recalling the three-step test on absent witnesses that the ECtHR has elaborated over many decades – and recently reviewed in the well-known *Al-Khawaja and Tahery* case. In a nutshell: for the untested statements to be read at trial and admitted as evidence there should be good reasons warranting the absence of the witness and, in so far as they may represent the sole or decisive basis for a possible conviction, the national system should provide for counterbalancing factors, 'including strong procedural safeguards, sufficient to compensate for the handicaps faced by the accused'.[46]

Gradually, but firmly, the ECJ imports the Strasbourg 'method' into EU law, a long-established sequence of judicial assessments to check the breach of Article 6(3)(d) ECHR, codifying many decades of tormented case law defining each step of the process. First, the absence of the witness from trial should be for a 'good reason'. A death, health-related reasons, the impossibility to locate them, a fear of the witness of retaliation if forced to appear at trial, can be considered good reasons. Even when those reasons occur, it is the duty of the trial court – *rectius*, of all the authorities involved, including the prosecutor – to pursue every reasonable effort to ensure the witness's presence at trial.[47] Second, the national court should assess whether the untested statements, if admitted at trial, would represent the sole or decisive basis for the conviction of the accused person. In mutualising the criterion of the 'sole or decisive evidence' from the ECtHR, the ECJ clarifies that a witness's statement should be regarded as a decisive element when 'it is of such a significance that it is likely to be determinative of the outcome of the case'.[48]

Until 2011, the ECtHR assessment would only require these two steps. With the *Al-Khawaja and Tahery* decision, the ECtHR 'abandoned its previous stance and introduced

[44] ibid, para 52.

[45] T Tridimas, 'Proportionality' in T Tridimas, *The General Principles of EU Law*, 2nd edn (Oxford University Press, 2009) 591 ff; G de Búrca, 'The Principle of Proportionality and its Application in EC Law' (1993) 13 *Yearbook of European Law* 105; N Emiliou, *The Principle of Proportionality in European Law: A Comparative Study* (Kluwer Law International, 1996).

[46] *HYA and Others* (n 29), para 55.

[47] *Schatschaschwili v Germany* (n 5), para 107; *Cafagna v Italy* App no 26073/13, ECLI:CE:ECHR:2017:1012JUD002607313, para 42: 'lorsque l'absence du témoin s'explique par la raison évoquée en l'espèce [ie l'impossibilité pour les juridictions internes d'entrer en contact avec le témoin concerné], elle exige du tribunal du fond qu'il ait fait tout ce que l'on pouvait raisonnablement attendre de lui pour assurer la comparution de l'intéressé'.

[48] *HYA and Others* (n 29), para 57.

an exception to the exception'.[49] A third step was then added by the ECtHR to compose the current trinity: when the incriminating statements do represent the sole or decisive element for the conviction, the presence of counterbalancing factors may compensate the breach of Article 6(3)(d) ECHR and re-establish the fairness of the proceedings as a whole.

Promptly recalled by the ECJ, the controversial nature of these counterbalancing factors is well-known. Scholars and some judges, including some dissenting voices within the Strasbourg court,[50] strongly – and correctly – criticised the unfortunate turn impressed by the *Al-Khawaja and Tahery* decision on the consolidated doctrine of the ECHR on pre-trial untested witness statements. Some clarity – though very limited, as some of the factors have been classified as tempting *trompe l'oeil*[51] – came with the *Schatschaschwili v Germany* case, where the ECtHR illustrated how the three-prong test has to be applied and offers indications on what may constitute a counterbalancing factor.[52] It remains true that, with the shift in question, the ECtHR retracted from its more activist stance of setting higher standards on criminal evidence imposing rigid exclusionary duties, such as the 'sole or decisive' rule. However, judges are now 'forced to engage more holistically with the effect of certain kinds of evidence on both the weight of the evidence as a whole and on the fairness of the proceedings as a whole'.[53] But the curtailing of defence rights is undeniable, as well as the uncertainty on what rules national court should apply when facing the absent witness dilemma.[54] Should the domestic court refuse to read out those statements in order to protect defence rights and prevent an infringement? Or should it anticipate a sort of holistic assessment, running somehow the risk of insufficient counterbalancing measures to compensate the disadvantage suffered by the defence as result of the inability to question the witness in the trial phase? Uncertainty and pitfalls of the ECHR holistic approach on untested witness' statements may only increase once that doctrine has been transposed into Union law by the ECJ.

IV. LIGHTS AND SHADES OF THE ECJ ALIGNMENT WITH THE ECHR HOLISTIC APPROACH ON PROCEDURAL FAIRNESS

With this decision, the ECJ takes a strong stance on two crucial issues. First, it intervenes on the interaction of Union law with the Convention framework of the Council of Europe, tormented since *Opinion 2/13* and not yet solved through decades of negotiations on the

[49] Mirandola (n 6).

[50] See joint partly dissenting and partly concurring opinion of Judges Sajó and Karakaş to the *Al-Khawaja* judgment.

[51] S Mirandola, 'Uso probatorio delle dichiarazioni di testi assenti e giurisprudenza europea: variazioni sul tema "Al-Khawaja"' (2017) *Cassazione Penale* 368, 379. A deeper analysis shows how with the *Schatschaschwili* case the ECtHR has excluded any hierarchy among the counterbalancing factors, mixing up measures of different nature.

[52] *Schatschaschwili v Germany* (n 5), paras 126–31. The list includes the caution of domestic courts in assessing the untested evidence of an absent witness as such evidence carries less weight; how detailed is the reasoning (*Przydział v Poland* App no 15487/08, ECLI:CE:ECHR:2016:0524JUD001548708, para 53; *Daştan v Turkey* App no 37272/08, ECLI:CE:ECHR:2017:1010JUD003727208, para 31; the eventuality of directions being given to the jury by the trial judge regarding the absent witnesses' evidence (*Simon Price v the United Kingdom* App no 15602/07, ECLI:CE:ECHR:2016:0915JUD001560207, para 130); or the availability at trial of corroborative evidence supporting the untested witness statement. Again, the ECtHR may consider the existence of a video recording of the absent witness's questioning at the investigation stage, or statements made at trial by persons to whom the absent witness reported the events immediately after their occurrence.

[53] Jackson (n 7): the aim of many of these rules has been to promote accurate fact finding, this is achieved by judges filtering out certain classes of unreliable evidence on an atomistic, piecemeal basis, without considering the impact of these items of evidence on the case as a whole.

[54] L Bernardini and G Ancona, 'HYA and Others: Reshaping Participation at Criminal Trials in Europe' (2023) 30 *Maastricht Journal of European and Comparative Law* 312.

accession marred with tension.[55] Despite this background, it paves the way towards a unitary conception of procedural fairness in criminal justice, promoting consistency between the two supranational systems. Fully integrating the current ECHR three-prong test into Union law, it completes the liaison between the Charter and the Convention via the mechanism of equivalence of rights.

Second, even more significantly, the ECJ shows no reluctance to directly address the admissibility of evidence in criminal trial, a clear message to the scepticism of the Commission, always aiming at reducing the potential of the directives on procedural safeguards.[56] Hence, the ECJ highlights the Charter's potential – in combination with the directives on procedural safeguards – as a solid path for expansion: the ECHR giving content to the rights and carving tolerable exceptions; the Charter absorbing the ECHR principles and methods, transforming them into operational tools and expanding the ECJ control in fields still unexplored by EU law – and hopefully inaugurating a new season of European judicial integration.

However, a deeper analysis shows some pitfalls and suggests caution in approaching the Union alignment with the ECtHR on criminal evidence in general, and on absent witnesses in particular. Hence, the ECJ cannot hide a crucial difference between the two supreme courts, a difference that alters the very nature of the ECHR assessment of fairness as a whole when transposed to the EU level. In the words of Advocate General Ćapeta in a recent case:

> the ECtHR is entrusted with the task of assessing *a posteriori* whether the way in which particular criminal proceedings were conducted infringed ECHR-based rights. The ECtHR can, therefore, assess retroactively, taking into consideration all the circumstances of the particular case.[57]

As a matter of fact, the peculiar nature of the scrutiny in Strasbourg – receiving applications based on closed cases, once internal remedies have been exhausted – allows the ECtHR to have a complete overview of all phases, of all evidence on which the final decision is based, including potential remedies intervened during the appeals, or compensation measures applied throughout the entire procedure.

In light of the different setting and timing of the ECJ intervention, the decision on the decisiveness of pre-trial witness' statements appears particularly problematic. The ECHR decides according to the probative value of the other evidence gathered during trial, or on how counterbalancing measures have influenced overall fairness. The latter are scrutinised against the entire proceedings, including anticipating the presence of the defence to the pre-trial questioning or the compensations allowed during appeal proceedings.[58]

[55] Major progress on the path to EU accession to the ECHR was announced on 31 March 2023, as negotiations concluded at technical level in Strasbourg. Once the EU ratifies the treaty, this would complete a process that began 70 years ago. P Craig, 'EU Accession to the ECHR: Competence, Procedure and Substance' (2013) 36 *Fordham International Law Journal* 1115. On specific issues related to criminal justice, see S Allegrezza, 'Towards a European Public Prosecutor' in K Ligeti (ed), *The Accession of the European Union to the European Convention on Human Rights* (Hart Publishing, 2012) 905; L Bay Larsen, 'Beskyttelsen af fundamentale rettigheder i EU og samspillet med. Den Europæiske Menneskerettighedskonvention set i lyset af Domstolens udtalelse i Avis 2/13' in E Ersbøll (ed), *EU's Charter: i et menneskeretligt krydsfelt* (Jurist-og Økonomforbundets Forlag, 2016) 41.

[56] See, among others, Opinion of AG Collins in *HYA and Others* (n 29), paras 37–43; Opinion of AG Bobek in Case C-646/17 *Moro*, ECLI:EU:C:2019:489, para 59; Opinion of AG Wathelet in Case C-310/18 *Milev*, ECLI:EU:C:2018:732, paras 54–55.

[57] Opinion of AG Ćapeta in C-175/22 *BK*, ECLI:EU:C:2023:436, para 65. For a comment, see L Bernardini, 'Turning Labels – A sound interpretation of the right to be informed in criminal proceedings that still holds some drawbacks' (EU Law Live, 29 November 2023), https://eulawlive.com/op-ed-turning-labels-a-sound-interpretation-of-the-right-to-be-informed-in-criminal-proceedings-that-still-holds-some-drawbacks-bk-case-c-175-22-by-lorenzo-bernardini/, accessed 29 April 2024.

[58] *Schatschaschwili v Germany* (n 5), para 123.

The ECJ, on the contrary, is called to interpret Union law and check the compatibility of domestic rules with European legislation when requested by national courts in the framework of proceedings still pending. The request for a preliminary ruling imposes on the ECJ the task of pronouncing *rebus sic stantibus*, on the basis of the factual and legal background described by the referring court, offering guidelines to the latter on how to solve the conundrum. In the majority of cases, preliminary rulings are requested pending proceedings in the first degree. Consequently, the possibility to scrutinise the procedure 'as a whole' is precluded, as the latter is still ongoing. Focusing on the issues at stake, when a national court is asking whether to read out untested statements – and use them as incriminating evidence – or rather exclude them, the ECJ's choice to adopt the ECtHR methodology may prove to be extremely hard, or precarious, or impossible. How can the national judge assess how decisive the untested statements may be? In the best scenario, it cannot be more than an *a priori* estimation on how the other evidence presented during trial may impact the final decision, not an *a posteriori* assessment based on the weight of the different elements according to the stream of judicial reasoning, because no judgment has been delivered and no reason yet stated. And similar considerations apply to the ECJ conclusion on the need to check for counterbalancing measures in order to assess 'fairness as a whole'. What compensating factors should the domestic court consider, given that the proceedings are still pending? The referring court will only have limited chances to conduct such a scrutiny. It may check whether the defence had the opportunity to question the witness during the investigation stage as a valid counterbalancing measure – potentially relevant but not decisive for the 'fairness as a whole'[59] – but any reference to additional measures intervening later on in the proceeding is precluded because the proceedings have not yet reached that stage.

Codifying general rules from the casuistic approach of the ECtHR is a risky operation. Transplanting them into the EU legal order without a sufficient reflection on how those principles should be applied throughout the criminal proceedings, and not for a final, holistic appreciation of fairness 'as a whole', can lead to misleading indications for national courts on how to proceed.[60] Conceding the necessity of a coherent interpretation of corresponding rights on procedural safeguards for suspects and accused persons, the simple alignment of Union law with the ECHR falls short of offering clear indications to national courts on how to comply with European law.

V. CONCLUSION: TOWARD AN EU AUTONOMOUS CONCEPT OF 'FAIRNESS' IN CRIMINAL PROCEEDINGS

The Union legal order has specific legal features to be regarded as distinctive from the ECHR, especially with reference to the way judicial scrutiny is organised. This is particularly true in respect of the preliminary ruling procedure and its outcomes. And the *HYA* case is the perfect example of how the limits of the preliminary ruling procedure may impact the way the ECJ conveys the legally binding content of its decisions.

After recalling the specific circumstances of the case, the ECJ concluded that Article 8(1) of Directive 2016/343 precludes national courts from applying domestic legislation which allows the basing of the final decision on the witness testimony collected before a judge in the pre-trial stage:

[59] *Gani v Spain* (n 7), para 44: 'Nonetheless, the Court holds that that fact is not decisive in concluding that the proceedings were fair'.

[60] Mirandola (n 51), 378.

> […] without the participation of the accused person or their lawyer, unless there is a good reason warranting the non-appearance of the witness at the judicial stage of the criminal proceedings, the testimony given by the witness does not constitute the sole or decisive basis for the conviction of the accused person, and there are sufficient counterbalancing factors to compensate for the handicaps faced by the accused person and their lawyer as a result of the taking into account of that testimony.[61]

As the three conditions are strictly interrelated and cumulative, the wording of the decision seems to exclude any possible use of witness' untested statements, which constitute the 'sole or decisive' basis for the conviction. The use of 'and' introducing the third condition of fairness – the presence of counterbalancing factors – seems to make the latter applicable only to cases in which untested testimony is not the sole or decisive evidence of guiltiness.

Consequently, some scholars defined the current decision as a 'significant departure from the previous case law of the ECtHR',[62] a bold example of autonomy of the ECJ in relation to the principles elaborated by the ECtHR. The scrutiny as restructured by *Al-Khawaja and Tahery* would then not be possible according to EU law, as no counterbalancing measure would compensate the infringement of Article 6 ECHR for using untested statements as the sole or decisive evidence.

This strong statement is surely justified in the light of the wording mentioned above and should be welcomed. As a matter of fact, it offers a clearer indication to domestic courts, offering a higher standard of protection for both the right to examine prosecutorial witnesses and to right to actively participate in their trial for the accused person. It also allows to emphasise how the right to question incriminating witnesses has 'an instrumental value that transcends the interests of the particular party: it serves the interests of justice by pursuing the epistemic objective of contributing to a more accurate fact-finding and thus enhancing the chances of a correct trial outcome'.[63] The right to examine prosecutorial witnesses may gain the full dignity of cross-examination as a legal engine to expose weaknesses of adverse witnesses not only for defence purposes but to serve justice in a more general way promoting a 'better truth'.[64]

Unfortunately, it is hard to avoid the suspicion that what lies behind the convoluted wording of the conclusions in the *HYA* case is nothing more than an error due to the peculiar structure of preliminary rulings, forced to adopt the negative formula of the 'must be interpreted as precluding'. However, an interpretation of the conclusions in light of the entire reasoning cannot but suggest that the ECJ, with the unfortunate wording, wanted to 'save' testimonies which are not sole or decisive from the stricter rules on participation rights, and not radically exclude the ones which are sole or decisive with no possible compensation via counterbalancing factors. Clarity would benefit from a less convoluted structure of the conclusions, as they are legally binding for all national courts of the Union. However, reaffirming the golden rule excluding untested statements as the 'sole and decisive' evidence for convictions is the rocky and steep way to go within the Union, for a better protection of the right to participation, and for better justice as a whole.

[61] *HYA and Others* (n 29).

[62] Bernardini and Ancona (n 54); partially, A Cabiale, 'Absent Witnesses and EU Law: A Groundbreaking Ruling by the CJEU' (2023) *European Papers* 55, 66.

[63] Mirandola (n 6), 2; Trechsel and Summers (n 2), 293, L Heffernan, 'Calibrating the Right to Confrontation' (2016) 20 *International Journal of Evidence and Proof* 103.

[64] See JR Spencer, 'Evidence' in JR Spencer and M Delmas-Marty (eds), *European Criminal Procedures* (Cambridge University Press, 2002) 618. It has been defined as 'the greatest legal engine ever invented for the discovery of the truth' by JH Wigmore, *Evidence in Trials at Common Law*, vol V, 4th edn (Little, Brown and Co, 1974) 32.

27

The Contribution of the European Court of Justice to the Definition of Refugee in International Law

HUGO STOREY*

I. INTRODUCTION

BY ANY GAUGE, the European Court of Justice's (ECJ) contribution to international refugee law is immense. Focus here is on just one aspect of this contribution, albeit undoubtedly a core one. It concerns the following question: How has the ECJ's case law contributed to a better international understanding of the refugee definition?[1]

Article 2(d) of the recast Qualification Directive (QD(recast))[2] gives a definition of refugee, which largely – but not entirely – replicates the definition set out in Article 1A(2) of the 1951 Refugee Convention.[3] Article 2(d) provides that:

> […] 'refugee' means a third-country national who, owing to a well-founded fear of being persecuted for reasons of race, religion, nationality, political opinion or membership of a particular social group, is outside the country of nationality and is unable or, owing to such fear, is unwilling to avail himself or herself of the protection of that country, or a stateless person, who, being outside of the country of former habitual residence for the same reasons as mentioned above, is unable or, owing to such fear, unwilling to return to it, and to whom Article 12 does not apply […]

In order to answer the question posed, it is necessary first to provide more context. This is the main purpose of the next section (Section II). Section III endeavours to analyse the ECJ cases that have had most bearing on the refugee definition and its meaning. It is then felt necessary

* Retired Judge of the Upper Tribunal (UK). Immediate past president and honorary president, International Association of Refugee and Migration Judges (IAMRJ) European Chapter.

[1] Noteworthy is that in a very significant number of the cases cited in this chapter, Vice-President Lars Bay Larsen was one of the judges, often as Rapporteur.

[2] Directive 2011/95/EU of the European Parliament and of the Council of 13 December 2011 on standards for the qualification of third-country nationals or stateless persons as beneficiaries of international protection, for a uniform status for refugees or for persons eligible for subsidiary protection, and for the content of the protection granted (recast) [2011] OJ L337/9. See further, S Peers et al, 'Qualification: Refugee Status and Subsidiary Protection' in S Peers et al (eds), *EU Immigration and Asylum Law (Text and Commentary)*, 2nd edn (Brill, 2014) 47–56; and H Dorig et al, 'Asylum Qualification Directive 2011/95/EU' in K Hailbronner and D Thym (eds), *EU Immigration and Asylum Law: A Commentary* (Beck/Hart/Nomos, 2016) 1229.

[3] Convention Relating to the Status of Refugees (Geneva, 28 July 1951). In Case C-91/20 *LW v Bundesrepublik Deutschland*, ECLI:EU:C:2021:898, the ECJ noted at para 31 that this definition 'reproduces, in essence, the definition in Article 1A(2)'.

in Section IV to consider, before concluding, a number of ongoing concerns about the present direction of the ECJ's case law. Against this backdrop the author ventures in Section V several closing reflections.

II. CONTEXT

It has always been clear, from the moment that asylum was moved to the first pillar of EU law,[4] that the ECJ would come to play an instrumental role in the development of international refugee law and in particular the definition of refugee.[5] Fuelling that was the primacy afforded in EU primary and secondary law to the Refugee Convention.[6] Also reinforcing that was the specific contents of the Qualification Directive,[7] which sought to resolve a number of issues relating to the refugee definition that had divided Member States, most notably whether there can be non-State actors of persecution.[8]

Given the closely corresponding definitions of refugee, the prime factor making ECJ impact predictable was the interpretive vacuum created by the narrow terms of Article 38 of the Refugee Convention. This provides for disputes as to interpretation to be settled by the International Court of Justice, but prescribes a purely inter-State mechanism for activating it. Unsurprisingly, this remains unactivated. No less surprisingly, this inactivation has resulted globally in an 'unacceptable degree of diversity in the interpretation of the Convention', which is seen to be at odds with a cluster of important legal principles, including the principle that like cases should be treated alike.[9]

Also always clear too, though, have been anxieties about the ECJ's role. One general anxiety in that regard resides in the ECJ's approach to interpretation. Despite Article 2(d)'s close correspondence, the Qualification Directive and its recast do not incorporate the Article 1A(2) definition of refugee as it stands. The ECJ has accepted that when provisions of the Directive correspond 'in substance' with provisions of the Refugee Convention it can interpret the latter's meaning.[10] The ECJ has also insisted that the objective of the Qualification Directive is 'to guide authorities in the application of [the Refugee] Convention'.[11] However, being an international treaty, the Refugee Convention falls to be interpreted in accordance with the rules of interpretation laid down in Articles 31–33 of the Vienna Convention on the Law of Treaties (VCLT). These embody an interactive approach that takes into account good faith, ordinary meaning, context, object and purpose, subsequent agreements and practice, other rules of international law and supplementary means of interpretation (most notably

[4] By the Treaty of Lisbon (Lisbon, 1 December 2009).

[5] H Lambert et al (eds), *The Global Reach of European Refugee Law* (Cambridge University Press, 2013).

[6] Arts 78(1) and (2) Treaty on the Functioning of the European Union (TFEU), state that the EU legislative instruments in the field of asylum must be 'in accordance with' the Refugee Convention: see eg Case C-57/09 *B and D*, ECLI:EU:C:2010:661, para 72. See further H Storey, *The Refugee Definition in International Law* (Oxford University Press, 2023) 117 and 357.

[7] Council Directive 2004/83/EC of 29 April 2004 on minimum standards for the qualification and status of third country nationals or stateless persons as refugees or as persons who otherwise need inter- national protection and the content of the protection granted [2004] OJ L304/12 (Qualification Directive). This was replaced by the QD(recast) in 2011.

[8] H Dorig, 'Asylum Qualification Directive 2011/95/EU (Articles 1–10)' in Hailbronner and Thym (n 2), 1229.

[9] AM North and J Chia, 'Towards Convergence in the Interpretation of the Refugee Convention: A Proposal for the Establishment of an International Judicial Commission for Refugees' (2006) 25 *Australian Year Book of International Law* 105. See also A Betts and P Collier, *Refuge: Transforming a Broken Refugee System* (Penguin, 2017) 43 and 46.

[10] *B and D* (n 6), para 72.

[11] Joined Cases C-175/08, C-176/08, C-178/08 and C-179/08 *Salahadin Abdulla and Others*, ECLI:EU:C:2010:105, para 52; Case C-31/09 *Bolbol*, ECLI:EU:C:2010:351, para 37.

the *travaux preparatoires*).[12] The ECJ approach to interpretation, by contrast, combines a purposive with a 'meta-teleological' dimension.[13] Its approach focuses not only on the object and purpose of the relevant provisions of the particular legal instrument concerned but also those of the EU regime as a whole, relying on the human rights standards contained in the EU Charter and the founding values of the organisation. As noted by Hemme Battjes, 'it is not the purpose of the provision but rather the purpose of the Treaty as a whole that guides the interpretation'.[14] This might be said to risk Eurocentrism. If the ECJ was strictly applying VCLT rules to the refugee definition in Article 1A(2), it would only be concerned with 'the general scheme and purpose' of the Refugee Convention, not of the EU treaties; and under VCLT rules any recourse it had to human rights or other treaty norms would ordinarily be to global human rights instruments, not, self-evidently, to the Charter.[15]

Another general concern stems from a key feature of the ECJ Rules of Procedure. Whilst on the one hand these confer a right on the Commission and as many Member States as wish to intervene, they do not (in contrast to the rules of the European Court of Human Rights (ECtHR)) permit third-party intervention.[16] Most notably, this feature shuts out the United Nations High Commissioner for Refugees (UNHCR) from any formal role in its proceedings, save when the national court has joined it at the national stage prior to reference.[17] It does this notwithstanding the ECJ's recognition that EU secondary asylum legislation expressly acknowledges the latter's supervisory role and that the ECJ has commended UNHCR sources of guidance in particular.[18]

But perhaps the greatest general anxiety is that the close legal and political unity of 27 EU Member States, coupled with the strongly precedential nature of ECJ jurisprudence, would work to drown out non-European State practice and perspectives and also weaken the global authority of UNHCR guidance. In a world in which – despite the UNHCR's – efforts there is no agreed understanding of the refugee definition, the existence of a regional State practice comprising 27 Member States plus several European countries closely tied to the EU inevitably puts pressure on non-European States to go along with ECJ rulings.[19]

Then there have been a range of specific anxieties to do with the particular terms in which the Qualification Directive and its recast seek to codify the meaning of key terms of the refugee definition and the ECJ's response to these. A cluster of such specific concerns relate to apparent deviations from the text of the Article 1A(2) definition. The greatest concern has been that,

[12] O Dörr and K Schmalenbach (eds), *Vienna Convention on the Law of Treaties* (Springer, 2012); JR Crawford, *Brownlie's Principles of Public International Law*, 9th edn (Oxford University Press, 2019).

[13] V Moreno-Lax, 'Of Autonomy, Autarky, Purposiveness and Fragmentation: The Relationship between EU Asylum Law and International Humanitarian Law' in D Cantor and JF Durieux (eds), *Refugee from Inhumanity? War Refugees and International Humanitarian Law* (Brill, 2014) 340–41 and 311.

[14] H Battjes, *European Asylum Law and International Law* (Martinus Nijhoff, 2006) 43. See eg *Bolbol* (n 11), paras 37–38. See further Storey (n 6), 117–21.

[15] Storey (n 6), 83.

[16] Rules of Procedure of the Court of Justice [2012] OJ L265/1, Art 96.

[17] See eg Cases C-349/20 *Secretary of State for the Home Department (Status of a refugee or stateless person of Palestinian origin)*, ECLI:EU:C:2022:151; and C-151/22 *S&A*, ECLI:EU:C:2023:688, para 36.

[18] QD(recast), Recital 22 states that consultations with UNHCR 'may provide valuable guidance for Member States when determining refugee status according to Article 1 of the Geneva Convention'. In Case C-528/11 *Halaf*, ECLI:EU:C:2013:342, para 44, the ECJ stated that UNHCR documents 'are particularly relevant in that assessment in the light of the role conferred on the UNHCR by the Geneva Convention, in consistency with which the rules of European Union law dealing with asylum must be interpreted (see, to that effect, *NS and Others*, paragraph 75, and Case C-364/11 *Abed El Karem El Kott and Others* [2012] ECR, paragraph 43).' See also *LW* (n 3), para 56. For reliance on the 1979 Handbook, see Cases C-280/21 *Migracijos departamentas (Reasons for persecution on the ground of political opinion)*, ECLI:EU:C:2023:13, para 27; and C-720/17 *Bilali*, ECLI:EU:C:2019:448, para 57.

[19] Lambert et al (n 5), 258–66.

in contrast to the latter's universal personal scope, the personal scope of the QD(recast) is confined to 'third-country nationals'. For some this could be seen as an 'illegitimate modification' of the Refugee Convention contrary to Article 41 VCLT.[20] The Article 2(d) definition also omits the second paragraph of Article 1A(2), dealing with multiple nationality.

As regards the codification of the meaning of some of the key terms of the refugee definition, concerns expressed include the following: the apparent adoption within the Article 9 definition of 'Acts of persecution' of an outmoded hierarchical approach to violations of human rights;[21] a too narrow preoccupation with 'acts' of persecution rather than on the predicament of 'being persecuted';[22] the Directive's incorporation in its Article 7 definition of 'Actors of protection 'and serious harm' of a narrow requirement of 'reasonable willingness' seeming to permit decision makers to find that protection exists even when a country of origin may in fact fail to protect;[23] its evident extension of the scope of 'Actors of protection' as defined by this same article to include not just States but international organisations;[24] and the apparent endorsement in Article 10 of a narrow and restrictive definition of particular social group (which requires an applicant to show *both* that the group is based on a protected characteristic and that it is one that is perceived to be set apart by the wider society').[25]

It must not be thought that specific anxieties pertain exclusively to restrictive codification. There has also been some debate about whether some of its provisions, at least as interpreted by the ECJ, are more generous than is required by the international meaning of key terms. The ECJ's possible Eurocentric divergence from VCLT rules has already been mentioned. Another possible example concerns the ECJ's ruling that the activities of civil society actors are irrelevant to whether protection is effective, discussed in Section IV below.[26]

III. THE CONTRIBUTION

Let us turn then to the ECJ case law on the refugee definition. It is impossible in a short chapter to cover all the ways in which the ECJ has further clarified this definition, but the following are among the main examples.

Although from what is said below it will be apparent that in the period from 2009 to 2023 the case law has traversed considerable ground, it cannot be ignored, of course, that for the most part the ECJ depends on questions being posed to it by national courts and tribunals in preliminary references and there remain some elements or aspects of the definition that have yet to be addressed, in particular nationality and statelessness and the Convention reasons of

[20] GS Goodwin-Gill and J McAdam (with E Dunlop), *The Refugee in International Law*, 4th edn (Oxford University Press, 2021) 66. See further discussion in Storey (n 6), 120–21.

[21] J Hathaway and M Foster, *The Law of Refugee Status*, 2nd edn (Cambridge University Press, 2014) 202–205 express concern about Art 9 QD(recast) limiting focus of the analysis to 'non-derogable' rights seen as having a higher normative status and also note with concern some suggestion in national case law (citing a UK case) that Art 9(1) is read in an exhaustive manner.

[22] M Scott, *Climate Change, Disasters, and the Refugee Convention* (Cambridge University Press, 2020) 129.

[23] ECRE, *The Impact of the EU Qualification Directive on International Protection* (ELENA, 2008); see further J Lehmann, 'Availability of Protection in the Country of Origin' in C Bauloz et al (eds), *Seeking Asylum in the European Union* (Brill Nijhoff, 2014) 120–26. Furthermore, see Hathaway and Foster (n 21), 317, fn 172 that the Directive 'still contains the original language that is more akin to due diligence'.

[24] This is not addressed further in this chapter but see Storey (n 6), 458–63.

[25] Hathaway and Foster (n 21), 429–32.

[26] For another example concerning cessation and Art 11(3) QD(recast) (which, despite substantial correspondence in wording with Art 1C of the Refugee Convention, permits allowance to be made for egregious past persecution in the Art 1A(2)/Art 2 context), see the critique by Hathaway and Foster (n 21), 490–94.

race and nationality. Nor must it be forgotten that Commission proposals for a Qualification Regulation remain pending, the content of which is likely to amend some existing, and add some further, codifying clauses.[27]

An initial obstacle to adjudging the ECJ contribution is that there can be no simple comparison between its interpretation of key elements of the refugee definition and a complete, universally agreed understanding of their meaning. As already noted, the latter is lacking. But it has become possible to at least compare the ECJ interpretation with a certain number of propositions about which there is wide agreement.[28] And although, beyond that, it is more a matter of considering trends, the ECJ's interpretative forays are helping refine the issues involved in ongoing debates.

The following constitute some of the ECJ's important clarifications.

The text of Article 9 QD(recast) was widely seen to encapsulate a human rights approach to the core concept of persecution,[29] but there was uncertainty as to what extent this rested on a hierarchical approach and also as to what was meant by 'acts' of persecution.

Whilst certain issues remain to be considered, it is apparent that the ECJ has turned its face against an overtechnical approach to the key ingredients of both Article 9(1)(a) and (b). As regards the concept of 'basic human rights', the ECJ held in *Y and Z* that the right to religion (which is not a non-derogable right) was a 'basic right'. It also held that:

> [...] it is apparent from the wording of Article 9(1) of the Directive that there must be a 'severe violation' of religious freedom having a significant effect on the person concerned in order for it to be possible for the acts in question to be regarded as acts of persecution.[30]

As observed by Lehmann, this means that 'it is the nature of the repression and its consequences rather than the substantive ambit of a right that forms the basis for identifying acts of persecution'.[31] Whilst clearly taking a structured approach to Article 9 (considering basic rights first), nothing in the ECJ's analysis suggests a hierarchical approach.

Further reinforcing this has been the ECJ's insistence that the pivotal severity criterion must eschew formalism and have regard to actuality. It vividly highlighted the need for evidence of actual application in the case of *Fathi*:

> [...] In the present case, it must be considered that the fact that legislation, such as the law on apostasy at issue in the main proceedings, imposes the death penalty or a custodial sentence, is capable, in itself, of constituting an 'act of persecution', within the meaning of Article 9(1) of Directive 2011/95, provided that such penalties are actually applied in the country of origin which adopted such legislation.[32]

Despite concerns that the focus in Article 9 on 'acts' of persecution was too narrow and at odds with a 'predicament' approach (which highlights the use of the passive tense in the Article 1A(2) definition ('being persecuted')), the ECJ has clearly adopted a broad approach to the concept of acts. In several judgments the ECJ has highlighted the fact that both Article 9(1) and (2)

[27] Now made more likely by the political agreement reached on 20 December 2023 by the European Parliament and the Council on the New Pact on Migration and Asylum: see further S Peers, 'The New EU Asylum Laws, Part 1: the Qualification Regulation' (2023) *EU Law Analysis Blog*, http://eulawanalysis.blogspot.com/2023/12/the-new-eu-asylum-laws-part-1.html#:~:text=The%20Regulation%20will%20change%20the,to%20rights%20is%20more%20effective, accessed 4 March 2024.

[28] What this author terms a 'working definition': see Storey (n 6), 37–38, 724–25 and 733–38.

[29] See eg Goodwin-Gill and McAdam (with Dunlop) (n 20), 69.

[30] Joined Cases C-71/11 and C-99/11 *Y and Z*, ECLI:EU:C:2012:518, paras 64–65.

[31] J Lehmann, *'Protection' in European Union Asylum Law* (Brill Nijhoff, 2020) 64.

[32] Case C-56/17 *Bahtiyar Fathi v Predsedatel na Darzhavna agentsia za bezhantsite*, ECLI:EU:C:2018:803, para 96.

refer to 'measures' and that 'acts' can include measures, conduct, sanctions and prohibitions, sometimes in the form of legislation.[33] If the ECJ follows the Advocate General Opinion in *AH and FN*, it is likely it will further underline that the second limb of Article 9(1)–9(1)(b) – can sometimes encompass general situations of oppression.[34]

One of the most widely noted achievements of the ECJ has been its strong rejection of the idea that persons can be expected to avoid persecution by concealing characteristics such as sexual identity, religion and political opinion. By the time of the ECJ's ruling in *Y and Z*,[35] the international jurisprudence was already shifting in that direction,[36] but the ECJ's imprimatur in this case and in *X, Y and Z*[37] has effectively settled previous debates. Continuing a trend observable in the international jurisprudence and building on the provisions of Article 9(2) QD(recast), the ECJ has recognised that persecutory acts are not just confined to acts of violence, physical and mental, and various uses of laws, but can include other types of harm.

As regards health-related harm, in *MP*, whilst rejecting the notion that shortcomings in health facilities could constitute either persecution or serious harm, the ECJ did not exclude that, at least in certain circumstances, applicants who on return could face a serious deterioration in their health could establish persecutory or serious harm – if there was a lack of care attributable to the State authorities. Even if the latter was not enough on its own, it could be in conjunction with other factors, eg other measures of discrimination.[38] As regards socio-economic harm, whilst in *OA* it stated that 'mere economic hardship cannot, as a general rule, be classified as 'persecution', within the meaning of Article 9 of Directive 2004/83',[39] this formulation clearly left open that there may be exceptional cases where socio-economic harm could constitute persecution. The ECJ will shortly have an opportunity to consider this matter in *AH and FN* and, if they follow the reasoning of the Advocate General, they will identify socio-economic harms as among those that taken cumulatively can give rise to persecution.[40]

Of particular moment has been the ECJ's approach to Article 4 QD(recast). This is a provision which on its face lays down a number of evidentiary indicators rather than legal standards. For the ECJ, however, it has come to be seen as an expression of the principle of individual assessment. This is well-illustrated by the case of *Ahemdebekova*. In this case, the ECJ ruled that the refugee definition requires that an applicant faces a well-founded fear of being 'personally persecuted' and that 'an application for international protection cannot be granted as such on the ground that one of the applicant's family members has a well-founded fear of being persecuted or faces a real risk of suffering serious harm'.[41] Thus, the principle set out in Recital 36 of the QD(recast) only creates a presumption which may be displaced by the particular circumstances of a case.[42]

[33] *Y and Z* (n 30), para 65; *Fathi* (n 32), paras 93 and 96; and Case C-542/13 *M'Bodj*, ECLI:EU:C:2014:2452, para 35.

[34] Opinion of AG De La Tour in Joined Cases C-608/22 and C-609/22 *AH and FN (Femmes afghanes)*, ECLI:EU:C:2023:856, para 73.

[35] *Y and Z* (n 30), para 78.

[36] *Appellant S395/2002 v MIMA* [2003] HCA 71, [40] (Kirby and McHugh JJ); see also *HJ (Iran) v Secretary of State for the Home Department* [2010] UKSC 31, [53].

[37] Joined Cases C-199/12 to C-201/12 *X and Others*, ECLI:EU:C:2013:720, paras 70–71. See also *S&A* (n 17), para 48.

[38] Case C-353/16 *MP*, ECLI:EU:C:2018:276, paras 51 and 58. Although primarily concerned with subsidiary protection, the ECJ in this case drew on its analysis of Art 6 which contains a uniform definition of actors of persecution applicable to both persecution and serious harm.

[39] Case C-255/19 *OA*, ECLI:EU:C:2021:36, para 49.

[40] *AH and FN* (n 34).

[41] Case C-652/16 *Ahmedbekova*, ECLI:EU:C:2018:801, para 50.

[42] This does not necessarily entail that there cannot be group or category persecution. It is likely the ECJ will address this issue in *AH and FN* (n 34).

One of the issues that has vexed the international jurisprudence concerns the interrelationship between persecution and protection. For some, these two concepts are independent, a view that might appear to be supported by the Directive's reference to 'protection against persecution' – wording that appears to treat the two terms as antinomies.[43] However, adoption of such an approach would have been difficult to square with the underlying human rights framework, which depends heavily on the notion that it is only States that can violate human rights. In *OA* the ECJ firmly endorsed the need to see both concepts as interdependent, and 'intrinsically linked'.[44]

There have now been two very important ECJ judgments dealing with the Convention reason of political opinion: *PI* and *S & A*. In addition to emphasising that this compound expression requires a broad interpretation, the ECJ notably emphasised that in assessing whether or not an opinion is political, much depends on the societal context, noting in *S & A* that decision-makers:

> [...] must carry out an exhaustive and thorough examination of all the relevant circumstances, relating to the specific personal situation of that applicant and of the more general context of his or her country of origin, from, inter alia, a political, legal, judicial, historical and sociocultural perspective, in order to determine whether the applicant has a well-founded fear of being personally persecuted on account of his or her political opinions, and in particular of those which potential actors of persecution in his or her country of origin might be led to attribute to him or her [...].[45]

As well as aligning itself with international case law developments of this notion,[46] the ECJ's emphasis on the importance of societal context may prove critical in further elaborations of other Convention reasons.

The ECJ has shown no signs of endorsing the traditional 'bipartite' approach to well-founded fear, which requires an applicant to satisfy two necessary conditions: that s/he has subjective fear; and that s/he has objective fear. Given that the bipartite approach is increasingly seen as untenable in the wider literature, it is pertinent that all that the ECJ has seen as essential is the establishment of 'reasonable fear'.[47]

Before seeking to draw together conclusions on the main cases that appear to have made a positive contribution to international understanding, it is important to have regard to some aspects that could be seen to detract from that contribution.

IV. ONGOING CONCERNS

It is difficult to assess the ECJ contribution in isolation from the possible changes in the EU legislation that will ensue if the EU institutions proceed to adopt the Commission's proposed Qualification Regulation, and, as illustrated by the submissions made by various bodies regarding that proposal, the number of concerns voiced so far are quite diverse. My aim here is to focus on just five of these.

[43] See eg D Wilsher, 'Non-State Actors and the Definition of a Refugee in the United Kingdom: Protection, Accountability or Culpability' (2003) 15 *International Journal of Refugee Law* 68, 80–81.

[44] *OA* (n 39), para 56. See further, Storey (n 6), 431–35.

[45] *S&A* (n 17), para 45; *Migracijos departamentas* (n 18), paras 33 and 38.

[46] See Storey (n 6), 638–53.

[47] *Y and Z* (n 30), para 72. See further Storey (n 6), 663–712.

A. Uncritical Reference to UNHCR Guidance

It was noted above that the ECJ has seen fit to highlight the special role afforded to UNHCR guidance under the secondary legislation. That has to be seen as a positive development, compensating somewhat from the lack of any third-party right to intervene in pending ECJ asylum cases. However, there now appears to be a danger of the ECJ going too far in this direction. In more than one judgment, the ECJ has gone out of its way to view the 1979 UNHCR Handbook as an authoritative guide to the meaning of the refugee definition. The problem with this is that, whilst much of this Handbook's guidance remains valid, it can no longer be safely said that all its paragraphs embody either State practice or best practice. The scholarship now identifies a significant number of observable shortcomings in its guidance.[48] Unqualified endorsement is also at odds with the ECJ's own case law, which has rejected some of the Handbook's positions on Article 1.[49] It also risks weakening the growing momentum for a comprehensive updating of this Handbook, which is now over 45 years old.

B. Non-Application of VCLT Rules of Interpretation

It must be open to question whether the ECJ is right not to align its approach to interpretation of the Refugee Convention more directly with VCLT rules, for four main reasons. First, its own primary law at Article 78 TFEU stipulates that its asylum legislation must be 'in accordance with' the Refugee Convention. Second, Article 3(5) TFEU requires strict observance of international treaties and, by Article 21(2)(b), the Union's actions on the international scene should be in order to 'consolidate […] the principles of international law'. Third, the VCLT rules have the status of customary international law and the ECJ itself has held that:

> even though the [VCLT] does not bind either the Community or all its Member States, a series of provisions in that convention reflect the rules of customary international law which, as such, are binding on the community institutions and form part of the Community legal order.[50]

Fourth, it might be thought that in the field of international refugee law, at least, the more the ECJ expressly applies VCLT norms of interpretation, the more likely it is that non-EU States will follow its interpretation and the better it can achieve its own stated objective of providing guidance on the Refugee Convention.

Several points may be argued to the contrary. First, the only essential requirement embodied in the VCLT rules is that the treaty interpreter reaches outcomes consistent with such rules and the ECJ's own conscious adoption of a doctrine of harmonious or conforming interpretation of EU materials with international law would appear to promote such consistency. Second, it is difficult to deny that the ECJ's interpretation of Article 1A(2) has often been in substance consistent with an approach based on VCLT rules law. It could also be pointed out that the ECJ's recourse to the Charter has in large part been, in substance, recourse to 'generic' international human rights law rights, which is essentially in line with the human rights approach applied in international refugee law.[51] It does not look as if applying a VCLT

[48] See survey and discussion in Storey (n 6), 41–45 and 741–43.

[49] Most notably, in *B and D* (n 6), paras 108–109, the ECJ expressly rejected recourse to the concept of proportionality (so as to balance criminality and risk) endorsed by the UNHCR Handbook at para 156.

[50] Case C-386/08 *Brita*, ECLI:EU:C:2010:91, para 42.

[51] On the human rights approach, see H Storey, 'The Human Rights Approach: Rising Sun or Falling Star' (2021) 33 *International Journal of Refugee Law* 379. On the interrelationship between VCLT and EU rules of interpretation, see further Storey (n 6), 117–21.

approach would have produced a different outcome. It remains, however, that for the non-EU world, preoccupation with the EU Treaty can undermine the value of ECJ guidance at the international level.

C. Possible Support for the Dubious Requirement of Persecutory Intent

It is an axiom of refugee law that persecution must emanate from human actors. For a considerable time, the predominant view in the common law world was that it also required intentionality, on the footing that harm that was not deliberate could not be persecutory.[52] Whilst that view is still espoused by some common law countries, most notably Australia,[53] it has come under increasing criticism. Among the main points that have been made are that the wording of the refugee definition, by its use of the passive voice ('being persecuted'), highlights not so much the act of inflicting harm as the exposure to harm and that what matters is the (threatened or actual) effects of a persecutor's conduct or actions, rather than his or her intention;[54] and that a requirement of persecutory intent fits badly with the reality of refugee determination procedure. If persecutory intent were accepted as a necessary condition, then decision makers would be obliged to be mind-readers, notwithstanding that conducting an inquiry into the motives of alleged persecutors who reside in a foreign country is a task which has properly been termed 'extremely difficult or impossible to perform'.[55]

Against this backdrop, it is worrisome that the ECJ analysis in *M'Bodj*[56] and *MP (Sri Lanka)*[57] appear to lend credence to the notion that it is always necessary to show persecutory intent. Neither case was concerned with the refugee definition, as such; rather the focus was on subsidiary protection; but the ECJ nevertheless sought to base its analysis on the meaning of Article 6 which provides a common definition of 'Actors of Persecution or serious harm'. It stated in *M'Bodj* that:

> the risk of deterioration in the health of a third country national suffering from a serious illness as a result of the absence of appropriate treatment in his country of origin is not sufficient, unless that third country national is intentionally deprived of health care, to warrant that person being granted subsidiary protection.[58]

Whilst the ECJ's analysis is broadly in line with established principles regarding human agency, it is problematic that they have cast matters in terms of 'intentional infliction' of harm, since ill treatment can arise without there necessarily having been infliction that is intentional. It may be that the ECJ only meant here to identify human conduct attributable to the authorities of a State. If, however, they meant to treat persecutory intent as a necessary condition for an act of persecution, that would conflict with the growing body of case law and wider literature rejecting that position.[59]

[52] Its *locus classicus* is the US Supreme Court decision in *INS v Elias-Zacarias* [1992] 502 US 478, which held that the refugee definition 'makes motives critical' and required claimants to establish the motives of alleged persecutors.

[53] *Ram v MIEA* [1995] 57 FCR, 565 and 568.

[54] *Refugee Appeal No 72635* [2002] NZRSAA 33, citing *Chen Shi Hai v MIMA* [2000] 201 CLR 293, paras 33 and 65.

[55] Kirby J in *Chen Shi Hai* (n 54), para 313.

[56] *M'Bodj* (n 33), para 35.

[57] *MP* (n 38).

[58] *M'Bodj* (n 33), paras 41 and 36; see *MP* (n 38), paras 51 and 58.

[59] See further, Storey (n 6), 391–96.

D. The Issue of Civil Society Actors and the Effectiveness of Protection

In *OA*, the ECJ held not only that private actors cannot qualify as actors of protection (which must indubitably be correct) but that any provision by private actors of social and financial support or security is 'irrelevant' to the issue of whether actors of protection provide *effective* protection.[60] But neither this judgment nor the prior Advocate General Opinion furnishes any clear reasons why. As to why protective functions or acts carried out by civil society actors in relation to social and financial support are considered irrelevant, the ECJ's only reason is a circular one – that such acts are:

> inherently incapable of either preventing acts of persecution or of detecting, prosecuting and punishing such acts and, therefore, cannot be regarded as providing the protection required by Article 11(1)(e) of Directive 2004/83, read together with Article 7(2) of that directive.

In relation to provision of security, the ECJ's principal reason for considering this irrelevant is that assessing well-founded fear of persecution requires verification,

> having regard to that refugee's individual situation, that the actor or actors in question who are providing protection, within the meaning of Article 7(1), have taken reasonable steps to prevent the persecution, that they therefore operate, inter alia, an effective legal system for the detection, prosecution and punishment of acts constituting persecution.[61]

However, if not also circular, that appears unduly dogmatic. Even assuming that the sine qua non of effective protection is such prevention, it is possible to hypothesise situations where social and financial support and/or security functions performed by civil society actors might play a role in at least preventing persecution. One example this author has given is that of a victim of domestic violence, now divorced, whose claim is she would face persecution at the hands of the ex-spouse's family. Bearing in mind that Article 4 requires decision-makers to take all circumstances into account, why would it therefore be irrelevant if, for instance, there was evidence that the woman concerned had remarried into a wealthy family that employs effective private security? Possibly such circumstances on their own would be far from establishing that she would receive effective protection, but to say they are 'irrelevant' appears absolutist and to run counter to the plainly holistic approach enjoined by Article 4 – requiring decision-makers to take account of all circumstances in the round.[62]

E. The Cumulative Test for Membership of a Particular Social Group (PSG)

Article 10(1) QD(recast) provides:

> […] a group shall be considered to form a particular social group where in particular:
>
> – members of that group share an innate characteristic, or a common background that cannot be changed, or share a characteristic or belief that is so fundamental to identity or conscience that a person should not be forced to renounce it, and
> – that group has a distinct identity in the relevant country, because it is perceived as being different by the surrounding society.

[60] *OA* (n 39), paras 48, 52–53 and 63.
[61] ibid, para 38.
[62] Storey (n 6), 466–71.

Whether or not it might have been possible for the ECJ to read the text of Article 10(1)(d) differently, it has now made clear that it considers the above criteria to be cumulative.[63] This has attracted considerable criticism, including from the UNHCR and leading scholars.[64] It must be said that the criticisms appear unusually pointed. The ECJ's current approach appears to be at odds with its own analysis of two other of the five Convention reasons, namely religion and political opinion, which has expressly stated that they require a broad reading.[65] Given that the Directive formulates the reasons of race and nationality in self-evidently broad terms, it must be questioned why, therefore, the ECJ should consider the membership of a particular social group reason, alone among the five, not to require a broad reading. The cumulative approach would appear to inevitably narrow its scope.

One suggestion that has been made is that decision-makers could seek to mitigate the rigours of the cumulative approach by placing reliance on the apparently non-exhaustive wording of Article 10(1)(d).[66] However, whilst the term 'in particular' in Article 10(1)(d) would appear to import a non-exhaustive, iterative approach, it is hard to see that any further iteration could expressly contradict the dual test set out in Article 10(1)(d), as it would render the latter as of no *effet utile*. It is possible, though, that the ECJ may be able to mitigate too rigorous a test by adopting the approach urged by Advocate General Collins in *K, L* of recasting the two tests as concerned with the 'internal' and 'external' aspects of the same phenomenon and in particular of relying on the fact that, although described in the literature as a 'protected characteristics' approach, the first limb clearly goes wider than innate characteristics and extends to 'beliefs' fundamental to identity and conscience and that 'beliefs' can include, eg a belief in gender equality. In his Opinion on *K, L* the Advocate General was prepared to accept on this basis that:

> [...] third-country nationals who are girls and women share an innate characteristic on account of their biological sex and, as a result of having lived in a Member State for a considerable period during the phase of their life in which they form their identity, may share a belief in gender equality that is so fundamental to their identity that they should not be forced to renounce it.[67]

Since that Opinion was given, the ECJ Grand Chamber has delivered its judgment in Case C-621/21 *WS and Intervyuirasht organ na Darzhavna agentsia za bezhantsite pri Ministerskia savet*, on 16 January 2024. In this case the ECJ ruled that:

> [...] depending on the circumstances in the country of origin, women in that country, as a whole, and more restricted groups of women who share an additional common characteristic may be regarded as belonging to 'a particular social group', as a 'reason for persecution' capable of leading to the recognition of refugee status. (para 62).

In one respect, this would appear to take too wide a view of the 'innate characteristic' component of the first condition. The ECJ confirmed at para 49 that 'the fact of being female

[63] *Ahmedbekova* (n 41), para 89. By contrast the UK House of Lords in *Fornah v Secretary of State for the Home Department* [2006] UKHL 46 followed the position taken in the UNHCR, *Guidelines on International Protection (Guidelines) No 2: Membership of a particular social group within the context of Article 1A(2) of the 1951 Convention and/or its 1967 Protocol relating to the Status of Refugees* (7 May 2002) UN Doc HCR/GIP/02/01, which considered the two tests as stated in Art 10(1)(d) to be alternatives.

[64] See eg A Zimmermann and C Mahler, 'Article 1A, para 2' in A Zimmermann and T Einarsen (eds), *The 1951 Convention Relating to the Status of Refugees and Its 1967 Protocol: A Commentary* (Oxford University Press, 2011) 394, who cite criticisms by Hruschka and Löhr.

[65] On religion, see *Y and Z* (n 30), para 63; on political opinion, see *Migracijos departamentas* (n 18), para 35.

[66] Opinion of AG Collins in Case C-646/21 *Staatssecretaris van Justitie en Veiligheid (Personnes s'identifiant aux valeurs de l'Union)*, ECLI:EU:C:2023:581 para 22, [in line with the approach generally taken] AG Collins considers 'in particular' in this context to mean 'non-exhaustive'.

[67] ibid, para 74; see also ibid, paras 25–48.

constitutes an innate characteristic and therefore suffices to satisfy that condition'. In terms of the debates in the wider refugee law literature, that would appear to establish that women satisfy the 'protected characteristics' condition per se in any society, anywhere, at any time. On the other hand, it could be read as reinforcing the approach taken by Advocate General Collins in *K, L* in essentially treating the 'protected characteristics' condition as concerned with largely internal aspects of the overall test, and the 'distinct identity' (or sometimes called the 'social perception) condition concerned with the external aspects. Read thus, in order to satisfy the cumulative test, it is obviously necessary to establish, in addition, that women in the particular society in question have a 'distinct identity in the relevant country' (Turkey in the *WS* case). If read thus, that is not so much a 'victory' for proponents of the protected characteristics approach as conventionally understood, but rather confirmation that this 'protected characteristics' test was never meant to have – or should never have been understood as having – a free-standing role sufficient in itself to establish a PSG. How the *WS* case and future ECJ cases on PSG play out in the wider sphere of international refugee law will depend crucially on whether it is read in the way just outlined or otherwise.[68] But a cumulative test still poses a real problem for groups that cannot meet the first condition under any of its three components, even though they may appear capable of being PSGs in certain situations – eg the wider literature has discussed philatelists and rollerbladers as examples of groups that can be socially distinct (within the legal meaning of that term) and in certain societies may face (sometimes even severe) discrimination.[69]

V. CONCLUSION

It will be recalled that the question posed in this chapter is: How has the ECJ's case law contributed to a better international understanding of the refugee definition? From the foregoing brief and selective analysis it is hopefully clear that the ECJ contribution has done much to clarify key aspects of the refugee definition, in particular as to the meaning of persecution; the importance of a factual approach to legislative persecution; adoption of a broad understanding of acts of persecution; rejection of a concealment requirement; an open-ended approach to forms of persecution; making central the principle of individual assessment; emphasising the interdependency of the concepts of persecution and protection; application of a broad approach to the Convention reasons of religion and political opinion; and lack of support for the (outmoded) bipartite approach to well-founded fear.

However, in light of the concerns discussed in Part IV, one must be cautious of automatically assuming that the increasingly weighty *acquis* of ECJ guidance on the refugee definition always furthers the advancement of an agreed international meaning of its key elements. These concerns – the uncritical referencing of UNHCR guidance, the non-application of VCLT rules of interpretation, the possible support for the dubious requirement of persecutory intent, the seemingly dogmatic rejection of any role for civil society actors when assessing the effectiveness of protection; and the seemingly narrow approach taken to membership of a particular social

[68] For further discussion, see Storey (n 6), 627–32. If an attempt were made to transpose the ECJ approach to innate characteristics as clarified in *WA* directly to some other jurisdictions that operate much the same two conditions as alternatives, not as cumulative conditons (eg Australia presently), the odd result would be that the PSG category could be established in relation to an infinitely wide number of innate characteristics, irrespective of whether they had any significance in a particular society.

[69] ibid, 630.

group – are potentially ones that blur, if not compromise, the current levels of agreement as to the international meaning of key terms of the refugee definition. Further progress towards greater agreement internationally may depend on there being more of a two-way street. On the one side, the ECJ needs to address apparent deviations from agreed international understandings and wider jurisprudential trends (which for well-known reasons depends crucially on engagement on the part of the Advocates General). On the other side, the courts and tribunals of non-EU countries need to be more prepared (when permitted by their national laws or practices) to engage in greater horizontal judicial dialogue, eg by both citing and analysing ECJ case law. Further progress may also, of course, depend on revisions by EU legislators of EU secondary law on qualification avoiding departures from widely agreed international understandings.

28

Reciprocal Influences between the European Court of Justice and the European Court of Human Rights in Asylum Matters: 'Un Quatrain Juridique'?

LEDI BIANKU*

I. INTRODUCTION

THE DIFFERENT NATURES of the two highest regional courts in Europe, the European Court of Justice (ECJ) and the European Court of Human Rights (ECtHR) have already been underlined and analysed.[1] Such differences can be explained by their respective origins, their initial raison d'être, their organisation and the judicial procedures before them. They are also different in view of the body of law they have to apply, though this difference is considered narrowed after the entry into force of the Charter of Fundamental Rights of the European Union (the Charter), on 1 December 2009. Although traces of reciprocal influences between the two European courts are to be found before that date, the entry into force of the Charter increased more than ever the potential that the two European courts would deal with similar legal bases, decide on the same issues, and eventually contradict or be influenced by each other. Asylum and migration matters have been one of the areas where such influence has been conspicuous. The implementation by the European Union (EU) Member States of the Dublin Convention and later of the Dublin Regulation had already been source of detailed analysis both in Strasbourg and in Luxembourg. However, the entry into force of the Charter and the migration crises the European shores faced repeatedly since 2009, have obviously increased the number of cases landing in Strasbourg and Luxembourg, therefore amplifying the possibilities for reciprocal influence between the two European courts. Against that background, this chapter focuses on how methods of interpretation used by the ECJ and the ECtHR in relation to removals within the Dublin system have influenced their reciprocal case law in this area and to a larger extent their respective case law in relation to fundamental rights protection in Europe.

* Former Judge at the European Court of Human Rights and an Associate Professor at the University of Strasbourg.

[1] See for example D Spielmann and P Voyatzis, 'L'étendue du contrôle du respect des droits fondamentaux à l'aune de l'expérience judiciaire comparée' (2017) *Revue trimestrielle des droits de l'homme* 897.

II. FROM STRASBOURG TO LUXEMBOURG

Building on the principle of practical and effective interpretation of the European Convention on Human Rights (the Convention or ECHR) also in cases of removals[2] and despite the fact that the right to asylum is not recognised as such by the Convention, the ECtHR has dealt with asylum cases since 1991.[3] Especially Articles 2 and 3 of the ECHR have become an important legal instrument in avoiding removals of asylum seekers to countries where the rights guaranteed by these two provisions could be violated upon return. Since then, the ECtHR has developed a massive body of case law in asylum cases, and this was done before the ECJ had any competence to deal with asylum issues under EU law. The ECtHR also had the possibility to deal with the foundations of the Common European Asylum System (CEAS) before the ECJ was entitled to do so under EU law.[4] This created the premise that when the ECJ was empowered to deal with asylum cases, it had the benefit of looking to the ECtHR's already considerable case law on the matter.

A. The Birth of the Systemic Deficiencies Test

The relationship between the ECHR system and the EU system is governed by what some authors call 'the Bosphorus modus vivendi'.[5] However, in relation to Dublin removals cases, in the case of *TI v the United Kingdom*, dealing with the application of the Dublin Convention,[6] the ECtHR had previously developed three criteria as the method of analysis in Strasbourg in relation to Dublin removals.[7] While in that case the ECtHR accepted the laudable objectives of the Dublin Convention, it underlined that 'its effectiveness may be undermined in practice by the differing approaches adopted by Contracting States to the scope of protection offered'.[8] In the *KRS v UK*,[9] a case concerning the Dublin removal of an Iranian asylum seeker from the UK to Greece in application of the Dublin Regulation II,[10] the ECJ did not find that the effectiveness of the Dublin system was undermined by the Greek authorities. The ECtHR referred to the presumption that the Greek authorities will abide by its obligations under the relevant EU directives.[11] However, in that decision, the ECtHR did not specify that this was a Bosphorus presumption, nor that it was irrebuttable.[12]

[2] *Soering v the United Kingdom* App no 14038/88, ECLI:CE:ECHR:1989:0707JUD001403888, para 87.

[3] *Cruz Varas and Others v Sweden* App no 15576/89, ECLI:CE:ECHR:1991:0320JUD001557689, paras 69–86; and *Vilvarajah and Others v the United Kingdom* App no 13163/87, no 13164/87, no 13165/87, no 13447/87 and no 13448/87, ECLI:CE:ECHR:1991:1030JUD001316387, paras 101–16.

[4] *TI v the United Kingdom* App no 43844/98, ECLI:CE:ECHR:2000:0307DEC004384498. See, in relation to the evolution of the CEAS, *An Introduction to the Common European Asylum System for Courts and Tribunals – A Judicial Analysis* (Publications Office of the EU, 2016) 13–24.

[5] See Spielmann and Voyatzis (n 1), 914.

[6] Convention determining the State responsible for examining applications for asylum lodged in one of the Member States of the European Communities, Dublin Convention [1997] OJ C254/1.

[7] *TI v the United Kingdom* (n 4), 15.

[8] ibid.

[9] *KRS v the United Kingdom* App no 32733/08, ECLI:CE:ECHR:2008:1202DEC003273308. See also on this point *Stapleton v Ireland* App no 56588/07, ECLI:CE:ECHR:2010:0504DEC005658807, para 30.

[10] Council Regulation (EC) No 343/2003 of 18 February 2003 establishing the criteria and mechanisms for determining the Member State responsible for examining an asylum application lodged in one of the Member States by a third-country national [2003] OJ L50/1.

[11] Respectively Council Directive 2005/85/EC of 1 December 2005 on minimum standards on procedures in Member States for granting and withdrawing refugee status [2005] OJ L326/13; and Council Directive 2003/9/EC of 27 January 2003 laying down minimum standards for the reception of asylum seekers [2003] OJ L31/18.

[12] *KRS v the United Kingdom* (n 9), 18, para 2.

The three *TI v UK* criteria in dealing with Dublin removals were confirmed by the ECtHR Grand Chamber in the case of *MSS v Belgium and Greece*.[13] The case concerned the application of the Dublin II Regulation in the case of the removal of an Afghani asylum seeker from Belgium to Greece. The ECtHR notes, as it did in *KRS*, that the Dublin system is based on the presumption that the EU Member States respect the principle of *non-refoulement* enshrined in the Geneva Convention and are considered as safe countries.[14] However, and contrary to the allegations of some governments in this case,[15] the ECtHR clarified at the outset that the Bosphorus presumption does not apply where the application of the Dublin Regulation II is concerned.[16] In such cases only a general presumption for respect of Convention rights applies.[17] The question was in which circumstances the effectiveness of the Dublin system has been undermined by the concerned EU Member State(s), leading to the conclusion that the presumption is rebutted in relation to the specific case.

The structure of the *MSS* judgment somehow introduces the methodology to be followed to find the answer to this question. Although the application is directed against Belgium and Greece, the Grand Chamber of the ECtHR operated first with the analysis of the situation of Dublin removals in Greece. It found that Greece has violated Article 3 of the ECHR, both in relation to detention conditions and living conditions of the applicant. The ECtHR also found a violation of Article 13 taken together with Article 3 of the ECHR in relation to asylum procedures in Greece.[18]

Then the ECtHR assessed whether, in view of that situation, the Belgian authorities should have regarded as rebutted the presumption that the Greek authorities would respect their international obligations in asylum matters.[19] The ECtHR decided that, in view of the numerous and consistent reports on the situation in Greece, including information directed to the Belgian authorities, the latter should not have proceeded with automatic Dublin removals of asylum seekers to that country. In view of such information on the general situation in Greece, the ECtHR concluded that the burden of proof for the risk upon removal to Greece could not be borne by the applicant alone. In this way the ECtHR has somehow reconstructed the criteria according to which it is in principle for the applicants to adduce evidence capable of proving that there are substantial grounds for believing that, if removed, they would be exposed to a real risk of being subjected to treatment contrary to Articles 2 and/or 3 of the ECHR.[20] In *MSS* the ECtHR clearly established that this burden is shifted, at least partially, when sufficient information on the general situation in the country of destination is available to the removing authorities[21] so they know – or ought to know – the dangers faced by the applicants upon removal.[22] In that judgment the ECtHR concluded, for the first time, that simply the fact of

[13] *MSS v Belgium and Greece* App no 30696/09, ECLI:CE:ECHR:2011:0121JUD003069609, para 343.

[14] ibid, paras 69 and 343.

[15] See the third-party intervention of the Government of the Netherlands in the case of *MSS v Belgium and Greece*, ibid, para 300.

[16] ibid, paras 338–40.

[17] ibid, paras 69 and 345.

[18] See especially ibid, para 300, where the Court notes that 'the asylum procedure is marked by such major structural deficiencies'.

[19] ibid, para 345.

[20] *JK and Others v Sweden* App no 59166/12, ECLI:CE:ECHR:2016:0823JUD005916612, para 91. See also the UNHCR's Handbook and Guidelines on Procedures and Criteria for Determining Refugee Status of 1979 and reissued in 2019, especially at para 196, and the UNHCR 1998 Note on Burden and Standard of Proof in Refugee Claims, para 6.

[21] *MSS v Belgium and Greece* (n 13); in para 352 of the judgment the ECtHR states that: 'In these conditions, the Court considers that the general situation was known to the Belgian authorities and that the applicant should not be expected to bear the entire burden of proof'.

[22] ibid, para 358, where the ECtHR affirms that: 'In the light of the foregoing, the Court considers that at the time of the applicant's expulsion the Belgian authorities knew or ought to have known that he had no guarantee that

being an asylum seeker in a country where the system is deficient, meets the burden of proof for a real and individualised risk.[23] However, it did not say that this, ie the general situation in the country of destination, was to be the new and exclusive criteria in deciding asylum cases under the ECHR.[24]

The judgment of *NS and Others*[25] gave the ECJ the opportunity to analyse the compatibility of Dublin removals to Greece from the standpoint of the EU law and of the Charter. Importantly, the ECJ states from the outset that the Dublin system presumption of compliance with fundamental rights cannot be considered as conclusive, as this could be regarded as undermining the safeguards which are intended to ensure compliance with fundamental rights by the EU and its Member States.[26] Therefore, the ECJ considers the Dublin presumption as rebuttable.[27] After these important findings the ECJ turns to the criteria that should be used by the national authorities in assessing whether the Dublin presumption is rebutted in cases of removal of asylum seekers from one EU Member State to another. The ECJ, by directly referring to the analysis used by the ECtHR in the *MSS* judgment,[28] confirms that the EU Member States had the possibility to evaluate the risks of removals to Greece, especially in view of the European Commission's reports and proposals for amendment of Regulation No 343/2003.[29] It seems that, in such circumstances, the ECJ too considers that the burden does not lay with the applicants alone in claiming risk upon removal to another EU Member State.

All in all, the ECJ indicates that the Member States, including the national courts, may not transfer an asylum seeker to the EU Member State responsible under the Dublin system, where they cannot be unaware that systemic deficiencies in the asylum procedure and in the reception conditions of asylum seekers in that Member State lead to the conclusion that the asylum seeker would face a real risk of being subjected to inhuman or degrading treatment.[30]

B. The 'Revival' of Individual Assessment Test

The conclusion by the ECJ in *NS and Others* might seem to sketch more distinctly the boundary between situations when EU Member States can proceed with Dublin removals with situations they cannot do so. While the ECtHR in its *MSS* judgment based the risk analysis of the applicant individually on the general situation of asylum seekers in Greece,[31] the ECJ, under the preliminary ruling procedure provided by Article 267 of the Treaty on the Functioning of the European Union, gave an a priori answer to questions raised by the national courts dealing with such proceedings at national level. The judgments of *MSS v Belgium and Greece* and in

his asylum application would be seriously examined by the Greek authorities. They also had the means of refusing to transfer him'.

[23] ibid, para 259. This line of reasoning was later confirmed in *JK and Others v Sweden* (n 20), para 98. On the concept of systemic deficiencies see A von Bogdandy 'Principles of a Systemic Deficiencies Doctrine: How to Protect Checks and Balances in Member States' (2020) 57 *Common Market Law Review* 705.

[24] On this judgment see P Gragl, 'The Shortcomings of Dublin II: Strasbourg's M.S.S. Judgment and its Implications for the European Union's Legal Order' (2012) *European Yearbook on Human Rights* 123.

[25] Joined Cases C-411/10 and C-493/10 *NS and Others*, ECLI:EU:C:2011:865.

[26] ibid, para 100.

[27] ibid, para 104.

[28] ibid, paras 88–90.

[29] ibid, para 92.

[30] ibid, para 106.

[31] See n 20 and the references therein.

NS and Others v Secretary of State were read by many, including the European Commission,[32] the ECJ,[33] some national courts[34] and to a certain extent the ECtHR,[35] as being the sole criteria for challenging Dublin removals and excluding in this way the criteria and the need for an individual assessment of the situation of the asylum seekers. This understanding was reinforced by the introduction of the systemic deficiencies criteria in the text of Article 3(2) of the Dublin III Regulation.[36] Particularly, the *Abdullahi* judgment of the ECJ seems to adopt a strict textual interpretation of the Dublin III Regulation,[37] limiting the grounds for justifying a stop in Dublin removals to the systemic deficiencies. With *Abdullahi*, the only door left open by the ECJ to call into question removals to another EU Member State, was by pleading systemic deficiencies in the asylum procedure and in the conditions for the reception of applicants for asylum in that Member State. In that judgment, it seems that the main preoccupation of the ECJ seems to be the working of the CEAS and of the principle of mutual trust and the assumption that all EU Member States respect the Geneva Convention and the ECHR.[38]

This reading of the required standard in cases of Dublin removals raised issues especially under the fundamental rights protection and the criteria applied consistently by the ECtHR in asylum cases. The judicial endeavour to find a workable way of operation of the Dublin system while respecting fundamental rights, risked putting into question the respect for fundamental rights in the framework of the Dublin system if the criteria was not clearly formulated and correctly understood. To elucidate the formulation and to avoid any

[32] Case C-578/16 PPU *CK and Others v Republika Slovenija*, ECLI:EU:C:2017:127, para 91, referring to the European Commission's understanding on this point.

[33] Case C-4/11 *Bundesrepublik Deutschland v Kaveh Puid*, ECLI:EU:C:2013:740; and especially Case C-394/12 *Abdullahi v Bundesasylamt*, ECLI:EU:C:2013:813, paras 60 and 62. See also *Opinion C-2/13 (Accession of the European Union to the ECHR)*, ECLI:EU:C:240:2454, para 191.

[34] See for example the decisions of the Federal Supreme Administrative Court of Germany BVerwG 10 B 6.14 OVG 4 L 44/13, 19 March 2014; and BVerwG 10 B 35.14 OVG 1 A 21/12.A, the decision of 18 November 2011 in *EM (Eritrea) and Others v the Secretary of State for the Home Department* [2011] EWHC 3012 (Admin), especially para 12 and the decision of the Court of Appeal for England and Wales in the same case at [2012] EWCA Civ 1336.

[35] See *Sharifi v Austria* App no 60104/08, ECLI:CE:ECHR:2013:1205JUD006010408, para 38; *Mohammed v Austria* App no 2283/12, ECLI:CE:ECHR:2013:0606JUD000228312, para 95, where the Chamber concluded that Austrian authorities, at the relevant period, did not know that Greece was facing systemic deficiencies in its asylum system and on this basis the applicant's claims were rejected. However, in another line of cases, the ECtHR did make a holistic analysis on risks upon return, analysing both systemic and individual deficiencies. See *Mohammed Hussein v the Netherlands & Italy* App no 27725/10, ECLI:CE:ECHR:2013:0402DEC002772510, para 69; *Daytbegova & Magomedova v Austria* App no 6198/12, ECLI:CE:ECHR:2013:0604DEC000619812, para 61; *Halimi v Austria & Italy* App no 53852/11, ECLI:CE:ECHR:2013:0618DEC005385211, para 57; *Abubeker v Austria & Italy* App no 73874/11, ECLI:CE:ECHR:2013:0618DEC007387411, para 49; *Miruts Hagos v the Netherlands and Italy*, App no 9053/10, ECLI:CE:ECHR:2013:0827DEC000905310, para 39; *Safaii v Austria* App no 44689/09, ECLI:CE:ECHR:2014:0507JUD004468909, para 50; *Mohammadi v Austria* App no 71932/12, ECLI:CE:ECHR:2014:0703JUD007193212, para 62; and *Hussein Diirshi v the Netherlands and Italy* App no 2314/10, ECLI:CE:ECHR:2013:0910DEC000231410, para 138.

[36] Regulation (EU) No 604/2013 of the European Parliament and of the Council of 26 June 2013 Establishing the Criteria and Mechanisms for Determining the Member State Responsible for Examining an Application for International Protection Lodged in One of the Member States by a Third-Country National or a Stateless Person, [2013] OJ L180/31. Its Art 3 (2) reads: 'Where it is impossible to transfer an applicant to the Member State primarily designated as responsible because there are substantial grounds for believing that there are systemic flaws in the asylum procedure and in the reception conditions for applicants in that Member State, resulting in a risk of inhuman or degrading treatment within the meaning of Article 4 of the Charter of Fundamental Rights of the European Union, the determining Member State shall continue to examine the criteria set out in Chapter III in order to establish whether another Member State can be designated as responsible.'

[37] *Abdullahi v Bundesasylamt* (n 33), paras 60 and 62: 'In a situation in which the Member State agrees to take charge of the applicant for asylum, and given [the assumption that all Member States observe fundamental rights and can have confidence in each other in that regard, and in order to avoid blockages and forum shopping,] the only way in which the applicant for asylum can call into question the choice of that criterion is by pleading systemic deficiencies in the asylum procedure and in the conditions for the reception.'

[38] See ibid, paras 48–59 in *Abdullahi*. See also Case C-245/11 *K v Bundesasylamt*, ECLI:EU:C:2012:685.

doubt in the understanding of the criteria applicable and the method to be used in Dublin cases,[39] the ECtHR sent to the Grand Chamber for examination of the case *Tarakhel v Switzerland*.[40] The case concerned the removal of a couple with six young children from Switzerland to Italy, the latter being the Member State responsible under the Dublin Regulation. The information available to the ECtHR on the reception conditions of asylum seekers in Italy at the time was rather worrying. Several national judges from other EU Member States had expressed their concerns about whether Italy also was facing systemic deficiencies in the accommodation of Dublin returnees, leading to the violation of the fundamental rights of asylum seekers in that country. On 12 February 2014 the Grand Chamber of the ECtHR held the hearing and the first deliberations in that case. Only one week later, on 19 March 2014 the UK Supreme Court delivered the judgment in *EM [Eritrea]*.[41] In that judgment the UK Supreme Court reviewed the test used by the lower courts in the same case by referring and, it must be said, correctly analysed the long-established case law of the ECtHR in asylum matters. The UK Supreme Court rightly underlined that the ECtHR has established, since its very first asylum cases, that both the general situation in the country of destination and the individual circumstances of the applicant shall be analysed in deciding the risk upon return for the purpose of Articles 2 and 3 of the ECHR.[42]

In *Tarakhel*, after recalling the general principles in paragraph 93 of the judgment, the ECtHR confirmed this approach. In that judgment the ECtHR clarified the test to be used in Dublin removals, by stating that this was indeed the approach it adopted in the *MSS* case, which consists in the examination of the applicant's individual situation in the light of the overall situation in the country of destination at the relevant time.[43] The Grand Chamber in *Tarakhel* found it useful to recall too, on the basis of the ECtHR and ECJ judgments respectively in *MSS* and *NS*, both mentioned above, that the presumption that a State participating in the 'Dublin' system will respect the fundamental rights laid down by the Convention can validly be rebutted where 'substantial grounds have been shown for believing' that the person whose return is being ordered faces a 'real risk' of being subjected to treatment contrary to that provision in the receiving country.[44] The structure of the judgment in *Tarakhel* is also quite explicit, with the aim of making clear the need for a holistic approach. The ECtHR first deals with the general situation with regard to the reception arrangements for asylum seekers in Italy,[45] then continues, in a second stage, with an analysis of the applicant's individual situation.[46] The judgment introduced a safeguard clause to allow the operation of the Dublin system in respect of the fundamental rights standards under the ECHR. The Grand Chamber concluded that the Swiss authorities could remove the applicants to Italy only after having obtained appropriate guarantees about their situation.[47]

[39] See E Tsourdi and C Costello, '"Systemic Violations" in EU Asylum Law: Cover or Catalyst?' (2023) 24 *German Law Journal* 982.

[40] *Tarakhel v Switzerland* App no 29217/12, ECLI:CE:ECHR:2014:1104JUD002921712.

[41] *R (on the application of EM (Eritrea)) v Secretary of State for the Home Department* [2014] UKSC 12.

[42] *Vilvarajah and Others v United Kingdom* (n 3), para 108 *in fine* where the ECtHR says the examination of the risk: 'focus on the foreseeable consequences of the removal of the applicants to Sri Lanka in the light of the general situation [...] as well as on their personal circumstances'.

[43] *Tarakhel v Switzerland* (n 40), paras 101 and 104–105.

[44] ibid, paras 103–104.

[45] ibid, paras 106–15.

[46] ibid, paras 116–22.

[47] ibid, para 122 and point two of the operative part of the judgment.

III. FROM LUXEMBOURG TO STRASBOURG

The *Tarakhel* judgment of the ECtHR, while clarifying the Strasbourg case law in relation to Dublin removals, raised the question of whether a conflict now appeared in the methodologies that the two highest regional jurisdictions were following in this area.[48] The *Tarakhel* judgment served somehow as an open invitation to the ECJ to clarify, in turn, its position concerning not only the compatibility of the Dublin removals, but also the compatibility of the cooperation in criminal matters under the European arrest warrant (EAW)[49] with the fundamental rights standards. Indeed, both situations – Dublin removals and EAW – raised the question of the relationship between mutual trust and respect for fundamental rights.

A. The Embodiment of the Two-Step Assessment in Luxembourg

The case that gave the opportunity to the ECJ to respond to the *Tarakhel*'s 'open invitation', was the already famous *Aranyosi and Căldăraru*.[50] As is known, the case concerned the compatibility of the execution of two EAW requests under Article 4 of the Charter. The German court[51] dealing with these two cases was concerned with the compatibility of the surrender, in execution of EAW requests, to the issuing EU Member State, where there are strong indications that detention conditions in that State infringe the detention conditions required by the person concerned.[52]

One can notice in *Aranyosi and Căldăraru* a different disposition of the ECJ compared with some of its earlier judgments dealing with this issue.[53] In *Abdullahi*, for example, mentioned above, the only door left open by the ECJ to call into question removal to another EU Member State, was by pleading systemic deficiencies in the asylum procedure and in the conditions for the reception of applicants for asylum in that Member State. In that judgment it seems that the main preoccupation of the ECJ seems to be the working of the CEAS and of the principle of the mutual trust and the assumption that all EU Member States respect the Geneva Convention and the ECHR.[54]

This does not seem to be the tone in *Aranyosi and Căldăraru*. In this later case it can be noted that the ECJ duly recalled that the principle of mutual recognition, which forms the 'cornerstone' of judicial cooperation in criminal matters, is founded on the mutual confidence between the Member States that their national legal systems are capable of providing equivalent and effective protection of the fundamental rights recognised at EU level, particularly in the Charter.[55] In *Aranyosi and Căldăraru* the ECJ also referred to the fact that an EAW might be refused, or its implementation be suspended, only on the basis of grounds exclusively listed in the EAW Framework Decision.[56] Up to that point the position of the ECJ in *Aranyosi and Căldăraru* is quite similar with that in *Abdullahi*.

[48] A Lübbe, '"Systemic Flaw" and Dublin Transfers: Incompatible Tests before the CJEU and the ECtHR?' (2015) 27 *International Journal of Refugee Law* 135.

[49] Council Framework Decision 2002/584/JHA of 13 June 2002 on the European arrest warrant and the surrender procedures between Member States [2002] OJ L190/1.

[50] Joined Cases C-404/15 and C-659/15 PPU *Aranyosi and Căldăraru*, ECLI:EU:C:2016:198.

[51] The questions, identical in both cases, were formulated by the Hanseatisches Oberlandesgericht in Bremen (Higher Regional Court of Bremen).

[52] *Aranyosi and Căldăraru* (n 50), paras 46 and 63.

[53] Compare especially with *Kaveh Puid* (n 33) and *Abdullahi* (n 33).

[54] See *Abdullahi*(n 33), paras 48–59.

[55] *Aranyosi and Căldăraru* (n 50), paras 75–79.

[56] ibid, paras 80–81.

However, in *Aranyosi and Căldăraru* the ECJ continued with a detailed analysis of the fundamental rights obligations for the EU Member States in executing the EAW.[57] This is a step the ECJ had not taken in some of its earlier judgments dealing with this issue.[58] In *Aranyosi and Căldăraru* the ECJ also recalled that, according to Article 1(3) of the Framework Decision, the EAW system is not to have the effect of modifying the obligation to respect fundamental rights.[59] It clearly underlined the binding nature of these obligations[60] and the absolute character of the rights at stake in that case under Article 4 of the Charter and Article 3 of the ECHR.[61] The conclusion of such analysis is that, where there is evidence of a real risk of inhuman or degrading treatment of individuals in the destination EU Member State, the judicial authorities in the EU Member State of the execution shall assess the existence of that risk under the standard of protection of fundamental rights guaranteed by EU law in order to avoid the possibility that the individual concerned suffers inhuman or degrading treatment.[62] It seems clear that in *Aranyosi and Căldăraru* the presumption that all EU Member States have assumed and will respect these obligations is no longer enough. The conclusion is that, when there is available evidence, EU Member States shall assess whether other EU Member States, to which the individual shall be sent, respect fundamental rights to that level that risk of inhuman or degrading treatment is excluded. This confirms the position taken in *NS and Others*, ie that the presumption for respecting fundamental rights is rebuttable for both EU Member States and the ECHR Contracting Parties.

The *Aranyosi and Căldăraru* judgment has the merit to go further and to detail the methodology to be used for assessing whether the destination EU Member State effectively respects fundamental rights. In paragraph 89 of the judgment the ECJ sketched the elements to be taken into account in this assessment. It identified the nature of the information to be used in that assessment by the executing judicial authorities, specifying that it should be 'objective, reliable, specific and properly updated' and obtained by reliable sources.[63] The ECJ further continued by indicating that the source of the risk for the fundamental rights deficiencies may be systemic or generalised, or it may affect certain groups of people, or certain places of detention.[64] Most importantly, the ECJ indicated that national jurisdictions should further assess whether there are substantial grounds to believe that such deficiencies faced by the EU Member State of destination will affect the individual concerned.[65] This methodology rightly combines the assessment of the individual situation in the light of the overall situation prevailing in the EU Member State of destination. This two-step assessment is indeed identical with the methodology adopted by the ECtHR in *Tarakhel v Switzerland*.[66] This means that for the ECJ the systemic deficiencies are no longer the only ground for justifying the removal of an individual to another EU Member State and this is true in cases of extradition under the EAW

[57] ibid, para 82.

[58] Compare especially with *Kaveh Puid* (n 33) and *Abdullahi* (n 33).

[59] *Aranyosi and Căldăraru* (n 50), para 83. It can be said that a similar language is used by the ECJ in *NS and Others* (n 25), paras 98–102.

[60] *Aranyosi and Căldăraru* (n 50), para 84.

[61] ibid, paras 85–87.

[62] ibid, para 88.

[63] ibid, para 89. In reading these elements, one can think of *Sufi and Elmi v the United Kingdom* App no 8319/07 and no 11449/07, ECLI:CE:ECHR:2011:0628JUD000831907, paras 230–34.

[64] *Aranyosi and Căldăraru* (n 50), para 89.

[65] Compare this reasoning with the very similar one in the ECtHR judgment in *Sufi and Elmi* (n 63), paras 216 and 218.

[66] *Tarakhel v Switzerland* (n 40). In paras 101–105, the ECtHR recalls the methodology consisting: first, the analysis of general situation in the country of destination; and, second, the individual situation of the asylum seeker. Then the ECtHR applies this methodology in that case by focusing first (in paras 106–15) on the general situation in the country of destination and then, in a second stage (in paras 116–22) examining the applicants' individual situation.

Framework Decision – as in *Aranyosi and Căldăraru*[67] – as well as in the Dublin removal cases. Indeed, in the case of *CK and Others v Republika Slovenija*,[68] the ECJ seized the opportunity to explain that Article 3(2) of the Dublin Regulation cannot be read, as suggested by the European Commission, as meaning that only the existence of systemic flaws in the Member State responsible is capable of affecting the obligation to transfer an asylum seeker to an EU Member State.[69] The ECJ was right to underline that such reading of that provision is:

> irreconcilable with the general character of Article 4 of the Charter, which prohibits inhuman or degrading treatment in all its forms [and …] would be manifestly incompatible with the absolute character of that prohibition if the Member States could disregard a real and proven risk of inhuman or degrading treatment affecting an asylum seeker under the pretext that it does not result from a systemic flaw in the Member State responsible.[70]

This can be considered a transformative moment in the ECJ philosophy as a guarantor of the fundamental rights in the EU legal order, by clarifying that risks to fundamental rights in cases of removals have to be assessed by following this two-step approach, ie analysing in turn the general situation in the destination and the individual circumstances of the persons concerned. The Member States and their authorities must keep their eyes open in that regard.[71]

B. The Adjustment of the Two-Step Formula in Strasbourg – Back to the Origins?

The methodological clarification made by the ECJ in *Aranyosi and Căldăraru* and in *CK and Others v Republika Slovenija* reflects indeed the position that the ECtHR has adopted since its first asylum-related cases. As mentioned above, the ECtHR since its very first asylum cases has consistently specified that 'the examination [in removal cases] must focus on the foreseeable consequences of the removal of the applicants [to the country of destination], in the light of the general situation there […] as well as on their personal circumstances'.[72] It had confirmed the same methodology also in *MSS*, stating that 'The fact that a large number of asylum-seekers in Greece find themselves in the same situation as the applicant does not make the risk concerned any less individual where it is sufficiently real and probable.'[73]

However, the ECtHR found it necessary to recall, as part of the identification of the main principles applicable in asylum cases, how the assessment of risk should be conducted in these cases. In two judgments delivered in the same period as *Aranyosi and Căldăraru*, the ECtHR clearly reiterated that the assessment of the existence of a real risk in asylum cases must necessarily be a rigorous one. This assessment must focus on the foreseeable consequences of the

[67] See E Bribosia and A Weyembergh, 'Arrêt "Aranyosi et Caldararu": imposition de certaines limites à la confiance mutuelle dans la coopération judiciaire pénale' (2016) *Journal de droit européen* 225.

[68] *CK and Others v Republika Slovenija* (n 32), especially para 63.

[69] ibid, paras 91–92.

[70] ibid, para 93. Compare with the language of the ECtHR in *Vilvarajah and Others v the United Kingdom* (n 3), para 108. See also for a more recent judgment Case C-163/17 *Abubacarr Jawo v Bundesrepublik Deutschland*, ECLI:EU:C:2019:218. See also Spielmann and Voyatzis (n 1), 920; and G Anagnostaras, 'The Common European Asylum System: Balancing Mutual Trust against Fundamental Rights Protection' (2020) 21 *German Law Journal* 1180.

[71] This philosophy is also reflected by the ECJ President in K Lenaerts, 'La vie après l'avis: Exploring the principle of mutual (yet not blind) trust' (2017) 54 *Common Market Law Review* 805.

[72] *Cruz Varas and Others v Sweden* App no 15576/89, ECLI:CE:ECHR:1991:0320JUD001557689, paras 77–83, and especially *Vilvarajah and Others v the United Kingdom* (n 3), paras 108 and 111. This analysis was followed later in *Chahal v The United Kingdom* App no 22414/93, ECLI:CE:ECHR:1996:1115JUD002241493, paras 97–98; *Ahmed v Austria* App no 25964/94, ECLI:CE:ECHR:1996:1217JUD002596494, paras 38–47; and *Saadi v Italy* App no 37201/06, ECLI:CE:ECHR:2008:0228JUD003720106, para 130 ff.

[73] *MSS v Belgium and Greece* (n 13), para 359 *in fine*.

applicant's removal to the country of destination, in the light of the general situation there and of his or her personal circumstances. In this connection, and where it is relevant to do so, the ECJ will have regard to whether there is a general situation of violence or systemic deficiencies existing in the country of destination, which, in view of the analysis in *MSS*, might dispense with the applicants pleading particular individual circumstances. In both these judgments the ECtHR recalled that if the existence of risk for Articles 2 and/or 3 of the ECHR is established, the applicant's removal would necessarily breach these provisions, regardless of whether the risk emanates from a general situation of violence, a personal characteristic of the applicant, or a combination of the two.[74]

In a more recent Grand Chamber case, *Khasanov and Rakhmanov v Russia*,[75] the ECtHR confirmed again the same approach and dedicated a substantial part of its analysis to this issue. The Grand Chamber dedicated a separate section to the scope of the assessment to be conducted in asylum cases. The Grand Chamber announced at the outset of the judgment a three-tier analysis.[76] It announced the introduction of the criteria of the membership of a targeted group, arguing that this ground is different from the assessment relating to the general situation of violence in a particular country, on the one hand, and to individual circumstances, on the other.[77] However, this criterion seems to belong conceptually to the individual situation of the asylum seekers, which is in many cases shared with others, such as membership of a religious, ethnic, sexual, political, etc minority, or which in exceptional cases might be unique.[78] This has been the approach adopted by the ECtHR in previous cases, the membership of a particular group being considered as an element distinguishing the applicants from the general population in the country of destination.[79] At the end, the analysis of the ECtHR in this case was focused on a two-step test comprising the general situation in the destination State and the individual circumstances of the person concerned.[80] What is most important for the purposes of this analysis, however, is that the ECtHR confirmed once more that in the assessment of risk in asylum cases both the general situation in the destination and the individual circumstances of the person concerned must be analysed, bringing another clarification to the debate briefly dealt with in this contribution, and offering an example of a judicial dialogue between the two European courts.

IV. CONCLUSION

Against that background, this chapter focuses on how methods of interpretation used by the ECJ and the ECtHR in relation to removals within the Dublin system have influenced their reciprocal case law in this area and to a larger extent their respective case law in relation to fundamental rights protection in Europe. I identified as particularly important the four moments by which this chapter is structured. The influence is indeed reciprocal, and it might be said that even deviations from the settled case law, which also depended on the nature of

[74] *FG v Sweden* App no 43611/11, ECLI:CE:ECHR:2016:0323JUD004361111, para 116; and *JK and Others v Sweden* (n 20), paras 85–86.

[75] *Khasanov and Rakhmanov v Russia* App no 28492/15 and no 49975/15, ECLI:CE:ECHR:2022:0429JUD002849215.

[76] ibid, 1.

[77] ibid, para 96.

[78] See EK Blöndal and OM Arnardóttir, 'Non-Refoulement in Strasbourg: Making Sense of the Assessment of Individual Circumstances' (2021) 5 *Oslo Law Review* 147.

[79] *JK and Others v Sweden* (n 20), paras 103–105, and the references therein.

[80] ibid, paras 95–101 of the judgment.

particular cases, at the end have contributed to the enrichment and fine tuning of the assessment criteria in asylum-related cases at European and national level.[81] The direct exchanges and dialogue between both Courts' judges, including the competent national judges, with Vice-President Lars Bay Larsen being an admirable contributor on such occasions, have contributed considerably to the clarification of the variations in the case law of the two European courts and to the refining of the protection of fundamental rights in Europe in this area. This increased cooperation through judgments and dialogues gives hope that the era of 'je t'aime, moi non plus' is definitely over.[82]

[81] Of course, such reciprocal influence goes far beyond the asylum cases. See in this regard K Lenaerts, 'The European Court of Human Rights and the Court of Justice of the European Union: Creating Synergies in the Field of Fundamental Rights Protection' (2018) *Il Diritto dell'Unione Europea* 9.

[82] D Simon, 'Des influences réciproques entre CJCE et CEDH: "je t'aime, moi non plus?"' (2001) 96 *Pouvoirs* 31.

29

The External Dimension of the Area of Freedom, Security and Justice: Member States' Cooperation with External Partners within and at the Margins of EU Law

CHLOÉ BRIÈRE*

I. INTRODUCTION

THE AREA OF freedom, security and justice (AFSJ) was officially recognised as an objective of the European Union (EU) with the Treaty of Amsterdam in 1997. Subsequent treaty revisions added further details about its different components, and expanded the EU's competences. They have been accompanied by very dynamic legislative developments, with the adoption of numerous instruments of EU secondary law, consistently updated and modernised, and by the ever-increasing case law of the European Court of Justice (ECJ).

If the AFSJ aims first to offer the benefit of free movement and a high level of security to EU citizens and residents, while ensuring effective migration management, it is inextricably linked to international cooperation with external partners. The awareness of its necessary external dimension can be traced through the references to international cooperation in early policy documents, or provisions included in the first EU instruments. Unti\l today, international cooperation remains considered a core component of the AFSJ by all EU institutions (European Council, Commission, Parliament and Council) and EU legislative instruments include provisions for supporting and promoting cooperation with external partners in strategic and operational matters.

The last 30 years have been instrumental in the development of the EU as an international actor in matters connected to the AFSJ, but not without complexities and hurdles. The AFSJ concerns matters that are particularly sensitive, due to their possible impact on the protection of the rights of vulnerable individuals, but also due to their connection with the sovereignty of the Member States and the exercise of government functions in migratory and criminal matters. Therefore, the EU's intervention has been exposed to extensive scrutiny by European

* Professor of EU Law at the Centre for European Law and an affiliated member of the IEE (Université libre de Bruxelles).

and national political actors, scholars, and judges alike, notably to monitor its compliance with EU constitutional principles, or to assess its respect for fundamental rights. Such scrutiny is further warranted considering the complex applicable legal framework, in which the Member States retain a capacity to act internationally. A detailed appreciation is required to determine the existence, scope and nature of the EU's competence, and the possibility for the Member States to develop their own international cooperation, in bilateral or multilateral settings, autonomously or within the limits determined by EU law.

The present contribution will focus on the persistence of the Member States' external actions and their role in the external dimension of the AFSJ. It aims to unpack the complexities and arrangements in place that allow them to retain an international role and to develop their cooperation with third countries. To attain such objectives, the contribution will be divided into two parts. First, it will analyse to what extent the recognition and exercise of the EU's competences in the AFSJ define a new framework and offer new opportunities for the Member States' cooperation with non-EU countries. Second, it will address how the Member States can rely on other avenues to develop their cooperation with third countries in the margins or outside the constraints of EU law. It concludes by stressing how – despite the evolutions of the AFSJ – the policy area remains strongly influenced by the Member States, and their reluctance to withdraw their capacity to act internationally.

II. EU LAW AS A VEHICLE FOR THE MEMBER STATES' INTERNATIONAL COOPERATION

Over the last 30 years, the EU has gained increasing competences in the fields of migration and criminal law, and has adopted a plethora of instruments, approximating standards, establishing innovative mechanisms of cooperation, and creating new actors to support cross-border cooperation within the AFSJ. The Member States have always been instrumental in such developments and have expressed their support for new initiatives, adopting certain instruments in record time,[1] or updating others in a frequent manner to answer operational needs.[2] In contrast, opposition and tensions have considerably slowed down the negotiation of new instruments, leading at times to their withdrawal by the European Commission,[3] or more drastically to an absence of proposals.[4]

In such a context of dynamic legislative activity, one may question whether the exercise of EU competences influences the way Member States cooperate with external partners. The following sections will analyse how EU secondary law instruments support the participation of third countries into EU mechanisms of cooperation (A), and then the way the EU has mobilised its external competences to define frameworks in which Member States can develop bilateral cooperation with third countries (B).

[1] See eg Council Decision (EU) 2022/2332 of 28 November 2022 on identifying the violation of Union restrictive measures as an area of crime that meets the criteria specified in Article 83(1) TFEU [2022] OJ L308/18.

[2] See the multiple revisions of the Regulations on Europol or Frontex since 2016.

[3] See the withdrawal and changes made by the Commission in 2020 to asylum proposals presented in 2016, Commission, 'Proposal for a Regulation of the European Parliament and of the Council on asylum and migration management and amending Council Directive (EC) 2003/109 and the proposed Regulation (EU) XXX/XXX [Asylum and Migration Fund] COM (2020) 610 final.

[4] An example is the Facilitators' Package, adopted in 2002 and with no revision proposed before November 2023 (Commission, 'Proposal for a Directive of the European Parliament and of the Council laying down minimum rules to prevent and counter the facilitation of unauthorised entry, transit and stay in the Union, and replacing Council Directive 2002/90/EC and Council Framework Decision 2002/946 JHA COM (2023) 755 final).

A. International Cooperation and its Support under EU Secondary Law

The EU legislation adopted to develop the AFSJ is inextricably linked to the objectives assigned to the EU and the competences it received from the Member States. Consequently, the different policy areas encompassed within the AFSJ have not all been the object of similar and parallel patterns of legislative activities. Additionally, for some policy areas, the focus of EU secondary law instruments is first and foremost internal, as they serve the purpose of establishing common standards applicable across the Member States, and eventually organising their cooperation and/or providing for burden-sharing mechanisms. This does not, however, prevent the EU from integrating – whenever it is relevant – provisions on cooperation with external partners, facilitating their cooperation with Member States.

This is noticeable in the field of EU criminal law, marked by the frequent transnational nature of crime, and the need to ensure that cooperation in criminal matters 'knows as few borders as possible'. Many mechanisms designed to foster cooperation between the Member States are 'open' to third countries, allowing them to participate and benefit from the new tools created. Such participation may be conditional, but it nevertheless indicates an ambition to cooperate with them as much as possible, and a recognition of the added value of such cooperation.

The Regulation establishing a collaboration platform to support the functioning of joint investigation teams (JITs) is a representative example of this trend.[5] Although JITs have been created by internal EU law instruments[6] and are primarily envisaged as a mechanism to boost cooperation between authorities of two or more Member States, they have increasingly involved authorities from non-EU countries and international actors.[7] As is reminded in Eurojust's Guidelines, several legal bases may allow a third country to participate in a JIT, ranging from provisions on international cooperation in multilateral agreements signed within the Council of Europe or the United Nations, ad hoc agreements between the EU and third countries, to bilateral agreements concluded by the Member States, or even national legislation.[8] Despite the complexities in associating a third country to a JIT, the statistics published annually demonstrate that their participation has become a regular practice, especially from authorities benefiting from a close relationship with the EU (eg UK, Switzerland, Norway and/or more occasionally candidate countries). More recently, JITs have been established involving third countries that are more geographically distant, such as the JIT established to investigate the crash of the MH17 flight, involving the Netherlands, Australia, Malaysia, Belgium and Ukraine. Lastly, for the first time, the Office of the Prosecutor of the International Criminal Court has participated since 2022 in the JIT established to investigate the war crimes committed in Ukraine.[9] The frequency and regularity of JITs involving external partners thus raised the question of the possibility of their accessing the new collaboration platform set up by the EU institutions. Unsurprisingly, their right to access the platform has been provided for, even

[5] Regulation (EU) 2023/969 of the European Parliament and of the Council of 10 May 2023 establishing a collaboration platform to support the functioning of joint investigation teams [2023] OJ L132/1.

[6] Convention on Mutual Assistance in Criminal Matters between the Member States of the European Union [2000] OJ C197/1; and Council Framework Decision of 13 June 2002 on joint investigation teams [2002] OJ L162/1.

[7] Eurojust, 'Third JIT Evaluation Report' (2020) 19; and Eurojust, 'Guidelines on JITs Involving Third Countries' (2022) (Eurojust Guidelines) 38.

[8] Eurojust Guidelines, ibid, 5.

[9] Eurojust, 'Highlights of the 2022 Annual Meeting of the Network of National Experts on JITs', Doc 16201/22.

though it is subject to specific conditions, especially relating to respect for data protection rules in case of transfer of personal data to a third country.[10]

Support to international cooperation is further evidenced by the automatic insertion of provisions foreseeing such cooperation for EU AFSJ actors. Most of the instruments defining the mandate and the tasks of these EU actors entrust them with supporting and promoting cross-border cooperation, and they include provisions forming a basis for the conclusion of cooperation agreements and/or arrangements with external partners, or for the posting of liaison officers or magistrates. The legal regime applicable has been streamlined with the Lisbon Treaty, with the necessity to apply the procedure applicable for the conclusion of international agreements (Article 218 the Treaty on the Functioning of the European Union (TFEU)). This has partially impacted the capacity and willingness of such actors to conclude formal cooperation agreements, but the increasing number of arrangements concluded with external partners shows that such cooperation is far from being neglected. Rather to the contrary, some actors favour working arrangements either because they do not require the application of the procedure foreseen in the TFEU, or because they are the only cooperation instruments envisaged, while the EU institutions negotiate and conclude agreements either defining the EU's cooperation with key international actors,[11] or better assisting the implementation of the technical tasks assigned to EU specialised actors. In these texts, the possibilities of cooperation between the Member States and third countries are not forgotten. This is, for instance, demonstrated by the regime foreseen under the Frontex Regulation, updated in 2016 and 2019,[12] in relation to the extraterritorial expansion of its operations through the conclusion of status agreements with third countries.[13] These agreements are related to the actions carried out by Frontex on the territory of a third country and in close collaboration with the national authorities of that State. The Member States may participate through their national staff in joint operations between Frontex and third countries implemented under such status agreements, and they may also develop their operational cooperation with third countries based on bilateral or multilateral agreements, other forms of arrangements or through regional networks.[14]

Additionally, the EU legislature is granting to EU AFSJ actors the role of intermediaries, who may assist the Member States in their collaboration with third countries. This is the case, for instance, when Eurojust is mobilised to support and accompany the establishment of a JIT involving a third country, or when the European Union Agency for Asylum supports a Member State in the implementation of resettlement schemes.[15] Conversely, EU AFSJ actors are also positioned as hubs or contact points for third countries seeking to cooperate with the Member States. Eurojust is entrusted under the revised Regulation (EU)

[10] Regulation (EU) 2023/969 of the European Parliament and of the Council of 10 May 2023 establishing a collaboration platform to support the functioning of joint investigation teams and amending regulation (EU) 2018/1726 [2023] OJ L132/1, Art 17.

[11] Council Decision (EU) 2021/1313 authorising the opening of negotiations for a cooperation agreement between the EU and Interpol [2021] OJ L287/6.

[12] Regulation (EU) 2019/1896 of the European Parliament and of the Council of 13 November 2019 on the European Border and Coast Guard [2019] OJ L295/1.

[13] F Coman-Kund, 'The Territorial Expansion of Frontex Operations to Third Countries: On the Recently Concluded Status Agreements in the Western Balkans and Beyond …' (*Verfassungsblog*, 6 February 2020), https://verfassungsblog.de/the-territorial-expansion-of-frontex-operations-to-third-countries-on-the-recently-concluded-status-agreements-in-the-western-balkans-and-beyond/, accessed 4 March 2024.

[14] Regulation (EU) 2019/1896 of 13 November 2019 on the European Border and Coast Guard (Frontex Regulation) [2019] OJ L295/1, Art 76(3).

[15] Regulation (EU) 2021/2303 of the European Parliament and of the Council of 15 December 2021 on the European Union Agency for Asylum [2021] OJ L468/1, Art 35(3).

2019/816 to act as a contact point for third countries and international organisations, asking for the consent of the individual Member State before providing the relevant information for obtaining extracts from criminal records.[16] Europol, to whom third countries and international organisations frequently provide information on third-country nationals suspected to be involved in terrorist offences or other serious crimes, is competent to propose to Member States that they enter information alerts into the Schengen Information System, and ensures the reliability of such alerts.[17]

These examples illustrate how international cooperation is envisaged, accompanied, and even promoted within EU secondary law instruments, even though they concern mostly the development of legislation and actors aiming to allow the smooth development of the AFSJ. The Member States can benefit from such an ecosystem to further develop their international cooperation, and even more so when the EU mobilises its external competences.

B. International Cooperation Framed by the Exercise of EU External Competences

The conferral of external competences to the EU in the AFSJ took place at a very early stage. In criminal matters, the Treaty of Amsterdam provided for the possibility to mobilise the legal basis for the conclusion of the Common Foreign and Security Policy (CFSP) agreements to conclude agreements in the field of police and judicial cooperation. Moreover, the capacity for the Community to engage in the negotiation and conclusion of international agreements relating to migration has been considered possible based on implicit external competences,[18] and has even in some cases led to the recognition of exclusive competence by exercise, such as in the field of visa-waiver agreements.[19] The Lisbon Treaty provided clarifications and granted explicit external competences to the EU in the field of migration, notably for the conclusion of readmission agreements with third countries (Article 79(2) TFEU) and the adoption of partnerships for the purpose of managing inflows of people applying for asylum (Article 78(2)(g) TFEU). Other external AFSJ activities remain under the regime of implicit external competences. The conferral and exercise of these EU external competences is not detrimental to the cooperation of Member States with third countries, nor to their capacity to develop their own international initiatives and conclude international agreements.

The capacity of the EU to act on the international scene may first boost the willingness of third countries to enter into negotiation of an agreement. They may find an appeal in negotiating with the EU rather than with individual Member States for reasons of efficiency or relevancy. This was particularly salient in the negotiation and conclusion of the EU–Japan Mutual Legal Assistance Agreement,[20] which was not preceded by bilateral agreements

[16] Regulation (EU) 2019/816 of the European Parliament and of the Council of 17 April 2019 establishing a centralised system for the identification of Member States holding conviction information on third-country nationals and stateless persons (ECRIS-TCN) [2019] OJ L135/1, Art 17.

[17] Regulation (EU) 2022/1190 of the European Parliament and of the Council of 6 July 2022 amending Regulation (EU) 2018/1862 as regards the entry of information alerts into the Schengen Information System (SIS) on third-country nationals in the interest of the Union [2022] OJ L185/1.

[18] P Garcia Andrade, 'The External Dimension of the EU Migration Policy: The Legal Framing of Building Partnerships with Third Countries' in E Tsourdi and P de Bruycker (eds), *Research Handbook on EU Migration and Asylum Law* (Edward Elgar, 2022) 368.

[19] ibid, 370.

[20] A Weyembergh and I Wieczorek, 'Norm Diffusion as a Tool to Uphold and Promote EU Values and Interests: A Case Study on the EU Japan Mutual Legal Assistance Agreement' (2020) 11 *New Journal of European Criminal Law* 439, 445.

concluded by the Member States. The possibility to negotiate only with the EU and conclude a single agreement organising cooperation with 27 Member States has been particularly appealing to the Japanese authorities. The Member States may also find an added value in relying on the EU, which may benefit from stronger bargaining power and ensure a better balance in the content of the agreements discussed. This also helps to push for the promotion of certain values,[21] notably in relation to the abolition of death penalty, a key aspect in agreements with countries that still apply it.[22]

The mobilisation of the EU's external competences may also participate in reducing fragmentation and incoherencies in fields in which the Member States are likely to have concluded bilateral agreements. The conclusion of an agreement by the EU can form a framework for the conclusion of bilateral agreements by individual Member States. This is, for instance, clearly foreseen in the two agreements concluded with the US,[23] which both contain provisions not opposing the conclusion of bilateral agreements between the US and Member States, upon the condition that they are consistent with the EU–US agreements.[24] In such a context, the EU-wide agreement does not replace previously existing agreements, nor prevent the negotiation of new agreements by the Member States.[25] Such a regime has been evaluated positively by the EU, its Member States and the US,[26] and is envisaged as one of the possibilities for the negotiation of a cooperation regime between the EU and the US in exchanging e-evidence.[27] A similar dynamic is envisaged in the Trade and Cooperation Agreement concluded between the EU and the UK, which allows the Member States to enter into negotiation with the UK to define bilateral and specific modalities of cooperation,[28] notably on procedural aspects. Bilateral negotiations were, for instance, initiated with Belgium in order to allow information exchange between British and Belgian law enforcement agencies without the need to obtain prior consent from a Belgian magistrate to enable faster information exchange.[29]

Such EU 'framework agreements' encouraging the conclusion of complementary bilateral agreements by the Member States also exist in the field of migration, in which the EU can conclude readmission agreements (EURA).[30] As of January 2024, the EU has concluded 18 EURAs, as well as six non-binding readmission agreements,[31] which take precedence over

[21] E Fahey and I Wieczorek, 'The European Parliament as a Defender of EU Values in EU-Japan Agreements: What Role for Soft Law and Hard Law Powers?' (2022) 47 *European Law Review* 331.

[22] See eg Agreement between the EU and Japan on mutual legal assistance in criminal matters [2010] OJ L39/20.

[23] Agreement on extradition between the EU and the United States of America [2003] OJ L181/27 (EU–US extradition agreement); and Agreement on mutual legal assistance between the EU and the United States of America [2003] OJ L181/34 (EU–US MLA agreement).

[24] EU–US extradition agreement (n 23), Art 18, or EU–US MLA agreement (n 23), Art 14.

[25] V Mitsilegas, 'The External Dimension of EU Action in Criminal Matters' (2007) 12 *European Foreign Affairs Review* 457, 475–76.

[26] Council, Review of the 2010 EU–US MLA Agreement – Examination of draft texts, 2016, doc 7403/16, Annex III, 15.

[27] T Christakis and F Terpan, 'EU–US Negotiations on Law Enforcement Access to Data: Divergences, Challenges and EU Law Procedures and Options' (2021) 11 *International Data Privacy Law* 81, 92–93.

[28] Answer by T Pursglove MP on 'Changes to cross-border police cooperation in the EU and to the Prüm rules: potential implications for the UK' (2022), https://committees.parliament.uk/publications/31567/documents/177095/default/, accessed 4 March 2024.

[29] ibid.

[30] See eg Council Decision of 18 January 2011 on the conclusion of the Agreement between the European Union and Georgia on the readmission of persons residing without authorization [2011] OJ L52/45 and the agreement in Annex, Art 19.

[31] European Commission 'A humane and effective return and readmission policy', home-affairs.ec.europa.eu/policies/migration-and-asylum/irregular-migration-and-return/humane-and-effective-return-and-readmission-policy_en, accessed 4 March 2024.

pre-existing bilateral agreements concluded by the Member States.[32] The EURAs provide for the possibility for the Member States to conclude implementing protocols with each third country to agree on more technical and operational aspects of their cooperation.[33] On that basis, during the period 2014–2020, all Member States (except Ireland and Finland) signed at least one bilateral implementing protocol, resulting in a total of 69 bilateral implementing protocols.[34] This illustrates the importance of the exercise of the EU's competence (or its non-exercise) on the capacity of Member States to develop their own external cooperation with third countries. Yet, as argued by Molnár, the EU can only claim an exclusive competence in readmission matters based on a country-by-country approach,[35] thus leaving to the Member States the competence to conclude their own agreements with third countries with whom the EU has not initiated negotiations of an EURA.

It thus appears that the international cooperation between Member States and third countries is shaped by EU law in areas covered by EU competences, whether internal or external ones. It translates in the openness to external partners of cooperation mechanisms designed to encourage cross-border cooperation between Member States, or the way EU AFSJ actors are placed in a strategic position to facilitate such cooperation. The recognition and exercise of the EU's external competence also provides frameworks and/or legal bases in favour of more advanced bilateral cooperation, to be developed in conformity with the standards set out in EU law instruments and/or under the control of the EU institutions. The mobilisation of EU external competences may also restrain, in application of their duty of loyal cooperation with the EU, the Member States' capacity to enter into new agreements that may undermine the EU's external actions. Yet the Member States have not completely lost their agency and are not forced to act only within the remit and the limits defined by EU law. They can maintain their own international activities, exercised autonomously, or in coordination with the EU.

III. THE CHOICES OPEN TO THE MEMBER STATES TO MAINTAIN THEIR INTERNATIONAL ACTIVITIES

The accession of a State to the EU does not put an end to its existence as a subject of international law, and its capacity to act on the international scene. The EU does not possess a competence to act that would extinguish by virtue of exclusivity the competences of the Member States. This is particularly true in the fields included within the AFSJ, which are close to their sovereignty, and Member States continue to act internationally, be it in participating jointly in agreements alongside the EU (A) or on their own.[36] They have used their treaty-making capacity to conclude international agreements outside the EU's legal framework, including among themselves (B), and their favour of informal arrangements, shared by the EU, further adds to their capacity to modulate their international cooperation with third countries (C).

[32] EU–Georgia Agreement (n 30), Art 20.

[33] T Molnár, 'EU Readmission Policy: a (Shapeshifter) Technical Toolkit or Challenge to Rights Compliance?' in Tsourdi and de Bruycker (n 18), 492.

[34] European Migration Network, *EMN Inform Bilateral Readmission Agreements* (2022) 2 and 4, https://emnbelgium.be/publication/bilateral-readmission-agreements-emn-inform, accessed 4 March 2024.

[35] Molnár (n 33), 497.

[36] See the migration agreement concluded between Italy and Albania, allegedly compatible with EU law falling within the competences of the Member States.

A. Mixed Agreements

The shared nature of the EU competences in most areas covered by the AFSJ often translates in the necessity to conclude international agreements as mixed agreements, concluded and ratified by both the EU and the Member States. This practice of mixity is well-known and particularly important for the conclusion of international agreements relating to crime prevention and international criminal justice. Many of the instruments developed in this field, either internationally within the United Nations, or regionally within the Council of Europe, are indeed negotiated and concluded jointly. In many instances, this configuration does not raise problems. The EU and the Member States agree on the division of their respective competences and responsibilities. The declaration of competences attached to the EU's ratification identifies the parts falling under the EU's competences and may even be updated to reflect their evolution.[37] Such mixed agreements are particularly important for international cooperation between EU and non-EU countries. The Conventions elaborated within the Council of Europe, for instance on mutual legal assistance or extradition, have proven their added value in that regard. They not only serve as a legal basis for establishing a minimum level of cooperation with countries often engaged in pre-accession negotiations,[38] but they also serve as fallback option guaranteeing a minimum level of cooperation when a Member State withdraws from the EU.[39]

However, in some cases, the mixity of certain envisaged agreements opens the door to a stronger influence of the Member States on their negotiation and conclusion. Such hurdles may be due to divergences among Member States on the instruments to be adopted, and the existence of ad hoc practices, not foreseen in Article 218 TFEU, that slow down or prevent the EU's participation in some agreements. The saga around the ratification of the Istanbul Convention is a representative example of such difficulties.[40] Since the adoption of the text in 2011 and its entry into force in 2014, it has crystallised certain social tensions around gender issues and violence against women. Several Member States (Bulgaria, the Czech Republic, Hungary, Latvia, Lithuania, and the Slovak Republic) have only signed the text, in some cases more than 10 years ago, without making any progress towards its ratification. This division impacted the ratification of the text by the EU. While the signature of the text was approved by the Council in 2017,[41] the adoption of the Decisions authorising its ratification was postponed, due to the lack of a 'common accord' of all the Member States to be bound by this Convention in the areas falling within their competence. Faced with this deadlock, the European Parliament asked the ECJ to review the compatibility with the Treaties of the Council's approach of securing the common accord of the Member States before concluding a mixed agreement, and the

[37] Example of the UN Convention against Corruption (UNCAC) and the update of the EU's declaration of competences in 2020 (Commission, Communication on the review of the EU under the Implementation Review Mechanism of the UNCAC, COM (2020) 793 final).

[38] Mitsilegas (n 25), 468.

[39] A Oehmichen and B Keith, 'Mutual Legal Assistance under the EU–UK Trade and Cooperation Agreement' (2021) 12 *New Journal of European Criminal Law* 222, 224.

[40] Council of Europe, Convention on preventing and combating violence against women and domestic violence (CETS No 210).

[41] Council Decision (EU) 2017/865 of 11 May 2017 on the signing, on behalf of the European Union, of the Council of Europe Convention on preventing and combating violence against women and domestic violence with regard to matters related to judicial cooperation in criminal matters [2017] OJ L131/11; and Council Decision (EU) 2017/866 of 11 May 2017 on the signing, on behalf of the European Union, of the Council of Europe Convention on preventing and combating violence against women and domestic violence with regard to asylum and non-refoulement [2017] OJ L131/13.

conclusion of a text in the absence of such agreement. In its Opinion, the ECJ stressed that while the Treaties do not prohibit the Council from waiting for the 'common accord' of the Member States, the Treaties do prohibit the Council from adding a further step to the conclusion procedure laid down in Article 218 TFEU.[42] Yet, despite such clarification, the Council Decisions were not adopted until June 2023,[43] and the EU deposited its instrument of approval on 28 June 2023, together with a particularly detailed declaration of competences, including a list of EU instruments conferring on it an exclusive competence.[44] Nevertheless, the non-participation of some Member States leads to difficulties, notably due to the variable geometry it creates.

This example illustrates the extent to which Member States can retain a role in shaping and influencing the EU's external actions. The consequences are even more felt in the field of migration, in which the divergences among Member States are stronger, leading to their division, even to support the adoption of non-binding commitments such as the Global Compact on Safe, Orderly and Regular Migration.[45] Through the shared nature of the EU's competences in the AFSJ, and the exclusivity by exercise obtained at a slow pace, the Member States manage to retain a margin of manoeuvre to develop their own external actions in fields covered by the AFSJ. They have additionally resorted to new avenues for establishing cooperation mechanisms among themselves – and open to third countries – and/or with third countries, thus managing to 'further emancipate themselves from the shackles of EU law'.

B. Reliance on their Autonomous Treaty Making Capacity

The Member States can mobilise their capacity to negotiate and conclude international law agreements among themselves in fields that are not covered by EU law and/or for which there is no consensus to develop such mechanisms within the framework provided by the EU Treaties.

A prime example of such mobilisation can be found in relation to the abolition of internal border controls between Member States that was made possible through the negotiation and conclusion of two agreements – the Schengen Agreement and the Convention Implementing the Schengen Agreement – outside the EC framework. This was not meant to circumvent the constraints provided in EU law, as the treaties included a clear legal basis for the pursuit of such objective. It was, however, the opposition of some Member States that led those committed to such ambition to sign separate agreements, with the aim to set up an experimental legal framework that could later integrate within the EU legal framework. This choice allowed them to develop the first cooperation mechanisms in migration and criminal matters, and to provide so in the legal form that allowed third countries to join. This notably allowed Norway and Iceland to join the Schengen Area in 1996, together with the Member States participating

[42] *Opinion 1/19 (Istanbul Convention)*, ECLI:EU:C:2021:198, para 274.

[43] Council Decision (EU) 2023/1075 of 1 June 2023 on the conclusion, on behalf of the European Union, of the Council of Europe Convention on preventing and combating violence against women and domestic violence with regard to institutions and public administration of the Union [2023] OJ L143I/1; and Council Decision (EU) 2023/1076 of 1 June 2023 on the conclusion, on behalf of the European Union, of the Council of Europe Convention on preventing and combating violence against women and domestic violence with regard to matters related to judicial cooperation in criminal matters, asylum and non-refoulement [2023] OJ L143I/4.

[44] Council of Europe, Reservations and Declarations for Treaty No 210, EU, https://coe.int/fr/web/conventions/full-list?module=declarations-by-treaty&numSte=210&codeNature=0, accessed 4 March 2024.

[45] P Melin, 'Two Years after the Adoption of the Global Compact for Migration: Some Thoughts on the Role Played by the EU' in W Douma et al (eds), *The Evolving Nature of EU External Relations Law* (Springer, 2021) 301.

in the Nordic Passport Union. It also prompted the development of specific arrangements to foster cooperation between some Schengen associated countries and Member States, such as the extradition agreement concluded between the EU, Norway and Iceland,[46] which sets up the 'Nordic arrest warrant', with a regime close to the European arrest warrant.[47] Such an openness to third countries was maintained after the 'repatriation' of the Schengen *acquis* in EU law with the Treaty of Amsterdam, and two other third countries, Switzerland and Liechtenstein, joined the Schengen area in 2004 and 2008.

The Prüm Treaty constitutes another example. The text was initially signed in 2005 by seven Member States outside the EU framework and integrated in 2008.[48] The Member States opted for a self-standing agreement, as the minimum number of States for an enhanced cooperation was not met and the process of establishing such scheme was considered too burdensome.[49] Its adoption promoted the interest of third countries closely collaborating with Member States to conclude similar agreements opening up access to security-related databases. The US developed, for instance, a policy linking its Visa Waiver Program to the conclusion of agreements enhancing the access of its national authorities to such databases, which resulted in several Member States concluding such agreements, which included a clear reference to the Prüm treaty in their preambles.[50] Since then, another 'Prüm-like' treaty, referred to as the Prüm Agreement for South-East Europe, has been concluded between Member States and third countries.[51] The revision of the EU Prüm regime took into consideration the exchange of data with third countries. The text notably makes third country-sourced data stored at Europol available to the Member States and allows the agency to search Member States' databases with data received from third-country authorities.[52] The revised text illustrates the trend discussed above of making EU agencies intermediaries for international cooperation but says nothing about the other agreements that the Member States have concluded, agreeing implicitly to maintain their discretion in that matter.

C. Informal Arrangements

International cooperation with third countries in sensitive fields covered by the AFSJ may lead to situations in which the establishment of cooperation mechanisms is at best delayed, and at worst abandoned, because of dissension on their purposes, content or the – (in)sufficient – guarantees they provide for safeguarding fundamental rights. Such difficulties are particularly vivid in migration matters, as demonstrated by the lengthy negotiation of the instruments reforming EU asylum law, and they also appear when international cooperation mechanisms, contributing to the externalisation of migration control, are being developed.

[46] Agreement on the surrender procedure between the Member States of the European Union and Iceland and Norway [2006] OJ L292/2.

[47] A Suominen, 'Brexit and EU Criminal Law – The Norwegian Approach' (2017) 28 *Criminal Law Forum* 251.

[48] Council Decision 2008/615/JHA of 23 June 2008 on the stepping up of cross-border cooperation, particularly in combating terrorism and cross-border crime [2008] OJ L210/1; and Council Decision 2008/616/JHA of 23 June 2008 on the implementation of Decision 2008/615/JHA on the stepping up of cross-border cooperation, particularly in combating terrorism and cross-border crime [2008] OJ L210/12.

[49] P Luif and F Trauner, 'The Prüm Process: The Effects of Enhanced Cooperation within Europe and with the United States in Combating Serious Crime' in RL Holzhacker and P Luif (eds), *Freedom, Security and Justice in the European Union* (Springer, 2014) 106.

[50] ibid, 112.

[51] Albania, Austria, Bulgaria, Hungary, Moldova, Montenegro, North Macedonia, Romania, and Serbia.

[52] Compromise text of the Regulation 'Prüm II', Council, Doc 16314/23, Arts 49 and 50 on Europol.

As a result, the EU as well as the Member States have opted for the development of informal arrangements with third countries, that may complement or replace more formal agreements. Many scholars have analysed such informalisation of the external dimension of the EU migration policy,[53] referring to it as 'formal informality'[54] or focusing on the use of 'soft law' or atypical instruments.[55] The Member States also engage in the adoption of similar informal bilateral arrangements.

These 'texts' are generally motivated by the aim of securing the cooperation of third countries in the management of migration flows towards the EU. Whereas such cooperation has existed since the early 2000s, the number of arrangements has increased since 2015, and they are often coupled with financial incentives to secure third countries' cooperation.

Such an approach gained visibility with the EU–Turkey Statement, accompanied by the EU Refugee Facility for Turkey.[56] Cooperation is based on a statement published as a press release after a meeting of the European Council, and has been criticised due to its content and objectives, and the way it was 'adopted'. It indeed circumvents the procedures applicable at national and European levels to guarantee the involvement of parliamentary actors and the political accountability of executives before them. The ECJ's refusal to recognise the admissibility of legal actions challenging its compatibility with EU law has further discouraged those who envisaged judicial accountability as a way to redress the circumvention of the applicable legal norms.[57]

Unfortunately, the Member States support the development of new informal mechanisms, and the EU institutions, in particular the Commission, are reluctant to stress their possible incompatibility with the EU Treaties. The Commission has – rather to the contrary – noted their added-value,[58] considering that the coordination of actions between the EU and the Member States, pooling resources through the creation of trust funds or facilities, and implementing a coordinated 'Team Europe' approach, is the way forward in migration policy.[59] The EU–Tunisia Memorandum of Understanding is a recent example of such an approach: it was announced on the occasion of a visit of the President of the Commission to Tunisia, where she was accompanied by two Prime Ministers from Italy and the Netherlands 'in a Team Europe spirit' even though they played no formal role.[60] The text combines economic and migration measures, and escapes scrutiny from the European Parliament as it is not a legally binding agreement.

These examples illustrate how the Member States can rely on various routes to develop cooperation mechanisms in AFSJ matters, within or outside the framework provided by the EU treaties. In the three hypotheses examined in this part, the Council, the Commission and the Parliament have expressed different positions with regard to the choices made by

[53] E Kassoti and N Idriz (eds), *The Informalisation of the EU's External Action in the Field of Migration and Asylum* (TMC Asser Press, 2022).

[54] PJ Cardwell and R Dickson, '"Formal Informality" in EU External Migration Governance: The Case of Mobility Partnerships' (2023) 49 *Journal of Ethnic and Migration Studies* 312.

[55] V Moreno-Lax, 'The Informalisation of the External Dimension of EU Asylum Policy: the Hard Implications of Soft Law' in Tsourdi and de Bruycker (n 18), 282–304.

[56] Commission Decision of 24 November 2015 on the Refugee Facility for Turkey [2018] OJ C407/8.

[57] Joined Cases C-208/17 P and C-210/17 P *NF, NG and NM*, ECLI:EU:C:2018:705.

[58] Commission, 'New Pact on Migration and Asylum' (Communication) COM (2020) 609 final, 17–18.

[59] E Tsourdi et al, 'Funding the EU's External Migration Policy: "Same Old" or Potential for Sustainable Collaboration?' (2023) EPC Discussion Paper, https://www.epc.eu/en/Publications/Funding-the-EUs-external-migration-policy-Same-old-or-potential-fo~4fb44c, accessed 4 March 2024.

[60] DG Near, Press release 'The European Union and Tunisia: Political Agreement on a Comprehensive Partnership Package', 16 July 2023.

the Member States. It is not surprising that the Council would tend to privilege intergovernmental approaches, or that the European Parliament would contest ad hoc procedural steps or informal mechanisms that deprive it of its prerogatives. However, the benevolence of the Commission, and its encouragement to 'innovative' cooperation mechanisms especially in migration matters, is more concerning. While it may be understood from pragmatic reasons and the need to reassure Member States, it undermines substantially the capacity for the EU to respect its own constitutional arrangements and creates loopholes in the accountability of the EU and its Member States before political and judicial actors.

IV. CONCLUSION

The contribution has focused on the international cooperation between the Member States and non-EU countries, a topic inextricably linked to the external dimension of the AFSJ. The Member States have been able to rely on the development of EU law, either through the adoption of EU secondary law instruments or the conclusion of EU-only international agreements, to further develop their international cooperation. Interestingly, the EU specialised actors are positioned as intermediaries and hubs for the cooperation and exchange of information with the authorities from third countries and/or international bodies. While this can be interpreted as a sign of maturity for the AFSJ and the trust the EU actors have acquired therein, it also raises some questions, and further justifies the exploration of their accountability before independent actors.[61]

Such accountability is even more necessary in the light of the Member States also having been keen to maintain the exercise of their own competences, either through the conclusion of mixed agreements, or through the conclusion of agreements outside the legal regime foreseen under the EU treaties. Such an exercise is understandable in areas not covered by EU competences, and it is more than welcome when it serves to push the adoption of new international agreements supporting an enhanced cooperation at global level.[62] It is, however, more problematic when Member States – and the European Commission – choose to resort to informal cooperation arrangements that raise numerous concerns in terms of transparency, political and judicial accountability. Such practices exist in other fields of international cooperation, and reflect the evolution of global governance mechanisms, that are less formal, less based on legally binding commitments, and more flexible in their composition. Yet, the political sensitivity and the possible infringements of fundamental rights that may occur in the framework of international cooperation in fields covered by the AFSJ calls for a continuous attention to and scrutiny of such developments.

[61] See eg M Schinina, 'What Balance between Eurojust and Europol from a Parliamentary Angle?' (2020) 11 *New Journal of European Criminal Law* 123.

[62] See for instance the role of Member States in the adoption in 2023 of The Hague – Ljubljana Convention to facilitate extradition and mutual legal assistance in the prosecution of international core crimes (Ljubljana, 26 May 2023).

Index

www.ingramcontent.com/pod-product-compliance
Ingram Content Group UK Ltd.
Pitfield, Milton Keynes, MK11 3LW, UK
UKHW050954290926
15470UKWH00006B/1811